U.S. HISTORY AND GOVERNMENT

Second Edition

Dr. Andrew Peiser
Graduate School of Education
Mercy College, New York

Michael Serber
Principal, Academy of American Studies,
New York

AMSCO

AMSCO SCHOOL PUBLICATIONS, INC.
315 Hudson Street   New York, N.Y. 10013

W9-BZU-935

Dr. Andrew Peiser, Graduate School of Education, Mercy College.
Dr. Peiser was Assistant Principal for Social Studies, Sheepshead Bay
High School, Brooklyn, N.Y.

Michael Serber, Principal, Academy of American Studies, New York.
Mr. Serber was Assistant Principal for Social Studies, Forest Hills
High School, Forest Hills, N.Y.

Dr. Andrew Peiser dedicates this book to his wife, Barbara,
his children, Richard, Jacqueline, and Brett and his mother, Marianne,
for all their love and support.

Michael Serber dedicates this book to his wife, Adele,
his children, Richard, Ellen, and Jeff, his grandchildren, Daniel and Noah,
and his mother, Faye, for all their love and support.

CONTRIBUTING AUTHORS

Stephen A. Shultz, Assistant Principal for Social Studies
Boys and Girls High School, New York City
Author of *Teacher's Manual for Global History and Geography* (Amsco)

Norman Lunger, writer, editor, reporter
Author of *Reviewing American History* and coauthor of *Global Geography* (Amsco)

Text design and cover by Howard S. Leiderman

Photo research by Tobi Zausner

Composition by Monotype Composition

When ordering this book, please specify:
R 036 H   *or*
U.S. History and Government Hardbound
or
R 036 P   *or*
U.S. History and Government Softbound

ISBN: 1-56765-613-7   /   *NYC Item 56765-613-6 Hardbound*

ISBN: 1-56765-612-9   /   *NYC Item 56765-612-8 Softbound*

Please visit our Web site at   *www.amscopub.com*

TEXT ACKNOWLEDGMENT
page 469: Words and music by Malvina Reynolds, from the song "Little Boxes,"
© 1962 by Schroder Music Co. (ASCAP), renewed 1990. Reprinted by permission.
All rights reserved.

Preface

This second edition of *U.S. History and Government* was prepared for students who are studying for the 11th grade New York State Regents examination. The book follows the course of study recommended by the New York State Education Department. As in the first edition, emphasis is on the period from the end of the Civil War to the present day. Many significant changes and additions have been made in the text to reflect the new course of study. These include increased attention to:

★ the physical geography and regional development of the nation. A new opening section describes the physical context of the continent in which the nation developed. Throughout, the arrival of new Americans, the exploration of the continent and the westward movement of the population, changing demographics, and the development of urban life and culture are emphasized.

★ the people of the nation, including Native Americans, African Americans, new emigrants, and women. The struggles for equal rights under the law, and for fair treatment of all Americans, have a prominent place in the text.

★ the development of democratic society from the colonial period to the present day. Included are the influences of Enlightenment thinkers on the writers of the Declaration of Independence, the Constitution, and the Bill of Rights. Special attention is given to the federal laws and constitutional amendments that define and protect the rights of African Americans.

★ the challenges and opportunities, both national and international, faced by the American people and their leaders in the 20th century—including two world wars, economic depression, the cold war, and the growth of the U.S. into a world political and economic leader. In Chapter 22, a special three-part section, "The American People: Challenges at the Millennium," describes the changes in population, households, and cities in the recent past.

Features that will encourage student interest and aid learning include

★ increased use of tables, graphs, maps, cartoons, and photographs as the basis for student exercises

★ in-chapter reviews to target important subjects and concepts

★ in-chapter readings and exercise documents from primary sources

To assist students and teachers in preparation for the Regents examination, all Chapter Reviews have Regents-style multiple-choice, thematic essay, and document-based questions. Many chapter-review questions test students' understanding and comprehension of the visual materials and readings in the text.

In addition to the text, teachers will find the Teacher's Manual of valuable assistance in preparing lessons, motivating students, and developing students' history skills. The manual also contains full answers to all the questions in the text and a Student Study Guide to assist in preparing for the Regents exam. The Answer Key is also available separately.

Dr. Andrew Peiser
Michael Serber

Contents

★ Graphs and Tables ★

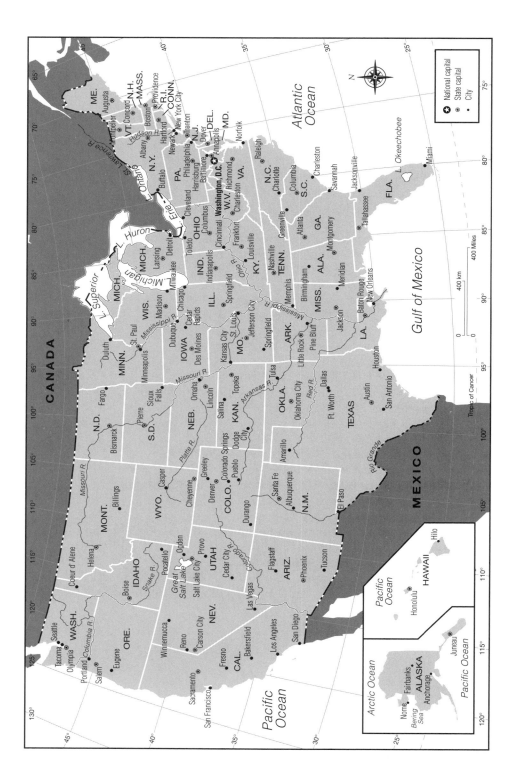

Introduction
Geography of the United States

★ **Objectives**

- ★ To understand how geography has helped to shape the experiences of the American people.
- ★ To identify the key geographic features of the United States.
- ★ To describe the relationships among landforms, climate, and vegetation.
- ★ To see how geographic factors help determine economic activities in different parts of the country.

You have probably seen images of the United States transmitted by weather satellites. In those fast-forward pictures, swirling masses of clouds skitter from west to east above the surface of the land. The country revealed through and between the clouds resembles a piece of a giant jigsaw puzzle plunked down between two oceans. At such a distance, most details are lost. The surface looks vaguely rippled, almost smooth.

Closer to Earth—say, from the layers of atmosphere traversed by airplanes—more details are visible, at least when no clouds interfere with the view. Lakes glitter in the sunlight. Streaks of light or dark reveal the shapes of farms, forests, lawns, and parks. You can identify hills and mountains, cities and highways.

Finally, from your perspective on the surface of the land, physical reality is in sharp detail. Walk along a city street, seeing and hearing the rush. Relax in a park as a breeze rustles the green grass. Swim across a pool or even a river. Feel the sting of wind-blown snow or the splash of a gentle summer shower.

These experiences can give you a feel for the geography of the United States. Exploring and understanding that geography will help prepare you to study the history and government of the United States. That history, as discussed in this book, and the decisions that, even now, are defining the nation's destiny have been greatly affected by geography—by resources, landforms, climate, and other features. This brief survey of the geography of the United States will help give shape and immediacy to events and sites mentioned in the chapters ahead.

Geography Shapes the American Experience

Geography is the study of the Earth and its inhabitants. It also reveals a given area's physical features, its biological makeup, and the culture of the people who live there. Look for connections: How do the features of the land affect how people live? How do people's actions affect the land? What uses do people make of an area's resources—minerals, vegetation, animals, wind, water, and so on? Where do people choose to live and why? Those are just a few of the questions that geographers ask.

The lyrics of "America, the Beautiful" describe the United States as sprawling "from sea to shining sea." Indeed, it stretches across the continent of North America from the Pacific Ocean on the west to the Atlantic Ocean on the east. Size and location are two of the country's defining features.

Immense Size of the United States

In area, the United States is the fourth largest nation in the world. *Area* is a measure of how much of the Earth's surface one place covers. It is often stated in square miles or square kilometers. Only Russia, China, and Canada cover larger areas than the United States. Immense size benefits the United States in many ways.

Variation in Climate and Vegetation The United States reaches from the icy fringes of the Arctic (in Alaska) to the balmy tropics (in Hawaii). The 48 *contiguous states*—those that share an uninterrupted expanse of territory—cover a range of climates from chilly to mild to hot and from dry to moist. Because of this variation, almost anything can grow somewhere in the United States.

Only a few other nations produce as wide a range of crops as does the United States. Bananas and coffee grow in Hawaii. Apples and potatoes grow in the colder climates of Washington State, New York, and Maine. Wheat and corn flourish in many states. Rice grows in relatively warm and wet places, such as South Carolina. Summer vegetables grow almost everywhere, and parts of California, Florida, and Texas produce them in winter, too.

Range and Abundance of Resources Big countries benefit most from natural resources. The larger a nation's area, the more likely it is to contain a wide variety of the resources on which people and industries depend. Because the land and water surfaces of the United States vary immensely, its natural resources range from oil and iron to forests and fish—not to mention rich soils for growing crops.

U.S. resources are not only varied but also abundant. Many have called the United States "a land of milk and honey" (a place that can lavishly supply what its people need). The United States is first or second in world production of such important energy resources as oil, natural gas, and coal. It is also a major producer of other minerals used by modern industries, such as lead, phosphate, and molybdenum.

Room to Grow Crossing a main street in a major U.S. city at rush hour will make you think that the United States is a very crowded place. But city centers make up only a small portion of the country. In fact, the United States, by current world standards, is quite lightly populated. Geographers measure *population density* to judge how crowded a place is. Population density is calculated by dividing the population of a place by its area, which gives the number of people living in each square mile or kilometer. With about 275 million inhabitants in the year 2000, the United States had a population density of 78 people per square mile (30 per square kilometer). China was twice as crowded, India 10 times, the Netherlands 12 times, and Korea 16 times.

Because of its low population density, the United States has had room to grow. It has accommodated not only the babies born within its boundaries but also people who have arrived from other lands. Many millions of immigrants have come to the United States, and more do so every year.

Fortunate Location

The United States has also been fortunately situated on the Earth. Unlike many nations, it does not share borders with unfriendly and aggressive neighbors. It is bordered only by Canada and Mexico. Wide oceans separate it from the major centers of world power in Europe and Asia.

Oceans Provide Both Security and Trade Routes On the one hand, the Atlantic and Pacific oceans have been effective barriers against military attack and invasion. On the other hand, they have given the American people easy access to peaceful trade.

Some nations must overcome such barriers as mountains and deserts to trade with the outside world, but not the United States. Moreover, it has long coastlines and deep harbors where ships can load and unload cargoes. From colonial times to the present, trade by sea has played a major role in the U.S. economy.

★ In Review

1. In what ways does the United States benefit from its great size?
2. Compare the United States to a country such as Switzerland, which lacks sea or ocean coastlines.

Physical Features of the United States

If you fly over Arizona's Grand Canyon, you can look down into a deep chasm—a giant-sized ditch. Then, as the airplane heads northeast away from the Grand Canyon, you may pass over the tall peaks of the Rocky Mountains. Canyons and mountains are among the many landforms found in the United States. *Landforms* are natural features of the Earth's surface. Don't be fooled by the "land" in landforms. They include such features as lakes and oceans—parts of the Earth's surface that are covered by water.

Forces That Have Helped Shape U.S. Landforms

Powerful forces have helped to create the landforms we see today.

Continental Drift Scientists believe that the Earth's continents were once a single land mass (or perhaps two), which began to break up and drift apart some 240 million years ago. According to the theory of *continental drift*, continents "float" on immense plates of rock. They move at only fractions of an inch a year and sometimes gain or lose land when they collide with

Physical Map of the United States

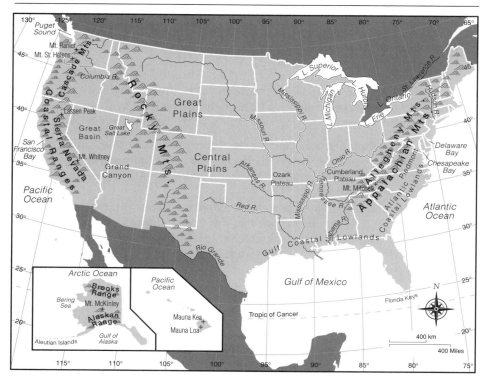

one another. Gradually, the continents reached their present positions. When plates collided, they pushed the surface together to form great mountains. When plates broke apart, deep oceans often filled the gaps.

Along the Pacific coastline of the United States, the North American Plate presses against the Pacific Plate. Plate collisions are believed to be responsible for the volcanoes and earthquakes that are part of the experience of living in California.

Volcanoes and Earthquakes Volcanoes and earthquakes occur frequently along boundaries between shifting continental plates. These violent phenomena play a key role in shaping the land.

Volcanoes occur when hot gases and *magma* (molten, or melted, rock within the Earth) build up pressure and spew forth from underground as *lava*. As volcanoes erupt again and again over many centuries, they can create cone-shaped mountains. Within the continental United States, two active volcanoes are Mount St. Helens in Washington State and Lassen Peak in California. Volcanoes also occur in Hawaii and Alaska.

Pressures beneath the Earth's surface also cause *earthquakes*, which can topple buildings and rip up the landscape. In recent years, powerful earthquakes have rocked both southern and northern California. Scientists keep a particularly close eye on the *San Andreas Fault*—an earthquake-prone fracture that runs roughly southeast to northwest from southern California to the San Francisco area.

Glaciers Many landforms in the United States—especially in Alaska, in mountainous areas, and near Canada—have been shaped by moving masses of snow and ice. These *glaciers*, common in polar regions, form where more snow falls in winter than can melt in summer. Glaciers spread out during periods called *ice ages*, when global temperatures dip sharply. During the last ice age, some 20,000 years ago, a mile-high mountain of ice stretched from west of what is now Chicago to New York City and south to the Ohio River valley.

Glaciers can slice off the tops of mountains, fill valleys with new soil, and gouge out depressions that become lakes. Because of the ancient actions of glaciers in Minnesota, the state is sometimes called "the Land of Ten Thousand Lakes."

Erosion The moving of rocks and soil by glaciers is one of many forms of *erosion*—the wearing away of land by wind, rain, or ice. The older a landform, the longer the forces of erosion have been at work grinding it down. The Appalachian Mountains of the eastern United States are relatively old and eroded mountains. That is why they are lower and less rugged than the younger Rocky Mountains of the West.

Mountain Ranges and Plateaus

Mountains are perhaps the most easily identified landforms. These elevated areas of peaks and crests rise high above the surrounding countryside. Other elevated landforms, *plateaus*, are flat or gently rolling expanses at high altitudes. *Altitude* measures the height of a landform above sea level or another surface, such as the ocean floor.

Appalachians The Appalachians are the most prominent range of mountains in the eastern United States. They stretch from Georgia and Alabama northward into Canada. Although nowhere near as rugged as the mountains of the West, the Appalachians long served as a barrier to westward expansion by European settlers. The highest point in the Appalachians is Mount Mitchell (6684 feet) in North Carolina.

Rockies The Rocky Mountains are the easternmost of three major mountain ranges in the western United States. The peaks of the Rockies reach over 12,000 or 13,000 feet in New Mexico, Utah, Wyoming, Idaho, and Montana and above 14,000 feet in Colorado. Prized now as a site for big-game hunting and downhill skiing, the Rockies once teemed with trappers in search of beaver and other animal pelts.

Other Western Mountains Two mountain ranges, along with extensive areas of high plateau, lie between the Rockies and the Pacific coast. Closest to the Rockies is a range with two names—the Sierra Nevada in California and the Cascades in Oregon and Washington. Farther west are the Coast ranges, which flank the Pacific coast and extend from Mexico to Alaska.

Alaska and Brooks Ranges The highest mountain in the United States is Mount McKinley (20,320 feet). It is part of the spectacular Alaska Range in south-central Alaska. The Brooks Range lies in the north.

Interior and Coastal Lowlands

Lowlands are valuable landforms because they are often flat or gently rolling and thus suitable for agriculture. The United States has many major lowlands.

Basin and Range Lowland deserts and areas of scrubby vegetation occupy part of the area between the mountain ranges of the West. In landforms called *basins*, flowing water with no outlet collects to form lakes that become very salty as water continually evaporates. (All water contains tiny amounts of various salts, and evaporation greatly concentrates them.) Utah's Great Salt Lake lies in the Great Basin.

Great Plains and Central Plains A *plain* is a large area of level or gently rolling land. The Great Plains and the Central Plains of the United States make up one of the most extensive lowlands in the world. These two plains reach through the central United States from Texas into Canada. From the edge of the Rockies, the plains slope gently eastward to the Mississippi River, with the drier western area, the Great Plains, giving way to the more humid Central Plains. The boundary between the two plains areas is defined by the amount of rainfall and runs from about the eastern edges of Texas and Oklahoma northward to the eastern edge of North Dakota.

Interior Lowlands East of the Mississippi River, another large lowland area extends through Illinois, Indiana, Michigan, and most of Ohio. Along with the plains, this became prime farming country as settlers cleared away its forests.

Coastal Plains and Piedmont Another major lowland area wraps around the southeastern edges of the United States beginning in Texas and extending northward to New York. Along the eastern Gulf and Atlantic coasts, flat or rolling coastal plains reach inland to the line where the Appalachian Mountains begin to rise. Between this lowland and the mountains lies the *Piedmont* (French for "foot" and "mountain"). As you travel up a river from the coast, you know you have reached the Piedmont when you encounter a series of rapids and waterfalls; water flowing from the mountains to the sea makes a sharp drop as the elevation of the land suddenly changes. This boundary between the Piedmont and the coastal plains is called the *fall line*.

The northernmost part of the Atlantic coastal plain reaches inland deep into New York State in the form of a narrow band of lowlands on either side of the Hudson River.

Major Water Features

Water is an important natural resource, and so are rivers and lakes— landforms defined by water. Rivers and lakes are useful for transportation, food (fish, shellfish, edible plants such as seaweed), and the removal of wastes.

Great Lakes Together, the five Great Lakes make up the largest body of fresh water in the world. They lie between the United States and Canada, bordering the states of Minnesota, Wisconsin, Michigan, Illinois, Indiana, Ohio, Pennsylvania, and New York. Only Lake Michigan is entirely within the United States. The four lakes straddling the U.S.–Canadian border are (from west to east) Lakes Superior, Huron, Erie, and Ontario.

Long before Europeans set foot in North America, Native Americans were fishing the Great Lakes and carrying people and goods across them by boat. Since the 19th century, cargo ships have crisscrossed the lakes carrying products needed for modern industry—iron ore, coal, and wheat, for example. The lakes are also a major source of food fish.

St. Lawrence River The Great Lakes empty into the Atlantic Ocean through the St. Lawrence River, one of two great rivers that drain the U.S. interior. Since 1959, ships have been able to pass from the Great Lakes to the ocean through a series of canals known as the *St. Lawrence Seaway*. The seaway, built jointly by the United States and Canada, widens and deepens the St. Lawrence so that ships can travel between Lake Ontario and Montreal in Canada's Quebec Province. From Montreal to the ocean, the St. Lawrence is *navigable* without the use of canals.

More than a century before the St. Lawrence Seaway opened, New York State dug another water route to serve as an outlet for the Great Lakes. The *Erie Canal*, which opened to shallow canal boats in 1825, connected Lake Erie near Buffalo to the Hudson River near Albany. By means of the Hudson, cargoes from the Midwest could reach New York City, which owes much of its growth as a port and center of industry to the Erie Canal.

Mississippi River   The greatest of all U.S. rivers is the Mississippi. With its *tributaries* (the rivers that flow into it), the Mississippi River drains almost the entire area from the Appalachians to the Rockies. It widens to as much as a mile and a half before pouring into the Gulf of Mexico near New Orleans, Louisiana.

The Mississippi itself is 2348 miles long—or 3860 miles long if its length is measured from where the Missouri River, a tributary, starts in the Rockies. Other important tributaries include the Ohio River (with its own tributary, the Tennessee River), the Arkansas River, and the Red River.

The Mississippi figures prominently in North American history, from its use as a "highway" by early Native Americans through its exploration by the Spaniards and French to its roles in the Civil War and as part of the modern U.S. industrial economy. Such major cities as Memphis and St. Louis arose largely because of their favored locations along the Mississippi.

Lesser Lakes and Rivers   Many other rivers have also played central roles in U.S. history. Most of the nation's largest cities grew up beside navigable rivers. A few examples include Boston, Massachusetts (at the mouth of the Charles and Mystic rivers); Richmond, Virginia (at the mouth of the James River); Mobile, Alabama (at the mouth of the Mobile River); Pittsburgh, Pennsylvania (where two rivers merge to form the Ohio River); and Portland, Oregon (on the Columbia River as it nears the Pacific Ocean).

Extensive Ocean Coastlines

Access to oceans is a great advantage for trade and travel, and 23 of the 50 United States benefit from ocean coastlines. At many points, arms of the sea poke inland to form protected inlets and bays. Such features include Chesapeake Bay and Delaware Bay (on the Atlantic coast) and San Francisco Bay and Puget Sound (on the Pacific coast).

Seacoast states often have important fishing industries. In the past, whaling also contributed significantly to the economies of coastal regions.

Atlantic Fisheries   The waters off the east coast of the United States and Canada contain some of the best fishing grounds in the world, especially along the Grand Banks off Newfoundland. Native Americans have fished in coastal waters for many centuries, as have Europeans. Many New England coastal villages made a living from the sea in colonial days, and some still do. Fishing boats bring back lobsters and finfish such as cod, haddock, and mackerel. Farther south, the Chesapeake Bay and other coastal regions also have commercial fishing industries as well as sports fishing for species such as tuna.

Gulf Fisheries   More good fishing is found in the Gulf of Mexico. Shrimp and other shellfish are a featured part of the cuisine in Louisiana and other Gulf states.

Pacific Fisheries   Fishing boats set off from the U.S. Pacific coast in search of tuna, sardines, anchovies, and many other types of fish. Salmon are abundant along the Northwest Coast. They spawn in rivers flowing into the sea and are a traditional harvest for Native Americans in the region.

Hawaii: An Archipelago   Hawaii is the only state completely surrounded by ocean waters. An *archipelago*, or chain of islands, was created over the centuries by volcanic activity. Most Hawaiians live on the island of Oahu. The world's largest active volcano, Mauna Loa, is on the big island of Hawaii.

Mineral and Energy Resources

Associated with U.S. landforms are a variety of mineral and energy resources. They were first tapped by early Native Americans, who learned to use them in their daily lives. Today, such resources are crucial to the operation of the U.S. economy.

True Minerals   Most minerals lack organic matter—by-products of living organisms. These minerals are solid substances occurring in nature, each with its own distinctive chemical composition. Since minerals do not replicate themselves as animals and plants do, they are called *nonrenewable resources*.

Metals have been especially useful to human societies. The three most important metals for modern industry are iron, copper, and aluminum, all of them found in the United States. Ancient societies used iron and copper to make tools and weapons. Relatively abundant and easy to work, iron is the main ingredient of steel and is used in products as varied as needles, kitchen appliances, and spaceships. Copper is a good conductor of electricity and is used in products ranging from soup kettles to computers. Aluminum, also an electrical conductor, is one of the lightest metals and is often used in automobiles as a substitute for steel to keep down overall weight.

Valuable mineral deposits occur in many parts of the United States. Today, U.S. iron ore comes mainly from Minnesota and Michigan. Copper is mined in such Western states as Arizona and Montana. Bauxite ore (for aluminum) is mined in Arkansas. A variety of other mineral deposits are highlighted in the map on page 10.

Energy Resources   Energy is vital in every aspect of modern life. The United States has a variety of resources that can be used to produce energy.

Coal, petroleum, and natural gas are *fossil fuels*: They originated from a combination of ancient organisms and ancient minerals. Like true min-

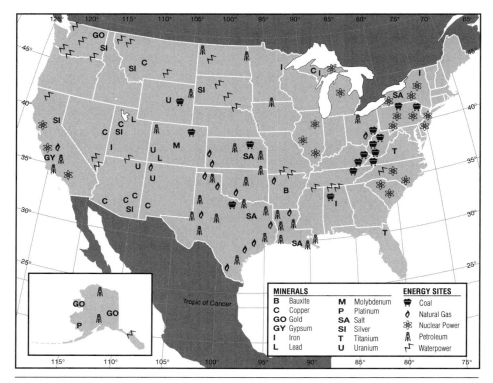

Selected Major U.S. Mineral Deposits and Energy Resources

erals, fossil fuels are nonrenewable, since they came about through a complex process lasting millions of years. Known U.S. coal resources are more extensive than those of any other nation, and the United States is the second largest producer of coal, after China. The United States is also a leading producer of petroleum (crude oil) and natural gas. The oil industry is a major presence in Texas, Oklahoma, and several other states. Much oil is produced from wells that have been sunk beneath the shallow ocean waters along U.S. coastlines—off Louisiana and California, for example. Since 1957, however, the United States has been unable to produce enough petroleum to satisfy its demand; in recent years, it has bought about as much crude oil from other nations as it has produced.

Electricity is another form of energy required by modern societies. Slightly more than half of U.S. electricity comes from coal. (At power plants, coal is burned to create heat; heat makes steam to turn turbines; turbines generate electrical current.) Another 20 percent of U.S. electricity comes from *nuclear power*; the decay of radioactive materials becomes the source of steam-producing heat. Uranium, a radioactive mineral used for the production of nuclear power, has been found in greater quantities in the United States than anywhere else. The United States also has many sites that are suited to producing *hydroelectric power*, which is generated when falling water turns turbines. Hydroelectric plants at dams built along rivers and other waterways produce about 10 percent of U.S. electric power. Two famous hydroelectric dams are Grand Coulee Dam (on the Columbia River in Washington) and Hoover Dam (on the Colorado River between Arizona and Nevada).

Since the 1970s, when the United States and other industrial nations experienced alarming, but short-lasting, energy shortages, serious efforts have been made to develop additional types of energy. Here are some of the main types of *alternative energy*:

★ *Solar power*, or energy from the sun, can be seen at work in one simple and familiar device, the greenhouse. It traps the sun's rays behind glass to facilitate the growth of flowers or vegetables out of season. Another solar device is the heat sink, which uses the sun's warmth to heat stone walls or liquid-filled containers that slowly release their heat after sundown. Solar batteries also use the sun's power to generate electricity. Space missions use solar batteries as a source of power. You may have a calculator run by such batteries.

★ *Alcohol*, produced from plants such as corn, can be burned by itself or mixed with gasoline (*gasohol*) to run automobile engines. Iowa and other states of the Midwest are major produces of gasohol.

★ *Methane* is an economical substitute for natural gas. It is made by allowing organic matter, such as manure, to rot; in the process, gases are emitted and then captured for use in such devices as cookstoves and space heaters.

★ *Geothermal energy* is heat from within the Earth. It can be used directly to heat homes or indirectly to generate electricity. Geothermal electricity plants are usually located in areas like Hawaii and California that are subject to volcanic activity.

★ *Windmills* are used in California and other parts of the country to generate electricity. Often, they are grouped in "windmill farms" located at passes between hills or mountains, where winds are strong and persistent.

★ *Shale oil* is a fossil fuel obtained by heating and crushing oil-bearing rocks.

Many of these alternative sources of energy are *renewable resources*. Some, like the sun's energy and the wind, can be used without diminishing the supply. Others, like alcohol and methane, use resources that can be planted and grown year after year. Shale oil, however, is a nonrenewable resource.

Importance to the Economy   Mineral and energy resources are the basis for many economic activities that give a distinctive character to regional life. Many Western states have developed mining industries based on their resources in copper, silver, gold, and other metals. Coal mining was a traditional activity in coal-rich parts of the Appalachians scattered from West Virginia and Pennsylvania to Alabama. Although less important today, mining still gives a distinctive atmosphere to such regions.

Often, industries have grown up where local resources are abundant or transportation routes give ready access to more distant resources. For example, Pittsburgh in western Pennsylvania and Birmingham in Alabama developed major steel industries based on nearby supplies of coal and iron. Great Lakes cities—Chicago, Detroit, and Gary, Indiana, for example—were midway between the coal of the Appalachians and the iron ore of Minnesota and Wisconsin. Ships and railroads brought together the raw materials, and those cities, too, became important centers of industry. Similar examples can be found in other parts of the country.

★ In Review

1. Define the following terms: landforms, continental drift, ice age, plateau, altitude, plain, Piedmont, fall line, tributary, archipelago, fossil fuel.
2. Give examples of *each* of the following natural features of the United States: (a) mountain ranges, (b) interior lowlands, (c) coastal plains, (d) lakes, (e) rivers.
3. What are the three most important metals mined in the United States? How are they used in today's economy?
4. Describe the energy resources of the United States, making a distinction between renewable and nonrenewable ones.

Major Geographic Zones of the United States

Landforms and mineral and energy resources are not the only geographic factors that influence life in a particular location. Other key factors include climate, vegetation, and natural resources. Together, these factors have influenced the development of different parts of the United States and the economic activities of their inhabitants.

Climate Zones

Depending on where you live in the United States, winter may be a good time to take a swim, throw snowballs, or stay dry indoors and read a book. The United States has a wide range of climates and, in most places, distinct differences from one season to another.

Snow and rain, heat and cold, and seasonal variations are characteristics of *climate*, the year-to-year weather conditions that prevail over long periods of time. Climate greatly affects our environment and, therefore, our way of life.

What Determines Climate?   The climate that people in a particular location enjoy or endure depends on a number of factors:

★ *Latitude* is the measure of how far a place is from the equator and from the Earth's poles. The United States is entirely north of the equator, in the *Northern Hemisphere*. The great bulk of the country lies in what are known as the middle latitudes, neither very near the equator nor very close to the north pole. Exceptions are northern Alaska, which extends above the Arctic Circle, and Hawaii, which is in the tropics and relatively close to the equator. The closer a place is to the equator, the more directly the sun's rays strike it and, therefore, the more its surface is heated.

★ Altitude, the distance above sea level or the ocean floor, also affects climate, since high altitudes are colder than low altitudes. You can observe this as you travel from the bottom to the top of a tall mountain. Even if you are sweltering in extreme heat at the start of the trip, you may feel downright chilled when you reach the top. At the highest altitudes, even close to the equator, snow may stay on the ground throughout the year.

★ A third influence on climate is the direction of *prevailing winds*— the normal direction from which high-altitude winds blow. High-altitude winds carry weather systems around the globe, bringing a succession of storms and fair weather. In the middle latitudes, the prevailing winds blow from west to east, so storms generally cross the United States from the Pacific to the Atlantic.

★ Landforms such as mountains interact with the prevailing winds to help determine climate. As storm systems gain altitude to cross over mountains or other high places, they generally release their moisture. (Moisture in air condenses, or turns from gas to liquid, as the air rises and cools.) Since U.S. storms typically move from west to east, the western sides of mountains receive the rain or snow, while the eastern sides can remain very dry. The driest areas in the United States lie east of the high mountain ranges in the West.

★ Seacoasts are also landforms that influence climate. Generally, the closer to an ocean a place is the more rain or snow it will receive. Heavy rains are common near the Pacific and Atlantic coasts.

  Oceans and lakes have a moderating effect on temperature. Such large bodies of water lose or gain heat only slowly, so they hold their heat into early winter and remain cool even in early summer. That is why people cool off in summer by going to the shore.

★ Oceans are not static; they have moving currents that circulate their water from one area to another. The *Gulf Stream*, an important feature of the Atlantic Ocean, carries warm waters from the Gulf of Mexico north along the east coast of the United States and then eastward toward northern Europe. The Gulf Stream keeps the eastern United States and much of Europe warmer than most other places at the same latitudes.

Ocean currents in the Pacific also affect U.S. climate. The waters of the tropical Pacific are periodically warm or cool. When the waters are warm, a condition known as *El Niño* contributes to strong storms and bitterly cold winters in the United States. When the waters of the tropical Pacific are cool, another condition, known as *La Niña*, tends to bring warm winters to the nation's Southwest, cool winters to the northern central regions, and mild winters to the East.

Temperature Variations Temperatures in the United States vary widely from day to day and season to season. The *growing season* is the period between the last frost of spring and the first frost of autumn. Because most parts of the United States have reasonably long growing seasons, farmers can raise a wide variety of crops.

Temperatures also influence the kinds of homes people live in. In cold regions such as Alaska and New England, dwellings need to be well insulated to hold heat in and keep cold out. In hot places such as Arizona, many traditional homes have thick walls of adobe (mud brick) to keep rooms cool during the summer heat.

Moisture Variations The amount of moisture that falls on an area helps to determine what kinds of crops can be grown there. Rain, snow, sleet, and hail are all forms of *precipitation*. Snow, sleet, and hail are melted before being measured; typically, ten inches of snow melts down to about one inch of precipitation.

Ocean Currents Affecting the United States

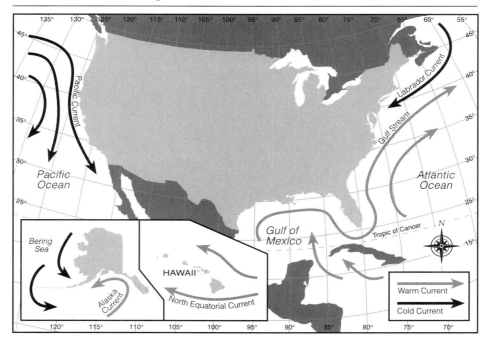

Key Climate Regions The United States has ten major climate regions, each with its own distinct features:

★ The north coast of Alaska along the Arctic Ocean has an *arctic climate*. Winters are long, dark, and cold, and the summers last only a few weeks. The temperature barely rises above freezing during a few months of the year. The region is treeless.

★ From its western coast to its interior, Alaska has a *subarctic climate*. The long, dark winters are less cold than in the arctic region. The summers, though short, are warm, and their long hours of daylight allow many types of crops to grow to maturity. (Alaska owes its long winter nights and long summer days to its high latitudes.)

★ From southern Alaska to northern California, a *marine West Coast climate* prevails. Winds blowing inland from the Pacific help to keep temperatures cool in summer and mild in winter. Annual rainfall is relatively high (40 to 80 inches or more) and comes mainly in late fall, winter, and early spring (October to May).

★ A good portion of California, including all but the northern coast and much of the interior lowlands, has a *Mediterranean climate*. This area has hot, dry summers and cool, rainy winters—conditions that are also

Ten Major Climate Regions of the United States

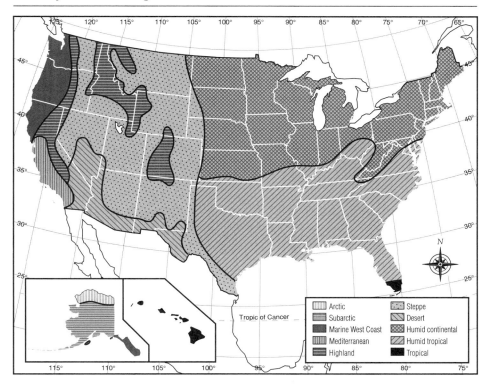

typical of lands bordering the Mediterranean Sea. The growing season lasts almost all year. Because the summers are dry, farmers often use *irrigation* (supplying water to crops by artificial means).

★ The interior mountain ranges of the western states (New Mexico, Arizona, Nevada, Utah, Colorado, Wyoming, Idaho, and parts of California, Oregon, and Washington) have a *highland climate*. It is characterized by cool to cold temperatures, depending on mountain altitudes, and much more moisture than the surrounding lowlands. (As mentioned earlier, mountains draw down moisture from passing weather systems.)

★ The western Great Plains and the lowlands between the mountains of the West generally have a *steppe climate*, with lots of sunshine and not much rain. (A steppe is an area that receives less than 20 inches of precipitation a year—enough to support grass but not enough to support trees.)

★ Most of the lowlands of the Southwest have a *desert climate*, even drier than the steppes. Here only scanty scrub vegetation can grow.

★ The northeastern quarter of the continental United States, from the edge of the Great Plains to the Atlantic, has a *humid continental climate*. "Humid" means moist, and annual rainfall in much of the region exceeds 40 inches, tapering off to around 20 inches in the western Great Plains. In this region, seasons are quite distinct; summers range from short and cool to long and hot, and winters from bitterly cold to mild. Such a climate tends to be very good for farming.

★ The southeastern United States, as far inland as Texas and Oklahoma, generally has a *humid subtropical climate*. Summers are hot, with frequent thunderstorms, while winters are mild, with frequent rain and occasional snow. The growing season is longer than farther north, and rainfall averages from about 30 to 80 inches a year.

★ The tip of Florida, the Florida Keys, and Hawaii all have a mild *tropical climate*. Because of Hawaii's location in the lower northern latitudes, prevailing winds, known in the tropics as *trade winds*, come from the northeast. Blowing off the Pacific Ocean, they help keep the islands' temperatures mild, averaging from 72 degrees Fahrenheit in the coolest month (February) to 79 degrees in the warmest month (August). Tropical Florida is usually a bit hotter in the summer.

Natural Vegetation Zones

Latitude, altitude, landforms, and climate combine to influence the natural vegetation that a place supports.

What Are Natural Vegetation Zones? "Natural vegetation" means the plants that would grow in an area even if humans did nothing. *Natural vegetation* *zones* are bands of territory in which climate and other natural conditions produce certain characteristic mixtures or communities of plants.

Major U.S. Natural Vegetation Zones Alaska and the 48 contiguous United States have eight major natural vegetation zones:

★ The *tundra zone* is a bleak, dry lowland stretching inland from Alaska's coasts. It has very low temperatures, little precipitation, and a short growing season. Typical plants are mosses, lichens, and a few stunted trees. In much of the zone, the summer sun melts only the uppermost part of the soil, leaving a frozen layer called *permafrost* underneath.

★ The *coniferous forest zone* stretches south from inland Alaska through western Washington and Oregon to northern California and also includes northern Minnesota, Wisconsin, and Michigan. In a coniferous forest, the dominant trees are evergreens bearing their seeds in cones.

★ The *broadleaf forest zone* reaches from the central Midwest to the southern Appalachians and into the Mid-Atlantic states. Its dominant trees are oaks, maples, and other *deciduous trees* (those that lose their leaves seasonally), with flat, broad leaves.

Eight U.S. Vegetation Zones

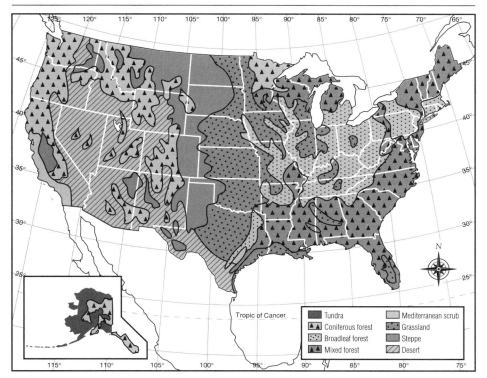

★ The *mixed forest zone* comprises coniferous and broadleaf trees and covers much of the northern and eastern United States. One band stretches through the upper parts of several states along the Great Lakes. Another band reaches from Maine through New England to the northern Appalachians. A third band crosses a series of southern states from Virginia to eastern Texas.

★ The *Mediterranean scrub zone* includes California's coastal terrain from the San Francisco region southward and the lowland interiors to the east. Here, hot dry summers and wet winters limit vegetation to low-growing shrubs and small trees.

★ The *grassland zone* covers most of the Great Plains. With relatively low rainfall (10 to 20 inches a year), this zone will not support forests. With water supplied by irrigation, however, it becomes an excellent territory for growing crops such as wheat.

★ The *steppe zone* occupies nonmountainous areas in northern New Mexico and western Colorado and parts of Utah, Nevada, Oregon, Washington, Idaho, Montana, and Wyoming.

★ The *desert zone* lies in a broad band from northern Nevada to the southwestern corner of Texas. This area includes much of the Basin and Range region described on page 6.

Conditions on the Hawaiian islands create two additional zones that occur nowhere else in the United States. A *tropical rain forest zone* predominates in the mountains, where year-round warmth and plentiful rain sustain many kinds of trees. Among them are extremely tall varieties that create a canopy over the dark, thick undergrowth. Neighboring lowlands experience several short dry seasons every year, which create a *tropical grassland zone*. This environment is characterized by scrubby shrubs and scattered trees.

Agriculture and Industry

Thousands of years ago, humans moved into what is now the United States and began to put their own imprint on the land and its vegetation. As early as 2000 B.C., Native Americans may have planted corn in what is now part of Arizona and New Mexico. That development marked the start in what is the present-day United States of *agriculture*, the raising of crops and livestock for human purposes. As agriculture spread over the centuries, natural vegetation was supplemented by new plant varieties developed through human experimentation and selection. In addition, people from outside the region introduced entirely new species of plants, a process that sharply accelerated after Europeans arrived in the 15th century.

Nature + Culture + Technology Many types of agriculture are practiced in the United States today. Like natural vegetation, agriculture depends on natural factors—latitude, altitude, landforms, climate. But agriculture also depends on culture and technology:

★ Culture: What kinds of food do people like to eat? (Do they want mainly grains? Do they raise animals for meat? For milk?)

★ Technology: What tools do they use to grow crops? (Simple wooden digging tools? Horse-drawn plows? Giant tractors?)

★ Culture *and* technology: What crops do they use for purposes other than food? (Do they raise cotton to make into cloth, or grain to blend into gasohol?)

Over the centuries, the answers to those questions have changed, and so has the distribution of agriculture within the United States.

Culture and technology also interact with nature in determining what kinds of industries are found in an area. Many industries depend on mineral or energy resources and tend to be located near necessary raw materials. Other industries use agricultural products (wheat for making bread or tobacco for cigarettes) and tend to be located where such products are grown or stored.

Other factors also affect both agriculture and industry:

★ Can products find buyers nearby? Over time, many cities have grown up, filled with consumers for the products of farms and industries.

★ How will the finished products be transported? Do oceans, rivers, railroads, or highways make transportation relatively easy? If so, an industry may choose a location closer to buyers than to raw materials.

U.S. Agriculture and Industry by Region The United States can be divided into seven main regions with their own typical blends of agriculture and industry:

★ *New England*, comprising Vermont, New Hampshire, Maine, Massachusetts, Connecticut, and Rhode Island, has lots of ups and downs—valleys and hillsides, as well as mountains. Because of the varied terrain, farms tend to be smaller than elsewhere. Much of the farmland is devoted to hay and pasture for dairy cattle. Specialized crops include potatoes in northern Maine, cigar tobacco in Connecticut, and cranberries on Cape Cod in Massachusetts. Orchards grow apples, cherries, and pears. Forested areas produce maple syrup.

With easy access to ocean transport, New England tapped into world trade early on. In the early 19th century, it became the first U.S. center of manufacturing. Shipbuilding, shoemaking, and textiles were among the pathbreaking industries. Early textile factories were often built along rivers and used the power of falling water to run their machinery. Later on, other industries developed—firearms, precision tools, aircraft engines, and, recently, computers and other high-tech products. Today, New England is also home to such service industries as banking and insurance. And it still has a large fishing industry.

Boston, the largest city in New England, has dominated the region since colonial times. Hartford, Connecticut, is a center of the insurance industry.

★ The *Mid-Atlantic region* comprises New York, New Jersey, Pennsylvania, Delaware, and Maryland. Those five states have fairly large areas of level land but also many mountains and valleys. Helped by a longer growing season than in New England, Mid-Atlantic farmers can raise more varied crops. Some farms specialize in dairy products, poultry, or fruit, while others produce green beans, tomatoes, and onions.

Like New England, the Mid-Atlantic region began to industrialize early. Large rivers such as the Hudson, Delaware, and Susquehanna served as avenues of transportation. During the 19th century, canals and then railroads improved the transportation mix. Coal and iron resources in Pennsylvania provided the basis for such key industries as steelmaking. Ocean ports such as New York and Baltimore gave the region ready access to imported raw materials, and oil refineries and chemical industries soon developed. Today, the region is one of the most industrialized in the nation. Its industries range from manufacturing to banking to advertising to publishing.

Among the other important cities of the region are Philadelphia and Pittsburgh (in Pennsylvania) and the nation's capital, Washington, D.C.

★ The *South* is an immense region comprising 14 states—Virginia, West Virginia, North Carolina, South Carolina, Georgia, Florida, Alabama, Mississippi, Louisiana, Texas, Oklahoma, Arkansas, Kentucky, and Tennessee. All by itself, Texas is larger than New England and the Mid-Atlantic region combined.

With generally high rainfall (tapering off to the west) and hot summers, the modern South grows a great variety of crops. At one time, cotton was "king," and its cultivation was based on slave labor. With slavery long gone, crop preferences have shifted, although cotton planting remains important from the Mississippi valley westward. Farmers grow such grains and other crops as corn, soybeans, peanuts, watermelons, tobacco, pecans, and citrus fruits. Rice and sugarcane are also southern crops.

Only lightly industrialized at the time of the Civil War (1861–1865), the South has since developed a strong industrial base. Oil and natural gas deposits in Texas, Oklahoma, and Louisiana have helped the region become a center of refining, petrochemicals, and plastics. Southern industries also include textiles (originally based on cotton but now using artificial fibers, too), papermaking (based on the region's large softwood forests), fishing, and fish processing. The areas around Birmingham, Alabama, and Wheeling, West Virginia, are major centers of iron and steel production.

Urban areas of the South include Richmond, Virginia; Charleston, South Carolina; Miami, Florida; Atlanta, Georgia; New Orleans, Louisiana; Houston and Dallas, Texas; Memphis, Tennessee; and Louisville, Kentucky.

★ The *Midwest* is a relatively flat expanse of 12 states—Ohio, Indiana, Illinois, Michigan, Wisconsin, Minnesota, North Dakota, South Dakota, Nebraska, Iowa, Kansas, and Missouri.

On these flatlands, farms may sprawl over hundreds of acres. Much of the nation's corn grows in the "corn belt" from Ohio to Nebraska, with numerous feedlots for the corn-feeding of pigs and cattle that are later slaughtered and processed into meat. Farther west, on the drier Great Plains, wheat is the leading crop—hard wheat for breads and pastas, soft wheat for cakes and cookies. The farms of the Midwest also produce soybeans and dairy products. The "dairy belt" of Wisconsin and Minnesota makes much of the nation's cheese, butter, and evaporated milk.

Like the Mid-Atlantic states, the Midwest has long been a center of heavy industry. By tapping the extensive deposits of iron near the Great Lakes, the area developed iron and steel mills and a variety of manufacturing plants. Detroit, Michigan, became the center of the U.S. auto industry. Factories in the Midwest also produce farm equipment, machine tools, computers, and many other products.

Chicago, the region's largest city, is a major center of manufacturing and finance, as well as a transportation hub where railroads, air routes, and highways converge.

Other key cities include St. Louis, Missouri; Minneapolis, Minnesota; Omaha, Nebraska; and Kansas City, Missouri.

★ The *West* covers a lot of ground and many landforms and climates. Its 11 states are Washington, Oregon, California, Nevada, Arizona, New Mexico, Utah, Colorado, Wyoming, Idaho, and Montana.

Except along the Pacific coast, much of the region is fairly dry, and farmers often depend on irrigation. On the western Great Plains, crops such as wheat, sugar beets, beans, and alfalfa predominate. In the basins and plateaus between mountain ranges, crops range from wheat and cantaloupes to potatoes (an Idaho specialty) and cotton. California farmers grow much of the nation's vegetables, as well as nuts, grapes, oranges, strawberries, cotton, rice, and sugar beets. In Oregon and Washington, apples and cherries are a big part of the crop mix.

A rich resource base gives the West many opportunities for industry. Mining is widespread, although the gold rushes of the 19th century are long past. Today's miners operate immense open-pit coal mines and use up-to-date machinery to extract copper, uranium, molybdenum, petroleum, and other minerals from numerous sites. Some industries are devoted to making equipment for the mining and oil industries. Others manufacture aircraft, ships, and consumer goods.

The West has a number of major cities. Los Angeles is a vast, sprawling place that includes Hollywood, the center of the nation's motion picture industry. Farther north in California, the region around San Francisco and San Jose includes "Silicon Valley," where high-tech industries specialize in turning out microchips, software, and other computer-related products. Seattle, Denver, and Phoenix also have concentrations of high-tech industries.

★ *Alaska* is off by itself in the far north. Despite the long winters and cool summers, farmers there raise various fruits and vegetables. Alaska also has dairy farms.

Logging and fishing are major industries, and so is gold mining. Since the 1960s, Alaska has developed an important oil industry based on petroleum deposits at Prudhoe Bay in the far north. A pipeline carries the oil across Alaska to Valdez, where it is loaded on ships and taken to refineries in California and elsewhere.

Alaska's largest city, Anchorage, has only about 250,000 inhabitants.

★ *Hawaii* lies even farther afield, in the mid-Pacific at roughly the latitude of central Mexico. For decades, Hawaii was a major producer of sugarcane and pineapples. Its plantations drew large numbers of workers from China, Japan, and the Philippines, and their descendants (along with native Polynesians and people from the U.S. mainland) became part of a rich mixture of races in Hawaii. Today, Hawaiian sugar and pineapple producers are challenged by world competition, and farmers are converting to new crops such as peanuts.

Taking advantage of its warm climate and extensive coastline, Hawaii has developed an important tourist industry. It also has factories that process sugar and pineapples and manufacture clothing and other consumer products.

The main city is Honolulu, the capital.

★ Review

1. What are six major factors that help determine a place's climate?
2. Name the country's eight main natural vegetation zones, and tell how they relate to climate.
3. In what region or regions of the United States would you be likely to find each of the following: (a) uranium mines, (b) the center of the U.S. auto industry, (c) pineapple plantations, (d) sugarcane, (e) the "corn belt," (f) a heavy dependence on irrigation, (g) the "dairy belt"?

★ UNIT 1 ★

The Constitutional Foundations of American Society

Chapter 1
Origins of the Constitution

★ Objectives

- ★ To explain the influence of 17th- and 18th-century Enlightenment thought on American political rights and institutions.
- ★ To describe the experiences of the various ethnic groups who populated the American colonies.
- ★ To explain the British-American conflict leading to the American Revolution.
- ★ To evaluate the importance of the Declaration of Independence.
- ★ To describe the strengths and weaknesses of the Articles of Confederation.

In the revolutionary year 1776, a young Virginian named Thomas Jefferson wrote: "We hold these truths to be self-evident: That all men are created equal. . . ."

These words are included in a document that declared the independent existence of a new nation, the United States of America. The government of this nation was unique because it was founded on the ideal of equal rights for all citizens. In practice, large numbers of Americans—especially women and people of African descent—did not enjoy the rights granted to white males. But the ideal of equal rights was never abandoned, and eventually those who believed in it changed the U.S. government to make it conform more closely to Jefferson's phrase, "all men are created equal."

This chapter will explain the revolutionary ideas contained in the Declaration of Independence (1776), and the major principles of the Articles of Confederation (1781). First, it will explain how and when these ideas originated.

Historical Foundations of Representative Government

Throughout world history, governments controlled by monarchs (kings, queens, and other hereditary rulers) have been far more common than governments ruled by elected representatives of the people. The origins of *representative government* in the United States were greatly influenced by philosophers of the Enlightenment as well as by events in England and colonial America.

17th- and 18th-Century Enlightenment Thought

European Philosophers In the 1700s, leading thinkers of Western Europe looked to the future with optimism. They thought that the future could be shaped and directed by reason. They believed that society was based on natural laws. As a result, they challenged the power of absolute monarchs and the idea that a monarch ruled by divine right. Historians have labeled this period the *Age of Enlightenment*.

In Great Britain, John Locke (1632–1704) was a leading Enlightenment figure. This English philosopher is best known for his work *Two Treatises of Government* (1690). Locke wrote that life, liberty, and property were *natural rights*, rights with which all persons are born. He stated that people gave up total freedom in return for protection from a ruler. Thus, it was the ruler's responsibility to protect the natural rights of the people. If a ruler failed to carry out this responsibility, the people have the right to overthrow the government.

Baron Montesquieu (1689–1755) was a French philosopher who is best remembered for his monumental work, *The Spirit of the Laws* (1748). He wrote that the ideal government should be separated into three branches. The legislative branch would pass the laws; the executive branch would carry out the laws; and the judicial branch would interpret the laws. The purpose of this separation was to prevent any one individual or group from becoming too powerful and thereby gaining total control of the government. Montesquieu's ideas became the basis for the separation of powers clauses in the U.S. Constitution.

Voltaire (1694–1778) was a French author and probably the most influential Enlightenment figure. Like Montesquieu, he was a great admirer of the English system of government. He wrote essays, plays, and letters that attacked injustices by the French monarchy. He condemned abusive power, class privilege, torture, slavery, censorship, and religious intolerance. Voltaire argued that the best form of government was a monarchy that had a constitution, a strong parliament, and civil rights for all.

Jean-Jacques Rousseau (1712–1778) was a Swiss writer who lived most of his life in France. In his most famous book, *The Social Contract*, he rejected the way that society was then governed. Rousseau proposed a different way of governing—one in which the will of the people would guide the decisions of the government. He wrote that people are born good but are corrupted by society: "Man is born free, and everywhere he is in chains."

The writers of the Enlightenment had a major impact on America. Their ideas formed the intellectual basis for the American Revolution. For example, Locke's ideas on natural rights and the right to overthrow one's government influenced American revolutionary leader Thomas Jefferson. Locke had written, "Man has the right to defend his life, liberty, and property against those who would take it away." Later, in the Declaration of Independence, Jefferson would write that all people had a right to "life, liberty, and the pursuit of happiness."

Key English Events Limiting Government   In 1215 a group of rebellious nobles compelled England's King John to agree to the terms of the *Magna Carta*. Among the rights guaranteed in this celebrated document were (a) the right to be tried by a jury of average citizens and (b) the right of the Great Council (a group of nobles) to approve the monarch's proposed taxes.

In later years, beginning in 1295, English kings periodically called upon representatives of both the English nobility and the middle class to meet as a *Parliament* (or advisory group) to consider laws and taxes. Over time, the Parliament acquired more power and became an established part of the English political system. For example, in 1679, Parliament passed the Habeas Corpus Act, which protected people from being thrown into jail without a valid reason. The act required that a jailed person be brought into court so that a judge could decide whether the person was being lawfully detained. If not, the judge could order the prisoner's release.

Another major step limiting the power of government was the *Glorious Revolution*. In 1688 Parliament forced King James II to give up the throne.

This revolt led to the drafting of the English Bill of Rights in 1689. The bill guaranteed a number of basic liberties, including the right to a speedy jury trial and protection against excessive bails and fines. Most important, the consent of Parliament was required for collecting taxes, suspending laws, and maintaining an army.

The People of the American Colonies

Native Americans

The United States has been called "a nation of immigrants" because all its citizens have ancestors who once emigrated from another land. The Native Americans are the descendants of an Asiatic people who probably migrated from Siberia to North America between 20,000 to 40,000 years ago.

The first contacts between Native Americans and Europeans occurred mainly in the Spanish colonies of Latin America during and after the voyages of Columbus in the 1490s. As a result of these voyages, Spain gained control over much of the land that had been controlled by Native American empires. In these colonies, the Native American people were forced to do heavy manual labor for landowners and missionaries as well as work in Spanish gold mines. The population declined rapidly as a result of deaths from (1) European diseases such as smallpox, and (2) harsh treatment by the conquerors.

In the British colonies of North America, the first contacts between the colonists and the Native Americans occurred in Jamestown, Virginia, in the early 1600s. Although relations were tense from the start, the colonists did receive needed corn from the Native Americans, which barely enabled them to survive. In the winter of 1609–1610, however, most of the colonists died of starvation. Conditions for the colonists began to improve after one of their leaders, John Rolfe, discovered that tobacco could be grown in the colony. This crop became a major export of Virginia in the years to come. John Rolfe also married the Native American princess Pocahontas. However, as the colonists expanded their settlements and intruded upon Native Americans' lands, warfare resulted.

Conflicts between colonists and Native Americans were also common in other parts of British North America. In New England, the Pilgrims were assisted by Squanto, a Native American who had some knowledge of English. Despite such assistance, the English colonists looked upon his people as uncivilized. Due in large measure to the deaths of many Native Americans from smallpox, the colonists were able to expand without much opposition. Those who did attempt to resist English expansion were defeated.

A notable exception in the relationship between the Native Americans and colonists occurred in Pennsylvania, which was settled mainly by Quakers. The Quakers were a religious group who believed in peaceful relations with all peoples. William Penn, who founded the Pennsylvania colony, pursued a policy of living peaceably with the Native Americans who inhabited the region. The relationship worked so well that many Native Americans who were forced from other colonies migrated to Pennsylvania.

Between 1756 and 1763, Great Britain and France fought for control of North America in the French and Indian War. In this war, both countries created alliances with the Native Americans. The British were allied with the Iroquois nation, while the French were allied with the Huron. As a result of this war, the British emerged victorious and gained control of much of North America, including Canada.

Africans

The Slave Trade A large number of African people were shipped to the British colonies against their will. They were captured in wars between West African kingdoms, sold to European slave traders, and forced to endure a frightening voyage across unknown waters to an unknown destination. African slaves labored in Spanish America as early as the 1500s, where they replaced the Native Americans who had died from disease and overwork. The slave trade to the British colonies in North America represented about 6 percent of the total number of slaves shipped to South America, Central America, the Caribbean, and North America.

The Global Slave Trade in the 1700s

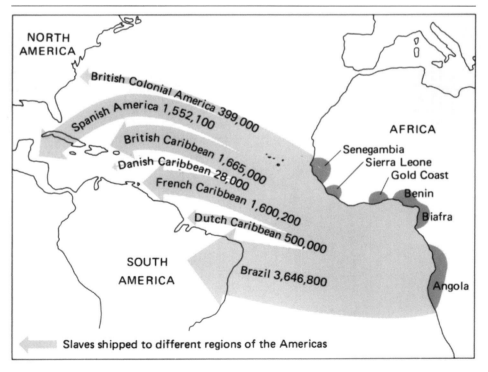

Slaves shipped to different regions of the Americas

For the Africans, the *middle passage*, the time spent aboard ships between West Africa and the Americas, was a horrendous journey. Most slaves on board the ships were given small food rations. Those who were sick or weak were often left to die. Ships were packed with as many slaves as possible, leaving little room to move about. Slaves (particularly men) were bound in chains. Disease spread rapidly. As a result, some Africans threw themselves overboard rather than face these inhumane conditions. An estimated 10 million to 11 million Africans were sold into slavery throughout all of the Americas.

Immigrants to the British Colonies

A majority of those who immigrated to the British colonies from 1607 to 1776 came from the British Isles: England, Scotland, Wales, and Northern Ireland. Some immigrated for religious reasons. The Puritans, for example, were persecuted because they demanded reforms in the Church of England. Many Puritans settled in the Massachusetts Bay Colony. The Quakers who settled in Pennsylvania under the leadership of William Penn sought religious freedom. Other immigrants were unemployed city dwellers and debtors who hoped to find economic opportunities in the American colonies. For example, under the leadership of James Oglethorpe, Georgia was settled by criminals, debtors, and the poor. Some immigrants came as *indentured servants*. These were people who agreed to work for a number of years (usually seven) in return for the payment of their passage to America.

A large number of immigrants to the British colonies did not speak English when they arrived. The Europeans among them came chiefly from France, Germany, Holland, and Sweden. (See the graph below.) Their reasons for emigrating were similar to those of the English and Scottish. They

Ethnic Groups in the U.S., in 1790

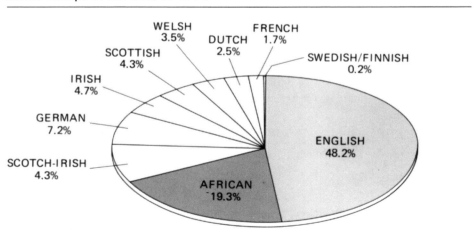

wanted to escape from religious intolerance and sought opportunities to own land on the frontier.

Immigrants in the early colonial period endured many difficulties. In Plymouth and the Massachusetts Bay Colony, early settlers learned how to survive from the Native Americans. The immigrants were separated from family, friends, and familiar surroundings. Those who were city dwellers had to learn how to farm the land. Disease was always a threat in the colonial communities, as were attacks from Native Americans. Supplies often had to be obtained from England and sent on the long journey to the colonies.

★ In Review

1. How did the ideas of the Enlightenment influence the development of the American nation?
2. Describe three important events in British history that limited the power of government.
3. Contrast the experiences of Native Americans, African Americans, and European Americans during the colonial period.

The Colonial Experience

Colonial Charters and Self-Government

The settlers in England's American colonies brought with them their country's tradition of representative government. In 1619 the settlers of Jamestown in Virginia founded the *House of Burgesses*, America's first representative assembly for making laws. In the following years, English Pilgrims aboard the *Mayflower* agreed that the laws for their colony at Plymouth in Massachusetts would be subject to the colonists' approval and consent. The document presenting their agreement is known as the *Mayflower Compact*. As a result of this Compact, citizens in many New England towns met regularly to discuss problems and vote directly on laws. These *town meetings* were an important element in the development of our democratic heritage.

During the next 150 years, English colonies were founded from New Hampshire in the north to Georgia in the south. The laws of each colony were made, in part, by a popularly elected assembly. The colonial governors, who were appointed by the king, were often successfully opposed by the assemblies. By 1760 it was generally conceded that the colonial assemblies controlled the vital *power of the purse*—the power either to approve or reject a proposal for a new tax.

Despite the power of the elected assemblies, none of the English colonies was fully democratic. After all, only a minority of the people

Ben Franklin's 1750s cartoon advocated colonial union.

owned property or were permitted to vote for representatives. Prohibited from voting were all women, all slaves, and the many white males who owned no property. Even so, considering that all white male property owners could vote, the basis for a future democracy was well established during colonial times.

In 1754, representatives from England, seven of the British colonies in America, and the Iroquois nation met in Albany to discuss a common plan of defense against France. At that meeting, Benjamin Franklin, the representative from Pennsylvania, proposed a plan to bring representatives from the colonies together in a council led by a British representative of the Crown (the king). This plan, based on the governing model of the Iroquois, failed to win support from either the colonial assemblies or the Crown. This *Albany Plan of Union* represented an early attempt to unite the British colonies in America.

The early colonists believed in both property rights and enforceable contracts. Thus, land was privately owned and purchased through legally binding contracts. Indentured servants were expected to serve their full terms. Certain businesses were given exclusive rights by the British Crown to trade in specific areas in the colonies. These businesses were *joint-stock companies*, in which individuals would invest their money in hopes of making a profit. For example, the Virginia Company provided supplies and additional settlers for the colony of Virginia. The colonies were also expected to produce only what England needed and to buy everything that they needed from England. This trade policy is known as *mercantilism*. However, England did not enforce the policy until the 1760s.

Native American Governmental Systems

Most Native American governmental systems consisted of loose confederations of villages or tribal clans. At first, the Native Americans were loyal to their village or clan. However, as time went on, villages joined together and formed tribal councils to better defend themselves. This led to increased loyalty to the confederacy or tribe rather than to the village. With a concern for defense, warriors became the most important group within the tribe. A Native American tribal unit could include a few hundred to many thousands of people. In the colony of New York, long before the American Revolution, the six nations of the Iroquois had formed a *confederate system* for cooperating for their mutual benefit. Their form of government was known as the *Haudenosaunee* political system. Colonial leaders knew about system, and it may have influenced the confederate plan of government adopted in 1781 by those who wrote the Articles of Confederation (see page 42).

Colonial Slavery

Slavery in the British North American colonies began with the first transfer of Africans in 1619 to the Jamestown colony in Virginia. Through the 1600s and 1700s, the slave trade continued to grow. By the time of the American Revolution, slaves in the original 13 states numbered between 750,000 and 850,000 and formed about 20 percent of the population. Thus, in George Washington's time, one American in five was of African ancestry.

Slavery in the United States first developed in what was known as Chesapeake, an area that included both Virginia and Maryland. The region's major crop was tobacco, which had become very popular in England and Europe. As a result, slavery grew as the demand for tobacco grew. This production of tobacco, based on a slave system, enabled Maryland and Virginia to become the leading states of the South. It was no accident that, when the British colonies became an independent nation, four of the first six presidents of the United States came from Virginia.

South Carolina and Georgia built a slave society based on producing and exporting rice. As rice exports to Europe grew from approximately 15,000 pounds in 1700 to 80 million pounds in the 1770s, both South Carolina and Georgia significantly increased their reliance on slave labor. Georgia, which had originally banned slavery, reversed itself in the mid-1700s. As rice production soared, the city of Charleston, South Carolina, became one of the most populous cities in the British colonies.

Slavery also developed in the lower Mississippi valley in the French territory of Louisiana. There, slaves were used in the production of both tobacco and rice. In the later colonial period, sugar also became a major crop. In Louisiana, slaves were employed not only in agriculture but also as skilled craftsworkers and domestic servants. This was especially true in the city of New Orleans, the main trading center on the Mississippi River. Many products that could not be sent overland were first shipped down the Mississippi River and then loaded on larger ships destined for major ports on the Atlantic coast. Thus, in North America, slavery developed in French as well as British territory.

Slavery in the northern British colonies developed on a much smaller scale than southern slavery since there were fewer large farms and plantations in the North. The large farms that did exist often employed slaves in

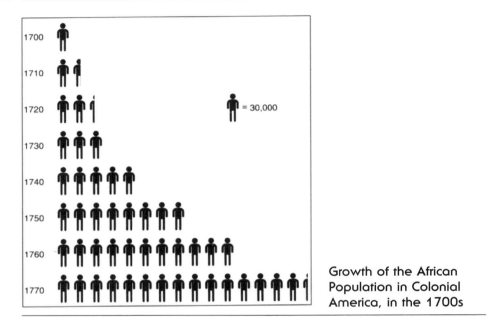

Growth of the African Population in Colonial America, in the 1700s

the production of wheat. Some large plantations in the North were "provisioning plantations" which produced food and lumber destined for sugar plantations in the West Indies. As a result, ships regularly sailed to the West Indies with meat, wheat, barrels, and lumber, and returned with molasses to make rum. Much of this rum was then shipped to Africa and traded for slaves who would be sent to the West Indies and the southern colonies.

In addition to working on the large wheat farms, slaves in the northern colonies also served as laborers and skilled artisans. However, the economics of slavery did not provide sufficient rewards for its use on small farms and in the towns. As a result, slavery never became the significant factor in the northern colonies that it was in the southern colonies.

The large number of slaves throughout the South helped to perpetuate African traditions and culture. Thus slave music with its "call and response" features was based on African music. Wood carvings and the use of folk medicines and charms were African in origin. Christianity would be intermingled with aspects of *animism*, which believes that spirits exist in natural objects such as trees, rocks, earth, and sky. Further, African names were often used for newborn children, although this practice declined as slavery passed from one generation to the next. Even in the northern colonies, with many fewer slaves, African cultural traditions were maintained. For example, the construction of slaves' houses was very similar to that of dwellings found in West Africa. In addition, pottery recently found at slave sites in the North is similar to the pottery found in the African nations of Nigeria and Ghana.

Most important was the contradiction between slavery and the emerging ideas of freedom and liberty in the colonial period. Slavery was a direct contradiction to the universal values expressed in the Declaration of Independence. During the Revolution, the English and their loyalist followers in America noted that those who would fight for their own freedom were willing to deny it to others. The British as well as some American revolutionaries promised freedom to those slaves willing to fight on their respective sides. As a consequence, some slaves were freed following the Revolutionary War. Between the end of the Revolution in 1781 and 1800, slavery was ended in the North. But, with the growing importance of cotton and the invention of the cotton gin in 1793, slavery expanded substantially in the South.

Freedom of the Press

Colonial political rights were expanded by a famous legal trial that became known as the *Zenger case*. John Peter Zenger was a printer who wrote an article criticizing the governor of New York. He was arrested and brought to trial in 1733. In his defense, he admitted that he was responsible for the article but argued that he had written the truth. The jury accepted his reasoning and declared him innocent of the charge of *libel* (writing a wrongfully unfavorable opinion of another person). The ruling established the principle of freedom of the press. This meant that the press had the right to be critical of the government. This freedom has withstood many challenges throughout American history and is an important part of the First Amendment to the Constitution.

Rights of English Citizens in America

For the most part, English citizens in America enjoyed the same basic rights as citizens in Great Britain. For example, prior to the French and Indian War, England allowed the colonies to govern themselves without much interference. Its colonial policy was one of *salutary neglect* (salutary meaning "beneficial"). For example, laws that required the colonies to trade only with England were not enforced, and taxes were not collected. Colonists also had the right to establish popular assemblies in the colonies, although they were not allowed to vote for representatives in the British Parliament.

The American Revolution

The British empire grew much larger as a result of the French and Indian War (1754–1763). Although Great Britain won the war and gained French Canada, its victory led almost immediately to growing conflict with its 13 American colonies. Eventually, the Americans' protests against British tax policies turned into full-scale revolution and war.

Causes of the Revolution

Change in British Policy of Governing and Settlement   After the French and Indian War, Great Britain, with an expanded empire to govern, decided to enforce its trade laws and station a permanent military force in the colonies. To stabilize the western frontier and prevent Native American rebellion, Britain in the *Proclamation of 1763* forbade the colonists from settling west of the Appalachian Mountains. The colonists were furious because they wished to settle west of the mountains. Even worse, from their point of view, was the *Quebec Act of 1774*, which set the southern boundary of the former French colony at the Ohio River. The American colonists had claimed lands in this area.

Resistance to British Taxes   The British Parliament and king also decided to tax the American colonies without the consent of their assemblies. The colonists protested vehemently against (1) a stamp tax (1765) on colonial newspapers and legal documents and (2) import taxes (1767) on shipments of British tea, glass, and other articles. Resistance to these taxes took the form of *boycotts* (refusal to buy British goods), riots (mob action against tax collectors), and dumping British tea into Boston Harbor (the *Boston Tea Party*).

The American Colonies, in 1763 and 1774

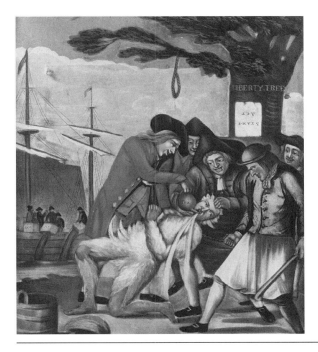

The American colonists took violent action against hated British taxes and tax collectors.

British Retaliation Acts of British retaliation angered the colonists further. Two events were especially alarming to Americans: (1) In the *Boston Massacre* (1770) British troops fired on a crowd of people, and five colonists were killed, including an African American, Crispus Attucks. Thus, a black colonist was one of the first Americans to die in what would grow into the American Revolution. (2) The *Coercive Acts* (1774) closed Boston to shipping as punishment for the Boston Tea Party, weakened the Massachusetts legislature, and nearly shut down Boston's economy. These acts and the *Quebec Act* were condemned as *"Intolerable Acts"* by the colonists.

Battles of Lexington and Concord The first shots of the American Revolution were exchanged in the Massachusetts towns of Lexington and Concord. On April 19, 1775, British troops marched into Lexington and fired upon a small band of armed Americans. Continuing to Concord, the British were driven back by farmers firing from behind trees and stone walls.

Revolutionary Ideology

Even after the bloody encounters at Lexington and Concord, most Americans thought of fighting the British only for the purpose of defending their rights. They rejected the idea of fighting for independence. But many changed their minds after reading "Common Sense," a pamphlet by Thomas Paine. Referring to tyrants as "royal brutes," Paine boldly set forth

The Boston Massacre, in 1770, engraved by Paul Revere

arguments for American independence. He wrote that it made no sense for a small island kingdom like Great Britain to rule over vastly larger American lands at such a great distance.

On two occasions, delegates from the different colonies met in Philadelphia to plan united action in defense of their rights. The *First Continental Congress* (1774) petitioned the British government to repeal its taxes and overturn other harsh measures. But the British made no concessions. The *Second Continental Congress* (1776) met after the British and Americans had clashed at Lexington and Concord and then at Bunker Hill outside Boston. On July 4, 1776, the congress announced its decision to declare the independence of a new nation, the United States.

Declaration of Independence   Congress's reasons for declaring independence were eloquently stated by Thomas Jefferson, the main author of the Declaration of Independence. His arguments were both general and specific. Drawing upon the theories of John Locke, the Declaration argues that governments must be (1) representative of the people and (2) limited in power by a recognition of basic human rights. Furthermore, when any government violates people's natural rights, then the people have the additional right to "alter or to abolish" that government.

A second section of the Declaration lists specific grievances against the British king in order to demonstrate that the colonists' rights were repeatedly violated. The grievances included: (1) dissolving colonial assemblies, (2) keeping British troops in the colonies, and (3) "imposing taxes without [the colonists'] consent."

The Battle of Lexington, in 1775—the opening of the Revolution

Continuing Importance of the Declaration The revolutionary ideas in the Declaration of Independence have had a profound effect on world history. Inspired by its principles of equal rights and popular consent, people in many nations have used the Declaration to justify their own struggles for independence against oppressive governments. In the United States, the Declaration served as an important document in the fight to end slavery, since it states that all men are created equal.

Revolutionary Leaders

The American Revolution could not have succeeded without the leadership of an extraordinary group of Americans. For example, Benjamin Franklin was a leading figure who developed the 1754 Albany Plan of Union, assisted in the writing of the Declaration of Independence, and represented the *Continental Congress* (the governing body for the American revolutionaries) in France during the Revolutionary War. Highly respected for his scientific achievements, he was a firm believer in a republican form of government. (A *republic* is a form of government in which the citizens elect the persons who run the government.)

George Washington served as the commander of the revolutionary army. His leadership during the war was critical to the revolution's success. Washington was known as the "soul and sword" of the American Revolution. He later became the first president of the United States and served for two terms.

Samuel Adams was another influential leader during the revolutionary period. He led the resistance to British taxes by organizing a boycott of

★ ★ ★ ★ ★

THE DECLARATION OF INDEPENDENCE

This excerpt from the 1776 document that gave birth to the United States argues that, under certain circumstances, people have a right to rebel against an established government.

We hold these truths to be self-evident: That all men are created equal; that they are endowed by their Creator with certain unalienable rights; that among these are life, liberty, and the pursuit of happiness. That to secure these rights, governments are instituted among men, deriving their just powers from the consent of the governed.

That whenever any form of government becomes destructive of these ends, it is the right of the people to alter or to abolish it, and to institute new government, laying its foundation on such principles and organizing its powers in such form as to them shall seem most likely to effect their safety and happiness. Prudence, indeed, will dictate that governments long established should not be changed for light and transient causes; and, accordingly, all experience hath shown that mankind are more disposed to suffer, while evils are sufferable, than to right themselves by abolishing the forms to which they are accustomed. But when a long train of abuses and usurpations, pursuing invariably the same object, evinces a design to reduce them under absolute despotism, it is their right, it is their duty, to throw off such government, and to provide new guards for their future security.

British goods. He then organized a *Committee of Correspondence* to make it easier for colonists in Massachusetts to communicate their opinions and activities with one another. Adams also served as a delegate from Massachusetts to the Second Continental Congress.

John Adams, later to become the second president of the United States, played a major role in opposing British actions in the colonies. As one of the delegates to the First Continental Congress in 1774, he argued strongly against Britain's right to tax the colonies. Together with Thomas Jefferson, Adams would later serve on the committee that wrote the Declaration of Independence.

Patrick Henry served as a delegate from Virginia to both the First and Second Continental Congresses. An eloquent speaker, Henry vigorously urged independence from Britain and defended individual freedom by proclaiming "Give me liberty, or give me death!" His words helped to sway many colonists in favor of revolution.

★ Actions and Reactions ★
(events leading to revolution)

British Action	Colonial Reaction	British Response
1. Attempt to collect stamp tax (1765)	Riots and protests; tax collectors "tarred and feathered"	Repeal of stamp tax (1766)
2. Attempt to collect import taxes on paint, lead, tea (1767)	Boycotts, riots, increased anger	British troops sent to Massachusetts
3. Arrival of British troops (1768)	More protests; citizens killed in Boston Massacre (1770)	Import taxes repealed, except for a reduced tax on tea
4. Tea Act (1773)	Destruction of British tea in Boston Tea Party (1773)	Decision to punish Boston by harsh measures
5. "Coercive Acts" close Boston Harbor (1774)	Meeting of First Continental Congress in Philadelphia to protest British acts (1774)	Orders to arrest resistance leaders
6. British march on Lexington and Concord to confiscate colonists' supply of gunpowder (April 1775)	Militia ("Minutemen") warned of British march by Paul Revere and William Dawes	Shots exchanged, military conflict; British retreat to Boston
7. British troops in Boston prepare for war	Meeting of Second Continental Congress (1776)	British reinforcements sent to Boston
8. British reject colonists' petition for recognition of their rights, King George III hires German (Hessian) troops	Thomas Paine publishes "Common Sense"; Congress adopts Declaration of Independence (1776)	After eight years of war, Britain signs peace treaty (1783) recognizing U.S. independence

The War for Independence (1776–1781)

Early Defeats   The first year of war was a desperate one for the largely untrained, disorganized troops led by General George Washington. Fighting a losing battle in defense of New York City (July 1776), Washington's army barely managed to escape disaster by retreating across the Hudson River to New Jersey. By the end of the first year, British troops, as well as hired troops from Hesse in Germany, occupied two of the colonies' most important cities, Boston and New York. The American capital, Philadelphia, fell to the British and Hessians the following year.

Turning Points Desperately needing a victory to keep American hopes alive, Washington launched a surprise attack on Trenton, New Jersey, on Christmas Night, 1776. The Hessian defenders of Trenton were routed. A second turning point was a decisive American victory at Saratoga, New York, in October 1777, against a British army commanded by General John Burgoyne. Americans showed enough strength in this battle to convince France to give them military and naval assistance. This news came as a welcome relief to Washington and his men, who were suffering from inadequate food and clothing while camped at Valley Forge in Pennsylvania, during the severe winter of 1777–1778.

Victory at Yorktown The last years of the war were fought in the South. Aided by French naval support and reinforced by French troops, Washington's army forced Britain's commanding general, Lord Cornwallis, to surrender his army at Yorktown, Virginia (1781). Two years later, in Paris, American and British diplomats signed a peace treaty ending the war. In the treaty, Great Britain recognized the existence of the United States as an

The United States in 1783

independent nation. The western border of the new American nation was to be the Mississippi River.

Contributions of African Americans   During the Revolutionary War, approximately 5,000 free blacks and slaves fought against Britain. A major cause for their involvement was the decision to offer freedom to slaves whose masters would allow them to fight in the war. This decision was a response to Britain's offer of freedom to any slaves who would fight against the colonists. Thus, African Americans fought on both sides during the Revolutionary War. After the war, some of the former slaves who had fought on the British side went to the West Indies or to England.

★ In Review

1. Identify three acts of the British Parliament that led to protest in the American colonies.
2. Explain how slavery influenced the economy of southern colonies.
3. Discuss the ways in which the Declaration of Independence expressed both the idea of representative government and the idea of limited government.

New York and Other State Constitutions

State Constitutions and Religious Freedom

Many states, including New York, adopted constitutions before the United States Constitution was written. Most of these constitutions (written plans of government) contained references to a *bicameral* (two-house) rather than a *unicameral* (one-house) legislature, an executive branch, a judicial branch, and even a bill of rights prohibiting the establishment of a religion. As a result, these constitutions guaranteed religious liberty and encouraged the growth of *religious pluralism* (toleration of more than one religious group). Constitutions of states such as New York, Massachusetts, and Maryland strongly influenced the writing of the U.S. Constitution. These state constitutions, like the U.S. Constitution to come, followed *republican* principles by providing that the final authority rested with the people.

Abolition of Slavery in the North

By 1800, all the northern states had passed laws to end slavery. The first of the states to do so were Vermont and Massachusetts. In 1799, New York abolished slavery by passing an act that would gradually free enslaved people. New York's law provided that future-born males would be freed at age 28, while females would be freed at age 25. By 1810, most northern African Americans were free citizens.

The Articles of Confederation

Both during and after the American Revolution, delegates from the 13 original colonies, which later became states, met as a congress to make laws for the United States. This congress drew up the Articles of Confederation in 1777. The states finally ratified the articles in 1781.

Major Principles

The Articles of Confederation was the first constitution for the United States. Government under the Articles soon proved unsatisfactory.

Organization and Powers of the Government The U.S. government under the Articles consisted simply of a one-house lawmaking body, the Congress (or Continental Congress). There was neither a separate executive branch to enforce the laws nor a separate system of national courts to interpret

★ ★ ★ ★ ★

POEM BY A YOUNG AFRICAN AMERICAN WOMAN

Born in Africa, Phillis Wheatley was kidnapped at the age of nine and brought to Massachusetts as a slave. Her master's wife taught her to read and write. In 1773, Wheatley published a volume of poetry, only the second book of poems to be published by a woman living in America. The following poem was addressed to a British noble, the Earl of Dartmouth.

No more *America* in mournful strain
of wrongs, and grievance unredress'd complain,
No longer shall thou dread the iron chain,
Which wanton *Tyranny* with lawless hand
Has made, and which it meant t'enslave the land.
Should you, my lord, while you peruse my song,
Wonder from whence my love of *Freedom* sprung,
Whence flow these wishes for the common good,
By feeling hearts alone best understood,
I, young in life, by seeming cruel fate
Was snatch'd from *Afric's* fancy'd happy seat:
What pangs excruciating must molest,
What sorrows labour in my parent's breast?
Steel'd was the soul and by no misery mov'd
That from a father seiz'd his babe belov'd
Such, such my case. And can I then but pray
others may never feel tyrannic sway?

them. Each state was equally represented in Congress by a delegation that could cast just one vote on each issue. The Congress was given the power to declare war, make peace, and conduct foreign affairs.

Strengths and Weaknesses

Congress under the Articles had two major achievements: (1) bringing the Revolutionary War to a successful end and (2) establishing a workable plan (the *Northwest Ordinance*, 1787) for governing the western lands between the Appalachian Mountains and the Mississippi River. A major feature of the Northwest Ordinance was the abolition of slavery in these lands.

But Congress lacked the power to collect taxes directly and relied upon grants of money from the states to pay its expenses. Laws required approval by a two-thirds majority of the states for passage. It could not regulate commerce between the states, and the paper currency it issued was nearly worthless. The Articles of Confederation could not be changed without the states' unanimous agreement.

In the 1780s economic troubles and political unrest caused many Americans to doubt whether their young country could long survive under a weak central government. Particularly alarming was a violent protest by Massachusetts farmers (*Shays's Rebellion*, 1786) against the collection of a state tax.

★ In Review

1. What features from the states' constitutions were incorporated into the United States Constitution?
2. Describe how the national government was organized under the Articles of Confederation.
3. Summarize how the state governments were stronger than the national government under the Articles of Confederation.

Chapter Review

MULTIPLE-CHOICE QUESTIONS

1. The development of a tobacco economy in Virginia, the marriage of Pocahontas and John Rolfe, and the assistance of Squanto show that

(1) relations between Native Americans and settlers were sometimes cordial
(2) the colonists and Native Americans had opportunities for interaction that never materialized

(3) Native Americans readily accepted British customs and traditions
(4) warfare between the colonists and Native Americans could have been avoided.

2. The map on page 34 shows that the Proclamation of 1763 and the Quebec Act of 1764
(1) promoted further expansion of American settlement into Native American territory
(2) permitted free travel between Britain's Canadian colonies and the 13 original British colonies
(3) defined the boundaries between Britain's newly acquired Canadian colonies, the original British colonies, Spanish Florida, and the Native Americans
(4) enhanced British control of the Mississippi River.

3. The illustration of the Boston Massacre on page 36 takes the position that
(1) the Boston crowd provoked the British soldiers
(2) British soldiers attacked a group of unarmed people
(3) the British government was placing its soldiers in a dangerous situation
(4) the British government could not control its overseas armies.

4. Which issue or event most directly led to the American Revolution?
(1) freedom of speech and press
(2) taxation of the colonies by Britain
(3) the African slave trade
(4) the French and Indian War.

5. The passage from the Declaration of Independence on page 38 illustrates that formal separation from Britain was derived mostly from the ideas of
(1) Voltaire
(2) John Locke
(3) Baron de Montesquieu
(4) Rousseau.

6. Which correctly explains the role of African Americans during the Revolution?
(1) They did not participate in the Revolutionary War.
(2) They fought primarily on the side of Britain.
(3) They fought on the side of the colonists when their masters allowed them to fight.
(4) They fought on both the British and colonial sides.

7. The map of the United States in 1783 on page 40 illustrates that
(1) the British promised to leave North America
(2) the Americans captured parts of Canada during the Revolution
(3) as a result of the Revolution, the United States gained a significant amount of territory
(4) the United States was surrounded by Spanish territories.

8. The New York State Constitution as well as those of Massachusetts and Maryland
(1) had to be changed as a result of the Revolution
(2) created single-house legislatures
(3) varied in their toleration of religious differences
(4) preceded the U.S. Constitution and promoted republican principles of government.

9. Which is the most accurate conclusion about the United States

government under the Articles of Confederation?

(1) The national government was totally powerless and accomplished nothing, with the exception of ending the Revolution.

(2) Order ceased to exist in some states but remained strong and powerful in others.

(3) The national government had little power but was successful in establishing a plan to settle the Northwest Territory.

(4) Paper currency was worthless while coined money was inflated in value.

10. The pie graph on page 28 illustrates that in 1790

(1) more than half of the people living in the early United States were English

(2) Africans comprised the second largest ethnic group in the United States

(3) almost half of the population was from places other than Western Europe

(4) there were few ethnic groups in the United States that were not English or African.

THEMATIC ESSAYS

1. **Theme:** American Colonial Democracy and Self-Government

The 13 British North American colonies established traditions of democracy and self-government long before the Declaration of Independence was written.

Task: Describe the extent to which democracy and/or self-government were found in colonial America prior to 1776.

You may use any example from your study of American history and government. Some suggestions that you might wish to consider include the Mayflower Compact in Plymouth, the House of Burgesses in Virginia, town meetings throughout New England, and the trial of John Peter Zenger in New York.

2. **Theme:** Immigration to Colonial America

People came to colonial America for a variety of reasons. Some immigrated for improved economic opportunity. Others made the voyage to obtain political or religious freedom. Still others came unwillingly.

Task: Choose two of the above reasons why people came to colonial America. For each reason, name the group that came to America and describe the circumstances that resulted in its people leaving their country of origin to immigrate to the British colonies.

DOCUMENT-BASED QUESTION

*Read or analyze each document and answer the questions that follows it. Then read the **Task** and write your essay. Essays should include references to most of the documents along with additional information based on your knowledge of United States history and government.*

Historical Context: By the 1760s and 1770s, a number of events occurred that, coupled with the colonial tradition of self-government, led to a debate over the benefits of independence from Britain.

Document 1   From John Locke, *Second Treatise on Civil Government:*

> Whenever the legislators endeavor to take away and destroy the property of the people, or to reduce them to slavery . . . they put themselves into a state of war with the people, who are thereupon absolved from any further obedience and are left to the common refuge which God hath provided for all men against violence.

Question: How does John Locke feel rulers should be treated when they disregard the rights of the people?

Document 2   From Thomas Paine, "Common Sense":

> Small islands not capable of protecting themselves are the proper objects for kingdoms to take under their care; but there is something very absurd in supposing a continent to be perpetually governed by an island. In no instance hath nature made the satellite larger than its primary planet; and as England and America, with respect to each other, reverse the common order of nature, it is evident that they belong to different systems. England to Europe: America to itself.

Question: Why does Thomas Paine feel that the American colonies should declare independence from Britain?

Document 3:   Lord Mansfield, Debate on the Repeal of the Stamp Act, in the British House of Lords, 1766:

> It must be granted that they migrated with leave as colonies and therefore from the very meaning of the word were, are, and must be subjects, and owe allegiance and subjection to their mother country [England].

Question: How does Lord Mansfield feel about the relationship between colonies and the "mother country"?

Task: Using information from the documents and your knowledge of the causes of the American Revolution, write an essay that discusses whether or not the American Revolution was inevitable.

Chapter 2
The Constitution and the Bill of Rights

★ **Objectives**

★ To identify and understand the importance of key clauses in the Constitution.

★ To define and illustrate basic principles of the U.S. Constitution, including federalism, separation of powers, and checks and balances.

★ To know the main provisions of the U.S. Bill of Rights.

★ To understand that the Constitution is a living document that has changed over time.

The form of government created for the United States in 1787 by the framers of the Constitution has endured for more than 200 years. No other written constitution in the world has been in force for so long. Let us examine the features of the Constitution that have made our government both stable and flexible enough to respond well to the changing needs of American society.

The Constitutional Convention

Delegates from the states met in Philadelphia in the summer of 1787. Although the original purpose of this meeting was to amend the Articles of Confederation, this plan soon changed.

Representation and Process

All the states except Rhode Island sent delegates to the Constitutional Convention. A majority of these delegates were lawyers. Approximately half had fought against Britain in the Revolutionary War. Most of the southern delegates owned slaves. Among the oldest delegates was Benjamin Franklin, and among the youngest was Alexander Hamilton. George Washington presided over the convention. The majority at this convention were persuaded by James Madison and other Virginia delegates to replace the existing plan of government (the Articles) with an entirely new constitution. The delegates agreed to take this constitution back to their states for ratification. The task of creating a new constitution had begun.

Conflict and Compromise

The delegates disagreed sharply on three issues: representation, slavery, and trade.

Representation The larger states like Virginia insisted that the number of each state's representatives in the newly organized Congress should be proportional to the size of its population. The smaller states like New Jersey wanted the number of representatives to be the same for all states.

Slavery Because slaves made up a large part of the South's population, southern delegates proposed that slaves be counted in a state's population for representation purposes but not for tax purposes. Northern delegates proposed just the opposite—counting slaves for tax purposes but not for representation.

Another disagreement over slavery concerned the slave trade. Most northerners at the convention hoped to end the slave trade, while southerners feared that such action could lead to the end of slavery.

Trade Southern delegates thought foreign commerce should not be taxed, because their region relied heavily on importing goods manufactured in Great Britain. A tax on *imports* would make foreign goods more expensive. Northerners thought foreign commerce should be taxed, since their region was beginning to manufacture goods that completed with imports. A tax on foreign goods might help these domestic "infant industries" grow. The southern states, which shipped large quantities of cotton and tobacco to Great Britain, also opposed taxing *exports*. Each conflict at the convention was resolved through compromise.

The *Great Compromise* created a Congress of two houses: the House of Representatives, where states would be represented in proportion to their populations; the Senate, where all states would be represented equally.

One compromise on slavery provided that three-fifths of a state's slave population would be counted for purposes of both taxation and representation. A second compromise provided that Congress could pass no law ending the slave trade for 20 years (until 1808). In addition, the tax on slaves entering the country could not exceed $10 a person. (It is interesting to note that the word "slave" never appears in the Constitution.)

A compromise on trade gave Congress the power to tax imports but not exports.

Signers of the Constitution, in Philadelphia, 1787

The Document: Structure of Government

The Constitution begins with its most famous paragraph, the Preamble. Then follows the main body of the document, which consists of seven major parts known as articles. Added to the document soon after it was written and ratified were ten amendments, known as the Bill of Rights. Seventeen other amendments have been adopted at different times in U.S. history.

The Preamble

Recall that the Constitution's creators—or Framers—wanted to improve upon the Articles of Confederation of 1781, which had established a loose association of states. Therefore, to give authority to the people of the entire nation, the Preamble asserts that the new U.S. government was being established by "we the people" rather than by the individual states. The Preamble identifies the goals of the new government as follows:

> We the people of the United States, in order to form a more perfect Union, establish justice, insure domestic tranquillity, provide for the common defense, promote the general welfare, and secure the blessings of liberty to ourselves and our posterity, do ordain and establish this Constitution for the United States of America.

The Three Branches of Government

The Constitution gives the powers of government to three separate groups, or branches: the legislative branch, the executive branch, and the judicial branch. This is known as the principle of *separation of powers*.

The Legislative Branch: Congress Article I describes the organization and powers of the legislative, or lawmaking, branch—the U.S. Congress. It says that Congress shall consist of two groups of lawmakers: the House of Representatives and the Senate. In addition to listing the *legislative powers* of Congress (the laws it may make), Article I also describes (1) the method for electing members of each house, (2) the qualifications for election, (3) terms of office in the House and Senate, and (4) the procedures for making laws.

The Executive Branch: President and Vice President Article II describes the law-enforcing, or executive, branch. It says that the *chief executive* (the official in charge of the law-enforcing branch) shall be the president. It also mentions the vice president but says little about this official's responsibilities.

Article II describes (1) the president's powers, (2) the president's four-year term of office, (3) the method of electing the president and vice president, and (4) the method for removing the president by *impeachment* (an accusation of wrongdoing, followed by a trial).

The Judicial Branch: Supreme Court and Lower Courts Article III describes the judicial branch—the federal court system that interprets the laws of Congress as they apply to specific cases. The Constitution mentions both "inferior" (lower) courts and a Supreme Court. It describes (1) the term of office for federal judges and (2) Congress's power to establish new courts. Concerning the *jurisdiction* (assigned area of responsibility) of the courts, it distinguishes between cases that go directly to the Supreme Court (the highest, most powerful court) and cases that may be heard first by lower federal courts.

Chapter 3 describes the operation of the three branches of government in greater detail.

The States, the Amendment Process, and the Supreme Law

The main body of the original Constitution (the part written in 1787) concludes with four short articles on miscellaneous matters.

Interstate Relations Article IV describes relations among the states and their obligations toward one another. The article says that a person charged with breaking the laws of one state and fleeing to another may be *extradited* (returned) to the original state. The article also describes (1) how U.S. territories may enter the Union as new states and (2) the responsibility of the federal government to protect states from invasion and "domestic violence" (rioting).

The Amendment Process Article V describes methods for amending the Constitution. (See pages 61–63.)

The Supremacy Clause According to the so-called *supremacy clause* in Article VI, "The Constitution, and the laws of the United States . . . shall be the supreme law of the land." (This clause was the basis for historic decisions of the Supreme Court by which it declared national laws to be supreme over states laws.) Another clause in Article VI says that a person's religion may never be a qualification for holding public office.

Ratification The seventh and final article of the original Constitution is no longer in force. It describes the method by which the Constitution was to be submitted to the states in 1787 for ratification, or approval.

Debate on Ratification

The Constitution describes a *federal system* of government. This is a system in which political power is divided more or less evenly between a central, or national, government and state governments. In September 1787, the Constitution was submitted to the states for their approval. A great debate followed on whether or not the new plan of government should be substituted for the Articles of Confederation. Favoring the ratification of the Constitution was a group called the *Federalists*. Opposing ratification were the *Anti-Federalists*.

Federalist Arguments A series of essays by three Federalists (James Madison, Alexander Hamilton, and John Jay) explained the need for a federal plan of government to replace the confederate plan (the Articles of 1781). Each essay presented reasons why the new Constitution would both strengthen the national government and protect personal liberties. When published as a book, *The Federalist* became a classic work in defense of a representative government whose powers are evenly distributed among three branches.

Anti-Federalist Arguments Opponents of ratification included two leaders of the American Revolution, Patrick Henry and Samuel Adams. They feared that the central government under the Constitution might become too strong and crush people's liberties. As originally written, the Constitution lacked a bill of rights. The Anti-Federalists pointed to this omission as proof that people's rights would not be respected.

Federalist Victory Each state called a special convention in which delegates voted for or against the proposed Constitution. The Federalists won the first three states by large majorities. But vigorous opposition in Massachusetts and Virginia was overcome only after the Federalists promised to add a bill of rights as the new government's first order of business. Even so, the vote to ratify the Constitution was far from unanimous. New York's convention, for example, voted to ratify by the slim majority of 30–27. Ratification by the required number of states (nine) was accomplished in June 1788.

How the Constitution Differed
From the Articles of Confederation

The Constitution created a central government for the nation that was considerably stronger than the one created by the Articles of Confederation. The new plan of government differed from the Articles in these respects:

A Separate Executive Branch   The president was to act as the leader of an executive branch for enforcing Congress's laws. (Under the Articles, there was no executive branch and no president with executive responsibilities.)

A Separate Judicial Branch   To settle cases of law under the Constitution, a separate U.S. court system, or judicial branch, was established. (Under the Articles, there was no national court system.)

A Two-House Legislature   The legislative branch, Congress, was to consist of two houses, a Senate and a House of Representatives. (Under the Articles, Congress had only one house.)

Greater Power for Congress   Congress was given the power to collect taxes on imports. (Under the Articles, Congress had no tax-collecting powers.)

Federal in Form (Not Confederate)   The powers of government were divided between a strong central government and strong state governments. Such an arrangement is known as a *federal system*. (Under a confederate form of government, the central government is generally weaker than the state governments.)

★ In Review

1. Describe two conflicts that arose at the Constitutional Convention, and the compromise that settled each conflict.
2. How did the Preamble to the Constitution give authority to the people rather than the states?
3. Describe the major function of each of the three branches of the federal government.

Basic Constitutional Principles

Following is a discussion of the basic principles that are the foundations for the U.S. Constitution. These include the *separation of powers*, *checks and balances*, and *federalism*.

Separation of Powers

The framers of the Constitution created a system for distributing the legislative, executive, and judicial powers of government among three separate branches. This is known as the *separation of powers*, since it gives each of the three branches of the federal government its own special area of responsibility. The Congress as the legislative branch was to be responsible for making the nation's laws. The president as the chief executive was to be responsible for enforcing the laws. The federal courts as the judicial branch were to be responsible for interpreting the laws.

By creating three branches, each with a different area of responsibility, the framers hoped to prevent one official or group of officials from acquiring all or most of the powers of government.

Checks and Balances

A second great principle of the Constitution concerns the system by which the three branches interact with one another.

Definition and Purpose The framers gave each branch some powers to participate in the decisions of the other branches. This fact forces *each* branch to try to gain *the approval* of the other branches for its policies and decisions. If it fails to win such approval, its policies may be defeated. Such a system of partially shared responsibility is called *checks and balances*, because each branch has the ability to check, or block, the actions of the other branches. Powers are distributed in a balanced way so as to prevent any one branch from dominating the others.

As an example of the checks-and-balances system, consider the process for enacting a federal law. Although Congress has primary responsibility for lawmaking, the president participates in the process by signing proposed laws passed by both houses of Congress. The president may also decide to *veto* (reject) an act of Congress. The president thereby checks Congress. Congress, however, has the power to countercheck. It may override the president's veto by passing the proposed law again with a two-thirds vote of approval in each house (rather than the simple majority required for original passage). If the override is accomplished, an act of Congress becomes law without the president's signature.

Suppose that a bill becomes law (either with or without the president's approval). Then the law may be challenged in the federal courts. The Supreme Court may be called upon to consider whether or not the law is allowed by the Constitution. If the Supreme Court decides that the law is unconstitutional, it is no longer considered a valid law. In this way the Supreme Court checks Congress (and checks the president as well, if the president had signed the original bill).

Other Examples In the statements below, each clause introduced by *but* represents a constitutional power given to one branch to enable it to check another branch's actions.

The president may:

★ nominate federal judges, including the justices of the Supreme Court, *but* the Senate must confirm (approve) such appointments by majority vote.

★ nominate cabinet officials and the heads of executive agencies, *but* the Senate must confirm such appointments by majority vote.

★ sign treaties with other nations, *but* the Senate must confirm such treaties by a two-thirds vote.

The president acts . . .		Another branch checks . . .
	1. Makes a treaty with a foreign government.	The Senate rejects the treaty (fails to ratify it by a two-thirds vote).
	2. Commits certain "crimes and misdemeanors."	The House impeaches the president; then the Senate votes to remove the president from office.
	3. Vetoes an act of Congress.	Congress overrides the veto by a two-thirds vote of each house.
	4. Makes an appointment to a cabinet post.	The Senate rejects the president's nominee.

Congress acts . . .		Another branch checks . . .
	1. Enacts a bill.	The president vetoes Congress's act.
	2. Enacts a bill that is signed by the president.	The Supreme Court declares Congress's act to be unconstitutional.

The Supreme Court acts . . .		Another branch checks . . .
	1. Declares an act of Congress unconstitutional.	Congress proposes a constitutional amendment.
	2. Declares an action of the president unconstitutional.	The president appoints a new justice to the Supreme Court (if there is a vacancy).

Checks and Balances in the Federal Government

★ propose laws, *but* Congress must agree to enact the proposed laws.

★ carry out duties stated in the Constitution, *but* if the president acts improperly, he or she may be impeached (accused) by a majority vote of the House of Representatives and removed from office by a two-thirds vote of the Senate.

Congress may:

★ attempt to influence the Supreme Court by voting to increase the number of justices, *but*, once selected, Supreme Court justices vote independently on all judicial questions.

★ *appropriate* (set aside) funds for a government program, *but* the president may delay spending the money.

The Supreme Court may:

★ declare an action of the president to be unconstitutional, *but*, if the president defies the Court's ruling, only Congress can initiate impeachment proceedings.

★ declare a law to be unconstitutional, *but* Congress may propose an amendment to the Constitution that would permit the law to stand if it is passed a second time.

Federalism: Powers of the Central and State Governments

Division of Powers The federal system of the Constitution replaced the confederate system established by the Articles of Confederation in 1781. Recall that the Articles provided for a weak central government (a one-house Congress) and much stronger state governments. As a result the central government of the 1780s was unable to govern effectively. The framers of the Constitution attempted to remedy this situation by increasing the powers of the central government while reserving other powers for the states.

Delegated Powers Powers given to the central government are those affecting the entire nation. Such powers—known as *delegated powers* or *enumerated powers*—are ones specifically named by the Constitution. They include collecting taxes, coining money, maintaining the armed forces, regulating trade, and making treaties.

Reserved Powers Those powers reserved to the states and to the people by the Tenth Amendment include any and all powers that the Constitution neither delegates to the central government nor denies to the states. Although not named by the Constitution, these *reserved powers* include the states' traditional authority over such matters as health and safety, marriage and divorce, the regulation of business, and the licensing of professions.

Concurrent Powers Powers that are exercised by both the federal government and the state governments are *concurrent powers*. Examples of these powers include building roads and highways, borrowing money, collecting taxes, and operating courts.

★ In Review

1. Define separation of powers, checks and balances, and federalism.
2. Describe one way in which each branch of the federal government may check the other two branches.

The Bill of Rights

A *bill of rights* is a document that sets forth the kinds of actions that government officials may not take. Its purpose is to prevent abuses of power and protect people's liberties. Soon after the Constitution was adopted, one of the first acts of the new Congress was to propose a series of amendments. The first ten amendments to the Constitution are the *Bill of Rights*. These amendments were proposed by Congress in 1789 and ratified as a group in 1791. Originally, they protected citizens from the powers of the federal government only. Later, the rights guaranteed by these amendments were applied to state governments as well. (See the section on the Fourteenth Amendment, page 58.)

Among the freedoms and rights guaranteed in the Bill of Rights are the following: freedom of religion; freedom of speech and the press; right to a fair trial; freedom from unreasonable searches by the police; and freedom from cruel and unusual punishments.

In the diagram on page 57, "Sources of Major Ideas in the Constitution and the Bill of Rights," observe how the U.S. Bill of Rights continues a long history going back to 1215 and the Magna Carta—the history of people forcing government to recognize strict limits on its powers.

Main Provisions

In the summary that follows, notice that most provisions of the Bill of Rights define something that government officials are *not* permitted to do.

Freedom of Religion   Congress may not interfere with a person's right to worship according to his or her own conscience. (First Amendment)

Separation of Church and State   Congress may not favor one religion over another by giving special support to any church, synagogue, or other religious institution. (First Amendment)

Freedom of Speech, Press, Assembly, and Petition   Congress may make no law that interferes with a person's freedom to express ideas in speech and writing. Officials of the U.S. government may not stop people from *assembling* (demonstrating in a peaceful manner). Nor may people be punished for *petitioning* (asking in writing) the government for a change in policy. (First Amendment)

Right to "Keep and Bear Arms"   Citizens may not be denied the right to carry weapons for use in a *state militia* (a group of volunteer soldiers trained for the common defense). (Second Amendment)

Right Against Unfair Police Searches and Seizures   Government officials must obtain a judge's permission—a *search warrant*—before they may conduct a search of a person's property. A warrant must describe "the place to be searched and the persons or things to be seized." It may be issued to a police officer only if a judge is convinced that there is "probable cause" of criminal evidence being found. (Fourth Amendment)

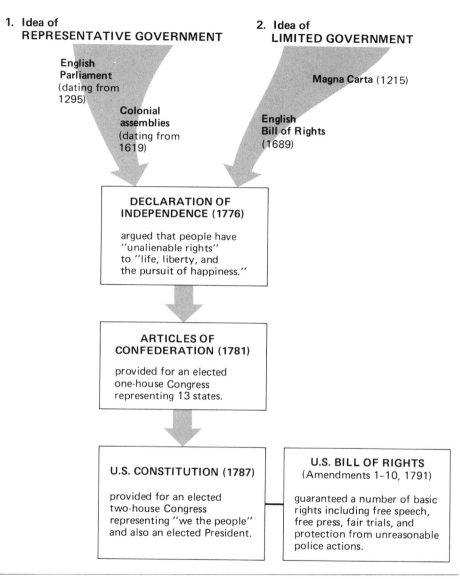

1. Idea of
   REPRESENTATIVE GOVERNMENT

2. Idea of
   LIMITED GOVERNMENT

English Parliament (dating from 1295)

Magna Carta (1215)

Colonial assemblies (dating from 1619)

English Bill of Rights (1689)

DECLARATION OF INDEPENDENCE (1776)

argued that people have "unalienable rights" to "life, liberty, and the pursuit of happiness."

ARTICLES OF CONFEDERATION (1781)

provided for an elected one-house Congress representing 13 states.

U.S. CONSTITUTION (1787)

provided for an elected two-house Congress representing "we the people" and also an elected President.

U.S. BILL OF RIGHTS (Amendments 1-10, 1791)

guaranteed a number of basic rights including free speech, free press, fair trials, and protection from unreasonable police actions.

Sources of the Major Ideas in the Constitution and the Bill of Rights

Rights of Persons Accused of Breaking U.S. Laws The following rights of an accused person are guaranteed in the Fifth Amendment and the Sixth Amendment.

★ The accusation, or indictment, of a federal court must be made by a grand jury.

★ A person acquitted by a jury cannot be tried again on the same charge (no *double jeopardy*).

★ No person can be forced to give testimony or evidence that may be used against him or her at a trial.

★ An accused person is guaranteed: "a speedy and public trial"; the right to a trial by an impartial jury; the right to be informed of the criminal charges against him or her; and the right to be represented by a lawyer and to have the government assist in producing witnesses on his or her behalf.

Right to Due Process   No person may be deprived of "life, liberty, or property without due process of law." (Fifth Amendment)

Rights Concerning Bail and Punishment for Crime   A person awaiting trial may not be charged an excessive amount for *bail* (a sum of money to obtain release from jail pending trial). A person convicted of a crime may not be punished for it in "cruel and unusual" ways. (Eighth Amendment)

Rights Reserved to the States   The powers neither delegated to the federal government nor denied to the states belong to the governments of the different states and to the American people. (Tenth Amendment)

Since the adoption of the Bill of Rights, the Constitution has been changed by amendment only 17 times from 1795 (adoption of the Eleventh Amendment) to 1992 (adoption of the Twenty-seventh Amendment). Among the most important of these amendments are:

★ The Twelfth Amendment modifies the system for electing the president and vice president.

★ The Thirteenth Amendment abolishes slavery.

★ The Fourteenth Amendment guarantees equal rights of citizenship to all groups.

★ The Fifteenth Amendment guarantees voting rights to citizens of all races.

★ The Sixteenth Amendment provides for the collection of a federal income tax.

★ The Seventeenth Amendment provides for the election of U.S. senators by direct popular vote (rather than by vote of the state legislatures).

★ The Nineteenth Amendment guarantees voting rights to women as well as men.

★ The Twenty-sixth Amendment guarantees voting rights to young adults aged 18 or older.

For a summary of all of the later amendments (11 to 27), see the table on page 62.

The Fourteenth Amendment

Adopted in 1791, the first ten amendments—or Bill of Rights—protected citizens from abuses of the federal government only, not from unfair state laws. This partial protection continued for more than 75 years, until 1868.

In that year the Fourteenth Amendment was added to the Constitution. After the Civil War, northerners wanted the amendment to be a means of protecting the rights of freed slaves. Of course, the amendment applied to all other Americans as well.

The Fourteenth Amendment provides that no state may deny its citizens either "due process of law" or "equal protection of the laws." Often, in the 20th century, the Supreme Court used the due process clause of the Fourteenth Amendment to expand the protections of the first ten amendments. Therefore, instead of applying only to federal laws, the Bill of Rights now applies to state laws as well.

Interpreting the Bill of Rights

In the 20th century many of the most important, or landmark, decisions of the Supreme Court involved various provisions of the Bill of Rights. Let us examine some of these landmark decisions and the bases for them.

Decisions on First Amendment Rights

The rights protected by the First Amendment are fundamental to a free society. The amendment guarantees every citizen's right to freedom of religion, freedom of speech, freedom of the press, freedom of assembly, and freedom of petition.

Separation of Church and State   The First Amendment states that Congress may "make no law respecting an establishment of religion." In other words, the government may not do anything to favor or give preference to any religious practice or group. Thomas Jefferson said that "a wall of separation between church and state" should keep government from interfering in religious matters. Important Supreme Court decisions have affirmed and clarified this idea. For example:

★ In the case of *Engel* v. *Vitale* (1962), the Supreme Court ruled that prayer in public schools was unconstitutional because it violated the principle of separation of church and state.

★ In *School District of Abington Township [Pennsylvania]* v. *Schempp* (1963), the highest court ruled that Bible reading in public schools violated the First Amendment.

Freedom of Speech and the Press   Freedom of speech and the press means that no one may be penalized for criticizing government officials and policies. However, under certain circumstances affecting the public safety, the right to express ideas freely may be limited.

★ In *Schenck* v. *United States* (1919), Justice Oliver Wendell Holmes said that speech could be limited if it presented a "clear and present danger." As an example of such a danger, he said, "free speech would not protect a man falsely shouting fire in a theatre and causing a panic."

★ In *Tinker* v. *Des Moines School District* (1969), the Supreme Court ruled that students could not be penalized for wearing black armbands to school to protest the Vietnam War. The Court argued that students do not "shed their Constitutional rights to freedom of speech or expression at the schoolhouse gate."

★ In a controversial 1989 case, *Texas* v. *Johnson*, the Supreme Court decided that a person who had deliberately set fire to an American flag as an act of protest could not be punished by state officials, because flag burning could be considered a form of symbolic speech protected under the First Amendment.

Freedom of Assembly   The First Amendment guarantees the right of people to assemble peacefully and to petition the government "for a redress of grievances."

★ In *Collin* v. *Smith* (1978), the Supreme Court agreed with an appeals court ruling that the American Nazi party had a right to march in the city of Skokie, Illinois, even if this act of "peaceable assembly" offended other people in the community.

From the above cases, we see that the Supreme Court uses its power of *judicial review* to define what each clause of the First Amendment means in a specific situation.

Decisions on the Fourth, Fifth, and Sixth Amendments

In the 1960s, under the leadership of Chief Justice Earl Warren, the Supreme Court decided a great number of cases that tested the meaning of the Fourth, Fifth, and Sixth amendments.

Search and Seizure   The Fourth Amendment protects citizens against police officers making "unreasonable" searches and seizures of personal property. Two decisions concerning search and seizure were especially important.

★ In *Mapp* v. *Ohio* (1961), the Supreme Court ruled that evidence obtained without a valid search warrant may not be admitted into a state court.

★ In *Katz* v. *United States* (1967), the Court ruled that wiretapping requires a search warrant. A person's privacy, not just property, is protected by the Fourth Amendment.

Rights of Accused Persons   The rights guaranteed in the Fifth and Sixth amendments concern the procedures that the courts and the police must use to ensure fair treatment of persons arrested for crimes.

★ In *Gideon* v. *Wainwright* (1963), the Supreme Court under Earl Warren ruled that if an accused person is too poor to hire a lawyer, a state is obligated to provide one at public expense.

★ In *Escobedo* v. *Illinois* (1964), the Court ruled that anyone taken to a police station for questioning has the right to be represented by a lawyer.

★ In *Miranda* v. *Arizona* (1966), the Court ruled that at the time of arrest, a person must be told his or her rights to remain silent and to have an attorney present.

Decisions Concerning "Cruel and Unusual Punishments"

Is it constitutional to execute a convicted criminal for violent crimes? Or are such executions forbidden by the Eighth Amendment's ban against "cruel and unusual" punishments? In two landmark cases of the 1970s, the Supreme Court ruled on this matter.

★ In *Furman* v. *Georgia* (1972), the Court ruled that the death penalty is not constitutional unless the state has clear and consistent rules for applying the penalty uniformly to people of all races and social classes.

★ In *Gregg* v. *Georgia* (1976), the Court ruled that the death penalty is constitutional if the nature of the crime is made the sole factor for imposing the sentence.

★ In Review

1. List three rights protected in the First Amendment.
2. Define separation of church and state, and due process of law.
3. Explain how the Fourteenth Amendment extended the protections of the Bill of Rights.

The Constitution as a Living Document

Scholars have called the U.S. Constitution a living document because it is flexible enough to change with the times. Our constitutional system may be changed in two ways: (1) by formal amendment and (2) by informal adjustments and decision making.

Formal Procedures of Amendment

Article V of the Constitution describes the formal procedures for proposing and ratifying amendments. Although several procedures may be used, the most common of them involves two steps:

Step One Congress proposes an amendment by a two-thirds vote of each house.

Step Two The proposed amendment is considered by the legislatures of the states. If approved or ratified by at least three-fourths of the states, the amendment is added to the Constitution.

Informal Methods of Change

Congress and the Elastic Clause The Constitution is a flexible, living document not only because it can be changed by formal amendment but also be-

★ Summary of Amendments 11 to 27* ★

Amendment	Year Adopted	Main Provisions
Eleventh	1798	Citizens of other states or of foreign countries cannot sue a state in federal court without that state's consent.
Twelfth	1804	Electors from each state shall cast two separate ballots—one for president, one for vice president.
Thirteenth	1865	Slavery in the United States is abolished.
Fourteenth	1868	All persons born in the United States are U.S. citizens, who are entitled to due process of law and equal protection of the laws.
Fifteenth	1870	No government in the United States may prevent citizens from voting because of their race.
Sixteenth	1913	Congress has the power to collect taxes on incomes without dividing the taxes among the states according to their population.
Seventeenth	1913	The two U.S. senators from each state shall be elected by a direct vote of the people of the state.
Eighteenth	1919	The manufacture and sale of intoxicating beverages in the United States is prohibited (also known as the Prohibition Amendment).
Nineteenth	1920	No government in the United States may prevent citizens from voting because of their gender.
Twentieth	1933	The terms of office of the president and vice president end at noon, January 20. The terms of office of members of Congress end at noon, January 3 (also known as the "Lame Duck" Amendment).
Twenty-first	1933	The Eighteenth Amendment is repealed.
Twenty-second	1951	No person can be elected more than twice to the office of president.
Twenty-third	1961	Residents of the District of Columbia may participate in the election for president and vice president by choosing three electors.
Twenty-fourth	1964	No government in the United States may collect a poll tax from citizens as a requirement for voting. (A *poll tax* is a tax collected from voters before they are issued ballots.)
Twenty-fifth	1967	If the cabinet and the Congress determine that the president is disabled, the vice president will temporarily assume the duties of president.
Twenty-sixth	1971	No government in the United States may prevent persons 18 or older from voting on account on their age.
Twenty-seventh	1992	A Congressional pay raise may not go into effect until an election of representatives has occurred.

*The first ten amendments, the Bill of Rights, were discussed earlier.

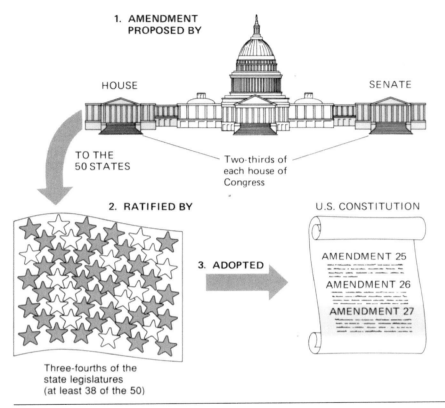

1. AMENDMENT PROPOSED BY

HOUSE

SENATE

TO THE 50 STATES

Two-thirds of each house of Congress

2. RATIFIED BY

3. ADOPTED

U.S. CONSTITUTION

AMENDMENT 25

AMENDMENT 26

AMENDMENT 27

Three-fourths of the state legislatures (at least 38 of the 50)

The Most Common Method of Amending the Constitution

cause it allows informal methods of change. Congress would be unable to cope with changing times if it were not for the *elastic clause* (or "necessary and proper" clause) in Article I of the Constitution. Thanks to this clause, Congress is empowered to legislate on a vast number of subjects that were unknown when the Constitution was written.

★ In Review

1. Explain the idea that the Constitution is a living document.
2. Describe the elastic clause.

The Strengths and Weaknesses of Our Constitutional System

How can we explain the remarkable fact that a constitution created more than 200 years ago is still the basis for one of the most successful and stable governments in the world? Some reasons are as follows:

★ The Constitution is a brief and flexible set of guidelines, allowing the government to adapt to change. Thus, each generation has been able to interpret the Constitution in terms of changing needs and conditions. At the same time, the traditional values and principles of the Constitution are still respected.

★ The Preamble emphasizes that the Constitution is a document of the people, not of the states.

★ The principles of separation of powers and checks and balances have helped to block the possibility of one of the three branches wielding absolute power.

★ The Bill of Rights has served to protect individual liberties.

★ Amendments to the Constitution have extended voting rights to all groups in the adult population.

Although the original Constitution had many strengths, it has been criticized for its omissions with regard to equality. These criticisms include the following:

★ The Constitution failed to guarantee that women receive equal treatment, including the right to vote. Other rights denied to women were the right to hold property in their own name, and the right of women to be the legal guardians of their own children.

★ Although African Americans had fought in the Revolutionary War, the Constitution failed to abolish slavery.

★ The Constitution failed to guarantee the right to vote to all white males, many of whom were denied that right by states that maintained property qualifications for voting.

Chapter Review

MULTIPLE-CHOICE QUESTIONS

1. At the Constitutional Convention of 1787, the issue of how to count slaves was settled by
   (1) northerners yielding to southerners
   (2) southerners yielding to northerners
   (3) blacks yielding to whites

   (4) a compromise involving concessions by both northerners and southerners.

2. Both the Articles of Confederation and the U.S. Constitution provided for
   (1) a Congress with legislative power

(2) a president with executive power
(3) a Supreme Court with judicial power
(4) local governments with veto powers.

3. The framers of the Constitution gave voters the most direct participation in the selection of the
(1) House of Representatives
(2) Senate
(3) president
(4) Supreme Court.

4. Why does the U.S. Constitution establish a system of checks and balances?
(1) to provide a means of electing members of Congress
(2) to keep one branch of government from becoming too powerful
(3) to allow the Supreme Court to judge cases of law
(4) to limit the term of office of the president.

5. All of the following situations illustrate the constitutional principle of checks and balances *except*
(1) the Senate rejects a presidential appointment
(2) the House of Representatives votes to impeach the president
(3) the Supreme Court declares a law unconstitutional
(4) the president acts as both chief of state and chief executive.

Base your answers to questions 6 and 7 on the statements below and on your knowledge of the ratification of the Constitution.

Speaker A: "We should reject any plan of government that makes no mention of such basic rights as freedom of speech and freedom of religion."

Speaker B: For every power granted to the executive branch there should be a comparable power granted to the legislative branch."

Speaker C: "Our nation should be viewed as a loose compact among the states. The chief concern of the central government should be the conduct foreign affairs."

Speaker D: "The laws of the national government and the state governments must both be subject to the supreme law of the land: the Constitution."

6. The kind of government created by the Articles of Confederation is described by
(1) Speaker A
(2) Speaker B
(3) Speaker C
(4) Speaker D.

7. Which two speakers would most likely have voted *against* the ratification of the U.S. Constitution in 1787?
(1) A and B
(2) B and C
(3) A and C
(4) C and D.

8. The fact that the U.S. Constitution can be interpreted differently at different times allows the government to
(1) take any action favored by the political party in power
(2) meet the needs of a changing society
(3) eliminate the system of checks and balances
(4) determine the circumstances under which war may be declared.

9. In the United States, informing suspects of their legal rights during an arrest procedure is required as a result of
(1) customs adopted from English common law
(2) state laws
(3) decisions of the U.S. Supreme Court
(4) laws passed by Congress.

10. The principle of federalism as established by the U.S. Constitution provides for the
(1) separation of powers of the three branches of government
(2) placement of ultimate sovereignty in the hands of the state governments
(3) division of power between the state governments and the national government
(4) creation of a republican form of government.

THEMATIC ESSAYS

1. Theme: Compromise as a Foundation of Our Constitution

The Constitution of the United States would never have been written without compromises by all sides. Our nation, therefore, was founded on the give and take of debate, discussion, and problem solving.

Task: Choose two areas of disagreement between the delegates to the Constitutional Convention.

For each of these areas of disagreement:

★ Describe the disagreement through a discussion of all sides of the problem.
★ Explain how the disagreement was resolved through compromise.

You may use any examples of compromise at the Constitutional Convention. These may include compromises over the following issues: representation, slavery, the slave trade, and foreign trade.

2. Theme: Interpreting the Bill of Rights

The Supreme Court has consistently had to make decisions over disputes involving the interpretation of the Bill of Rights. These disputes often involve issues of freedom of speech, separation of church and state, the right to assemble, freedom from illegal search and seizure, rights of accused persons, and freedom from cruel and unusual punishment.

Task: Choose two of the above issues.

For each issue:

★ Describe a dispute over the issue.
★ Discuss how the Supreme Court interpreted the Bill of Rights in order to resolve each dispute.

You *must* use a different issue and a different case in answering the question. You may, however, use any example from your study of the Supreme Court cases in this chapter.

DOCUMENT-BASED QUESTION

Read or analyze each document and answer the question that follows it. Then read the Task and write your essay. Essays should include references to most of the documents along with additional information based on your knowledge of United States history and government.

Historical Context: A critical period followed the success of the American Revolution. As a result, a new Constitution was created to replace the original organization of government known as the Articles of Confederation.

Document 1 Patrick Henry, at a debate in the Virginia ratifying convention, June 5, 1788:

> The Confederation . . . carried us through a long and dangerous war, it rendered us victorious in that bloody conflict with a powerful nation; it has secured us a territory greater than any European monarch possesses: and shall a government which has been thus strong and vigorous, be accused of imbecility and want of energy? Consider what you are about to do before you part with the government. . .

Question: Why does Patrick Henry feel that the Articles of Confederation should not be replaced?

Document 2 James Madison, in the *Federalist*, Number 10, 1787:

> Complaints are everywhere heard . . . that our governments are too unstable . . . it may be concluded that a pure democracy . . . can admit of no cure for the mischiefs of faction . . . A republic . . . promises the cure for which we are seeking . . .
> The effect is . . . to refine and enlarge the public views, by passing them through the medium of a chosen body of citizens, whose wisdom may best discern the true interest of their country. . . On the other hand, men of factious [dissenting] tempers, of local prejudices may . . . betray the interests of the people. . . The influence of factious leaders may kindle a flame within their particular States, but will be unable to spread a general conflagration [revolution] through the other States.

Question: Why does James Madison feel that the new constitution will better serve the people than the Articles of Confederation?

Document 3   Benjamin Franklin, on the actions of politicians:

Few men in public affairs act from a mere view of the good of their country, whatever they may pretend; and though their activity may bring real good to their country, they do not act from a spirit of benevolence.

Question: What dangers does Benjamin Franklin feel exist in any form of government?

Task: Using the information from the documents and your knowledge of the issues surrounding ratification of the Constitution of the United States, write an essay in which you:

★ Compare and contrast the arguments for and against the new Constitution.
★ Write an argument favoring either the arguments for or against ratification of the Constitution.

Chapter 3
The Federal Government
and the State Governments

★ Objectives

★ To understand how the legislative, executive, and judicial branches of the U.S. government are organized.

★ To know how the persons filling the positions in government are elected or chosen.

★ To evaluate the importance of selected landmark cases of the Supreme Court.

★ To know how the principle of separation of powers is carried out by state and local governments.

The Constitution gives the powers of the federal government to three separate groups, or branches: the legislative branch (Congress), the executive branch (the president), and the judicial branch (the courts).

The Congress

As the legislative branch of government, Congress has the major responsibility for making the nation's law.

Bicameral Organization

The Congress is *bicameral*. It is divided into two houses: a House of Representatives and a Senate. Each house must vote separately on all bills. The chart on page 70 summarizes differences between the two houses.

Apportionment of Seats in Congress A chief difference between the House and the Senate is that the House is affected by population change, while the

69

Senate is not. Every ten years, in the year ending in zero, a *census* (count) is taken to determine the population of the 50 states. In a process called *reapportionment*, a state that has gained population relative to other states will gain seats in the House. At the same time, a state that has lost population relative to other states will lose seats. The total number of House seats, however, remains the same (435) from one census year to the next. The number of Senate seats remains two for each state, no matter how a state's population changes.

Special Powers and Rules of the Senate The Constitution gives to the Senate certain lawmaking powers that it alone exercises. Only the Senate gives its "advice and consent" to treaties made by the executive branch. Only the Senate votes on whether or not to accept the president's nominations of high-level federal officials.

Each house determines its own rules for conducting business. A rule peculiar to the Senate allows for unlimited debate on the Senate "floor" (chamber where all members meet). Because of this rule, a small group of senators may attempt to defeat a bill favored by the majority simply by *filibustering*. This is the technique of speaking endlessly, thereby delaying a vote on the bill and weakening the majority's determination to pass it.

★ The Two Houses of Congress ★
A Comparison

	House of Representatives	Senate
Number of members	435; seats apportioned to each state according to the size of that state's population.	100; each state represented by two senators.
Term of each member	Two years; may be reelected to an unlimited number of terms; all members subject to election at the same time.	Six years; may be reelected to an unlimited number of terms; only about one-third of Senate seats subject to election in the same year.
Member's qualifications	At least 25 years old; U.S. citizen for at least seven years; resident of the state from which he or she was elected.	At least 30 years old; U.S. citizen for at least nine years; resident of the state from which he or she was elected.
Member's constituency (the people represented by each member)	Citizens residing within a congressional district (part of the state).	All citizens of the state.
Presiding officer	Speaker of the House	Vice president of the United States

Elections to Congress Elections to Congress are held in every even-numbered year—2000, 2002, and so on. All members of the House are subject to election at the same time. In the Senate, where members serve for six years, only one-third of the senators are elected at one time. The second third are elected two years later and a final third are elected two years after that. Because terms are staggered in this way, the Senate is more an ongoing body than the House.

Powers of Congress

The powers delegated to Congress by Article I of the Constitution include the power to collect taxes, borrow money, regulate trade, coin money, declare war, raise and support armed forces, and establish a post office.

Elastic Clause The final legislative power listed in Article I is known as the *elastic clause* because it gives Congress the ability to expand, or, stretch, its specific powers to meet a variety of circumstances. According to this clause, Congress may make "all laws that are necessary and proper" for carrying out its other powers. Because of the elastic clause, Congress can adapt to change by legislating on matters that were unknown back in 1789 (for example, regulating TV broadcasting or Internet contracts). Powers derived from the elastic clause are known as *implied powers*.

Limits of Power Besides granting certain powers to Congress, the Constitution also denies Congress certain powers. For example, Congress may not pass laws that allow it to (a) impose taxes on exports, (b) grant titles of nobility, (c) favor the ports of one state over those of another state, or (d) suspend the writ of *habeas corpus* except in an emergency. Such a writ is a document issued by a judge to protect citizens from being thrown into jail without a valid reason. The writ requires that the jailed person be brought promptly into court so that a judge can decide whether the person is being lawfully detained. (If not, the judge orders the prisoner's immediate release.)

Procedures for Making Laws

Congress could not possibly deal with the thousands of *bills* (proposals for laws) that come before it each year. Therefore, it relies upon committees to screen out bills that are unworthy of attention.

Committees and Subcommittees Committees of both the House and the Senate specialize in different areas of lawmaking. There are *standing* (permanent) *committees*, for example, on agriculture, foreign affairs, the armed services, commerce, and labor. Before any bill is voted upon by either the House or the Senate, it is first considered by the committee that specializes in the subject of the bill. Committees often divide into smaller working

Representative introduces bill by placing it in hopper. Speaker refers bill to proper committee.

Committee studies bill, holds hearings, and may change provisions. If approved, bill goes to Rules Committee.

Rules Committee places bill on calendar for discussion by entire House.

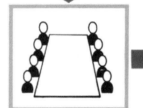

The bill is introduced in Senate, considered by committee, and debated by entire Senate. If Senate passes bill different from House version, bill goes to conference committee.

House debates bill and may pass it as is or with further change. If passed, bill goes to Senate.

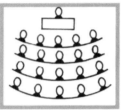

If conference committee of House and Senate members resolves differences, compromise bill is submitted to both House and Senate.

If both House and Senate pass compromise bill, it goes to President for signature.

If President signs, bill becomes law; if he vetoes, Congress may override veto by two-thirds vote of both House and Senate.

How a Bill Becomes a Law

groups, or subcommittees, that study bills in depth and report back to the full committee. Guided by a subcommittee's written report, the full committee votes on whether to approve the original bill as is, defeat the bill as is, or approve an *amended* (changed) version of the bill.

Floor Votes   If a bill is approved by committee, it then goes to the floor of the full House or Senate for debate and vote. The senators or representatives may debate the merits of the bill and propose amendments. To be *enacted* (passed), the bill must receive the "yea" (yes) votes of a majority of those present. After passage of a bill by one house, the bill then goes to the other house for its consideration and vote.

Conference Committee   The House and the Senate pass bills that are often very similar but not identical. For these bills to merge into one, the differences in them must be ironed out by a *conference committee*, consisting of members from both houses. If this committee agrees to a compromise, two identically worded bills go back to the full House and full Senate for a final vote.

Action by the President   If a bill is enacted by both houses—known at this stage as an *act of Congress*—it goes to the president, who may either sign it or veto it.

★ If it is signed, it becomes a law.
★ If it is unsigned, whether or not the act becomes a law depends on how long Congress continues in session.

(1) If Congress is in session longer than ten days after passing an act, a president wishing to veto the act must promptly return it to Congress with an explanation for vetoing it. Congress then has an opportunity to override the president's veto by a two-thirds vote. (See page 54.)

(2) If Congress is in session fewer than ten days after passing an act, the president can defeat the act simply by not signing it. This method of vetoing is known as the *pocket veto*.

Influence of Pressure Groups

How a member of Congress votes on a certain bill depends in part on whether the bill is favored or opposed by voters in the lawmaker's home district. Voters who wish to influence the lawmaking process may do so either as members of *special interest groups* or as individuals.

Group Action   Many businesses, labor unions, and other organizations have a special interest in influencing the decisions of Congress because certain laws directly affect them. (For example, farmers have a special interest in agriculture bills; senior citizens have a special interest in Social Security bills.) To oppose or support bills that affect them, special interest groups organize letter-writing campaigns, place advertisements, and hire *lobbyists* (professional representatives) to visit members of Congress in their offices. Many special interest groups form *political action committees (PACs)* to contribute money to the election campaigns of people running for Congress.

Individual Action   Also influencing government policy are those citizens who take the trouble to communicate their views to their elected representatives. They may either write letters to the representative or senator or visit the lawmaker's district office in their home state. Also, members of Congress may send out a mass mailing to their *constituents* (the voters in their district), asking their opinions on public issues. Of course, the final expression of public opinion comes on election day, when voters decide by majority vote whether those who currently represent them in government should be reelected.

The President

When the Constitution was written, the executive branch was meant to have the same amount of power as the other two branches. However, many historians believe that in the later 20th century, the presidency became more powerful than either Congress or the Supreme Court. In this section we will examine the growth of presidential power as well as the rules of the Constitution relating to the presidency.

Presidential Leadership

The president has many roles to play: chief executive, military leader, legislative leader, diplomatic leader, and ceremonial leader.

Chief Executive The Constitution states that the president shall be "chief executive," or head of government. In this capacity, the president directs the work of cabinet heads and supervises agencies that make up the executive branch. The enforcement of all federal laws and programs is ultimately the president's responsibility.

Among the dozens of government agencies that directly assist the nation's chief executive are:

★ The Office of Management and Budget (OMB), which prepares a spending plan each year for the government

★ The Central Intelligence Agency (CIA), which gathers information on foreign matters affecting national security

★ The National Aeronautics and Space Administration (NASA), which directs exploration in space.

Those officials who head the major departments of the federal government form a *cabinet* of advisers to the president. George Washington, the first president, had a cabinet that consisted of four members. Today, the cabinet has more than three times that number. Cabinet positions include the secretaries of agriculture, commerce, defense, education, energy, health and human services, housing and urban development, interior, justice, labor, state, transportation, treasury, and veterans' affairs.

Today, the executive branch employs some 3 million government workers (or civil servants) and spends more than $1 trillion a year. The president's chief responsibilities include giving leadership to this immense organization and recommending a workable budget to Congress.

Military Leader: Commander in Chief The president is the commander in chief of the armed forces. Although a civilian, the president outranks every general and admiral. The president must approve the most important military decisions. For example, when U.S. troops were sent into Bosnia in 1995 to oversee the peace treaty ending the war with Croatia and Serbia, the action had the approval of President Clinton.

Legislative Leader In the role of legislative leader, the president recommends new laws in an annual State of the Union address. For example, President Lyndon Johnson recommended to Congress an ambitious Civil Rights Act, which he persuaded Congress to pass and then signed into law in 1964. Another legislative power is the president's ability to call Congress into special session after it has adjourned for the year. The president either signs or vetoes acts of Congress.

Diplomatic Leader The Constitution gives to the president the power to (1) make treaties (with the approval of two-thirds of the Senate), (2) receive ambassadors from other countries (and thereby recognize those governments), and (3) nominate U.S. ambassadors to other countries (with the approval of a majority of the Senate). For example, in 1803 President Thomas Jefferson arranged a treaty with France by which that country's huge Louisiana Territory was added to the United States. Because of these diplomatic powers, the president is the chief maker of U.S. foreign policy.

Ceremonial Leader: Chief of State In many nations, the *chief of state* (a ceremonial leader) is different from the *chief executive* (head of government). Great Britain, for example, has both a prime minister who acts as the political leader and a monarch who acts as the ceremonial chief of state. In the United States, the president serves in both roles. In the chief of state's role, the president speaks for the nation when traveling abroad and at home tries to inspire the American people to honor their traditions and live up to their ideals.

Judicial Role Occasionally, the president participates in the judicial process by granting either a *pardon* (forgiveness for a federal crime) or a *reprieve* (delay of punishment). When a vacancy occurs on the Supreme Court, the president nominates a new justice, submitting the choice to the Senate for its *confirmation* (approval).

The Election Process

Every four years, on the second Tuesday in November, millions of eligible voters 18 years and older enter voting booths to elect a president and vice president. Of course, the election process begins not on the day of election but many months earlier. Let us review the main stages of the long campaign for the presidency.

Nominating Candidates for President and Vice President Those wishing to be president begin their campaign by seeking the nomination of either the Democratic party, the Republican party, or one of several minor parties. In the summer of the presidential election year, each political party holds a national convention at which delegates from the 50 states nominate (vote for) the party's candidates for president and vice president.

How are convention delegates chosen? Most of the delegates to a party's convention are elected by the voters belonging to that party. Such pre-convention elections are known as *primaries*. Each party holds its own primary.

The candidate who wins his or her party's primary election in a state receives most or all of that state's delegate votes at the national convention. In recent elections, a single candidate in each party won enough primaries to be assured of winning nomination at the party's convention. After the convention votes for a presidential nominee, this person usually selects a running mate who is the party's candidate for vice president.

The Fall Campaign Following the conventions, the campaign moves to the final stage. Campaigning together, the presidential and vice presidential nominees of each party travel the nation seeking votes in the November election. They also devote much time to appearing on television—a medium that now plays a decisive role in the campaign process.

The Electoral College People who vote on election day may think that they are voting directly for a president and a vice president. In fact, they are voting for a number of *electors* (either Republican electors or Democratic elec-

Presidential Campaign 2000: Texas Governor George W. Bush and Vice President Al Gore greeting their supporters.

tors) who are authorized by the Constitution to cast ballots for president and vice president.

Electors are assigned to the 50 states according to the size of a state's delegation in Congress. Nevada, for example, had two representatives and two senators in 1996, giving it four electors. California had 52 representatives and two senators, giving it 54 electors.

The candidate who wins a majority of a state's *popular votes* (those cast by the people) wins all of that state's electoral votes. The winning group of electors in each state makes up that state's *electoral college*. The electors cast ballots for president and vice president about one month after the popular election in November. Almost always, the electors can be counted upon to cast their ballots for the candidates favored by a majority of the voters.

If There Is No Majority   If there are more than two major candidates in the race for president and no one wins a majority (more than 50 percent) of the electoral ballots, the Constitution provides that the election be decided by a special vote in the House of Representatives. In the House, the delegation of each state is given just one vote. The candidate who wins a majority of the House vote is elected president.

Unusual Elections

Election of 1800: Tie vote broken by the House. Electoral Vote: Jefferson, 73; Burr, 73.

Since no candidate had an electoral majority, the election was decided by the House of Representatives. The winner: Jefferson.

Election of 1824: Defeat of the most popular candidate

Candidate	Popular Vote	Electoral Vote
Andrew Jackson	153,544	99
John Quincy Adams	108,740	84
William H. Crawford	46,618	41
Henry Clay	47,136	37

Since no candidate had an electoral majority, the election was decided by the House. The winner: John Quincy Adams.

Election of 1876: Defeat of the more popular candidate

Candidate	Popular Vote	Electoral Vote
Samuel J. Tilden	4,284,020	184
Rutherford B. Hayes	4,036,572	185

This disputed election was resolved by a special commission in favor of Hayes.

Election of 1888: Defeat of the more popular candidate

Candidate	Popular Vote	Electoral Vote
Benjamin Harrison	5,447,129	233
Grover Cleveland	5,537,857	168

The winner, Harrison, had less than a majority of the popular vote.

Election of 1912: Three-way race

Candidate	Popular Vote	Electoral Vote
Woodrow Wilson	6,296,547	435
Theodore Roosevelt	4,118,571	88
William H. Taft	3,486,720	8

The winner, Wilson, had less than a majority of the popular vote.

Arguments for and Against the System Our election system has long been a subject for debate. Some people argue that the system should be kept unchanged. Others advocate a variety of methods for either eliminating the electoral college or modifying it. (See the table below, The Electoral College.)

Debating the Electoral College

Examine the arguments for and against the electoral college system in the following table. Then decide which position you support and why.

★ The Electoral College ★

Arguments For	Arguments Against
1. The system is democratic since electors vote according to the will of each state then in majority.	1. A far more democratic system would be one in which people vote directly for a president and vice president. There is no need for a second election involving only a small number of electors.
2. The federal system emphasizes the importance of the states. As the electoral college permits voting to be expressed state by state, the federal principle is carried out.	2. Although it rarely happens, electors can vote contrary to the wishes of the majority of voters. In a democracy, this is a dangerous possibility.
3. The system is good for minority groups, since candidates must appeal to them in order to win election in a large urban state.	3. If three or more candidates compete for the presidency, there is a good chance that the election will be decided—not by the people—but by the House of Representatives.
4. The system is good for lightly populated states since it guarantees each of them at least four electoral votes.	4. The system is too good for a lightly populated state like Nevada; its four electoral votes give it greater weight in the election total than its population justifies.

Rules of Succession

Every nation must be concerned with developing orderly procedures for re-placing its chief executive if that person should fall seriously ill or die. In the United States the *rules of succession* are spelled out in an act of Congress and two amendments to the Constitution.

Act of Presidential Succession   A 1947 act of Congress states that the vice president shall automatically become president if the president dies. It then lists those officials who become president if both the president and vice president died at the same time. Next in line after the vice president is the Speaker of the House, then the president pro tempore of the Senate, and then the department heads in the cabinet in the order in which the departments were created, beginning with the secretary of state.

Twenty-second Amendment   Adopted in 1951, the Twenty-second Amendment provides that no person may serve more than two elected terms as president. This amendment was adopted after Franklin D. Roosevelt had won election to the presidency four times, causing some people to worry about a president becoming too powerful.

Twenty-fifth Amendment   This amendment, adopted in 1967, describes what happens if the president is disabled by illness or injury. It allows for three possibilities: (1) The disabled president may prepare a written statement saying that he or she is unable to carry out presidential powers and duties. After this statement is received by leaders of both houses of Congress, the vice president then temporarily serves as acting president. (2) The vice president, if supported by a majority of the cabinet, may submit a written declaration to the leaders of Congress stating that the president is unable to "discharge the powers and duties of his office." Then the vice president serves as acting president. (3) In a third circumstance, the president may believe that he or she is capable of carrying out presidential duties, while the vice president and a majority of cabinet members think the president is incapable. Congress would then have the power to decide the issue. If the president's view is to be overruled, a two-thirds vote of Congress is required.

Removal of President by Impeachment

The Constitution says that a president who commits "high crimes and misdemeanors" may be forced to leave office by a procedure known as *impeachment*. First, the House of Representatives decides by majority vote whether or not to impeach (accuse) a president of acting either dishonestly or unlawfully. If the impeachment bill is passed, the Senate then meets as a trial court presided over by the chief justice of the Supreme Court. Two-thirds of the senators must vote for conviction if an impeached president is to be removed.

Two presidents, Andrew Johnson (in 1868) and Bill Clinton (in 1998), were impeached by the House but then acquitted by the Senate. Richard Nixon resigned from office in 1974 before the House could vote on a bill of impeachment.

The Presidency and the Unwritten Constitution

The *unwritten constitution* refers to traditions that have become part of our political system. For example: (1) Most elected offices are filled by members of two major political parties, the Republicans and the Democrats, even though there is no mention of political parties in the Constitution. (2) After George Washington, the first president, declined to serve more than two terms, later presidents made the same decision. The "two-term tradition," as it was called, was finally broken in 1940, when Franklin Roosevelt ran successfully for a third term. He also won a fourth term in 1944. (In 1947, supporters of the two-term tradition persuaded the nation to adopt the Twenty-second Amendment, which limits the president to two elected terms.) (3) The Constitution says nothing about the president's cabinet. But early in his presidency, George Washington made a habit of meeting with a cabinet of four advisers. Since then, presidents have asked Congress to add new cabinet positions to meet the needs of changing times.

Growth of Presidential Power

The office of U.S. president is today considered the most powerful elected position in the world. However, it was not always so powerful. In 1789, the United States was a nation of only 4 million people. It had a new and untried government, an agricultural economy, and a tiny army and navy. Today, it is a mighty industrial nation with one of the largest armed forces in the world. As the power of the nation has grown, so has the power of the presidency. The growth of presidential power in both domestic affairs and foreign affairs can be traced to the beginning years of the 20th century.

President's Leadership in Domestic Affairs   In the early 1900s, three successive presidents—Theodore Roosevelt, William H. Taft, and Woodrow Wilson—responded vigorously to public demands for honest and efficient government. Reforms championed by these presidents (see Chapter 10) won the admiration of millions of citizens. Vigorous leadership was provided by Franklin D. Roosevelt in the 1930s and 1940s in meeting the economic crisis of the Great Depression and then leading the nation to victory in World War II. In the 20th century, no other president did more than Roosevelt to increase the power and prestige of the presidency. Adding further to the central role of modern presidents was the civil rights movement in the 1950s and 1960s. Four presidents—Truman, Eisenhower, Kennedy, and Johnson—generally supported the struggle of African Americans to obtain relief from discriminatory laws.

President's Leadership in Foreign Affairs   The increased role of the president in domestic affairs has been matched by an increased role in international affairs. As a leader of the world's strongest nation, the president meets often with other world leaders at global economic summit conferences.

The necessity for quick decision making in a crisis has further added to presidential power. In the fast-paced age of jet planes, nuclear weapons, and computer-controlled missile-delivery systems, the awesome responsibility of deciding how to respond to a perceived military attack must usually be entrusted to a single leader, rather than to the much slower deliberation of Congress's 535 members.

Additional Factors Modern technology allows presidents to speak to and be viewed by the entire nation. On television the president is seen almost daily (unlike the average member of Congress, who appears on national TV news infrequently, if at all).

Because the federal government has expanded to include agencies that affect all aspects of our lives, from health to Social Security to housing, the president's ability to influence our lives through presidential appointments and policies has also expanded.

★ In Review

1. Describe three differences between the Senate and the House of Representatives.
2. List two limits on the powers of Congress.
3. How does a bill become a law?
4. Describe three important powers of the president of the United States.

The Supreme Court and Lower Courts

In Article III the framers of the Constitution established a federal *judiciary* (court system) as the third branch of government. Article III gives certain powers to a Supreme Court but leaves to Congress the responsibility of organizing the lower courts. Let us examine the jurisdiction of the Supreme Court, the organization of the federal courts, and some significant early Supreme Court decisions.

Jurisdiction of the Supreme Court

The Supreme Court is the only court in the federal system that has both *original jurisdiction* and *appellate jurisdiction*. In a small number of cases, the Supreme Court is authorized by the Constitution to act as a trial court (a court with original jurisdiction). Such cases include those involving (1) ambassadors and (2) disputes between the states. The Supreme Court also has the authority to review cases appealed to it from lower courts. In these cases it has appellate jurisdiction. It may decide either to uphold the decision of the lower court or to overturn that decision.

Justices of the Supreme Court Congress has the power to determine the number of justices who shall sit on the Supreme Court. The first Supreme Court had six justices; today there are nine (one chief justice and eight

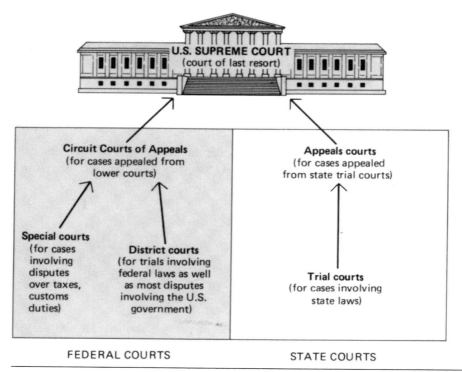

U.S. SUPREME COURT
(court of last resort)

Circuit Courts of Appeals
(for cases appealed from
lower courts)

Appeals courts
(for cases appealed
from state trial courts)

Special courts
(for cases
involving
disputes
over taxes,
customs
duties)

District courts
(for trials involving
federal laws as well
as most disputes
involving the U.S.
government)

Trial courts
(for cases involving
state laws)

FEDERAL COURTS   STATE COURTS

Federal Courts, State Courts, and the Appeals Process

associate justices). Cases are decided by majority vote. One of the justices in the majority is assigned the task of writing the constitutional reasons for the Court's decision. A judge who does not agree with the majority may write a *dissenting opinion*.

Life Tenure   According to the Constitution, Supreme Court justices and all other judges in the federal government "shall hold their offices during good behavior." Thus, there is no fixed limit on a judge's term of office. In effect, a federal judge may be in office for life or until she or he voluntarily retires. As a result of this rule, a federal judge feels no pressure to make decisions to win the favor of politicians or the popularity of voters.

Organization of the Federal Courts

In 1789 Congress passed the Federal Judiciary Act, which organized the *federal court system*. It set up a district court (or lower court) in each state. Three circuit courts (or appeals courts) were created with the power to review the district courts' decisions. Since then, as the nation has grown, so has the number of courts. In 2000 there were 94 district courts and 13 circuit courts, in addition to the highest court—the U.S. Supreme Court.

Trial Courts Most trials for cases involving federal laws are held in district courts. Such courts have original jurisdiction for conducting trials.

The Appeals Process A lawyer who believes that a trial has been unfair may appeal the district court's decision to a circuit court. Courts that hear appeals cases have what is known as appellate jurisdiction. If unsuccessful there, the lawyer may make a further appeal to the Supreme Court, "the court of last resort." Cases begun in a state court may also be heard by the Supreme Court following a hearing by that state's appeals court. However, the Supreme Court is not required to hear all of the many cases that are appealed each year. It has the power to decide either to hear a case on appeal or not to hear it.

Landmark Decisions of John Marshall

John Marshall served as chief justice of the United States from 1801 to 1835. He was remarkably successful in establishing the Supreme Court as an independent and influential force in the federal government. Three of Marshall's most important decisions are summarized here.

Marbury v. *Madison* (1803) Just before leaving office, President John Adams appointed William Marbury as a federal court judge. Thomas Jefferson, the next president, ordered his secretary of state, James Madison, not to carry out the appointment. Marbury appealed to the Supreme Court, arguing that a 1789 law granted the Supreme Court the power to force

Chief Justice John Marshall

Madison to give Marbury his appointment. But Chief Justice Marshall, writing the majority opinion of the highest court, argued that the 1789 law of Congress applying to Marbury's case was not authorized by the Constitution. Thus, the law was *unconstitutional*—null and void.

The Supreme Court's decision in this case established the principle of judicial review. *Judicial review* is the power of the Supreme Court to rule on the constitutionality of federal and state laws. Each case decided by the highest court involves a question of how the words of the Constitution apply to a unique set of circumstances. Of course, the circumstances keep changing. In the 1880s and 1890s, many cases involved the issue of regulating railroads and oil companies—institutions that were unknown to the Constitution's framers. In the future, issues involving computer technologies will probably make up a large number of Supreme Court cases. No matter what the issue, the Supreme Court uses its power of judicial review to adapt the Constitution to changing circumstances.

McCulloch v. Maryland (1819)   At issue in this case was whether a state government (Maryland) could collect a tax from a bank that had been chartered by the U.S. government. Marshall argued that the states could not tax a federal agency because, according to the Constitution, the federal government was meant to be supreme. Marshall stated that "the power to tax is the power to destroy." On another question, Marshall argued that Congress's powers could be interpreted loosely to authorize the creation of a national bank.

★ ★ ★ ★ ★

McCULLOCH V. MARYLAND

Could the state of Maryland tax a bank created by the U.S. Congress? Did Congress have the constitutional power to create such a bank? Here is John Marshall's answer to these questions in the landmark case of *McCulloch* v. *Maryland* (1819).

We admit, as all must admit, that the powers of the government are limited, and that its limits are not to be transcended. But we think the sound construction of the Constitution must allow to the national legislature that discretion, with respect to the means by which the powers it confers are to be carried into execution, which will enable that body to perform the high duties assigned to it, in the manner most beneficial to the people. Let the end be legitimate, let it be within the scope of the Constitution, and all means which are appropriate, which are plainly adapted to that end, which are not prohibited, but consistent with the letter and spirit of the Constitution, are constitutional. . . .

This case established the idea that a state law could be *nullified* (declared void) if it was found to be in conflict with a federal law.

Gibbons v. Ogden (1824)   At issue in this case was whether a state (New York) could grant to one steamship company the exclusive right to operate on an interstate waterway (the Hudson River). In his decision Marshall stated that trade is commerce, that commerce between states was controlled by the U.S. Congress, and therefore that New York's law was invalid.

The ruling clarified the concept of interstate commerce and increased the authority of the federal government to regulate businesses that operate in more than one state.

Impact of Marshall's Decisions   Taken as a whole, the many cases decided by Chief Justice Marshall increased the power of the national government in relation to that of the states. Also, by the repeated application of judicial review, Marshall greatly expanded the power and influence of the Supreme Court.

Separation of Powers in a Federal System

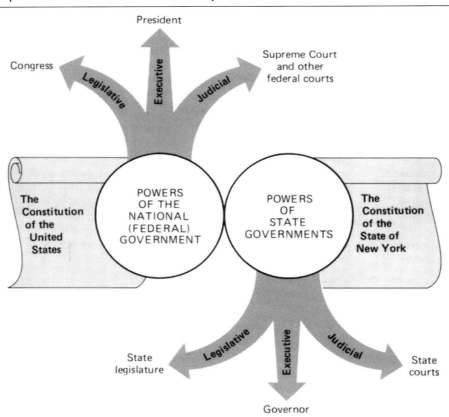

The States in the Federal System

Citizens of the United States are also citizens of the states in which they reside. While the U.S. government takes responsibility for national problems and foreign affairs, the states have authority for dealing with such local issues as education, public safety, and public health. The organization of state governments is similar to that of the national government. Each of the 50 states has its own constitution, which provides for the separation of powers among a legislative branch, a judicial branch, and an executive branch headed by a governor.

Admission of New States   Thirty-seven of the present 50 states were admitted to the Union after the Constitution was written in 1787. The Constitution in Article IV provides that new states may be admitted to the Union, and Congress was given the power to make rules and regulations regarding the territories of the United States. First, a territory formally applies to Congress for statehood. The territory must submit a proposed state constitution that has been approved by the people of the territory. By majority vote, Congress may either accept or reject a territory's application for statehood. At times Congress may attach conditions to statehood. In 1896, for example, Utah was admitted as a state on the condition that it forbid *polygamy* (the practice of being married to two or more persons at the same time). The last two territories to apply for admission, Hawaii and Alaska, won statehood in 1959.

New York State Government

The Legislative Branch

Like the U.S. government, New York State's government has a representative legislature whose members debate and vote upon proposed laws for the state. Representing the citizens who elect them, state lawmakers vote on issues such as these:

★ How much money should be spent for education, human services, and the environment?

★ Should penalties for serious crimes be changed?

★ How much money should be set aside for mass transit and highways?

Bicameral Organization   Like Congress, almost all the state legislatures have two houses, both of which must approve bills by majority vote. In New York State the larger of the two houses is called the assembly and the smaller house the senate.

The Politics of Redistricting   Periodically, district lines for the houses of the state legislature are changed to reflect shifts in population. The New York

State legislature has the power to vote on how the new district boundaries shall be drawn. Often, by a common practice called *gerrymandering*, politicians belonging to the majority party in the legislature draw district lines that favor their party. To restrict this practice, the U.S. Supreme Court ruled in *Baker* v. *Carr* (1962) that legislative district lines must reflect the principle of "one man, one vote." In other words, districts must be roughly equal in population to ensure that residents of the districts are equally represented. Despite this requirement, district lines can still be twisted out of shape—or gerrymandered—to make it easier for the candidates of one political party to win an election.

The Executive Branch

New York State's chief executive is the governor. Just as the president enforces the laws of Congress, the governor's primary role is to carry out, or enforce, the laws of the state. To assist in this complicated task, the governor directs a number of executive departments and agencies, each responsible for a different function. For example, a highway department maintains state roads, and an education department supervises state schools.

The Governor's Influence on Legislation The governor provides legislative as well as executive leadership. He or she proposes a legislative *program* (series of bills) and tries to persuade a majority of state lawmakers to vote for it. The governor, like the president, has the power to veto bills.

Every year, the governor of New York (and all the other states) recommends a state *budget* (taxing and spending plan) to the legislature. To persuade the legislatures to approve their proposed budgets, governors make full use of their executive authority, access to the media, and political influence as party leaders.

Other Duties The governor nominates the heads of executive departments and agencies. In many states the governor also appoints state judges. Usually, a governor's appointments require the approval of one of the two houses of the legislature. The governor also is commander in chief of the state's *national guard* (a military force consisting of citizen volunteers). In times of emergency, natural disaster, or riot, the governor may order national guard units into action. If necessary, the governor may also request that the president call federal units into service.

The governor may grant a *pardon* (forgiveness for a crime) or a *reprieve* (postponement of a punishment) to a person convicted of a state crime.

The Judicial Branch

New York State has its own court system, consisting of both lower courts for trying cases and higher courts for hearing appeals. The lower court is called the New York State Supreme Court. The higher court is called the New York State Court of Appeals.

Functions The three main functions of state courts are to (1) hear criminal cases involving violations of state laws, (2) settle legal disputes between citizens, and (3) resolve cases involving the interpretation of the state constitution.

The Judicial Process Before any criminal case goes to trial, a group of citizens called a *grand jury* (large jury) decides whether there is enough evidence to indict, or accuse, a certain person of committing a crime. If so, the indicted person stands trial in a state trial court, where a *petit jury* (smaller jury) decides the person's guilt or innocence. If found guilty, the convicted person may appeal the case to a state appeals court. If the case involves a federal issue or an interpretation of the Constitution, a final appeal may be made to the Supreme Court.

In making their decisions, state courts must be guided not only by the rules of the state constitution, but also by the rights guaranteed by the Constitution.

Interstate Relations

Because each state is free to make laws and regulations of its own, there could be a problem of states competing with one another rather than working together for their mutual good. But two factors help to alleviate the problem: provisions of the U.S. Constitution and interstate agreements, or compacts.

"Full Faith and Credit" Imagine, for a moment, these possibilities:

★ Your automobile license is not recognized as valid when you drive out of state.

★ Your high school diploma is considered legitimate only by your own state.

Fortunately, neither event could occur because Article IV of the Constitution requires that states give "full faith and credit" to each other's laws, licenses, and official documents. For example, the state of Florida must honor the drivers' licenses granted by New York State to New Yorkers traveling in Florida. However, the scope of the "full faith and credit" clause is limited. A state may require that its lawyers and teachers meet its own licensing standards and may refuse to acknowledge out-of-state certificates in these professions as valid.

Interstate Compacts States that share a common border often recognize that they have a mutual interest in solving a common problem. By signing *interstate compacts*, the governors of neighboring states establish *regional agencies* managed by officials from those states. An example is the Port Authority of New York and New Jersey, which operates interstate bridges and tunnels on either side of the Hudson River.

Local Governments Within the states, there are smaller units of government for counties, villages, towns, and *municipalities* (cities). Each unit has its own governing bodies for carrying out duties within its jurisdiction. Most municipalities, for example, have their own police, fire, sanitation, and health departments.

Local officials such as mayors, city managers, and county executives act in the role of chief executive, supervising the departments of the municipal or county government. Members of city councils and county boards of supervisors (or freeholders) have legislative powers for making local regulations called *ordinances*. In making their decisions, both legislative bodies and executive officials must be careful to conform to state laws.

Funding the public schools and other local institutions comes mainly from property taxes collected on the value of residents' homes and local businesses. These tax revenues are supplemented by grants of money from both the state and federal governments.

Chapter Review

MULTIPLE-CHOICE QUESTIONS

1. The illustration on page 85 shows that
   (1) New York State government works in conflict with the federal government
   (2) both the federal and New York State governments employ a system of checks and balances
   (3) few powers are shared by New York State and the federal government
   (4) New York State has no equivalent to the U.S. Congress.

2. The illustration of the most common method of amending the Constitution (page 62) shows that the

(1) process is fairly simple and easy
(2) president may veto any proposed amendment
(3) states have a significant role in the amendment process
(4) Supreme Court may declare an amendment unconstitutional.

3. Which situation in the United States is an illustration of lobbying?
   (1) A defeated candidate for the Senate is appointed a member of the president's cabinet.
   (2) A special interest group hires a person to present its views to certain members of Congress.

(3) Federal public works projects are awarded to a state.
(4) Two members of Congress agree to support each other's bills.

4. In the United States, the electoral college system influences presidential candidates to
(1) make personal appearances in every state
(2) campaign extensively in states with large populations
(3) state their platforms in *very* specific terms
(4) seek endorsements from state governors.

5. A power shared by both the state governments and the federal government is the power to
(1) regulate interstate commerce
(2) issue money
(3) declare war
(4) collect taxes.

6. In a presidential election, the electoral vote was distributed as follows:

Candidate	A	B	C	D
Percentage of electoral vote	38	38	16	8

Based on this information, which is a valid statement about the outcome of the election?
(1) Candidate A was declared the winner immediately after the election.
(2) Candidate A became president and Candidate B became vice president.
(3) Another presidential election was held in order to determine a winner.
(4) The president was chosen by a vote of the House of Representatives.

7. The principle of federalism as established by the U.S. Constitution provides for the
(1) separation of powers of the three branches of government
(2) placement of ultimate sovereignty in the hands of the state governments
(3) division of power between the state governments and the national government
(4) creation of a republican form of government.

8. How did the Supreme Court under Chief Justice John Marshall influence U.S. history?
(1) The Court stimulated the states' rights movement by supporting the idea that states could reject acts of Congress.
(2) The Court's decisions in many cases helped to strengthen the federal government.
(3) The Court weakened the judiciary by refusing to deal with controversial issues.
(4) The Court became deeply involved with foreign affairs.

9. The fact that the U.S. Constitution provides for federalism and a system of checks and balances suggests that
(1) the original 13 states sought to dominate the national government
(2) its writers desired the national government to rule over the states
(3) its writers feared a concentration of political power
(4) the American people supported a military government.

10. Which statement is the most accurate about the role and function of the president?

(1) The president holds the most power in the federal government.
(2) The office of president has a variety of functions that include influencing legislation, conducting foreign affairs, and appointing justices to the Supreme Court.

(3) Laws may not be passed without the approval of the president.
(4) The president does not have as much power as the Supreme Court but has more power than Congress.

THEMATIC ESSAYS

1. **Theme:** The Powers of the President

   The powers of the president have increased over time in order to meet the challenges posed by developments in the nation and the world.

   Task: Choose two instances in which a problem, crisis, or an emergency demanded an increase of presidential powers.

   For each situation:

   ★ Describe the problem, crisis, or emergency.

   ★ Demonstrate how the solution increased the power of the president.

   You may utilize any two situations from your study of the Constitution, the presidency, and American history. Some situations that you might wish to include involve civil rights, economic depression, the need for honest and efficient government, and national emergencies, such as war or rebellion.

2. **Theme:** State and Federal Powers

   Our Constitution provides for a federal system of government that delegates certain powers to the national (federal) government, reserves other powers for the states, and provides for concurrent, or shared, powers between the federal and state governments.

   Task: Choose one power that illustrates each of the following:

   ★ Powers that are delegated to the federal government.

   ★ Powers that are reserved for the various state governments.

   ★ Powers that are concurrent, or shared, between federal and state governments.

   Explain why the writers of the Constitution created each power that you have selected as a national, state, or shared power.

DOCUMENT-BASED QUESTION

*Read or analyze each document and answer the question that follows it. Then read the **Task** and write your essay. Essays should include references to most of the documents along with additional information based on your knowledge of United States history and government.*

Historical Context: The writers of the Constitution created a government that was designed to meet the needs of the new nation while at the same time avoiding becoming abusive in its power.

Document 1   From the Constitution of the United States:

> The Congress shall have the power to make all laws which shall be necessary and proper for carrying into execution the foregoing powers and all other powers vested by this Constitution in the government of the United States, or in any department or officer thereof.

Question: How does the elastic clause of the Constitution help the Congress to pass needed laws?

Document 2   Refer to the reading on page 84.

Question: What decision did the Supreme Court, in the case of *McCulloch* v. *Maryland*, reach about the power of Congress?

Document 3   From the Supreme Court's decision in *Gideon* v. *Wainwright*, 1963:

> We accept *Betts* v. *Brady's* assumption . . . that a provision of the Bill of Rights which is "fundamental and essential to a fair trial" is made *obligatory* [binding] upon the States by the Fourteenth Amendment. We think the Court in *Betts* was wrong, however, in concluding that the Sixth Amendment's guarantee of counsel is not one of those fundamental rights. . . .
>
> Reason and reflection require us to recognize that in our . . . system of criminal justice, any person [brought] into court, who is too poor to hire a lawyer, cannot be assured a fair trial unless counsel is provided for him. . . .
>
> The judgment is reversed. . . .

Question: Why did the Supreme Court reverse the decision of a lower court?

Task: Using the information from the documents and your knowledge of United States history and government, write an essay that illustrates how our Constitution has been flexible enough to adapt to the needs of changing times yet secure enough to ensure that it does not abuse its power.

Chapter 4
Implementing Principles
of the New Constitution

$\mathbf{T}$he U.S. political system consists of much more than the words of the Constitution. Continually shaping and reshaping that system are the day-to-day actions of leaders in all three branches of government. The first presidents to lead the executive branch strongly affected not only their own times but also the future development of the U.S. government. This chapter tells of the problems they confronted, the decisions they made, and the long-term effects of their decisions.

Policies of Five Presidents

After the Constitution was ratified, steps were taken in each state to elect senators and representatives to the first Congress (that is, the first one to meet under the new Constitution). In addition, a group of electors (special voters for president and vice president) were chosen by the 13 states. The electors agreed by unanimous vote that George Washington should be the first president. By April 1789, both the first president and the first Congress had been sworn into office. Thus, the Constitution drafted in 1787 went into effect less than two years later.

Would the federal system of government created by the Constitution work well or poorly? Because the system was new and untried in the 1790s, no one could be certain of the answer.

Domestic Policy: Hamilton's Financial Plan

In order to get the nation started on a sound financial basis, Washington selected Alexander Hamilton as secretary of the treasury. Hamilton proposed a series of measures for strengthening the finances of the newly created U.S. government. Hamilton's financial plan was eventually enacted by Congress after a bitter struggle with Secretary of State Thomas Jefferson and James Madison. Included in the plan were: (1) a means for repaying the debts of the states and the national government; (2) the establishment of a national bank for depositing both tax revenues and merchants' loans to the U.S. government; and (3) tariffs to protect new American industries from foreign competition. Jefferson and Madison opposed Hamilton's plan because his policies favored business interests and the North rather than agrarian interests and the South. In addition, Jefferson believed that the federal government would gain too much power at the expense of the states. Hamilton's plan, however, provided financial stability for the new nation and contributed to its economic growth.

Development of Unwritten Constitutional Government

George Washington served two terms as president (1789–1797). More than any later president, Washington made decisions and adopted policies that profoundly influenced the nature of American government. In his first term Washington decided to (1) form a cabinet and (2) put down a rebellion (see page 96). Other major policy decisions that became part of the unwritten constitution were made by John Adams, the second president, and his successor, Thomas Jefferson.

The First Cabinet (1789) A cabinet consists of high-level officials who meet as a group to advise the chief executive. Cabinet meetings are not mentioned in the Constitution. But Washington's decision in 1789 to appoint a secretary of state (Thomas Jefferson), a secretary of the treasury (Alexander Hamilton), a secretary of war (Henry Knox), and an attorney general (Edmund Randolph) established the cabinet as a permanent institution of the executive branch.

Political Parties Although Washington expected to receive conflicting advice from various cabinet members, he hoped to avoid the formation of political parties. These parties are not mentioned in the Constitution, yet they form the basis for U.S. elections. The two major political parties in the United States today are the Democratic and the Republican parties.

Establishing a Stable Political System

Formation of Political Parties: The Federalists Conflict over Hamilton's financial plan was one reason that two political parties emerged in the 1790s. Leading the two parties were rival members of Washington's cabinet, Alexander Hamilton and Thomas Jefferson. Hamilton's party, the Federalists, favored government policies that would serve the interests of northern merchants and, to a lesser extent, of southern planters. The merchants approved Hamilton's program for the following reasons:

★ They thought it would help the national government to become strong and stable. (Stable government promotes a healthy economy.)

★ They wanted a national bank to serve as a source of loans for new businesses.

★ They hoped that tariffs would protect new, or "infant," industries in the United States from foreign competition.

On constitutional issues, the Federalists argued for *loose construction*—the idea that government had many powers that were implied by the Constitution's "necessary and proper," or elastic, clause.

George Washington, first president, and his first cabinet: Henry Knox, Thomas Jefferson, Alexander Hamilton, and Edmund Randolph

★ America's First Political Parties ★

	Federalists	Democratic-Republicans
Leaders	Alexander Hamilton John Adams John Marshall	Thomas Jefferson James Madison James Monroe
Geographic strength	Strongest support among merchants of the Northeast	Strongest support among farmers of the South and West
Position on Hamilton's financial plan	Favored all parts of the plan (establishing central bank, funding the debt, protecting infant industries)	Opposed all parts of the plan
Position on constitutional issues	Favored loose construction of the Constitution to give the national government maximum power	Favored strict construction of the Constitution to limit the national government's power and safeguard the independent powers of the states
Position on foreign policy	Though partial to the British, supported Washington's Proclamation of Neutrality	Though partial to the French, supported Jefferson's attempts to maintain U.S. neutrality during the Napoleonic wars

The Democratic-Republicans   Opposing the Federalists was a second political party, the Democratic-Republicans. Led by Thomas Jefferson, this party favored government policies that would promote the interests of farmers and the common people. It opposed Hamilton's financial plan for several reasons.

First, full payment of the national debt by buying back government bonds would benefit *speculators* (those who buy and sell bonds and other property in the hope of making huge profits). Many bondholders had obtained government bonds at a reduced rate and stood to make a fortune if the government bought them back at full value.

Second, a national bank would provide loans for northern merchants, but it would be less likely to lend money to western and southern farmers.

Unlike the Federalists, Jefferson and the Democratic-Republicans argued for strict construction of the Constitution, meaning that the federal government should do no more than what specific clauses of the Constitution allowed. (However, Jefferson would later reverse his position when, as president, he had the opportunity to purchase the vast Louisiana Territory from France. For a full discussion, see Chapter 6.)

During the Federalist era, the two-party system became an important and enduring part of American government.

The Whisky Rebellion (1794)   To raise revenue, Congress placed a federal excise tax on the distilling of whisky. (An *excise tax* is a tax on the sale of a product made within the country collecting the tax.) News of the whisky tax provoked an armed revolt among whisky-producing farmers in western Pennsylvania. Washington's decision to send troops to put down the rebellion demonstrated that the federal government had real power to act effectively in a crisis, unlike the confederate government of the 1780s, which could do nothing about Shays's Rebellion. Not everyone approved Washington's use of a large army to deal with the rebellion. Thomas Jefferson, the secretary of state, said the government's action was like using "a meat axe to kill a spider."

Alien and Sedition Acts (1798) Conflict between the two parties was particularly bitter during the presidency of Washington's successor, John Adams (1797–1801). A Federalist majority in Congress enacted two laws whose chief purpose was to intimidate the supporters of the Democratic-Republicans. The *Alien Act* authorized the president to deport foreigners residing in the United States who were thought to be dangerous to the public safety. The *Sedition Act* authorized the government to fine and imprison newspaper editors who printed any "scandalous and malicious writing" about the government.

The state legislatures of Virginia and Kentucky passed resolutions that protested these acts and claimed the right to *nullify* (disregard) them as

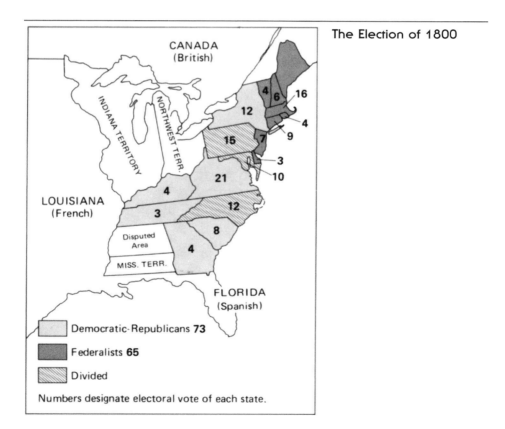

The Election of 1800

CANADA (British)

INDIANA TERRITORY

NORTHWEST TERR.

LOUISIANA (French)

Disputed Area

MISS. TERR.

FLORIDA (Spanish)

Democratic-Republicans **73**

Federalists **65**

Divided

Numbers designate electoral vote of each state.

unconstitutional. These resolutions expressed the views of Thomas Jefferson, who argued that the Alien and Sedition Acts violated citizens' basic rights.

End of the Federalist Era: The Election of 1800 The first 13 years of U.S. government under the Constitution were dominated by three leaders: George Washington, Alexander Hamilton, and John Adams. That era ended in 1800 when Adams was defeated for reelection by two candidates of the Democratic-Republican party—Thomas Jefferson and Aaron Burr. Because Jefferson and Burr were tied with the same number of electoral votes, the election was decided by a vote of the House of Representatives. Jefferson finally emerged as the winner, but only after much confusion in Congress and suspense in the nation at large.

To avoid tie votes in the future, Congress proposed changing the electoral college system by means of the Twelfth Amendment (adopted by the states in 1804). The original Constitution had provided that each elector was to cast two ballots, both for president. Now, according to the Twelfth Amendment, each elector would cast one ballot for president and a second ballot for vice president. (The amendment has worked well; since its adoption there have been no tie votes like that of 1800.)

★ In Review

1. Contrast Hamilton's and Jefferson's views of the Constitution.
2. Explain how the Alien and Sedition Acts caused controversy.
3. How did the election of 1800 lead to changes in the Constitution?

Foreign Policy:
Neutrality and National Security

Compared to other countries of the world, the United States in the 1790s was in a unique position. Unlike the kingdoms of Europe, the United States was a republic with a written constitution. (Recall that a republican form of government is one in which officials are elected by vote of the people.) Unlike the Spanish colonies to the south (including Florida and Mexico) and the British colony to the north (Canada), the United States before 1800 was the only sovereign nation in the Western Hemisphere. Through the early years of the American republic, the foreign policies of five presidents were shaped by the following goals:

★ *Neutrality* (giving support to neither side in a foreign war)
★ Defense of U.S. rights as a sovereign republic
★ Support of the people of Latin America in their struggle for freedom from foreign rule

President Washington recognized that the new nation, separated from Europe by the Atlantic Ocean, should not become involved in European conflicts. Moreover, the United States at the time was not a strong nation and had a small army and navy. It was bordered on the north by Canada, a British colony; on the south by Florida, a Spanish colony; and on the west by the Mississippi River, which was controlled by Spain. Given these conditions, Washington believed it was best to follow a policy of neutrality. (See the map, page 40.)

Washington and the French Revolution In France a revolution overthrew the French monarchy in 1789 (the same year that the Constitution went into effect). Viewed as a threat to the monarchies of Europe, the revolutionary government of the French Republic fought for its survival against invading armies of Britain, Austria, and Spain. In the United States, public opinion was sharply divided on whether or not to give assistance to the French Republic. Through his two terms as president, George Washington followed a policy of neutrality. In his Farewell Address to the American people, Washington urged that the United States "steer clear of permanent alliances with any portion of the foreign world."

John Adams and the XYZ Affair (1797) The next two presidents, John Adams and Thomas Jefferson, adopted Washington's policy of neutrality toward the conflict in Europe. During Adams's presidency, the French navy seized American ships at sea. French diplomats (identified only as X, Y, and Z) demanded bribes for their assistance in stopping the French government's abuses of U.S. rights. Angered by the XYZ Affair, many Americans called for war. Their slogan was, "Millions for defense but not one cent for *tribute* (bribery)." Adams avoided an open declaration of war against France. Even so, in 1798, French and American naval forces fought on the high seas. When Napoleon Bonaparte took control of the French government, he and Adams negotiated a settlement, although it did not resolve all differences.

Jefferson and the Napoleonic Wars During Jefferson's presidency, Napoleon crowned himself emperor of France, thereby ending the French experiment with republican government. To fight Napoleon at sea and cut off supplies to Napoleon's empire, British warships often stopped and searched U.S. merchant ships, removed cargo, and *impressed* (forced) American sailors into service in the British navy. The French also stopped American shipping and violated U.S. rights as a neutral nation. To prevent further violation of U.S. rights, Jefferson persuaded Congress to place an *embargo* (a prohibition on trade) on the shipment of American goods to Europe. But New England merchants and shipbuilders protested bitterly because the embargo badly hurt their business. The embargo was lifted after a two-year trial (1807–1809).

The War of 1812

Madison and the War of 1812 The fourth president, James Madison (1809–1817), also attempted to defend U.S. rights at sea without going to war. But

Cartoon of President Jefferson threatened by King George III of England (left), and Emperor Napoleon Bonaparte, of France

another issue arose in the West, which increased tensions between Great Britain and the United States. Reacting to the pressure of Americans settling on their lands, the Native Americans of the Great Lakes region were persuaded by their leader, Tecumseh, to fight a war against the settlers. Westerners complained bitterly that the weapons used by Tecumseh's forces had been supplied by Britain. Furthermore, a faction of young southerners and westerners in Congress—the so-called *war hawks*—thought that a war with Britain might give the United States an opportunity to acquire British Canada.

Congress declared war against Great Britain in 1812. At first, the war went badly for the United States. An attempted invasion of Canada failed. Later, British forces captured Washington, D.C., and set fire to government buildings, including the Capitol and the White House. But these defeats were offset by a U.S. naval victory on Lake Erie (1813) and a military victory led by Andrew Jackson at New Orleans (1815). A treaty ending the war did not say a word about U.S. neutral rights and did not award any *compensation* (territory or money) to either side. (Also in 1815, peace was restored in Europe when Napoleon was defeated in battle and sent into exile.)

The snapping turtle "Ograbme" ("embargo," spelled backwards) prevents the shipment of goods from the U.S. to Britain.

After the War of 1812 (also called the "second war for independence"), Great Britain ended its much resented policy of stopping American ships and seizing their cargoes. The United States emerged from the war as a respected member of the community of nations.

Consequences of War   A chief consequence of the war was the boost it gave to the spirit of nationalism.   Examples of wartime patriotism were many. For his victory at New Orleans in 1815, Andrew Jackson became a national hero. A witness to one of the war's battles, Francis Scott Key, was inspired to express his national pride in the poem "The Star-Spangled Banner." It was later adopted as the U.S. national anthem. People recognized that the treaty of peace gave nothing to either side. But many Americans felt proud simply to have fought the mighty British Empire to a draw.

Sectionalist Protest in New England   Not everyone was elated by the war news, however. In New England, members of the Federalist party were so opposed to the war that they called a convention to protest it. Meeting in Hartford, Connecticut, from December 15, 1814 to January 5, 1815, convention delegates seriously considered pulling the New England states out of the Union. No action was taken, but this sectionalist outburst warned of worse troubles to come from a different region: the South.

Tecumseh, Native American leader

The Era of Good Feelings

After the War of 1812, the United States was united as never before, as a tide of nationalist feeling swept through all sections—North, South, and West. The Federalist party was widely condemned for its antiwar convention in Hartford. Soon afterward, the party ceased to be a major force in American politics. The Democratic-Republican candidate for president, James Monroe, was practically unopposed in his two campaigns for president (1816 and 1820). The eight years of his presidency (1817–1825) have been called the *Era of Good Feelings*.

Monroe and Latin American Independence Inspired by the examples of the American Revolution and the French Revolution, rebel groups in South America and Central America led successful revolts against the colonial rule of Spain, Portugal, and France. President Monroe and Secretary of State John Quincy Adams feared that the monarchies of Europe might try to reconquer the newly established Latin American republics. As a warning to Spain and other European powers, Monroe in 1823 sent to Congress a message later known as the *Monroe Doctrine*. It stated:

★ The Western Hemisphere was closed to any further colonization by a European power.

★ The United States would firmly oppose attempts by a European power to intervene in the affairs of the Western Hemisphere.

★ The United States would not involve itself politically in the affairs of Europe.

The burning of Washington, D.C., during the War of 1812

Monroe's policy had the full support of Great Britain and the new nations of Latin America. For more than one hundred years, the Monroe Doctrine was viewed by American leaders as the foundation for U.S. policy toward Europe and Latin America.

The Monroe Doctrine is often viewed as reflecting isolationist-neutrality sentiment, since it reaffirmed that the United States would not become involved in European affairs. The document also reflects U.S. national concerns by seeking to keep the strong nations of Europe from obtaining and maintaining colonies in the Western Hemisphere. Finally, the document also protected the interests of the new Latin American republics by stating that the U.S. would firmly oppose any attempt by a European power to intervene in the Western Hemisphere.

Sectional Disputes   Two disputes in the Era of Good Feelings revealed that sectional resentments lay just beneath the surface of the nationalist calm. The first dispute concerned slavery. (For the Missouri Compromise, see Chapter 5.) The second dispute concerned party politics. By 1824, at the end of Monroe's presidency, the Democratic-Republican party had split into several groups, each hoping to elect a different candidate to the presidency. Of the four candidates, Andrew Jackson, hero of the War of 1812, had the

Latin America: Dates of Independence from European Rule

largest number of popular votes. But no candidate received the majority of electoral votes required to win election. As the Constitution provided in these circumstances, the House of Representatives decided the election. After much political wrangling, the House voted in favor of the candidate from Massachusetts, John Quincy Adams. Jackson and his supporters were outraged, charging that the election had been stolen. They formed a new political party, thus ending the brief Era of Good Feelings in which there had been only one national party.

★ In Review

1. To what extent did Adams and Jefferson follow Washington's policy of neutrality?
2. Explain the major causes and results of the War of 1812.
3. To what extent did the Monroe Doctrine reflect isolationist-neutrality sentiment?

Cartoon showing the United States enforcing the Monroe Doctrine, later in the 19th century

★ ★ ★ ★ ★

THE MONROE DOCTRINE

This statement of U.S. foreign policy toward Europe and the Western Hemisphere was included in President Monroe's State of the Union message to Congress in 1823.

In the wars of the European powers in matters relating to themselves we have never taken any part, nor does it comport with our policy so to do. It is only when our rights are invaded or seriously menaced that we resent injuries or make preparation for our defense. With the movements in this hemisphere we are of necessity more immediately connected. . . . We owe it, therefore, to candor and to the amicable [friendly] relations existing between the United States and those powers to declare that we should consider any attempt on their part to extend their system to any portion of this hemisphere as dangerous to our peace and safety. With the existing colonies or dependencies of any European power we have not interfered and shall not interfere. But with the Governments who have declared their independence and maintained it . . . we could not view any interposition for the purpose of oppressing them, or controlling in any other manner their destiny, by any European power in any other light than as a manifestation of an unfriendly disposition toward the United States. . . .

Chapter Review

MULTIPLE-CHOICE QUESTIONS

Base your answers to questions 1 and 2 on the statements made by the speakers and your knowledge of the early years of the United States.

Speaker A: The federal government must be permitted to do whatever it has to do to establish a sound economy.

Speaker B: If the federal government does not follow the Constitution to its exact letter, tyranny and the loss of individual freedom will result.

Speaker C: There is no provision in the Constitution that permits the establishment of a national bank.

Speaker D: The elastic clause gives Congress broad legislative powers.

1. Which speaker or speakers promote(s) the ideas of Alexander Hamilton?
   (1) Speaker A only
   (2) Speakers B and D
   (3) Speakers C and D
   (4) Speakers A and D.

2. The speaker or speakers most likely to support the Democratic-Republicans is/are
   (1) Speakers A and B
   (2) Speakers B and C
   (3) Speakers C and D
   (4) Speaker D only.

3. Which of the following best illustrates the "unwritten Constitution"?
   (1) President George Washington signed the national bank bill into law.
   (2) The Federalist and Democratic-Republican parties were established.
   (3) Congress approved the Jay Treaty with Britain.
   (4) John Adams made judicial appointments during the final months of his presidency.

Use the map on page 97 to answer questions 4 and 5.

4. Which generalization about the election of 1800 is accurate?
   (1) The Federalist party was strongest in the Northeast.
   (2) The Federalist party was strongest in the South.
   (3) Democratic-Republicans lost the election.
   (4) Democratic-Republicans had greater support in the North than in the South.

5. Which of the following did *not* participate in the election of 1800?
   (1) the state of New Jersey
   (2) people of New England
   (3) people living in the Indiana, Northwest, and Mississippi territories
   (4) the state of Georgia.

6. The Whisky Rebellion demonstrated that the federal government
(1) established tyrannical authority
(2) had the power to enforce its laws
(3) needed the assistance of the state militia of Pennsylvania to stop the uprising
(4) established the authority to ban the sale and consumption of alcoholic beverages.

Base your answer to question 7 on the following statement and your knowledge of U.S. history and government.

"The Alien Law . . . affects only foreigners who are conspiring against us, and has no relation whatever to an American citizen. . . . The Sedition Act . . . prescribes a punishment only for those pests of society and disturbers of order and tranquillity. . . ."

—Timothy Pickering,
Secretary of State under
John Adams

7. The quotation is arguing that the Alien and Sedition Acts
(1) are necessary and proper for the security of the United States
(2) apply only to foreign conspirators
(3) are unconstitutional and a violation of the First Amendment
(4) should be strengthened.

8. The foreign policies of Washington, Jefferson, and Monroe were similar in that they
(1) aided the French Republic
(2) favored England

(3) were hostile in England
(4) sought to avoid involvement in European affairs.

9. The main purpose of the Monroe Doctrine was to
(1) exclude Portugal from Latin America
(2) encourage France to protect the Western Hemisphere
(3) create an alliance of Latin American nations
(4) warn European nations not to interfere in the affairs of nations in the Americas.

Base your answer to question 10 on the following statement:

"The United States of America . . . [are] fostering revolutions wherever they show themselves . . . they lend new strength . . . and reanimate the courage of every conspirator. If this flood of evil doctrines . . . should extend over the whole of [North and South] America, what would become of our [European] . . . institutions?"

—Prince Metternich of
Austria commenting
on the Monroe Doctrine

10. Prince Metternich takes the position that the Monroe Doctrine is
(1) in the best interests of the nations of Latin America
(2) a plea on the part of the United States to allow it to remain neutral
(3) helpful to Austria but not the rest of Europe
(4) harmful to the interests of most of the powers of Europe.

THEMATIC ESSAYS

1. **Theme:** Neutrality as a Foreign Policy

   Our first president, George Washington, decided that it was in the best interests of the new nation to pursue a foreign policy of neutrality. This policy was followed by succeeding presidents, with varying degrees of success.

   Task: Show how two situations required that U.S. presidents enforce the policy of neutrality.

   For each situation:

   ★ Describe the events that led the president to enforce the policy of neutrality.
   ★ Evaluate the degree of success or failure in keeping the United States neutral.

   You may utilize any event that you have studied. Some presidents and events that you may wish to use in your answer are John Adams and the XYZ Affair, Thomas Jefferson and the Napoleonic wars, James Madison and the War of 1812, and James Monroe and the issuance of the Monroe Doctrine.

2. **Theme:** The Unwritten Constitution

   The government of the United States operates through an unwritten Constitution as well as a formal, written Constitution.

   Task: Choose two examples of the unwritten Constitution.

   For each example:

   ★ Explain why this example of the unwritten Constitution came into use.
   ★ Discuss how the example helps our government function.

   You may use, but are not limited to, the following examples: the presidential cabinet, political parties, judicial review, and lobbying.

DOCUMENT-BASED QUESTION

*Read or analyze each document and answer the question that follows it. Then read the **Task** and write your essay. Essays should include references to most of the documents along with additional information based on your knowledge of United States history and government.*

Historical Context: Even though our early presidents followed a policy of neutrality, they could not ignore the rest of the world.

Document 1   From George Washington's Farewell Address:

Europe has a set of primary interests which to us have no or a very remote relation . . . therefore it must be unwise to implicate ourselves by artificial ties . . . it is our true policy to steer clear of permanent alliances with any portion of the foreign world. . . .

Question: Why did George Washington feel the United States should not be involved in the affairs of Europe?

Document 2   Anonymous Author, "Open Letter to George Washington," 1793:

Had you . . . consulted the general sentiments of your fellow citizens, you would have found them . . . firmly attached to the cause of France. . . . Had even no written treaty existed between France and the United States, still would the strongest ties of amity [friendship] have united the people of both nations; still would the republican citizens of America have regarded Frenchmen, contending for liberty, as their brethren.

Question: Why does the writer tell George Washington that the nation should support France in its war against Britain?

Document 3   Thomas Jefferson on France's possible acquisition of the Louisiana Territory:

The day France takes possession of New Orleans . . . we must marry ourselves to the British fleet and nation. . . . This is not a state of things we seek and desire.

Question: What would Jefferson have to do if France took control of New Orleans?

Document 4   Refer to the map of the Louisiana Purchase, on page 143.

Question: How did the purchase of the Louisiana Territory prevent the United States from "marrying" the fleet of England?

Document 5   Study the cartoon "Ograbme," on page 101.

Question: How does the cartoonist feel the embargo is affecting New England? (Note that "Ograbme" is "Embargo" spelled backwards.)

Document 6   From James Madison, War Message to Congress, 1812:

British cruisers have been in the continued practice of violating the American flag on the great highway of nations [the Atlantic Ocean], and of seizing and carrying off persons sailing under it. . . . British cruisers have been in the practice also of violating the rights and peace of our coasts. They hover over and harass our entering and departing commerce . . . our commerce has been plundered in every sea, the great staples [products] of our country have been cut off from their legitimate markets. . . .

Question: Why was President Madison recommending that Congress declare war on England?

Task: Using the information from the documents and your knowledge of early American foreign affairs, write an essay in which you explain

★ why the United States followed a policy of neutrality.

★ the difficulties created by public opinion that made maintaining neutrality difficult.

★ how world affairs placed the policy of neutrality in jeopardy.

Chapter 5
The Constitution Tested:
Nationalism and Sectionalism

★ To identify the geographic and economic factors that contributed to sectional differences.

★ To identify the roles of early immigrant groups in the United States and their impact on the nation.

★ To identify the most important policies of Andrew Jackson and evaluate their effect on the U.S. political system.

★ To describe the various democratic-humanitarian reform movements during the Age of Jackson.

★ To explain the conditions of life under slavery for African Americans.

★ To describe the impact of U.S. expansion on Native Americans.

★ To compare and contrast attempts at compromise to preserve the Union.

Between 1789 and 1861, several forces contributed to national unity. For example, the Supreme Court rulings of John Marshall (see Chapter 3) established that the federal government was supreme over the state governments and had the power to regulate interstate commerce. By strengthening the national government, the Marshall Court helped to unite the country. The development of the two-party system owes its origins to the differences between Hamilton and Jefferson. These differences led to the formation of the Federalists and the Democratic-Republicans. In the 1820s, this first two-party system was replaced by a second two-party system: the Democratic party and the National Republican party, a party later known as the Whigs. The tradition of a two-party system proved to be a unifying force, since most Americans belonged to one of the two parties. Finally, the War of 1812 led to increased industrialization and building of roads and canals, thereby contributing to growing economic interdependence within the United States.

Although these forces contributed to national unity, there were also forces that resulted in sectional conflict, which finally led to the Civil War between North and South in 1861. Nationalism and sectionalism are the main subjects of this chapter.

Growing Sectional Differences and Philosophies of Government

Political change is often driven by economic forces. This is clearly seen in the young American nation where, in the early 1800s, three regions, or sections, developed different economies. The economic differences between the North, the South, and the West caused political strains and growing conflict.

Urban and Industrial Patterns of Life in the North

In the early 1800s the building of new factories in the North began to change that region into a center of industrial growth. Why did the North industrialize more rapidly than other sections?

Transportation and Technology   Geography was an important factor aiding industrial growth. Many rivers in the North (1) provided waterpower for driving machinery and (2) served as natural highways for transporting goods. Connecting the rivers was a network of roads and canals. The completion of the Erie Canal in 1825 enabled merchants and farmers to ship goods in one continuous voyage between New York City and ports on Lake Erie. Also, the North had a number of excellent ocean ports that made trade with Europe easy and profitable.

Major Canals and Roads, 1820–1850

Another factor in the growth of industry was technological progress. The invention and development of the steamboat by Robert Fulton and others in the early 1800s increased the speed of water transportation. The building of railroads in the 1830s and 1840s greatly improved the speed and efficiency of transporting goods by land.

National Bank and Tariffs Alexander Hamilton of New York used his political influence to encourage the North's industrial growth. Partly because of Hamilton's efforts, Congress established a national bank whose activities benefited northern merchants. Then, after the War of 1812, Congress passed a tariff act (1816) that taxed foreign imports and made it easier for new American textile mills to compete against British mills. In 1816, to replace Hamilton's first national bank, Congress chartered a second Bank of the United States, which provided loans to businesses and helped industry grow.

The Factory System Following the War of 1812, the United States became more self-sufficient. A nation with abundant natural and human resources, it had the base for developing a factory system. The growth of these facto-

The Erie Canal, in the 1830s

ries was aided by the new system of using *interchangeable parts* in manufacturing invented by Eli Whitney. As a result, factories and textile mills increased throughout the North and especially in New England, where there were abundant sources of waterpower. Thousands of immigrants arriving at the ports of Boston and New York yearly provided a supply of cheap labor. The major products of this early industrial revolution were clothing and furniture. Since these items were produced by machines and cost less than handmade ones, many Americans now sought to purchase rather than make these products themselves.

Working Conditions of Women and Children As early as the 1820s, it was clear that the life of a machine operator in a New England textile mill was far different from the life of a skilled craftworker in an old-fashioned home workshop. Most of the wage earners in New England's textile mills were women and children under the age of 12. Many of these women migrated from farms to factories to take advantage of the newly created textile jobs. For example, in Lowell, Massachusetts, women formed the majority of workers who produced cotton cloth. The early working conditions for these women were reasonable. The workers had their own homes and lived as a community. However, this soon changed. The mill owners now required that the women work 12 to 14 hours a day, six days a week. Wages were so low and working conditions so bad that a mill worker's life was compared to that of a slave. Critics of the factory system—especially southerners—said that factory workers were nothing but "wage slaves." In general, how-

An 1840s cartoon contrasting slavery in the American South with "wage slavery" in the American North and in England

ever, working conditions in U.S. factories were considerably better than those in England. Some American mill owners took an interest in the welfare of their workers, providing housing and meals. The cost of these benefits was deducted from the workers' pay, however.

★ Population of the United States by Region, 1790–1860 ★

Year	Northeast[1]	North Central[2]	South[3]	West[4]
1790	1,968,040	—	1,961,174	—
1800	2,635,576	51,006	2,621,901	—
1810	3,486,675	292,107	3,461,099	—
1820	4,359,916	859,305	4,419,232	—
1830	5,542,381	1,610,473	5,707,848	—
1840	6,761,082	3,351,542	6,950,729	—
1850	8,626,951	5,403,595	8,982,612	178,818
1860	10,594,268	9,096,716	11,133,361	618,976

[1] Northeast includes Maine, New Hampshire, Vermont, Massachusetts, Rhode Island, Connecticut, New York, New Jersey, and Pennsylvania.
[2] North Central includes Ohio, Indiana, Illinois, Michigan, Wisconsin, Minnesota, Iowa, Missouri, and the territories of Kansas and Nebraska.
[3] South includes Delaware, Maryland, Virginia, North Carolina, South Carolina, Georgia, Florida, Kentucky, Tennessee, Alabama, Mississippi, Arkansas, Texas, Louisiana, and the Oklahoma Territory.
[4] West includes all areas west of the states and territories listed for Northeast, North Central, and South.

Urban Problems   The growth of the factory system led to the growth of cities. As workers migrated from rural areas and immigrants came from Europe seeking jobs, eastern U.S. cities such as Baltimore, New York, Philadelphia, and Boston greatly increased in population and problems. For example, unsanitary conditions were typical in the poor areas of the cities. Fresh pure water was often difficult to obtain; as a result, disease spread rapidly. Bathing was considered a luxury. Rows of houses saw no sunlight. Overcrowded streets served as playgrounds. As poor whites competed with free blacks for jobs, race riots occurred in cities such as Philadelphia. With the influx of many new people, often poor, those with higher incomes left for new sections of the city. Consequently, cities were divided into wealthy and poor neighborhoods.

Middle-Class and Working-Class Life in the Pre–Civil War North

Families and Gender Roles   A wide gap existed between middle-class and working-class families in the pre–Civil War (1860) North. Middle-class families lived in comfortable homes, whereas working-class families lived in cramped surroundings with little privacy. Every member of middle-class families had a specific role, based on gender. For example, men were expected to earn the money to pay their families' expenses, while women ran the household and raised the family. Children were expected to learn values needed for their roles as adults. In contrast, in working-class families, men, women, and children were often forced to work at jobs that had little or no security.

Education   Until the 1830s, most children did not go to school. Education was primarily for privileged boys whose parents paid for them to attend private schools. Recognizing that democracy depended upon citizens who could read, write, and reason, reformers like Horace Mann and Henry Barnard advocated systems of public education paid for by the states. Massachusetts and New York led the way by establishing state systems of elementary schools. Attendance was free of charge and compulsory for children ages eight to fourteen. By 1850 New York had extended its public education system to offer instruction from grades one to twelve.

Status of Free Blacks   Although a majority of blacks in the United States were slaves, most in the pre–Civil War North were free. However, these free blacks did not have the full rights of citizenship. Most cities and towns denied blacks the right to vote. Only in the New England states did blacks have the right to vote. Throughout most of the North, African Americans were segregated. Black children could not attend schools with white children. Churches often refused to accept black members. As a result, many blacks formed their own churches. In some northern states, blacks were not allowed to serve on juries or testify in criminal cases. Too often, African Americans faced the hostility of white mobs who resented the competition for jobs.

Immigration in the Pre–Civil War Period

The immigrant ships that arrived in U.S. ports after 1800 brought three main groups: the British, the Germans, and the Irish.

Immigration of British, Germans, and Irish   Thousands of British people decided to leave their homeland mainly for economic reasons related to the Industrial Revolution. They had gone to London and other cities looking for employment, but there were not enough jobs for all the people seeking them. Desperately poor, these immigrants hoped to do better in the fast-growing American republic.

After a revolution in 1848—a revolution that failed—Germans emigrated to the United States in large numbers. Among them were many Jews. The Germans came for both political reasons (defeat of their revolution) and economic reasons (opportunities for farming and employment). As a group they added their voices to the antislavery movement, supported the growth of public education, and established successful farms in the Midwest.

The largest immigrant group before the Civil War were the Irish. In 1846 a blight killed the potato crop upon which the Irish relied for food. Hundred of thousands starved to death. For thousands of others, emigrating to the United States seemed the only way to survive the effects of the potato famine. The wave of Irish immigration was the first large-scale entry of Roman Catholics into U.S. society. Many Irish earned their wages through hard labor by building canals and roads. Irish immigrants also helped build the Union Pacific Railroad in the 1860s. Following the Civil War, they worked in America's coal mines, where they campaigned for better working conditions.

New citizens, an Irishman and a German, steal the ballot box, in a nativist cartoon of the 1800s.

Nativist Reactions to the New Immigrants A *nativist* is someone who believes that foreign-born people pose a threat to the majority culture and should be stopped from entering the country. At different times in the 19th century, nativists made organized attempts to exclude certain immigrant groups, especially Irish Catholics, east European Jews, Italians, Chinese, and Japanese.

The first target of nativist anger were the Irish Catholics who emigrated to America in record numbers in the 1850s. Groups of American-born Protestants organized a secret society nicknamed the Know-Nothings. As a political party, it tried to elect candidates who would promise to restrict, or limit, immigration. (Members of the society were called "know-nothings" because, when asked about the society's activities, they would answer, "I know nothing.")

Patterns of Development in the South

In colonial times the South's economy depended far more on farming than on commerce. This emphasis became even greater in the early 1800s when southern planters grew rich by growing a single crop: cotton. Why did cotton suddenly emerge as the South's most important crop?

Growth of Cotton Cultivation To supply their booming textile mills, British manufacturers of the 1780s and 1790s needed ever greater quantities of cotton. Cotton was easily grown in the American South. But removing the seeds from cotton plants had been a slow and laborious hand process. In 1793, Eli Whitney invented the cotton gin, which did the separating mechanically. This machine made it extremely profitable for southerners to grow cotton for the textile mills springing up in both Great Britain and the American Northeast.

As the demand for cotton increased and land used for cotton growth became costly or unavailable, southern farmers began to move west into such territories as Alabama, Mississippi, Louisiana, Arkansas, and Texas. As a result, southern wealth and leadership passed to the large-plantation own-

Slaveholding Southerners—and Those With No Slaves

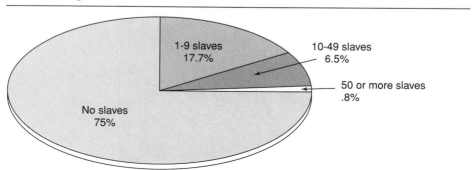

1-9 slaves
17.7%

10-49 slaves
6.5%

50 or more slaves
.8%

No slaves
75%

ers in the new regions that supplied cotton to the northern textile mills. Slavery consequently became more entrenched in the South with each passing year, and the nation became more divided.

Women on Plantations Women on plantations were expected to supervise the large home on the plantation, entertain relatives, friends, and business associates, and provide a "woman's touch" to all events. Their style of living depended to a great extent on the efforts of their slaves.

Life Under Slavery

Laws on Slavery Life under slavery was very different and far worse than life for free Americans. Southern laws protected the plantation owner and allowed him free reign over his slaves. Thus, beatings and whippings were common. Children born into slavery were considered the property of the plantation owners. The sale of slaves and the separation of families were legal. Under slavery, families could be forcibly separated and sold to other owners.

Women Under Slavery Slave women worked equally as hard as slave men in the fields, with the added responsibility of maintaining their home and raising their family. In the plantation houses, slave women performed vital services as cooks, seamstresses, and caretakers of the white owners' children. Black women often became concubines of male slaveholders. Many historians now believe that Thomas Jefferson had at least one child through a long relationship with Sally Hemmings, a slave on his plantation. In her famous speech "Ain't I a Woman?", the abolitionist and former slave Sojourner Truth spoke forcefully about women as slaves.

Children Under Slavery In their early years, slave children on the plantation were often allowed to engage in play. By the ages of six or eight, however, they were expected to become part of the labor force. Thus, childhood ended early for slave children. In his autobiography, Frederick Douglass writes of his childhood in slavery. He speaks of eating "cornmeal mush" from a trough, using shells as spoons, and wearing only a thin linen shirt.

★ United States Labor Force, 1800–1860 ★
(in thousands)

Year	Free	Slave	Total
1800	1,330	530	1,860
1810	1,590	740	2,330
1820	2,185	950	3,135
1830	3,020	1,180	4,200
1840	4,180	1,480	5,660
1850	6,280	1,970	8,250
1860	8,770	2,340	11,110

There were no beds or warm blankets to protect children from cold nights. Most important, he explained that, unlike white children, he never knew his father or his brothers. Slave children were not taught to read or write. Frederick Douglass escaped from slavery in 1838 at the age of 20.

Slave Labor Greater demand for cotton had the terrible result of increasing the use of slaves to plant and pick it. Congress banned the importation of slaves in 1808, as required by the Constitution. But the law was largely ignored in the South, where cotton growers now considered slaves to be an economic necessity. Slaves continued to be bought and sold at auction. Besides working in the cotton fields, slaves also provided the skilled labor (such as carpentry, blacksmithing, and barrelmaking) that enabled plantations to operate as nearly self-sufficient economic enterprises.

Slavery and Religion Sunday was often a day of rest for slaves. Although they were not allowed to learn to read or write, and therefore could not read the Bible, they attended religious services for slaves led by preachers or visiting ministers. Although they practiced Christianity, many slaves also retained elements from their African religions. These included charms, love potions, and folk medicines. Most important, slaves favored religious leaders who stressed freedom over obedience. Most blacks became Baptists or Methodists, the major religions in the South. Although blacks and whites often attended the same church, blacks sat in segregated pews.

Resistance to Slavery Because only Africans and their descendants were held as slaves, whites tended to view themselves as a superior race while treating both slaves and free blacks as social inferiors. Racist attitudes hardened in the 1800s and became extremely difficult for later generations to overcome.

Cotton Production and Slave Population, 1790–1860

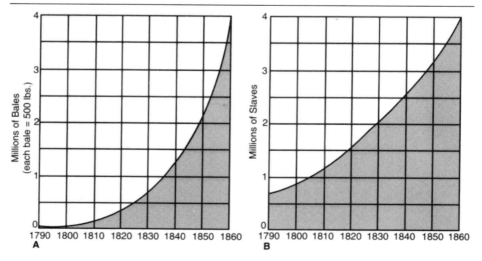

Some slaves found their condition of lifelong bondage so intolerable that they revolted against it. They did so even while recognizing that there was little hope of success and that the penalty for revolt was death. Some uprisings, such as the one planned by Denmark Vesey in South Carolina in 1822, were discovered before being carried out. Other revolts, such as the one led by Nat Turner in Virginia in 1831, were soon halted and brutally suppressed, after 59 whites were killed. Nat Turner was not captured for two months, after which he was tried and executed.

Freedom, though denied, was greatly desired. One outlet for expressing this desire was in the religious songs composed by African Americans—songs known as *spirituals*. Slaves who sang such spirituals as "Swing Low, Sweet Chariot" and "Michael, Row the Boat Ashore" gave vent to deep yearnings for freedom that were not allowed to be spoken. In addition, music was used to pass along secret messages.

Resistance was noted in the daily life of the slave. Often, slaves deliberately worked at a slow pace when picking cotton in the fields. They were sometimes able to win greater rewards and promises of free time if they would complete their tasks in a shorter time. Slaves at times refused to carry out the demands placed upon them. They did this despite knowing that they would be beaten or whipped.

The Underground Railroad, showing routes and "stations" on the way to freedom

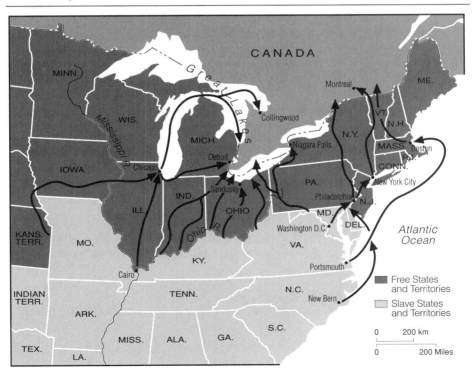

Cartoon of Henry "Box" Brown arriving in the North

Slaves also demonstrated resistance by running away. The deeper into the South, the more likely a runaway slave would be caught. Some who lived closer to the North, such as Frederick Douglass, escaped by railroad using various disguises. For example, Douglass dressed as a seaman and was assumed to be a free black. One slave, later called "Box Henry," escaped by placing himself in a box and shipping himself to a northern address. Most slaves, however, escaped through what has become known as the *Underground Railroad*. Undertaking a long and difficult journey on foot, and with inadequate food and supplies, these individuals attempted to flee to the north or Canada. At times, these individuals were led by guides known as "conductors." For example, the former slave Harriet Tubman returned to the South many times, risking her life to lead others to freedom.

★ In Review

1. Compare and contrast patterns of life in the North and the South.
2. How did the nativist movement impact on the new immigrants?
3. How did African Americans resist slavery?

Equal Rights and Justice

In the presidential election of 1828, Andrew Jackson won both the popular vote and the electoral vote by an impressive margin. Jackson was consid-

Fugitive slaves arriving at an Underground Railroad "station" in the North

ered a man of the people and was the first president who came from a state other than Massachusetts or Virginia—he came from Tennessee. Jackson's dynamic leadership during his two-term presidency (1829–1837) stamped itself on his era: the *Age of Jackson*. Although remembered for its democratic reforms, the Jacksonian era was also marked by the expansion of slavery, the denial of rights to and removal of Native Americans, and sectional conflicts.

Political Democratization

Throughout U.S. history, there have been periods when people campaigned widely for reforms in society and government. The first period of such reforming effort occurred during the Age of Jackson. Reformers embraced a number of causes: votes for women, improved treatment of the mentally ill, free public education for children, abolition of slavery, and more democratic procedures for nominating candidates for office.

In George Washington's time (1780s–1790s), most state laws required that voters own a certain amount of property. Those lacking sufficient property were barred from voting. But in the new century, between 1800

Nelson-Atkins Museum of Art, Kansas City, Missouri

"Canvassing for a Vote": politicians from the Jacksonian era onward sought the vote of the common man

and 1830, state after state removed property requirements for voting. By the time Jackson was elected president in 1828, virtually all white males aged 21 and older were permitted to vote.

New Democratic Campaigns for Election As voting rights were extended to the masses, candidates for office adopted new techniques for reaching great numbers of votes. Political parties conducted elaborate campaigns for their candidates, using banners, rallies, speeches, and debates. Political parties also changed their methods for nominating candidates. Instead of *caucuses* (meetings among party leaders only), Andrew Jackson's Democratic party and Henry Clay's Whig party held nominating conventions in which party delegates from different states voted to select party candidates.

The Rise of Mass Politics

The Spoils System President Jackson adopted as his motto: "Let the people rule." As the victor in the election of 1828, Jackson dismissed from federal employment some officials who were not Democrats and replaced them with his own Democratic supporters. The rewarding of political supporters with government jobs is known as the *spoils system*. Later presidents, whether Whig or Democrat, followed Jackson's example. Those who supported the spoils system considered it democratic at the time, because it meant that government jobs would go to ordinary people ("the common man"), not to a specially educated and privileged group.

The Bank Issue   Another conflict in the Age of Jackson pitted merchants of the Northeast against farmers of the West. The dispute involved the second Bank of the United States. The bank's 1816 charter was up for renewal. Jackson accused the bank of serving only the interests of wealthy easterners. At the same time, he thought the bank discriminated against ordinary people—especially western farmers. He accused the bank of readily granting loans to merchants and manufacturers while denying loans to western farmers. In 1832 Jackson vetoed an act of Congress that would have renewed the bank's charter. He boldly defended his controversial decision in his 1832 campaign for reelection. Henry Clay, the Whig candidate for president, supported the bank and thought that Jackson had made a disastrous mistake by attacking it. But Jackson proved the extent of his popularity with the people by winning reelection with a huge majority.

Native Americans

For nearly 250 years (1607–1850), the frontier had been the scene of frequent fighting between Native Americans (the original settlers of North America) and the *pioneers* (newcomers to the land). As Europeans emi-

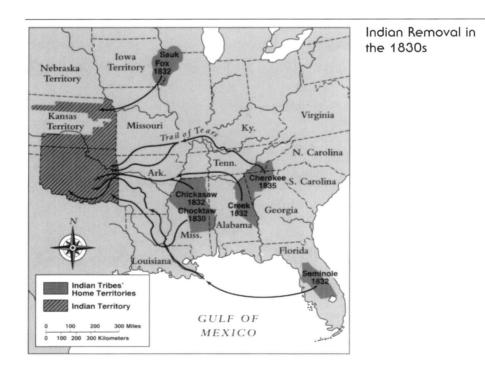

Indian Removal in the 1830s

grated to the United States in ever larger numbers, Native Americans were pushed farther west. In addition to their growing numbers, Europeans also had an advantage in military weapons. As a consequence, the Native Americans adopted various survival strategies. Some Native Americans believed that survival depended upon adopting the culture of the Europeans. Others believed in maintaining and strengthening their cultural heritage. At times, groups of Native Americans joined together in an attempt to resist the expansion of the U.S. government into their territories.

Policy of Removal

Despite their attempts to resist U.S. expansion, the Native Americans found themselves being forced to move farther west. One such period occurred during the Jackson's presidency. Jackson was a champion of democracy for people of his own social class and thus favored western farmers and pioneers. However, he had little sympathy for people who were nonwhite. Jackson reasoned that a policy of *Indian removal* would put an end to conflict between whites and Native Americans. This explains, in part, his decision concerning the Indian Resettlement Act (1830) and the forced removal of Native Americans from their lands east of the Mississippi River. Under the terms of the act, the U.S. government signed more than 90 removal treaties with Native American groups. Some Native Americans left peacefully for the lands set aside for them in the *Indian Territory* west of the Mississippi River (later to become the state of Oklahoma). Others fought before being forced to submit.

Trail of Tears The most tragic of the forced removals occurred in 1838, when some 15,000 Cherokees from Georgia (men, women, and children)

"The Trail of Tears"—the Cherokees' forced journey to an unknown land

trekked westward for 800 miles through cold and rain. On this *Trail of Tears*, many died from starvation. Earlier, in the Supreme Court case *Worcester* v. *Georgia* (1832), Chief Justice John Marshall had ruled that the state of Georgia had no jurisdiction over the Cherokees' lands and thus could not force them to leave. But President Jackson ignored the Court's ruling and supposedly said, "Marshall made his decision, now let him enforce it."

Birth of the American Reform Tradition

Women's Rights Movement

Even though they were barred from voting, women were extremely active in the reform movements of the 1830s and 1840s. One group of reformers declared at a convention at Seneca Falls, New York (1848), that "all men and women are created equal." Among the rights listed in their declaration were the following: the right of women to vote and hold office, the right of married women to hold property in their own names, the right of women jobholders to manage their own incomes, and the right of women to be the legal guardians of their own children.

Elizabeth Cady Stanton was 33 years old when she called the Seneca Falls convention. Joining Lucretia Mott and other reformers, she objected to being kept out of male-only political meetings. Until her death in 1902, Stanton worked tirelessly for laws that would grant women the rights long denied them, including the right to vote. From 1869 to 1890, she led the National Woman Suffrage Association as its president.

Movement for Controlling the Sale of Alcohol

In the 1840s women took the lead in an antidrinking campaign called the *temperance movement*. Women reformers were concerned about husbands and other male relatives who spent their wages on liquor rather than on useful goods for their families. Temperance advocates persuaded lawmakers in several states to prohibit the production and sale of alcoholic beverages.

Movement for State Institutions for the Mentally Ill

A former schoolteacher, Dorothea Dix, discovered that the mentally ill were often chained, beaten, and abused. Dix worked tirelessly to call public attention to these horrors and to establish state institutions where the mentally ill could receive decent care. She persuaded several states to supervise the care given to patients in special "asylums" set aside for them.

★ ★ ★ ★ ★

DECLARATION OF SENTIMENTS

More than a hundred women and men traveled to the home of Elizabeth Cady Stanton in Seneca Falls, New York, in 1848. There, they drafted a declaration about women's rights that in style and form closely imitated the Declaration of Independence. But instead of accusing a king of tyranny, this document accused men of many offenses against women.

> The history of mankind is a history of repeated injuries and usurpations on the part of man toward woman, having in direct object the establishment of an absolute tyranny over her. To prove this, let facts be submitted to a candid world.

> He has never permitted her to exercise her inalienable right to the elective franchise [voting].

> He has compelled her to submit to laws, in the formation of which she had no voice. . . .

> Having deprived her of this first right of a citizen, the elective franchise, thereby leaving her without representation in the halls of legislation, he has oppressed her on all sides. . . .

> He has taken from her all right in property, even to the wages she earns. . . .

> He has monopolized all the profitable employments, and from those she is permitted to follow, she receives but a scanty remuneration. . . .

The Seneca Falls Convention of 1848

Elizabeth Cady Stanton

Political Conflict Over Slavery

Before the invention of the cotton gin, some southerners as well as northerners wanted slavery to be abolished by law. But in the 1800s, as slave labor became more important, southern whites were nearly unanimous in supporting slavery. They argued that slaves were a form of property and that the Constitution itself permitted slavery. In the North, however, one state after another prohibited its citizens from owning slaves. A small but dedicated group, mostly northerners, were called *abolitionists*. They demanded that slavery be abolished everywhere in the United States. A more moderate group of antislavery northerners wanted to stop slavery from spreading into the western territories beyond the Mississippi. Conflict over the slavery question caused North and South to view each other with increasing distrust.

The Abolitionist Movement: Leaders

Harriet Beecher Stowe A white woman from Connecticut, Stowe was the author of one of the most influential novels ever written: *Uncle Tom's Cabin*. It tells the story of a kind-spirited elderly slave, Uncle Tom, who is savagely beaten and killed by a vicious slave overseer, Simon Legree. The book's publication in 1852 caused a sensation in both the North and the South. Northerners were morally outraged by its depiction of the evils of slavery. Southerners were deeply offended by the book, complaining that it presented a false picture of southern society. After the Civil War erupted,

Lucretia Mott

President Lincoln, meeting with Harriet Beecher Stowe, remarked that she was "the little woman whose book made such a great war."

Harriet Tubman As a young woman, Harriet Tubman in 1849 escaped slavery and then spent a decade leading others to freedom. She was one of an estimated 50,000 people who escaped slavery by journeying to the North over secret routes and stopovers on the Underground Railroad. Tubman was a principal activist in the secret "railroad." Because of her heroic efforts for her people, she has been called the "Moses" of the antislavery movement. Tubman also helped free hundreds of slaves during the Civil War and was an advocate of women's rights after the war.

Frederick Douglass After escaping slavery, Frederick Douglass dedicated himself to the cause of African American freedom and equal rights. He spoke to large crowds about the injustice of slavery and argued forcefully for its abolition. He also published his arguments in the *North Star*, a newspaper he founded in Rochester, New York. The newspaper was written by African Americans. He helped recruit black soldiers for the Union army during the Civil War. Douglass also wrote an autobiography.

William Lloyd Garrison A white reformer named William Lloyd Garrison helped to launch the abolitionist movement by publishing an antislavery newspaper, *The Liberator*, beginning in 1831. His writings and speeches demanded an immediate end to slavery without compensating the slave owners for their loss. Because slavery was permitted by the Constitution, Garrison condemned that document as "a covenant with death and an agreement with Hell."

Abolitionists (left to right): Harriet Beecher Stowe, Frederick Douglass, Sojourner Truth (top), John Brown, and Henry Lloyd Garrison

John Brown White abolitionist John Brown believed in using violence to fight slavery. In Kansas in 1856, Brown and his sons murdered five supporters of slavery in retaliation for the deaths of antislavery settlers. Then, at Harpers Ferry, Virginia, in 1859, Brown led an attack on a federal arsenal, probably with the hope of arming slaves for a revolt against their masters. But the plot failed, and Brown was captured, tried, and hanged. Northern abolitionists hailed Brown as a martyr, while southerners viewed him as a fanatic. Sensational newspaper accounts of the raid on Harpers Ferry added to the growing hostility between North and South.

★ Review

1. How did democracy expand in the first half of the 19th century?
2. How did Andrew Jackson resolve issues with regard to banks and Native Americans?
3. How did abolitionists attempt to end slavery?

The Great Constitutional Debates

States' Rights vs. Federal Supremacy

Nullification Until the end of the Civil War, one of the great constitutional debates concerned the issue of nullification, the belief that states had the right to *nullify* (disregard) laws passed by the national government. One of the first examples of nullification occurred in 1798 after a Federalist majority in Congress passed the Alien and Sedition Acts. State legislatures in Virginia and Kentucky passed resolutions that protested these measures and claimed the right to nullify them as unconstitutional. After the debate over the Alien and Sedition Acts subsided, the country entered a period of expansion and consolidation. (See Chapter 4.)

Tariffs The nullification debate heated up again during Jackson's presidency. This time the issue was an economic one—the tariff. When the United States went to war in 1812, Americans were stopped from importing factory goods from Great Britain (the wartime enemy). Without competition from abroad, new American factories sprang up in the North and made handsome profits. In peacetime, Congress tried to maintain the good times for the infant U.S. industries by raising tariff rates in 1816, 1818, 1824, and 1828.

The effect of high tariffs on northern industry was generally positive. Tariffs not only lessened foreign competition but also enabled northern manufacturers to raise the prices of goods sold to U.S. consumers. But the effect of high tariffs on the South was doubly negative. First, the tariffs made manufactured goods more expensive to buy. Second, the tariffs reduced the market for British-made cotton cloth. This meant that the South would sell less raw cotton to Britain, its chief customer. Many southerners had already been hurt by earlier tariffs. The passage of even higher tariffs in 1828 seemed to them good cause for revolt. They said they could not stand for this *Tariff of Abominations* (hated tariff).

Leading the southern resistance to high tariffs was John C. Calhoun of South Carolina. While serving as vice president under Andrew Jackson, Calhoun wrote and published an essay championing the right of the states to defy national law. He argued that every state had a right to ignore, or nullify, any act of Congress that in the state's judgment violated the Constitution. The right of nullification applied to the Tariff of 1828, said Calhoun, because it benefited one section of the country at the expense of another.

To President Jackson, Calhoun's nullification ideas seemed treasonable. Angrily opposing the vice president's words at a political dinner in 1830, the president made a short speech that warmed the hearts of nationalists. "Our Union," he said, "it must be preserved."

In 1832 Congress eliminated some parts of the Tariff of 1828, but this mostly benefited northern manufacturers. Many southerners were still dissatisfied. South Carolina called a special state convention, which declared the tariffs of 1828 and 1832 "null, void, and no law." In its *Ordinance of Nullification*, South Carolina threatened to withdraw from the Union if the federal government tried to enforce the collection of tariffs in southern ports. In other words, South Carolina talked of *seceding* (leaving the Union to become an independent republic).

President Jackson threatened to send troops into South Carolina to uphold the Union and enforce the tariff law. But then Senator Henry Clay saved the day by proposing a compromise. Clay persuaded Congress to pass a new tariff act in 1833, which provided for a gradual reduction of tariff rates. South Carolina then repealed its Ordinance of Nullification. For the moment, violent conflict between the sections was avoided.

Growing Sectional Conflict (1850–1861)

During the first half of the 19th century, the nation expanded westward at an ever-increasing pace. Expansion came at a price, however. As new territories were added, arguments over whether to allow slavery in the West became more and more heated. Various compromises were proposed, and two of them were tried. But as we shall see, despite these compromises, the South eventually seceded and the Civil War began. Slavery was more difficult to resolve than the differences over the tariff.

The Missouri Compromise in 1820

Southern slaveowners who moved to the Missouri Territory brought their slaves with them. In 1819 the people of Missouri applied for admission to the Union as a new state—a state permitting slavery. There was much debate. Both northerners and southerners were well aware that Missouri's admission would end the fragile balance of power between slave states of the South and free, or nonslave, states of the North. Finally in 1820 Congress passed a compromise measure. According to this *Missouri Compromise*:

★ Missouri would enter the Union as a slave state.

★ Maine would enter the Union as a free state.

★ All territory north of the 36°30' line of latitude in the lands of the Louisiana Purchase would be closed to slavery.

This agreement of course did not apply to western lands (such as California or New Mexico) that the United States did not yet own. Thus, the crisis over slavery in the West was not solved, only put off to a later time.

The Compromise of 1850

In 1850, following war with Mexico (see Chapter 6), a compromise was reached that called for a state's residents to vote to determine if the state would or would not allow slavery. After the war with Mexico and the addition of the California territory to the United States, the Missouri Compromise was no longer acceptable to either northerners or southerners. Congress therefore worked out a second compromise—the *Compromise of 1850*. (To compare the slavery compromises of 1820 and 1850, see the maps on pages 134 and 135.)

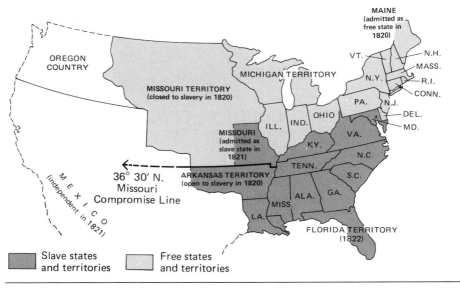

MAINE
(admitted as
free state in
1820)

OREGON
COUNTRY

VT.

MICHIGAN TERRITORY

N.H.

MASS.

N.Y.

R.I.

MISSOURI TERRITORY
(closed to slavery in 1820)

CONN.

PA.

N.J.

OHIO

DEL.

ILL.

IND.

MD.

MISSOURI
(admitted as
slave state in
1821)

VA.

KY.

N.C.

TENN.

36° 30' N.
Missouri
Compromise Line

ARKANSAS TERRITORY
(open to slavery in 1820)

S.C.

M E X I C O
(independent in 1821)

ALA.

GA.

MISS.

LA.

FLORIDA TERRITORY
(1822)

Slave states
and territories

Free states
and territories

The Missouri Compromise of 1820

The Issue of California   Because of its rapid settlement during the gold rush (see page 149), California was the first of the new territories to apply for admission as a state.   The South was alarmed because California insisted on being admitted as a free (nonslave) state.   This would upset the balance of free states and slaves states established by the Missouri Compromise.   It would increase the representation in Congress of the northern, nonslave states and give the North an absolute majority in the Senate as well as the House.   Southern cotton farmers feared that the northerners in Congress might try to block them from taking their slaves into the Southwest territories won from Mexico.   They threatened to defy any antislavery law that the North might attempt to pass.

To settle the dispute, Senator Henry Clay of Kentucky proposed another compromise:

★ California would be admitted to the Union as a free state.   In other parts of the *Mexican Cession* (lands given by Mexico to the United States after the 1848 war, including what would be the states of Arizona, New Mexico, Utah, and Nevada), settlers would decide by majority vote whether or not to allow slavery.   The issue, in other words, would be decided by *popular sovereignty*.   (See the discussion of the Mexican War in Chapter 6.)

★ The practice of buying and selling slaves at public auction in Washington, D.C., would be abolished.

★ Government officials in the North would assist in the capture of escaped slaves and return them to their masters in the South.   This *Fugitive Slave Act* would be strictly enforced, with heavy fines for those who

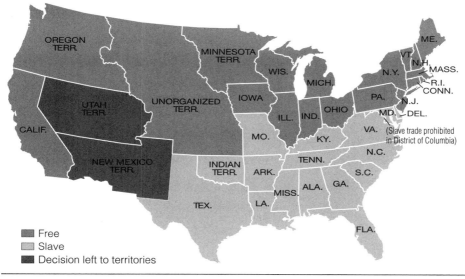

The Compromise of 1850

Free
Slave
Decision left to territories

disobeyed. Although Congress voted for Clay's compromise, there was widespread resistance among northern abolitionists to the Fugitive Slave Act.

Dred Scott v. Sanford (1857)

The antislavery writings and speeches of the abolitionists increased sectional tensions. The Supreme Court's decision in the Dred Scott case of 1857 increased tensions even further.

Facts of the Case   Dred Scott had lived in Missouri as a slave before being taken by his owner to Illinois, a free state. Returning to the slave state of Missouri, Scott went to court to sue for his freedom. He argued that he had lived in free territory and therefore should be declared a free citizen. His case eventually was appealed to the U.S. Supreme Court.

Supreme Court Decision   In 1857 the Supreme Court ruled that Scott's petition was not valid. The reason the Court gave was extremely controversial. Chief Justice Roger Taney, a southerner, argued as follows:

★ Even free African Americans could not sue in a federal court, since they were not citizens of the United States.

★ Slaves brought into free territory remained slaves because they were a form of property. Owners would not be denied their property rights without due process of law.

★ The Missouri Compromise, which had excluded slavery from free territory, was unconstitutional because it denied slave owners their property rights.

Public Reaction Southern slave owners were pleased that the Supreme Court's decision completely confirmed their views. In the North, many people were shocked to think that all western territories were now thrown open to slavery. Although conditions were tense following the Dred Scott decision, both the North and the South remained within the Union. By the late 1850s, however, the preservation of the Union was in jeopardy.

★ In Review

1. How did the tariff issue heat up the nullification debate during Jackson's administration?
2. How did each of the following attempt to resolve the issue of slavery? (a) Missouri Compromise; (b) Compromise of 1850?
3. What were the facts and issues and the decision in *Dred Scott* v. *Sanford* (1857)?

Chapter Review

MULTIPLE-CHOICE QUESTIONS

1. Refer to the map of canals and roads, 1820–1850, on page 113. Which is the most accurate conclusion that can be made from this map?
(1) Travel between states and territories was becoming more difficult.
(2) Most canals went in a "north–south" direction while most roads went in an "east–west" direction.
(3) Most roads and canals linked the east with the west.
(4) Travel was difficult because most roads and canals were not connected.

Examine the population table on page 115. Answer questions 2 and 3 based on the statistics found in the table.

2. Which is a conclusion that may be reached about the population of the United States between 1790 and 1860?
(1) The number of people living in all areas rose with the exception of the North Central region.
(2) The South had fewer people than the Northeast between the years 1790 and 1810, but this trend reversed itself between 1820 and 1860.
(3) By 1850, population in the North Central region lagged behind that of the West.
(4) Population was declining in the Northeast from 1840 to 1860.

3. An explanation for the difference in population in the West be-

tween 1850 and 1860 would be that
(1) the population declined as a result of disease and harsh living conditions
(2) the discovery of gold caused a migration of settlers from the West to the South
(3) some of the territories in the West became states
(4) many of the roads and canals built in the 1820s were destroyed by natural disasters.

4. A conclusion that can be reached from the graph on page 118 is that
(1) some southern states had no slavery
(2) 25 percent of southerners had no slaves
(3) most southerners owned 50 or more slaves
(4) the majority of slaveholders held between one and nine slaves.

5. The map on page 125 shows that in the 1830s, Native Americans
(1) generally migrated from the North to the South
(2) were forced to move to designated western territories
(3) were free to move wherever they wished
(4) returned to their original home states in the East after abandoning their western reservations.

6. Which belief was essential to the doctrine of nullification?
(1) The states had created the federal government and could therefore overturn federal laws.
(2) The federal government had been created by federal interests.
(3) Individuals could decide for themselves whether or not to obey a law.

(4) The southern states had made a mistake in joining the union.

7. One reason why westerners opposed the Bank of the United States was that they
(1) feared inflation
(2) believed the bank favored debtors
(3) believed deposits were mismanaged
(4) believed that eastern business interests received most of the benefits.

8. During the Age of Jackson, the Native Americans
(1) moved to urban areas in large numbers
(2) sought to form alliances with other minority groups
(3) were forced to move westward
(4) chose to adopt the culture of European settlers.

Base your answers to questions 9 and 10 on the discussion below and your knowledge of U.S. history and government.

Speaker A: On all sides we see the threat of the national government becoming all-powerful and crushing the liberties of the states.

Speaker B: The time will come— and I rejoice to think of it—when the United States will stretch from sea to shining sea.

Speaker C: The tariff laws are an abomination to our section, and we must resist them with all our strength.

Speaker D: Because the union is one and inseparable, we cannot permit the states to defy the laws of Congress.

9. Which speakers are most likely to stress the importance of states' rights?
(1) A and B
(2) A and C
(3) C and D
(4) B and C.

10. Which speaker is most likely to be an advocate of westward expansion?
(1) A
(2) B
(3) C
(4) D.

THEMATIC ESSAYS

1. Theme: Sectionalism in the North and South

During the years 1800 to 1850, the United States became a nation increasingly separated by distinct sectional differences in the North and the South.

Task: Explain three ways in which the sections differed from each other, and give reasons for the differences. Refer to historical events that contributed to the growth of these sectional differences.

In answering the question, consider such factors as people, geography, work, and life-styles.

2. Theme: Expansion as a Cause of Nationalism and Sectionalism

The expansion of the western frontier resulted in events that encouraged both the unity of nationalism and the disunity of sectionalism.

Task: Describe one circumstance that promoted nationalism and a second that resulted in sectionalism. For each example, be sure to include the following:

★ the background of the circumstance
★ how nationalism or sectionalism became an outcome of each circumstance.

You may use any example from what you have learned, including Eli Whitney's cotton gin and system of interchangeable parts, the Missouri Compromise, the Compromise of 1850, the annexation of Texas, and the Mexican Cession.

DOCUMENT-BASED QUESTION

*Read or analyze each document and answer the question that follows it. Then read the **Task** and write your essay. Essays should include references to most of the documents along with additional information based on your knowledge of United States history and government.*

Historical Context: While the period between the 1820s and 1840s saw the expansion of democracy, there were still many people who either had no control of their lives or were second-class citizens.

Document 1 Refer to the illustration of Henry "Box" Brown's escape to freedom, on page 122.

Question: What does the illustration show about the means to which some African Americans would go to gain their freedom?

Document 2 From Lucretia Mott and Elizabeth Cady Stanton, "Declaration of Sentiments" (The Seneca Falls Manifesto, 1848):

> The history of mankind is a history of repeated injuries . . . on the part of man toward woman, having in the direct object the establishment of an absolute tyranny over her. To prove this, let facts be submitted to a candid world:
>   He has never permitted her to exercise her inalienable right to the elective franchise.
>   He has compelled her to submit to laws, in the formation of which she had no voice. . . .

Question: What complaints did Lucretia Mott, Elizabeth Cady Stanton, and other women have about men's treatment of women throughout history?

Document 3 Examine the painting "the Trail of Tears" on page 126.

Question: What does the painting show about the U.S. government's treatment of Native Americans?

Document 4 Refer to the cartoons of American slaves and English and American working people on page 115.

Question: What attitude does the artist express in the comparison of factory labor in England (and in the North) and slavery in the South?

Document 5 Look at the cartoon of an Irish immigrant and a German immigrant, on page 117.

Question: How does the cartoon illustrate the view of some Americans about immigrants during the early to mid-1800s?

Document 6   Harriet Martineau, a British author, describes her 1834 visit to the United States:

> I had been less than three weeks in the country and was in a state of something like awe at the prevalence of not only external competence but intellectual ability. The striking effect upon a stranger of witnessing, for the first time, the absence of poverty, of gross ignorance, of all servility, of all insolence of manner cannot be exaggerated in description. I had seen every man in the towns an independent citizen; every man in the country a landowner. I had seen that the villages had their newspapers, the factory girls their libraries. I had witnessed the controversies between candidates for office on some difficult subjects, of which the people were to be the judges.
>   With all these things in my mind, and with evidence of prosperity about me in the comfortable homesteads which every turn in the road and every reach of the lake brought into view, I was thrown into painful amazement by being told that the grand question of the time was "whether the people should be encouraged to govern themselves, or whether the wise should save them from themselves."

Question: How did British writer Harriet Martineau feel about life in the United States in 1834?

Document 7   Look at the painting "Canvassing for a Vote," on page 124.

Question: What does the painting show about election campaigns in the Jacksonian era?

Task: Using the information in the documents and your knowledge of the United States during the early and mid-1800s, write an essay in which you show how the period had both democratic and undemocratic aspects.

Chapter 6
Westward Expansion and Civil War

★ **Objectives**

- ★ To explain the impact of expansion in the West upon Native Americans and Mexicans.
- ★ To examine how a dispute over Oregon was settled peacefully, while another dispute over Texas and the Southwest resulted in war.
- ★ To identify the causes and consequences of the U.S. war with Mexico.
- ★ To compare the points of view of northerners and southerners on the slavery issue.
- ★ To identify the causes and consequences of the Civil War.

Territorial Expansion and Manifest Destiny

As a Democratic-Republican, President Thomas Jefferson was committed to the idea of states' rights and strict construction of the Constitution. And yet Jefferson's policies as president did not differ greatly from those of his Federalist predecessors. He discovered that in his role as U.S. president, his first duty was to strengthen the nation. To do this, he reluctantly changed his view of the Constitution. The issue that prompted a change of mind was this: Should he consent to purchase from France the vast western territory called Louisiana?

The Louisiana Purchase

By 1800 pioneer families had moved beyond the Appalachian Mountains into Kentucky, Tennessee, and Ohio. These lands were already part of the United States. On the Mississippi River, however, the city of New Orleans as well as the unexplored lands of Louisiana to the west were under French rule. In 1803 the French emperor Napoleon Bonaparte made the extraordinary offer to sell New Orleans and the Louisiana Territory to the United States for a bargain price (about $15 million).

Jefferson's Constitutional Dilemma In considering whether or not to buy New Orleans and the Louisiana Territory, Jefferson faced a constitutional dilemma. No clause in the Constitution authorized the national government to expand the country's borders. As a strict constructionist, Jefferson could not justify making the purchase. But to turn down the offer of Louisiana would be to miss out on the greatest land sale in history.

Decision for Loose Construction Jefferson's opponents in the Federalist party argued for a loose construction of the Constitution. According to this view, the national government had many powers that were implied by the "necessary and proper" clause of the Constitution. Reluctantly, Jefferson adopted the loose construction view when, in 1803, he asked the Senate to ratify the treaty with France for the purchase of Louisiana.

Exploring and Settling the West

The history of the West is the story of constant movement, growth, and change. The *frontier* (an imaginary line dividing settled areas from the wilderness) was pushed ever westward to the Appalachian Mountains (by 1790); to the Mississippi River (by 1820); and finally across the Great Plains to the Pacific Ocean (by 1850). (See the map in Chapter 9, page 253.) Settlers in the western territories formed governments and soon won admission to the Union as new states.

President Jefferson's purchase of the Louisiana Territory from France in 1803 more than doubled the land area of the United States and extended U.S. boundaries far beyond the Mississippi all the way to the Rocky Mountains. Thus, a vast new frontier beckoned to explorers, trappers, traders, pioneering farmers, and missionaries.

With the full support of Congress, Jefferson sent an expedition led by Meriwether Lewis and William Clark from St. Louis in 1804 to explore the newly acquired lands and to look for a water route to the Pacific. The next year, Lewis and Clark reached the Columbia River and finally the Pacific Ocean. These explorations enabled the United States to claim the whole Oregon region and prepared the way for later settlement of the American West. In addition, the rocks, plants, and animals that the explorers discovered and brought back were of great value for naturalists.

After the Lewis and Clark expedition, Americans became interested in the fur trade in the Oregon Country. Fur trappers known as mountain men explored the region, discovering trails and mountain passes. They made friends with the Native Americans, learning their language and customs. Each year, traders from St. Louis, the center of the fur trade, would meet with the mountain men and Indians and exchange goods for beaver pelts. The pelts were

The Louisiana Purchase

then sold in the East and in Europe. By discovering new trails and routes, the mountain men became trailblazers for pioneers moving west.

In addition to fur traders, missionaries traveled to the Oregon Country to convert the Native Americans to Christianity. They built missions and schools, and sent for more settlers from the East. As a result, by the 1840s, several thousand American farmers and pioneers resided in the Oregon Country.

One of the largest groups to settle the West was the Mormons. The Mormon Church, also known as the Church of the Latter-Day Saints, was founded in the 1820s in western New York State by Joseph Smith. As thousands of converts joined the new religion, the Mormons attempted to set up their own communities in the Midwest. However, they were persecuted for their beliefs, which included the practice of *polygamy* (having more than one spouse at one time). In 1844, Joseph Smith was killed by an Illinois mob, and the Mormons were forced to move. Led by Brigham Young, they founded Salt Lake City in Utah, hundreds of miles from the nearest settlement. The Mormons also sent out missionaries and transported converts to their new community in Utah.

The Spanish, Mexican, and Native American West

The present-day states of Texas, New Mexico, Arizona, and California were originally explored and settled by the Spanish. Spreading northward from

Lewis and Clark, assisted by Sacagawea, meet Native Americans in the Louisiana Territory

Mexico City, the Spanish founded Santa Fe in 1609, in what is now New Mexico. They claimed and occupied much of what has become the southwestern United States, establishing forts, missions, ranches, villages, and towns throughout the region.

The missions were an important part of Spanish colonization. Their purposes were to convert the Native Americans to Christianity, teach them Spanish culture, and make them loyal subjects. The center of each mission was the Catholic Church, and the mission was enclosed within an adobe (sun-dried brick) or stone wall. The mission was surrounded by farming lands, where the Native Americans might be given land of their own if they had converted to Christianity and learned Spanish culture. These missions became important centers of community life, and some of the old missions have survived to this day. Spanish control, however, did not go unchallenged by the Native Americans. In 1680, the Spanish were driven from Sante Fe, New Mexico, by the Pueblos. This represented the first Native American victory over a European power. Within a dozen years, however, the Spanish had regained control of the region.

★ In Review

1. How did the Louisiana Purchase present Jefferson with a constitutional dilemma?
2. Discuss the long-term effects of Jefferson's decision in 1803 to purchase the Louisiana Territory.
3. Describe the significance of the Lewis and Clark expedition.

Motives for Expansion and Western Settlement

In the 1800s many Americans came to believe that their country was destined to expand westward. They spoke of the *manifest destiny* of the United States to expand at least as far as the Pacific coast and to be the dominant nation in North America.

> [The American claim] is by the right of our manifest destiny to overspread and to possess the whole of the continent which Providence has given us for the development of the great experiment of liberty. . . .
>
> —John L. O'Sullivan, *Democratic Review*

Large parts of the West, however, were already occupied and settled by Mexicans. From the Mexicans' point of view, the U.S. idea of manifest destiny posed a challenge and a threat to their control of the Southwest.

Congress passed a number of laws to encourage the settlement of the West. Senator Henry Clay of Kentucky proposed in 1816 an ambitious plan for linking the economic fortunes of East and West in a scheme he called the *American System*. Adopting Clay's idea, Congress voted to finance the building of western roads and canals. Also, for the easterners' benefit, Congress voted for a high tariff on European imports that would encourage westerners to buy their supplies from eastern manufacturers. Thus, by aid-

Settlers traveling through the Cumberland Gap in the early 1800s

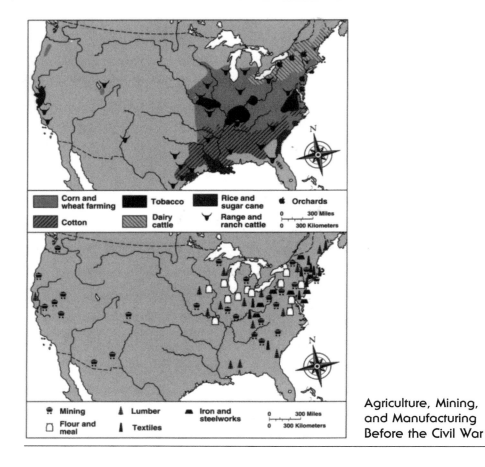

Agriculture, Mining, and Manufacturing Before the Civil War

ing both West and East, Clay hoped to tie the nation together as one economic unit.

The Politics and Strategies of Westward Expansion

Four western territories were added to the United States between 1845 and 1853:

★ Texas (annexed by an act of Congress in 1845)

★ Oregon (added by a treaty with Britain in 1846)

★ California and much of the Southwest (ceded by Mexico in 1848)

★ southern Arizona and New Mexico (purchased from Mexico in 1853).

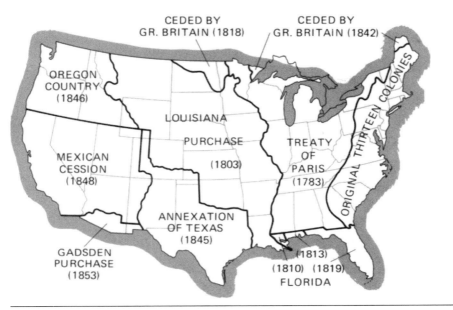

Lands Added to the United States, 1783-1853

Annexation of Texas

The first new territory added to the United States in the 1840s was Texas. In colonial times, Texas, California, and the lands in between had been part of the Spanish empire. When the Mexicans revolted against Spanish rule in 1821, Texas and California became the northern part of the new nation of Mexico.

Texan Independence   In the 1820s Texas was settled by only a few thousand Mexicans. As a result, the Mexican government did not object when the open land attracted pioneer families from the United States. Most were from the South and many owned slaves. By the mid-1830s, however, there were more American settlers in Texas than Mexicans. The Americans often defied Mexico's laws, including its ban against the holding of slaves. When Mexico tried to stop further American immigration, the American settlers revolted and declared Texas an independent nation (1836).

Determined to put down the revolt, Mexican president Antonio López de Santa Anna led troops into Texas. His forces overwhelmed and killed the Texan defenders who were occupying the Alamo, a church mission turned into a fort. Soon afterward, however, during a battle on the San Jacinto River, the Texans captured Santa Anna, who was forced to grant their demand for independence.

Annexation   For nine years (1836–1845), Texas was a completely separate and independent nation: the Lone Star Republic. Its leaders applied for admission to the Union as a state. But for years the proposed *annexation* (formal addition) of Texas failed to receive a favorable vote in Congress. The chief obstacle was slavery. Northerners opposed annexation of Texas because slavery was well established there. Solidly supporting Texas annexation were the slave states of the South. Finally, in 1845, the issue was settled in the South's favor when Congress passed a joint resolution admitting Texas to the Union as the 28th state. This annexation led to worsening relations with Mexico.

Fighting for Texas and California: War With Mexico (1846–1848)

After its loss of Texas, Mexico still held vast lands in the Southwest (what are today Arizona, New Mexico, Utah, Nevada, and California). Many Americans looked upon these lands as part of their country's "manifest destiny" to expand. But Mexico was angered by the United States' annexation of Texas and refused to discuss offers to purchase Mexican lands. Tensions grew and war threatened.

The Annexation of Texas, Mexican Cession, and Gadsden Purchase

Causes of War A Democratic president, James K. Polk, believed strongly in expansion. His desire to gain western lands was largely responsible for the outbreak of a war with Mexico. The immediate cause of the war was a disputed boundary between Texas and Mexico. Was this boundary marked by the Nueces River, as Mexico claimed? Or was it farther south on the Rio Grande, as the United States claimed? When Mexican troops fired upon U.S. troops within the disputed territory, President Polk asked Congress for a declaration of war. As his reason, Polk said that Mexico had "shed American blood on American soil."

Invasion of Mexico Two U.S. armies struck south into Mexican territory. One army, under Zachary Taylor, occupied northern Mexico, while a second army, under Winfield Scott, forced the Mexicans to surrender their capital, Mexico City, in 1848.

Revolt in California A third American army under Stephen Kearny marched westward to California. There it joined a band of American settlers, who had earlier revolted against Mexican rule. Mexican defenders were quickly overcome, and California in 1848 became American territory.

Peace Terms In the treaty ending the Mexican War (Treaty of Guadalupe Hidalgo, 1848), the United States paid the token sum of $15 million to Mexico for the huge territory extending from Texas's western border all the way to the California coast. In addition, the United States agreed to relieve Mexico of responsibility for paying $3.2 million in debts to U.S. citizens. The Rio Grande was established as the U.S.–Mexican border.

Gold Rush in California Soon after the war, an American settler in California discovered gold on his land. News of the discovery touched off excitement in the East and throughout the world. Fortune hunters poured into California in search of golden nuggets. "California or bust" was the slogan of thousands of people who joined the great 1849 gold rush. Most met with

"Plucked"—the bird symbolizing Mexico, before and after its territories were taken by the United States

disappointment. Even so, California's population grew so rapidly that it soon qualified to apply to Congress for statehood. But because California proposed to be a nonslave, or free, state, the South strongly opposed its admission.

Gadsden Purchase The last section of land acquired from Mexico was won without violence. This land—the so-called *Gadsden Purchase*—was bought from Mexico in 1853 for $10 million. (James Gadsden was the American diplomat who arranged the transfer.)

Dispute Over Oregon

President Polk and other expansionists were eager to possess not only the rock-and-desert country of the Southwest, but also the forested lands of the Northwest: the territory known as Oregon. The obstacle to U.S. possession of Oregon was Great Britain, which also claimed the territory as far as the 54°40' line of latitude in northern Canada. (See map.) A U.S. war with Britain loomed as a real possibility.

Conflicting Claims Since the early 1800s, the United States and Great Britain had agreed to joint occupation of the vast Oregon Country. But in

The Oregon Country, in 1848

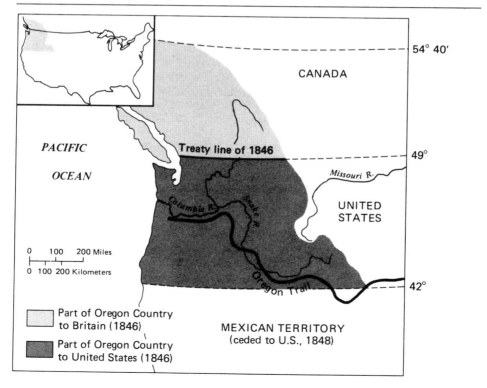

English cartoon of "John Bull" (England) laughing at the nerve of "Yankee Doodle" (the United States) in the Oregon dispute

1844 many Americans wanted control of the entire territory and would no longer accept joint occupation. They heartily approved of the Democratic campaign slogan: "Fifty-four forty or fight!" which meant: make Great Britain give up all of Oregon to the 54°40' line.

Although both nations wanted control of Oregon, both also had strong reasons for avoiding war. Great Britain wanted to preserve its good trade relations with the United States. The United States, at war with Mexico in 1846, had no desire to see Great Britain go to Mexico's aid.

Settlement   Diplomats on both sides managed to work out a compromise. A British–American treaty of 1846 divided the Oregon Country into two roughly equal halves. The northern half went to Great Britain. The southern half (below the 49th parallel of latitude) went to the United States. Two long-term results of the treaty were (1) the border between Canada and the United States was extended to the Pacific and (2) relations between Great Britain and the United States were much improved.

Impact of Western Expansion Upon Mexicans and Native Americans

As a result of the Mexican War, Mexico lost much of its land and natural resources, and thousands of Mexican citizens became citizens of the United States. Most Mexican Americans lost their lands, and many former landowners took low-paying jobs as farmworkers or as laborers in mines or on railroads. In addition, many Americans looked down upon the culture of the Mexicans, resulting in prejudice and discrimination. Resentment by Mexico over U.S. conquest of the Southwest in the Mexican War would linger for many generations.

Western expansion also disrupted Native American life. The contacts with settlers resulted in the spread of diseases such as measles and small-pox, against which Native Americans had no immunity. As a result, the Native American population was severely reduced. Western expansion also resulted in the destruction of much of the wildlife, such as the great buffalo herds of the Plains, that Native Americans depended upon for survival. Finally, settlers increasingly took the Native Americans' lands, resulting in a series of wars as Native Americans fought to defend their territory. To make room for the settlers, the government forced Native Americans to give up their lands and move to reservations. (See pages 258–260.)

★ In Review

1. How did the idea of manifest destiny lead to western expansion and settlement?
2. Identify the causes of conflict between each of these: (a) Mexico and American settlers of Texas in 1836; (b) Great Britain and the United States in 1845; and (c) the United States and Mexico in 1846.
3. Summarize the impact of western expansion upon Mexicans and Native Americans.

The 1850s: United States Society Divided

In the 1850s, divisions between North and South sharply increased as sectional interests and views polarized the nation. In 1861, the American Constitution and the nation were put in jeopardy when 11 southern states seceded from the Union. This led to a great Civil War, which cost more lives than any other war in American history. Below we will examine the events and wartime actions associated with that terrible conflict.

Kansas-Nebraska Act (1854)

As you recall from Chapter 5, the Compromise of 1850 called for popular sovereignty in the western territories gained from Mexico. Only four years after Congress agreed to the Compromise of 1850, another proposal was made about slavery in the western territories. This time the proposal concerned territories on the Great Plains: the Kansas Territory and the Nebraska Territory.

Changing the Law Both Kansas and Nebraska were located north of the 36°30' line. According to the Missouri Compromise of 1820, slavery would not be permitted north of the line. But in the 1850s, southerners objected to this restriction and hoped to do away with it by amending the law. Stephen A. Douglas, a U.S. senator from Illinois, encouraged southern hopes. Douglas proposed that settlers in Kansas and Nebraska decide for themselves whether or not to allow slavery in their territories. Congress voted in favor of Douglas's proposal, and the Kansas-Nebraska Act became law. Its most important provisions were these:

★ The terms of the Missouri Compromise no longer applied to Kansas and Nebraska.

★ Instead, the people of these territories would exercise popular sovereignty by voting on whether or not to allow slavery.

Violent Outcome Voting is one way to settle an issue; fighting is another. In Kansas, after the passage of Senator Douglas's bill, fighting broke out between southern, proslavery settlers, and northern, antislavery settlers. Armed clashes between northerners and southerners in "Bleeding Kansas" warned of the nationwide civil war that would soon follow.

Disintegration of the Whig Party

From the early to mid-1800s, the Whig party was one of the two major parties of the United States. Its leaders included such famous Americans as

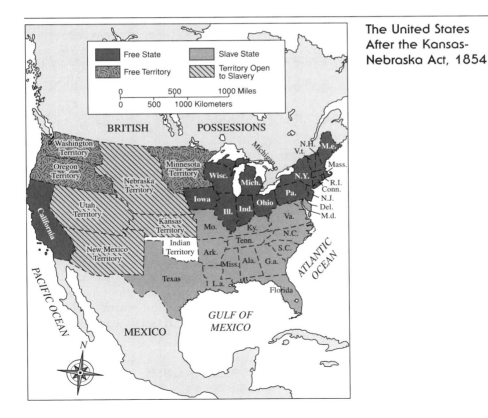

The United States After the Kansas-Nebraska Act, 1854

Daniel Webster and Henry Clay. It supported high tariffs to protect business, a national bank to control the currency, and internal improvements on roads and canals. With supporters in both the North and the South, the Whig party at first took no stand on the issue of slavery.

In the 1840s, however, slavery began to divide the party. Legislation such as the Compromise of 1850 and the Kansas-Nebraska Act in 1854 showed the deep divisions among northern and southern Whigs over the issue of slavery and its expansion.

In 1852, the Whig candidate for president, General Winfield Scott, won only four states. As Whigs divided, many in the North joined the American party, also known as the Know-Nothings, who campaigned on a platform of anti-immigration and anti-Catholicism. However, it would be the newly formed Republican party that would replace the Whigs as they declined in popularity.

Rise of the Republican Party

Founded in 1854, the Republican party drew all of its support from the North and the West. In the South it was looked upon with suspicion and hostility as an antislavery, antisouthern party. It was founded by various antislavery groups (Whigs, northern Democrats, and abolitionists) who came together in the 1850s to form the new party. As a result of its growth, the Republican party was able to challenge the Democratic party throughout the North. The Democratic party, however, was a national party with strength in all three sections: North, West, and South. As stated in the Republican platforms of 1856 and 1860, the new party stood for the following:

★ Keeping slavery out of the western territories. (The abolition of slavery in the South was a goal of only a minority of Republicans; it was not an official goal of the party.)

★ Enacting a high protective tariff to encourage northern industries

★ Building a *transcontinental*, or nationwide, *railroad* stretching from the Atlantic coast all the way to the Pacific.

The attraction of many people in the North to the Republican party increased with the warfare in Kansas and the hardening of sectional feelings. For example, as you recall from Chapter 5, the Dred Scott decision and John Brown's raid on Harpers Ferry inflamed divisions between the North and South. These issues added to the growing popularity of the Republican party in the North. In the election of 1856, the Republican candidate for president, John C. Frémont, came in second in national voting and first in the North. This election proved that the Republican party was now one of the two major parties in the nation.

Abraham Lincoln and the Secession Crisis

Abraham Lincoln, the man who would become the 16th president, began his life on a small homestead in Kentucky. When he was three years old, his father moved the family to Indiana where Abe grew up on the family farm teaching himself to read and write. Although he had some primary school instruction, Lincoln was largely self-taught. When Lincoln was 21 years old, his father moved the family to Illinois, a relatively new state. It was here that Lincoln began his career as a lawyer and legislator. His political beliefs included opposition to the expansion of slavery, internal improvements, and a high tariff. On a personal and moral level, Lincoln opposed slavery. Lincoln launched his political career as a Whig. As the Whig party began to disintegrate, Lincoln joined the newly formed Republican party. By 1858, having served as a state legislator, Lincoln became the Republican candidate for the United States Senate.

Lincoln-Douglas Debates The person holding the Senate seat and running for reelection was the famed Democratic leader in the Senate, Stephen Douglas. In various towns in Illinois, Lincoln, the tall Republican, debated the much shorter Democrat (the "Little Giant," as Douglas was called) on the slavery issue. Douglas defended his position on popular sovereignty; Lincoln attacked it. Said Lincoln in one debate: "The Republican party looks upon slavery as a moral, social, and political wrong. They insist that it should be treated as a wrong; and one of the methods of treating it as a wrong is to make sure that it should grow no longer."

It was during this race for the Senate that Lincoln gave his famous "house divided" speech.

> A house divided against itself cannot stand. I believe this government cannot endure permanently half slave, and half free. . . . I do not expect the Union to be dissolved. I do not expect the house to fall; but I do expect it will cease to be divided. It will become all one thing, or all the other.

A Lincoln-Douglas debate

In the 19th century, U.S. senators were elected by the legislature in their state. Since more Douglas supporters than Lincoln supporters were elected to the Illinois state legislature, Lincoln lost the Senate election. However, Lincoln's strong arguments in the debates and the closeness of the election had won him national attention.

Election of 1860

Angry feelings between northerners and southerners dominated politics in 1860 as Republicans and Democrats met in national conventions to choose their candidates for president. The Republicans nominated Lincoln after several ballots when it became apparent that the well-known William H. Seward would not win enough support at the convention to gain the nomination. A majority of Democrats nominated Stephen Douglas, a moderate on the slavery issue. But southern Democrats wanted a candidate of their own, who would be committed to the proslavery interests of their section. These southerners nominated John Breckinridge as a third candidate. A fourth candidate, John Bell, was nominated by a new party, the Constitutional Union party. In this four-way race, Lincoln emerged as the winner although he won only 40 percent of the popular vote. However, he won the

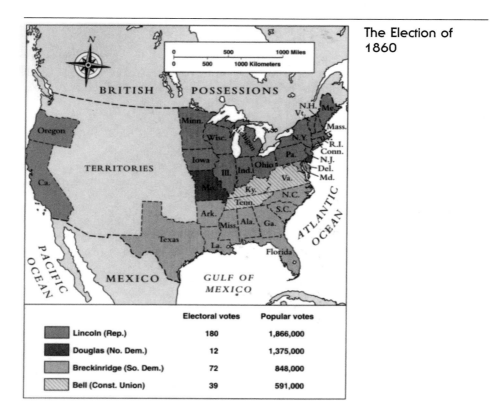

The Election of 1860

	Electoral votes	Popular votes
Lincoln (Rep.)	180	1,866,000
Douglas (No. Dem.)	12	1,375,000
Breckinridge (So. Dem.)	72	848,000
Bell (Const. Union)	39	591,000

heavily populated states throughout the North, thereby winning the electoral vote. From the South's point of view, it was the worst possible outcome.

Southern Secession

Only one month after Lincoln's election, South Carolina announced its decision to secede from the Union. Other southern states followed South Carolina's example. By March 1861, northern states and southern states were acting as two separate nations. The Union had come apart.

Why did the South secede? Historians who have studied the coming of the Civil War point to several forces that built to a climax in 1860.

Cultural and Economic Differences The plantation South differed greatly from the industrial North. The way of life on a southern plantation was based on a single family's ownership of land worked by a large number of slaves. The courtly manners of the owners of the plantation house represented the customs of an older age. In contrast, the more commercial North was rapidly developing new customs and values in keeping with a new industrial age.

The two regions' differing economies meant that they were often at odds on important political questions, such as the tariff.

Regional Loyalties Nationalism was weaker in the South than in the North. Southerners felt a great attachment to their own region and jealously guarded states' rights. They were convinced that the states had every right to secede from the Union if the national government tried to interfere too much with local matters.

Southerners' Belief in Easy Victory Many southerners believed that secession could be achieved peacefully and that the North would not go to war over it. Even if war came, southerners were confident that the industrial world's need for their cotton would bring support from abroad for their independence. If the South won the backing of just one nation, Great Britain, it was felt that the southern cause would surely triumph in peace or war. As one southerner put it: "Should the South produce no cotton for three years, England would topple headlong and carry the whole civilized world with her except the South. No, you dare not make war on cotton. No power on earth dares to make war upon it. Cotton is king."

Lack of National Leadership The presidents of the 1850s (Millard Fillmore, Franklin Pierce, and James Buchanan) were not strong leaders. In Congress, too, leadership was lacking when it was most needed. Hopes for holding the Union together suffered a setback when two nationalist senators, Henry Clay and Daniel Webster, both died early in the 1850s.

Slavery as a Moral Issue The issue of slavery aroused strong feelings on both sides. Although most southern whites owned no slaves, they supported slavery as part of the southern way of life. In the 1850s, more and more northerners began to view slavery as a moral issue and also as an institution that could not live side by side with democracy.

Events Related to the Issue of Slavery In the 1850s one incident after another related to slavery kept stirring up feelings of suspicion and hostility. After the publication of *Uncle Tom's Cabin* (1852) came John Brown's raids in Kansas (1856), the Dred Scott decision (1857), the hanging of John Brown at Harpers Ferry (1859), and the election of Lincoln, an antislavery Republican, as president (1860). The disputes over slavery and the hostility of southerners to Lincoln's election made clear that the main issue that led to the Civil War was slavery.

Efforts at Compromise After Lincoln's election, there was a major effort to reach a compromise over slavery that could save the Union. The compromise plan was known as the *Crittenden Proposal*. It called for federal protection for slavery in any United States territory below the 36°30' line of latitude. Thus, slavery would be allowed in any southern territory. Any territory north of this line would be denied slavery. Upon becoming a state, any territory north or south of the line could choose to enter the Union as a slave or free state. Lincoln, who always opposed the expansion of slavery into the territories, rejected the compromise. Thus war became more likely.

Firing on Fort Sumter The secession of South Carolina and other southern states did not necessarily mean war. All depended on the response of the federal government and its new leader, President Lincoln. A month after Lincoln's inauguration, an incident occurred that was the immediate cause of civil war. Fort Sumter, an island fortress in the harbor of Charleston, South Carolina, was held by U.S. forces. South Carolina insisted that the fort be surrendered to the South. Lincoln refused, and sent food and supplies to the fort. Southern guns then bombarded the fort, and thus the war began.

★ In Review

1. Explain the major reasons for the decline of the Whigs and the rise of the Republican party.
2. List key reasons for Lincoln's victory in the election of 1860.
3. Describe the major reasons that led to the Civil War.

The Civil War

The 11 southern states that seceded were loosely joined under their own national constitution and central government. They called their nation a confederacy (the Confederate States of America). For four years (1861–1865),

The United States at the Outbreak of the Civil War, in 1860

the Confederate army of the South fought for independence against a northern army committed to preserving the Union and putting down the "rebellion."

Advantages of Each Side

In general, the South had a better army for fighting a short war, but the North's vast economic resources gave it the advantage in a longer war.

Military Strategy, Battles, and Human Toll

Victory for the North was not inevitable. In fact, both the North and South believed that the war would end in their favor within a short period of time. The South thought that, if it could defend itself against northern assaults on its own territory, Union troops would soon quit the field. The North believed that, given its huge advantage in manpower, it would quickly bring the rebellious states into line.

Military Strategy   Lincoln's strategy centered on dividing the South's forces by capturing the Mississippi River, thereby making it easier to defeat sepa-

★ North and South in the Civil War ★

Union Advantages

1. Population. The North's population (22 million in 1860) was more than twice that of the South (6 million free citizens, 3 million slaves).

2. Economic resources. The Union's numerous factories and farms were capable of producing the massive amount of war goods and food supplies needed for victory. In contrast the South had little industry, and its farms produced chiefly cotton, not food. In addition, the North's railroad system was far superior to the South's.

3. Political leadership. Though hard-working and dedicated, the Confederate president, Jefferson Davis, did not have the leadership ability of the Union president, Lincoln.

4. Foreign relations. The United States was recognized throughout the world as a legitimate nation. The South's efforts to win the support and recognition of Great Britain and other nations ended in failure.

5. Naval superiority. The South had very few ships of war compared to the North's strong navy. Thus, the North was able to blockade southern ports and cut off vital supplies.

Confederate Advantages

1. Strategic position. In war it is generally easier to defend a position than it is to attack it. Instead of launching risky offensives, the Confederacy needed only to beat back northern assaults.

2. Preparation for war. Southerners had a stronger military tradition than northerners. Most of them knew how to shoot and ride and needed less training than the raw recruits in the Union army.

3. Military leadership. On the whole southern generals like Robert E. Lee and Thomas J. ("Stonewall") Jackson were much superior to northern generals.

4. Morale. Because southern troops were fighting in defense of their homeland, their morale, or fighting spirit, was usually greater than that of northern troops.

rate southern armies in the West and in the East. A second aspect of Lincoln's strategy was to blockade southern ports in order to stop the exportation of cotton and the importation of supplies and weapons from other nations. A final aspect of Lincoln's strategy was to use the North's larger population to field bigger armies than the South in the hope of inflicting major manpower losses on the smaller southern army.

Battle of Antietam   In the first years of the war, 1861–1862, the South won most of the important battles. For example, in the first Battle of Bull Run, the larger Union army, just 30 miles from Washington, D. C., was defeated by a smaller southern army led by Thomas (Stonewall) Jackson. In 1862, a second Union army lost again at Bull Run. However, on September 17, 1862, General McClellan stopped an advance by General Lee and the army of Virginia in Maryland at the Battle of Antietam.

Halting the southern army had important consequences for both sides. First, England and France decided not to involve themselves in the conflict at this time although they appeared to sympathize with the South. Further, Lincoln would use the occasion to issue the Emancipation Proclamation (see page 165).

Battle of Gettysburg With war supplies running low, the South's brilliant general, Robert E. Lee, decided to take the offensive in a bold, do-or-die invasion of the North. In the Pennsylvania farm town of Gettysburg, three days of fighting (July 1–3, 1863), ended in a desperate charge across an open field by the South's General George Pickett. Both sides suffered thousands of deaths at Gettysburg. But the Union army was clearly the victor, as the surviving remnant of Lee's army marched wearily back to Virginia.

The North and the South in the Civil War

The northern victory halted any hopes of intervention by England or France on behalf of the South. The loss of life at Gettysburg was such that a national cemetery was dedicated at the site and was the location for Lincoln's famous Gettysburg Address (see page 166).

Siege of Vicksburg Only one day after Gettysburg, July 4, 1863, Union troops under General Ulysses S. Grant forced the surrender of a strategic fortress at Vicksburg on the Mississippi River. This victory gave the North complete control of the Mississippi River and thus split the South in two. Three Confederate states on the west side of the river (Texas, Arkansas, and western Louisiana) were separated from the rest of the Confederacy.

After Gettysburg and Vicksburg, the Civil War continued to consume thousands of lives, as opposing armies under Grant and Lee fought each other in bloody combat in a densely wooded region in Virginia. At the same time, in 1864, an untold number of southern farmhouses were put to the torch by Union troops marching through Georgia and South Carolina.

Sherman's March to the Sea The northern army was led by William T. Sherman on a campaign of destruction eastward from Tennessee to the Georgia coast and then northward to the Carolinas. For the first time in the war, civilian property was deliberately destroyed as an act of policy. "War is hell," said Sherman, and he made the South feel the full truth of his statement.

Richmond and Appomattox As the capital of the Confederacy, Richmond in central Virginia was a target of northern military campaigns throughout the war. For four years Confederate armies saved the capital from being taken. But, finally, on April 2, 1865, Lee's battered army gave way and a Union army marched into Richmond. Seven days later, Lee surrendered his army to Grant at Appomattox Court House. The war was over.

★ In Review

1. Explain why each of the following events is considered a turning point in the Civil War: (a) the Battle of Antietam, (b) the Union victory at Gettysburg, and (c) the Union victory at Vicksburg.
2. Discuss the importance of each of these to northern victory in the Civil War: (a) Lincoln's leadership, (b) the northern economy, and (c) the freeing of slaves by Union troops after the Emancipation Proclamation.

Impact of War on the Home Front

The Civil War had a major impact on both civil liberties and the role of women.

Civil Liberties During the war, civil liberties suffered as Lincoln made the defeat of the South his priority. Thus, in Maryland, hundreds of people were arrested but not placed on trial, as the writ of habeas corpus was suspended. Lincoln feared that individuals loyal to the South would take over the state, thereby threatening Washington, D.C. As a result, federal army officers arrested the mayor and police chief of Baltimore as well as members of the state legislature. The charge was "giving aid and comfort in various ways to the insurrection." By the end of the war, at least 15,000 individuals had been arrested and imprisoned without formal trials. In addition, some civilians were tried and convicted by military courts. After the war ended, a Supreme Court decision (*Ex Parte Milligan*) held that military courts could not place civilians on trial where state and federal courts are functioning.

Disagreement regarding Lincoln's actions continues today. Supporters note that the nation was threatened by a rebellion that aimed to destroy the country. They believe that under such circumstances the chief executive has the right to suspend civil liberties since the Constitution provides that the writ of habeas corpus may be suspended "when in cases of rebellion or invasion the public safety may require it" (Article I, Section 9). Opponents of Lincoln's actions believe that only Congress has the right to suspend habeas corpus, and that such a power in the hands of a president could lead to one-man rule. Most historians agree that Lincoln's actions were very limited and were necessary in the context of the times.

Women's Roles Before the war, women were accustomed to working long hours on farms and as wage-earning mill workers. During the war, as hundreds of thousands of men left home to wear a uniform, women had to work even longer hours to fill the labor gap. Employed in factories for wages as low as 25 cents a day, women provided much of the labor force needed to produce uniforms, weapons, and other war goods.

The need for nurses in the war opened up an important profession for women. Under the energetic leadership of Dorothea Dix and Clara Barton, women volunteers took to the battlefield to care for the wounded. After the war Clara Barton continued her pioneering efforts in the nursing field by organizing the American Red Cross in 1877.

An examination of letters from soldiers on both sides to their wives and mothers as well as those going from women to their men in war reveal that most women supported the soldiers' decision to stand and fight. Most letters use terms such as "honor" and "duty" to explain loyalty in both armies. Thus women played a major role in supporting the war effort.

★ In Review

1. Explain how Lincoln's wartime strategies were related to northern advantages.
2. Was Lincoln right or wrong to limit civil liberties during the Civil War? Explain.

3. Although women did not engage in combat, they played a major role during the Civil War. Would you agree or disagree with this statement? Explain.

Government Financial Policy During the War

Wartime Finances   Like all wars, the Civil War cost not only lives and property but also money. In the North, with its strong industrial base, money to finance the war effort was gained through increased tariffs, increased excise taxes on goods produced in the United States (such as alcoholic beverages), the issuance of greenbacks (paper money), and the sale of government bonds. It was the sale of government bonds that brought in the greatest amount of money. Of course, the value of these bonds went up or down, depending on the relative success of the Union army.

The South had fewer options for raising money. The Union blockade stopped foreign goods from entering the Confederacy, thereby limiting tariff collection. In addition, the southern states believed in states' rights and opposed the authority of even the Confederate government to collect taxes. As a result, the South was forced to print large amounts of paper currency with little gold backing. Thus, Confederate money lost its value as the southern cause worsened. By the end of the war, Confederate notes had virtually no value.

Creating a National Currency   The passage of the National Banking Act in 1863 led to the creation of a standard national currency. Banks that were part of the national banking system could issue paper money backed by government bonds. The relative success of the national government in selling Treasury bonds allowed for the introduction of a sound currency.

The Transcontinental Railroad

A great achievement of northern industry during and after the Civil War was building a transcontinental railroad across the western plains to the Pacific coast. Undertaken by two private companies, the project was authorized by and received funding from the federal government.

Land Grants   The route of the proposed railroad passed over almost totally unsettled territory. To encourage railroad companies to risk their money on the colossal venture, the Republican majority in Congress voted to grant huge sections of land all along the route to the railroads. As shown on the map on page 219, sections of land were arranged in the checkerboard pattern, half the land squares going to the railroad companies, half to be kept by the government for sale to would-be settlers.

The Race to Lay Track   Starting from Sacramento, California, crews hired by the Central Pacific Railroad cut tunnels through the Sierra Nevada, the great Pacific coast mountain range. Heading in the opposite direction, from Omaha, Nebraska, crews of the Union Pacific Railroad fought off hostile Native Americans on the Great Plains and then blasted tunnels through mountain passes in the towering Rockies. After three years of work, the rival crews came together in 1869 in Promontory, Utah, where they hammered the last spike—a spike of solid gold.

The Immigrant Contribution The grueling labor of building the first transcontinental railroad was undertaken by two groups of immigrants. The Central Pacific crew consisted of 10,000 men from China who were specially recruited for the task by agents of the railroad company. Many lost their lives in the dangerous work of building bridges and dynamiting tunnels. Another 10,000 men from Ireland, working for the Union Pacific, performed the feat of laying as much as four miles of track a day.

Homestead Act (1862) The laws passed by Congress that gave grants of land to western railroads encouraged the railroads to sell land to farmers at very low prices. With farmers purchasing land from the railroads, Congress in 1862 enacted The *Homestead Act*, which provided available public lands at no financial cost to those willing to settle on them. By the terms of this law, any citizen or immigrant intending to become a citizen could acquire 160 acres of federal land simply by farming it for five years. Labor, not money, was the price of a homestead.

Lincoln and Emancipation

Although Lincoln personally opposed slavery, he waited through almost two years of war before taking action on the issue. He issued a preliminary proclamation in September 1862 after the Battle of Antietam. In this document, he stated that a final emancipation order would be issued in the new year. True to his word, on January 1, 1863, under his authority as commander-in-chief of the armed forces, Lincoln issued the Emancipation Proclamation. In this document, Lincoln declared that slaves in the Confederate states were now free men and women.

Although the border states, which had remained loyal to the Union, were allowed to keep slavery and the Confederate states did not recognize Lincoln's authority, most people understood that slavery would probably be abolished throughout the nation if and when the North won the war. For slavery, it was the beginning of the end as enslaved people throughout the South made their way to Union lines seeking freedom. In addition, the emancipation provided a moral basis to the war. Thus, Great Britain, which had abolished slavery in the 1830s, was reluctant to aid the South despite its need for cotton.

The Gettysburg Address

As you read on page 161, thousands of soldiers died at the Battle of Gettysburg. Throughout the summer, the town of Gettysburg had to deal with the acrid smell of death and the chore of burying the dead. It was then decided that a military cemetery should be built at Gettysburg to honor those who had given their lives for the Union cause. The chief speaker at the dedication of the cemetery was Edward Everett. Everett had been president of Harvard University, governor of Massachusetts, and a senator. He was known as one of the best orators (speakers) of his generation. Although Lincoln was invited to speak, he was asked to make only a few brief remarks. Those brief remarks have become known as the Gettysburg Address. This two-minute speech ranks among the most memorable and inspiring speeches in American history. In this speech, Lincoln was able to

★   ★   ★   ★   ★

THE EMANCIPATION PROCLAMATION

Lincoln's proclamation of January 1, 1863, extended only to those states that were then "in rebellion against the United States." Unaffected by it were five states still in the Union where slavery was legal: Missouri, Kentucky, Maryland, Delaware, and West Virginia.

Tell whether or not you think Lincoln's proclamation should have applied to the "loyal" states as well as the "rebellious" ones.

And, by virtue of the power and for the purpose aforesaid, I do order and declare that all persons held as slaves within said designated states and parts of states are, and henceforward shall be, free; and that the executive government of the United States, including the military and naval authorities thereof, will recognize and maintain the freedom of said persons.

And I hereby enjoin upon the people so declared to be free to abstain from all violence, unless in necessary self-defense—and I recommend to them that, in all cases when allowed, they labor faithfully for reasonable wages.

And I further declare and make known that such persons of suitable condition will be received into the armed service of the United States to garrison forts, positions, stations, and other places, and to man vessels of all sorts in said service.

And upon this act, sincerely believed to be an act of justice, warranted by the Constitution upon military necessity, I invoke the considerate judgment of mankind and the gracious favor of Almighty God.

demonstrate that the Union was fighting not only for a military victory but for universal values such as those expressed in the Declaration of Independence. The speech ends in a series of simple yet stirring phrases:

> . . . that we here highly resolve that these dead shall not have died in vain; that this nation, under God, shall have a new birth of freedom; and that government of the people, by the people, for the people, shall not perish from the earth.

African American Participation in the War

When the war began, neither the North nor the South allowed African Americans to enlist in its armed forces. Thousands of free blacks in the North attempted to enlist but were turned away. As the war progressed, the U.S. government changed its policy to permit both emancipated southern slaves and free northern blacks to serve in racially *segregated* (separate) army units. At first they were assigned to tasks other than fighting—for example, cooking meals and building fortifications. But beginning in 1863 African American troops (usually under the command of white officers) were trained to fight and then sent into battle. They served with distinction. By war's end, over 180,000 African Americans had joined the Union armed forces and about 38,000 had lost their lives. Twenty-two were awarded the nation's highest military honor, the Medal of Honor (sometimes known as the Congressional Medal of Honor). The actions of these heroes of the battlefield were highlighted by Colonel Robert Shaw and his African American troops in the 54th Massachusetts. Led by Shaw, these gallant soldiers attacked Fort Wagner which guarded Charleston, South Carolina's harbor. Shaw and approximately 40 percent of his unit were killed in the battle.

African American Civil War soldiers

Enlistment in the Union army was voluntary until 1863, when Congress passed a law that *drafted* (compelled) young men of a certain age into military service. In New York City, whites who did not want to serve rioted against the draft law. They took out their anger against African Americans, who competed with them for factory jobs. During four days of street violence, countless African Americans were beaten by the raging mob, and many were lynched.

The Thirteenth Amendment

The Thirteenth Amendment, passed by two-thirds of Congress in 1864 and approved by three quarters of the states in 1865, provided that slavery was illegal in every state of the Union. As a consequence of the Thirteenth Amendment, people who had been enslaved all of their lives were now free. In addition, the institution of slavery, which had begun in the British colony of Virginia in 1619, had now ended.

Lincoln's Leadership

Lincoln was reelected president in 1864. But only one month into his second term (April 1865), he was assassinated by an embittered actor and southern sympathizer, John Wilkes Booth. Why do historians consider Lincoln to have been one of the nation's greatest presidents? The explanation lies in his firm beliefs and excellent judgment.

Firm Political Purpose Lincoln made it clear from the beginning that his one goal as president was to save the Union. All of his actions and decisions were directed at achieving this overriding purpose.

Political Shrewdness and Courage Lincoln was subject to much criticism from the press, the public, and even Republican politicians. As a politician himself, he had a keen sense of when to give in to political pressures and when to take the risk of making an unpopular decision. Patiently, he tried out different generals until one of them, Grant, emerged as the most capable.

Lincoln had a number of achievements as president. He maintained the war against the Confederacy where others might have compromised with the South. In the end, he succeeded in keeping the Union together. Further, the challenge of sectionalism had been defeated. Never again would any state declare its right to leave the Union. Thus, the United States emerged as one nation. Finally, as a result of Lincoln's actions, 4 million people were freed from bondage.

Lincoln had dreamed of his own death prior to his assassination. He dreamed that he walked through the White House and saw a body surrounded by mourners. When he asked, "Who is dead?", he was told, "The President; he was killed by an assassin." Lincoln's assassination shocked the nation and added to his mystique. As was said at the moment of his death, "Now he belongs to the ages."

★ In Review

1. What advantage did the Union have over the South in financing the war effort?
2. Explain why the Emancipation Proclamation and Gettysburg Address are among the greatest documents in the history of the United States.
3. Lincoln is often considered one of the greatest of United States presidents. Would you agree or disagree with this assessment? Explain.

Chapter Review

MULTIPLE-CHOICE QUESTIONS

Use the map on page 143 to answer questions 1 and 2.

1. The map shows that the Louisiana Purchase
(1) gave control of the Mississippi River and the port of New Orleans to the United States
(2) included the territories of Oregon and Florida
(3) immediately added several new states to the union
(4) led to a conflict between the United States and the settlers in British Canada.

2. Which is the best conclusion that can be reached about the Louisiana Purchase through study of the map?
(1) The purchase was unconstitutional.
(2) The boundaries of the Louisiana Purchase were somewhat unclear.
(3) The United States paid too much money for a small amount of land.

(4) Mexico received payment for some of the land in Louisiana.

3. The maps on page 146 show that before the Civil War
(1) a large amount of manufacturing was done in the Southeast
(2) ranching existed only in the far western territories
(3) cotton growing was an important activity in the Southwest
(4) most agriculture, mining, and manufacturing took place east of the Mississippi River.

4. The labor force table on page 119 shows that
(1) slavery caused unemployment among those who were free
(2) the free labor force was consistently larger than slave labor force
(3) slavery forced free people to leave the South for the North and West
(4) the free labor force decreased as the slave labor force increased.

Refer to the map on page 147 to answer questions 5–7.

5. According to the idea of manifest destiny, the United States
   (1) had to acquire all new land through treaties
   (2) had no right to purchase Louisiana from France
   (3) respected all Mexican land claims in North America
   (4) claimed a right to control all of the land shown on the map.

6. In 1783, the United States extended from the Atlantic Ocean to the
   (1) Appalachian Mountains
   (2) Mississippi River
   (3) Rocky Mountains
   (4) Pacific Ocean.

7. As a result of the Mexican War and Oregon settlement, the United States
   (1) approximately doubled in land size
   (2) lost land west of the Mississippi River
   (3) extended to the Pacific Ocean
   (4) gained Texas.

8. The cartoon on page 151, published in the British magazine *Punch*, is referring to the dispute with the United States over the
   (1) Mexican War
   (2) Oregon Country
   (3) Louisiana Purchase
   (4) Florida Territory.

9. The map on page 153 shows that by 1854
   (1) few territories were still open to slavery
   (2) the eastern states had already declared themselves to be slave or free states
   (3) the far West was completely open to slavery
   (4) the Utah territory would be free.

10. The map and table on page 156 show that
    (1) Stephen A. Douglas came in last in both the number of electoral and popular votes
    (2) the Constitutional Union party won three states in the upper South
    (3) Abraham Lincoln received few votes in the far West
    (4) John C. Breckinridge and the Southern Democrats received no votes in the northern states.

THEMATIC ESSAYS

1. **Theme:** Slavery and the Civil War

   Slavery and the controversy over its moral justification and expansion into new territories led the United States into sectional conflict and ultimately to a civil war.

   Task: Choose two events that caused serious controversy and helped lead the nation toward the Civil War. For each event:

   ★ Describe the circumstances causing the event.

★ Explain how the results of the event helped lead the nation into the Civil War.

Some of the events that you may use are the results of the Mexican War, the Compromise of 1850, the Kansas-Nebraska Act, the Dred Scott decision, and John Brown's raid on the federal arsenal at Harpers Ferry, Virginia.

2. **Theme:** States' Rights and the Civil War

Although the Civil War was fought over the morality of slavery, it also was fought to determine if the powers of the federal government (the Union) were greater than the rights of the various states.

Task: Choose two issues that created great controversy and helped lead the nation toward the Civil War. For each issue, *specifically* discuss how the opposition of states' rights and federal powers played a part in leading to Civil War.

Some ideas that you may wish to discuss involve the Fugitive Slave Act, popular sovereignty, and the Dred Scott decision.

DOCUMENT-BASED QUESTION

*Read or analyze each document and answer the question that follows it. Then read the **Task** and write your essay. Essays should include references to most of the documents along with additional information based on your knowledge of United States history and government.*

Historical Context: Although the United States was originally an Atlantic coast nation, its future rested in its expansion in a westerly direction.

Document 1 Study the map of the Louisiana Purchase, on page 143.

Question: How did the United States change as a result of the Louisiana Purchase?

Document 2 Study the map of Indian removal in the 1830s, on page 125.

Question: How was the United States government able to remove Native American groups from their tribal homelands?

Document 3 Study the map of the addition of western and southwestern territories, on page 148.

Question: How did war with Mexico affect the territory of the United States?

Document 4   Look at the cartoon of the Mexican eagle before and after the Mexican War, on page 149.

Question: How does the cartoonist feel about what happened to the Mexicans as a result of the war with the United States?

Document 5   Study the map of the United States in 1854, on page 153.

Question: How did the acquisition of western lands further aggravate the controversy over slavery?

Document 6   Study the map of U.S. expansion from 1783 to 1853, on page 147.

Question: How did the United States change from the end of the Revolutionary War in 1783 through the Gadsden Purchase from Mexico in 1853?

Task: Using the information in the documents and your knowledge of United States history, write an essay in which you

★ describe the variety of opportunities that the acquisition of land in the West provided for the United States.
★ explain how the territorial expansion of the United States also resulted in issues that had serious consequences for the nation.

UNIT II

The Industrialization of the United States

Chapter 7
The Reconstructed Nation

★ To evaluate different plans for bringing the southern states back into the Union after the Civil War.

★ To understand the changing nature of American society—and especially southern society—from 1865 to 1895.

★ To describe the factors that prevented full freedom for African Americans after their emancipation from slavery.

★ To describe the long-term social, political, and economic consequences of the Civil War and Reconstruction.

General Lee's surrender to General Grant at Appomattox Court House in 1865 brought the Civil War to an end. The South lay in ruins. The Confederacy was no more. The triumphant northerners who controlled the U.S. government now faced the problem of "reconstructing," or reshaping, the governments of the defeated southern states so that they might rejoin the Union. For 12 years after the war (1865–1877), northern troops occupied parts of the South. These postwar years are known as the *Era of Reconstruction*.

The Era of Reconstruction

Except for Antietam and Gettysburg, every battle of the Civil War had been fought in the South. After four years of armies marching over the land, the South's economy was in a pitiful state. The wartime destruction of property was vast and incalculable. In addition, southern planters and farmers faced the loss of their labor force, as Union armies carried out Lincoln's Emancipation Proclamation and set free 4 million slaves in the former Confederacy.

In the North, the Republican government in Washington had to resolve two major questions: (1) On what terms should southern states be readmitted to the Union, and (2) how were the rights of former slaves to be protected? Different plans for answering these questions were proposed and heatedly debated.

Lincoln's Plan of Reconstruction

President Lincoln favored lenient treatment of the South. He wanted the seceded states to rejoin the Union, not as conquered territories, but as states equal in status to those of the North. Lincoln proposed two conditions for a seceded state's readmission. (1) Ten percent of the state's voters would be required to take an oath of allegiance to the United States, and (2) the new state government would be required to guarantee the abolition of slavery. Lincoln's hopes for putting this plan into effect were abruptly ended in April 1865 by an assassin's bullet.

Andrew Johnson's Plan of Reconstruction

After Lincoln's murder, Vice President Andrew Johnson became president. Many northern Republicans deeply distrusted Johnson because he had been a Democrat from Tennessee, one of the southern slaveholding states.

The new president proposed a plan of reconstruction similar to Lincoln's. He proposed three conditions for readmitting a seceded state to the Union: (1) Ten percent of the state's voters would be required to take an oath of loyalty to the U.S. Constitution; (2) the state must ratify the Thirteenth Amendment abolishing slavery; and (3) it must deny the right to vote to a few Confederate leaders, while granting that right to all other southern white men.

Congressional Reconstruction

Many Republicans in Congress supported an entirely different Reconstruction plan from that of Lincoln and Johnson. They thought the South should be punished for its role in the war and that the seceded states should be treated as conquered territories. They also believed that the newly freed slaves should be given political rights. Thus, the plan favored by abolitionists like Senator Charles Sumner of Massachusetts and Congressman Thaddeus Stevens of Pennsylvania was harsh toward southern whites but helpful to southern blacks. The Republicans in Congress who supported such a plan were known as *Radical Republicans*. Their plan of Reconstruction proposed the following:

★ No state would be allowed to deprive anyone born on American soil of the rights of citizenship. No state could deprive a person of the right to vote because of that person's race or former status as a slave. (These guarantees were written into the Fourteenth and Fifteenth amendments to the U.S. Constitution.)

★ No military leader or political officeholder of the defeated Confederacy would be permitted to hold state or federal office in the postwar period. (This provision was included in the Fourteenth Amendment.)

★ The South would be occupied by federal troops and governed by army generals. The troops would be withdrawn from a state after it had adopted a new state constitution acceptable to Congress.

Post–Civil War Amendments:
Protecting the Civil Rights of African Americans

During Andrew Johnson's presidency (1865–1869), the Radical Republicans dominated Congress. So great was their power that they were able to enact their Reconstruction plan despite the president's opposition and repeated vetoes. By far the most important measures passed by the Radical Republicans were three Constitutional amendments guaranteeing the rights of the freed slaves.

Thirteenth Amendment (1865) Going well beyond Lincoln's Emancipation Proclamation, this amendment declared slavery illegal in every state of the Union. Through the Thirteenth Amendment, northern abolitionists fully achieved their objective.

Fourteenth Amendment (1868) This amendment defined the rights of American citizenship as follows: "All persons born or naturalized in the United States, and subject to the jurisdiction thereof, are citizens of the United States and of the state wherein they reside." In addition, the Four-

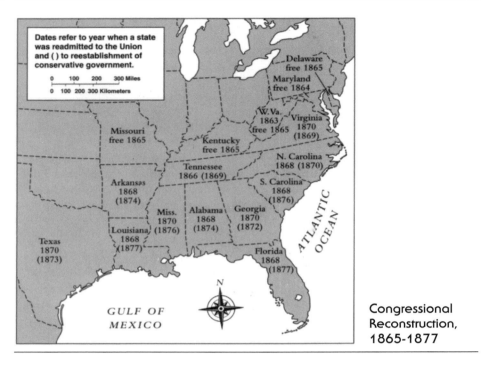

Dates refer to year when a state was readmitted to the Union and ( ) to reestablishment of conservative government.

0   100   200   300 Miles

0   100   200   300 Kilometers

Delaware free 1865

Maryland free 1864

W.Va. 1863 free 1865

Virginia 1870 (1869)

Missouri free 1865

Kentucky free 1865

N. Carolina 1868 (1870)

Tennessee 1866 (1869)

S. Carolina 1868 (1876)

Arkansas 1868 (1874)

Miss. 1870 (1876)

Alabama 1868 (1874)

Georgia 1870 (1872)

Louisiana 1868 (1877)

Texas 1870 (1873)

Florida 1868 (1877)

GULF OF MEXICO

N

ATLANTIC OCEAN

Congressional Reconstruction, 1865-1877

teenth Amendment prohibited the states from interfering with the "privileges and immunities" of citizens of the United States. Thus, all African Americans (including freed slaves) were to be U.S. citizens with rights equal to those of other citizens.

The Fourteenth Amendment also prohibited the states from depriving a person of life, liberty, or property without due process of law. Nor could the states deny a citizen the equal protection of the laws. The rights protected by the Constitution now applied to the state governments as well as the federal government.

Fifteenth Amendment (1870) This amendment said that voting rights could not be denied to a person because of that person's "race, color, or previous condition of servitude." In effect, the Fifteenth Amendment guaranteed voting rights to African Americans.

Impeachment and Trial of Andrew Johnson

Andrew Johnson was an unpopular president. He antagonized the Radical Republicans in Congress by repeatedly using his veto power to try to block their Reconstruction plan. The lawmakers managed to override each veto by the required two-thirds vote.

In 1867 Congress passed, over the president's veto, an act that would have changed the constitutional system of checks and balances in Con-

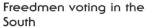
Freedmen voting in the South

gress's favor. The Tenure of Office Act prohibited the president from firing a cabinet officer without the Senate's approval. After the act was passed, Johnson defiantly announced the firing of his secretary of war, Edwin Stanton. In 1868 the House of Representatives responded by voting to impeach the president.

At Johnson's trial on impeachment charges, the Senate fell just one vote short of the two-thirds majority required to remove an official from office. Thus, barely saved from removal, Johnson continued as president until the end of his term.

★ In Review

1. How were congressional Republicans' plans for Reconstruction more "radical" than those of Abraham Lincoln and Andrew Johnson?
2. Summarize the provisions of the Thirteenth, Fourteenth, and Fifteenth amendments.
3. Why did the Radical Republicans impeach Andrew Johnson? How did this conflict between Congress and President Johnson illustrate the principle of checks and balances?

Views of Reconstruction

Because of their defeat in the war, southerners reluctantly conceded that the national government and the U.S. Constitution were supreme. Never again would a southern state threaten to secede from the Union. (Even so, the southern states continued to champion the idea of states' rights.)

The state governments organized in the South after 1867 were extremely controversial. Southern whites and southern blacks looked at Reconstruction from entirely different points of view. For whites, already embittered by Confederate defeat, northern control of their state governments was an insult. For blacks, on the other hand, Reconstruction was an all-too-brief period of potential freedom and equal opportunity (enforced by federal law).

Let us look at Reconstruction from the differing points of view of northerners and southerners.

Northerners' Point of View

In the postwar years, thousands of northerners moved to the South, seeing opportunities for both economic gain and political power. Shielded by federal troops, the northerners campaigned for election to seats in the legislatures created by the South's new state constitutions. They ran as Republicans and counted upon southern blacks to vote Republican on Election Day.

Republican Victories In 1868 elections were held in seven southern states. Aided by the nearly unanimous support of freed blacks, northern Republicans won four of the seven governorships, ten (out of 14) seats in the U.S. Senate, and 20 (out of 35) seats in the U.S. House of Representatives.

Extravagant Use of Public Funds The chief task of the newly organized state legislatures was to help rebuild all that had been destroyed during the war. For this purpose large sums of money were voted by the Republican legislators. However, some of the money intended for rebuilding was taken by the legislators for their personal profit.

Southerners' Point of View

The chief interests of southern whites during Reconstruction were to (1) revive their war-torn economy, (2) regain control of their state governments, and (3) reduce the political power of southern blacks. They viewed the Reconstruction governments as hateful and scorned the northern whites and southern blacks who took part in them.

"Carpetbaggers" and "Scalawags" Northerners who went south were accused of profiting from the region's economic distress and political weakness. They were scornfully nicknamed *carpetbaggers* (fortune hunters who carry all their belongings in a single travel bag). Even worse in the eyes of Confederate loyalists were those southern whites who cooperated with the northerners. These *scalawags*, as they were called, were thought to have only one motive: to share in the northerners' corrupt, moneymaking schemes.

Cartoon championing
the white-supremacist
Ku Klux Klan

Terrorist Raids   Many whites were so hostile to blacks in the South that they decided to use violent means to attack them.   In every southern state, groups of whites formed secret societies such as the Knights of the White Camellia and the Ku Klux Klan (KKK).   They often beat and killed African Americans.   Scalawag whites were also intimidated.

Economic and Technological Impact
of the Civil War

The Civil War accelerated industrial production in the North but had a devastating effect on factories in the South.   After the war, northern manufacturing firms broke all records for output, invention, and business growth.   Some historians argue that the postwar business boom would have happened even if there had been no war.   Others argue that the war acted as a major stimulant for business investment.   But nobody questions that a postwar boom did in fact occur and that it changed the nation. As you will read in the next chapter, new industries developed in steel, oil, and consumer goods. Furthermore, electrification would change U.S. industry.

Expanding World Trade After the Civil War

Trade With Europe After the Civil War, trade was vital both to the United States and to the nations of Europe. In fact, as time passed and the United States and Europe became more industrialized, trade became ever more important. After all, industrialism meant an increasing amount of factory-made goods and an increasing need to find buyers or markets for those goods. At the same time each nation needed more materials (such as cotton, coal, iron, and oil) to keep manufacturing more clothing, machines, and other industrial products. The United States was rich in these resources and was thus able to build its industries at a rapid pace. Many of these resources were exported to Europe. As a result, U.S. exports to Europe increased from 60 percent in 1865 to 75 percent by 1900.

Trade With Asia Throughout the 1800s, trade with Europe was much greater than trade with China. American merchants had difficulty exporting U.S. goods to the Chinese empire because the Chinese viewed their civilization as superior to any other. High officials at the emperor's court had little interest in the cheap factory-made goods that Western traders wanted to sell. However, Chinese teas, porcelains, and silks were in great demand in the United States.

For many years, Japan was even less interested than China in trading with Europeans and Americans. It became more open to trade after 1853, the year that Commodore Matthew Perry arrived in Japan with an American fleet. Perry wanted not only to open trade with Japan but also to gain assurances that Japan would assist shipwrecked U.S. sailors. He brought gifts demonstrating the benefits of industrial technology and, in a show of force, fired off the fleet's guns. Japanese officials were sufficiently impressed to sign a trade treaty with the United States. Soon afterward, new leadership in Japan adopted a policy of learning western technologies and making Japan into a modern industrial nation. As a result, trade with Japan increased in the post–Civil War period. However, U.S. imports from Asia were significantly greater than U.S. exports to Asia.

Growing Need for Labor

The industrial growth of the United States depended upon the labor of immigrants. They provided the labor for the building of the first transcontinental railroad; turned the prairies and forests of the Middle West into prosperous farms; helped to make New York City the center for a booming garment industry; opened small retail stores that would later grow into large department stores, such as Macy's and Gimbel's; and worked in the steel mills of Pittsburgh, Pennsylvania and Birmingham, Alabama.

Immigrants and their children became the technicians, inventors, and scientists who helped to turn the dream of a mighty industrial empire into a reality. In addition to immigrants, many farmers began to leave the land and settle in urban areas where factory jobs were available. Women also entered the labor force in larger numbers. The jobs available to working-class women in the early years after the Civil War were limited to low-paying work in factories and laundries, and to domestic work as cleaners and cooks in middle-class homes. But new technologies of the 1880s and 1890s opened up thousands of jobs in business for women as typists and telephone operators. Women often entered the labor market because men's wages were not high enough to pay the rent and buy necessities for their families.

★ In Review

1. Define carpetbagger. Describe how carpetbaggers were viewed by (a) southern whites and (b) southern blacks.
2. In what ways did the North benefit economically from the Civil War?
3. How did trade with Europe and Asia increase after the Civil War?

The New South

Southern Agriculture: Land and Labor

What was to replace the great cotton plantations and the slavery system of the prewar period? Who was to plant and harvest the crops? Who was to own and manage the land? During and after Reconstruction, the economic system that developed in the South gave whites ownership of most of the land, while blacks worked the land as tenants and sharecroppers.

Farm Owners   After the destruction of wartime, only a few plantation owners could afford to keep their huge properties intact. Other planters divided their estates into small sections, which they sold as farms. Most of the land went to white buyers, although a small number of blacks also managed to become landowning farmers.

Tenant Farmers   Instead of selling the land, plantation owners often rented sections of it to tenants. In order to live and work on the land, tenant farmers provided their own seed, mules, and provisions.

Sharecroppers   The poorest southerners (whites as well as blacks) lacked the money either to pay rents or to buy mules for plowing. In return for farming a piece of land, they paid a certain share of the crop to the landlord. *Sharecroppers*, as they were called, were often unable to pay their debts for many reasons—wornout land, low prices for their cotton, and relatively high prices for farm supplies. Thus, many African Americans were still economically in bondage (even though, legally, they were free from slavery).

Status of Freedmen

For southern blacks, making the transition from slavery to freedom was an enormous challenge. At first they had high hopes that the U.S. government would protect their rights and help them to take their place in southern society as landowning farmers.

Economic Hopes In the early years of Reconstruction, it was widely rumored that every black family in the South would be given a chance at economic independence by receiving 40 acres and a mule from the government. Blacks' hopes were encouraged by Congressman Thaddeus Stevens and other Radical Republicans, who favored the idea of distributing land to freed slaves.

Political Hopes The adoption of the Fifteenth Amendment gave African Americans solid grounds for believing that the U.S. government would do all in its power to protect their civil rights as voters.

Economic and Political Reality The reality was a bitter disappointment. Congress never acted on the idea of providing 40 acres and a mule. Also, the Fifteenth Amendment's guarantee of voting rights proved to be misleading. At first northern troops tried to protect the right of blacks to vote. But, as we shall see, many southern whites were determined to stop blacks from voting.

Participation in Reconstruction Governments In the early years of Reconstruction (1868–1872), blacks had the full support of northern Republicans

Senator Hiram Revels

and U.S. troops. In this period many African Americans won election to seats in southern legislatures. In one house of South Carolina's legislature, blacks were in the majority. Black citizens may have been better represented in the lawmaking process during Reconstruction than at any time before or since.

African Americans in Congress During Reconstruction, 14 African Americans from the South served in the U.S. Congress. Among them were Senator Hiram Revels of Mississippi, Congressman Robert Smalls of South Carolina, and Congressman Jeremiah Haralson of Alabama. Half of the black lawmakers were former slaves; half had attended college. As a group they championed a number of causes including protection of civil rights and federal aid to education.

From Exclusion to Segregation

From the days of slavery, both in the North and the South, many whites tended to regard blacks as their social inferiors. In some cities in both regions, they expressed this racial prejudice by forbidding blacks to mix with whites in public places (railroad cars, streetcars, restaurants, and hotels). Laws that segregated, or separated, the races in this way were known as *Jim Crow laws*.

The Civil Rights Act of 1875 prohibited owners of railroads, restaurants, and other public places from discriminating against African American customers. For a few years, the law was generally obeyed. Beginning in 1881, however, one southern state after another adopted Jim Crow laws. By the 1890s, segregation was the rule everywhere in the South. African Americans were strictly prohibited from entering public places that had been reserved "for whites only."

Congressman Robert Smalls

Struggle for Political Control in the New South

Black Codes   The first year after the Civil War, 1865, was a time of terrible confusion.   Southerners held state conventions in order to organize new postwar governments for their respective states.   President Johnson accepted the conventions as legitimate if they complied with the terms of his Reconstruction plan.   From South Carolina to Texas, each convention drew up a list of measures for limiting the movements and restricting the rights of former slaves.   These measures, known as *Black Codes*, prohibited blacks from doing the following: carrying firearms; starting businesses; appearing on the streets after sunset; renting or leasing farmland; and traveling without a permit.

Southern whites argued that the codes were necessary to keep order. But to other Americans, it seemed all too obvious that the codes were meant to deprive freed blacks of their civil rights.

Radical Republican Laws   Radical Republicans condemned the Black Codes and argued that the state conventions in the South were not legitimate.   To accomplish their two goals (protecting southern blacks and punishing southern whites), Radical Republican leaders pushed a series of Reconstruction laws through Congress.

A new agency of the U.S. government, the Freedmen's Bureau (1865), was given the ambitious task of aiding nearly 4 million former slaves (freedmen) in adjusting to freedom.   It built and operated schools in the South for blacks, recognizing that as slaves, they had been deliberately deprived of the skills of literacy.   As a result, thousands of former slaves took advan-

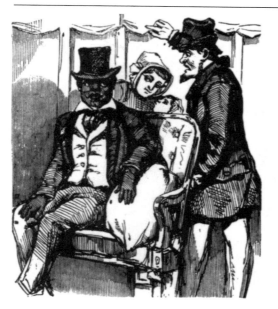

Cartoon of a segregated southern railroad car

tage of the educational opportunities provided by the Freedmen's Bureau by attending schools and colleges for the first time. The bureau also provided emergency aid in the form of clothing, food, and medical supplies. The Civil Rights Act of 1866 combatted the Black Codes, by giving the federal government the authority to protect the civil rights of blacks.

Military Reconstruction (1867)   Congress divided the South into five military districts. Each district was occupied by federal troops and commanded by a military governor (instead of an elected civilian governor). In 1867 Congress also set conditions for readmitting a seceded state to the union. The state conventions of 1865 were deemed illegitimate. A state wanting to be readmitted to the Union had to draw up a constitution that accepted the terms of the Fourteenth Amendment. One part of this amendment disqualified former Confederate leaders from holding office. The Force Acts of 1870–1871 authorized federal troops to break up terrorist organizations such as the Ku Klux Klan formed by southern whites to intimidate black voters.

Supreme Court Interpretations of the New Amendments (*Civil Rights Cases*, 1883)

Black citizens went to court to challenge the constitutionality of the Jim Crow laws. They argued that such laws violated the Fourteenth Amendment's clause guaranteeing equal protection of the laws. But the Supreme Court ruled otherwise.

Civil Rights Cases (1883)   In a series of cases, the Supreme Court concluded that Jim Crow practices in the South were allowed by the Constitution. The

The Freedmen's Bureau, where former slaves and their children received an education

Court said that individual property owners had the right to keep out customers if they wished. The Fourteenth Amendment applied only to the actions of government officials, not to those of private citizens.

Debate Over the Role of African Americans

For a time, African Americans were forced to obey the Jim Crow laws as an unpleasant reality of southern life. Between 1890 and 1910 two leaders arose who took opposite positions on segregation.

Booker T. Washington's Arguments   One of the leaders freed from slavery in 1865 was a nine-year-old boy named Booker T. Washington. As a young man, in 1881, Washington founded the Tuskegee Institute in Alabama, a school dedicated to giving industrial and vocational training to African Americans. Washington took the position that blacks should not seek to be accepted into white society. A more realistic and important goal, he said, was to win economic opportunity by filling skilled, high-paying jobs. In a famous speech delivered in Atlanta in 1895, Washington said, "In all things that are purely social we can be separate as the fingers, yet one as the hand in all things essential to mutual progress."

W. E. B. Du Bois's Arguments   A younger man than Washington, Du Bois grew up in Massachusetts, where he excelled as a scholar, earning a Ph.D. degree from Harvard. In his book *The Souls of Black Folk* (1903), Du Bois challenged Washington's views on segregation. He agreed that vocational education for blacks was one important avenue of economic opportunity. But he strongly disagreed with the idea that economic gains were more important than civil rights. He urged African Americans to insist on their rights and to oppose the Jim Crow laws with all their strength.

★ In Review

1. What economic changes were brought about in the South in the years after the Civil War?
2. What new forms of discrimination against African Americans developed in the years following the Civil War?
3. Compare and contrast the strategies of Booker T. Washington and W. E. B. Du Bois to achieve equal rights.

The End of Reconstruction

Northern Republican control of state governments in the South began to weaken in 1869. In that year, Tennessee became the first southern state to elect a postwar government dominated by Democrats. One by one, other southern states also elected Democratic majorities. By 1877 there were no more Reconstruction governments.

Southern Democratic Domination of Governments

Change in Public Opinion   As time passed, many northern whites grew tired of the Reconstruction issue. They became less concerned about protecting the rights of African Americans and more interested in private pursuits. By 1875 the Civil War lay ten years in the past. Many people wanted to put the war behind them by withdrawing troops from the South.

Amnesty Act (1872)   As public opinion shifted, Radical Republicans lost their grip on Congress. Toward the end of Ulysses S. Grant's first term as president, a more moderate Congress enacted the Amnesty Act, which restored voting rights to about 160,000 former Confederates.

Increase in Terrorist Pressure   Secret societies like the Ku Klux Klan increased in number and strength. Despite the Force Acts, federal troops had little success in capturing and bringing to justice those responsible for the KKK's beatings and lynchings. Though some blacks took up arms in defense of their homes and families, they were eventually forced to submit to white pressure. In time, it became clear that the federal government either could not or would not enforce its own civil rights laws. Rather than

The Election of 1876

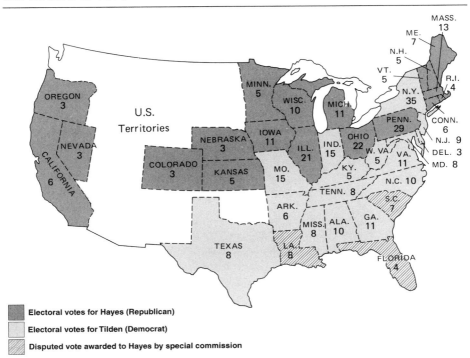

Electoral votes for Hayes (Republican)

Electoral votes for Tilden (Democrat)

Disputed vote awarded to Hayes by special commission

jeopardize their lives, many southern blacks stopped going to the polls to vote.

Disputed Election of 1876

Election Results in Three States During the 1876 election year, federal troops occupied just three southern states: South Carolina, Florida, and Louisiana. In all other states of the South, the troops had left and the Democrats had returned to power. In these southern states without troops, the Democratic candidate for president, Samuel Tilden of New York, won every electoral vote. Only in the three states with federal troops was the Republican candidate, Rutherford Hayes, able to claim a victory. But Tilden also claimed victory in these states, pointing to a set of Democratic voting returns that contradicted the Republican returns. A special commission was called to investigate whether the election had been won by Hayes or Tilden. Since Republicans on the commission outnumbered Democrats, the decision went for Hayes—declared the winner by just one electoral vote. So angry were the southern Democrats at this point that some talked of taking up arms and fighting another civil war if necessary.

End of Military Occupation

Compromise of 1877 The political crisis was solved by compromise. Meeting in secret, Republican and Democratic leaders agreed that Hayes (Republican) would be the next president. In exchange, Hayes would immediately order the last federal troops to leave the South. By withdrawing these troops, Republicans were in effect abandoning southern blacks to rule by the white majority. Northern commitment to Reconstruction was over.

★   Methods Used to Disenfranchise African Americans   ★

Method	Voting Law	How the Law Discriminated Against African Americans
1. Literacy test	Voters must take a test demonstrating an ability to read and write.	Slaves had not been taught the skills of literacy. State examiners could deliberately pass whites and fail blacks.
2. Poll tax	Citizens must pay a tax to the state before being allowed to vote.	Most blacks were poorer than most whites and could not afford to pay the tax.
3. "Grandfather clause"	A person whose grandfather had voted before 1867 could vote without having to pass a literacy test.	Only whites had grandfathers who voted before 1867.

★ ★ ★ ★ ★

TESTIMONY OF A BLACK CONGRESSMAN

Born a slave in 1847, John R. Lynch of Mississippi enrolled in a school as soon as federal troops freed his family. He won election to the reconstructed legislature of Mississippi and went to Washington in 1872 as a member of the U.S. House of Representatives. This account of racial prejudice was printed in the Congressional Record.

. . . Think of it for a moment; here am I, a member of your honorable body, representing one of the largest and wealthiest districts in the State of Mississippi, and possibly in the South; a district composed of persons of different races, religions, and nationalities: and yet, when I leave my home to come to the capital of the nation, to take part in the deliberations of the House and to participate with you in making laws for the government of this great Republic, . . . I am treated, not as an American citizen, but as a brute. Forced to occupy a filthy smoking-car both night and day, with drunkards, gamblers, and criminals; and for what? Not that I am unable or unwilling to pay my way; not that I am obnoxious in my personal appearance or disrespectful in my conduct; but simply because I happen to be of a darker complexion. If this treatment was confined to persons of our own sex we could possibly afford to endure it. But such is not the case. Our wives and our daughters, our sisters and our mothers are subjected to the same insults and to the same uncivilized treatment. . . . The only moments of my life when I am necessarily compelled to question my loyalty to my Government or my devotion to the flag of my country is when I read of outrages having been committed upon innocent colored people and . . . when I leave my home to go traveling.

Congressman John Lynch

Restoration of White Control in the South (1870s and 1880s)

The South that emerged from the Civil War and Reconstruction was profoundly different from the antebellum (prewar) South. In all areas of southern life, institutions arose that endured for generations.

The Solid South   Southern whites generally blamed the Republican party for the hardships they suffered from war and Reconstruction. After Reconstruction, they made sure that the Democratic party in their region would be strong enough to win every southern state and local election. In a short time the South became virtually a one-party region. It was the *Solid South* (solidly for the Democratic party). From 1880 to 1924, Democratic candidates for president won all the electoral votes of the southern states.

Disenfranchisement of African Americans   To *disenfranchise* is to take voting rights away from a person or group. Confederate officers had been briefly disenfranchised by the Fourteenth Amendment. After Reconstruction, the South disenfranchised black citizens in order to ensure the control of the Democratic party. Each southern state passed a number of laws that made it either difficult or impossible for African Americans to vote. (See the chart on page 188.)

Plessy v. *Ferguson* (1896): "Separate but Equal"

Homer Plessy, a black citizen of Louisiana, sued a railroad company for preventing him from entering a railroad car set aside for whites. Once again, in a landmark decision, the Supreme Court ruled in favor of the property owner and against the African American petitioner. Because the railroad provided "separate but equal" facilities for blacks, the Court decided that the equal protection clause of the Constitution had not been violated. One justice, John Harlan, disagreed. In his dissenting opinion, Justice Harlan argued that segregation threatened personal liberty and equality of rights. But for many years the majority on the Court used the standard of "separate but equal" to justify racial segregation.

★ In Review

1. Explain the significance of the election of 1876.
2. How did the Compromise of 1877 contribute to segregation?
3. How did the Supreme Court's ruling in *Plessy* v. *Ferguson* (1896) establish a legal basis for segregation?

The Impact of the Civil War and Reconstruction: Summary

On Political Alignments

Following the Civil War, the Republican party grew in strength in the South, as millions of freed slaves won the right to vote and run for elective office. This right was protected by federal troops stationed in the South. By 1877, however, Reconstruction in the South had ended. A major factor that led to the end of Reconstruction was the Compromise of 1877. This compromise ended the dispute over electoral votes in three southern states. Those electoral votes were awarded to the Republican candidate Hayes in return for the removal of the remaining federal troops in the South. As a result, African Americans had their right to participate in the political process taken from them. Southern states led by white voters returned to the Democratic party. Thus, the southern states became known as the *Solid South*, since only Democratic party candidates had a chance to win both state and national elections.

On the Nature of Citizenship

Citizenship is a dearly held value for all Americans. Prior to the Civil War, most African Americans were slaves and denied citizenship. Following the Civil War, the Thirteenth Amendment ended slavery and the Fourteenth Amendment provided citizenship for all people "born or naturalized within the United States." For African Americans, the road from slavery to citizenship had taken almost 250 years. Along that road, African Americans had fought in both the Revolutionary War and the Civil War seeking freedom. Citizenship, however, did not mean true equality, since a series of court rulings following the Reconstruction period held that "separate but equal" did not violate the Fourteenth Amendment.

On Federal-State Relations

Prior to the Civil War, some states had asserted their right to leave the Union. Their chief argument held that since the states had approved the Constitution, they had a right to nullify federal laws and even secede from the United States. This right was asserted by New England Federalists, who were emphatically opposed to the War of 1812. It was also asserted by South Carolina in 1832 when high tariffs were the issue. The most extreme example was the secession of the southern states that occurred following Lincoln's election in 1860. Those who opposed nullification and secession noted that the Constitution begins with the words "We the people" and not "We the states." They further noted that while the Constitution provided that territories may become states, but it did not provide a method for states to leave the Union. Finally, opponents of secession point to Article VI, Section II, of the Constitution, which provides for federal supremacy.

The Civil War finally ended all talk of nullification and secession. The victory of the U.S. government forever ended the possibility that any state would again attempt to leave the Union. The placement of federal troops in the South during Reconstruction was further evidence of national supremacy.

On the Development of the North as an Industrial Power

The Civil War served as a major force in the ongoing industrialization of the United States. The need to produce weapons and materials greatly expanded the nation's industrial base. Following the Civil War, new opportunities for industrial growth were created by the availability of natural resources, the arrival of many new immigrants, the growth of railroads, the settlement of the West, and increased investment by Europeans. The Republican party and the Republican presidents, who would serve for all but eight years from 1860 to 1900, supported industrialization. As you recall, the Republican party platform prior to the Civil War supported high tariffs, a transcontinental railroad, and the creation of a national banking system. These policies would go far in aiding the growth of the United States as an industrial power following the Civil War.

On American Society

The northern victory in the Civil War and the ending of slavery provided an opportunity for freed slaves to move to both the North and the West. In addition, Reconstruction policies provided an opportunity for African Americans in the South to seek economic advancement, acquire an education, and gain some social equality. The protection of these rights by the federal government during the Reconstruction period represented no less than a second American revolution.

In the early days of the nation, Alexander Hamilton and Thomas Jefferson offered different views of the future of American society. Hamilton developed policies that supported industrialization, while Jefferson viewed the future as agricultural. While Hamilton lived in New York City and favored urbanization, Jefferson lived in Monticello, Virginia, and saw American society as essentially rural. The Civil War and the policies of the Republican party ensured that American society would move more in the direction of Hamilton's vision than that of Jefferson.

Another important result of the Civil War was that the United States could now focus on westward expansion. Westward expansion would help the United States obtain the natural resources and the farm products to feed the growing workforce in the eastern cities. With war no longer a factor, the settlement of the West and the conquest of Native Americans would become a major objective of the United States government.

MULTIPLE-CHOICE QUESTIONS

1. Which was a major result of the Civil War?
   (1) Disputes between the North and the South were ended.
   (2) Whites accepted blacks as social equals.
   (3) Slavery was ended through the passage of an amendment to the Constitution.
   (4) The South returned to the way it was before the war.

2. Which statement accurately compares Andrew Johnson's Reconstruction plan with that of the Radical Republicans?
   (1) Both plans aimed to punish southern whites severely.
   (2) Johnson's plan was more lenient than that of the Radical Republicans.
   (3) Radical Republicans wanted to provide aid to southern whites, while Johnson wanted to provide aid to southern blacks.
   (4) Both plans welcomed the secessionist states back into the Union with few conditions.

3. A major feature of Reconstruction was that
   (1) new federal laws and constitutional amendments attempted to ensure equal rights and opportunities for African Americans
   (2) the South rapidly developed into the nation's major industrial center

   (3) a spirit of cooperation existed between the president and Congress
   (4) new state governments in the South concentrated on ending corruption.

4. The Fourteenth Amendment is important because, in addition to awarding citizenship to former slaves, it
   (1) guarantees women the right to vote
   (2) abolishes the poll tax
   (3) guarantees equal protection of the laws
   (4) provides protection against illegal searches and seizures of property.

5. During Reconstruction, African American voters in the South generally
   (1) voted for Republican candidates
   (2) voted for Democratic candidates
   (3) showed no preference for either Republicans or Democrats
   (4) refused to participate in elections.

6. A difference between the way that the Ku Klux Klan is portrayed in the poster on page 179 and the actual practices of the Klan is that the Klan
   (1) failed to achieve a popular following

(2) only occasionally used violence
(3) operated in secret
(4) was rarely successful.

7. The map on page 187 shows that, in the presidential election of 1876,
(1) westerners split their votes between Rutherford B. Hayes and Samuel Tilden
(2) the states of New York and Indiana voted for Tilden while the rest of the northern states voted for Hayes
(3) the South was solidly behind Hayes
(4) the territories split their vote between Hayes and Tilden.

8. Reconstruction ended when Democrats agreed to the election of Rutherford Hayes, and Republicans promised to
(1) withdraw federal troops from the South
(2) give each freedman forty acres and a mule
(3) do away with the electoral college
(4) repeal the Fifteenth Amendment.

9. The purpose of Jim Crow laws was to
(1) give full civil rights to African Americans
(2) keep African Americans in a separate and inferior position
(3) give economic incentives for business growth
(4) provide equal opportunities for all citizens.

10. In *Plessy* v. *Ferguson*, the Supreme Court argued that
(1) states could pass laws separating people on the basis of race as long as equal facilities were provided
(2) segregation on the basis of race was unconstitutional
(3) the Fourteenth Amendment outlawed practices that emphasized racial distinctions
(4) separate but equal laws would create separate but unequal facilities.

THEMATIC ESSAYS

1. **Theme:** Reconstruction and Balance of Power

An intense struggle for power between President Andrew Johnson and the Radical Republicans of Congress took place between 1865 and 1868.

Task:

★ Compare and contrast the Reconstruction plans of President Andrew Johnson and the congressional Radical Republicans.

★ Show how the dispute between President Andrew Johnson and the Radical Republicans in Congress ended in the impeachment of the president and describe its outcome.

You may include in your answer the differing views on secession, amnesty, pardon, and procedures for the readmission of former states of the Confederacy. In addition to this, describe the controversy over the Tenure of Office Act, which led to the impeachment of President Johnson.

2. **Theme:** Outcomes of the Civil War and Reconstruction

The Civil War and the following period of Reconstruction resulted in change but left many serious problems unresolved.

Task:

★ Describe one change that took effect as a result of the Civil War and/or Reconstruction.
★ Show how one problem remained unsolved after the period of Reconstruction concluded.
★ Based on the information you have given, react to the following statement: "In some ways the Civil War was both a victory for the North and a draw for the South."

In answering the above questions, you may refer to relations between the federal and state governments, the development of northern industry, the Compromise of 1877, *Plessy* v. *Ferguson* (1896), sharecropping, and tenant farming.

DOCUMENT-BASED QUESTION

*Read or analyze each document and answer the question that follows it. Then read the **Task** and write your essay. Essays should include references to most of the documents along with additional information based on your knowledge of United States history and government.*

Historical Context: In spite of emancipation, many former slaves were given only a brief period of freedom. As Reconstruction ended, African Americans who remained in the South became segregated from white society, with no real rights as citizens of the United States.

Document 1 The Thirteenth and Fifteenth Amendments:

Amendment 13: Abolition of Slavery (1865)

[Slavery Forbidden] Neither slavery nor involuntary servitude [compulsory service], except as a punishment for a crime whereof the party shall have been duly convicted, shall exist within the United States, or any place subject to their jurisdiction.

[Enforcement Power] Congress shall have power to enforce this article [amendment] by appropriate [suitable] legislation.

Amendment 15: Right of Suffrage (1870)

[African Americans Guaranteed the Right to Vote] The right of citizens of the United States to vote shall not be denied or abridged by the United States or by any state on account of race, color, or previous condition of servitude [slavery].

[Enforcement Power] The Congress shall have power to enforce this article by appropriate legislation.

Question: According to the Thirteenth and Fifteenth amendments, what responsibilities was Congress given on behalf of the freedmen?

Document 2   Refer to the illustration of freedmen voting, on page 177.

Question: How does the illustration show the change in the South that had taken place by 1867?

Document 3   From the writings of southerner "Pitchfork" Ben Tillman:

. . . We reorganized the Democratic Party with one plank, and only one plank, namely that "this is a white man's country, and white men must govern it. . . .

. . . President Grant sent troops to maintain the carpetbag government in power and to protect the Negroes in the right to vote. He merely obeyed the law. . . . Then it was that "we stuffed ballot boxes" because desperate diseases require desperate remedies and having resolved to take the state away, we hesitated at nothing. . . .

I want to say now that we have not shot any Negroes . . . on account of politics since 1876. We have not found it necessary. Eighteen hundred and seventy-six happened to be the hundredth anniversary of the Declaration of Independence, and the action of the white men . . . in taking the [government] away from the Negroes we regard as a second declaration of independence from African barbarism.

Question: How did southern whites of the Democratic party justify their actions?

Document 4   An excerpt of the Supreme Court's *Plessy* v. *Ferguson* decision (1896):

Legislation is powerless to eradicate racial instincts or to abolish distinctions based upon physical differences, and the attempt to do so can only result in accentuating the difficulties of the present situation. If the civil and political rights of both races be equal, one cannot be inferior to the other civilly or politically. If one race be inferior to the other socially, the Constitution of the United States cannot put them upon the same plane.

Question: What was the decision of the Supreme Court regarding segregation in *Plessy* v. *Ferguson*?

Document 5   Refer to the illustration of a segregated railroad car, on page 184.

Question: How does the photograph show a result of the Civil War, Reconstruction, and the period immediately following?

Task

★ Show in what ways former slaves obtained temporary freedom and equality.

★ Explain how the post–Reconstruction Era left southern African Americans in a segregated and inferior status.

Chapter 8
The Rise of American Business, Labor, and Agriculture

★ **Objectives**

★ To understand how industrialization in the United States was part of a worldwide economic revolution.

★ To know the ways in which American business changed from 1865 to 1920.

★ To understand the response of the federal government to industrialization and business growth.

★ To recognize the struggle of labor and labor organizations to achieve improved working conditions.

★ To explain the causes of farmers' discontent and evaluate their political program.

Economic Transformation of the United States

In Chapter 7 we saw the dramatic changes in southern society brought about by the Civil War. In this chapter we shall see the even more sweeping and lasting changes in the American economy brought about by the Industrial Revolution. What was this revolution, and how did the United States jump to a position of economic leadership in the world in the decades following the Civil War? How did business organize itself to take advantage of the changes created by this revolution?

To understand what happened after the Civil War, we must first go back in time to the colonial period about a century earlier. During the 1700s, before the United States existed as a separate nation, the Industrial Revolution had its beginnings in the world's first industrial nation, Great Britain.

The Industrial Revolution

The word "manufacture" originally meant "to make something by hand" (*manu* comes from a Latin word meaning "hand"). For centuries, manufacturing had indeed been done slowly by hand, usually in a home workshop. Workers did not come together in large groups to labor at machinery provided by factory owners. Factories as we know them did not exist.

The *Industrial Revolution* refers to an extended period of economic change, beginning about 1750 and continuing to the present, in which people invented not only new machines but also new systems for producing goods on a mass scale for *mass markets* (large numbers of people). As a result of this revolution, manufacturing is now carried out in large factories, not in home workshops. The change in methods for producing goods revolutionized all aspects of life, including how we think about the world.

In the first hundred years of the Industrial Revolution, new methods of production were invented by the British and adopted by others, including Americans.

Beginnings in Great Britain The making of cotton cloth, or textiles, was the first industry to be revolutionized by machinery and methods of mass production. Several British inventors created machines for producing cotton thread. In 1785 a power loom was invented for rapidly weaving thread into cloth. The power for the mechanized loom was supplied by another invention, the steam engine, developed by James Watt in 1765.

Because each yard of machinemade cloth could be produced at less cost than a yard of handmade cloth, it could be sold cheaply not only in Great Britain but throughout the world. Enterprising businesspersons could hope to make huge profits. But first they had to invest large sums of money for purchasing textile machines, building factories to house the machines, and paying workers to operate them.

Rapid Development in the United States Americans were quick to adopt the revolutionary methods of British industrialists. Recall from Chapter 4 that merchants of the Northeast were eager to compete with the British and sell inexpensive American textiles both at home and abroad. Recall too that Secretary of the Treasury Alexander Hamilton devised government programs that encouraged the development of American industries. His ideas for a U.S. bank and high tariffs were generally supported in the industrial North, but they were opposed in the agrarian (farming) South.

U.S. Advantages in the Race to Industrialize More than most nations on earth, the United States was richly endowed with the three resources needed for rapid industrial growth. Economists call these three types of resources *land* (raw materials), *labor* (human energy and skill), and *capital* (tools, machinery, and money for investment).

Critical Importance of Capital A capitalist system is one in which *capital goods*—tools, machinery, and factories—are privately owned and managed by competing businesses. Consider these advantages of the U.S. economy, in terms of capital alone:

★ *Strong tradition of business enterprise.* Colonial merchants in Boston, New York, and Philadelphia had long been accustomed to risking capital in hopes of making a profit. The profits they earned from their business successes enabled U.S. banks to finance costly new ventures for the new industrial age.

★ *Patent laws to encourage invention.* The U.S. Constitution gives to Congress the power to "promote the progress of science and useful arts" by issuing patents to inventors. A *patent* is a government document giving to the creator of an original object the exclusive right to make and sell that object for profit. Thousands of Americans recognized that a good idea for a useful gadget or machine could make their fortune. Of course, not all of the would-be inventors succeeded. But those who did not only enriched themselves but also contributed to the Industrial Revolution.

Growth of American Industry After the Civil War

Northern industry made great strides in the 1850s, the decade just before the Civil War. By 1860 the nation's cities were linked by more than 30,000 miles of railroad track (three times the mileage of 1850). Every year the production of pig iron (crudely cast iron) set new records. The invention of the telegraph by Samuel F. B. Morse in 1844 speeded business communications. Perhaps the most revolutionary change since standardized parts was the assembly line developed by Henry Ford in the early 1900s. Using this process, automobiles moved along on conveyor belts with each worker assigned a specific task that would be repeated on each car. Thus workers became *specialized* and could work faster. This ability to produce more in a given period of time is called "productivity" and leads to lower cost.

Proprietorships, Partnerships, and the Rise of Monopolies

In early America, businesses were usually organized as proprietorships or partnerships. But both methods had major disadvantages for large-scale business organization. In both, the proprietor or partner was liable for all the debts of the business. Thus, in any enterprise involving risk, it was difficult to raise money. As you shall see, by 1900, U.S. businesses moved from proprietorships and partnerships to corporations and then *monopolies* (a situation in which one producer controls an industry, thereby controlling production and prices).

Incorporation

Corporate Form of Business Organization Nineteenth-century business owners were encouraged by state laws that enabled them to form corporations. A *corporation* is a business chartered, or formed, under state law. To raise capital, a corporation may sell shares of ownership (stock) to the public. Anyone buying stock in a corporation is subject to lose no more than the sum originally invested in the stock. If the corporation cannot pay its debts and goes bankrupt, its stockholders (owners) are not personally *liable*, or responsible, for paying its debts. In other words, they may keep their homes and other personal property instead of losing everything to pay business debts. (Owners of the other forms of businesses—proprietorships and partnerships—do in fact risk all that they own.)

Investment in Transportation   Another advantage of the corporate form of business is the amount of investment money that corporations may raise for ambitious and costly industrial projects such as building a railroad or digging a canal. Nineteenth-century railroad and canal companies sold their stock to the public to *capitalize*, or finance, building these costly enterprises. People who bought stock in a railroad had faith in its money-making potential. They recognized that railroads and the rapid hauling of freight over long distances were the key to the industrial future.

Capital Concentration and Consolidation

Theory of Laissez-Faire   According to the Scottish philosopher-economist Adam Smith, the surest road to economic progress was to allow businesses to compete freely and without legal restriction. Any government attempt to regulate business would only reduce the economic benefits to be gained from competition. Therefore, said Smith, the best government policy was one of *laissez-faire*—leave businesses alone, without laws to restrict or regulate them. Although Adam Smith lived at the time of the American Revolution, his theory had wide influence a century later.

There was one central flaw in the argument for laissez-faire. If business leaders had their way, the final result of completely free competition would be no competition at all. The goal of every business leader was to eliminate his or her competitors. Whoever succeeded would be the one and only seller of the product. Then the business would be a monopoly. One consequence of monopoly control is monopolists' ability to charge high prices for their products. In the 1870s and 1880s, the trend toward monopoly control was all too clear. In every industry it seemed that businesses were becoming less and less competitive, as more and more *consolidated* (joined together).

Expanding National and International Markets

National Markets   Recognizing that goods could be shipped by rail all over the country, inventors and business leaders began to create products that could be sold nationwide (rather than sold mainly to local customers, as in the past). Goods manufactured in eastern factories were shipped west. Meat and wheat produced in the West were shipped east to feed the growing number of workers in major cities. Urban populations increased as a result of increasing immigration from overseas and the migration of former

Cartoon of "King Monopoly" and his subjects

slaves to areas with new jobs and opportunities. Both groups settled in northern cities.

International Markets The Industrial Revolution led to increased global trade. Western European nations and Japan competed with the United States to sell textiles, steel, machinery, and ships. *Imperialism*, the practice of European nations and Japan of gaining control over overseas areas for their own economic benefit, led to increased railroad building and the shipment of consumer goods throughout the world. Thus, the Industrial Revolution led to new markets for American goods.

Changes in Merchandising: Department Stores, Mail-Order Catalogs

Department Stores for Urban Consumers Until the 1860s, small specialty stores in the cities catered to the rich. Middle-class consumers felt out of place in such shops. But they delighted in wandering from department to department of a large New York City store erected by A. T. Stewart in 1862. This *department store*, as it was called, was widely imitated in other major cities. For the first time, shopping for consumer goods became a popular pastime for large numbers of urban Americans.

Mail-Order Catalogs for Rural Consumers Most potential buyers of consumer goods lived on farms far from any city store. To reach these millions of rural Americans, Chicago businessman Montgomery Ward mailed catalogs picturing his merchandise and invited people to mail back their orders

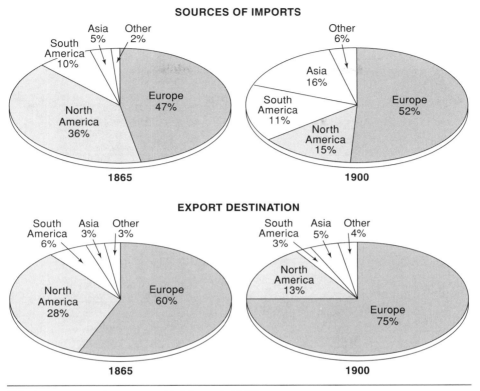

SOURCES OF IMPORTS

1865

Asia 5%
Other 2%
South America 10%
North America 36%
Europe 47%

1900

Other 6%
Asia 16%
South America 11%
North America 15%
Europe 52%

EXPORT DESTINATION

1865

South America 6%
Asia 3%
Other 3%
North America 28%
Europe 60%

1900

South America 3%
Asia 5%
Other 4%
North America 13%
Europe 75%

U.S. Imports and Exports, 1865 and 1900

for advertised items. The first catalogs were mailed in 1871 and drew orders from far and wide. Two other Chicagoans, Richard Sears and Alvah Roebuck, also built a hugely successful business in the 1890s. The Sears, Roebuck catalogs offered everything from mousetraps to pianos.

Major Areas of Growth in Business and Industry

In the decades following the Civil War, one of the most important factors in the growing industrialization of the United States was the growth of transportation.

Transportation

Prior to the Civil War, roads, rivers, and canals were the vital parts of the transportation system in the United States. In the early part of the 19th century, settlers and traders followed the Cumberland Road from Maryland to

Page from a late-19th-century Sears, Roebuck catalog

West Virginia. They traveled by steamboat on the Mississippi River and utilized the Erie Canal for the shipment of goods from the Hudson River through Lake Erie to Ohio. Slowly but surely, the United States was building a transportation system to link the West with the East.

Railroads

Although these developments were important, it was the railroad that truly united the growing nation. The development of the railroad is one of the great achievements of the United States. First invented in 1814 in England, the steam locomotive soon led to vast new transportation networks. On the eve of the Civil War, railroads ran through major cities of the United States, linking East and West. As noted earlier, the first transcontinental railroad was completed in 1869.

After the completion of the first transcontinental railroad, other western railroads followed in rapid succession. Between 1865 and 1900 railroad tracks in the United States went from 35,000 miles to 260,000 miles—an eightfold increase in just 35 years. By the end of the century, the United States was tied together by many more miles of railroad track than existed in all of Europe, including Russia.

Transcontinental Railroads, 1865–1900

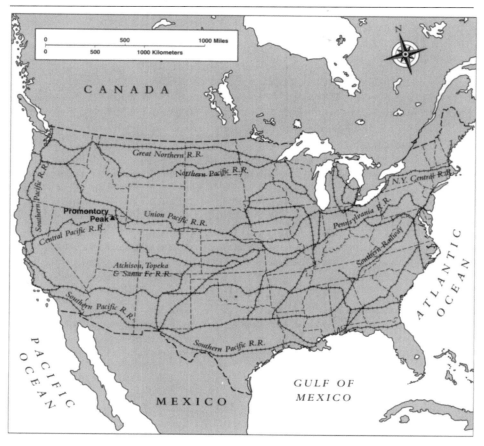

Building Materials

Steel   Another industry that boomed in the post–Civil War years was the manufacture of steel. Before the war, iron was the chief metal of the Industrial Revolution. It was known for a long time that steel was stronger and more durable than iron, but the process for making it was slow and costly. All this changed in 1856 when British industrialist Henry Bessemer invented a process for blowing cold air through molten iron, thereby producing steel that had no impurities. The Bessemer process for making steel was adopted by American industrialist Andrew Carnegie in 1867. Soon the United States led the world in steel production, with an output of 13.5 million tons in 1901.

Energy Sources

Coal   Coal has served the United States as both a source of fuel and a source of heat. Coal as a fuel became important when it replaced wood to power locomotives in the early 1800s. As railroads and factories grew, so did the need for coal. Coal was mined in the Allegheny Mountains from Pittsburgh, Pennsylvania, to Birmingham, Alabama. Growing industrialization led to an increase in coal production from approximately 30 million tons in 1870 to more than 200 million tons by 1900.

Oil   Before the Civil War, homes were lighted mainly by small lamps that burned either whale oil or vegetable oil. In the 1850s it was discovered that kerosene made from petroleum was a relatively clean fuel for home lighting. But where was petroleum to be found in quantity? The answer came in 1859 when Edwin Drake dug a deep well in Titusville, Pennsylvania, and underground oil gushed to the surface. The digging of oil wells and the processing of oil to yield kerosene became a big business in the United States, particularly when Cleveland businessman John D. Rockefeller entered the field (see page 207).

Electricity   One creative genius who changed American life with his ideas was Thomas Edison, the "Wizard of Menlo Park." This New Jersey town was the site of Edison's most famous invention, a lightbulb whose bamboo filament glowed brightly when an electric current passed through it. Edison hired a team of scientists and engineers to assist him in his search for new products. Even more important than his hundreds of individual inventions (including the Victrola phonograph and the motion picture camera) was Edison's system for bringing talented people together to work jointly on a research project, His *invention factory* of the 1870s and 1880s is the direct forerunner of modern industrial laboratories.

Communications

Telegraph and Telephone   In the new industrial age, using electricity to send messages greatly speeded up communications between businesses.

Thousands of miles of telegraph wires already connected American cities before the Civil War. After the war, the invention of the telephone (1874–1876) by Alexander Graham Bell, a Scottish immigrant, gave people the ability to talk with each other over long distances. By 1900, some 1.3 million telephones were in use in American homes and businesses.

★ In Review

1. Define Industrial Revolution, capital, corporation, laissez-faire.
2. What advantages did the United States have in its ability to industrialize?
3. What were the effects of railroads on United States industrial growth?

Representative Entrepreneurs

John D. Rockefeller (1839–1937) A native of Cleveland, Ohio, John D. Rockefeller invested his savings in an oil-refining company in 1865. Oil refining was then a fiercely competitive industry, and the chances of business failure seemed much greater than the chances of success. To ensure the survival of his own company, Rockefeller aimed to take control of the entire industry and drive all competitors out of business. He nearly succeeded. In 1870, when Rockefeller organized the Standard Oil Company, he had 200 competitors. Ten years later, only a few competitors were still in business,

John D. Rockefeller

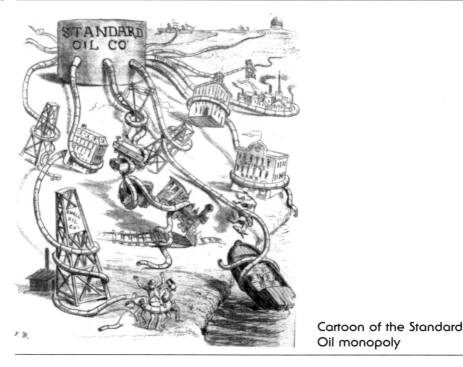

Cartoon of the Standard
Oil monopoly

and Standard Oil accounted for 90 percent of the oil refined in the United States. Rockefeller crushed his competitors by using the following tactics:

★ He persuaded railroads to give *rebates* to Standard Oil—that is, to return to his company a portion of the railroad's shipping charges. This enabled him to charge the lowest prices for oil until his competitors were forced out of business.

★ Whenever a competitor was struggling, Rockefeller moved in with an offer to buy out the firm.

★ To avoid paying railroads' freight charges, Rockefeller increased his competitive advantage by shipping oil more cheaply through pipelines built and owned by Standard Oil.

Andrew Carnegie (1835–1919) Born in Scotland, Andrew Carnegie was one of thousands of immigrants who came to the United States in the 1840s with much hope but no money. As a teenager he worked in a cotton mill nine hours a day, six days a week, for only 20 cents a day. His good fortune and unusual ability won him a job working directly for the president of the Pennsylvania Railroad. In a short time, he was a millionaire, because of investments in railroad sleeping cars, iron mills, and finally steel.

As the hard-driving owner of his own steel company in the 1870s, Carnegie paid his workers low wages, drove tough bargains with railroad

Andrew Carnegie

companies on their prices for shipping steel, and did all in his power to bankrupt competitors. In 1901 Carnegie sold his huge steel company for nearly $500 million to a group of bankers led by J. P. Morgan. From a humble beginning, Carnegie had risen to become one of the world's richest and most successful men.

The Work Ethic: Cotton Mather to Horatio Alger

Cotton Mather (1663–1728) There had long been a strong emphasis on the *work ethic* in the United States. The arrival of the Pilgrims and Puritans from England in the 1620s and 1630s helped to forge this work ethic. Both the Pilgrims and Puritans followed the beliefs of John Calvin. These beliefs included *predestination*, the belief that the afterlife for each individual was determined before the person's birth. Hard work and material success were considered as signs that a person was predestined for a good afterlife. Thus, in the late 17th and early 18th centuries, individuals such as the minister Cotton Mather in Boston preached and wrote about the importance of good behavior and a strong work ethic.

Horatio Alger (1832–1899) In the post–Civil War era, Horatio Alger wrote immensely popular books for children and young adults. His stories told of poor boys who, by hard work and lucky breaks, rose from rags (poverty) to riches. The amazing career of Andrew Carnegie made many Americans think that Horatio Alger's success stories actually happened in real life.

Public Good vs. Private Gain

The conflict between public good and private gain was most noted in the actions of Andrew Carnegie and John D. Rockefeller. These business leaders made the industries they dominated bigger and more productive than any that had existed before. To do so, they risked large amounts of money with no guarantee of success. In addition, both men were philanthropists who donated large amounts of money for the building of libraries, schools, hospitals, and other institutions. The impressive results of their efforts support those who call them *captains of industry*.

On the other hand, Carnegie and Rockefeller—as well as other business leaders of their age—did not concern themselves with fairness. Workers received low wages, and strikes were not tolerated. Competitors were put out of business by whatever means a big business chose to use, including secret agreements with railroads and temporary price cuts. These practices lend support to the charge that industrial leaders of the late 1800s were *robber barons*.

New Business and Government Practices

The growth of large-scale industry and monopolies led to demands that government take action to break up these businesses and limit their growth.

Laissez-Faire and Interpretation of the Fourteenth Amendment

Earlier, you read about Adam Smith and the development of laissez-faire. You also read about the growth of monopolies and their impact on smaller businesses and consumers. One reason for the growth of large-scale business and the corporate form of business organization was the Supreme Court's interpretation of the Fourteenth Amendment as favoring business. The original purpose of the amendment had been to extend citizenship to the freed slaves and to protect the rights of all citizens by providing that no state may "deprive any person of life, liberty, or property without due process of law." However, the Supreme Court later broadened the meaning of "person" to include corporations. Thus, corporations received the same protections as individuals and received favorable rulings in judicial decisions.

Railroad Pooling and Rate Differences

Railroad companies at first tried to suppress competition by a method called *pooling*. Railroad lines that once cut their fares in order to attract more business secretly agreed to charge exactly the same high fares. The railroads would also divide the total market for their transportation services, Railroad A serving one territory and Railroad B a different territory.

Furthermore, railroads often charged more for a short haul than a long haul, recognizing that small towns, unlike large cities, could not choose from among competing railroads. In fact, a single railroad often had a monopoly on lines that served small towns. As a result, although trips from one town to another may have been shorter than trips from one large city to another, businesses and consumers were forced to pay higher prices for shorter trips.

Competition and Absorption

Mergers   In the 1870s and 1880s the trend toward monopoly control was all too clear. In every industry it seemed that businesses were becoming less and less competitive, as more and more *merged* (joined together). First, let us see how big business firms became bigger. Then we shall see how government responded to the trend.

Trusts   Rockefeller devised an ingenious method for bringing many former competitors under his control. The stock certificates of competing firms were traded for *trust certificates* in a new supercorporation called a *trust*. After his competitors were near ruin, Rockefeller persuaded them to join his Standard Oil Trust, formed in 1882. If they refused, he threatened to drive them out of business. Other leading business firms in other industries were quick to follow the Standard Oil example. Soon, in addition to an oil trust, there was a steel trust, a tobacco trust, a sugar-refining trust, and many more. Trusts came to influence lawmakers in state legislatures and Congress to pass laws favorable to big business.

Cartoon showing that business trusts controlled the U.S. Senate

Holding Companies In the 1890s business leaders discovered a third method of consolidation. They formed corporations whose only function was to hold the stocks of several firms in the same industry. *Holding companies*, as they were called, held a majority of stocks in each company and thus had the power to dictate a common policy for all.

Government Attempts to Control Trusts

Sherman Antitrust Act (1890) The Sherman Act provided that "every contract, combination in the form of a trust or otherwise, or conspiracy, in restraint of trade or commerce . . . is hereby declared to be illegal." The law, however, was poorly and vaguely written. Terms such as trust, conspiracy, and restraint of trade were not defined. As a result no trusts were success-

★ **Changes in Business and Industry, 1825–1900** ★

	Age of Jackson (1825–1845)	Midcentury (1845–1865)	After Civil War (1865–1900)
Organization of business and advances in manufacturing	Growth of textile mills Increased number of corporations	Isaac Singer's plant for making sewing machines, 1853 Bessemer process for making steel, 1856	Standard Oil Trust organized, 1882 Trend toward bigger, consolidated business firms
Inventions in transportation and communication	Peter Cooper's first locomotive, 1830 Samuel F. B. Morse's telegraph, 1844	First oil pipeline, 1865 Laying of transatlantic cable, New York to London, 1866	Cable streetcar in use in San Francisco, 1873 Alexander Graham Bell's telephone, 1876 Thomas Edison's phonograph, 1878
Inventions in agriculture	John Deere's steel plow, 1837 Cyrus McCormick's reaper, 1831	Introduction of grain elevators, 1850s Mowing, threshing, and haying machines, 1850s	Giant combine harvester and thresher, 1880s Corn-shucking machine, 1890s

fully prosecuted in the 1890s. Weak as it was, however, the Sherman Antitrust Act established the principle that government should act to break up trusts and other forms of monopoly.

United States v. *E. C. Knight* (1895)   The government's lack of success was particularly noted in its attempt to break up the sugar trust. E. C. Knight and Company controlled over 95 percent of the sugar-refining industry in the United States. Despite this, the Supreme Court ruled that the federal government had no authority to break up the sugar monopoly. The Court based its ruling on an interpretation of interstate commerce that defined it as a business involved in trade or transportation. Since the sugar refinery was located within the borders of a state, it was not considered interstate commerce.

★ In Review

1. Define pooling, mergers, trusts, holding companies.
2. What methods did John D. Rockefeller use to maximize profits, reduce costs, and eliminate competition?
3. How did Supreme Court rulings affect efforts to regulate business?

Labor's Response to Economic Change

The growth of industry and big business created problems for industrial workers. To minimize their labor costs, most manufacturers believed in keeping wages as low as possible. They saw nothing wrong with demanding from their workers a 60- to 70-hour workweek. Factories were often cold in winter and hot in summer. Ventilation was poor. Machines had few safeguards to prevent accidents. If an accident injured or killed a worker, it was considered the worker's fault, not the employer's. Overworked and poorly paid, factory workers found that they could do nothing as individuals to persuade giant corporations to treat them better. Therefore, in response to the organization of large corporations, workers organized into large labor unions.

Efforts to Organize National Labor Unions

The Knights of Labor (1869)   The first union to become a major economic force was the *Knights of Labor*, organized in 1869. Unlike earlier unions, the Knights of Labor invited both *craft* (skilled) and *industrial* (unskilled) *workers* of all kinds to join. No one was excluded. So African Americans and whites, women and men, foreign-born and native-born all joined the union.

Under the leadership of its president, Terence Powderly, the Knights of Labor avoided strikes for many years. Until 1885 it tried to settle labor disputes through *arbitration* (the judging of a dispute by an impartial person). It established cooperatives, in which workers owned and operated their own businesses. Most important to the Knights of Labor was the goal of winning employers' consent to an eight-hour workday.

Abandoning its antistrike policy, the Knights of Labor surprised the nation by winning a major strike against a railroad company in 1885. Following the strike, membership in the union shot up to 700,000. But its triumph was short-lived. In 1886, in the Haymarket section of Chicago, someone threw a bomb into a crowd, killing several police officers and civilians. The Knights of Labor was wrongly blamed for the incident because one of the bomb throwers belonged to the union. After the Haymarket Riot, workers left the Knights of Labor in droves. By the 1890s, membership had dwindled to a small number.

Those responsible for the Haymarket bombing in Chicago in 1886 were *anarchists*. They believed that the capitalist system and the political system that supported it could not be reformed, and violent means should be used to end them.

As a union, the Knights of Labor had weaknesses that were as much responsible for its downfall as the Haymarket disaster. (1) Prejudices were difficult to overcome. Many skilled workers did not like being associated with unskilled workers. Many whites did not like being on equal terms with blacks. (2) The Knights of Labor probably gave too much attention to political goals (a graduated income tax, for example) and too little attention to bread-and-butter economic issues (higher wages and better working conditions).

The American Federation of Labor (1886) A second national union, the *American Federation of Labor* (A.F. of L.), lasted much longer than the Knights of Labor. In fact, in altered form, it survives to this day as the largest union in the United States.

The founder of the A.F. of L., Samuel Gompers, was a British immigrant who arrived in New York City as a teenager. As the leader of a union of cigar makers, he had the idea of bringing other crafts unions together in a single organization. The *federation*, or loose association, of unions that he organized in 1886 permitted the member unions (a union of cigar makers, a union of carpenters, and so on) to continue their separate existence. The A.F. of L. leadership set overall policy for achieving the objectives held in common by the various crafts unions. Membership in the A.F. of L. grew steadily. By 1900, half a million workers belonged to crafts unions in the A.F. of L.

Under Gompers's leadership, the A.F. of L. focused strictly on bread-and-butter goals: higher wages, shorter working hours, and better working conditions. Once asked what he wanted for members of his union, Gompers replied simply "more." If Gompers thought a strike was a practical

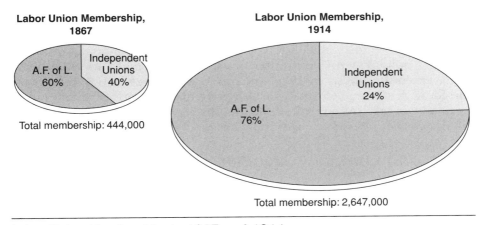

Labor Union Membership, in 1867 and 1914

means of attaining an A.F. of L. objective, he approved it. If it was judged impractical, other tactics were tried.

Unions in the A.F. of L. tended to discriminate against black workers, excluding them from membership simply because of their race. The few unions that admitted African Americans forced them to meet in segregated units. The unfortunate result of this policy was that the excluded blacks were often used by employers to fill the jobs of striking union members. Their reputation as "strikebreakers" only increased the racial prejudice of the A.F. of L. membership.

Women were also discriminated against in the male-dominated A.F. of L. Yet women were commonly exploited by their employers even more than men. Conditions of work were notoriously bad in *sweatshops*, where women sat at sewing machines for long hours stitching clothing at break-neck speed, earning very low pay under crowded and unsafe conditions.

One of many young women who became active in the labor movement was Mary Kenney O'Sullivan. This energetic Irish American persuaded thousands of garment workers in New York City and Troy, New York, to join local unions. Then in 1903 she founded a national organization for women similar in purpose to the A.F. of L. Attracting members from both the middle class and working class, the National Women's Trade Union League concentrated on trying to improve wages and working conditions in those industries where women were employed in large numbers.

The International Ladies' Garment Workers' Union (1900) Representing workers in the women's clothing industry, the International Ladies' Garment Workers' Union (ILGWU) was formed in 1900 to protest low pay, long hours, and unsafe working conditions. Most of its members were Jewish immigrants employed in sweatshops. In 1909, the ILGWU organized the first garment strike, which consisted of 20,000 shirtwaist makers, mostly women and children. In the end, the garment workers won a pay raise and a reduction of hours of work per week. In 1910, the ILGWU organized a second large strike, this one of 50,000 cloak makers. Taking their lead from the women, the mostly male strikers won equal wages, a shorter workweek, and paid holidays. An arbitration board was established to settle labor-management disputes. In 1911, one of the worst fires in U.S. history occurred at the Triangle Shirtwaist Company in New York City, killing 146 garment workers. As a result of the fire, the New York State legislature established strict fire safety codes in factories.

Union and Company Struggles and Conflicts

Workers' strikes were extremely common in the late 19th- and early 20th-century era. Many ended in violence, as strikers clashed with police and state troopers. These strikes involved labor disputes with some of the nation's biggest corporations.

Homestead Strike (1892) The Homestead strike was one of the most violent labor strikes in U.S. history. It was called in 1892 by the Amalgamated Association of Iron and Steel against the Homestead, Penn., steel plant (owned by Andrew Carnegie's steel company), after the union refused to accept a wage reduction. Henry Clay Frick, the chairman of Carnegie Steel, responded to the strike by calling in guards from the Pinkerton National Detective Agency to protect the plant and the workers hired to replace the strikers. Fierce fighting broke out between the Pinkerton guards and the strikers, and many on both sides were killed. The governor then called out the state militia, and the strike was broken as workers went back to work at lower wages. In the end, the steel workers' union was crushed, and unionization of the steel industry was set back until the 1930s.

Pullman Strike (1894) George Pullman was the inventor and manufacturer of the Pullman sleeping car for comfortable railroad travel. In 1894 he announced a 25 percent reduction in wages, but he did not lower the rents or groceries in the company town. (In a *company town*, a community is dependent on one firm for most of the necessities, such as employment, housing, and stores.) In protest the workers at Pullman went on strike, and they were supported by their union, the American Railway Union, led by Eugene V. Debs. To enforce their demands, the workers picketed Pullman's railway cars and would not allow them either to enter or leave Chicago. Debs then called for a boycott of all Pullman cars. As a result, railroad workers throughout the country refused to handle trains that included Pullman cars. In doing this they stopped interstate commerce and also the cars carrying U.S. mail. The company was granted an *injunction* (court order) by a federal court against the union picketing. President Grover Cleveland then sent federal troops to end the strike. He justified his action on the grounds that U.S. mails were delayed by the strikers' action. When the court order was not carried out, Debs and other officers of the union were convicted and jailed, and the railway union was broken. In 1895, in a case

★ ★ ★ ★ ★

A BROOKLYN GARMENT WORKER IN 1900

A magazine called *The Independent* printed this account of a young woman's daily routine working at a garment factory in Brooklyn, New York, around the year 1900.

Two years ago I came to this place, Brownsville, where so many of my people are, and where I have friends. I got work in a factory making underskirts—all sorts of cheap underskirts, like cotton and calico for the summer and woolen for the winter, but never the silk, satin, or velvet underskirts. I earned $4.50 a week and lived on $2 a week. . . .

At seven o'clock [A.M.] we all sit down to our machines and the boss brings to each one the pile of work that he or she is to finish during the day, what they call in English their "stint." This pile is put down beside the machine and as soon as a skirt is done it is laid on the other side of the machine. . . .

The machines go like mad all day, because the faster you work the more money you get. Sometimes in my haste I get my finger caught and the needle goes right through it. It goes so quick, though, that it does not hurt much. I bind the finger up with a piece of cotton and go on working. We all have accidents like that. Where the needle goes through the nail it makes a sore finger, or where it splinters a bone it does much harm. Sometimes a finger has to come off. Generally, though, one can be cured by a salve.

All the time we are working the boss walks about examining the finished garments and making us do them over again if they are not just right. So we have to be careful as well as swift. . . .

known as *In Re Debs*, the Supreme Court upheld the injunction by ruling that the federal government may prevent "all obstructions to the freedom of interstate commerce or the transportation of the mails."

Lawrence Strike (1912) Lawrence, a city in Massachusetts, developed as one of the largest woolen textile centers in the United States during the second half of the 19th century. In 1912, Lawrence was the scene of a strike by the Industrial Workers of the World (IWW) against the American Woolen Company. Founded in 1905, the IWW was a *radical* labor organization. It opposed capitalism and promoted *socialism*—the belief that all major in-

Government troops were called in to put down the Pullman Strike, in 1894.

dustries should be owned and operated by the national government. The issue of the Lawrence strike was low wages, and it was led by Joseph Ettor, "Big Bill" Haywood, and Elizabeth Gurley Flynn. The governor called upon the state militia to protect strikebreakers and keep order. The strike was settled when the American Woolen Company offered raises and no punishment against those who had struck.

Public Policy and Public Opinion   Most Americans generally supported the government's use of troops to break strikes. They viewed strike leaders as revolutionaries who challenged the traditional values of society. But a growing minority sympathized with the unions and pointed to the unhappy plight of the workers—their low wages, long hours, and unhealthy working conditions. Government in the 1800s consistently sided with business against unions. But as you shall see, it would change its policies to support both business and labor in the 20th century.

★ In Review

1. Explain how the growth of labor unions was a response to the growth of business.
2. How did the Knights of Labor and the American Federation of Labor differ?
3. For the following three strikes, prepare a chart listing the (a) conditions that led to the strike, (b) tactics used by both sides, (c) union leadership, (d) role of state or federal government, and (e) outcome of the strike: (1) Homestead, (2) Pullman, and (3) Lawrence.

Agrarian Response to Economic Change

For farmers, the post–Civil War era was both the best of times and the worst of times. Because of advances in science and technology, American farmers were more productive than ever before. At the same time the prices that farmers received for each pound of cotton and each bushel of wheat were discouragingly low. In short, farmers succeeded as never before—and also failed as never before.

Availability of Cheap Land

When the Republican party came to power in 1861, one of its primary goals was to support agricultural progress by practically giving away public lands in the West. For this purpose Congress gave land grants to western railroads. The lawmakers assumed, correctly, that the railroads would sell land to farmers at almost giveaway prices. Congress also enacted two laws for disposing of public lands.

The Homestead Act (1862)   By the terms of this law, any citizen, or immigrant intending to become a citizen, could acquire 160 acres of federal land simply by cultivating it for five years. Labor, not money, was the price of a homestead.

The Morrill Act (1862)   This act provided that huge tracts of federal land would go to the states. The one condition was that the states build colleges on the land for teaching "agricultural and mechanical arts." These *land-grant colleges* were extremely influential in teaching farmers how to use new technology to increase their crop yields.

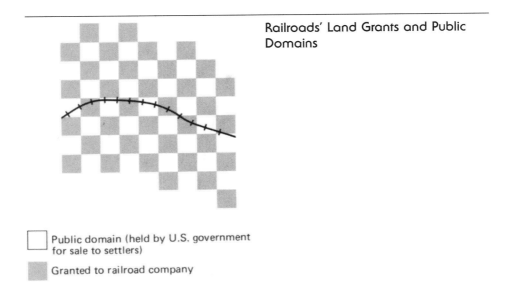

Railroads' Land Grants and Public Domains

☐ Public domain (held by U.S. government for sale to settlers)

▨ Granted to railroad company

Farmers' Dependence on Railroads, Merchants, and Banks

While land was cheap, everything else about a farmer's business was expensive: farm machinery, tools, buildings, seed, horses, and mules. Another major expense was paying railroads to store the farmer's crop temporarily in grain elevators and then haul it to city markets. In other words, a farm family started out with good land and dependable labor (their own) but lacked capital (the money with which to buy farm equipment and supplies).

Capital was provided to farmers in the form of merchants' credit and bankers' loans. Of course, every farmer hoped to repay the creditor or bank by selling a good-sized crop for a good price. But every year there was also the possibility of little rain, poor crops, and low prices. If this happened several years in a row, a farmer's debts could grow to the point that a bank would lose patience and *foreclose* on (take possession of) the farm.

Naturally, farmers resented being always at the mercy of railroads, merchants, and banks. They were particularly upset when they succeeded in growing a large crop only to receive prices far below those of previous years. This condition—good crop, poor price—happened year after year in the 1870s, 1880s, and 1890s. As prices sank, farm debts soared.

Twice farmers turned to politics to solve their problems. Midwestern farmers battled the railroads in the Grange movement of the 1870s. Then farmers of the South and West campaigned against northeastern bankers in the Populist movement of the 1890s.

The Grange Movement as Agrarian Protest

The Patrons of Husbandry, otherwise known as the *Grange*, was founded in 1867 as a society for bringing farm families together for social purposes.

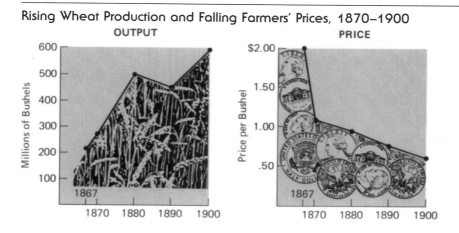

Rising Wheat Production and Falling Farmers' Prices, 1870–1900

Soon, however, Grange meetings focused on the economic issues troubling the farmers: how to cope with falling grain prices and rising railroad rates.

Grangers' Grievances Farmers complained about the common railroad practice of charging low rates for a long haul (for example, Chicago to New York) and a much higher rate for a short haul (for example, Springfield, Illinois, to Chicago). Railroads competed with one another for business on the long routes. They commonly made up for their losses by overcharging farmers for the less competitive shorter hauls.

Farmers also complained about the high charge for the storage of their wheat and corn in grain elevators. Farmers could choose to sell their grain directly to the elevator company, which then would sell it to the public. But the price farmers were offered was usually very low. How could farmers break free from the crushing rates charged by others?

Farmers' Cooperatives One solution was for farmers themselves to build and operate their own grain elevators. The new elevators were financed with money contributed by Grange members to businesses known as *cooperatives*. A cooperative is an enterprise owned and operated by those using its services. Besides operating the grain elevators at reasonable rates, Grange cooperatives lowered prices for needed supplies by buying from merchants in great quantities.

Granger Laws To fight high railroad rates, the Grangers took political action. They persuaded several state legislatures in the 1870s to pass laws

Cartoon of the effects of the railroad monopoly on the farmers

regulating both the freight rates of railroad companies and the storage rates of elevator companies.

Supreme Court Decisions For and Against Regulation   Companies facing regulation under the so-called Granger laws challenged the laws in court. In the landmark case of *Munn* v. *Illinois* (1877), the Supreme Court decided that a state could set maximum rates for the storage of grain. But the Supreme Court reversed itself in 1886 in the case of *Wabash, St. Louis, and Pacific Railway* v. *Illinois* by declaring that railroad rates set by state laws interfered with Congress's exclusive power to regulate interstate commerce. The next year, Congress enacted the *Interstate Commerce Act*. (See page 225.)

Populism: A Political Response to Economic Change

Farm prices rose briefly in the early 1880s, and Grange membership declined. But later in the decade, prices again dropped lower and lower. At one point farmers burned their own corn for fuel rather than sell it at the prevailing low price. Embittered farmers in all parts of the country joined a movement that eventually became a new political party—the People's party, also known as the *Populist party*.

Origins of the Populist Movement

The first organized response to falling farm prices was the formation of farmers' associations called *alliances*. They were (1) the Northern Alliance, with 2 million farmers of the Middle West and Northwest, (2) the Southern Alliance, with 3 million white farmers of the South, and (3) the Colored Farmers' National Alliance, with about 1 million African American farmers. In the South, an effort was made to include farmers of both races in a single alliance. But white-alliance leaders feared that the presence of African Americans might deter many white farmers of the South from joining the movement.

In 1890 leaders of the Northern Alliance organized independent parties to champion farmers' interests. The next year, members of both the Northern and Southern alliances met in Cincinnati, where they founded the Populist party.

The Populist Platform of 1892   Populist delegates assembled in Omaha, Nebraska, in the summer of 1892 for their party's first national convention. Included in their new party's *platform* (statement of political ideas) were a number of reform ideas that caused a sensation when they were reported in the nation's newspapers. For the time, Populists' ideas sounded radical. They wanted the following:

★ A graduated income tax—a tax on the incomes of rich people (the higher the person's income, the higher the tax rate)

* ★ Establishment of savings banks in U.S. post offices
* ★ Government ownership and operation of the railroads
* ★ Government ownership and operation of telephone and telegraph companies
* ★ Election of U.S. senators by direct vote of the people rather than by state legislatures
* ★ An eight-hour workday for all factory workers
* ★ State laws granting the *initiative* (voters' power to initiate ideas for new laws) and the *referendum* (voters' power to mark their ballots for or against proposed laws).

Populists' Plan for Inflated Money

American democracy benefited the most from the Populists' ideas listed above. But the Populists were most excited about a financial reform that, at the time, seemed to offer a surefire solution to their economic troubles.

★   ★   ★   ★   ★

PLATFORM OF THE POPULIST PARTY IN 1892

In their platform of 1892, the Populists accused both major parties of neglecting the interests of the common people.

We have witnessed for more than a quarter of a century the struggles of the two great political parties for power and plunder, while grievous wrongs have been inflicted upon the suffering people. We charge that the controlling influences dominating both these parties have permitted the existing dreadful conditions to develop without serious effort to prevent or restrain them. Neither do they now promise us any substantial reform. They have agreed together to ignore, in the coming campaign, every issue but one. They propose to drown the outcries of a plundered people with the uproar of a sham battle over the tariff, so that capitalists, corporations, national banks, rings, trusts, watered stock, the demonetization of silver and the oppressions of the usurers [moneylenders who charge high rates of interest] may all be lost sight of. They propose to sacrifice our homes, lives, and children on the altar of mammon [worship of riches]; to destroy the multitude in order to secure corruption funds from the millionaires.

Assembled on the anniversary of the birthday of the nation . . . we seek to restore the government of the Republic to the hands of the "plain people," with which class it originated.

Between 1873 and 1890, no silver coins had been minted and circulated by the U.S. government. Only gold coins were minted, and because gold was a more valuable precious metal than silver, these coins were often *hoarded* (kept and not spent). Money, therefore, was scarce. Farmers saw a direct connection between the scarcity of money and the low prices they received for cotton and corn. The Populists' solution was to raise farm prices by making the government coin more money—silver money.

In other words, the Populists wanted the U.S. government to bring about inflation (a regular increase in prices). The way to do it, they said, was to coin 16 silver dollars for every one gold dollar. Naturally, the farmers' fondness for silver coins was fully shared by silver miners, who became enthusiastic Populists in 1892.

Early Populist Triumphs The coinage of silver and other reforms promised by the Populists in 1892 drew many votes. The Populist candidate for president, James Weaver, received over a million votes (almost 9 percent of the total) as well as 22 electoral votes. Other Populists were elected to the U.S. Congress and to state legislatures in the South and West. For a brand-new party, it was an impressive showing.

The president elected in 1892, however, was Grover Cleveland, a Democrat. In his four years in office, he became known for his support of gold as the only metal for U.S. coins. Most Democrats of the North and East agreed with Cleveland that gold represented "sound money," and business confidence would suffer a terrible blow if silver coins were issued. The "gold-bug" Democrats, as they were called, were opposed by Democrats of the South and West, who favored the "free and unlimited coinage of silver."

The Election of 1896

At the Democratic convention of 1896, the so-called silver Democrats were thrilled by the rousing speech of a young U.S. congressman from Nebraska, William Jennings Bryan. His speech (known as the cross-of-gold speech) declared that farmers would prevail over the bankers of the cities. Bryan brought the convention to its feet with his last sentence: "You shall not press down upon the brow of labor this crown of thorns, you shall not crucify mankind upon a cross of gold." In the vote for a presidential candidate, the conservative, "gold-bug" Democrats were defeated by the supporters of the "silver-tongued" candidate, William Jennings Bryan.

Populists' Nomination of Bryan At the Populists' convention of 1896, a majority favored the idea of nominating the Democrats' choice, Bryan. After all, they reasoned, who could match Bryan's ability to rally the nation behind the Populists' favorite cause, silver? To satisfy those who opposed Bryan's nomination, the Populists chose a vice presidential candidate different from the one picked by the Democrats.

Republican Victory Even with the support of both the Democrats and the Populists, Bryan lost the election. He was defeated by the Republican candidate, William McKinley, who supported the use of gold and opposed the use of silver as currency. Although Bryan carried the South and much of the West, he failed to win the crucial electoral votes of the East. Many eastern workers feared inflation and were persuaded by McKinley's campaign that silver money would cause high prices, which in turn would bring on a depression and the loss of jobs.

The Populists' Contribution

The defeat of Bryan and improved farm prices after 1896 caused a rapid decline of the Populist party. After 1900 no more were Populists elected to Congress. Nevertheless, many of the reforms in the Populist platform of 1892 were eventually adopted by the two major parties. In fact, two Populist ideas became the basis for constitutional amendments:

Populist Idea	Amendment
Graduated income tax	Sixteenth Amendment (adopted 1913)
Direct election of U.S. senators by popular vote	Seventeenth Amendment (adopted 1913)

We see, then, that third parties, even if they fail to elect many candidates, can have a major influence on national policy.

National Government Response to Economic Change

To some extent, state governments regulated businesses that operated within their borders. But until 1887 the federal government generally followed a policy of laissez-faire. Its laws encouraged business growth through tariffs, land grants, and patents. But it did very little to regulate business practices. In the 1880s, however, the voting public became more and more alarmed about companies using unfair methods for eliminating competition. Responding to public pressures, Congress enacted a law that marked the beginning of business regulation by the U.S. government.

Interstate Commerce Act (1887) To regulate certain practices of railroad companies, Congress created the Interstate Commerce Commission (ICC) to enforce the following regulations:

★ Railroad rates had to be "reasonable and just."

★ Pools were illegal.

★ Returning rebates to favored customers was illegal.

★ Railroads could not charge more for a short haul than for a long haul.

At first the commission's powers were limited, but they were expanded by later amendments to the law.

★ In Review

1. What were the problems experienced by small farmers?
2. To what extent was the Populist party successful in resolving the problems of the farmers?
3. What aspects of the Populist agenda were eventually legislated?

MULTIPLE-CHOICE QUESTIONS

1. "The problem of our age is the proper administration of wealth, that the ties of brotherhood may still bind together the rich and poor in harmonious relationship. . . ."
   —Andrew Carnegie

   Which of the following quotations best describes the above statement?
   (1) "The rich have an obligation to contribute to the betterment of society."
   (2) "There needs to be a constitutional amendment providing for a graduated income tax."
   (3) "Government should never tax what is inherited."
   (4) "Anyone who is wealthy must have become so through corrupt means."

2. Which of the following would have been most likely to write a letter to the editor opposing the viewpoint expressed in the cartoon on page 201?
   (1) Terrence Powderly
   (2) John D. Rockefeller
   (3) Samuel Gompers
   (4) "Big Bill" Heyward.

3. A conclusion that may be reached from an examination of the advertisement on page 204 that is that
   (1) to increase sales, the manufacturer of the graphophone reduced its selling price
   (2) the graphophone was utilized primarily in offices
   (3) by 1898 there was a great amount of recorded music
   (4) most people in the United States were able to afford a graphophone.

4. Which is a conclusion that may be made from a study of the two pie graphs on page 215?
   (1) The A.F. of L. was taking control of all unions in the United States.
   (2) In 1867 few workers joined the A.F. of L.
   (3) By 1914, most American workers were members of a labor union.
   (4) The A.F. of L. organized 76 percent of all U.S. union members in 1914.

5. The graphs on page 220 show that from 1870 through 1890

(1) farmers earned tremendous profits as the production of wheat increased
(2) the price of wheat dropped as production increased
(3) value for the dollar increased
(4) as the price of wheat fell, farmers produced other crops.

6. The map on page 205 illustrates that, during the post–Civil War era, the transcontinental railroads served to
(1) continue the promotion of sectional interests
(2) further detach states in the North and South
(3) extend U.S. influence into Mexico and Canada
(4) connect most of the sections of the nation.

7. Which of the following titles could be substituted for the title expressed in the 1889 political cartoon on page 211?
(1) "The People's Court"
(2) "The Senate Runs the Country"
(3) ". . . of the Trusts, by the Trusts, for the Trusts"
(4) "Checks and Balances in Action."

8. "Show me the country in which there are no strikes and I'll show you the country in which there is no liberty!"
The above statement was probably made by
(1) Samuel Gompers
(2) Grover Cleveland
(3) George M. Pullman
(4) William Vanderbilt.

9. During the late 1800s farmers supported free and unlimited coinage of silver mainly because they believed that it would lead to
(1) the establishment of government farm price supports
(2) the lowering of rates charged by railroads
(3) lower prices for consumer goods
(4) higher prices for farm products.

10. A major aim of both the Grange movement and Populist movement was
(1) the establishment of a gold standard for currency
(2) mandatory government policies to end inflation
(3) passage of laws for the public control of railroads
(4) unlimited immigration of Asians.

THEMATIC ESSAYS

1. **Theme:** The Federal Government as a Partner of Big Business

   In spite of its hands-off policy toward business (laissez-faire), the federal government actively cooperated with and assisted in the growth and development of private business.

   Task

   ★ Discuss *two* specific ways that the federal government assisted the expansion of private business.

★ Evaluate how each example chosen had a positive impact or a negative impact on a *specific* group of people in the United States.

You may discuss land grants, subsidies to railroads, and tariff and monetary policies, with their impact on any group of people, including farmers, Native Americans, consumers, and industrial workers.

2. **Theme:** Impact of Railroads on the Nation

The completion of the transcontinental railroad in 1869 marked a major change for the people living in the United States and its territories.

Task: Choose two groups of people and show how railroads caused major changes in their lives.

Examples of groups you may choose are farmers, immigrants, city dwellers, and Native Americans.

DOCUMENT-BASED QUESTION

Read or analyze each document and answer the question that follows it. Then read the **Task** *and write your essay. Essays should include references to most of the documents along with additional information based on your knowledge of United States history and government.*

Historical Context: Because of the excesses of businesses, banks, and even the federal government, industrial workers and farmers organized into both unions and political parties to make their voices heard.

Document 1 Refer to the illustration of soldiers at the Pullman Strike, on page 218.

Question: For what purpose did President Grover Cleveland use the United States army during the Pullman Strike?

Document 2 An infamous sign posted in a sweatshop:

IF YOU DON'T COME IN SUNDAY,
DON'T COME TO WORK MONDAY!

Question: How were the owners of the factory that posted the above notice taking advantage of their workers?

Document 3 Samuel Gompers, Letter on Labor, in *Industrial Society Forum*, September, 1894:

Year by year man's liberties are trampled under foot at the bidding of corporations and trusts, rights are invaded and laws perverted. In all ages wherever a tyrant has shown himself he has always found some willing judge to clothe that tyranny in the robes of legality, and modern capitalism has proven no exception to this.

Question: How does Samuel Gompers feel about the attitude of government to labor and the common people?

Document 4 Refer to the cartoon about the Grange, on page 221.

Question: How does the cartoonist feel about the way the railroads were treating the farmers?

Document 5 From a speech by Mary Lease, a Populist orator, in 1890:

This is a nation of inconsistencies. The Puritans fleeing from oppression became oppressors. We fought England for our liberty and put chains on four million blacks. We wiped out slavery and by our tariff laws and national banks began a system of white wage slavery worse than the first.

Wall Street owns the country. It is no longer a government of the people, by the people, and for the people, but a government of Wall Street, by Wall Street, and for Wall Street. . .

. . . Kansas suffers from two great robbers, the Sante Fe Railroad and the loan companies. The common people are robbed to enrich their masters. . . .

Question: How was Mary Lease comparing the problems of farmers in Kansas to those of slaves?

Document 6 From the cross-of-gold speech, by William Jennings Bryan, at the Democratic National Convention, 1896:

You come to us and tell us that the great cities are in favor of the gold standard; we reply that the great cities rest upon our broad and fertile prairies. Burn down your cities and leave our farms, and your cities will spring up again as if by magic; but destroy our farms and the grass will grow in the streets of every city in the country. . . .

. . . We will answer their demand for a gold standard by saying to them: You shall not press down upon the brow of labor this crown of thorns, you shall not crucify mankind upon a cross of gold.

Question: Why does Bryan say that the gold standard will destroy both the farms and the cities?

Task: Using the documents and your knowledge of United States history, write an essay in which you describe how, between the late 1800s and early 1900s, farmers and factory workers organized themselves into labor unions and political parties to gain an effective voice in politics.

Chapter 9
The Impact of Industrialization

★ Objectives

★ To understand the impact of industrialization and urbanization on American life.

★ To trace the changing role of women in response to industrialism.

★ To appreciate the immigrant contribution to American life and the development of a pluralistic society.

★ To examine episodes of prejudice and discrimination from the point of view of ethnic minorities.

★ To understand the impact of western settlement on Native Americans and U.S. society.

Urban Growth After the Civil War

The increasing industrialization of the United States after the Civil War encouraged millions of people to move to the cities of the East and Middle West. These newcomers included native-born Americans from rural areas, freed slaves from the South, and immigrants from Europe and Asia.

Attractions of Urban Life

People moved to cities for both economic reasons (jobs) and cultural reasons (schools, museums, theaters, and sports).

Jobs In the industrial age, cities grew larger mainly because of the factories that were built in them. In order to ship goods, industrialists located their factories near transportation centers, such as railroad terminals and steamship ports. Workers moved in to take advantage of the factory jobs. Near the factories, owners of real estate saw opportunities to rent housing to the workers and open shops catering to their needs. Thus, as cities grew in population, the variety of goods and services available to the public also grew.

Education   City schools were larger and better equipped than the one-room schoolhouses of rural America. They offered a more varied and complete course of study. Also all the cultural resources of the city—libraries, museums, and concert halls—greatly enriched the education of city children.

Culture   Many people were drawn from the farm to the city by the cultural excitement associated with urban life. In a city like New York, the rich and the middle class could dine in a restaurant or attend a new play at the theater whenever they wished. People of all classes could enjoy going to the city's beaches and parks, sporting events, and amusement centers.

Public Education System   In the same period, schools increased in number and improved in quality. More teachers received professional training. Cities raised money for new elementary schools and high schools. Between 1865 and 1900, enrollments at the elementary school level more than doubled. The number of high schools in the country rose from about 400 in 1860 to more than 6,000 in 1900. The general public approved the building of new schools, recognizing that an educated citizenry benefited everyone.

In response to the needs of a new industrial age, educators defined their goals differently. Formerly, they had concentrated on teaching basic literacy: reading, writing, and arithmetic. But after 1900, "progressive" educators believed that it was equally important to offer occupational-training courses and to prepare students for citizenship.

Urban Problems

City life also had its problems. Among them were urban slums, violent crime, and bad sanitation.

Urban America in 1900

5,000 to 100,000 inhabitants
100,000 inhabitants and over

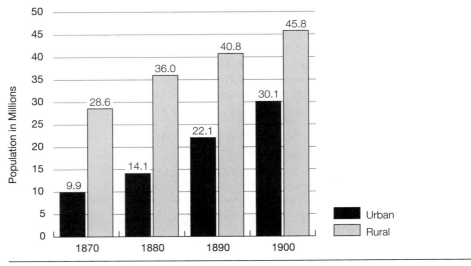

Urban and Rural Population, 1870–1900

Slums Although poverty conditions existed in rural areas, the "slum" became the setting for the urban poor. As immigrants and African Americans from the South crowded into the cities, they tended to live in poor, ethnic, working-class neighborhoods noted for their crowded streets and buildings. For example, the Lower East Side in New York City became home to Jews, Poles, Italians, the Chinese, and others. In an age before television and air-conditioners, street life provided the major source of news and entertainment for those with little money. Pushcarts, rather than stores, provided many of the inexpensive goods.

Increased Crime Urban poverty encouraged urban crime. As cities grew in size, so did the number of violent crimes—murders, burglaries, and robberies. In tenement neighborhoods, youths organized rival gangs that sometimes fought one another with weapons.

Inadequate Water and Sanitation Services Disposing of garbage was another problem. Cities commonly dumped sewage into the same rivers and lakes that provided drinking water. As a result, there were frequent outbreaks of typhoid fever, a disease transmitted by polluted water. Lacking bathtubs and running water, tenement dwellers had trouble keeping clean. Factory smokestacks polluted the air. Before the automobile was invented, droppings from thousands of carriage-pulling horses added to the city's foul odor and unsanitary condition.

New Urban Architecture

Skyscrapers and Elevators The first skyscraper was built in Chicago in 1884. Ten stories high, it was widely imitated in other cities. The invention

★ ★ ★ ★ ★

GROWING UP IN NEW YORK CITY IN THE MID-1850S

Gene Schermerhorn was a man of 44 in 1886 when he began writing to a cousin about his memories of childhood growing up in New York City. In the excerpt below he compares the city of the 1850s with the city of the 1880s.

It seems hard to believe that Twenty-third Street—which is the first street in the city of which I remember anything, could have changed so much in so short a time. The rural scenes, the open spaces, have vanished; and the small and quiet residences, many of them built entirely of wood, have given place to huge piles of brick and stone, and to iron and plateglass fronts of the stores which now line the street.

I was six years old when we moved to New York from Williamsburg [Brooklyn] in 1848. We went to live in a house in this street just west of Sixth Avenue. . . .

This will give you an idea of the house: right next door was a small farm or truck-garden extending nearly to Seventh Avenue. Across the way were the stables of the 6th Ave Omnibus line; the stages starting here and going down Sixth Avenue, 8th Street and Broadway to the Battery. They afterwards started from Forty-sixth Street. I shall have more to tell about these Stage Lines for at this time there were no horse cars. Twenty-third Street and in fact all the streets in the neighborhood were unpaved. Here was my playground and a good one it was. There certainly was plenty of room, plenty of dirt (clean dirt) and plenty of boys; what more could be desired!

of electric elevators made it possible for people to shop on different floors of big-city department stores.

Tenements and Walk-ups Before unions became strong, factory workers received low wages—only a few cents an hour. They could afford to pay only very low rents for housing. Landlords therefore built cheaply constructed buildings called *tenements*. Designed to hold as many families as possible, each tenement was five or six stories high. Tenants had to walk up stairs since there were no elevators in these buildings. Apartments were small and dark, with perhaps one toilet per floor. Each house was built so close to neighboring tenements that a fire could spread through an entire neighborhood in minutes. Overcrowded tenements were breeding grounds for rats, roaches, and disease. Many residents died of tuberculosis and other diseases.

Jacob Riis, a New York City reporter, described one such tenement: "Here is a door. Listen! That short hacking cough, that tiny helpless wail—what do they mean? . . . Oh! a sadly familiar story. . . . The child is dying with measles. With half a chance it might have lived; but it had none. That dark bedroom killed it."

Urban Social Classes

Social Darwinism British biologist Charles Darwin advanced the theory that lower forms of life evolved into higher and higher forms as a result of an ongoing struggle for survival. Those who survived the struggle were the "fittest" of the species. British philosopher Herbert Spencer applied Darwin's theory to the competitive world of business. In a theory known as *social Darwinism*, Spencer argued that those businesses that were strongest, fittest, and most efficient would survive. Weaker businesses deserved to fail and die out. Spencer wrote: "The American economy is controlled for the benefit of all by a natural aristocracy, and the leaders of this aristocracy were brought to the top by a competitive struggle that weeded out the weak, incompetent, and unfit and selected the wise and able."

Increased Class Division Families in the crowded cities of the late 1800s had to adapt to changing conditions of the industrial-urban age. Also, city neighborhoods arose that showed a sharp division between three economic and social classes: the working class, the middle class, and the wealthy class.

Working-Class Families On a farm, members of the family worked together and saw one another from morning to night. But factory workers in the

The Gilded Age: the very rich (left) and the very poor

cities were seldom home. The daily routine among members of a worker's family was to split up during the day. For men working in factories and other trades, the home became merely an evening refuge from the day's labor. One man's wages were seldom enough to pay the rent and expenses, so the women and children of the household also had to find work. Since women and children were paid lower wages than men, they sometimes found it easier than men to hold a job in a time of economic depression.

Middle-Class Families   As cities grew, so did the numbers of Americans who belonged to society's *middle class*. (This class consists of people who have sufficient income to live in modest comfort.) In the period after the Civil War, the emerging middle class included shopkeepers, well-educated professionals (doctors, lawyers, teachers, and others), and salaried office workers who wore white collars and business suits to work. Office workers were known as *white-collar workers* to distinguish them from *blue-collar* (factory) *workers*. The values of people in the middle class tended to be conservative—honoring the nation, upholding polite manners, and regularly attending religious services in a church or synagogue.

Conspicuous Consumption   The smallest class in society—the wealthy— were also the most visible. Those who made great fortunes from running successful corporations and trusts (men like Andrew Carnegie, J. P. Morgan, and John D. Rockefeller) displayed their wealth so that all would notice and admire it. In New York City and elsewhere, they built enormous mansions, hired scores of household servants, entertained friends on yachts and private railroad cars, bred racehorses, and paid huge sums for masterpieces of European art. The buying habits of the rich were called *conspicuous consumption* by Thorstein Veblen, an economist and keen observer of the time. He said that the wealthy bought costly items, not because they were useful, but because they showed off the owner's success. The humorist Mark Twain called the late 19th century the *Gilded Age* because of the showy objects collected by millionaires. (To *gild* is to cover objects with a thin layer of gold.)

Social Conscience and Philanthropy   Although the rich spent lavishly on their private amusements, they also donated millions for public causes. Rockefeller, Carnegie, Morgan, and others devoted the later years of their lives to enriching American culture by financing libraries, hospitals, museums, universities, and medical research. Those who donate large sums of money for worthwhile causes that benefit society are known as *philanthropists*.

Work and Workers

Immigrant Workers' Patterns of Settlement

Both before and after the Civil War, many factory workers were immigrants. Prior to the Civil War, most immigrants came from western Europe and included such nationalities as the British, Irish, and Germans. From 1865 to 1900, immigration patterns changed. Most immigrants now came from eastern and southern Europe and Asia. While some immigrants moved out west to farm, most remained in the large urban centers such as New York, Boston, and Chicago, where they worked in factories and industries. When they arrived, most immigrants moved into neighborhoods which were made up of people from their own ethnic group. Thus, in New York City, people referred to certain neighborhoods as Little Italy or Chinatown. Most immigrants had low-paying jobs and therefore lived in urban slums. Often political leaders would emerge who provided services for the urban poor in return for their support in elections. In most large cities, it was the Democratic party that provided such services and won the support of the various ethnic groups.

Working Conditions

After 1865, as business firms grew larger, the plight of factory workers tended to worsen. Long hours and low pay were the norm for thousands of workers. How were workers to combat these conditions? If they joined a union or participated in a strike, employers would almost certainly turn them out of their jobs. The daily grind was bad enough, but fear of unemployment was a nightmare. New workers were easy to find as Americans from rural areas poured into the cities. New immigrants worked for whatever they were offered.

There were other sources of worker insecurity. First, jobs could be eliminated as employers substituted the tireless work of machines for the more costly labor of human beings. Second, business booms (prosperous times) would come to a crashing halt in sudden depressions and panics. At such times, hundreds of thousands of jobless people faced the awful prospect of many months of no wages or income. Government aid in the form of unemployment insurance did not exist.

Women, Families, and Work

Traditional Roles—Ideal and Reality

Women had long been idealized in western society. In western Europe during the later Middle Ages, the code of chivalry for knights held that the "good knight" must go to the aid of a "damsel in distress." In the Victorian Age (from the mid- to late 1800s), the view that women needed protection continued. In this period, it was believed that women could best serve their families as wives, mothers, and homemakers. All the important decisions were considered to be the responsibility of the male head of the family. Married middle-class women, however, were generally discouraged from working. Instead of earning income, they were expected to devote themselves to the care of a family and also to engage in civic and charitable activities in the community. Many single middle-class women pursued careers as teachers—the one profession in which women greatly outnumbered men.

Working-class women had long worked to provide needed income for their families. In rural areas, women worked beside their husbands and brothers in the fields. In urban areas, women had double drudgery, both outside and inside their home. Working in textile mills, or as domestics and laundresses by day, women were still expected to take care of their families in the evenings.

Emerging Problems   The long hours worked by women in working-class families led to strains on family ties. It was difficult for women to maintain an exhausting job and then come home to take care of the house. In addition, women's income became increasingly important as working-class men earned very low salaries. Sometimes, a man would lose much of his salary as the result of gambling and drinking. It was not uncommon for a man to arrive home without his full pay, thereby creating strains on his relationship with his wife and children.

Prior to the Civil War, children under the age of 12 worked in textile mills where they earned pennies a day. As industry grew, children were employed in the new factories. In 1900, about 1.7 million children between the ages of 10 and 15 worked for pennies an hour in mines and factories (especially cotton mills and canning plants). Many child wage earners were as young as six and seven.

Unprotected by law, the elderly and the disabled often found themselves without employment. As a result, they constituted one of the poorest segments of American society. Often, they had to rely on family members for support. Many found themselves destitute and in need of charitable services. African American women were often stereotyped and could generally find employment only as domestics in northern urban areas.

Religion in a Pluralistic Society

Although early settlers such as the Pilgrims and Puritans had come to America seeking religious freedom, religious tolerance grew slowly. Quakers, in the early years of settlement, were sometimes forced to leave the Massachusetts Bay Colony or hanged. In the 1800s, Americans of British descent viewed their culture as superior to that of other nationalities, and their Protestant faith as the true religion. As Jews and Irish Catholics entered the United States in larger numbers in the 1840s, they felt the sting of Protestant reaction. After 1880, however, the problem of religious intolerance grew as large numbers of Catholics from Italy, Jews from Russia and Poland, and Eastern Orthodox Christians from Greece entered the nation.

Religion and Party Politics

From the founding of our nation through the 20th century, Protestants have maintained their position as the largest religious group in the United States. Throughout the 1800s, elected leaders on both national and state levels were Protestant. It was not until 1928 that a Roman Catholic, Alfred E. Smith, the governor of New York, ran for the presidency on the Democratic party ticket.

As more and more Catholics and Jews emigrated to the United States in the late 1800s and early 1900s, they began to influence the Democratic party in large cities such as New York, Boston, and Chicago. Party leaders often provided financial assistance and social welfare programs for new immigrants in order to win their loyalty and support at the polls. In New York City, Irish Catholic politicians gained control of Tammany Hall, the organization that controlled the Democratic party in the city.

As immigration increased in the late 1800s, Protestants throughout the country became more concerned with the newly arrived Catholics and Jews from eastern Europe as well as the increasing Chinese and Japanese immigration. Some believed that Catholics, led by the pope in Rome, wanted to take over the United States. Thus, some Protestants joined the American Protective Association, just as others had joined the Know-Nothing party decades earlier. Most Protestants, however, rejected these extremist ideas and organizations.

As most Catholics and Jews settled in northern cities, Protestants began to fear a loss of influence. In order to maintain such influence, Protestants established religious reform groups that aimed to eliminate or reduce many of the evils associated with urbanization, such as overcrowding, poor working conditions, and *machine politics* (organized control of elected officials by a small group of political party leaders). These ideas would influence the emerging Progressive movement of the early 1900s.

The Growing Middle Class

As the urban middle class grew larger, new methods of selling and buying goods took hold. Inventions such as the Singer sewing machine could be purchased on "time" by those who could not pay the entire price at once. Thus, credit and time payments encouraged middle-class families to enjoy many of the new products created by the Industrial Revolution.

City people had fewer opportunities for recreation and amusement, such as fishing, hunting, and picnicking, which rural dwellers enjoyed. In addition to the stage shows that had long been popular, city people in the late 1800s started cheering the "home team" in professional baseball games.

Sports and Recreation   An amateur baseball game, one of the first on record, was played in Hoboken, New Jersey, in 1846. But the sport did not fully come into its own until after the Civil War. Cincinnati was the first city to have a professional team—the Red Stockings (now the Cincinnati Reds), formed in

1869. Football began attracting crowds of spectators on college campuses in the 1870s. To give city youths some team exercise in the winter months, a teacher in Springfield, Massachusetts, invented basketball in 1892. In these new sports, people soon became fans of one team or of certain players.

The age of urban growth coincided with an age of scientific discovery. City doctors were challenged to find cures for diphtheria and other contagious diseases that, in urban crowds, turned into epidemics. City hospitals were built to meet the needs of a growing population. As a result of improved health care, the average life expectancy in the United States in 1900 was 47.3 years, compared to only 35.5 years a century earlier.

Literature, Music, and the Penny Press

A growing urban population made it possible for talented Americans to make a living as professional artists, musicians, and writers. As the author of *The Adventures of Tom Sawyer* (1876) and *The Adventures of Huckleberry Finn* (1884), Samuel Clemens became a Gilded Age celebrity under the pen name Mark Twain. Early in the 20th century, Willa Cather achieved fame for *My Antonía* (1918), a novel of midwestern life. Henry James's *Washington Square* (1880) and Edith Wharton's *The Age of Innocence* (1920) depicted the customs of upper-class New Yorkers.

Going to the opera and musical theaters became a popular pastime in the cities. In New York City the ornately decorated Metropolitan Opera House opened its doors in 1883. An original, distinctly American music of the period was composed by an African American and former slave, Scott Joplin. His music for the piano, including "Maple Leaf Rag" (1889), was known as *ragtime*, a lively and rhythmic music that influenced the development of jazz. In the 20th century, Joplin's music enjoyed a revival in the 1970s and as the background for a popular movie, *The Sting* (1973).

Penny Newspapers and Dime Novels   Other forms of inexpensive entertainment were the one-penny and two-penny newspapers that circulated daily in every city. New York publishers William Randolph Hearst and Joseph Pulitzer appealed to the urban masses by featuring articles on team sports and sensational crimes. Other publishers found that books sold well if they were on exciting subjects (like the outlaws of the West) and priced at only ten cents.

★ In Review

1. Describe the attractions as well as the problems that came with city life.
2. How were the lives of working-class women and children affected by industrialization?
3. Compare the impact of industrialism on a working-class family with its impact on a middle-class family.

Immigration (1850–1924)

In the 50-year period after the Civil War (1865–1915), more immigrants arrived than ever before. They played a vital role in the settling of both the western frontier and the eastern cities.

New Sources of Immigration

During the 1860s and the decades following, the nature of the foreign-born population began to change. Immigrants from Italy, Austria-Hungary, Greece, Russia, and other countries of eastern and southern Europe arrived in increasingly large numbers. They were called "new immigrants" because their cultures were different from those of the earlier ("older") groups from western Europe.

In addition to European immigrants, who settled mainly in the East, large numbers of Chinese and Japanese immigrants settled on the West Coast. By 1910 more than 300,000 Chinese and 150,000 Japanese immigrants had crossed the Pacific to live and work in the United States. Most were young men who had left their families and hoped to return home after having saved a large sum of money.

Italian Immigration Italians, attracted by the promises of successful lives in America, began a mass emigration in the late 19th century. Some 205,000 emigrated per year by 1888, a number that increased to about 750,000 a year between 1898 and 1914. The main cause of this huge migration was poverty. Between 1870 and 1900, the standard of living in Italy declined. Food had become the biggest cost for an Italian family, with many peasants

Peak Period of the "New" European Immigration

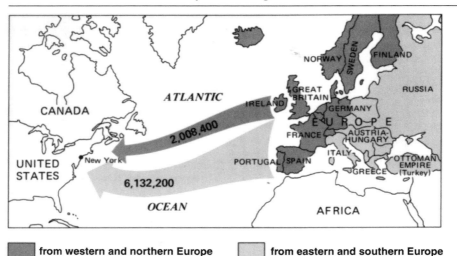

from western and northern Europe   from eastern and southern Europe

spending about 75 percent of their incomes on food. Another important factor was an agricultural crisis in the 1880s, due in part to increased competition of crops from the United States. The price of Italian wheat and other products fell, and unemployment increased, as Italian landowners and peasants could no longer trade profitably. Other factors in Italian emigration included a lack of democracy (few Italians had the right to vote) and a low literacy rate. Emigration was greatly assisted by improved rail and steamship transportation.

Chinese Immigration   The discovery of gold in California resulted in a great gold rush in 1849 as thousands of people sought fortunes. The earliest Chinese immigrants arrived in California during this time, full of hope about discovering riches and then returning home. The Chinese were the first non-Europeans who arrived in large numbers under their own free will, unlike African Americans who were brought over as slaves. These Chinese immigrants met with suspicion and hostility and were barred from owning property or becoming citizens.

Despite this treatment, Chinese labor became an essential factor in developing the United States. For example, agents of the Central Pacific Railroad company recruited thousands of men from China for the grueling task of building the western half of the first transcontinental railroad. The Chinese built one of the most difficult parts of the railroad by dynamiting tunnels through the Sierra Nevada range. They were forced to work from dawn to dusk in very dangerous conditions and sleep in tents in the middle of winter, without any protection against the cold or avalanches. Many Chinese lost their lives in this dangerous work.

A nationwide depression in the 1870s resulted in growing anti-Chinese feelings. Chinese laborers became the scapegoats. (A *scapegoat* is someone who is unjustly made to bear the blame for other people's misfortune). During this period, there were also increasing labor troubles, and Chinese laborers were repeatedly used as replacement labor, creating further resentment. This anti-Chinese sentiment led to the passage of the Chinese Exclusion Act (1882), which halted the further immigration of any Chinese. This act also prevented Asians already living in the United States, including their American-born offspring, from becoming naturalized citizens.

The Chinese Exclusion Act was a turning point in United States immigration policy. The first major restriction on immigration to America, it was not fully repealed until 1943, when China was America's wartime ally. However, Chinese immigrants learned to use the U.S. court system to challenge exclusion and many other forms of discrimination. For example, an 1897 U.S. Supreme Court decision established for the first time the legal right of citizenship by birth for all Americans.

The antiforeign attitudes of many native-born Americans were again reflected in the National Origins Act of 1924, which established quotas for immigrants from each country. However, the law prohibited the immigration of all Chinese, Japanese, and other Asians.

★ ★ ★ ★ ★

IMMIGRANTS TO CALIFORNIA

This description of San Francisco after the gold rush was published in 1855 in Frank Soulé's *The Annals of San Francisco*. After remarking that German and French immigrants were commonly seen, the author focuses on the thousands arriving yearly from China.

Upward of 20,000 Chinese are included in the general number of arrivals [in 1852]. Such people were becoming very numerous in San Francisco, from whence the recent immigrants from their country scattered themselves over the various mining regions of California. At one period of 1852 there were supposed to be about 27,000 Chinese in the state. A considerable number of people of "color" . . . also arrived. These were probably afraid to proceed to the mines to labor beside the domineering white races, and therefore they remained to . . . make much money and spend it in San Francisco, like almost everybody else. Mexicans from Sonora and other provinces of Mexico, and many Chileans, and a few Peruvians from South America, were likewise continually coming and going between San Francisco and the ports of their own countries. The Chinese immigrants had their mandarins [high-ranking scholars], their merchants, rich, educated, and respectable men, in San Francisco; but all the Mexicans and Chileans, like the people of Negro descent, were of the commonest description. . . .

Russian/Jewish Immigration   After arriving from Russia in 1882, Abraham Cahan adjusted quickly to American life. He published a novel about the experience of Russian Jews in the 1890s and wrote an article about his New York City neighborhood. The following passage is from Cahan's 1888 article, "The Lower East Side in 1898," in the *Atlantic Monthly*.

Sixteen years have elapsed [since Cahan's arrival in New York City]. The Jewish population has grown from a quarter of a million to about one million. Scarcely a large American town but has some Russo-Jewish names in its directory, with an educated Russian-speaking minority forming a colony within a Yiddish-speaking colony, while cities like New York, Chicago, Philadelphia, and Boston have each a ghetto [Jewish neighborhood] rivaling in extent of population the largest Jewish cities in Russia, Austria, and Rumania. The number of Jewish residents in Manhattan borough is estimated at 250,000, making it the largest center of Hebrew population in the world. . . .

The grammar schools of the Jewish quarter are overcrowded with children of immigrants, who, for progress and deportment, are raised with the very best in the city. At least 500 of 1,677 students at the New York City College, where tuition and books are free, are Jewish boys from the East Side. . . .

The 5,000,000 Jews living under the czar in Russia had not a single Yiddish daily paper even when the government allowed such publications, while their fellow countrymen and coreligionists who have taken up their abode in America publish six dailies (five in New York and one in Chicago), not to mention the countless Yiddish weeklies and monthlies, and the pamphlets and books which today make New York the largest Yiddish book market in the world. [Yiddish is a language spoken by many European Jews.]

Reasons for Emigration

From one country to the next, the reasons for emigration varied. In general, however, every person's or family's decision to emigrate was based on two conclusions—one negative and the other positive.

★ Negative conclusion: Conditions in the home country were bad and could no longer be tolerated.

★ Positive conclusion: Conditions in the United States were likely to be much better than those at home.

Let us identify the conditions that caused different groups of Europeans to board ships for America.

The Lower East Side, New York City, in 1900

Population Pressures In the Industrial Age, Europe was becoming over-crowded. A population of 140 million in 1750 grew to 260 million in 1850 and to 400 million in 1914. Farmland was scarce compared to the abundance of land on the western frontier of the United States.

Recruitment Campaigns Railroad companies with western lands to sell and steamship companies seeking passengers sent agents to Europe to promote the idea of emigration. Recruiters gave the impression that, after a few years of work, everyone could expect to become rich in the United States. Steamship lines offered tickets for the ocean voyage to New York City for as little as $25 a person.

Economic Conditions After 1880 In southern Italy and in the Scandinavian countries of Sweden and Norway, it became more and more difficult for poor farmers to earn a living. From one generation to the next, the farms in Italy and Scandinavia were divided and subdivided to provide the sons of a family with land. Most farms had become too small to raise a profitable crop. Many Italians, Swedes, and Norwegians were landless and desperately poor.

Immigrants' Life in the United States

Labor Needs Recognizing that the United States was industrializing at a rapid rate, many Europeans thought U.S. factory jobs might be easier to find and pay better wages than those near home. As one historian wrote, "The new machines [in the United States] provided jobs for the millions, so the millions appeared."

Liberty and Freedom Harsh laws could be as bad as economic troubles. As a religious and ethnic minority, Jews in Russia and Poland lived in fear of *pogroms*—sudden attacks on their communities in which Jews would be beaten and killed and their homes set on fire. In many countries of eastern Europe, people resented laws requiring boys of 15 and 16 to serve in a monarch's army.

Ghettos As different groups of immigrants moved into a city, they gathered in neighborhoods with people of their own nationality and ethnicity. (An *ethnic group* are people who share a common cultural background.) These sections of a city became known as *ghettos*, and were crowded with poor working people living in tenements. The residents of these ethnic neighborhoods found their main job opportunities in the city's factories.

Tenement apartments were known as "railroad flats" because they were arranged in a straight line, one room after the other. Families often had to share an already crowded apartment with relatives and friends recently arrived from Europe. Many apartments had no bathroom. A single toilet might be available for an entire floor. The grim living conditions of the typical immigrant family in New York City were fully described by Jacob Riis in his 1890 book, *How the Other Half Lives*—a book that shocked many middle-class readers.

The Americanization Process   The experience of leaving one's native country and traveling to live in an unknown place is usually a difficult and painful one. Certainly it was difficult for the Italians, Scandinavians, Greeks, and eastern Europeans, whose way of life in the "old country" was far different from the one in their adopted country, the United States. While living in ethnic neighborhoods, immigrants tried to preserve the customs and language that they had known in Europe. At the same time they tried hard to learn English and adopt American ways. Usually, the immigrants' children learned English and adopted American ways far more easily than their parents. Schools taught only in English and sometimes changed an immigrant student's name to make it easier for native-born Americans to pronounce. At times immigrants or their children changed their own names in order to blend in more easily with the majority culture.

Religion and Culture   In religion, immigrants of an earlier time had been much alike. Except for Irish Catholics and German Jews they were mainly Protestants. But very few of the "new immigrants" (those arriving after 1880) attended Protestant churches. The Italians were mainly Roman Catholics. The Greeks were Eastern Orthodox Christians. The Poles and Russians were largely Jewish.

   The culture of the new immigrants was also different from that of the American majority. For example, the new arrivals did not speak English, and wore clothing and cooked foods that seemed strange to many native-born Americans. As a result, schools attempted to Americanize the immigrants by teaching only in English and teaching only the language, history, and beliefs of the dominant culture.

   Most immigrants supported the Democratic party, which provided services for the urban poor in return for their votes. Since many urban areas had large immigrant populations, Democratic politicians usually won elections.

Immigrants' Contributions to American Society

The western frontier and eastern cities alike depended upon the labor of immigrants. They provided the labor for the building of the first transcontinental railroad. They turned the prairies and forests of the Middle West into prosperous farms. They helped to make New York City the center for a booming garment industry. They opened small retail stores that would later grow into large department stores such as Macy's and Gimbel's. They provided the necessary labor for the steel mills of Pittsburgh, Pennsylvania, and Birmingham, Alabama. They became the technicians, inventors, and scientists who helped to turn the dream of a mighty industrial empire into a reality.

Diversity of Population   The greatest influx of immigrants to the United States occurred between the 1840s and the 1920s. During this era, approximately 37 million immigrants arrived in the United States. Of these, about

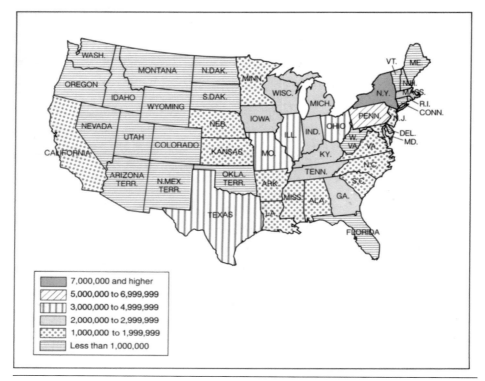

Population Distribution in the United States, in 1900

6 million were German, 4.5 million Irish, 4.75 million Italian, 4.2 million from England, Scotland, and Wales, 4.2 million from the Austro-Hungarian Empire, 2.3 million from Scandinavia, and 3.3 million from Russia and the Baltic states. Between the 1840s and the 1870s, German and Irish immigrants predominated. Beginning in 1896, immigrants from southern and eastern Europe, such as Italians, Jews, and Slavic people from the Austro-Hungarian Empire, were the most numerous.

Reactions to the "New" Immigration

The U.S. population has always represented a blend of two groups: (a) foreign-born people from many lands and (b) native-born Americans whose colonial ancestors had been immigrants but who had lost touch with their families' immigrant past. Because the second group (the native-born) formed a majority, they tended to dominate U.S. society and to determine the prime cultural values of the nation. Although these values differed from one region to another, the traits explained below described American society in general in the 19th century.

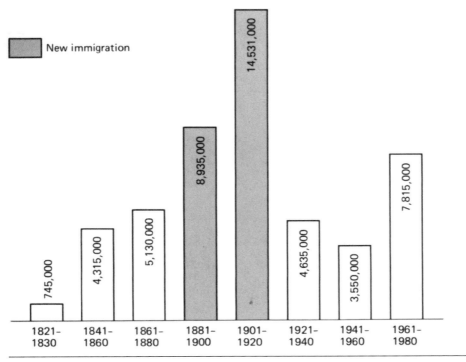

New immigration

745,000	4,315,000	5,130,000	8,935,000	14,531,000	4,635,000	3,550,000	7,815,000
1821–1830	1841–1860	1861–1880	1881–1900	1901–1920	1921–1940	1941–1960	1961–1980

Immigration, 1821–1980

Individualism   This was the belief that each person was completely responsible for his or her own actions. If a person was successful, it was assumed that the chief reasons were hard work and strength of character. Similarly, if a person failed, it was thought to be because of some character fault or weakness.

Rough Social Equality   Native-born people of European descent tended to view each other as social equals, especially on the western frontier. They stressed the importance of being neighborly and helpful to others.

Belief in White Superiority   Throughout the 1800s, many white Americans in the North as well as the South believed that their "race" was superior to other groups (Africans, Asians, Latin Americans, and Native Americans). They believed that the United States had a mission to bring the benefits of Western civilization to other regions and people. Americans of British descent viewed their culture as superior to the culture of other nationalities. Also, many Protestants regarded their faith as superior to others.

The cultural values of native-born European Americans influenced their attitudes toward foreign-born newcomers. The native-born became concerned after 1890 when the number of people arriving from southern and eastern Europe began to exceed the numbers from other regions. Between 1900 and 1910 total immigration averaged close to a million people a year (compared to less than 300,000 a year in the 1860s). Of the total arriving in 1910, about 700,000 people were from the countries of southern and eastern Europe and only about 300,000 from all other countries.

Americans who spoke English and worshipped in Protestant churches considered themselves to be the guardians of the dominant U.S. culture. Even though they were descended from immigrants, they distrusted the "new immigrants" who arrived in the United States in the post–Civil War era. They were afraid that these immigrants would not assimilate easily into the English-speaking culture of the majority. Beginning in the 1870s, the question of whether or not to admit foreign-born people from all lands became a major issue in U.S. politics.

Assimilation, the Melting Pot, and Cultural Pluralism

To what extent should immigrants be expected to adopt the customs and the language of the American majority? To what extent should they preserve and cherish the culture of their birth? In a "nation of immigrants" such as ours, the question is a vital and continuing one. During the peak years of immigration (1901–1910), Americans debated three opposing points of view on the issue.

Total Assimilation, or Americanization Assimilation is the slow process by which a minority culture learns the customs of the dominant culture. According to this viewpoint, immigrants should learn to speak English and become Americanized by adopting all aspects of American culture as quickly as possible. They should make an effort to rid themselves of customs derived from a foreign (non-American) culture.

"Melting-Pot" Theory According to this idea, immigrants from various nations would gradually and naturally blend into a single nation—the American nation. The culture of this *melting-pot* nation would combine the best elements of the many cultures and nationalities of the foreign-born. Although based on these foreign cultures, the new American culture would be different from them—and also superior to them, since it would combine their best features. The theory was democratic in that it respected elements from all cultures. It was also nationalistic, since it regarded American culture as superior to others. Believers in the melting-pot theory thought that English should be the common language for everyone: native-born and foreign-born alike.

Cultural Pluralism According to cultural pluralists, an English-speaking culture is not superior to any other culture. Instead, all cultures and languages of the foreign-born population should be respected as valuable. Each ethnic group should practice its own customs while also adjusting to the ways of the larger society. Today many cultural pluralists favor the idea of bilingualism—using Russian, Korean, or Spanish to teach science, math, and other subjects to foreign-born children rather than requiring them to cope in English. Their new language would be learned in periods set aside for English and also outside the classroom in the cafeteria and gym.

Nativist Opposition to Immigrants

A *nativist* is someone who believes that the foreign-born pose a threat to the majority culture and should be stopped from entering the country. At different times in the 19th century, nativists made organized attempts to exclude certain immigrant groups—especially Irish Catholics, eastern European Jews, Italians, Chinese, and Japanese. How can we explain the nativists' dislike for these groups?

★ An economic reason was competition for jobs.

★ A cultural reason was the tendency of people belonging to a dominant culture to protect that culture against outside or "foreign" influences.

★ A psychological reason was the nativist's desire to feel superior to others. This desire often takes a *racist* and *nationalist* form—the feeling that one's own race or nationality is superior to all others. Nativists expressed racist ideas by asserting that the newcomers from eastern and southern Europe were racially inferior and would produce a class of criminals and paupers.

Cartoon showing a nativist judge urging Uncle Sam to stop permitting the immigration of "undesirable" people

★ A political reason was a common fear among native-born Americans that many new immigrants might be connected with radical and revolutionary causes.

Nativist reaction was countered by those Americans who recognized the essential contributions of the immigrants. New York writer Emma Lazarus expressed this positive point of view in a poem that concludes:

. . . "Give me your tired, your poor,
Your huddled masses yearning to breathe free,
The wretched refuse of your teeming shore.
Send these, the homeless, tempest-tossed, to me,
I lift my lamp beside the golden door!"

Lazarus's poem is inscribed at the base of the Statue of Liberty, whose lamp started welcoming immigrant ships to New York Harbor in 1886.

Asians Excluded   In the 1870s there was talk of Asian people coming to the United States by the millions and overwhelming American culture. In western states and territories, anti-Chinese riots broke out to protest the so-called *yellow peril*. Two laws were passed in response to the nativist fears and prejudice.

★ The Chinese Exclusion Act (1882) declared that no more Chinese would be permitted to immigrate to the United States.

★ In the schools of San Francisco, Japanese children were required to attend segregated classes. The Japanese government was deeply offended by this practice. President Theodore Roosevelt persuaded California's

Early 20th-century immigrants arriving at Ellis Island in New York City

local governments to end their offensive school policies. In return Japan agreed to stop the further immigration of Japanese workers into the United States. This diplomatic understanding of 1907 and 1908 was known as the *Gentlemen's Agreement*.

Literacy Testing   Many lawmakers in Congress favored a literacy test as a device for limiting immigration. Such a test would disqualify those immigrants who could not read in any language. In 1917, after several earlier presidents had vetoed a literacy test bill, Congress overrode President Wilson's veto and passed a literacy test law. It provided that those unable to pass a reading test in their native language (or any other language) were prohibited from immigrating.

Red Scare   (See Chapter 11.)

Quota Acts of 1921 and 1924   The antiforeign attitudes of many native-born Americans were reflected in the Quota Acts of 1921 and 1924. The first of these laws (the Emergency Quota Act, 1921) limited the yearly immigration from any country to just 3 percent of the number arriving from that country in 1910. The second quota law (the Immigration Restriction Act, 1924) limited the yearly immigration from any country to just 2 percent of the number arriving from that country in 1890.

One purpose of the quota laws of the 1920s was to reduce to a bare minimum the number of immigrants arriving from Italy, the Soviet Union

Cartoon depicting anti-immigrant citizens and their "shadows"—their own immigrant ancestors

(formerly Russia), and other countries of southern and eastern Europe. A second purpose was to halt all immigration from Asia. The laws did in fact drastically reduce immigration to the United States. Earlier, during the peak period of immigration (1901–1910), more than 8 million immigrants (mostly from Italy, Austria-Hungary, and Russia) had arrived. Because of the restrictive immigration laws, fewer than 350,000 immigrants arrived in the 1930s.

★ In Review

1. How did the new immigrant groups differ from earlier immigrant groups?
2. What difficulties did the new immigrants face?
3. What conflicts between American ideals and reality are illustrated in the following immigration laws? (a) Chinese Exclusion Act, (b) Gentlemen's Agreement (c) Literacy Test (1917) (d) Emergency Quota Act (1921) (e) Immigration Restriction Act (1924).

The Changing Frontier (1850–1900)

The *frontier* is an imaginary line that separates settled areas from the wilderness. As trappers, miners, and farmers moved west, the frontier moved with them.

The Frontier Before 1850

Use the map on page 253 to review the main stages of the steady westward movement that, year after year, changed the location of the frontier.

First Colonial Century (1607–1700) After almost 100 years of settlement, the first frontier extended only about 300 to 400 miles inland from the Atlantic coast.

Founding of the Nation (1776–1790) Settlement advanced rapidly in this period. During the American Revolution, Daniel Boone opened a trail through the Appalachian Mountains into Kentucky. But for the most part the Appalachians still defined the western frontier when George Washington became president in 1789.

Early Republic (1790–1820) Flatboats and rafts on the Ohio River helped pioneering farm families move beyond the Appalachians to the wooded region that included Kentucky, Tennessee, Ohio, and Illinois. During the presidency of James Monroe (1817–1825), one section of the frontier lay just west of the Mississippi River.

Expansion to the Pacific (1830–1850) The next western lands to be settled were Texas, California, and Oregon. After the California gold rush of 1849,

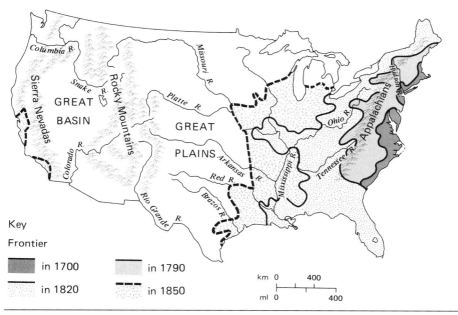

Key

Frontier

in 1700

in 1790

in 1820

in 1850

km 0   400

ml 0   400

Westward Movement of the Frontier, 1700–1850

a small section of the Pacific coast was settled, but the huge area between the Far West (Oregon and California) and the region just west of the Mississippi River was still unsettled. How did this "last frontier" of the American West (the lands between the settlements) finally yield to miners' pickaxes, cowboys' cattle, and farmers' plows?

Land West of the Mississippi

Rolling Plains and Great American Desert   Before 1850 the vast stretch of land between Missouri and California was popularly known as the Great American Desert because it seemed dry, barren, and impossible to farm. The region consisted of two main parts: (1) the flat grasslands of the Great Plains, stretching about 400 miles from the banks of the Missouri River to the steep slopes of the Rocky Mountains, and (2) the desert lowland known as the Great Basin, stretching about 700 miles between two mountain ranges (the Rockies and the Sierra Nevada).

The Plains People   Of course, the Native Americans had an entirely different view of the Great Plains. For them the Plains were filled with plants and animals that richly supported their way of life. Millions of shaggy buffalo provided almost all that the Plains Indians needed: meat for food, pelts for clothing, skins for shelter, bones for tools, and dried manure for fuel. The buffalo-hunting tribes (including the Blackfeet, Cheyenne, Comanche, and Sioux) viewed the Plains with religious awe and respect. To them the land and the life it supported were sacred.

Starting about 1850, easterners began to view the so-called Great American Desert in a new light. The settling of this region occurred in three stages. First came people hoping to strike rich deposits of gold and silver in the western mountains. Then came people who hoped to make their fortune raising and selling cattle. Finally came the homesteaders (farm families) who hoped for enough rain to raise wheat and corn for a profit.

Mining Frontier The news of a gold strike in the Rocky Mountains touched off a rush westward in 1859 similar to the rush to California ten years earlier. More than 100,000 people crossed the Great Plains in wagons and searched for gold near Pike's Peak in Colorado. In later years, thousands of others were lured into the western mountains by news of silver in Nevada, copper in Montana, and gold in the Black Hills of the Dakotas. In hundreds of remote places, mining towns sprang up almost overnight.

Cattle Frontier In Texas in the 1860s and 1870s the most promising way to make a living on the frontier was to hire a crew of cowboys for driving cattle to market. Millions of acres of the grassy plains were regarded by cattle owners as open grazing land. In other words, cattle herds were privately owned, but the open range was used by all.

Farming Frontier The passage of the Homestead Act in 1862 invited eastern farmers to try their luck settling on the Great Plains. Those who did so were often referred to as homesteaders. Anyone who wished could acquire 160 acres of western land simply by settling on it. Although intended for homesteaders, much of the land made available under the act was grabbed by speculators (those who buy something not for use, but only for later sale to others at a higher price).

Violent Conflict in the "Wild West"

The 25-year period after the Civil War (1865–1890) is the period most often dramatized in western movies and TV shows. Gunfights did occur in the mining towns and cow towns of the newly settled West, but the fights did not erupt every minute, as in the movies. Let us try to separate the reality of western life from the myth.

Ranchers Against Farmers One cause of violent conflict was the barbed wire that farmers used to fence in their homesteads. The fencing angered cattle owners, who had always treated the grasslands as open range. Cowboys used wire cutters to open a path through the farmers' fences and let their cattle through. Gun battles, or "barbed-wire wars," broke out between farmers and cattle ranchers. In the 1880s the ranchers conceded defeat by fencing in their own grazing lands. After that the days of the open range were over.

Vigilantes Against Outlaws Mining camps and cattle towns attracted many young men who were in a hurry to make their fortunes. Many found that it was easier to steal another miner's gold or rustle (steal) another rancher's cattle than to obtain them by honest work. To defend themselves and their property, most westerners carried guns. Sometimes they used them to settle personal quarrels in shootouts (later made famous in Western movies).

In a remote town, honest citizens could not always rely on government officials to capture cattle thieves and bank robbers. Therefore they carried out the law in their own way as *vigilantes* (a self-appointed police force). A suspected outlaw might be hanged without a full trial—or any trial at all. These crude procedures for dealing with crime on the frontier were known as vigilante justice.

Industrialization and the Frontier

Role of the Railroads Railroad companies were even more eager than the U.S. government to encourage farmers to go west. After all, a railroad's chief business was hauling freight from one place to another. If there were no settlers on the empty plains, there would be no business for a western railroad. To recruit settlers, railroad companies sent agents to Europe as well as to U.S. cities. Railroads' land grants from the U.S. government were offered for sale to would-be settlers at bargain prices. (See pages 164–166.)

Potential for Profit Railroads were crucial to the cattle drivers from Texas that altered life on the Plains. The end of the cowboys' long journey was the railroad depot in Abilene, Kansas. Here the cattle were herded into railroad cars for shipment to the slaughter pens in Chicago and from there (as meat) to the restaurants and butcher shops of the East. In the 1860s a long-horned steer bought in Texas for $3 could bring between $30 and $40 when sold to a Chicago meatpacker. Without the railroads as the connecting link, the cattleman's profitmaking enterprise would have been impossible.

Role of New Technology Farming the hard sod of the plains posed a double problem. For one thing, rainfall was slight. For another, there were no trees from which to make the rail fences commonly used in the East to enclose sheep and other farm animals. An old idea and a new invention went a long way toward solving both problems. (1) Windmills on a homesteader's land provided the power for pumping up underground water. (2) Barbed wire (invented in 1874) enabled farmers to fence their lands without using much wood. In addition, improved steel plows enabled farmers to cut deep into the hard ground.

Life on the Frontier

The first homesteaders to settle the Great Plains coped daily with a daunting number of hazards and hardships of life on the frontier.

Sod Houses and Dugouts Because of the absence of trees, homesteaders built their first homes out of bricks made from the prairie sod. If the ground was hilly, they might simply dig a room out of the hillside for shelter. Doors and windows were covered with blankets and hides. If it rained, water seeped through the sod roof and formed puddles on the dirt floor of the typical one-room cabin. If it did not rain for months at a time, crops withered, and dust covered everything the family owned.

Farmers on the Great Plains were separated by great distances. Occasional neighborly get-togethers provided the only social life. After several seasons of disappointing harvests, dust storms, hot summers, cold winters, and uncomfortable living, many farm families gave up and moved back east.

The Role of Women For women especially, life on the frontier was difficult and lonely. They performed a never-ending round of daily chores. They worked the land, fed the chickens, churned the butter, cooked the food, sewed the linens, made the clothing, and tended the children. The number of children to be tended was often ten or more. Little time was taken for giving birth. It was common for a woman to do a full morning of work, give birth in the afternoon, and return to her chores the next morning.

Women were a civilizing force on the frontier. When they arrived in the rough-and-tumble mining camps and cow towns originally populated by men, they managed to build more settled and peaceful communities. They made sure their towns had libraries, schools, even theaters. They acted as teachers, missionaries, librarians, and occasionally as doctors and dentists.

It was in the western territory of Wyoming that women first achieved the right to vote, in 1869. By 1910 women in most western states voted in large numbers, while most women in the East were still denied voting rights. One reason for the West's leadership was men's realization that

Farm family on the Great Plains, in the 1880s

western women had made many sacrifices and had played a crucial role in settling the last frontier.

Impact of the Frontier on American Life

The U.S. Bureau of the Census reported in 1890 that the frontier had ceased to exist. Taking note of this fact, historian Frederick Jackson Turner wrote about the passing of the frontier in an essay that received much public attention. He argued that the frontier had served the American nation as both a democratizing force and an outlet, or safety valve, for people seeking new economic opportunities.

Turner observed that life on the frontier tended to be more democratic than life in settled areas. People on the frontier judged each other not according to social rank, but according to their abilities and strength of character. There was a sense on the frontier that everyone had an equal chance to succeed.

Furthermore, according to Turner, the western frontier provided people living in crowded eastern cities with a safety valve—a means of starting life over by moving to unsettled lands. While the frontier lasted, cheap land was always available to those seeking new opportunities.

Other scholars have pointed out weaknesses in Turner's thesis. They argue that American democracy owed far more to British influences in colonial times than to the frontier. Disputing the safety-valve theory, they point out that the trip west was costly, and the poor could hardly afford to pay for a covered wagon and supplies.

Whether it was or was not a democratizing force, the frontier helped shape the American character. The passing of the frontier marked the end of a unique period in American history.

Native Americans
and Advancing White Settlement

As more and more Europeans arrived in the United States during the 1800s, Native Americans were forced to retreat westward. As you recall, a policy of removal was adopted by President Andrew Jackson in the 1830s. Native Americans of the East, including the Cherokees, were forced to leave their lands for territory set aside for their use—the territory known then as the Great American Desert.

During the gold rushes of 1849 and 1859, settlers pushed west in ever-greater numbers. The Homestead Act, the end of the Civil War, and the growth in railroads led to millions of new settlers crossing into the rolling Plains and the Great American Desert. This movement would have severe consequences for Native Americans. Unlike white settlers from the East, the Native Americans could not conceive of dividing the land into privately owned plots and using it for personal gain. In their view, the land and its wealth belonged to all.

By 1890, the Native Americans would be placed on reservations and would have lost their rights to the land. Indian peoples of the Plains lost not only their lands but also the buffalo herds upon which their way of life depended. The herds made an easy target for travelers who made a sport of killing buffalo from train windows. Hunting parties slaughtered buffalo for their furry hides, sold in the East as buffalo robes. By 1890 the great herds of buffalo, once numbering in the millions, had dwindled to less than a thousand.

Treaties and Legal Status   U.S. treaties guaranteed the Native Americans right to this land for "as long as the rivers shall run and the grass shall grow." But in the 1850s, as settlers started building mining towns and cattle towns in this region, the people's way of life was again threatened. Despite treaty rights, Native Americans had their land taken from them as the Europeans moved west in larger and larger numbers. Often the U.S. military supported the takeover of Native Americans' lands. In fact, Native Americans referred to African American troops as the "buffalo soldiers." Thus, the treaties offered little protection for Native Americans.

Native American Wars (1850–1900)

For more than 200 years (1607–1850) the frontier had been the scene of frequent fighting between Native Americans (the original settlers of North America) and pioneer families (newcomers to the land). As the frontier moved west to the Mississippi River and beyond, the setting for the Indian–U.S. wars also shifted westward. The final chapter in the long conflict was fought on the last frontier—the Great Plains.

The Sioux, who hunted buffalo on the plains of Wyoming, were the first of many Plains people to attack U.S. military posts in the region. The high point of their war was a battle on the Little Bighorn River in Montana in 1876. Led by Chief Crazy Horse, the Sioux killed 210 U.S. soldiers including Lieutenant Colonel George Custer. But in 1890 the U.S. army took a terrible revenge, killing about 300 Sioux at Wounded Knee Creek in South Dakota. The fighting was less a battle than a massacre of people, including women and children, who were cut down as they fled from the scene. This event ended the Sioux's resistance. Reluctantly, they moved to a reservation in South Dakota. (A *reservation* is an area with fixed boundaries for Native Americans' use alone.)

Other Native Americans fought against the loss of their hunting grounds to white settlers. But for them, too, it was a losing battle. In Oregon in 1877 a tribe of about 500 Nez Percé tried to escape the fate of being forced onto a reservation by journeying over mountain trails to Canada. But U.S. troops caught up with them, forcing the Nez Percé to surrender. It was a sad moment for their heroic leader, Chief Joseph, who said:

My people ask me for food, and I have none to give. It is cold, and we have no blankets, no wood. My people are starving. Where is my little

Native Americans in the West in the Late 1800s

daughter? I do not know. Perhaps even now she is freezing to death. Hear me, my chiefs. My heart is sick and sad. I have fought. But from where the sun now stands, I will fight no more, forever!

The Apache of Arizona were the last Native Americans to fight U.S. troops. After they submitted in 1900, the Native Americans lived peaceably but unhappily on reservations.

Why Native Americans Lost the Wars   Although Native Americans challenged white settlers and U.S. troops, they never won a war against them. They lost for three reasons. First, they fought as separate tribes rather than a single, united nation. Second, most tribes were small, often numbering fewer than a thousand people. Third, though they were equipped with rifles as well as bows and arrows, Native Americans lacked their foe's advanced weapons, such as the cannon and machine gun.

Legislating Native American Life

The lands assigned by the U.S. government to different tribes of Native Americans were not their native lands. Reservation lands were often barren and poorly suited to supporting life. Unable to hunt for their food as in the past, Native Americans were reduced to lives of poverty and hopelessness. Agents of the U.S. government who ran the reservations were often corrupt, pocketing the funds intended for Native Americans' welfare.

The Dawes Act In the 1880s many U.S. citizens began to recognize that Native Americans were not being treated fairly. The reformer Helen Hunt Jackson published *A Century of Dishonor* (1881), a book that described the many times that Native Americans had been deceived and cheated when the U.S. government violated its treaties with them.

Reform-minded lawmakers in Congress hoped to improve conditions on the reservations by encouraging Native Americans to adopt the lifestyle of American farmers. In 1887 Congress passed the Dawes Act, which offered 160-acre plots on the reservations to the heads of households. It was assumed that Native American farmers would become self-supporting and "Americanized." An official appointed to enforce the Dawes Act said, "We will make of them American citizens and render future conflicts between them and the government impossible." But people with a hunting culture did not become model farmers overnight. Rather than taking homesteads for themselves, many rented or sold them to white settlers for cash.

Chief Joseph of the Nez Percé, around 1870

★ ★ ★ ★ ★

THE TESTIMONY OF STANDING BEAR

Standing Bear was the chief of the Poncas, a Native American tribe that had been ordered to leave its homeland in the Dakotas for the Indian Territory to the south. The Poncas had great difficulty adapting to the change. Many died, including Standing Bear's son. Standing Bear violated army rules when he left the reservation to bury his son in his former homeland to the north. He was placed under arrest. At his trial in 1879, he made a speech that was recorded by a witness and white friend of the Poncas, Thomas H. Tibbles. The excerpt is from Tibbles's book, *Buckskin and Blanket Days.*

Standing Bear rose. Half facing the audience, he stretched his right hand out before him, holding it still so long that the audience grew tense. At last, looking up at the judge, he spoke quietly. "That hand is not the color of yours, but if I pierce it, I shall feel pain. If you pierce your hand, you also feel pain. The blood that will flow from mine will be of Standing Bear, the same color as yours. I am a man. The same God made us both."

Half facing the audience again, he let his gaze drift far out through a window. His tone grew tense.

"I seem to stand on the bank of a river. My wife and little girl are beside me. In front the river is wide and impassable, and behind are perpendicular cliffs. No man of my race ever stood there before. There is no tradition to guide me."

Then he described how a flood started to rise around them and how, looking despairingly at the great cliffs, he saw a steep, stony way leading upward. . . . Finally he saw a rift in the rocks and felt the prairie breeze strike his cheek.

"I turn to my wife and child with a shout that we are saved.

"We will return to the Swift Running Water that pours down between the green islands. There are the graves of my fathers. There again we will pitch our tepee and build our fires.

"But a man bars the passage. He is a thousand times more powerful than I. Behind him I see soldiers as numerous as the leaves of the trees. They will obey that man's orders. I too, must obey his orders. If he says that I cannot pass, I cannot. The long struggle will have been in vain. My wife and child and I must return and sink beneath the flood. We are weak and faint and sick. I cannot fight."

He paused with bowed head. Then, gazing up into Judge Dundy's face with an indescribable look of pathos and suffering, he said in a low, intense tone:

"You are that man."

No one who merely reads the speech can possibly imagine its effect on those people who knew of the Poncas' sufferings when they heard it spoken by the sad old chief in his brilliant robes.

The U.S. judge ruled in favor of Standing Bear. He said the Poncas and their chief could return to their homeland in the Dakotas.

Civil Rights for Native Americans

The Native Americans had lived in poverty ever since the 1870s and 1880s when they had been forced to live on reservations. The Dawes Act did little to change their conditions.

Early in the 20th century, however, the status of Native Americans was changed by two laws. By an act of Congress of 1924, all Native Americans were granted full U.S. citizenship. By a 1934 law, the Indian Reorganization Act, the former policy of dividing reservation lands into individual plots was abandoned. The new policy permitted Indian peoples to own land in common as tribal property rather than as separate farms. [Instead of individuals owning plots of land on the reservations, the U.S. government now stressed tribal ownership and tribal authority.] At the same time the reservation schools began to stress methods of scientific farming. These changes were for the better. Even so, most Indians were still desperately poor.

In the 1960s, inspired by the civil rights movement begun by African Americans, Native Americans from different reservations joined forces in an attempt to assert *red power*. An organization called the National Congress of American Indians complained bitterly about the government agency that supervised Indian life on the reservations. The U.S. Bureau of Indian Affairs (BIA) had failed for decades to raise the people's standard of living. A study in 1960 found that Native Americans had a life expectancy of only 46 years, compared with 70 years for the U.S. population as a whole. More than any other ethnic minority, Indians suffered from high rates of malnutrition and unemployment.

Activists in the movement for Native Americans rights wanted the following:

★ Less supervision by the BIA and greater freedom in reservation life as Native Americans saw fit. As one Native American put it, "We simply want to run our lives our own way."

★ The return of fishing and hunting rights that Native Americans had once enjoyed, even if this meant changing state game laws for their benefit.

★ Greater economic assistance in combating problems of poverty.

★ The return of lands that had belonged to the Native Americans' ancestors, which U.S. treaties had guaranteed would not be taken from them but were.

Protest at Wounded Knee   Though united in their goals, Native Americans disagreed on how best to achieve them. Some favored peaceful protest, while others resorted to the use of armed force. In 1972 a radical group, the American Indian Movement (AIM), occupied the offices of the BIA in Washington, D.C., and demanded that the U.S. government honor treaties signed a century or more earlier. The next year more than 200 members of AIM took up arms and gained control of the village of Wounded Knee on a Sioux reservation in South Dakota. Wounded Knee had been the site of a massacre by U.S. troops in 1890. For two months the invaders of Wounded

Knee filled the village and demanded that old treaty rights be reinstated. Even though they won no concessions, they may have prepared the way for the court victories later won by Native American tribes. In addition, in 1975, Congress passed the Indian Self-Determination and Education Act, which was designed to increase the role the people played on their own reservations and in their education.

Victories in Court   Through the 1970s, Native Americans from Maine to California went to court to sue for lands promised to them by treaties in earlier centuries. One court granted the Narragansett Indians of Rhode Island the return of 1,800 acres. As a result of their suit, the Penobscots of Maine won both thousands of acres and millions of dollars. The Sioux of South Dakota won another case, in which the court ruled that 7 million acres of land had been taken from their people illegally.

★ In Review

1. What are the geographic differences between the Great Plains and the Rocky Mountains regions of the West?
2. How did the Industrial Revolution contribute to the economic development of the Great Plains?
3. Summarize the federal government's attempts to address Native Americans' rights from 1887 to the present.

Chapter Review

MULTIPLE-CHOICE QUESTIONS

1. Which was most responsible for the rapid economic growth of cities during the 19th century?
   (1) presence of theaters and libraries
   (2) growth of industry
   (3) rise of urban mass transportation
   (4) the development of mass communication.

2. How did the "new immigrants" who came to the United States between 1880 and 1920 differ from earlier immigrants?
   (1) They were considered physically and mentally superior to earlier immigrants.
   (2) They arrived before the closing of the frontier in the West.
   (3) The countries they came from differed from those of the earlier immigrants.
   (4) They came chiefly from northern and western Europe.

Base your answer to question 3 on the Emma Lazarus poem quoted on page 250 and the poem below, by Thomas Bailey Aldrich.

Wide open and unguarded stand
    our gates,
And through them presses a wild
    motley throng —
Men from the Volga and the Tartar
    steppes,
Featureless figures of the Hoang-
    Ho,
Malayan, Scythian, Teuton, Kelt
    and Slav,
Flying the Old World's poverty and
    scorn;
These bringing with them unknown
    gods and rites,
Those, tiger passions, here to
    stretch their claws.
In street and alley what strange
    tongues are loud,
Accents of menace alien to our
    air,
Voices that once the Tower of Babel
    knew!
O Liberty, white Goddess! is it well
To leave the gates unguarded? . . .

3. Emma Lazarus and Thomas Bailey Aldrich
    (1) agreed that American-style democracy should be extended to other nations
    (2) felt that immigration should be limited
    (3) desired an immigration-quota system
    (4) disagreed about U.S. immigration policy.

4. The photographs on page 234, taken in the late 1800s, show that
    (1) most American families had a great amount of leisure time
    (2) while some Americans were very well off, others lived in poverty

(3) the divorce rate in America was high
(4) few children went to public schools.

5. The bar graph on page 232 tells us that
    (1) between 1870 and 1900, the number of people living in cities was gradually approaching the number living in the country
    (2) urban population would never be able to catch up with rural population
    (3) urban population would surpass rural population by 1910
    (4) agricultural output could be expected to outperform industrial output in 1900.

6. The artist of the cartoon on page 251 believed that those who wished to limit immigration were
    (1) cynical
    (2) correct
    (3) hypocritical
    (4) practical.

7. The graph on page 247 indicates that
    (1) the number of immigrants arriving in the United States tripled by 1861
    (2) immigration was severely limited in 1911
    (3) United States immigration officials limited the entry of immigrants from England, Ireland, and Germany
    (4) between 1881 and 1920, the nature of immigration to the United States changed.

8. "U.S. society may be described as a stew in which each ingredient adds to the stew's flavor but still retains its own distinct identity." This statement best describes the concept of
    (1) ethnocentrism

(2) cultural pluralism
(3) nativism
(4) social control.

9. What effect did U.S. population growth have on the Native Americans in the 19th century?
(1) It caused Indians to move to urban areas in ever increasing numbers.
(2) It forced Indians to move westward.
(3) It led most Indians to adopt the culture of the settlers.

(4) Most Indians formed alliances with other minority groups.

10. The passage of the immigration acts of 1921 and 1924 indicated that the United States wished to
(1) restrict the flow of immigrants
(2) continue the immigration policies followed during most of the 19th century
(3) encourage cultural diversity
(4) play a larger role in international affairs.

THEMATIC ESSAYS

1. **Theme:** Urbanization

    The gradual shift of the population of the United States from rural to urban areas created new problems that demanded new solutions.

    Task: Choose one change resulting from the growth of cities in the United States that created a problem. For the change that you have selected:

    ★ Describe the details of the problem that the change created.
    ★ Show how people attempted to solve the problem.
    ★ Evaluate the success of the attempted solution for the problem.

    Some of the changes that you may wish to consider could be in the areas of housing, immigration, and working conditions.

2. **Theme:** The Shrinking Frontier

    As the American frontier moved to the west, it shrank and ultimately disappeared.

    Task

    ★ Define the term "frontier" and show how its westerly movement resulted in its disappearance.
    ★ Explain two factors that caused the frontier to shrink and finally disappear.
    ★ Describe one outcome of the shrinking frontier.

    Some of the factors to consider in explaining the causes of the shrinking frontier are: the discovery of gold in California, the Homestead Act, the development of railroads, and the role of technology.
    Outcomes of the shrinking frontier might include its impact on the Native Americans, immigrants, the environment, and styles of living. You are not limited to these suggestions.

DOCUMENT-BASED QUESTION

Read or analyze each document and answer the question that follows it. Then read the Task and write your essay. Essays should include references to most of the documents along with additional information based on your knowledge of United States history and government.

Historical Context: The new immigration that began in the 1880s presented special challenges for the newcomers in New York and other United States cities.

Document 1 Refer to the graph of immigration, 1821–1980, on page 247.

Question: What happened to the number of people immigrating to the United States from 1881 through 1920?

Document 2 Refer to the map of European immigration, on page 240.

Question: Where did most of the immigrants to the United States during the period shown on the map come from?

Document 3 Refer to the illustration of immigrants arriving in New York, on page 250.

Question: What feelings do you think the artist was attempting to convey in this depiction of immigrants and the Statue of Liberty?

Document 4 Refer to the photograph of immigrants and urban life in 1900, on page 243.

Question: What conditions did many immigrants have to live in when they arrived in cities such as New York?

Document 5 Read the excerpt "The Lower East Side in 1898," on page 242.

Question: In the writer Abraham Cahan's view, how does life in the United States compare with that in Czarist Russia?

Task: Using the documents and your knowledge of United States history,

★ Describe some of the challenges faced by immigrants who came to American cities during the late 1800s and early 1900s.

★ Describe why most immigrants decided to remain in the United States in spite of the challenges with which they had to deal.

★ UNIT III ★

The Progressive Era

Chapter 10
Reform in America

★ Objectives

★ To identify and evaluate the reforms achieved by the Progressive movement.

★ To be aware of the origins of movements to protect consumers, workers, the environment, and the rights of women and minorities.

★ To describe the efforts of women and African Americans to bring about democratic reforms.

★ To compare the reform politics of three presidents: Theodore Roosevelt, William Howard Taft, and Woodrow Wilson.

One of the most remarkable periods of reform began shortly before 1900 and reached a climax in the presidential election of 1912. The reformers called themselves "progressives" and gave a name to the era they dominated—the *Progressive Era*.

Pressures for Reform

As the American nation became more industrial and urban, serious problems arose that cried out for attention. The Progressive movement that began in the 1890s was an attempt to bring under control the problems created by industrial growth and change.

Progressive Support for Government-Sponsored Reform

Should government regulate business, or should it leave business alone? This question was at the heart of the debate between citizens who favored progressive reforms and those who opposed them.

Conservative View People who took a conservative, anti-progressive view thought that businesses should be free to compete as they saw fit. In their view, businesses should not be regulated by government commissions and agencies. In other words, conservatives believed that the policy of laissez-faire (hands off business) should continue into the 20th century.

Progressive View People who sided with progressive politicians thought the time had come to abandon laissez-faire. They wanted laws that would (1) stop businesses from competing in unfair ways and (2) provide some protection for consumers and the general public from the unpleasant effects of industrialism. In their view, government should act toward businesses as a good police officer—making them obey rules that would ensure safety and fair treatment for all.

Effects of Developing Technologies

The growth of industry in the period from 1865 to 1914 was based partly on the developing technologies of the late 19th century. Much of this technology aided the railroads. For example, Andrew Carnegie, founder of the Carnegie Steel Company, was quick to utilize the Bessemer process for steel making, thus producing higher-quality steel than his competitors. Tracks made of this higher-quality steel replaced iron tracks as railroads expanded westward across the heartland of the United States. Steel tracks did not break as easily as iron tracks. Making railroads even safer was the use of the Westinghouse air brake. The development of the Pullman car made train travel more comfortable. The development of the refrigerated car enabled railroads to carry large shipments of food for long distances without fear of spoilage.

Cartoon: Conservative view (left) and progressive view of government's role in business

Improved transportation helped increasing numbers of farmers and miners move west. At the same time, immigrants poured into America's growing cities. The redistribution of population brought about the increasing urbanization of the nation. By 1920, more people lived in cities than in rural areas.

Technological developments such as the typewriter, Dictaphone, and telephone opened up additional jobs for women in the newly created industries. Women entered the workforce in record numbers and became full wage earners. This created a foundation for social and political change.

Struggle for Fair Standards in Business With more women in the workforce, reformers now became concerned about the effects of long hours of work on their health. Florence Kelley, a social worker in Chicago, was mainly responsible for an Illinois law prohibiting employment of women for more than eight hours a day. Women reformers in Massachusetts persuaded the legislature to enact a minimum wage law in 1912.

The courts, however, posed an obstacle to reform. Business firms and their lawyers argued in court that state regulatory laws were unconstitutional because they infringed on a property owner's rights. Lawyers cited the due process clause of the Fourteenth Amendment (". . . nor shall any state deprive any person of life, liberty, or property, without due process of law"). Two landmark Supreme Court cases examined the issue. Conservatives won one case; progressives won another.

Case of *Lochner* v. *New York* (1905) A New York law prohibited bakers in the state from working more than a 60-hour week or a 10-hour day. The U.S. Supreme Court decided that the New York law violated a business owner's right under the Fourteenth Amendment not to be deprived of the use of property without "due process of law." The Court therefore ruled the state law to be unconstitutional.

Case of *Muller* v. *Oregon* (1908)   An Oregon law provided that women could not work more than ten hours a day in factories and laundries. Defending the law before the U.S. Supreme Court, a brilliant lawyer named Louis Brandeis used scientific studies of women workers to demonstrate that women's health could be injured by overly long hours of physical labor. His arguments persuaded the Court to permit Oregon's law to stand. Brandeis later became the first American of the Jewish faith to serve on the U.S. Supreme Court.

Increasing Inequalities

The period from 1865 through the early 1900s created great inequalities between the wealthy and the poor. Railroad building had created millionaires such as Edward Harriman, Leland Stanford, and Cornelius Vanderbilt. The latter two would provide large sums of money to help found universities that bear their names. Men such as Rockefeller and Carnegie enjoyed unparalleled wealth as the founders of the large-scale oil and steel industries. Eventually, Carnegie would sell his steel company for the unheard-of sum of $400 million to a group led by the banker J. P. Morgan. Carnegie's steel company would then be combined with other steel companies to form U.S. Steel, the largest steel company in the world. Carnegie would donate most of the money from this sale to institutions such as libraries, which were established throughout the nation. The 42nd Street Public Library and Carnegie Hall in New York City stand as monuments to his philanthropy. Other multimillionaires included Gustavas Swift and Philip Armour in the newly developed meatpacking industry.

The new millionaires were supported in their quest for wealth by the philosophy of Social Darwinism (see page 234). Social Darwinists believed that wealth was an outcome of the fittest and best rising to the top.

In stark contrast to the rising group of wealthy stood the millions who labored long hours for low wages. In the late 1800s, steelworkers worked 12-hour shifts, often seven days a week. Immigrant women and children labored in clothing factories in New York's garment industry. In Chicago, immigrants worked for low wages in dangerous jobs in the meatpacking industry. From 1880 to 1900, the number of women working in the marketplace increased from approximately 2.5 million to almost 9 million, often for pennies a day. Thus, progressive reformers, taking note of the great disparity in wealth, resolved to change the political and economic systems.

Rising Power of the Middle Class and Newspapers

Progressive candidates for office depended on the backing of (1) middle-class voters and (2) publishers of city newspapers. Since the Civil War, both groups had grown more important in U.S. society as a result of industrial change and the growth of cities.

Social and economic progress was due in large part to the middle class. One of the chief characteristics of members of the middle class was their practice of reading popular books, newspapers, and magazines. These publications influenced the readers' economic and political views. Most members of the middle class took their civic duties seriously, the men by voting regularly and the women by participating in clubs and charities and sometimes joining reform movements. Most were native-born citizens who took pride in their country's traditions and growing strength.

Inventions in the publishing business kept pace with inventions in other industries. By the 1870s, city newspapers rolled off immense machine-driven presses. The goal of every newspaper publisher was to increase daily readership and advertising pages. Two of the most successful publishers owned rival newspapers in New York City. Joseph Pulitzer owned the *New York World*, and William Randolph Hearst owned the *New York Journal*. Both reached an enormous public by selling newspapers for only a penny and running feature stories that appealed to people's appetite for scandal and sensation. The methods used by Pulitzer and Hearst were known as *yellow journalism*. (The name derives from a popular cartoon, the "Yellow kid," featured daily in the *New York World*.)

Consumer Protection

Journalists were critically important to the Progressive movement. Their books and magazine articles gave millions of Americans an interest in righting the wrongs of society.

"Muckrakers" and Reform

Monthly magazines like the *Ladies Home Journal* and *McClure's* carried lengthy articles about corruption in city government and shocking conditions in factories and slums. The writers of these articles played up dirty politics, or "muck"—all that seemed dishonest, immoral, and ugly. Theodore Roosevelt referred to these writers as *muckrakers*.

Magazine Writers The most influential magazine writers who were considered muckrakers were:

★ Lincoln Steffens: His magazine articles and book, *The Shame of the Cities* (1904), revealed how thoroughly corrupt the city politicians of his time were.

★ Ida Tarbell: Her thorough investigation of the monopolistic methods of John D. Rockefeller was published as a series of magazine articles and then as a book, *History of the Standard Oil Company* (1904).

Novelists The most influential novelists who were considered muckrakers were:

★ Frank Norris: His novel *The Octopus* (1901) dealt with the struggle of California wheat growers against a monopolistic railway corporation. The book emphasized the control of "forces" such as wheat and railroads over individuals.

★ Upton Sinclair: His novel *The Jungle* (1906) exposed the dreadful conditions in Chicago meatpacking plants. The public outcry following publication led directly to a U.S. law providing for federal inspection of meat (the Meat Inspection Act, 1906). A related law, the Pure Food and Drug Act (1906), regulated the manufacture of foods.

Long after the era of progressive reform ended, the muckrakers continued to influence later generations of journalists who, in our time, are known as investigative reporters.

★ ★ ★ ★ ★

CONDITIONS IN A SAUSAGE FACTORY

The following quotation is one of the most nauseating paragraphs in American literature. It is a description of a sausage factory in Upton Sinclair's muckraking novel *The Jungle*. If you had been in Congress in 1906, would you have voted for a meat inspection law on the basis of this paragraph alone?

> There was never the least attention paid to what was cut up for sausage; there would come all the way back from Europe old sausage that had been rejected, and that was moldy and white—it would be dosed with borax and glycerine, and dumped into the hoppers, and made over again for home consumption. There would be meat that had tumbled out on the floor, in the dirt and sawdust, where the workers had tramped and spit uncounted billions of consumption germs. There would be meat stored in great piles in rooms, and the water from leaky roofs would drip over it, and thousands of rats would race about on it. It was too dark in these storage places to see well, but a man could run his hand over these piles of meat and sweep off handfuls of the dried dung of rats. These rats were nuisances, and the packers would put poisoned bread out for them; they would die, and then rats, bread, and meat would go into the hoppers together. This is no fairy story and no joke; the meat would be shoveled into carts, and the man who did the shoveling would not trouble to lift out a rat even when he saw one—there were things that went into the sausage in comparison with which a poisoned rat was a tidbit.

Legislation

★ The Pure Food and Drug Act (1906) banned the manufacture and sale of impure foods, drugs, and liquors and required commercially bottled and packaged medicines to be truthfully and fully labeled.

★ The Meat Inspection Act (1906) gave U.S. officials the power to check the quality and healthfulness of meats shipped in interstate commerce.

Social and Economic Reform

Some progressives were most concerned about the welfare of people living in urban slums. They were at the forefront of what was called the social justice movement. Included in their ranks were Jacob Riis, a New York City newspaper reporter and author of *How the Other Half Lives*, and Jane Addams, founder of Hull House, a settlement house in Chicago.

Poverty and the Social Settlement Movement

The grim living conditions of the typical immigrant family in New York City were described by Jacob Riis in his 1890 book, *How the Other Half Lives*. This book shocked many middle-class readers and prompted efforts to reduce overcrowding and unsanitary conditions in tenements.

A *settlement house* was a building located in a poor immigrant neighborhood where women and children could go for help in adjusting to American life. Both Jane Addams's Hull House in Chicago and Lillian Wald's Henry Street Settlement in New York City provided activities for poor chil-

Cartoon of dreadful tenement conditions—in this case, cholera confronting a slumlord

dren to keep them from the dangers of unsupervised play on city streets. Their immigrant parents were offered free classes in English as well as classes in the arts, literature, and music. Addams, Wald, and other social workers became experts on the problems of urban poverty. They used their knowledge to persuade state legislatures to enact laws to protect children—especially laws to abolish child labor.

Women's Rights

Suffrage Movement For almost 100 years after the United States declared its independence in 1776, only men were permitted to vote. Recall that the movement for woman's suffrage (voting rights) had officially begun at the Seneca Falls Convention in New York in 1848. (See Chapter 5.) Participants in the movement, men and women alike, were known as *suffragists*. Their leaders included Susan B. Anthony, Elizabeth Cady Stanton, and Lucy Stone.

Some suffragists concentrated on trying to persuade each state legislature to grant equal voting rights to women. Most of their triumphs came in the new states of the West—Utah, Wyoming, Colorado, and Idaho. The first women to vote in a U.S. election lived on the western frontier as residents of the territory of Wyoming. They cast their ballots in 1869, 21 years after the Seneca Falls Convention.

The movement for woman's suffrage that began in 1848 continued into the Progressive Era. The approach favored by Susan B. Anthony was to win support for an amendment to the U.S. Constitution that would guarantee voting rights for women in *all* the states. This amendment was first introduced in Congress in 1878, but the male lawmakers rejected it. Suffragists persisted by reintroducing the amendment in every session of Congress for the next 40 years.

Some men in the Progressive movement supported the women's crusade for voting rights. But many men, though reform-minded on other issues, thought women should not become involved in politics.

The suffragists kept up the pressure on state legislatures, asking how the United States could be a democracy if women could not vote. The older leadership (Susan B. Anthony and Elizabeth Cady Stanton) was replaced by a new generation of suffragists led by Alice Paul and Carrie Chapman Catt. Finally, in 1919, the amendment giving women the right to vote was passed by Congress. In 1920 it was ratified by the states as the Nineteenth Amendment.

Early Fight for Birth Control Working as a nurse among immigrant families in New York City, Margaret Sanger observed many women of the working class risking their lives and suffering increased poverty because of frequent pregnancies and births. She believed that women should be given information on ways to prevent pregnancy, if they wished. In 1914 she started publishing a magazine on birth control and opened the first birth-control clinic in Brooklyn. Her clinic and her book *What Every Girl Should Know* (1916) launched a movement for informed parenthood that gained strength in later decades.

Black Movement and Reform

Recall from Chapter 7 the Jim Crow laws that established racial segregation in the South in the 1880s and 1890s. During the Progressive Era, African American leaders challenged these laws and tried to win the support of white reformers.

The best-known leader of African Americans in the Progressive Era was Booker T. Washington. (For Washington's background and point of view toward segregation, see Chapter 7.) Many white business leaders and politicians conferred with Washington about the education and training of African Americans for skilled industrial jobs. Washington was frequently called to the White House to advise Theodore Roosevelt. After one such meting in 1908, Washington ate lunch with the president. News of this event touched off a storm of criticism in the South.

The chief leader of the movement for African American rights was a Harvard-educated scholar, W. E. B. Du Bois. In 1905 he launched the movement at a meeting of reformers in Niagara Falls, Canada. (They met there because hotels on the New York side of the border refused to give them rooms.) The *Niagara Movement*, as it was called, focused on publicizing and protesting acts of injustice against African Americans.

Formation of the NAACP In 1909, members of the Niagara Movement joined with white reformers in organizing the National Association for the Advancement of Colored People (NAACP). Dedicated to protecting the civil rights of African Americans, the NAACP stood ready to defend those accused of crimes merely because of their race. It also published a magazine, *The Crisis*, edited by Du Bois.

Except for the white reformers in the NAACP, most whites failed to consider the issue of civil rights for African Americans. Even so, during the Progressive Era, NAACP lawyers managed to win a number of civil rights

Reformer and educator
Booker T. Washington

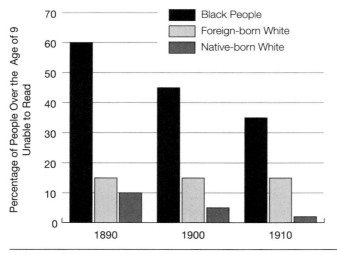

Illiteracy by Race, 1890–1910

cases in the Supreme Court. Between 1915 and 1917, the Court declared the following to be unconstitutional:

★ The "grandfather clause"

★ A segregated housing law

★ The practice of denying African Americans the right to serve on juries

★ The practice of denying African Americans the right to run for office in party primaries

Anti-Lynching Movement One of the NAACP's founders was an African American reporter from Tennessee, Ida B. Wells. She was appalled by the number of African Americans who were lynched, or hanged, by mobs of whites. There were more than 1,100 deaths of this brutal nature between 1900 and 1914. Wells wrote a muckraking book about the lynching evil and dedicated her career to the cause of racial justice.

Marcus Garvey While the NAACP worked for integration, a Jamaican immigrant named Marcus Garvey worked for the exact opposite. Coming to the United States in 1916, Garvey was deeply offended by the second-class status of African Americans. He decided that African Americans needed to take pride in their African heritage. In Jamaica, he had organized the Universal Negro Improvement Association (UNIA), which sponsored a "Back to Africa" movement. In the United States, UNIA attracted about 500,000 members. Garvey urged African Americans not to seek acceptance by the white majority. Instead, he believed that they should build their own institutions and leave the United States for Africa, their ancestors' homeland.

Garvey's leadership ended in 1925 when he was convicted of using the mails to defraud investors. In 1927 the U.S. government deported him to Jamaica.

W. E. B. Du Bois, African American leader against racial discrimination

Other Areas of Concern

Two other areas—the consequences of overindulgence in alcohol and prejudice by native-born Americans against minority cultures and religions—became the focus of progressive reformers.

Temperance/Prohibition Fighting alcohol abuse was another movement that attracted the energies of many women. Reformers in the *temperance movement*, as it was called, urged people not to drink alcoholic beverages and wanted to abolish the sale of alcoholic drinks in public places called saloons. They argued that excessive consumption of alcohol increased the poverty of working-class families. The most famous of the temperance crusaders were Frances Willard and Carrie Nation. Wielding a hatchet, Carrie Nation would march into the saloons of Kansas in the 1890s and destroy shelves of bottled liquor.

The temperance movement achieved its goal with the adoption in 1919 of the Eighteenth Amendment. Until its repeal in 1933, this amendment prohibited the manufacture and sale of alcoholic beverages in the United States.

Anti-Defamation League Jewish immigrants from Europe were often the target of native-born Americans' religious and cultural prejudices. To combat the unfair statements made about them, Jewish Americans organized the Anti-Defamation League in 1913.

★ In Review

1. How did the Supreme Court both assist and retard progressive reform at this time?
2. Define progressivism, muckraker, social justice, settlement house, and suffragist.

3. Describe the efforts of women and African Americans to bring about democratic reforms.

Progressivism and Governmental Action

In the early days of progressivism (from about 1890 to 1900), reformers focused on enacting progressive laws at the local and state levels. They did not become activist at the federal level until a progressive president, Theodore Roosevelt, came to power in 1901. In state and local politics, progressives sought reforms that would help the poor, regulate factory conditions, and expand democracy in the voting booth. Although their efforts began in the 1890s, they had their greatest successes between 1900 and 1916.

Political Reform

Whereas the Populist party was associated with issues and problems related to rural life, progressives were more concerned with reform in the cities. The growth in immigration had led to significant growth in urban population. In 1900, approximately 30 million Americans out of a population of 75 million lived in urban areas. Just 100 years earlier, America's urban population totaled no more than 5 percent of the people. Just as the urban population was growing, so was the middle class. Increasing numbers of lawyers, doctors, middle-management employees, teachers, and clerical workers swelled the ranks of the middle class. Many middle-class, native-born Americans opposed the alliance between political machines and immigrants in the large cities. Also, the middle class wanted mayors and governors to lower taxes, reduce the cost of government, and improve public services.

Municipal Reform Many cities in the late 1800s were controlled by party bosses and political machines. In cities such as New York and Boston, local party leaders provided financial aid to the recently arrived immigrants in exchange for loyalty at the polls. In an age when government did not yet provide an economic safety net in the form of unemployment insurance or welfare, the local party boss provided needed money for rent and food. At the same time, these local political leaders took bribes and kickbacks in return for contracts and jobs. Progressive reformers with middle-class support now attempted to break the power of local party bosses in order to reduce the cost of government, lower taxes, and end corruption.

The progressive movement was in part a response to the need for fiscal responsibility at a time when the need for services by local government was on the increase. In the larger cities, there was a growing need for bridges, subways, electric trolley cars, gas and electricity, and telephone service. Reformers were concerned that the growth in services would lead to graft and corruption.

In the early 1900s, progressive mayors in several large cities succeeded in winning electoral support to remove from power politicians associated with political machines. For example, mayors such as Tom Johnson in Cleveland and Samuel ("Golden Rule") Jones in Toledo, Ohio, provided efficient transportation services and honest government after being elected to office. Too often, though, reform politicians were unable to hold on to power when they failed to meet the needs of the growing ethnic minorities within their cities.

State Reform A great leader in the fight for state reform was the governor of Wisconsin, Robert ("Battling Bob") La Follette. In Wisconsin, as elsewhere, the railroads, political bosses, and business interests were hard to beat, but La Follette managed to rally voters to his cause and overcome opposition in the legislature. The direct primary, tax reform, curbs on businesses, and the use of technical experts were among many reforms that gave Wisconsin a nationwide reputation as a "laboratory for democracy."

Oregon was the first state to use the initiative and referendum (see below).

★ The *direct primary*: Instead of state conventions nominating candidates for office, the voters would nominate them by direct popular vote in a primary election (an early election before the general election in November).

★ The *initiative*: By signing a petition, a small percentage of voters could force the state legislature to consider a proposed law.

★ The *referendum*: A proposed law could be submitted directly to the people to be voted on in an election.

★ The *recall*: In a special election, people could vote on whether to remove an elected official from office before the end of his or her term.

Together with these reforms, many states adopted the *Australian ballot*, or secret ballot. Instead of openly marking a ballot issued by a political party, voters would enter a curtained booth and vote in secret using an official ballot printed by the state government.

In New York State, Theodore Roosevelt, who would later serve as the first progressive president, won election as governor in the late 1890s. As governor, he angered several major political leaders in New York with his sympathy for civil service reform. As a result, these leaders succeeded in having him selected as the vice presidential candidate on the Republican ticket under William McKinley. Prior to serving as governor, Roosevelt had served as president of the New York board of police commissioners where he sought to end police corruption.

Economic, Environmental, and Social Reforms

In addition to political reform, progressives also engaged in economic, environmental, and social reforms.

Progressives in every state in the country campaigned vigorously to stop employers from exploiting children. By 1914, child labor laws had been enacted by nearly all the states, although some of the laws were weak and easily evaded. For public health improvement, engineers and urban planners were called in to help develop new methods for sanitation and garbage removal. These engineers designed and built bridges and tunnels and put up street lighting to make cities safer at night. Building codes were established to increase safety in the new housing under construction in large cities. Mandatory education requirements grew as an increasing number of children attended public schools. Some progressives intervened directly in the lives of the urban poor by establishing settlement houses (see page 273).

Theodore Roosevelt and the Square Deal (1901–1909)

At 42 years of age, Theodore Roosevelt, affectionately called "Teddy" or T. R. by his many admirers, became the youngest president in U.S. history. He had been a progressive governor of New York in the 1890s, a hero of the Spanish-American War in 1898, and a successful candidate for vice president in the election of 1900. The Republican president in 1901, William McKinley, was known for his conservative policies during a previous term (1897–1901). When an assassin shot and killed McKinley shortly after his second term began, Theodore Roosevelt became president.

Almost immediately, the young president showed a bold style of leadership that excited the imagination of the voting public. He promised a *Square Deal* to all groups in the American population: labor as well as business, the poor as well as the rich. Said Roosevelt: "While I am president I want the laboring man to feel he has the same right of access to me as the capitalist has. Our doors swing open as easily to the wage workers as to the heads of the big corporation." As a champion of reform, Roosevelt acted on many fronts—dismantling trusts, pushing for new regulatory laws, settling labor disputes, and conserving the American wilderness.

The prevailing philosophy of government throughout the late 1800s was laissez-faire. Government was not expected to intervene in the economic activities of big business. At times, however, presidents in the late 1800s did intervene on the side of big business. For example, Grover Cleveland intervened in the Pullman strike of 1894 (see page 216). Roosevelt, however, believed in the *stewardship theory*—that presidents had an obligation to guide the nation's economic and political affairs. Since a depression in the 1890s caused business to slump and many workers to lose their jobs, Roosevelt felt that it was the responsibility of presidents to take action to create better conditions.

As president, Roosevelt demonstrated his activism by settling a strike of Pennsylvania coal miners in 1902. Recall that earlier presidents had used troops to support big business and break strikes. Roosevelt showed an unusual respect for the cause of labor by inviting to the White House the leaders of both the coal miners' union and the mining company. The strike was settled when the company agreed to a shorter workday and a 10 percent increase in miners' wages. This action was an example of Roosevelt's Square Deal philosophy.

Business Regulation and Consumer Protection

Roosevelt was also the first president to persuade Congress to enact a number of reform laws concerning railroads:

★ The Elkins Act (1903) strengthened the Interstate Commerce Commission (created in 1887) by providing for the punishment of railroads that granted *rebates* (special reductions in price) to favored customers.

★ The Hepburn Act (1906) gave the Interstate Commerce Commission the power to fix the rates that railroads charged for their services. It also strictly limited the free passes that railroads gave out to politicians and business owners.

In addition, Roosevelt persuaded Congress to pass consumer protection laws such as the Pure Food and Drug Act (1906) and the Meat Inspection Act (1906). (See pages 272–273.)

"Trust-Busting" Court Cases   Roosevelt was the first president to make a serious effort to enforce the Sherman Antitrust Act of 1890. People were amazed when he announced his decision to prosecute the Northern Securities Company, a powerful holding company that controlled several western railroads. In its decision in *Northern Securities Co. v. United States* in 1904, the Supreme Court concluded that the president's move to break up Northern Securities was proper and constitutional. After this victory, Roosevelt broke up other business combinations, including the Standard Oil Company.

Although Roosevelt was popularly known as a *trust buster* (a breaker of monopolistic businesses), he was not an enemy of big business. He always distinguished between "good trusts" (those that acted responsibly) and "bad trusts" (those that ignored the public interest). Only the latter were targets for his trust busting. This differentiation was often called the "rule of reason."

Conservation

Perhaps the most important of Roosevelt's reforms were his efforts to protect the nation's natural resources. Having hiked and camped in the West, Roosevelt appreciated the beauty of wilderness areas and did not want to see them exploited recklessly by mining and lumbering companies. He stated that "the forest and water problems are perhaps the most vital inter-

Cartoon of "Teddy" Roosevelt, trust buster

nal problems of the United States." From the beginning to the end of his presidency, Roosevelt tried to win public support for *conservation*—the wise management and careful use of the natural environment.

Federal Legislation and Projects Inspired by his leadership, Congress passed two major conservation laws:

★ The Newlands Reclamation Act (1902) provided that money from the sale of desert lands in the West be used to finance irrigation projects.

★ The Inland Waterways Act (1907) provided for the appointment of a commission to study the use of the nation's major rivers.

In addition, President Roosevelt used a previously existing law, the Forest Reserve Act, to establish 149 national forests totaling more than 190 million acres. All such forests were publicly owned and strictly controlled by officials in the U.S. Forest Service.

Gifford Pinchot and John Muir Two men who helped Theodore Roosevelt formulate his conservation policies were Gifford Pinchot and John Muir.

Roosevelt appointed Gifford Pinchot head of the National Forest Service. He had long attempted to persuade private lumber companies to use appropriate environmental methods when cutting down trees. He demanded that lumber companies replant trees to replace those that had been cut down. He also insisted that only fully grown trees could be cut down.

John Muir, a conservationist, was a long-time supporter of national parks. Prior to Roosevelt's administration, he had supported bills to create a national park in Yosemite Valley in California. During Roosevelt's administration, he supported the setting aside of additional forestlands and the establishment of national parks in Mesa Verde in Colorado and the Grand Canyon in Arizona.

Controversy Under President Taft (1909–1913)

Roosevelt chose a trusted member of his cabinet, William Howard Taft, to be the Republican nominee for president in 1908. Roosevelt hoped that his progressive policies would be continued by Taft. Taft won the election easily. Although he believed in progressive ideas, Taft lacked Roosevelt's energetic style of leadership. Progressive Republicans in Congress—and even Roosevelt himself—soon grew impatient with him.

In one respect, Taft proved even more aggressive than his predecessor. He ordered the Justice Department to prosecute 90 businesses for violating the antitrust law (compared to 44 such cases prosecuted under Roosevelt).

On two issues—tariff reform and conservation—Taft failed to give the leadership that reformers expected from him. They were disappointed with the results of a struggle to lower tariff rates. Instead of lowering prices on imports, as progressives had wanted, the new Payne-Aldrich Tariff (1909) raised prices on many products. Taft signed the tariff act into law over the protests of progressive members of Congress.

Progressives were even more upset when Taft fired Gifford Pinchot, the head of the Forest Service. As a friend of Pinchot, Roosevelt was especially angered by Taft's action. It seemed to many progressives that Taft was secretly going along with selfish business interests rather than fighting for conservation and low tariffs. Unhappy reformers in the Republican party invited Roosevelt to seek the Republican nomination for another term as president. The popular ex-president accepted.

Woodrow Wilson
and the New Freedom (1913–1921)

Wilson was only the second Democrat to be elected president since the Civil War. (Grover Cleveland had been the first.) In his inaugural address in

1913, he announced a sweeping program of economic reform, which he called the *New Freedom*. He proposed reforms of three kinds: a lower tariff, more effective regulation of big business, and a reformed system of banking.

Progressivism and the 1912 Election

The election of 1912 was one of the most unusual and exciting elections in U.S. history. It involved three major candidates for president (Roosevelt, Taft, and Wilson) and a fourth candidate of a minor party (Eugene V. Debs).

Taft Conservatives in the Republican party rallied around the president. They nominated Taft rather than Roosevelt.

Roosevelt Angered by their defeat in the Republican national convention, progressive supporters of Theodore Roosevelt decided to form a new political party. The Progressive party, as they called it, was also known as the *Bull Moose party* after its candidate, Roosevelt, described himself as "strong as a bull moose."

Wilson Born in Virginia, Woodrow Wilson had moved to New Jersey as a college professor and won national attention as a progressive governor of

The Election of 1912

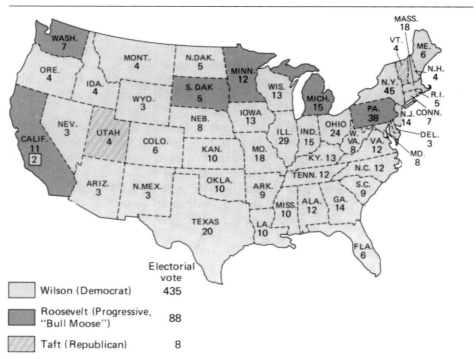

	Electorial vote
Wilson (Democrat)	435
Roosevelt (Progressive, "Bull Moose")	88
Taft (Republican)	8

that state. He was a newcomer in Democratic national politics in 1912 but managed to win the nomination of his party after a long and bitter struggle on the convention floor.

Debs Since 1900, the Socialist party had steadily gained in strength and numbers. It championed the interests of industrial workers and put forth the radical idea that all major industries should be owned and operated by the U.S. government. Its presidential candidate, Eugene Debs, the labor leader from Indiana, campaigned with great energy and zeal.

Election Results Wilson won with 435 electoral votes. Neither Taft nor Roosevelt had much chance of victory because they divided the Republican vote between them. Roosevelt won 88 electoral votes, far better than Taft's 8 electoral votes. Debs received not a single electoral vote, even though he polled nearly a million popular votes. Because all the candidates claimed to be reformers—even Taft—it seemed that the entire nation was now eager for reform.

Underwood Tariff/Graduated Income Tax

Addressing a special session of Congress, the new president said: "The tariff duties must be altered." When Congress balked, Wilson appealed to the American people to put pressure on their representatives. They did, and the Underwood Tariff became law (1913). One effect of the lower tariffs was to lower the price of many consumer goods. Another effect was to remove the special protection that big business had enjoyed for more than 20 years (since the enactment of the very high McKinley Tariff of 1890).

The Sixteenth Amendment (1913) gave Congress the power to collect a tax on incomes and removed an earlier requirement that such a tax be apportioned according to a state's population. The tax was considered democratic because, at first, it was collected only from people with extremely high incomes. It was also a *graduated income tax*, or progressive income tax. Such tax has a rate schedule that goes higher as a person's reported income increases.

Clayton Antitrust Act

President Wilson insisted on a stronger antitrust law and a federal commission to ensure fair business practices. From his struggle with Congress emerged the Clayton Antitrust Act (1914). This act greatly strengthened the Sherman Antitrust Act of 1890.

Instead of the vague clauses of the original act, the new act listed specific business practices that would now be illegal. It said businesses could not grow bigger by organizing holding companies. Further, the new law said that the same people could not sit on the boards of directors of several companies. In other words, *interlocking directorships* were now illegal. Also illegal were secret agreements among companies to "fix" prices (charge the same prices for the same products).

One clause of the Clayton Act pleased union leaders. It provided that labor unions, which had been prosecuted as monopolies under the Sherman Act, could no longer be prosecuted on charges of breaking the antitrust laws.

Federal Trade Commission Act

President Wilson also fought for the Federal Trade Commission Act, which Congress passed in 1914. The federal agency created by this act—the Federal Trade Commission (FTC)—was given power to (1) investigate business practices suspected of being unfair and (2) issue orders demanding that companies "cease and desist" from acting in illegal ways, as defined by the antitrust laws.

Thus, while the Clayton Antitrust Act sought to limit the growth of monopolies, the Federal Trade Commission Act sought to regulate the practices of big business.

The Progressive Movement: Causes and Effects

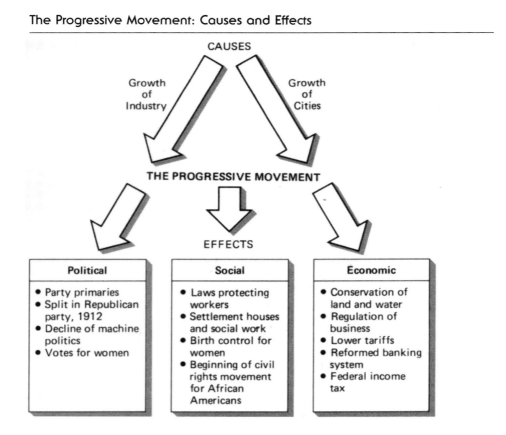

CAUSES

Growth of Industry

Growth of Cities

THE PROGRESSIVE MOVEMENT

EFFECTS

Political	Social	Economic
• Party primaries • Split in Republican party, 1912 • Decline of machine politics • Votes for women	• Laws protecting workers • Settlement houses and social work • Birth control for women • Beginning of civil rights movement for African Americans	• Conservation of land and water • Regulation of business • Lower tariffs • Reformed banking system • Federal income tax

Federal Reserve System

Before Wilson's administration, there had been no federal system for expanding or contracting the nation's supply of currency (money) when businesses' need for currency expanded or contracted. Wilson recognized that the growing industrial nation required an organized banking system.

In the past, private banks often had too little money in *reserve* (kept in their vaults). If hundreds of customers demanded the withdrawal of their money at the same time, a bank with a low reserve of currency might collapse and fail (go bankrupt). Many banks failing at once would cause the whole U.S. economy to sink into a depression.

The progressive solution to this problem, supported by Wilson, was to create a system of central banks called the *Federal Reserve System*. Private banks now kept their cash reserves in 12 Federal Reserve regional banks. The general policy for these banks would be made by a small group of U.S. officials—the Federal Reserve Board. The regional banks could make loans to private banks around the country at interest rates set by the governing board. The loans consisted of a paper currency printed by the U.S. government as Federal Reserve notes (dollar bills). This is the currency that Americans have used ever since the Federal Reserve Act was passed by Congress in 1913.

The Federal Reserve System makes it possible for the supply of currency to expand or contract according to the changing needs of business. Also, the interest rates charged by the Federal Reserve regional banks indirectly affect the interest rates of all banks and thus give the U.S. government the power to influence the entire national economy.

Expanding and Contracting Democracy

Direct Election of Senators (1913) The Seventeenth Amendment required that the senators from every state be elected by the voters of the state (not by state legislatures, as in the past). This helped reduce the influence of special interests, particularly big business, in the selection of senators.

Women's Suffrage Amendment (1920) As you recall from Chapter 10, women had worked for many years to gain voting rights. Their efforts were finally rewarded with the passage of the Nineteenth Amendment, which was nicknamed the "Susan B. Anthony Amendment" in honor of the leader who had first championed it. It stated: "The right of citizens of the United States to vote shall not be denied or abridged by the United States or by any state on account of sex." Suddenly, the number of people eligible to vote in U.S. elections nearly doubled.

Segregation Policies of Woodrow Wilson Though progressive in other ways, Wilson did not appear to be concerned about the civil rights of African Americans. He ordered the washrooms in federal buildings in the nation's

Suffragists celebrating the Nineteenth Amendment

capital to be strictly segregated. In each building, African Americans were limited to using only one washroom. When a group of African Americans came to the White House to protest Wilson's policies, the president angrily dismissed them.

World War I and Domestic Reform

In 1917, the United States entered World War I. During wartime, there was an emphasis on cooperation between government and big business in order to produce the greatest amount of war supplies in the shortest amount of time. Thus, government stopped regulating big businesses and began working with them. After the war, few citizens wanted to return to reform efforts. They were more interested in acquiring goods and services. As a result, the three Republican presidents who followed Woodrow Wilson promoted conservative rather than progressive policies. A new age of laissez-faire was at hand.

★ In Review

1. Define initiative, referendum, recall, direct primary, and Australian ballot.
2. For each of the following concerns, describe a specific reform of the Progressive Era that is associated with it: (a) consumer safety, (b) trusts, (c) natural resources, (d) tariffs, and (e) banks.

3. Describe the main features of Theodore Roosevelt's Square Deal program and Woodrow Wilson's New Freedom program.

MULTIPLE-CHOICE QUESTIONS

Use the cartoon on page 269 to answer questions 1 and 2.

1. The cartoon takes the position that
   (1) the progressive view of the proper relationship between government and business correctly meets the needs of the most people
   (2) a policy of laissez-faire is the best means of protecting both the public and business from corruption
   (3) workers should take part in the running of American corporations
   (4) a combination of business practices from the early and late 19th century is needed for a strong economy.

2. Which of the following would most likely disagree with the viewpoint expressed in the cartoon?
   (1) John D. Rockefeller and Andrew Carnegie
   (2) Samuel Gompers and Eugene V. Debs
   (3) Theodore Roosevelt and Robert La Follette
   (4) Upton Sinclair and Lincoln Steffens.

3. Which person might correctly be called a muckraker?
   (1) a cartoonist with strong conservative biases
   (2) a reporter during the Age of Jackson
   (3) a conservationist in the time of Theodore Roosevelt
   (4) a writer who investigates corruption in politics.

4. What problem did Elizabeth Cady Stanton and Susan B. Anthony hope to correct?
   (1) scarcity of free public schools
   (2) few legal and political rights for women
   (3) inadequate medical care
   (4) unfair treatment of ethnic minorities.

5. The main purpose of the initiative, referendum, and recall was to
   (1) reduce federal control over local government
   (2) enlarge citizens' control over state and local governments
   (3) stimulate economic growth
   (4) restore the balance between state and federal power.

Use the map on page 284 to answer questions 6 and 7.

6. Which is a conclusion that can be drawn from the map?
   (1) Third parties rarely have political influence.
   (2) The Progressive ("Bull Moose") party received more votes than did the Republican party.
   (3) The nation had become tired of progressive ideas.
   (4) Theodore Roosevelt carried the popular vote but lost the election.

7. An explanation of the results of the election of 1912 is that
   (1) President William Howard Taft failed to pursue the trust-busting policies of Theodore Roosevelt
   (2) Woodrow Wilson ran on a platform that, for the first time, appealed to African American voters
   (3) the Republican party split between followers of William Howard Taft and Theodore Roosevelt
   (4) people did not want to vote for Theodore Roosevelt because he would have served for a third term.

Use the chart on page 286 to answer questions 8 and 9.

8. The chart shows that the Progressive movement was
   (1) brought about by a group of ambitious politicians from cities and private industries
   (2) primarily a western rural experience
   (3) a result of the abuses that developed from rapid industrial and urban development
   (4) started by corporations and political organizations such as the New York Central Railroad and Tammany Hall.

9. Which best reflects the beginnings of the civil rights movement for African Americans, as expressed in the chart?
   (1) the passage of antilynching legislation
   (2) court decisions that outlawed Jim Crow laws
   (3) the policies of President Woodrow Wilson
   (4) the work of W. E. B. DuBois and Booker T. Washington.

10. A chief function of the Federal Reserve System was to
    (1) make loans to farmers
    (2) regulate international trade
    (3) balance the federal budget
    (4) regulate the amount of money in circulation.

THEMATIC ESSAYS

1. **Theme:** The Progressive Era and Reform

   The Progressive Era in the United States involved a broad span of reform that had far-reaching effects on the society at large.

   Task: Choose two areas in which reform was attempted during the Progressive Era. For each reform chosen:

   ★ Describe the problem that the reform attempted to correct.

★ Show how the reform attempted to correct the problem.

★ Evaluate the success of the reform in correcting the problem.

You may wish to include in your answer such topics as consumer protection, poverty and immigration, women's rights, and the attempts of African Americans to gain their civil rights.

2. **Theme:** The Progressive Era and Presidential Power

The Progressive Era in U.S. history was brought about largely through the activism of Presidents Theodore Roosevelt and Woodrow Wilson.

Task: Select one example of presidential activism on the part of Theodore Roosevelt and another by Woodrow Wilson.

★ Show how each president was trying to correct a specific existing problem. (Do not treat the same problem for both presidents.)

★ Demonstrate how each president expanded the power of the federal government.

You may select such topics as trust busting and conservation for Theodore Roosevelt, and tax reform and monetary policy for Woodrow Wilson.

DOCUMENT-BASED QUESTION

*Read each document and answer the question that follows it. Then read the **Task** and write your essay. Essays should include references to most of the documents along with additional information based on your knowledge of United States history and government.*

Historical Context: The reforms of the Progressive Era were a response to the many problems resulting from the Civil War, industrialization, and urbanization.

Document 1 From *Lochner* v. *New York*:

Statutes of the nature of that under review, limiting the hours in which grown and intelligent men may labor to earn their living, are mere meddlesome interferences with the rights of the individual, and they are not saved from condemnation by the claim that they are passed in the exercise of the police power and upon the subject of the health of the individual whose rights are interfered with, unless there be some fair ground, reasonable in and of itself, to say that there is material danger to the public health, or to the health of the employees, if the hours of labor are not curtailed.

Question: Why did the Supreme Court declare the New York State law limiting the hours of bakers to be unconstitutional?

Document 2   From *Muller* v. *Oregon*:

> . . . as healthy mothers are essential to vigorous offspring, the physical well-being of woman becomes an object of public interest and care in order to preserve the strength and vigor of the race. . . .
>   . . . Differentiated by these matters from the other sex, she is properly placed in a class by herself and legislation designed for her protection may be sustained, even when like legislation is not necessary for men and could not be sustained.

Question: Why did the Supreme Court protect female workers?

Document 3   Refer to the excerpt from Upton Sinclair's *The Jungle* on page 272.

Question: What was muckraker Upton Sinclair showing his readers about the meatpacking industry?

Document 4   Refer to the cartoon on page 273.

Question: Why does the cartoonist feel that the disease of cholera might spread?

Document 5   Refer to the graph on page 276.

Question: How does the graph show *both* progress and problems for African Americans living between 1890 and 1910?

Document 6   Refer to the cartoon on page 282.

Question: How does the cartoon illustrate what President Theodore Roosevelt did about monopolies that hurt the public (bad trusts)?

Task

★ Describe two of the problems that existed at the end of the 19th and the beginning of the 20th century.
★ Choose one of the problems that you have selected and show to what extent it was either solved or remained a problem.

Chapter 11
The Rise of American Power

★ **Objectives**

★ To analyze reasons for increased U.S. involvement in Asia and Latin America from 1890 to 1920.

★ To evaluate arguments for and against intervention in the affairs of Latin American nations.

★ To identify the causes of World War I.

★ To describe and explain the change in U.S. foreign policy from neutrality to involvement.

★ To understand the impact of wartime on the civil liberties of Americans.

★ To appraise U.S. contributions to peace and arms control after World War I.

★ To evaluate whether or not the United States made the right choices during and after the war.

From Old Diplomacy to New

The period from 1865 to 1900 saw the United States become increasingly involved in global affairs.

The end of the Civil War in 1865 and the growth of industrialization led to increasing American power and a change in U.S. diplomacy.

Communications Technology

A revolution in communications technology began to bring the world closer together between 1865 and 1900. The development of the telegraph and the Morse Code prior to the Civil War led to speedier communication over long distances. In the post–Civil War period, Cyrus Fields, after four failures, successfully completed a transatlantic cable in 1866. It allowed messages to travel through cables at the bottom of the ocean floor between Europe and the United States. At the same time, improved steamships made passage between Europe and the United States faster. As a result of these improvements in communication, Europe no longer seemed so distant from the United States.

American Attitudes Toward Internationalism

There was much disagreement about whether the United States should expand its power and take on a greater role in international affairs by adopting *imperialism* (expansionist policies). It was obvious that the United States, like the nations of Europe, was rapidly industrializing. It was also obvious that U.S. trade was growing. But did this mean that the United States had to enter the race for overseas colonies?

Arguments for Expansion Many U.S. businesses favored expanding U.S. power for economic reasons. Until about 1890, the settlement of the West had provided businesses with new markets for farm machinery and other products. It also opened up rich sources of copper, silver, and other needed materials. But after the physical frontier had been settled, some business leaders looked for new economic frontiers—new markets, new investment opportunities—in the vast, nonindustrialized world beyond U.S. borders. Many Americans also believed that the manifest destiny that had justified expansion from ocean to ocean now justified increasing the U.S. role in world affairs.

Some people also proposed cultural reasons for expansion. Protestant missionaries believed it was their moral duty to spread the message of Christianity to all parts of the world. Josiah Strong, an influential minister and author, argued that less developed regions of the world would benefit from being governed by the "advanced" civilizations of the West. He believed that the benefits of Christianity and U.S. civilization were practically one and the same. This belief was based on Social Darwinism. The idea of superior individuals and companies was replaced by the idea of superior nations such as the United States. Thus, Social Darwinism supported cultural superiority.

Arguments Against Expansion Some Americans opposed expansion for both moral and practical reasons. They thought the United States should follow President Washington's advice and focus on trade without political involvement. In their view, democracy would suffer if the United States took over foreign places and thereby denied native peoples their political rights and independence. In addition, opponents believed that manifest destiny had ended with American expansion to the Pacific. In their view, manifest destiny did not justify military expansion to Asia and Latin America.

Some feared that foreign involvement would lead to foreign wars. Even some businesspeople questioned the need for territorial gains, arguing that wars would harm rather than help overseas trade.

The United States (Theodore Roosevelt) as the world's policeman, in a 1905 cartoon

Growth of Naval Power

Some Americans wanted to acquire overseas territories for strategic reasons. Alfred Thayer Mahan, a U.S. naval captain, published a book in the 1890s pointing out the importance of sea power to a nation like Great Britain. He argued that U.S. security also depended on having a strong navy. Because ships of the industrial age were powered by coal-burning steam engines (not wind), the U.S. Navy needed to establish bases in the Atlantic and Pacific oceans where ships could pick up coal at strategically located islands. Furthermore, Mahan argued, increased U.S. trade with Asia and Latin America would depend on a larger navy to protect that trade against European rivals.

"Opening" of Japan

For many years, Japan was even less interested than China in trading with Europeans and Americans. It became more open to trade after 1853, the year that Commodore Matthew Perry arrived in Japan with an American fleet. Perry wanted to open trade with Japan and gain assurances that Japan would assist shipwrecked U.S. sailors. He brought gifts demonstrating the benefits of industrial technology and, in a show of force, fired off

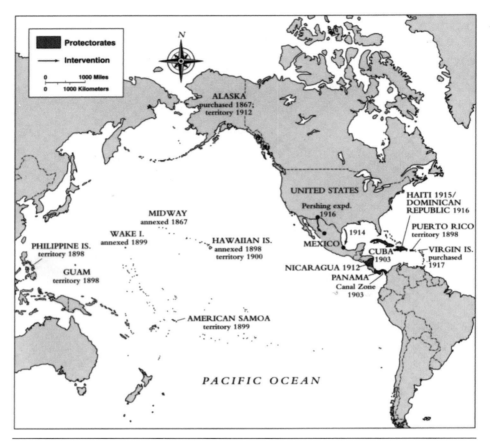

U.S. Territories and Protectorates in 1917

the fleet's guns. Japanese officials were sufficiently impressed to sign a trade treaty with the United States in 1854. Soon afterward, new leadership in Japan adopted a policy of learning Western technologies and making Japan into a modern industrial nation.

United States and China

In 1895, Japan defeated China in the Sino-Japanese War. The Japanese army and navy crushed the much weaker forces of the Chinese. It was clear that China could not defend itself against the imperialist ambitions of stronger rivals. It was also clear that Japan had become a major power in East Asia because of its successful efforts to industrialize.

After Japan defeated China, its armies occupied Korea and the Chinese island of Taiwan. Japan also won overall economic control of Manchuria in northern China. Manchuria became known as Japan's *sphere of influence*, which meant that Japan enjoyed special privileges in the region and more or less controlled its trade and industrial growth. Russia disputed Japan's control of Manchuria until 1904, when Russia's defeat in a war with Japan forced it to give up its claim.

Competition for Spheres of Influence

Following Japan's example, France, Germany, Russia, and Great Britain forced the Chinese government to grant other spheres of influence. It appeared as if all of China might be divided into such spheres. The U.S. government feared that America's long-standing trade with China might be cut off completely.

"Open Door" Notes

John Hay was the secretary of state for two presidents, William McKinley and Theodore Roosevelt. To oppose the spheres of influence in China and

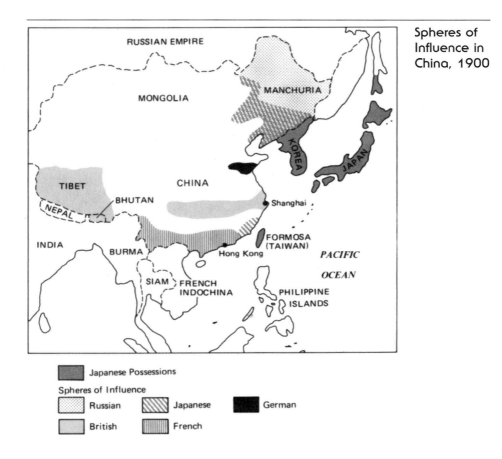

Spheres of Influence in China, 1900

keep the door open for U.S. businesses, Hay composed two diplomatic notes, one in 1899, the other in 1900. The first note called on the European powers and Japan to agree to an *Open Door policy* in China. Such a policy would mean that all nations would have "equal trading rights" in China and that none would have to pay higher port fees or taxes than any other. The second note suggested that all powers in East Asia respect the territorial integrity of China. In other words, no nation would compel China to give up the control of any of its own territory.

The various replies to Hay's notes were intentionally vague and evasive. But the U.S. government stood firmly committed to an Open Door policy in China. It would remain committed to that policy through the 1930s and early 1940s, when Japanese troops occupied much of China. U.S. involvement in World War II was partly a response to Japan's violation of the Open Door.

Boxer Rebellion

The people of China resented the imperialist policies of the Western powers. Many joined a nationalist organization named the Society of Righteous and Harmonious Fists—also known as the Boxers. The aim of the Boxers was to drive the "foreign devils" out of China. In 1900, the Boxers took action. They killed Chinese who supported Westerners and some European and Americans, especially Christian missionaries. They also attacked Western embassies in the Chinese capital of Peking (now Beijing). The United States, Japan, and the European powers put together an international army to rescue those trapped in the embassies. This force crushed the Boxer Rebellion.

The foreign powers forced China to pay them an *indemnity* (a sum of money to cover damages and deaths). But the United States stood by its commitment to respect the territorial integrity of China and insisted that the other powers do likewise. The U.S. Congress voted to return the U.S. portion of the indemnity to China. This gesture of friendship greatly impressed China's government. It used most of the returned money to pay for scholarships for Chinese students to attend U.S. colleges and universities.

Other Pacific Overtures

Acquisition of Hawaii

The acquisition of the Hawaiian islands in the Pacific is a good example of U.S. imperialism—and also of one president's opposition to imperialism. In the late 1800s, a group of American sugar growers in Hawaii made several attempts to overthrow the native Hawaiian ruler. Finally, in 1893, with the help of U.S. Marines, the sugar growers succeeded in overthrowing Hawaii's Queen Liliuokalani. But President Grover Cleveland opposed an imperialist policy and rejected the sugar growers' plan for turning over

Hawaii to the United States. Hawaii remained independent for a few more years. But the next president, William McKinley, was strongly influenced by imperialists in the Republican party and pushed to make Hawaii a U.S. territory.

In 1900 a treaty providing for the annexation of Hawaii was approved by the Senate. (Hawaii entered the Union as the 50th state in 1959.)

Naval Bases in Samoa

Far to the southwest of Hawaii lie a group of Pacific islands called Samoa. A few Americans thought Samoa would make a good U.S. naval base. But Germany and Great Britain also expressed interest in taking over the islands. At one point in the 1880s, it appeared that Germany and the United States might go to war over these small islands, which few people knew existed. However, the threat of war passed.

In the late 1890s, Germany and the United States agreed to divide Samoa, each taking control of different islands.

Spanish-American War

In 1895, a revolt against Spanish rule broke out in Cuba. Three years later, the United States came to the support of the Cuban people by declaring war against Spain. More than any other event, this war represented a turning point in U.S. foreign policy. The swift and decisive U.S. victory in that war demonstrated that the United States was truly a major military power as well as a leading economic power. How did this brief but important war come about?

Causes of War

The American people's sympathy for the Cuban rebels played a large role in bringing about the U.S. war with Spain. Americans' sympathies were fanned almost daily by sensational headlines in the newspapers.

"Yellow Journalism" The newspapers of the 1890s attracted readers by playing up scandalous and sensational news. News stories that used big headlines, dramatic pictures, and emotional writing were known as *yellow journalism*. Especially influential were the New York City newspapers owned by William Randolph Hearst and Joseph Pulitzer. Both publishers squeezed all the sensation they could out of the violent conflict in Cuba. Their reporters wrote of the terrible suffering of the Cuban people and the brutal acts of Valeriano Weyler, a Spanish general nicknamed "Butcher" Weyler. Reports of Spanish atrocities were often greatly exaggerated.

De Lôme Letter Early in 1898, Hearst's *New York Journal* caused a sensation by printing a stolen letter that seemed to insult U.S. President William McKinley. The author of the letter was the Spanish minister to the United States, Dupuy de Lôme. Many Americans were outraged by the minister's description of the president as "weak and a bidder for the admiration of the crowd."

Sinking of the *Maine* Only a few days later came even more shocking news. The U.S.S. *Maine*, an American battleship anchored in the harbor of Havana, Cuba, had mysteriously exploded and sunk, killing about 250 of its crew. It was not known then—or even today—what caused the explosion. But the newspapers made it seem as if Spain had deliberately blown up the U.S. ship. After this incident, editorials in the yellow press urged that the U.S. government go to war to help liberate Cuba from Spanish rule.

Additional Reasons Besides the public emotions stirred up by sensational news stories, there were other reasons for war. A strategic reason was that military and naval planners thought Cuba might provide an ideal naval base for U.S. ships. They also argued that an island only 90 miles from Florida should not belong to a European power. An economic reason was that Americans had invested $50 million in Cuba's sugar and tobacco plantations. One way to protect that investment was to drive out an unfriendly Spanish government and substitute a friendlier Cuban one.

Decision for War

Not everyone favored the idea of a war with Spain. Some business leaders feared that such a war might lead to the destruction of American-owned

Cartoon showing Cuba as a pawn in the U.S.–Spanish power play

properties. There was also a good diplomatic reason for avoiding war. After the sinking of the *Maine*, Spain agreed to virtually all of the U.S. demands concerning Cuba. Spain pledged, for example, that it would eventually grant Cuba its independence.

Even so, President McKinley decided that most Americans expected him to take the country to war. In April 1898, he asked Congress for a declaration of war against Spain. Congress readily complied.

In April 1898, President William McKinley wrote a lengthy message to Congress explaining why he believed the United States should declare war against Spain. The excerpt below from the president's message briefly summarizes the grounds for intervention in Cuba.

A "Splendid Little War"

The Spanish-American War lasted only about four months, and Americans won every major battle. From the U.S. point of view, it seemed a "splendid little war," as one American called it. It was fought on two fronts—the islands of Cuba and Puerto Rico in the Caribbean and the Philippine Islands in the Pacific.

In Cuba, a troop of U.S. volunteers known as the Rough Riders won instant fame and glory by following their leader, Theodore Roosevelt, in a bold and successful charge up San Juan Hill. African Americans in the reg-

★ ★ ★ ★ ★

MCKINLEY'S WAR MESSAGE TO CONGRESS, 1898

First, in the cause of humanity and to put an end to the barbarities, bloodshed, starvation, and horrible miseries now existing there, and which the parties to the conflict are either unable or unwilling to stop or mitigate. It is no answer to say this is all in another country, belonging to another nation, and is therefore none of our business. It is specially our duty, for it is right at our door.

Second, we owe it to our citizens in Cuba to afford them that protection and indemnity for life and property which no government there can or will afford, and to that end to terminate the conditions that deprive them of legal protection.

Third, the right to intervene may be justified by the very serious injury to the commerce, trade, and business of our people, and by the wanton destruction of property and devastation of the island.

Fourth, and which is of the utmost importance, the present condition of affairs in Cuba is a constant menace to our peace, and entails upon this government an enormous expense.

ular U.S. Army participated in the charge and spearheaded another attack in the Battle of El Caney. The battles of San Juan Hill and El Caney led to the Spanish surrender of the Cuban port of Santiago. At the same time, the neighboring island of Puerto Rico—a Spanish colony since 1508—fell to the invading Americans.

In the Pacific, the U.S. Navy distinguished itself in a devastating attack against the Spanish fleet in Manila Bay, near the Philippine capital of Manila. Commander George Dewey's overwhelming victory in this naval battle made him an American hero (he was promoted to admiral by Congress in 1899). But the attack, so far from Cuba, took most Americans by surprise. Many, including President McKinley, had to search to find the Philippines on a map. Only by reading the newspapers did Americans learn that the Philippines had been a Spanish possession since the 1500s. The Filipinos—like the Cubans—had been fighting for their independence from Spain when U.S. troops arrived. The Filipinos celebrated the U.S. victory at Manila Bay, fully expecting independence to be the result. Instead, they were bitterly disappointed by the terms of the U.S.–Spanish treaty of peace.

Results of the War

The terms of the treaty, signed in December, 1898, were as follows:

★ Spain gave two islands to the United States: Puerto Rico in the Caribbean and Guam in the Pacific. (See map, page 296.)

★ Spain granted Cuba its independence.

★ Spain "sold" the Philippines to the United States for the bargain price of only $20 million.

United States Empire

For economic reasons, the people of Puerto Rico thought it would be to their advantage to be included in the U.S. empire. By the terms of a U.S. law (the Foraker Act, 1900), Puerto Ricans were allowed to elect representatives to their own legislature, but their governor was appointed by the U.S. president.

Although Spain had already granted Cuban independence, the U.S. position was unclear. President McKinley and Congress finally decided that Cuba should be permitted its independence, but with certain conditions attached. In 1901, these conditions were included in an amendment to a military bill. The *Platt Amendment*, as it was called, provided that:

★ Cuba would sell or lease a piece of land to the United States for use as a naval and coaling station.

★ Cuba would not allow any foreign power other than the United States to acquire Cuban territory.

★ Cuba would allow the United States to intervene in the country whenever it was necessary to protect American citizens living in Cuba.

Cubans strongly protested these terms. But, by a treaty of 1903, they finally accepted the Platt Amendment when the United States insisted upon it as the condition for removing its troops.

Debate Over Acquisition of the Philippines

American public opinion was sharply divided between those who wanted to govern the Philippines as a U.S. territory and those who wanted the islands to be independent.

Anti-Imperialist Argument Those arguing against U.S. control of the Philippines were known as *anti-imperialists*. Their leader was William Jennings Bryan, the Democratic candidate for president in 1900. Anti-imperialists warned that the United States would be abandoning its own commitment to democracy and the ideals of the Declaration of independence if it ruled territory on the other side of the Pacific. Furthermore, they were afraid that the possession of islands near Asia would inevitably involve the United States in Asian politics and wars.

Imperialist Argument Those favoring an imperialist policy, including Theodore Roosevelt, thought the United States had a duty to involve itself actively in world affairs. They argued that the acquisition of Pacific islands like Hawaii, Guam, and the Philippines was necessary for building the reputation of the United States as one of the world's great powers. Also, the argument went, the Philippines were bound to fall under the influence of one Western power or another. If that was so, they were better off under U.S. rule than under a nondemocratic power like Germany or Russia.

Suppressing the Filipino Revolution The Philippine people could not accept the idea of being traded from one colonial power to another. In 1899, the rebel troops that had fought against Spain turned their weapons against U.S. forces. To put down the uprising, President McKinley sent 70,000 additional troops to the Philippines. After nearly three years of fighting, U.S. forces finally prevailed as the last rebel band surrendered in 1902.

Disposition of Territories

As a result of the Spanish-American War, the following territorial changes had taken place:

★ Cuba became a U.S. *protectorate* (a nation whose foreign policy is partly controlled by a foreign power).

★ The Philippines remained a colony of the United States until July 4, 1946, when it was granted independence.

Constitutional Issues The major issue concerning colonies was the question of whether the Constitution followed the flag. Did citizens of colonial territories have the rights of American citizens? Were they entitled to the same protections as American citizens? In a series of cases known as the *Insular*

Cases, the Supreme Court in 1901 ruled that the Constitution did not fully cover colonial possessions. The extent to which the Constitution applied to colonies would be determined by Congress.

Latin American Affairs

Even as early as the 1820s, the United States was the strongest nation in the Western Hemisphere. Because of the relative strength of U.S. military forces, presidents tended to view countries to the south as needing U.S. protection from internal disorder as well as European control. But this point of view was often bitterly resented by Latin Americans, especially when U.S. troops were sent into their countries to "protect" them.

Roosevelt Corollary to the Monroe Doctrine

Recall that the Monroe Doctrine of 1823 had warned Great Britain, France, Spain, and other European nations not to interfere in the internal politics of Latin American nations. (Review Chapter 4.) Implied in this warning was the idea that the United States would protect the countries of Latin America from outside interference. Also implied was the assumed right of the United States to send troops into any threatened country to the south.

The Platt Amendment that made Cuba a U.S. protectorate was an example of this policy. In the first 20 years of the 20th century, the policy of *intervention* would be applied again and again by the three presidents of the Progressive Era—Theodore Roosevelt, William H. Taft, and Woodrow Wilson.

Roosevelt used the Monroe Doctrine to justify his interventionist policy in Latin America. He even added to the famous doctrine by issuing a *corollary* (logical extension) to it. The problem that led him to do this was the failure of several Latin American nations to pay their debts to Great Britain, Germany, and other European nations. (The debts resulted from the use of borrowed funds to purchase European imports.)

Roosevelt recognized that Europeans might become impatient and use force to collect these debts. He was afraid that Europeans who wanted to colonize Latin America might use the debt problem as an excuse for taking political control of indebted countries. To avoid this possibility, he said that the United States might intervene in a Latin American country if its debts were far overdue. The *Roosevelt Corollary* to the Monroe Doctrine read:

> Chronic wrongdoing . . . may in America, as elsewhere, ultimately require intervention. . . . In the Western Hemisphere the adherence of the United States to the Monroe Doctrine may force the United States, however reluctantly, in flagrant cases of such wrongdoing . . . , to the exercise of an international police power.

From Latin Americans' viewpoint, however, the Roosevelt Corollary was an unfair expansion of the military power of the United States into the affairs of independent nations. The corollary, they reasoned, was not for their protection but to help maintain the dominant position of the United States.

West Indies Protectorates

Roosevelt was fond of saying, "Speak softly and carry a big stick." This quotation is part of an African proverb that reads "Speak softly, carry a big stick, and you shall go far." However, Roosevelt chose not to speak softly.

Applying his corollary in 1904, President Roosevelt sent U.S. troops to occupy the capital of the Dominican Republic, an island country in the Caribbean. The troops remained long enough to make sure that the Dominican Republic paid its debts. This occupation was an example of Roosevelt's "big stick" policy.

In addition to the Dominican Republic, other areas in the West Indies were also treated as American *protectorates* (nations considered to be independent but controlled by the United States). These nations included Haiti and Cuba.

Panama Canal

A foreign policy of intervention achieves political goals through military and naval power. A prime example is the story of the building of the Panama Canal.

Early Attempts   As early as the 1850s, there had been ambitious plans to dig a canal through a narrow, 30-mile-wide strip of land in Central America—the region known as Panama. Such a canal would cut in half the sailing time from New York to San Francisco. It would greatly help the trade of all nations of the world and also eliminate the dangerous voyage over stormy seas at the tip of South America. In the 1880s, a French business firm began work on a canal, but jungle diseases and inadequate funds put a stop to the venture. Another route for a canal was also considered—one through Nicaragua (north of Panama).

Roosevelt's Quarrel With Colombia   In 1901, when Theodore Roosevelt became president, Panama belonged to the South American republic of Colombia. Roosevelt was extremely eager to begin digging a canal through either Panama or Nicaragua. He preferred the Panama route and offered to pay Colombia $10 million for the right to lease the land through which the canal would pass. But Colombia refused his offer. Roosevelt was furious. Because Colombia would not cooperate, he decided to support an uprising in Panama against Colombian rule.

Acquisition   In 1903 the uprising in Panama took place as planned. It lasted only a few hours. U.S. naval forces were on hand in Panama to prevent

Colombian troops from stopping the so-called revolution. Roosevelt wasted no time in recognizing the government of the new Republic of Panama. Of course, this government quickly agreed to U.S. terms for leasing a canal zone through the country. Work on the canal began soon afterward.

Roosevelt's Intervention: An Evaluation Did the president act correctly? He himself was proud of moving so boldly in Panama and later boasted: "I took Panama." But Colombians were outraged. They called U.S. actions a form of imperialist robbery. Years later, President Woodrow Wilson persuaded Congress to award Colombia $25 million as compensation for its loss of Panama. Many historians consider Roosevelt's intervention another example of his "big stick" policy.

Construction The building of the Panama Canal was one of the engineering marvels of the 20th century. A wide strip of dense tropical vegetation had to be cleared from a canal zone ten miles wide. A huge dam had to be built to control the canal's water level. Entire towns had to be erected to house all the workers. Overseeing these awesome projects was Army engineer Colonel George W. Goethals.

The worst obstacles to the enterprise were the tropical mosquitoes that carried two lethal diseases—malaria and yellow fever. During the Spanish-American War, Dr. William C. Gorgas had learned to eliminate the breeding places of the deadly mosquitoes whose bites had been responsible for the deaths of thousands of American soldiers in Cuba. Gorgas went to Panama to apply his knowledge to controlling the jungle mosquitoes. He succeeded well enough to save the lives of most canal workers. Even so, thousands died of malaria and yellow fever. Most of the victims (4,500 out of a total of 5,500) were African Americans.

After seven years of human toil, the "big ditch" was completed in 1914. Theodore Roosevelt lived to see ocean-going ships move through the canal that was begun under his administration.

Disposition Ever since 1903, when Panama gained its independence, the United States has had a special relationship with that country. At first, the people of Panama welcomed U.S. efforts to build and protect the canal. Beginning in the 1960s, however, many Panamanians protested the U.S. presence in their country. The time had come, they said, for the United States to give control of the canal to Panama.

As a Democrat, President Jimmy Carter (1977–1981) favored the Good Neighbor policy of a Democratic predecessor, Franklin Roosevelt. He believed that U.S. troops in the Panama Canal Zone not only angered the Panamanian people but also offended other Latin Americans. Therefore, Carter negotiated two treaties with Panama. In the first, the United States promised to transfer ownership of the canal and canal zone to Panama by the year 2000. In the second treaty, the United States and Panama agreed that the canal would always be neutral territory. If the canal was threatened by an outside power, the United States could use military force to defend it.

The Panama Canal treaties stirred much controversy in the United States. Many Americans did not want their country to give up the canal. President Carter, however, managed to persuade two-thirds of the Senate to ratify both treaties. It was one of the major political victories of his presidency. In a special ceremony in 1999, former President Carter returned to Panama to officially turn over the canal to the people of Panama.

Taft and Dollar Diplomacy

President William Howard Taft continued Roosevelt's policy of intervention by sending U.S. Marines into Nicaragua in 1912. His reasons were slightly different from Roosevelt's. Taft believed that the United States should protect the many American businesses that invested in Latin America. He also believed that the United States had the right to force a Latin American country to repay loans it owed to U.S. banks. These monetary reasons for intervention were given the name *dollar diplomacy*. In the case of Nicaragua, Taft ordered in the Marines when a civil war there threatened to prevent repayment of a large U.S. bank loan.

Woodrow Wilson and Intervention

When Woodrow Wilson became president in 1913, he said that he did not believe in dollar diplomacy. But believed in keeping order, especially in troubled areas close to the United States. In 1915, he sent Marines to Haiti when a civil war erupted there. Two years later, similar disorders in the Dominican Republic caused Wilson to send more Marines to that country. U.S. military forces remained in the Dominican Republic until 1925 and in Haiti until 1934. Latin Americans throughout the region deeply resented the U.S. policy of intervention.

Wilson's most serious problem in Latin America was the result of a 1910 revolution in Mexico. After the revolution began, opposing armies of Mexicans fought for control of their country's government. Wilson wanted to support a Mexican government that respected civil rights and permitted free elections. He was often disappointed by the various governments that briefly came to power in Mexico.

"Watchful Waiting" Wilson especially disliked the ruthless methods of a Mexican dictator named Victoriano Huerta. Rather than recognize Huerta's government as fully legitimate, Wilson followed a policy of *watchful waiting*. In other words, he pledged to wait and see whether forces opposed to Huerta would soon overthrow him.

Intervention in Mexico In 1914, the jailing of several U.S. sailors in Mexico provided Wilson with a reason for taking action against Huerta. On the president's orders, U.S. troops occupied the Mexican port of Vera Cruz. The Mexican people were so offended by this U.S. action that even Huerta's political enemies rallied to his support. Wilson withdrew the troops after the

"ABC Powers" of South America (Argentina, Brazil, and Chile) urged Huerta to resign from office. Huerta finally did so. The new Mexican government of Venustiano Carranza was immediately challenged by rebel forces under Pancho Villa.

Villa's Raids In 1916, Villa tried to make himself a popular Mexican hero by raiding a U.S. town in New Mexico and killing 19 Americans. Wilson retaliated by sending a punitive expedition into northern Mexico. He avoided going to war, however. Early in 1917, he ordered the removal of U.S. troops and formally recognized the Carranza government as legitimate. Mexicans' bitter memories of U.S. intervention in their country had a negative effect on U.S.–Mexican relations for many years.

★ In Review

1. Define sphere of influence, Open Door policy, Boxer Rebellion, De Lôme Letter, Platt Amendment, anti-imperialists, protectorates, Roosevelt Corollary, and watchful waiting.
2. Evaluate (a) the decision to go to war with Spain and (b) the decision to take possession of the Philippines.
3. Describe the reaction by Latin Americans to U.S. intervention in Nicaragua, Mexico, Haiti, and the Dominican Republic.

U.S. Restraint and Involvement in World War I

Before the outbreak of World War I, U.S. troops had fought overseas in Latin America (Cuba and Mexico) and in Asia (the Philippines), but they had never fought in Europe. How and why did the United States become involved in 1917 in a terribly destructive European war? What were the consequences of U.S. involvement?

"The Great War," as it was called at the time, began in August 1914, and ended in November 1918. The United States participated in the war on the side of Great Britain and France only in the final 20 months, beginning in April 1917. Before analyzing how the United States became involved, let us review how the war came about in Europe.

Long-Range Causes of World War I

All wars have both long-range and short-range causes. The chief long-range causes of World War I were the forces of nationalism, militarism, and imperialism. In addition, a system of alliances made it likely that a war between any two nations of Europe would result automatically in a much larger war involving the many allies of those two nations.

In the 20 years before 1914, tensions between rival powers had been steadily building in Europe. Great Britain worried not only about Germany's ambitions for colonies and a strong navy but also about its growing industrial economy. Austria-Hungary worried more and more about the rebellious attitude of Serbs and other Slavic peoples in its empire. The aging Austrian monarch also worried about support for Serbia by the world's largest Slavic nation, Russia. Russia, in turn, worried about Germany's support for its ally, Austria-Hungary.

Short-Range Causes of World War I

The spark that ignited World War I was an assassination on the streets of Sarajevo—now the capital of Bosnia and Herzegovina, but then a city in Austria-Hungary. The victims of the shooting were the heir to the throne of Austria-Hungary, the Archduke Franz Ferdinand, and his wife. The assassin was a citizen of neighboring Serbia and a member of a band of Serbian nationalists. The group hoped to bring about the collapse of Austria-Hungary so that Serbs within the empire could join independent Serbia.

Austria-Hungary blamed Serbia for the attack and presented Serbia with an *ultimatum* (a list of final demands). Serbia agreed to most of the demands. Even so, Austria-Hungary declared war on Serbia and began bombarding Belgrade, the Serbian capital, on July 29, 1914.

The allies of the Austrians and the Serbs quickly called their armies into a state of readiness for war. A huge Russian army moved to defend Serbia. Recognizing that Germany would defend Austria-Hungary against Russia, France and Great Britain prepared for war in defense of themselves and their Russian ally. Germany declared war on Russia on August 1, on France on August 3, and marched into Belgium on the same day. Great Britain declared war on Germany on August 4.

Neutrality

The United States in 1914 was not allied with any European nation. Since fighting against Great Britain in the War of 1812, it had remained strictly neutral and uninvolved in Europe's conflicts. Both President Woodrow Wilson and the American people hoped to keep the United States neutral from the beginning to the end of "the Great War."

Years of Neutrality (1914–1916) In 1914, most Americans, including the president, believed that the war in Europe did not involve U.S. interests. They viewed the Atlantic Ocean as a great barrier that separated their nation from the problems of Europe. Also, many respected George Washington's advice not to become involved in permanent alliances.

As a neutral nation, the United States continued to trade with the countries of Europe. But Germany's chances for victory in the war depended in large part on keeping supplies from reaching its enemies. It could achieve this goal by using a weapon new to warfare—the submarine.

Germany had by far the greatest number of submarines and used them with deadly effect against British ships. Beginning in early 1915, Germany also used its submarines to sink any ships—even passenger liners and merchant ships—if they crossed into waters close to Great Britain. Many of the ships carried American cargo and American passengers.

In May 1915, a British passenger liner named the *Lusitania* steamed into the "war zone" near Ireland where it was torpedoed and sunk by a German submarine. More than 1,000 people lost their lives, including 128 Americans. News of the tragedy shocked the American people into recognizing that their nation might be drawn into the war after all. Several strongly worded messages of protest from President Wilson persuaded Germany to abandon its policy of sinking unarmed ships without warning. Germany's promise was known as the Sussex pledge (named for another torpedoed ship).

"Preparedness" Throughout the years of neutrality, Theodore Roosevelt called for a policy of preparedness. No longer president, Roosevelt campaigned very hard for a United States military buildup and even raised funds for summer training camps.

Although President Wilson worked hard for neutrality, he began to accept the need for preparedness after German submarines sank a number of passenger ships. Thus, even Wilson asked Congress for more funds to build up the army and navy. In addition, Wilson established a Council of National Defense to increase cooperation between the U.S. military and private industry.

Long-Range Causes of U.S. Involvement

Sympathy for Great Britain and France As citizens of an English-speaking nation, most Americans felt strong ties to Great Britain. They also sympathized with the French, remembering that France had helped win U.S. independence. Also, Americans recognized that both France and Great Britain had democratic governments. Their enemies, on the other hand, were both ruled by monarchs—Germany by a kaiser, Austria-Hungary by an emperor.

Economic Ties The British navy effectively blockaded German ports. Therefore, most of U.S. trade during the war was with the British and the French. In fact, the United States sold millions of dollars of war materials to both nations.

Fear of German Power Policymakers in the U.S. government feared German victory in the war for two reasons. First, the German economy before the war showed great strength, and its products competed strongly with U.S. goods in international markets. Second and more important, U.S. military leaders worried about threats to U.S. security if Germany won both the war and control of the Atlantic Ocean. German control of the Atlantic might hurt U.S. trade and would surely increase Germany's ability to intervene in Latin America.

British and French Propaganda   When the war began, German armies invaded the neutral country of Belgium in order to strike next at France. Americans viewed this invasion as cruel and unfair—the action of a bully. Skillful propagandists in Great Britain and France made the most of Germany's reputation as a military aggressor. They invented stories of German cruelty that were widely printed in U.S. newspapers. Pictures of the German kaiser, Wilhelm, made him appear especially villainous.

Desperate Conditions in Europe   As the war dragged on, people in all the belligerent (warring) nations suffered greatly. The death tolls on both the Eastern Front (Russia) and the Western Front (France) were staggering. By the end of 1916, millions had died from artillery fire, poison gas, tank attacks, and machine-gun bullets—and all in vain. There were no significant gains by either side. Civilians suffered almost as much as the soldiers, especially in Germany, where shipments of food supplies were cut off by the British blockade. The German people were hungry, nearly starved. Conditions in Russia were even worse. There the only hope for relief from desperate poverty and suffering lay in revolution.

Short-Range Causes of U.S. Involvement

Unrestricted Submarine Warfare   In January 1917, Germany decided that the time had come for desperate measures. It announced that its submarines would once again sink without warning all ships entering British waters. The military and political leaders who made this decision recognized that they were risking the entry of the United States into the war on the British side. But they hoped that submarine damage to British shipping would end the war before U.S. troops could be trained for combat.

Zimmermann Telegram   Early in 1917, the British had managed to intercept and decode a telegram sent by the German foreign secretary, Arthur Zimmermann, to a German diplomat in Mexico. The telegram instructed the German diplomat to tell Mexico that Germany might help it win back territories in Texas, Arizona, and New Mexico (territories lost to the United States in the 1840s). It would do so if Germany and Mexico both decided to declare war against the United States. The British sent the Zimmermann telegram to the U.S. government. Its publication in American newspapers caused a sensation.

Revolution in Russia   In March 1917 came news of the overthrow of the Russian czar, Nicholas II. Americans were excited by the news because they expected the new government in Russia to be democratic. President Wilson was especially pleased. As a leading champion of democracy, Wilson was willing to fight for democracies in Europe such as France and Great Britain. Now that their ally, Russia, was more democratic, Wilson could lead the United States to war on the side of democracies without exception.

Decision for War

On April 21, 1917, the president went to Congress to deliver one of the most eloquent and memorable speeches in U.S. history. He called Germany's submarine policy "warfare against mankind." He said: "It is a fearful thing to lead this great peaceful people into war, into the most terrible and disastrous of all wars." However, "the world must be made safe for democracy." Members of Congress stood up and cheered. Four days later, they voted almost unanimously for a U.S. declaration of war against Germany. (One of the few who voted against war was Jeannette Rankin, the first woman to serve in the House of Representatives. Another oppositionist was Senator Robert La Follette, the progressive reformer from Wisconsin.)

Mobilizing for War

Never before had the United States fought in a war on European soil. To help win the war, Wilson and his advisers recognized that all the resources of the nation—farms, factories, businesses, labor unions, men, women, even children—had to participate in a determined national effort. Daily sacrifices would have to be made by everybody.

1917 cartoon depicting the German kaiser honoring Senator La Follette for his antiwar stance

For an entire year, the main U.S. contribution to the Allied forces in France was to keep them supplied with food, guns, ships, airplanes, and other goods. This economic contribution was vital.

Organizing Factories Called to the nation's capital to coordinate the war effort were a number of American business leaders. Chief among them was Bernard Baruch, who was asked by Wilson to head a new war agency, the War Industries Board. Baruch sent telegrams and mailed instructions to thousands of corporation presidents, explaining how they could change both their products and their methods for wartime needs. Partly because of Baruch's abilities, U.S. factories turned out vast quantities of war materials. Especially impressive was the spectacular growth of the U.S. chemical industry, which produced gunpowder and explosives for the war.

Organizing the Food Supply Another dedicated manager, Herbert Hoover, accepted Wilson's call to head up the Food Administration. Hoover went to work sending out millions of pamphlets telling how every American could contribute to U.S. victory by eating less food. He explained that the British were nearly out of food and needed every ounce of bread and beef that could be saved in American homes. Americans soon grew accustomed to one "meatless" day and one "wheatless" day every week. The conservation effort made a huge difference in the amount of food shipped overseas in 1917 and 1918. When Hoover insisted that food would win the war, he exaggerated only slightly.

New Jobs for Women and Minorities War changed the nature of the American workforce. As young men entered the armed forces, young women took their places in shipyards and factories. African Americans also filled factory jobs vacated by departing troops. The migration of African Americans to northern cities, which had begun before the war, was significantly increased by the new job opportunities of wartime.

On the farms of the Southwest, workers were needed to plant and harvest crops. Between 1917 and 1920, about 100,000 Mexicans came to settle permanently in Texas, New Mexico, Arizona, and California.

Fighting the War

Weapons of World War I On land, the two most deadly weapons were (1) the machine gun, used to defend trenches against enemy attackers, and (2) poison gas, which was carried by wind currents into the enemy's trenches. Mustard gas attacked the skin, causing huge blisters, horrible pain, and death. Armored tanks were also used for the first time in World War I. At sea, Germany nearly crippled the British merchant fleet with another new weapon, the submarine. In the air, for the first time in the history of warfare, airplanes spied on enemy positions and fought each other in aerial "dogfights." (Bombing was not a major factor until World War II in the 1940s.)

Pershing's Troops "Over There" In a popular song of World War I, George M. Cohan's "Over There," soldiers in U.S. training camps sang enthusiastically of "going over . . . we're going over . . . and we won't come back 'til it's over over there." In 1917, only a few thousand were ready to be sent to the trenches in France (the place "over there" where troops were meant to go). But in the summer of 1918, they arrived in France by the hundreds of thousands. Unlike the war-weary troops of Europe, the Americans jumped into the trenches fresh and ready for action. Commanding them was American General John J. Pershing.

U.S. soldiers in France wrote home about the sights and sounds of life (and death) in the trenches. The letter quoted below tells of one young soldier's experience preparing for his first battle. Why do you think almost every attack in World War I was preceded by an artillery barrage?

Last Big Push An all-out German offensive in March 1918 almost succeeded in reaching its target, Paris. The drive was finally halted and beaten back.

★ ★ ★ ★ ★

A SOLDIER'S LETTER FROM THE WESTERN FRONT

This was war; I was finally in it. I can not say that I was not excited; but I don't think I was afraid; only sort of apprehensive. Thank God! It was night, and I overlooked a great many horrors. . . .

"Please step high and over here. Thanks."

"What's matter? Wounded?"

"No. My pal is dying."

A little farther on a fellow lying on his back and looking straight up—and many such. Something seemed to grip me; I wanted to run, but those fellows ahead of me were cool enough; they were not afraid. Then we reached the "jumping-over" trench. Our battalion was scheduled to start at 6:30 A.M.

We were to have a barrage. Now I knew all about a barrage, but had never seen one in action. Everything was quiet after 3 A.M.; not a shell was fired. Fritz [the German enemy] was sending up lots of star shells, but that's his way. Six-fifteen, 6:25, 6:30, My God! All hell turned loose; my heart lost several beats and then caught up and overdid itself. Someone shouted, "Let's at them!"

Oh, it was a dandy barrage, and we walked over behind it without much opposition and took our objective. I threw my grenades at a couple of Huns in a bay and when they exploded (both Huns and grenades) I slid into a trench.

Most U.S. troops arrived in time for a massive counterattack that eventually won the war. The first great thrust by U.S. troops occurred between September 12 and 16 along a section of the front-line trenches called the St. Mihiel Salient. This was followed by another assault (beginning September 26), which drove the exhausted and demoralized Germans through the Argonne, a forest in northwestern France. By early November, the retreating Germans had been pushed back almost to the border of their own country.

Armistice Then the war ended. Curiously, the end came on the eleventh hour of the eleventh day of the eleventh month—November 11, 1918. Germany signed an armistice and conceded defeat. The world war was over. In the United States, crowds went wild with excitement and joy.

U.S. Reaction to the Russian Revolution

President Wilson initially welcomed the Russian Revolution. However, in November 1917, a second revolution in Russia overthrew the democratic government that had come to power in March. This time, the revolutionaries were *Bolsheviks*—or Communists. They promptly ended Russian suffering in the war by making peace with Germany. With Russia out of the war, Germany and Austria-Hungary could concentrate all their remaining strength on the Western Front. In 1918, U.S. troops landed in Russia to aid forces known as the "Whites," who were attempting to overthrow the new Communist government, the "Reds." The effort failed, and U.S. troops were withdrawn.

In 1921, policymakers adopted a more humanitarian approach. Recognizing that the Russian people were starving after years of war, the United States sent them millions of tons of food. Organizing the relief effort was the wartime food manager, Herbert Hoover.

In 1922, the Communist government of Russia renamed the country the Soviet Union.

★ In Review

1. Describe the U.S. response to Germany's submarine policy from 1915 to 1917.
2. Identity the two causes of U.S. involvement in World War I that you think were most important. Explain each choice.
3. Describe the effects of U.S. participation in World War I on each of the following: (a) women and minorities and (b) industry.

Wartime Constitutional Issues

Although most Americans supported the war, a few made speeches against it and refused to cooperate with the government's policies. The opponents of war were *dissenters*—people who actively oppose the majority view. In times of peace, the First Amendment of the Constitution protects a dissenter's rights to speak out boldly on any issue. But in wartime, when the national security is at stake, might the Constitution be interpreted differently?

Draft Issue

An army can be recruited by (1) calling for volunteers and (2) compelling service by a procedure known as the draft. Woodrow Wilson believed that the latter method was both more efficient and more democratic (since members of every social class and ethnic group would be required to serve).

At Wilson's request, Congress passed the Selective Service Act in May 1917. All male citizens ages 21 to 30 were required to register for military service. Those called to service, if they passed a medical examination, were in the army—and in the war. By war's end, a total of 2.8 million young men were drafted out of the 24 million who registered.

Some opposed the draft because they believed that it threatened democracy and might cause Americans to glorify military life. Others, including many socialists and anarchists, thought the war was little more than a capitalist scheme for making money. Still others, known as pacifists, opposed fighting in any war because they regarded war as a form of legalized murder.

In a 1917 poster, Uncle Sam backs up the draft

Espionage and Sedition Acts

Congress passed the Espionage Act in 1917 and then the much harsher Sedition Act in 1918. These laws imposed heavy fines and prison sentences for the following antiwar actions: (1) spying and aiding the wartime enemy, (2) interfering with the recruitment of soldiers, (3) speaking against the government's campaign to sell bonds to finance the war, (4) urging resistance to U.S. laws, and (5) using "disloyal, profane, scurrilous, or abusive language" about the American form of government, flag, or military uniform. In addition, the U.S. Post Office was given the right to remove any antiwar materials from the mails.

About 1,500 who spoke out against the war were arrested under the Espionage and Sedition acts. Eugene Debs, who had been the Socialist party's candidate for president, was sentenced to ten years in prison for making an antiwar speech. Emma Goldman, an anarchist, received a two-year prison term for her antiwar activities. After serving her sentence, she was deported to the Soviet Union.

Schenck v. *United States* (1919)

Another dissenter who went to jail was the general secretary of the Socialist party, Charles Schenck. Schenck had mailed about 15,000 leaflets urging men who had been drafted into military service to oppose the law. After being tried and convicted under the Espionage Act, Schenck appealed to the U.S. Supreme Court. He argued that his First Amendment rights to freedom of speech and the press had been violated.

In the case of *Schenck* v. *United States* (1919), the Supreme Court ruled against Schenck and upheld the constitutionality of the Espionage Act. Justice Oliver Wendell Holmes, writing the decision of an unanimous court, noted that the right to free speech was not absolute. In ordinary times, wrote Holmes, the mailing of Schenck's leaflets would have been protected under the First Amendment. However, Holmes went on, every act of speech must be judged according to the circumstances in which it was committed. For example, "the most stringent protection of free speech would not protect a man in falsely shouting fire in a theatre and causing a panic." Furthermore, speech that might be harmless in a time of peace might injure the public safety in a time of war.

The question to be asked, according to Holmes, was whether or not an act of speech posed a "clear and present danger" to the public. If it did, then Congress had the power to restrain such speech. The "clear and present danger" test, first stated in the Schenck case, was often applied in later Supreme Court cases involving the issue of free speech.

Red Scare

The Communist revolution in Russia in 1917 fueled nativist fears about the loyalties of the huge foreign-born population. Nativists thought foreign-born radicals might attempt to overthrow the U.S. government. Their fears turned to action in the *Red Scare* of 1919 and 1920. Attorney General A. Mitchell Palmer organized a series of raids—the so-called *Palmer raids*—to arrest and deport immigrants suspected of disloyalty. Federal agents were told to enter homes, businesses, and the offices of political groups and search for damaging evidence. Often they did so without search warrants. Before the raids ended, nearly 600 people were forced to leave the United States as unwanted "Reds" (radical thinkers).

Search for Peace and Arms Control

Women's Peace Movement

The Women's International League for Peace and Freedom (WILPF) was founded in 1915 to protest World War I. Jane Addams was elected president of the new organization. Its aim was to unite women in helping abolish the causes of war and to work for a constructive peace. In 1919, the organization denounced the harsh terms of the treaty that ended the war. The WILPF maintained that the treaty created the conditions for a future war, and that even though the war was over, there was no peace or security in the world. During the 1920s, the WILPF called for the convening of a world congress to draw up a new agreement for a genuine peace, urged scientists to refuse to engage in research for war purposes, and demanded total and universal disarmament.

The Fourteen Points

Woodrow Wilson was an idealist. He wanted the war to result not just in military victory but in a lasting peace settlement that was fair to all people and nations. In January 1918, Wilson listed his goals for a peace settlement. This statement of goals became known as the *Fourteen Points*. The key points were:

★ An end to the practice of making secret treaties
★ Recognition of every nation's right to freedom of the seas in peace and war (especially, a neutral nation's rights to use the seas for trade and travel)
★ Reduction of weapons
★ Changing the borders of European countries according to the principle of *self-determination* (the many peoples of Austria-Hungary, for example, being allowed to decide to form nations of their own)
★ Establishment of a new international organization, the *League of Nations*, to keep the peace by fairly resolving disputes between nations
★ Placing European colonies in Africa, Asia, and Latin America under the control of the League of Nations.

Wilson explained the purpose underlying all points of his peace plan: "An evident principle runs through the whole program I have outlined. It is the principle of justice to all peoples and nationalities, and their right to live on equal terms of liberty and safety with one another. . . ."

Wilson and the Treaty of Versailles

The Fourteen Points were so important to Wilson that he did something no earlier president had ever done. He traveled to a foreign country—France—to meet with other leaders and negotiate the terms of a treaty of peace. The losers of the war, Germany and Austria-Hungary, did not participate in the victors' discussions, which took place in the palace at Versailles, near Paris. At first, Wilson had great influence because the people of Europe greeted him as a hero and even as a saint. But as the conference continued through the early months of 1919, the hard realities of European politics overwhelmed Wilson's idealistic plan for peace.

Allies Seek Revenge   Unlike Wilson, the leaders of France, Great Britain, and Italy wanted a peace treaty that would punish their wartime enemies. (Italy had entered the war on the side of the Allies in 1915.) The victorious European powers had suffered huge losses of life and property. They wanted to make sure that Germany would never rise again as a major mil-

Allied leaders at Versailles, from left to right: Lloyd George (Britain), Orlando (Italy), Clemençeau (France), and Wilson (United States)

itary power. They also wanted a treaty that would force Germany to pay for war damages.

Treaty of Versailles The treaty that finally emerged from the conference, the *Treaty of Versailles*, contained the following provisions:

★ Alsace-Lorraine (German territory since 1871) would again be part of France.

★ Poland, whose independence had been lost for more than a hundred years, would again be an independent nation. It would receive from Germany a piece of territory, the so-called Polish Corridor, that would connect Poland to the Baltic Sea.

★ Germany would lose all of its colonies, including three large colonies in Africa (Cameroon, German West Africa, and German East Africa).

★ Germany's Saar Basin, a major coal-producing region in western Germany, would be controlled by France for 15 years.

★ Germany would be required to pay a huge amount of money in *reparations* (payments for war damages).

★ Germany would be made to disband its armed forces and agree never to have a future army of more than 100,000 men.

★ Germany would be forbidden to manufacture and import war materials.

★ Germany would accept full responsibility for causing the world war. (This provision was known as the *war guilt clause*.)

★ A peacekeeping organization, the League of Nations, would be created to reduce the chance of future wars.

A separate treaty with Austria declared the old Austro-Hungarian Empire to be dissolved. It reduced Austrian territory to less than a third of its former size and recognized the existence of four new republics: Yugoslavia, Czechoslovakia, Austria, and Hungary.

Analysis of the Treaty The Treaty of Versailles was very harsh on Germany (although less harsh than France and Great Britain had originally wanted). Wilson succeeded in softening the treaty slightly and in seeing a few of his Fourteen Points carried out in modified form. He recognized that the treaty was more vengeful than fair and might cause Germany to rebel against its terms. Even so, he was happy about one diplomatic victory. He had succeeded in persuading others at the conference to include the League of Nations as part of the treaty. All signers of the treaty would be committed to joining the League. Wilson hoped the League would eventually correct the treaty's faults.

League of Nations and the United States Senate

Unfortunately for President Wilson, politics in the United States proved every bit as difficult as politics in Europe. Members of his own Democra-

New Nations of Eastern Europe, 1919

tic party generally supported the treaty that Wilson brought home with him from Paris. But Republicans in Congress were much less enthusiastic. Some were firmly opposed. To win approval of the Versailles treaty, Wilson had to win the votes of both Republican and Democratic senators.

Isolationists and Reservationists The Constitution provides that two-thirds of the Senate must ratify all treaties. Wilson could count on a majority of senators supporting the treaty, but a two-thirds vote was uncertain. Republicans opposing the treaty included two groups: (1) *isolationists*, who rejected the treaty outright because it would involve too many commitments abroad, and (2) *reservationists*, who would accept the treaty only if certain clauses were added to it—clauses called reservations. The leading reservationist in the Senate was Henry Cabot Lodge of Massachusetts, a bitter enemy of the president.

The chief issue in the struggle over the Versailles treaty was a clause providing that each member of the League of Nations would "respect and preserve as against external aggression the territorial integrity and existing political independence of all members of the League." In the opinion of the treaty's opponents, this clause meant that the United States might be drawn into a war that its own Congress did not approve.

Wilson's Breakdown   Wilson took his case to the public. Traveling by train from town to town around the country, he gave dozens of speeches in defense of the League and the treaty. But after a speech in Colorado, the president fell seriously ill. After returning to the White House, he had a stroke that paralyzed one side of his body. For several months, his poor health weakened his ability to provide leadership.

Votes in the Senate   In 1920, the Senate voted on whether to ratify the Treaty of Versailles. A majority voted in favor of the treaty with Senator Lodge's reservations. A two-thirds vote would have been possible if Wilson had supported these reservations. Instead, he instructed Democratic senators to vote no. A vote for the treaty without reservations also failed to win two-thirds approval.

End of the Debate   Had Wilson been willing to compromise, the treaty (with reservations) probably would have passed. Instead, the United States, which had proposed the League of Nations, was the only major power to vote against it. A separate U.S. peace treaty with Germany was signed by Republican president Warren Harding in 1921. Because it contained nothing about the League of Nations, it passed the Senate easily.

Washington Naval Disarmament Conference

In 1921, President Warren Harding and Secretary of State Charles Evans Hughes invited to Washington, D.C., representatives from all the major powers of the world except Russia. The subject of their talks was battleships and other ships of war. The question was how to limit the costly and potentially dangerous competition among the world's great naval powers.

1918 cartoon "Interrupting the Ceremony": U.S. congressional opposition to Wilson and the League of Nations

The five nations with the largest navies agreed in 1922 to limit ship construction according to a certain ratio: United States (5), Great Britain (5), Japan (3), France (1.67), and Italy (1.67). The U.S. Senate approved the agreement.

The Washington Conference helped the United States and Great Britain to keep down their governments' expenses on shipbuilding. But Japan was disappointed with its middle position. It wanted full *parity* (equality) with its Western rivals. In the 1930s, the military leaders of Japan ignored the limits imposed by the Washington Conference and built a navy strong enough to challenge both U.S. and British naval forces.

Reparations and War Debts

How much money should Germany be forced to pay the Allies in reparations? The Allies' answer was the crushing amount of $33 billion. The sum might have been more reasonable had the United States agreed to participate in the Allies' meetings on the issue. But because U.S. foreign policy

Hopes for world disarmament swallowed up by the tiger of militarism, in a 1926 cartoon

was dominated by a strong feeling of isolationism, the United States preferred to stay out of the discussions.

To carry out the war, the European Allies had borrowed more than $10 billion to purchase war materials. U.S. policymakers believed that other nations should promptly repay their debts to the United States. Because of its loans to Great Britain and France during the war, the United States in the 1920s was the world's greatest creditor nation (one to whom debts are owed). The French government argued that such debts should be canceled since the French had lost many more lives in the war than the Americans and had fought much longer. But U.S. presidents of the 1920s insisted that the Allies pay back at least a sizable portion of their war debts.

Kellogg-Briand Pact

In 1928, the United States signed a treaty with France known as the *Kellogg-Briand Pact*. The pact invited all nations of the world to declare a common policy of never fighting an aggressive war. Eventually, 63 nations signed the pact, which was said to "renounce war as an instrument of national policy." Unfortunately for the cause of world peace, the pact was only a written statement. There was no real commitment to stop an aggressor (warmaker). If a nation chose to wage war, nothing in the treaty required the United States to act. In the isolationist 1920s, that was the way most Americans wanted it.

Establishment of the World Court

One of the special branches of the League of Nations was the Permanent Court of International Justice, or World Court. The purpose of this court was to permit nations to settle their disputes peacefully by arguing their cases before a board of judges. The United States could have joined the World Court without joining the League itself. However, isolationists in the U.S. Senate defeated every proposal for joining the World Court. They feared that even an "advisory opinion" given by the court might draw the United States into a war.

★ In Review

1. Explain the significance of the following: the draft, dissenters, *Schenck* v. *United States*, Red Scare.
2. What factors contributed to the Senate's failure to ratify the Treaty of Versailles?
3. To what extent did the Treaty of Versailles and subsequent diplomacy from 1920 to 1928 reflect Wilsonian principles?

MULTIPLE-CHOICE QUESTIONS

Use the cartoon on page 295 to answer questions 1 and 2.

1. The cartoon demonstrates that in 1905, the United States was
   (1) following a policy of neutrality
   (2) making war on European nations violating the Monroe Doctrine
   (3) settling disputes that took place between nations
   (4) limiting foreign involvement to Latin America.

2. The president depicted in the cartoon is
   (1) Theodore Roosevelt
   (2) William McKinley
   (3) Grover Cleveland
   (4) William Henry Harrison.

Use the map on page 297 to answer questions 3 and 4.

3. The map shows that, at the time when Secretary of State John Hay issued the Open Door policy, the United States
   (1) was extensively involved in China
   (2) controlled Japan
   (3) had no sphere of influence in China
   (4) planned to create a shipping company between the Philippine Islands and Shanghai.

4. The map shows that a grievance of the Boxer rebels involved
   (1) Chinese isolation

(2) foreign dominance
(3) a desire to trade with the United States
(4) disputes over the border with Korea.

Use the cartoon on page 300 to answer question 5.

5. The main idea of the cartoon is that
   (1) a heroic United States was correcting Spanish atrocities
   (2) the United States should not have intervened on behalf of the Cuban revolutionaries
   (3) an overly aggressive United States government was attacking Spain
   (4) neither Spain nor the United States was truly interested in improving the lives of the Cuban people.

Base your answers to questions 6 and 7 on the statements made by the following speakers:

Speaker A: By the sheer genius of this people and the grow of our power, we have become a determining factor in the history of mankind; and after you become a determining factor, you cannot remain isolated.

Speaker B: Wars between nations come from contacts. A nation with which we have no contact is a nation with which we should never fight. . . .

Speaker C: Nations need to respect and preserve the territorial integrity and existing political independence of others.

Speaker D: We cannot meddle in European affairs and expect that Europe will not interfere in ours.

6. Which speakers would most agree with the establishment of the League of Nations following World War I?
   (1) Speakers A and D
   (2) Speakers B and C
   (3) Speakers A and C
   (4) Speakers C and D.

7. Which speakers would endorse isolationism?
   (1) Speakers A and B
   (2) Speakers C and D
   (3) Speakers A and D
   (4) Speakers B and D.

Use the cartoon on page 322 to answer questions 8 and 9.

8. The cartoon illustrates that
   (1) there was widespread U.S. support for the League of Nations
   (2) the Senate blocked U.S. membership in the League of Nations

(3) many foreigners were able to immigrate to the United States as a result of marriage to U.S. soldiers
(4) in 1918, the federal government was taking over the reserved state power of creating marriage laws.

9. Which constitutional principal is best reflected by the cartoon?
   (1) federalism
   (2) the unwritten Constitution
   (3) judicial review
   (4) checks and balances.

Use the cartoon on page 323 to answer question 10.

10. The artist who drew the cartoon feels that
    (1) there should be more attention to wildlife conservation
    (2) attempts at disarmament during the 1920s were unsuccessful
    (3) the armies of the world cannot be controlled
    (4) since peace is impossible, each nation should maintain a large standing army.

THEMATIC ESSAYS

1. **Theme:** The Spanish-American War

   The Spanish-American War was, to a great extent, a "newspaperman's war," which led to the acquisition of overseas territory for the United States.

   Task

   ★ Describe how newspapers influenced the decision of the federal government to declare war on Spain.
   ★ Explain how the results of the Spanish-American War represented the achievement of a second phase of manifest destiny.

2. **Theme:** Emerging Global Involvement of the United States

Overseas involvement on the part of the United States manifested itself primarily in Latin America, the Caribbean, and Asia.

Task: Select one example of U.S. overseas involvement that took place in the Latin American/Caribbean area and another from Asia. For each example:

★ Describe the circumstances leading to U.S. involvement.
★ Show whether the involvement of the United States had a positive or a negative impact on each of the two areas chosen.

You may use, but are not limited to, Panama and the canal, the use of the "big stick," and "dollar diplomacy" for Latin America and the Caribbean. Commodore Matthew C. Perry's opening of Japan, the Open Door policy in China, and the U.S. acquisition of the Philippines may be used as examples for Asia.

DOCUMENT-BASED QUESTION

*Read each document and answer the question that follows it. Then read the **Task** and write your essay. Essays should include references to most of the documents along with additional information based on your knowledge of United States history and government.*

Historical Context: The entry of the United States into World War I marked a unity and even conformity that was unprecedented in the history of our nation.

Document 1 Refer to the poster on page 316.

Question: How did the poster encourage young men in the United States to support the war effort?

Document 2 Senator Robert La Follette as recorded in the Congressional Record, 65th Congress, First Session (1917):

The President proposes alliance with Great Britain, which . . . is a hereditary monarchy, with a hereditary ruler, with a hereditary House of Lords, with a hereditary landed system, with a limited and restricted suffrage for one class and a multiplied suffrage power for another, and with grinding industrial conditions for all the wageworkers. The President has not suggested that we make our support of Great Britain conditional to her granting home rule to Ireland, or Egypt, or India. We rejoice in the establishment of a democracy in Russia, but it will hardly be contended that if Russia was still an autocratic government, we would not be asked to enter this alliance with her just the same. Italy and the lesser powers of Europe, Japan in the Orient; in fact, all of the countries with whom we are to enter into alliance, except France and the newly revolutionized Russia, are still of the old order. . . .

. . . This war is being forced upon our people without their knowing why and without their approval.

Question: Why does Senator Robert La Follette oppose U.S. entry into World War I?

Document 3 Refer to the cartoon on page 312.

Question: How does the cartoonist feel about Senator Robert La Follette's opposition to U.S. entry into World War I?

Document 4 From a release by George Creel, Director of the U.S. Committee for Public Information, 1918:

Now let us picture what a sudden invasion of the United States by these Germans would mean; sudden because their settled way is always to attack suddenly.

First they set themselves to capture New York City. While their fleet blockades the harbor and shells the city and the forts from far at sea, their troops land somewhere near and advance toward the city in order to cut its rail communications, starve it into surrender and plunder it. . . .

. . . They pass through Lakewood, a station on the Central Railroad of New Jersey. They first demand wine for the officers and beer for the men. Angered to find that an American town does not contain large quantities of either, they pillage and burn the post office and most of the hotels and stores. Then they demand $1,000,000 from the residents. One feeble old woman tries to conceal $20 which she has been hoarding in her desk drawer; she is taken out and hanged (to save a cartridge). Some teachers in two district schools meet a fate which makes them envy her. The Catholic priest and Methodist minister are thrown into a pig-sty, while the German soldiers look on and laugh. Some of the officers quarter themselves in a handsome house on the edge of the town, insult the ladies of the family, and destroy and defile the contents of the house.

By this time some of the soldiers have managed to get drunk; one of them discharges his gun accidentally, the cry goes up that the residents are firing on the troops, and then hell breaks loose. Robbery, murder, and outrage run riot. Most of the town and beautiful pinewoods are burned, and then the troops move on to treat New Brunswick in the same way. . . .

This is not just a snappy story. It is not fancy. The general plan of campaign against America has been announced repeatedly by German military men. *And every horrible detail is just what the German troops have done in Belgium and France.*

Question: What is George Creel telling his readers could happen if Germany invades the United States?

Task

* ★ Describe how the United States government promoted and encouraged conformity among its population in order to make victory in World War I more likely.
* ★ Explain how some people who opposed U.S. entry into World War I were treated.

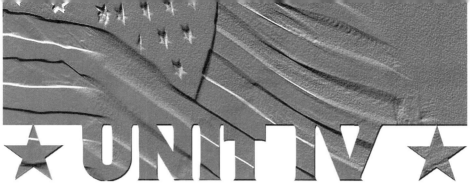

★ UNIT IV ★

Prosperity and Depression
At Home and Abroad

Chapter 12
War and Prosperity: 1917–1929

★ **Objectives**

- ★ To describe social changes in the postwar decade of the 1920s.
- ★ To examine both positive and negative changes in the lives of women, African Americans, and other minorities.
- ★ To examine the economic policies of the 1920s.
- ★ To understand the effects of mass consumption on cultural values.
- ★ To describe constitutional and legal issues that arose between 1917 and 1929.

$\mathbf{F}$rom 1900 to 1917, political life in the United States had moved under the banner of progressive reform. After World War I, however, most Americans ceased to care about promoting reform. They wanted to forget the war and enjoy the new prosperity. The U.S. government returned to the 19th-century policy of laissez-faire. For most of the 1920s, the United States enjoyed a period of prosperity.

Impact of War

World War I ended in 1918. In the election of 1920, the Republican candidate, Warren G. Harding, defeated his Democratic opponent by a huge majority. Harding's victory also represented a victory for postwar conservatism in place of the prewar policy of progressivism.

Women, African Americans, and Other Minorities

During World War I, both white and African American women entered the workforce to replace the men who went off to war. Some 300,000 African American men also joined the military fight to make the world "safe for democracy." When peace came, both women and African Americans were reluctant to accept their pre–World War I status. Women's rights advocates increased their protests to gain the right to vote. When African American soldiers returned home from the war, they had difficulty going back to being treated as second-class citizens. Thus, the 1920s saw increased confrontations between blacks and whites as well as the formation and strengthening of organizations that challenged second-class citizenship.

Many of the confrontations between blacks and whites occurred in southern cities. One of the most serious took place in Tulsa, Oklahoma, in 1921. As was true in other parts of the South, blacks in Tulsa were not allowed to live or own businesses in the white part of the city. As a result, African Americans lived and worked in their own segregated community. The cause of the Tulsa riot was similar to the cause of racial strife in other cities. Rumors had spread about a black male attacking a white woman. An army of whites forced their way into the black section of the city where deadly combat took place. When the rioting was over, many black-owned homes and businesses had been burned to the ground, and many people, mostly black, had been killed.

The 1920s also proved to be a difficult time for the foreign-born from eastern Europe and Asia. Many from eastern Europe were thought to be Communist sympathizers. Those from Asia, especially China and Japan, continued to face discrimination on the West Coast, where their increasing numbers were feared by the white population.

Movement of African Americans to the North

Between 1910 and 1930, the number of African Americans in the North more than doubled, going from one million to 2.5 million. Southern blacks moved to northern cities for two main reasons. First, they wanted to escape the segregation, or Jim Crow, laws of the South. Their resentment of these laws increased after World War I. If they boldly defied whites' prejudice against them, they risked being jailed or even lynched (killed by a mob, usually by hanging). In 1927 alone, there were 24 lynchings throughout the South. Most of them occurred because of suspected or rumored sexual encounters between black males and white females.

A second reason for moving to the North was the hope of finding a steady job for good pay.

Many whites in the North felt threatened by the arrival of blacks in large numbers. In Chicago in 1919, riots broke out between blacks and whites on a segregated beach. A total of 38 people of both races died in the fighting. Race riots broke out in other northern cities as well. In northern communities, as in the South, African Americans found segregation not only on beaches but also in housing, schools, and clubs. The goal of racial fairness was far from being realized in any section of the country.

Return to "Normalcy"

In his presidential campaign, Harding promised that he would lead the American nation back to *"normalcy."* In other words, he suggested a return to the quieter time before the war and before the progressive politics of Woodrow Wilson. Once in office, Harding showed his conservatism by doing very little to regulate business. He followed a laissez-faire policy like that of conservative presidents of the 1880s and 1890s.

The Twenties

The government's return to "normalcy" failed to recognize the realities of modern life. Society and the economy changed rapidly in the 1920s even if government did not.

Postwar Recession

During World War I, prices of many American-made goods increased because most were exported or used by the military. Fewer goods were available in the home market. During this period, wages did not keep pace with rising prices. By 1920, unemployment had increased from 2 percent during the war to more than 12 percent, as exports and the production of armaments declined. As the demand for goods decreased, businesses went bankrupt. Both the unemployed and those whose wages did not keep pace with prices could no longer afford to purchase goods and services. Added to this was the decline in farm income, as European farmers once again began to grow products that had been imported from the United States during the war. These conditions caused the United States to fall into a recession, which lasted from 1920 to 1922.

Greed and Scandal

Harding's presidency was marked by one of the worst scandals in U.S. history, known as the *Teapot Dome scandal*. Teapot Dome was the name of federally owned lands in Wyoming that contained huge reserves of oil. Secretary of the Interior Albert Fall secretly leased the oil-rich public lands to several oil companies. In return for his cooperation, Fall received from the companies secret and illegal payments (bribes) totaling about $325,000.

Harding knew nothing about the corrupt dealings of Fall and other high-ranking officials, but he bore the responsibility for having appointed untrustworthy politicians to office. Before the scandals were fully investigated by Congress, Harding died suddenly in 1923.

Prosperity Under Coolidge

Vice President Calvin Coolidge became president when Harding died. Coolidge was then elected to office in his own right in 1924. He declined to run again in 1928. Coolidge was a man of few words. His speeches were short. Often, in social situations, he said nothing at all. Reporters referred to him as "Silent Cal."

Coolidge did say something memorable: "The business of America is business." This statement expressed Coolidge's policy of supporting big business rather than regulating it. He favored high tariffs to protect American businesses and less government spending to permit lower taxes. He relied on the economic advice of Secretary of the Treasury Andrew Mellon—a banker and business leader. Thus, Coolidge and the Republican party were viewed as supporters of big business rather than as supporters of workers and farmers. During the Coolidge administration, big business and the wealthy gained the greatest share of wealth.

Farmers and Minorities in Trouble

In the midst of the general prosperity of the 1920s, people in the rural areas, as well as some in the cities, were finding life increasingly difficult.

Expansion, Mortgages, Advancing Technology Farm production had increased during World War I to meet the needs of both the United States and its European allies. With farmland in Europe turning into battlefields, U.S. farmers expanded production to meet the growing demand for their crops. Thus, in 1914, farm income rose to new heights. After 1921, however, farm-

"It Works Both Ways,"
a cartoon critical of high
tariffs in the early 1920s

ers suffered from falling prices caused by the return to production of European farms. There was less demand for U.S. food products in Europe. Moreover, better farm machinery produced surpluses of wheat and corn, which lowered their prices further.

To buy the new farm machinery and even the seeds for planting, farmers often borrowed money against the value of their land and homes. (They mortgaged their property.) The low prices that they received for their crops made it impossible to pay back the loans. When this happened, banks took the farmers' property in payment.

Nonsharers in the General Prosperity Burdened with heavy debts, many farmers were too poor to purchase the great quantities of consumer goods that U.S. businesses were selling. Minorities living in urban areas also failed to share in the economic benefits of the 1920s, as government no longer took an activist role in improving their living conditions and wages. Efforts by unions to force factory owners to increase wages also usually failed. Thus, the policy of laissez-faire hurt both farmers and workers.

Productivity, Investment, and the "Bull Market"

During the 1920s, there was no more trust busting by the government. Big businesses flourished and grew bigger and more powerful every year. By 1929, the 200 largest U.S. corporations controlled 49 percent of all corporate wealth in the country.

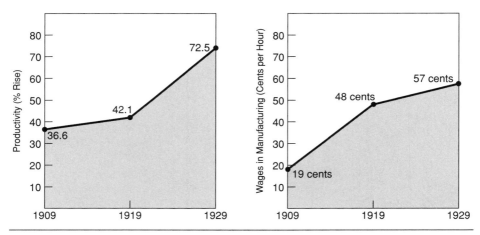

Gains in Productivity and Wages, 1909–1929

When workers spend less time accomplishing the same amount of work, we say that their productivity rises. New machinery and the use of assembly-line methods resulted in impressive gains in productivity during the 1920s, thus making it cheaper to manufacture goods. Although workers' wages also increased, they were far below the increases in productivity. An average factory worker earned $1,350 a year in 1929, compared to $1,100 a year in 1919.

Business was so good that average Americans with average incomes began buying the stocks of major corporations. As they invested larger sums in the stock market on New York City's Wall Street, the prices of most stocks went up and up. Month after month in 1928, people watched stock prices climb to record highs. It was a great *bull market* (the condition on a stock exchange when public confidence in stocks causes stock prices to rise).

★ In Review

1. Describe the effects of World War I on women and African Americans.
2. What were the causes and effects of South-to-North migration after World War I?
3. How did the uneven distribution of wealth and farm overproduction demonstrate that the prosperity of the 1920s did not include everyone?

Mass Consumption and Cultural Values

It was clear that an urban culture was fast emerging in the 1920s. Residents of rural areas felt that their more traditional culture was threatened by the new ways.

While prosperity lasted, most Americans cared less about politics than about the exciting amusements that were then coming into fashion. Young people in the cities and suburbs had automobiles, phonographs, radios, movies, major league sports, new dance steps, and a fast-paced, African American–inspired music called jazz. Their fun, which lasted for about a decade, gave a name to their times: the *Roaring Twenties*.

The Automobile

Henry Ford's Assembly Line   Henry Ford, an automaker in Detroit, Michigan, had the idea of mass-producing his Model T cars so that they could be sold cheaply to people with average incomes. The method used in manufacturing the Model T was as important as the car itself. Instead of workers moving about to pick up various automobile parts, Ford had them stand in one spot as the car being assembled moved past them on a moving conveyor belt. Without moving from their places in the assembly line, workers repeated the same operations over and over. The assembly-line method saved time, cut production costs, and enabled Model T's to be sold in 1916 for a price of only $400. Ford's methods were copied in other industries. By 1920, U.S. factories everywhere had switched to the assembly-line method for mass-producing goods.

The automobile did for the 20th century what the railroad had done for the 19th. It boosted the American economy and transformed American society. In only ten years, the number of cars manufactured by U.S. companies increased more than threefold—from 1.5 million in 1919 to 4.7 million in 1929. By the end of the decade of prosperity, Americans owned more than 25 million cars.

Economically, the millions of automobiles sold in the 1920s stimulated the growth of other industries. The rubber industry expanded to produce tires. The oil and gasoline industry provided fuel. The steel industry produced millions of tons of metal for auto bodies. Roadside hotels and restaurants were built all over the country to take advantage of the motorists' fondness for travel and tourism.

Of course, the automobile brought problems as well as benefits: drunken driving, fatal highway accidents, parking problems on city streets—and later, polluted air. But in the 1920s, most Americans were delighted with the automobile and the more mobile way of life it made possible.

Installment Buying

The telephone and phonograph had been invented in the 1870s. The first movies, the first automobiles with gasoline engines, and the first device for transmitting radio messages all appeared in the 1890s. At first, however, these inventions were merely curiosities. Ownership of telephones and automobiles was limited to the rich. Only in the postwar decade of the 1920s did the many marvels of the modern age become available to millions of American consumers.

To encourage people to buy new toasters, refrigerators, cars, and other products, businesses extended credit through *installment buying*. Rather

ESSEX COACH $1295

All-year Comfort and Dependable Service

With all the noted qualities of the Essex chassis, the Coach combines closed car utility, comfort and distinction, at an unrivalled price.

Note how little more it costs than the open car. That is made possible by great production. More Essex Coaches are now built than any other fine closed car.

You must see, examine and drive it to realize what is offered at this price.

Built to Endure Hard Service

The type of body construction is the newest. It gives a durable, comfortable type, of appealing distinction. But, perhaps more important, is the far quieter car that results. The Essex Coach construction absorbs and annuls practically all "drumming" noises of the closed compartment.

And the Coach is a product that will endure in good useful service for

Touring, $1095   Cabriolet. $1195

years. Come see, and drive it before you buy any car.

What Owners Say the Real Proof

There is a simple way to get the real truth about any car. Why buy blindly?

You have the all-important advantage of being able to ask owners. Make use of it. Find out how any car you think of buying has served others. What mileage does it give on gasoline and tires? What are upkeep costs? Is the second or third 10,000 miles just as satisfactory as the first? What is the future expectancy of good service after twenty or thirty thousand miles?

Just ask owners of the Coach how solid and quiet and free from rattles the body stays. How comfortable and easy it rides and handles. The satisfaction of owners is the best proof of all. We want you to know what Coach owners think because we believe their enthusiasm will win you, too.

Coach, 1295   Freight and Tax Extra

ESSEX MOTORS, DETROIT, MICHIGAN

Advertisement in a 1920s magazine

than paying the entire price of the product upon purchase, consumers had the opportunity to spread out their payments in installments, even as they used the product. However, millions of people went into debt to finance purchases. After a while, so much debt accumulated that a family had to stop buying new products just to make the monthly debt payments on all that it owed.

Real Estate Boom/Suburban Development

During the 1920s, millions of city dwellers moved to new housing in the suburbs. There they came to rely on the family car for transportation as well as recreation. A new suburban way of life developed around the possession and use of an automobile.

Public transportation in the cities also improved during the early years of the 20th century. Shoppers and workers could now move about the city on subways, buses, and electrified trolley cars. Cities continued to grow rapidly. The 1920s was the first decade in U.S. history in which residents of urban areas outnumbered residents of rural areas.

Even so, as cities increased in population, many people moved to the suburbs. Because many suburban dwellers worked in large cities nearby, road building to speed transportation from the suburbs to the cities became more of a priority than trolley and subway construction. In addition, new railroad lines connected suburban areas with urban centers. The new and faster means of transportation encouraged businesses to follow the movement of people from the cities to the suburbs.

New Regional, Political, and Economic Units The growth of smaller cities and towns beyond the larger urban centers led to alternate forms of government. For example, in some regions, such as Suffolk County in Long Island, New York, county government took over the administration of the region. Thus county boards and executives regulated matters such as property taxes, road building, environmental codes, and schools. They also provided services such as police protection, welfare, access to clean water, and garbage pickup. The new governments gave political parties new areas in which to exercise influence.

With the movement to the suburbs, *zoning regulations* became increasingly important. (Such regulations determine where businesses and homes may be established, how land may be used, and how much acreage each

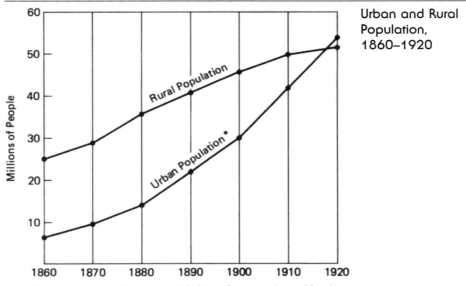

Urban and Rural Population, 1860–1920

*Urban areas were defined by the U.S. Census Bureau as places with at least 2,500 inhabitants.

house must have.) In the new suburbs of the 1920s, zoning regulations often required the purchase of a specific amount of land on which to build a home. In some towns, zoning regulations became a means to limit housing to those with higher incomes. Though challenged at the time, zoning regulations were upheld by the Supreme Court in a 1926 case, *Village of Euclid, Ohio* v. *Ambler Realty Company*, in which the Court agreed that municipalities had the right to regulate health and safety through zoning ordinances.

Entertainment and Cultural Homogenization

By 1920, popular forms of entertainment had undergone a revolution. There were now movies to see and phonograph records and radio shows to hear. Phonograph records preserved the voices of opera singers such as Enrico Caruso and popular singers such as Al Jolson. The practice of broadcasting shows on the radio—programs paid for by advertisers—began in the 1920s. For the first time, people heard election results, major news stories, and sporting events at the moment that they happened.

In the 1920s, the movie industry, which had begun in the East, found a new home on the West Coast. From studios in Hollywood, California, came hundreds of comedies, Westerns, and romances starring Charlie Chaplin, Mary Pickford, Rudolph Valentino, and others. The brief era of silent movies came to an end in 1927 when Al Jolson starred in *The Jazz Singer*, the first "talking movie."

Charles Lindbergh and his *Spirit of St. Louis*, 1927

The new forms of popular entertainment created a common culture for all Americans. Whether they lived in cities or on farms, people from East to West and North to South saw the same movies, listened to the same phonograph records, and adored the same celebrities. Everybody in the Roaring Twenties talked of aviators like Charles Lindbergh, who made the first solo flight from the United States to Europe, sports heroes like baseball's Babe Ruth and football's Red Grange, and publicity-seeking "flagpole sitters" and dance-marathon contestants.

Advertising in the mass media also became part of the popular culture. People from coast to coast saw the same magazine ads for cigarettes, soft drinks, cars, and appliances. The repetition of these ads gave Americans everywhere the sense of belonging to a common national culture. Some feared that the uniqueness of each region of the country would be lost. The differences would be homogenized, or blended, into one overall way of life.

Constitutional and Legal issues

Life in the 1920s was generally good for people of the middle class, who were largely native-born, white Americans. It was not so good for ethnic minorities and the foreign-born. Especially in rural communities, there was distrust of big cities where large numbers of Italian and Jewish immigrants had settled. Although most immigrants were hardworking and law-abiding, many people accused the foreign-born of being responsible for city slums and crime.

"The Only Way to Handle It," a cartoon depicting U.S. immigration quotas of the 1920s

Threats to Civil Liberties   The Communist revolution in Russia in 1917 fueled nativist fears about the loyalties of the huge foreign-born population. Nativists thought foreign-born radicals might attempt to overthrow the U.S. government.   Their fears turned to action in the Red Scare of 1919 and 1920. (See page 317.)   Federal agents trampled on the civil rights of a great many people.   Fear of Communists, or Reds, persisted throughout the 20th century.

Recall that the Ku Klux Klan (KKK) was a secret society of southern whites who had terrorized newly freed slaves after the Civil War.   In the 1920s, the Klan made a comeback.   Millions of people in small towns of the North, South, and Middle West joined the society and wore the KKK's white hoods in town parades.   The revived Klan tried to intimidate many groups—African Americans, Roman Catholics, Jews, and immigrants.   In the early years of the decade, its growing membership made it an important force in the politics of many states.   Oregon and Indiana, for example, both had governors who owed their election to the Klan's support.

Liberals blamed the antiforeign prejudices of many Americans for the deaths of two Italian immigrants.   In 1921, Nicola Sacco and Bartolomeo Vanzetti had been convicted in a Massachusetts court of armed robbery and

Grim cartoon summing up fear of foreign terrorists during the Red Scare

murder. As liberals pointed out, the evidence in the *Sacco-Vanzetti case* was weak, and the judge appeared to be biased against them. For years after the trial, there were worldwide protests and appeals for clemency. In 1927, however, both men were executed.

Prohibition and the Volstead Act   Many citizens were also alarmed by the unexpected result of the Eighteenth, or *Prohibition*, Amendment. This amendment, adopted in 1919, was the chief goal of Carrie Nation and other reformers in the temperance movement. (Review Chapter 10.) It prohibited the manufacture and sale of wines, beers, liquors, and other alcoholic beverages in the United States. After the amendment was ratified, Congress passed the National Prohibition Act—more popularly known as the Volstead Act, after Representative Andrew J. Volstead of Minnesota—which provided for the enforcement of Prohibition.

Supporters of Prohibition argued that banning alcohol would improve the country's morals, lower crime rates, reduce alcohol consumption, especially among the young, and increase the health of Americans. Instead, Prohibition had the opposite effects.

The new amendment failed to achieve its objective and caused millions of otherwise law-abiding citizens to obtain drinks illegally. The alcoholic beverages were either manufactured illegally in the United States or smuggled across the border from Canada and other foreign sources. *Bootleggers* (those who made a business of supplying illegal beverages) made huge prof-

Prohibitionist disposing of a dandelion that might be processed into homemade wine its. In large cities like New York and Chicago, bootleggers organized criminal gangs that often managed to evade the law by corrupting the police. Thus, Prohibition was largely responsible for a huge increase in organized crime. In addition, because there was no quality control in this illegal market, many Americans were poisoned or suffered other ill effects from contaminants and impurities in the liquor.

Federal officials continued their losing battle to enforce Prohibition until 1933. In that year, the Eighteenth Amendment was repealed (erased) by another amendment, the Twenty-first.

Scopes Trial The clash between urban and rural cultures expressed itself in a spectacular and much publicized trial in Tennessee in 1925. The defendant was a biology teacher named John Scopes. He had purposely defied a Tennessee law against the teaching in public schools of Charles Darwin's theory of evolution. The law had been passed because Darwin's ideas offended Protestant groups that interpreted the Bible strictly.

A famous lawyer named Clarence Darrow defended Scopes. The prosecutor was a politician from an earlier era—William Jennings Bryan, the Democratic Populist candidate for president in 1896 and former U.S. secretary of state. At one point in the trial, Darrow called Bryan as a witness and challenged Bryan's literal interpretation of the Bible. Reading about the trial in their newspapers, city people tended to side with Scopes and Darrow. Rural, church-going Americans tended to side with the prosecution. Although Scopes was convicted, he was fined only $100. A higher court in Tennessee later reversed the trial court's verdict.

The following excerpt from the trial is a portion of Darrow's examination of Bryan as a witness:

Mr. Darrow: Do you claim that everything in the Bible should be literally interpreted?

Mr. Bryan: I believe everything in the Bible should be accepted as it is given there; some of the Bible is given illustratively. For instance: "Ye are the salt of the earth." I would not insist that man was actually salt, or that he had flesh of salt, but it is used in the sense of salt as saving God's people.

Mr. Darrow: But when you read that Jonah swallowed the whale—or that the whale swallowed Jonah—excuse me please—how do you literally interpret that? . . .

Mr. Bryan: One miracle is just as easy to believe as another. . . .

Mr. Darrow: Perfectly easy to believe that Jonah swallowed the whale? . . .

Mr. Bryan: Your honor. I think I can shorten this testimony. The only purpose Mr. Darrow has is to slur at the Bible, but I will answer his question. I will answer it all at once, and I have no objection in the world, I want the world to know that this man, who does not believe in God, is trying to use a court in Tennessee—

Mr. Darrow: I object to that.

Mr. Bryan: [Continuing] to slur at it, and while it will require time, I am willing to take it.

Mr. Darrow: I object to your statement. I am examining you on your fool ideas that no intelligent Christian on earth believes.

Is it right or wrong to suppress the teaching of scientific ideas that conflict with traditional interpretations of the Bible? This issue was at the heart of the Scopes trial and continues to stir controversy in our own times.

Restrictions on Immigration Recall from Chapter 9 that immigration from eastern and southern Europe was severely restricted by quota laws enacted by Congress in 1921 and 1924. Another immigration law of 1927 limited total immigration to just 150,000 per year. (It went into effect in 1929.) Each country was assigned a small percentage of that total—a percentage (or quota) based on the number of people from that country who lived in the United States in 1920. In addition, the 1927 law prohibited any immigration from countries in Asia.

Shifting Cultural Values

During the 1920s, more liberal urban cultural values began to replace the traditional rural cultural values in the United States.

Fads, Flappers, and Freud During the 1920s, new forms of expression came into being. These forms, known as *fads*, lasted for a limited period of time. For example, a dance craze called the "Charleston" was popular only during the decade of the 1920s. Other fads included slang expressions such as "23 skidoo" (goodbye) and women putting rouge on their knees and wearing short skirts.

Many young women in high school and college experimented with a new style of dress. They raised hemlines above the knee and danced to the swinging beat of popular music. These young *flappers*, as they were called, shocked the older generation by wearing one-piece bathing suits and smoking cigarettes in public.

Many older Americans, both men and women, worried about the new flapper fashions and fads. They feared that greater freedom and full-time employment for women would lead to a breakdown of the traditional family. Traditional values seemed to be in serious danger.

Sigmund Freud was a pioneer in the field of *psychoanalysis*. While he did his work in his native Austria, his ideas became very popular in the United States. Freud held that individuals could resolve their emotional problems through talking about them in a process called *free association*. The treatment involved probing unconscious memories through interpretation of past events and dreams of the patient. Freud's theory that sexual repression was a major problem among the middle classes found a receptive audience during the newly liberated decade of the 1920s.

Women's Changing Roles

Between 1917 and 1929, women began to challenge old assumptions about their role in society.

Effect of World War I   World War I created new employment opportunities for women. With millions of men in the armed forces, women began filling jobs once thought suitable only for men. They became factory workers, railroad conductors, and farmers. They made shells in munitions plants, and enlisted in the Nurses Corps of the army and navy. The war increased the need for telephone operators, secretaries, and sales personnel. Women soon made up a majority in these occupations.

The Nineteenth Amendment   The adoption of the Nineteenth Amendment enabled women in every state to vote for presidents and other officials. In addition, during the struggle for its adoption, women organized public demonstrations and used such tactics as petitioning, picketing, and hunger strikes in their campaign to achieve equal political rights with men. They realized that they had the capability to influence public policy.

Women in the Workforce   Refrigerators, washing machines, vacuum cleaners, and other household appliances became commonplace in the 1920s. These time-saving devices reduced the household chores traditionally assigned to women. They made it possible for women of the middle class to enter the workforce in record numbers. But many jobs available to women were limited to support services—working for a man as a secretary or typist. The greatest expansion of jobs was in white-collar occupations such as telephone operator, clerk, stenographer, secretary, and teacher. Women were expected to leave the job market after marriage and often received lower wages than men for the same work. The ability to find jobs, however, enabled many young women to move away from their families and live on their own. This added to their independence and social freedom.

The health conditions of women generally improved as they moved from rural to urban areas. One major reason was that the physical labor once required on the farm was no longer necessary. A second reason was the increased number of doctors and medical facilities available in large urban areas.

The Literary and Musical Scene

Novels and American Diversity   During the 1920s, a number of talented writers wrote about Americans at home and abroad. For example, Sinclair Lewis, in his novel *Main Street* (1920), satirized the attitudes of small-town America and its feelings of superiority toward the large urban centers. Ernest Hemingway, one of the most interesting personalities of the 1920s, lived the life of an adventurer. His most famous novel, *The Sun Also Rises* (1926), depicted Americans abroad who have no clear view of themselves or the world around them. In *The Age of Innocence* (1920), Edith Wharton

Women workers in ship construction, Puget Sound, Oregon, 1919

traced the social manners, arrogance, and presumed superiority of upper-class New Yorkers. Willa Cather achieved fame for *My Antonía* (1918), a novel about the difficulties of western life on the harsh frontier. Finally, F. Scott Fitzgerald, another great personality of the 1920s, wrote about materialism and social climbing in his novel *The Great Gatsby* (1925).

Harlem Renaissance Many of the African Americans who moved to New York City between 1900 and 1930 settled in a neighborhood called Harlem. In the 1920s, a number of talented African Americans settled there and rose to fame as writers, performers, and musicians. Their creativity during this period was called the *Harlem Renaissance*. Best known of the Harlem poets were James Weldon Johnson, Langston Hughes, and Countee Cullen. Langston Hughes used the black vernacular in expressing the frustrations and difficulties faced by African Americans living in an age of discrimination and segregation.

  Among the celebrated actors living in Harlem was Paul Robeson, star of a number of Eugene O'Neill's plays as well as *Showboat*. Written by Jerome Kern and produced in 1927, *Showboat* was the first American musical to highlight the problems faced by black Americans. The show also brought together black and white performers on the same stage. Josephine Baker sang and danced her way to fame in night clubs in Philadelphia, New York, and Paris. Eubie Blake and W. C. Handy composed songs that are still heard today.

Jazz African American musicians were the principal creators of the most popular music of the 1920s—jazz. They first played the music in New

Orleans around 1900. By the 1920s, jazz had traveled north to Chicago and New York City. Its vibrant, fast-moving beat expressed the spirit of the times. Among the greatest of the jazz musicians were the bandleader and songwriter Duke Ellington, the trumpet player and singer Louis Armstrong, and the blues singer Bessie Smith.

Discrimination Talent and ability did not lead to acceptance. Movies rarely used African Americans in other than stereotyped roles (servants, maids). Chorus lines were generally all-white. Even in Harlem at the famous Cotton Club, African Americans would entertain, but were rarely seen as customers. African American entertainers continually faced discrimination—from not being allowed to stay in certain hotels or eat in certain restaurants to not having opportunities to display their talents.

★ In Review

1. Explain the significance of the following: installment buying, the Eighteenth Amendment, Sigmund Freud, the Nineteenth Amendment, the Harlem Renaissance.
2. How did the growth of the automobile industry stimulate the growth of other industries? How did it influence American lifestyles?
3. How did each of the following contribute to the literary scene during the 1920s: Sinclair Lewis, Ernest Hemingway, Edith Wharton, Willa Cather, F. Scott Fitzgerald, Langston Hughes?

Chapter Review

MULTIPLE-CHOICE QUESTIONS

Use the cartoon on page 335 to answer questions 1 and 2.

1. The cartoon
   (1) endorses U.S. trade policy during the 1920s
   (2) is critical of U.S. tariff policy
   (3) demands that Europeans be isolated as punishment for causing World War I
   (4) shows that the United States is self-sufficient and does not need foreign trade.

2. An argument that the cartoonist would probably make is that
   (1) the United States needs to retaliate against foreign tariffs
   (2) restrictions on immigration go hand in hand with high tariffs
   (3) high tariffs hurt American business
   (4) the United States should be totally isolated.

Use the graphs on page 336 to answer question 3.

3. What conclusion can be drawn from an examination of the two graphs?
(1) Higher productivity lowered the price of products between 1909 and 1929.
(2) During the periods shown, productivity and wages rose in proportion to each other.
(3) Although both productivity and wages rose between 1909 and 1929, they were not always in proportion to each other.
(4) There was little relationship between productivity and wages between 1909 and 1929.

Study the advertisement on page 338 and answer question 4.

4. The advertisement shows that during the 1920s, automobiles were
(1) still considered a luxury
(2) becoming more affordable
(3) only used in urban areas
(4) uncomfortable and unreliable.

5. "The nation became urbanized, a process to which the automobile especially, as well as the radio, the moving picture, and the newspaper, contributed." Which is the first period in U.S. history to which this statement might have been applied?
(1) 1890 to 1900
(2) 1901 to 1910
(3) 1910 to 1920
(4) 1920 to 1928.

Refer to the photograph on page 340 and answer question 6.

6. The photograph of Charles Lindbergh and his plane the *Spirit of St. Louis* was taken to honor the

(1) invention of the airplane
(2) first solo flight to Europe
(3) opening of the first modern airport
(4) first flight across the United States.

Use the cartoon on page 341 to answer question 7.

7. The cartoon shows that the United States
(1) continued its previous immigration policies into the 1920s
(2) limited immigration during the 1920s
(3) cut off all immigration
(4) stopped admitting immigrants from eastern and southern Europe.

Study the cartoon on page 343 and answer question 8.

8. The cartoonist feels that people who supported Prohibition were
(1) cynical
(2) intelligent
(3) practical
(4) extremist.

Read the following excerpt from a Brooklyn, New York, newspaper during the 1920s, and answer question 9:

And the pistol's red glare,
Bombs bursting in air
Gave proof through the night
That Chicago's still there.

9. The excerpt is referring to
(1) protests against immigration quotas
(2) the rise of organized crime in Chicago
(3) Ku Klux Klan violence in the Midwest
(4) strikes by unions following World War I.

Reread the dialog from the Scopes trial of 1925 on pages 344–345 and answer question 10.

10. The dialog is taken from a court case that decided whether
    (1) prohibition was constitutional
    (2) a teacher had broken the law by teaching evolution in a public school
    (3) the book *On the Origin of Species* should be removed from public libraries in Tennessee
    (4) fundamentalists had the right to teach creationism in public schools.

THEMATIC ESSAYS

1. **Theme:** Tradition Versus Change

   The 1920s were years that saw many great changes take place in the United States. These changes were, however, coupled with a backlash from people who resisted change and longed for "the good old days."

   Task

   ★ Choose one change that took place during the 1920s. Describe the cause of the change and the impact of the change on the United States.
   ★ Give one example of how some Americans tried to resist a change, and evaluate the success that they had in stopping or slowing the change. (You may use as your example the same change or a different one.)

   You may wish to discuss the changes involving the migration of African Americans, women's roles, and mass consumption.

   Some examples of Americans resisting change may be found in attitudes toward immigrants, Prohibition, and the fundamentalist response towards science.

2. **Theme:** The Return to "Normalcy"

   During the presidential election of 1920, the soon-to-be-elected Republican candidate, Warren G. Harding, promised a return to "normalcy."

   Task

   ★ Describe what Warren G. Harding meant by "normalcy" in the aftermath of World War I.
   ★ Choose two events or circumstances from the decade of the 1920s. For each event chosen, explain how it stemmed, in part, from U.S. participation in World War I.
   ★ Use each example given to evaluate if the United States had, in fact, returned to "normalcy."

You may use, but are not limited to, the following examples: treatment of immigrants, stock speculation, foreign policy, mass consumption, and changing cultural values.

3. **Theme:** Laws and Social Change

The 1920s proved that although legislation can create important and even momentous change, it can also prove to be ineffective if it runs counter to the desires and will of the people.

Task

★ Describe one way in which a law effectively instituted an important change in U.S. society.

★ Demonstrate how another law was opposed by many people and rendered ineffective in creating a lasting change in the way people of the United States live.

★ You may utilize, but are not limited to, New York State education law, federal immigration legislation, and constitutional amendments involving suffrage and prohibition.

DOCUMENT-BASED QUESTION

*Read each document and answer the question that follows it. Then read the **Task** and write your essay. Essays should include references to most of the documents along with additional information based on your knowledge of United States history and government.*

Historical Context: World War I left an aftereffect of fear among some and hope among others.

Document 1 Refer to the cartoon on page 342.

Question: What does the cartoon, published shortly after World War I, say about immigrants and foreigners?

Document 2 Hiram W. Evans, Imperial Wizard of the Ku Klux Klan, as quoted in *North American Review*, 1926:

The greatest achievement so far has been to formulate and gain recognition for an idea—the idea of preserving and developing America first and chiefly for the benefit of the children of pioneers who made America. . . . The Klan cannot claim to have created this idea—it has long been a vague stirring in the souls of the plain people. But the Klan can fairly claim to have given it purpose, method, direction. . . .

. . . there are three great racial instincts . . . condensed into the Klan slogan: "Native, white, Protestant supremacy."

Question: Who does Hiram W. Evans feel that the nation was created to benefit?

Document 3 Refer to the photograph on page 347.

Question: How does the photograph show that the role of women had started to change by the end of World War I?

Document 4 James Weldon Johnson in *Harper's*, November, 1928:

> . . . [T]here is a common, widespread, and persistent stereotyped idea regarding the Negro, and it is that he is here only to receive; to be shaped into something new and unquestionably better. The common idea is that the Negro reached America intellectually, culturally, and morally empty, and that he is here to be filled—filled with education, filled with religion, filled with morality, filled with culture. In a word, the stereotype is that the Negro is nothing more than a beggar at the gate of the nation, waiting to be thrown the crumbs of civilization.
>
> Through his artistic efforts the Negro is smashing this immemorial stereotype faster than he has ever done through any other method he has been able to use. He is making it realized that he is the possessor of a wealth of natural endowments and that he has long been a generous giver to America. He is impressing upon the national mind the conviction that he is an active and important force in American life; that he is a creator as well as a creature; that he has given as well as received; that he is the potential giver of larger and richer contributions.
>
> In this way the Negro is bringing about an entirely new national conception of himself; he has placed himself in an entirely new light before the American people. I do not think it too much to say that through artistic achievement the Negro has found a means of getting at the very core of the prejudice against him by challenging the Nordic superiority complex. A great deal has been accomplished in this decade of "renaissance."

Question: Why does James Weldon Johnson feel that there was a change in attitude toward African Americans during the period following World War I?

Task

★ Describe why Americans were *both* fearful and hopeful during the years immediately following World War I.

★ Show how one of the fears or hopes that you described is still important in the America of the new millennium.

Chapter 13
The Great Depression

★ **Objectives**

★ To examine the causes of the Great Depression and its effects on people and institutions.

★ To understand the interdependence of the world's financial and economic systems.

★ To examine the responses to the Depression by Herbert Hoover and Franklin D. Roosevelt.

★ To evaluate the impact of the New Deal on the U.S. economy.

★ To examine the cultural and intellectual life during the Depression.

Economic boom in the 1920s was followed by economic bust in the 1930s. The disaster known as the *Great Depression* awakened political leaders to the need for more reform laws. Under the leadership of President Franklin D. Roosevelt, the U.S. government became more actively involved in the economy than ever before.

Onset of the Depression

The term *depression* refers to a severe economic decline marked by business failures, high unemployment, low production, and low prices. By the middle of 1930, the signs of a worsening depression were everywhere. Farmers were deeper in debt than ever. Consumers were cutting back on the purchase of cars, radios, and other items. Businesses were laying off workers. Europeans and Canadians were buying fewer U.S. goods. Every month, from October 1929 to March 1933, the economic news seemed to grow worse. These were difficult years indeed—especially because Americans did not know when, if ever, the depression would end.

Weakness in the Economy

There were a number of basic weaknesses in the economy that contributed to the economic collapse that became known as the Great Depression. In addition, very few safeguards existed to soften the impact on the average person of an economic downturn.

Overproduction/Underconsumption   A nation's economic strength depends on the ability of millions of citizens to buy the things that factories and farms produce. If wages are low relative to all on offer for sale, many goods will go unsold and businesses will fail. In fact, wages in the 1920s lagged far behind increases in production, as we have seen. Therefore, workers' purchasing power (ability to buy goods and services) was too weak to sustain many years of prosperity. In other words, more goods were being produced than people could afford to buy.

Much of the wealth in the United States in 1929 was in the hands of a small number of people. The richest 5 percent of the population had 25 percent of the total income. The combined income of the 36,000 wealthiest families equaled that of the poorest 12 million families.

Overexpansion of Credit   Another problem of the period was the risky practice of taking out a loan to purchase stocks. It was common practice to pay a small percent of a stock's purchase price with one's own money and finance the rest with a bank loan. Such a practice was called buying stocks *"on margin."*

Take as an example a man who invests his entire savings of $1,000 to buy $10,000 worth of stock. This investor is buying on 10 percent margin, that is, borrowing $9,000, or 90 percent of the price of the stock. But what if the stock's market price goes down by 10 percent or more. The bank that made the loan would probably ask for more money from the investor. But the investor has no more money. The bank would then sell the investor's stock for whatever the stock is worth. The investor would thereby lose all of his savings. If the stock has fallen very far, the bank would lose part of its loan of $9,000. To see the implications of this type of investment nationally, multiply this one example by millions of investors and thousands of banks. Such were the potential dangers to the U.S. economy of investors in the 1920s going into debt to buy stocks on margin.

Stock Market Crash

When Coolidge decided not to run for reelection, the Republicans nominated Herbert Hoover as their candidate in 1928. Time and again, throughout his career, Hoover had demonstrated unusual abilities as a leader. He

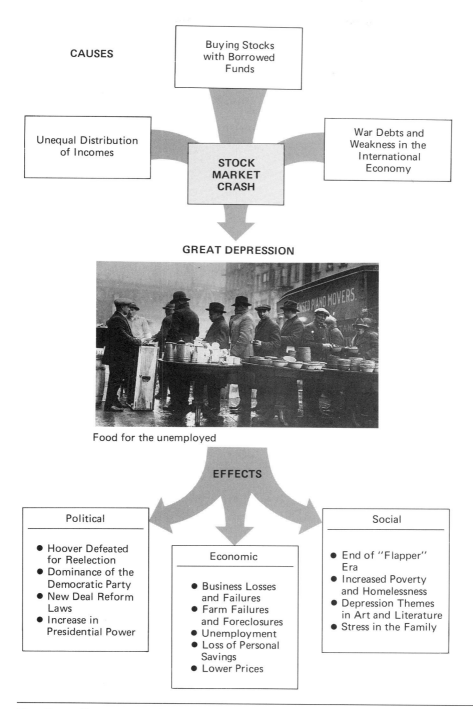

CAUSES

Buying Stocks
with Borrowed
Funds

Unequal Distribution
of Incomes

STOCK
MARKET
CRASH

War Debts and
Weakness in the
International
Economy

GREAT DEPRESSION

Food for the unemployed

EFFECTS

Political

- Hoover Defeated
  for Reelection
- Dominance of the
  Democratic Party
- New Deal Reform
  Laws
- Increase in
  Presidential Power

Economic

- Business Losses
  and Failures
- Farm Failures
  and Foreclosures
- Unemployment
- Loss of Personal
  Savings
- Lower Prices

Social

- End of "Flapper"
  Era
- Increased Poverty
  and Homelessness
- Depression Themes
  in Art and Literature
- Stress in the Family

The Great Depression: Causes and Effects

had succeeded brilliantly as an engineer, a business leader, an administrator of war relief following World War I, and a cabinet member under Harding and Coolidge. Much was expected of the new president when he took the oath of office in March 1929.

Through President Hoover's first six months in office, economic prosperity continued, and the president capably managed the government's executive branch. The bull (or rising) market on Wall Street reached its highest point in September 1929. After that the prices of stocks started to go down—sometimes slowly, sometimes in frightening drops. Bankers tried to save the market from losing any more ground. But on October 29, thousands of people panicked and ordered their brokers on Wall Street to sell at any price. On that "Black Tuesday" a record 16.5 million shares of stock were traded, almost all of them at prices far below what people originally paid. After that, prices continued to sink. By the end of December, the combined prices of Wall Street stocks had lost one-third of their peak value in September.

The *Great Crash* on Wall Street had three consequences, all bad. First, the billions of dollars in savings that people had used to buy stocks were largely wiped out. Second, many individuals and businesses that owned stock on margin could not pay their debts and went bankrupt. Banks failed because loans were not repaid. Third, and perhaps most serious of all, people lost confidence in the economy. For years after the crash, they preferred to save what they could rather than to risk investing in new business ventures.

Worldwide Repercussions

World War I had brought boom times to the U.S. economy. During the war, American farms had fed much of Europe, and farm prices had risen to impressive levels. American industries had mobilized for war and produced vast quantities of military equipment. The United States, which had been a debtor nation prior to World War I, emerged from the war as a creditor nation.

But the war also produced an imbalance in the world economy that eventually led to a worldwide depression. Recall that the peace treaty of 1919 forced Germany to pay the Allies a crushing sum of money in reparations. At the same time, the victorious Allies (Great Britain, France, and others) owed vast sums to the United States for their wartime consumption of American-made foods and military supplies. The United States in the 1920s was the one nation to whom many other nations owed a huge debt. This fact produced the economic imbalance that was one cause of the economic collapse of 1929.

By 1930, the nations of the world were financially interdependent (tied together). International debts could only be repaid with loans from the United States. For example, the United States lent money to Germany so that Germany could pay reparations to England and France. England and

France, in turn, could then repay loans to the United State made during World War I. The process went round and round in a cycle to everyone's benefit.

Interdependent Banking Systems   U.S. banks and businesses provided general loans to Europeans so that they could pay war debts owed to the United States. Such an arrangement could sustain prosperity only so long as U.S. banks were strong enough to keep making foreign loans. But if banks made too many loans to too many people, U.S. dollars might no longer be available to prop up the European economy. Suddenly, the cycle of debt payments both in the United States and Europe came to a stop when stock market prices on Wall Street collapsed.

International Trade   In times of panic, people sometimes do things that only make matters worse. That is what happened during the year following the Great Crash. It was understood that the U.S. economy was part of an international economy. The lifeblood of that larger economy was trade between nations. Tariffs that interfered with that trade could damage all nations, including the United States.

   Many politicians in Congress hoped to protect American industries from foreign competition by raising tariff rates. In 1930, they enacted a new tariff law—the *Hawley-Smoot Tariff*—that increased import taxes on more than a thousand items. The result was disastrous. European nations followed the U.S. example by raising their own tariffs. The volume of trade between the United States and Europe dropped to half of its peak level.

How U.S. Loans Financed International Prosperity, 1924–1929

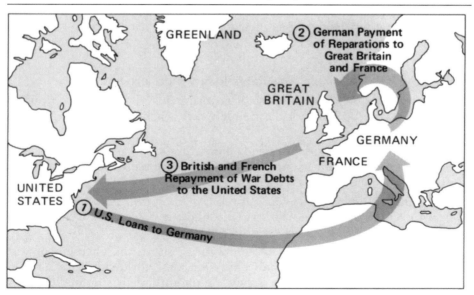

(Even today, those who oppose the idea of a protective tariff point to the negative effects of the tariff of 1930.)

After 1930, the economies of Europe and the United States sank deeper and deeper into a depression. Higher tariffs were not the only cause of the depression, but they were no help at all.

Domestic Political Repercussions

There were four major political repercussions of the Depression within the United States. First, Herbert Hoover was defeated by Franklin D. Roosevelt in the presidential election of 1932.

Second, the Republican party, which had won three consecutive presidential election during the 1920s, would fail to win another presidential election until 1952 when General Eisenhower won the presidency. Thus, for twenty years (1932–1952), only Democrats would occupy the White House.

Third, the administration of Franklin Roosevelt, together with a Democratic House and Senate, would pass far-reaching legislation to help provide relief to individuals, begin the process of recovery, and reform the economy.

Fourth, with a major worldwide crisis confronting the United States, Franklin Roosevelt would win election to the presidency four times and, in the process, greatly expand the power of the chief executive. Roosevelt would be the only American to be elected to the presidency more than twice.

Hoover's Response

The worst years of the Great Depression, 1930–1932, corresponded to the years when Herbert Hoover was president. Hoover tried hard to revive the economy. Drawing on his economic experience and past successes, he attempted to halt the Depression as follows:

★ Cutting taxes to enable consumers to buy more products

★ Greatly increasing the amount of government money spent on public projects—the building of dams, highways, harbors, and other public projects

★ Persuading Congress to provided federal funds to struggling banks, railroads, and insurance companies in order to keep them from going bankrupt

★ Persuading Congress to establish the *Federal Farm Board* to help farmers through hard times. This agency had the power to purchase farm goods in order to keep prices from falling

★ Declaring a *debt moratorium* (temporary halt on the payment of war debts). Recognizing that the Depression was worldwide, Hoover told European nations in 1931 that they could temporarily stop making payments on their debts.

Rugged Individualism Despite the president's efforts, economic conditions did not improve. Many Americans accused Hoover of doing nothing to give direct relief to the poor and unemployed. His policies gave the impression that he cared more about aiding businesses than aiding the common people.

Hoover disagreed with the idea of giving aid directly to the poor. He believed instead in what he called "rugged individualism." In his view, government was less important to economic recovery than the decisions of private businesses and individuals. His belief in limited government action was in keeping with the beliefs of earlier presidents. According to their views, if businesses succeeded, everyone would benefit indirectly from profits "trickling down" to wage earners.

Reconstruction Finance Corporation (RFC) Established in 1932, the RFC was an innovative concept. It involved the government directly in giving federal relief to businesses, particularly banks. The RFC also financed public works projects. This agency proved to be one of the most successful and long-lasting of Hoover's programs.

Impact of the Depression

Unemployment In 1932, about 12 million workers—25 percent of the labor force—were unemployed. (In contrast, the unemployment rate in 2000 was under 5 percent.) Those fortunate enough to keep their jobs worked for much lower wages than in the 1920s. Prices paid to farmers were desperately low. Factories produced only half of their 1929 output. By 1932, about 5,000 banks had closed their doors, forever cutting off customers from their savings.

"Bonus Army" One of the saddest events of the Great Depression occurred in the summer of 1932. About 17,000 unemployed veterans of World War I marched from their homes across the country all the way to Washington, D.C., to persuade the president and Congress to pay immediately the bonuses due them at a later time. The *Bonus Army*, as they were called, set

Falling Prices and Rising Unemployment, 1929–1932

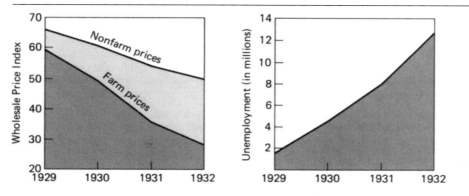

up makeshift shacks near the Capitol. President Hoover ordered them to leave. When they refused, federal troops moved in with tanks and tear gas and broke up the encampment.

A writer on the staff of the *New Republic* offered a ride to two war veterans who had joined the Bonus Army on its march to Washington in 1932. The writer's account of what they told him is below. Why were the men so angry at the U.S. government? How do you think the government should have treated the marchers when they finally arrived in Washington?

"Hoovervilles" Jobless persons who could not pay even the lowest rents were forced into the streets. For food they had no choice but to line up for free meals served by private charities and churches. The homeless slept in tents and shacks clustered in areas called *Hoovervilles*. They also found shelter in railroad boxcars and traveled about on freight trains. Jobless men and women sold apples on street corners in every large city to earn money for food. A sense of despair was settling over the population.

Impact on Women, Minorities, and Migrants The freedom and fun that young women had as flappers of the 1920s did not last into the 1930s.

★ ★ ★ ★ ★

ON THE ROAD WITH THE "BONUS ARMY," 1932

Mile after mile we passed the ragged line as we too drove northward to the camp at Ideal Park. We were carrying two of the veterans, chosen from a group of three hundred by a quick informal vote of their comrades. One was a man gassed in the Argonne . . . ; he breathed with an effort, as if each breath would be his last. The other was a man with family troubles; he had lost his wife and six children during the retreat from Camp Marks and hoped to find them in Johnstown. He talked about his service in France, his three medals, which he refused to wear, his wounds, his five years in a government hospital. "If they gave me a job," he said, "I wouldn't care about the bonus. . . . Now I don't ever want to see a flag again. Give me a gun and I'll go back to Washington."—"That's right, buddy," said a woman looking up from her two babies, who lay on a dirty quilt in the sun. A cloud of flies hovered above them. Another man was reading the editorial page of a Johnstown paper. He shouted, "Let them come here and mow us down with machine guns. We won't move this time."—"That's right, buddy," said the woman again. A haggard face—eyes bloodshot, skin pasty white under a three days' beard—suddenly appeared at the window of the car. "Hoover must die," said the face ominously. "You know what this means?" a man shouted from the other side. "This means revolution."

Some even lowered the hemlines on their skirts and dresses to the ankle again, symbolizing the change to more serious and traditional values. In the Great Depression, there were fewer job and career opportunities for women. Many women again concentrated on the needs of their families.

Perhaps even more than whites, African Americans suffered the full impact of the Depression. The last to be hired, they were usually the first to be fired.

Native Americans had lived in poverty ever since the 1870s and 1880s when they had been forced to live on reservations. From their point of view, the economic depression had been a reality 50 years before the stock market crash. The Great Depression was nothing new—except that whites now shared in the hard times.

Immigrants fared no better in the Depression decade than they had in the 1920s. Recall that a series of quota laws to reduce immigration had been passed during that decade. Native-born Americans' opposition to immigration continued in the 1930s when few jobs were available.

In the midst of the Great Depression, farmers from Oklahoma, Arkansas, Kansas, and other areas of the Great Plains found that their land had turned to dust. In the *Dust Bowl*, poor farming practices, a long-lasting drought, and high winds pulled the moisture out of the ground. Soil

New York City Depression scenes: Hooverville shacks in Central Park and (inset) women and men receiving bread and coffee at St. Peter's Mission, 1930

that had produced crops now produced nothing except dust. As a result, many of these poor farmers lost their income and land. They took to the open road looking for work as migrant farmworkers in California, believed to be the "land of plenty." So many of the migrants came from Oklahoma that the nickname "Okie" stuck to all of them.

★ In Review

1. Summarize the basic weaknesses in the economy that contributed to both the stock market crash and the general economic collapse that became known as the Great Depression.
2. Explain how Herbert Hoover responded to the Depression.
3. Identify the following: rugged individualism, trickle-down economics, Reconstruction Finance Corporation, Bonus Army, Hoovervilles.

Franklin D. Roosevelt and the New Deal

In 1932, most Americans were impatient with policies that did not seem to work. They expressed their impatience by voting overwhelmingly for a change in leadership. In the election of 1932, Hoover as the Republican candidate lost by a huge margin to his Democratic challenger, Franklin D. Roosevelt.

Roosevelt believed that government should do whatever it could to help people overcome economic hardship. His approach differed from that of Hoover, who believed in a trick-down theory for rescuing the economy by primarily aiding businesses. Roosevelt was more inclined to help people directly by giving them government jobs. The federal paychecks, in Roosevelt's view, would give people hope and put money in the economy to make possible the buying of more goods and services.

Above all, Roosevelt believed in trying out many ideas for solving the economic crisis. In his 1932 campaign, he promised a "new deal" for the American people. Through his first term and part of his second term as president (1933–1938), the government programs that he favored were known as the *New Deal*.

Roosevelt and his many advisers (a group called the "Brain Trust") had three main goals—*relief*, *recovery*, and *reform*. First, they wanted to provide relief to the poor and unemployed. Second, they wanted to bring about the recovery of business. Third, they wanted to reform the economic system to correct the mistakes that had caused the Depression.

Relief of Human Suffering

In Roosevelt's first three months in office—almost exactly 100 days—more important laws were enacted than during the entire decade of the 1920s. Rec-

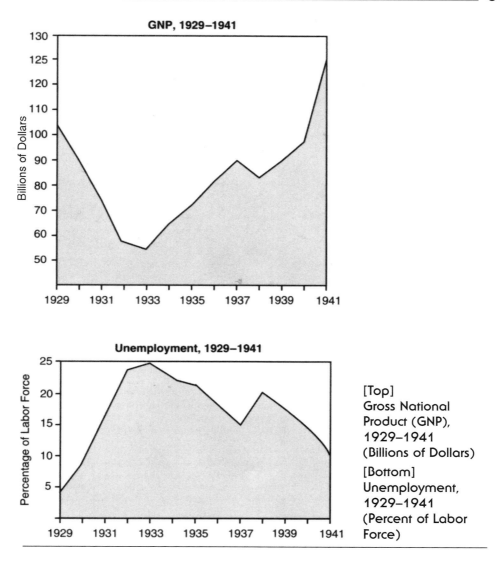

GNP, 1929–1941

Unemployment, 1929–1941

[Top]
Gross National
Product (GNP),
1929–1941
(Billions of Dollars)

[Bottom]
Unemployment,
1929–1941
(Percent of Labor
Force)

ognizing that the times called for bold measures, the Democratic majority in Congress gave the president almost all that he asked for. The legislation of the "Hundred Days" had a dramatic and long-lasting effect on the country.

Bank "Holiday" After the stock market crashed, great numbers of people lost their faith in banks and began to withdraw their money. As a result, bank failures rose sharply, as the banks could not produce all the cash that their depositors wanted. After Roosevelt took office in 1933, he declared a nationwide *bank holiday*. Within a few days, Congress passed the *Emergency Banking Act*, which allowed for the reopening of sound banks. The

Anxious depositors gather outside the closed doors of a New York City bank, 1931.

run on the banks stopped, and public confidence in them was restored. Soon, most of the nation's banks were in business again.

Federal Emergency Relief Act   The *Federal Emergency Relief Act* of 1933 created the Federal Emergency Relief Administration (FERA). It provided direct relief for the unemployed by giving federal money to the states. They used the money to set up projects that gave people jobs.

Unemployment: PWA, CCC, WPA   The *Public Works Administration (PWA)*, set up in 1933, provided relief by using federal money to put people to work in construction projects. They build roads, bridges, libraries, hospitals, schools, courthouses, and other public projects.

The *Civilian Conservation Corps (CCC)*, established in 1933, provided relief for unemployed young men between the ages of 18 and 25. They worked on conservation projects: flood control, soil conservation, forest replanting, and park construction. The idea was to combine work relief with the preservation of natural resources.

A troubling equity issue was that only one member of a family could qualify for a *Works Progress Administration (WPA)* job. It was usually the man, who was considered the head of the household. In rare instances when a woman headed the household, she was usually given a job sewing old clothes. Workers were not eligible for government jobs if they had been offered private employment, even at a lower wage.

Recovery of the U.S. Economy

NRA: "Codes of Fair Competition" The *National Recovery Administration (NRA)*, set up in 1933, provided for the recovery of business by encouraging leaders of business and labor in every industry to draw up codes of fair practices. These included maximum hours of work, minimum wages, how many goods should be produced, and at what price. The codes were designed to help businesses control production and raise prices, and to help labor by putting people back to work and raising wages. To win the support of labor, a provision in the NRA act gave workers the right to organize into unions.

Mortgage Relief Many owners of homes were out of work or had lowered earnings and could not meet their mortgage payments. To help them avoid foreclosure and the loss of their homes, Congress created the *Home Owners Loan Corporation (HOLC)* in 1933. It provided for low-interest, long-term, fixed-rate mortgages.

The HOLC was followed by the *Federal Housing Administration (FHA)* in 1934 to aid the recovery of the housing industry. The FHA insured loans made by banks for the construction of new housing and the repair of old homes, and reduced the required down payment for buying homes.

First AAA, Scarcity and Parity The *Agricultural Adjustment Act (AAA)* of 1933 provided for the recovery of agriculture by paying farmers to take land out of production as a means of limiting production and raising farm prices. The money for these payment was to come from a "processing tax" on the industries that made the raw products into finished goods. These industries included mills that processed wheat into flour and cotton into cloth. In addition, the act provided that farmers should destroy a portion of their crops and livestock. The purpose of this act was to raise the real income of farmers to "parity," that is, the higher price level that farmers had enjoyed before World War I.

Search for Effective Reform

Banking The *Glass-Steagall Act* of 1933 created the *Federal Deposit Insurance Corporation (FDIC)* and changed some banking practices. FDIC gave government backing and insurance for bank deposits up to a certain amount so that depositors would not risk loss of their money.

Stock Market The *Securities and Exchange Commission (SEC)* was set up in 1934. It reformed the stock market by regulating pricing practices and requiring that basic data on stocks and bonds offered for sale be made public. A major goal was to curb margin buying and speculation.

Social Security One of the most significant reforms of the New Deal came with the passage of the *Social Security Act* (1935). It established old-age insurance paid for by a joint tax on employers and employees. This would

★ New Deal Agencies and Their Purposes ★

Agency (Year Established)	Purpose
Federal Emergency Relief Administration (FERA) (1993)	*Relief for the unemployed:* Gave federal money to the states, which used the money to help people in need.
Works Progress Administration (WPA) (1935)	*Relief for the unemployed:* Put unemployed workers on the federal payroll and organized special projects for them to do (raking leaves, painting murals, repairing schools, etc.).
Civilian Conservation Corps (CCC) (1933)	*Relief for the unemployed:* Provided young people with jobs in conservation (flood control, soil conservation, forest replanting, etc.).
Agricultural Adjustment Administration (AAA) (1933)	*Recovery of agriculture:* Paid farmers to destroy a portion of their crops and livestock as a means of limiting production and raising farm prices.
National Recovery Administration (NRA) (1933)	*Recovery of business:* Encouraged business firms in every industry to agree upon prices and to draw up codes of fair practices.
Public Works Administration (PWA) (1933)	*Recovery and relief:* Used federal money to put people to work building bridges, dams, highways, and other public projects.
Federal Housing Administration (FHA) (1934)	*Recovery of housing industry:* Insured loans for the construction of new housing.
National Labor Relations Board (NLRB) (1935)	*Reform for labor unions:* Enforced the right of all workers to organize unions.
Social Security Board (SSB) (1935)	*Reform for the disabled, the unemployed, and the elderly:* Provided insurance benefits for those receiving no income because of old age, a physical handicap, or sudden loss of a job.
Securities and Exchange Commission (SEC) (1934)	*Reform of the stock market:* Regulated the stock market and required sellers of stocks to supply truthful information to the public.
Federal Deposit Insurance Corporation (FDIC) (1933)	*Reform of banking:* Provided government backing and insurance for bank deposits so that depositors would not risk loss of their money.

give workers a monthly income when they reached age 65. The act also established unemployment compensation to give laid-off workers some income for a number of weeks while they were looking for a new job. Finally, the Social Security Act provided for federal grants to the states to assist in caring for the disabled, the blind, and dependent children.

TVA   One of the most ambitious New Deal programs was an attempt to rescue an entire region from conditions of extreme poverty.

The southern region watered by the Tennessee River was often flooded. The farmers living near the river had no electric power and were desperately poor. In 1933, Congress created an agency to deal with these problems. The *Tennessee Valley Authority (TVA)* was given the power and the money to accomplish the following:

★ Build dams to control floods

★ Build power plants and provide electricity for the region

★ Charge fair prices for the use of TVA-generated electricity

★ Build reservoirs to hold needed water.

In a few years, the TVA experiment was a proven success. Throughout the region it served, people received relief in the form of TVA jobs. Recovery was evident in the farms that now had electric power. Reform was achieved through flood control and conservation.

Labor and Unions   Named for its sponsor, Senator Robert Wagner of New York, the *Wagner Act* of 1935 launched a new era for American labor unions. It guaranteed to all workers the right to join the union of their choice and thus to "bargain collectively" with their employer on such issues as wages, hours, and factory conditions. To enforce the act, a *National Labor Relations Board (NLRB)* was empowered to supervise elections and compel employers to deal with whatever union the majority of workers chose to join. Firing anyone for joining a union was made illegal. The NLRB could also prevent unfair labor practices by employers against unions.

The *Fair Labor Standards Act* of 1938 set minimum wages and maximum hours for workers in industries engaged in interstate commerce. At first, the minimum wage and maximum workweek established by this law was 25 cents an hour and 44 hours per week. (The act provided that the minimum wage was to gradually increase to 40 cents an hour, while the length of the workweek was to gradually be reduced to 40 hours.) Time and a half was to be paid for overtime. The law also prohibited children under 16 from working in interstate commerce.

Factory workers suffered during the Depression from wage cuts, frequent layoffs, and the daily fear of being unemployed. In the long run, however, workers benefited from the New Deal reforms that greatly strengthened unions. For example, immediately after the Wagner Act became law, union membership shot upward. In just five years, from 1935 to 1940, more than 5 million workers joined unions, doubling the total union membership and greatly increasing unions' bargaining power.

As unions grew more powerful, they started to compete among themselves. In 1935, the most powerful single union within the A.F. of L. was the United Mine Workers. Its aggressive leader, John L. Lewis, became impatient with the A.F. of L.'s policy of favoring unions of skilled crafts workers over the less skilled workers employed in automobile plants, steel mills, coal mines, and other industries. Lewis favored the organization of *industrial unions*, to which all workers in an industry—the unskilled and the skilled, African Americans and whites—could belong. Toward this end, he organized the *Congress of Industrial Organizations (C.I.O.)*, which included his own miners' union, an auto workers' union, and others. In 1938, Lewis broke with the A.F. of L. completely, and the C.I.O. became a separate and rival organization.

Industrial unions in the C.I.O. carried out strikes in the 1930s that shut down production for many months and resulted in major gains for labor. They devised the tactic of the "sitdown" strike, in which striking workers would simply occupy a factory and refuse to leave until their demands were met. The most dramatic and successful of such strikes shut down the automobile factories of General Motors in the winter of 1936–1937. The company finally yielded to almost all the demands of the automobile workers union.

Controversial Aspects of the New Deal

Constitutional Issues

Supreme Court and the NRA In the case of *Schechter Poultry Corp.* v. *United States* (1935), a company in the chicken-raising industry complained about the law that had created the National Recovery Administration (NRA). (See page 366.) The company's lawyer argued that the industry codes established under this law wrongly gave legislative power to the executive branch of government. The Supreme Court agreed that the NRA codes were too much like laws. Therefore, the National Industrial Recovery Act of 1933 was declared unconstitutional.

Supreme Court and the AAA In 1936, the Supreme Court considered whether a special processing tax could be collected to pay farmers under the Agricultural Adjustment Act of 1933. (See page 366.) It ruled against both the tax and the law. As a result, Congress passed a new Agricultural Adjustment Act in 1938. The new act replaced the processing tax with direct federal payments to farmers. Second, the act tried to stabilize farm prices by putting farm products in storage during years of surplus and releasing them during years of scarcity. Third, the act provided for a soil conservation program, allowed marketing quotas for certain crops, and insured wheat crops against natural disasters.

1936 Election: "Mandate" for Action

Roosevelt changed the nature of his party. Before the 1930s, the Republicans had usually been in the majority in national politics. The Democratic party had long relied on the solid support of southerners, whose views were generally conservative. But Roosevelt's New Deal appealed to great numbers of people in the northern cities. It appealed to industrial workers, immigrants, African Americans, ethnic Americans, and people with liberal views. It also appealed strongly to all farmers who were helped by New Deal programs. In the 1930s, members of these different groups formed a majority. Their votes could be counted on to elect Democratic majorities in Congress as well as a Democratic president, Franklin Roosevelt. As a result, in 1936, Roosevelt was reelected president by a landslide.

Roosevelt's "Court-Packing" Proposal During his first term as president, Roosevelt had a fairly easy time persuading a Democratic Congress to pass New Deal laws. But he had a much harder time with the conservative justices of the Supreme Court, most of whom had been appointed by Republican presidents.

Angered by the Supreme Court's decisions that declared the National Recovery Administration and the Agricultural Adjustment Act unconstitutional, Roosevelt proposed a scheme for increasing the number of justices from 9 to 15. This would have enabled him to appoint justices who shared his liberal point of view. But the president was denounced by conservative critics for attempting to "pack" the Court. In 1937, Roosevelt's plan was defeated in Congress.

"The Spirit of '37": FDR berates the Supreme Court for opposing the New Deal.

Third-Term Controversy   In 1940, Roosevelt was elected to a third term and in 1944 to a fourth term. No president before him had ever served more than two terms. When Roosevelt ran for a third term, Republican critics accused him of breaking a two-term tradition that had been respected as part of the unwritten constitution since the time of George Washington.

After Roosevelt's death, Congress proposed a constitutional amendment to prevent any future president from serving more than two full terms. The Twenty-second Amendment establishing this two-term limit was adopted in 1951.

Opposition to the New Deal

Franklin Roosevelt was a controversial president. Most Americans admired him as a great leader. Some critics, however, attacked him for doing too little about the economy while others said that he attempted too much.

Roosevelt was strongly criticized by business leaders and conservative politicians in both the Democratic and Republican parties. They accused New Deal programs like the TVA of undermining the free enterprise system. They thought such programs were hostile to business. "Creeping socialism," they said, was being substituted for the "rugged individualism" that had made the United States great. These critics included Alfred E. Smith, Alfred M. Landon, Huey Long, Father Charles Coughlin, and Dr. Francis Townsend.

Alfred E. Smith   Alfred E. Smith was the first Roman Catholic candidate to be nominated for president by a major party (1928). At the time, he was also New York's popular governor. In a strongly Republican decade (1920s), a Democrat like Smith had little chance of winning. Hurting Smith's chances even more was the prejudice of many voters against both Roman Catholics and New Yorkers. Hoover, the Republican candidate, won the election by a landslide (a very large majority of the vote). In 1932, Smith gave the nominating speech for Franklin D. Roosevelt at the Democratic convention. However, by 1934, Smith had turned against Roosevelt and the New Deal and helped form the Liberty League, a conservative, antilabor organization. Subsequently, Smith had little influence in American politics.

Radical Reformers   Because people were desperate in the 1930s, many wanted more radical changes than the reforms of the New Deal. At one extreme were Communists and Socialists who wanted the government to take over all major industries. (Socialists believed that radical change could be achieved peacefully through elections, while Communists looked forward to a violent revolt of the working class.) Norman Thomas, a well-known Socialist of the time, ran for president in 1928, 1932, and 1936. As a third-party candidate, his highest total was approximately 2 percent of the vote in 1932.

Huey Long   At the other extreme were racist and nationalist groups who thought the government should be run by a dictator. Probably the most serious challenge to Roosevelt's leadership came from a popular politician named Huey Long, who stirred up voter discontent. A long-time governor of Louisiana, Long called for the rich to give up their fortunes in order to provide every American family with an estate of $5,000. Through this "Share Our Wealth" program, each family would also be guaranteed an annual income of $2,500. Few families at the time had this kind of money. Long's ambitions for national power were cut short in 1935 when an assassin killed him.

Father Coughlin   Father Charles Coughlin, a Roman Catholic priest, attacked the New Deal in his national radio show. In so doing, he made anti-Semitic appeals, accusing the Jews of controlling banks throughout the world and causing the Depression. Although these charges were false, he gained some popularity at the time. Eventually, the Catholic Church took away his radio broadcast.

Dr. Townsend   A retired physician from California, Dr. Francis Townsend gained popularity with his proposal to provide monthly payments of $200 to all unemployed citizens over 60 years of age. At that time, $200 a month was an impressive sum of money. Dr. Townsend proposed that all people receiving these funds would have to spend the money within the same month. Although impractical, Dr. Townsend's plan was a forerunner of the concept of Social Security.

Support for the New Deal

Liberals defended the New Deal by arguing that Roosevelt had saved both democracy and the free enterprise system. In their view, extremist groups (Communists, Socialists, Fascists, and Populists like Huey Long) might have torn the nation apart if Roosevelt had failed to enact programs of economic relief. Liberals also argued that the reforms of the New Deal (the Social Security system, the regulation of the banking system, the minimum wage law, and others) simply extended the reforms of the Progressive Era. The purpose of these reforms was to avoid some of the bad effects of capitalism (such as bank failures, economic insecurity, and the possibility of depression) while preserving the good effects (such as freedom of choice, inventiveness, and economic growth).

The Roosevelts: Keeping the People in Mind

The new president was part of the same wealthy New York family as Theodore Roosevelt, a distant cousin. But unlike Theodore (a Progressive Republican), the second Roosevelt in the White House was a Democrat.

In 1920, Franklin Roosevelt had been the Democrats' unsuccessful candidate for vice president. Soon afterward, he contracted polio, an often crippling disease, and his legs became paralyzed. For the rest of his life, he worked in a wheelchair and wore heavy braces to support himself when he stood. But Roosevelt's personal charm and courage were unaffected by the handicap. He continued his career in politics, winning election as New York's governor in 1928 and 1930 and then as the U.S. president in 1932.

FDR as Communicator

By words and deeds, the new president demonstrated an eagerness to fight the Depression with all his strength. In his first inaugural address, for example, he declared: ". . . the only thing we have to fear is fear itself. . . ." Millions of Americans were also reassured by the president's messages explaining his New Deal programs. To communicate his ideas as widely as possible, Roosevelt used the radio. He called his radio talks "fireside chats." Through such lines of communication, the president attempted to calm the American people and restore confidence in the government.

Eleanor Roosevelt

Eleanor Roosevelt, wife of the president, helped him determine what needed to be done. She went even further than her husband in championing liberal causes. She traveled around the nation as the president's "eyes and ears," visiting those hard-hit by the Depression. She spoke out boldly and often on public issues. Soon, she came to symbolize the "new woman" who was actively involved in national and world affairs.

The New Deal and Women

Individual women of the 1930s achieved fame and high position in various fields. Amelia Earhart became world-famous after flying a plane across the Atlantic—the first woman to accomplish this feat. (In the 1920s, Charles Lindbergh had been the first person to do so.)

Another public-spirited woman of the 1930s was Secretary of Labor Frances Perkins. As the first woman cabinet member, she had a distinguished record of service spanning 12 years. She administered many of the relief programs of the New Deal and helped bring about the abolition of child labor.

The New Deal and Minorities

For the first time since the presidency of Abraham Lincoln, African Americans had the support of the president. "Among American citizens there should be no forgotten men and no forgotten races." So said President Roosevelt, expressing his awareness that blacks had long been neglected by the U.S. government. Backing the president's words were New Deal programs that gave African Americans what they most needed—jobs. Many thousands of jobs were made available by the WPA and CCC.

Roosevelt also brought to the White House a "Black Cabinet," consisting of distinguished African American leaders. Among them were Robert Weaver, an expert on urban housing problems, and Mary McLeod Bethune, an expert in education.

Perhaps most significant of all was the response of Eleanor Roosevelt to an incident of racial discrimination. In 1939, the great African American contralto Marian Anderson had been denied the right to sing at an important concert in Washington, D.C. When Eleanor Roosevelt learned of this, she invited Anderson to sing at the Lincoln Memorial.

The Roosevelts thus won a reputation for supporting the cause of racial justice. As a result, many thousands of African American voters left the Republican party and became loyal Democrats.

Despite gestures of sympathy and support by the Roosevelts, African Americans continued to suffer from racism and discrimination. Even New Deal agencies discriminated against them. Under the industrial codes of the NRA (National Recovery Administration), white workers were allowed higher wage rates than black workers. Whites who sought employment from the TVA were far more likely to be put on the payroll than African American applicants.

Indian Reorganization Act (1934)

The status of Native Americans did change. In 1934, Congress passed the *Indian Reorganization Act*. Instead of allowing individuals to own plots of land on the reservations, the U.S. government now stressed tribal ownership and tribal authority. It also urged the preservation of Native American cultures. At the same time, teachers in the reservation schools began to stress methods of scientific farming.

Many saw these changes as improving conditions for Native Americans. Even so, most Indians were still desperately poor. During the Great Depression there were few job opportunities outside the reservations and not enough income-earning opportunities on them.

Culture of the Depression

Gifted American artists and writers were inspired by the Great Depression to depict the lives of ordinary people struggling with hardship.

Literature

The novelist William Faulkner and the playwright Lillian Hellman portrayed psychological and social tensions in southern society. The writer who most directly and vividly depicted the human misery of the Great Depression was John Steinbeck. In his novel *The Grapes of Wrath* (1939), Steinbeck created an unforgettable picture of Oklahoma sharecroppers ("Okies") being driven off their land and trying desperately to find work as peach pickers in California. It is a story of human beings swept away by cruel and impersonal economic forces.

The WPA engaged researchers and writers in an interesting project of historical importance. They interviewed elderly former slaves and the children of slaves to better document slavery in America.

Music

The "hot jazz" of the Roaring Twenties gave way to the big bands and "swing" of the 1930s. Young people crowded into dance halls to dance to the new music. Big bands led by individuals such as Benny Goodman and Glenn Miller became very popular. During this period, most bands were segregated. Thus, bandleaders such as Cab Calloway, Duke Ellington, and Count Basie led popular bands composed of African American musicians. It was Benny Goodman, "the king of swing," who integrated his band by including such great African American musicians as Lionel Hampton and Teddy Wilson.

Popular Culture

People did not stop going to the movies in the Great Depression. In fact, while other industries fell on hard times, the movie industry was never more glamorous or prosperous than in the 1930s. One reason was that for only a few cents, people could briefly forget their troubles watching the great stars of Hollywood (for example, Shirley Temple, Clark Gable, James Stewart, and Judy Garland) perform in a make-believe world. Most movies of the time, such as *The Wizard of Oz* (1939), served people's needs for fantasy, adventure, romance, and fun. There were also great movies on serious social themes—movies that have become classics. The 1930s are considered the Golden Age of Hollywood.

In the 1930s, comic books first appeared in the United States. In fact, such comic books as *Superman* paved the way for generations for new comic book heroes. These included *Batman*, *Captain Marvel*, *Wonder Woman*, and *Spiderman*.

★ In Review

1. Explain how each of the following New Deal acts or programs contributed to relief, recovery, or reform: (a) Emergency Banking Act; (b) Federal Emergency Relief Act; (c) Works Progress Administra-

tion; (d) Public Works Administration; (e) Civilian Conservation Corps; (f) National Recovery Administration; (g) Home Owners Loan Corporation; (h) Federal Housing Administration; (i) Agricultural Adjustment acts; (j) Federal Deposit Insurance Corporation; (k) Securities and Exchange Commission; (l) Social Security Act; (m) National Labor Relations Board; (n) Fair Labor Standards Act; and (o) Tennessee Valley Authority.

2. Summarize the effects of the Great Depression and the New Deal on each of the following: labor unions, women, African Americans, Native Americans.

3. Describe the programs of three leading opponents of the New Deal. Why were these ideas popular?

Chapter Review

MULTIPLE-CHOICE QUESTIONS

Refer to the graphs on page 363 to answer question 1.

1. The two graphs illustrate that, between 1929 and 1941,
   (1) the Gross National Product and unemployment were unrelated
   (2) as the Gross National Product increased, so did unemployment
   (3) when people found employment, they were able to afford more goods and services
   (4) the Great Depression was aggravated because industry continued full production in spite of high unemployment.

Use the map on page 357 to answer questions 2 and 3.

2. Which of the following conclusions can be drawn from the map?

(1) Loans from the United States prevented the stock market from crashing earlier than 1929.
(2) The cycle of payments created the groundwork for making the Great Depression worldwide.
(3) Credit was tight and difficult to obtain during the latter part of the 1920s.
(4) American banks granted preferential loan rates to Germany.

3. Which component is missing from the cycle illustrated on the map?
(1) German repayment of Americans loans
(2) reparation payments to Germany
(3) U.S. loans to France and Britain
(4) reparation payments to the United States.

Use the chart on page 355 to answer questions 4 and 5.

4. The chart shows that the belief that the 1920s were a decade of great wealth was
   (1) completely false
   (2) untrue for many segments of the population
   (3) true for rural areas
   (4) partially true for skilled workers.

5. The chart shows that the
   (1) stock market crash was the most important cause of the Great Depression
   (2) Great Depression was predominantly a result of global economic weakness
   (3) ease of obtaining loans coupled with "get rich quick" stock schemes were the true causes of the Great Depression
   (4) Great Depression was generated from both international and domestic economic weaknesses.

Refer to the table on page 366 and answer questions 6 and 7.

6. The table shows that Franklin D. Roosevelt's New Deal
   (1) successfully utilized a laissez-faire policy in combating the Great Depression
   (2) endorsed a large degree of government action
   (3) was a compromise between leaders of the Democratic and Republican parties
   (4) immediately solved the problems created by the Great Depression.

7. The creation of the agencies listed in the table
   (1) limited federal power
   (2) increased the power of the executive branch

   (3) was declared constitutional by the Supreme Court
   (4) united the nation behind President Roosevelt.

Read the following debate about the 1930s New Deal and then answer questions 8 and 9.

Speaker A: Our nation's economy has been ruined by costly government programs that destroy freedom of enterprise and individual initiative.

Speaker B: I strongly disagree. Our economy will be helped by public works projects, unemployment insurance systems, and old-age retirement insurance. The New Deal is a peaceful and much-needed revolution.

Speaker C: We have had no revolution. We are simply witnessing the evolution of an idea that began in the days of Populism and Progressivism.

Speaker D: We need not concern ourselves with whether these changes are revolutionary or evolutionary. The important thing is to conserve our resources and to do so through the democratic process.

8. The idea referred to by Speaker C is
   (1) a regulatory role for the government
   (2) the free and unlimited coinage of silver
   (3) civil rights for minorities
   (4) an income tax amendment.

9. Speaker A is most likely a
   (1) farmer
   (2) corporate executive
   (3) union member
   (4) African American.

Refer to the cartoon on page 369 and answer question 10.

10. What point of view is expressed by the cartoon?
(1) The New Deal was a military as well as a political force.
(2) Congress accepted most of President Franklin Roosevelt's plans for dealing with the Great Depression.
(3) President Roosevelt strictly followed the concept of checks and balances.
(4) The judicial branch of the 1930s was controlled by the executive branch.

THEMATIC ESSAYS

1. Theme: Causes of the Great Depression

The business boom of the 1920s masked a number of weaknesses in the U.S. economy that ultimately helped to trigger the Great Depression.

Task

★ Choose two areas of U.S. economic weakness during the 1920s. Specifically show how each of these weaknesses contributed toward leading the United States into the Great Depression.
★ Describe how developing world interdependence in the post–World War I period contributed to making the Great Depression a global crisis.

You may wish to select economic weaknesses such as overproduction, easy credit, and the unequal distribution of wealth in your discussion regarding the U.S. economy. A discussion of international trade and banking may be of assistance in illustrating how the Great Depression grew to worldwide proportions.

2. Theme: The New Deal

President Franklin D. Roosevelt's New Deal was marked by dramatic action on the part of the federal government to fight the ravages of the Great Depression.

Task: Select two programs of the New Deal. For each program chosen:

★ Describe the specific problem that it was designed to correct.
★ Evaluate the effectiveness of the program.

You may include programs dealing with banking, labor, the stock market, or any other aspect of the U.S. economy.

3. Theme: The New Deal and Constitutional Issues

Although the New Deal did much to alleviate the effects of the Great Depression, there was controversy over its constitutionality.

Task: Choose two ways in which the New Deal caused controversy. For each way selected:

★ Describe the controversy.
★ Explain how the controversy was resolved.

Areas to consider in your essay may involve issues over checks and balances, federalism, presidential power, and the proper role of government.

4. **Theme:** Change During the 1930s

The 1930s are remembered for being a time of change as well as an era of economic depression.

Task: Select two changes that took place in the United States between 1930 and 1939. For each change:

★ Describe how the change occurred.
★ Explain the results that were created by each change.

You may wish to consider, but are not limited to, change in the role of women, environmental conditions, the arts, culture, government, and politics.

DOCUMENT-BASED QUESTION

*Read each document and answer the question that follows it. Then read the **Task** and write your essay. Essays should include references to most of the documents along with additional information based on your knowledge of United States history and government.*

Historical Context: The issues of the 1932 election for president entailed a fundamental disagreement over the degree of federal involvement in solving the severe problems caused by the Great Depression.

Document 1 From a speech given by President Herbert Hoover at Madison Square Garden, New York City, October 31, 1932:

> . . . you can not extend the master of government over the daily lives of a people out somewhere [,] making it master of people's souls and thoughts.
>
> Expansion of government in business means that the government, in order to protect itself from the political consequences of its errors, is driven . . . to greater and greater control of the Nation's press and platform. Free speech does not live many hours after free industry and free commerce die. . . .

Even if the Government conduct of business could give us the maximum of efficiency instead of least efficiency, it would be purchased at the cost of freedom.

Question: Why did Herbert Hoover choose to avoid most direct federal involvement with private business during the Great Depression?

Document 2   Refer to the larger photograph on page 361 and answer the question.

Question: Why did people call the Great Depression settlement shown in the photograph a "Hooverville"?

Document 3   From President Franklin D. Roosevelt's first inaugural address, March 4, 1933:

... Plenty is at our doorsteps, but a generous use of it languishes in the very sight of the supply. . . .
. . . Our greatest primary task is to put people to work. This is no unsolvable problem if we face it wisely and courageously. It can be accomplished in part by direct recruiting by the government itself, treating the test as we would treat the emergency of a war, but at the same time, through this employment, accomplishing greatly needed projects to stimulate and reorganize the use of our national resources.

Question: How did Franklin D. Roosevelt propose to fight the unemployment caused by the Great Depression?

Task

★ Describe the different philosophies of President Herbert Hoover and his presidential challenger, Franklin D. Roosevelt.
★ Explain why Franklin D. Roosevelt won the election of 1932 by an overwhelming majority of the popular vote.

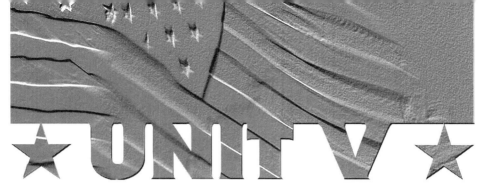

★ UNIT V ★

The United States
In an Age of Global Crisis

Chapter 14
Peace in Peril: 1933–1950

Throughout the 1930s, the American people were absorbed by issues close to home: how to cope with the Great Depression and how to react to the New Deal. At the same time, they were aware of events in Europe and Asia that might lead to another war similar to the "Great War" of 1914 to 1918. In fact, war did erupt when Japan invaded China in 1937 and Germany invaded Poland in 1939. The German invasion of Poland touched off a second world war even more destructive than the first. Once again, the United States entered the war only after one of the warring nations, Japan, forced it to do so.

This chapter will examine why the United States hesitated to become involved in World War II and why, after becoming involved, it did not return to the isolationist policy of the past.

Isolation and Neutrality

Recall from Chapter 10 that the United States did not expect to get involved in the "Great War" when it broke out in 1914. Until that time the traditional U.S. policy toward Europe had been one of *isolationism* (or noninvolvement) and *neutrality* (not taking sides in a foreign war).

Causes of Disillusion and Pacifism

The outbreak of World War I plunged U.S. policymakers into a crisis. In just six years, 1914 to 1920, U.S. policy went from isolationism (avoidance of war) to internationalism (Wilson in Paris leading a peace conference) and back to isolationism (U.S. rejection of the League of Nations).

In 1914 when war in Europe began, recall that Woodrow Wilson's first move was to proclaim U.S. neutrality. Only after German submarines attacked American shipping did he reluctantly ask Congress for a declaration of war. Wilson became a full-fledged internationalist after the war when he dedicated all his energies to winning public approval of the League of Nations.

But after the U.S. Senate in 1920 voted against the League and the Treaty of Versailles, most Americans grew tired of international politics. They even became disillusioned with the results of the war. In the 1920s, public opinion generally favored a return to the traditional U.S. policy of isolationism. Presidents during the 1920s (Harding, Coolidge, and Hoover) were content to follow the isolationist mood of the country.

The idea that war or fighting should not be used to settle disputes appealed to many. These *pacifists* did not approve of building up the military or supporting warring nations.

The Rise of Dictatorships

The type of government called *fascism* glorifies war, preaches an extreme form of nationalism, and follows the commands of an all-powerful dictator.

In Italy the Fascist party led by Benito Mussolini seized power in 1922. Anyone who criticized Mussolini's regime risked severe punishment.

After its defeat in World War I, Germany was faced with economic ruin, runaway inflation, and severe unemployment. As the Germans well knew, their country's economic plight stemmed largely from the penalties imposed by the Treaty of Versailles. This treaty forced Germany to pay a crushing sum of money in reparations and to surrender to France the coal mines of the Saar Valley. The treaty not only crippled Germany's economy but also wounded German national pride by forcing Germany to accept complete responsibility for causing World War I.

Many embittered Germans found an outlet for their hatred in the emotional speeches of Adolf Hitler, who led a Fascist-style party called the *Nazi party*. Hitler turned the rage and frustration of the German masses against a minority group, the Jews. In 1933 Hitler became chancellor (or prime minister) of Germany's government and then seized absolute power as the Nazi leader and dictator.

Neutrality Acts of 1935–1937

Through the 1930s the majority of the American people wanted their country to remain neutral in order to avoid involvement in another world war.

Hitler (left) and Nazi troops in Berlin

Members of Congress were well aware of isolationist feelings. Between 1935 and 1937, Congress enacted several laws to assure U.S. neutrality in the event of war. These *Neutrality Acts* provided for the following:

★ No sale or shipment of arms to *belligerent nations* (nations involved in war)

★ No loans or credits to belligerent nations

★ No traveling by U.S. citizens on the ships of belligerent nations

★ Nonmilitary goods purchased by belligerent nations to be paid for in cash and transported in their own ships.

This last provision was known as the *cash-and-carry principle*.

Spanish Civil War (1936–1939)

A troubling event to the democracies of the world was a vicious civil war in Spain. Beginning in 1936, Fascist forces in Spain, led by Francisco Franco, attempted to overthrow Spain's republican government. Defenders of the government received military aid from the Soviet Union, while the Fascists received aid from Hitler's Germany and Mussolini's Italy.

The civil war served as a testing ground for newly developed weapons. Germany sent tanks and airplanes to the Fascists. The republican government, which included Communists and Socialists, looked to the Western democracies for help. Some Americans formed a volunteer unit called the Abraham Lincoln Brigade to fight on the side of the republicans. Limited Soviet assistance and volunteer fighters, however, were no match for the help provided by Germany. In 1939, Spain fell to fascism.

FDR's "Quarantine" Speech (1937)

By 1937 President Roosevelt was growing more and more concerned about the aggressive acts of Japan, Germany, and Italy, and the Fascist threat in Spain. These acts included: invasion of Manchuria by Japan in 1931, invasion of Ethiopia by Italy in 1935, occupation of the Rhineland by Germany in 1936, and invasion of China by Japan in 1937.

Responding to the Japanese invasion of China, Roosevelt, in an address known as the *"Quarantine" speech*, proposed that democratic nations join together to "quarantine" aggressor nations. The purpose of such a policy, he explained, would be "to protect the health of the [international] community against the spread of the disease." Isolationists were quick to criticize Roosevelt's Quarantine speech. They warned that the president's proposed policy might lead to American involvement in war. Public opinion polls showed that most Americans agreed with the isolationists, not with the president. The largely negative reaction to Roosevelt's speech restrained the president from giving active assistance to the democracies of Europe. (In making foreign policy, even the strongest presidents hesitate to oppose the forces of public opinion.)

Failure of Peace—Triumph of Aggression

The rise of dictatorships in Nazi Germany and Fascist Italy, and the timid policies of the democracies, led to the triumph of aggression and the failure of peace efforts.

Aggressions of Japan, Germany, Italy: 1932–1940 The 1930s was a time of depression at home and aggression abroad. Though Germany and Japan posed threats to world peace, Americans were determined to remain neutral and uninvolved.

Hitler violated the terms of the Treaty of Versailles in 1936 by ordering German troops into the Rhineland, a neutral, demilitarized territory. Two years later, he sent troops into Austria and announced his intention of seizing a territory in Czechoslovakia known as the Sudetenland.

In Asia there were similar acts of aggression throughout the 1930s. The chief victim was China. The aggressor was Japan. A group of Japanese military leaders had come to dominate their country's government. Their nationalist beliefs and strong-arm methods resembled those of the Fascists of Europe. They wanted Japan to be the supreme power in East Asia. In line

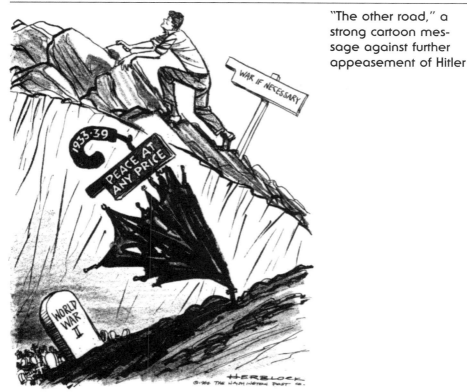

"The other road," a strong cartoon message against further appeasement of Hitler

From STRAIGHT HERBLOCK (Simon & Shuster, 1964)

with this goal, Japanese troops marched into Manchuria in 1931 and then invaded China's heartland in 1937.

Mussolini adopted a policy of military expansion. He ordered his Italian army to bring glory to the Fascist cause by conquering territory in Africa. The African kingdom of Ethiopia, long an independent nation, made a valiant effort at resistance but fell to the Italian invader in 1936.

Appeasement: The Munich Conference (1938) While Italy, Germany, and Japan followed a policy of military aggression, Great Britain and France followed a policy of *appeasement*. Appeasement is the policy of yielding to the demands of a rival power in order to avoid armed conflict. British and French leaders applied this policy at the Munich Conference in 1938 by giving in to Hitler's demand to annex the Sudetenland. The Sudetenland was a region in northern Czechoslovakia where there was a large German-speaking population. In appeasing Hitler, the British and French hoped they could trust his assurance that he wanted only the Sudetenland and nothing more.

But only a few months after Munich, German troops occupied all of Czechoslovakia and then threatened Poland. By 1939 it was all too clear that appeasement had failed to stop Hitler and that the only way to stop him in the future would be through the use of armed force.

Start of World War II in Europe: German Invasion of Poland

Germany invaded Poland in September 1939. This time, instead of continuing to appease Hitler, Great Britain and France both declared war against Germany. World War II had begun.

During the first two years of World War II (1939–1941), the democracies (Great Britain, France, and their allies) suffered a series of crushing defeats. Slamming across the Polish border, wave after wave of German tanks and planes forced Poland to surrender within only 30 days. So rapid and overwhelming was the German method of attack that it was called a *blitzkrieg* (a German word meaning lightning war). Next, German armies swept over Denmark and Norway. France managed only brief resistance before it too fell to the Nazi invader in June 1940.

Just before the war, in 1939, Soviet leader Joseph Stalin had signed a nonaggression pact with Hitler. The two dictators had pledged that, if war broke out, their countries would not attack each other. Thus, when war did break out, the Soviet Union was neither a friend nor a foe of Germany.

With France beaten and the Soviet Union pledged to remain uninvolved, Great Britain in 1940 was the only nation with a chance of stopping Germany and its ally Italy from conquering all of Europe. Hitler planned to invade England in mid-September, 1940. To weaken his enemy beforehand, he ordered thousands of German planes to bomb London and other British cities. Nightly, the wailing of British air raid sirens warned civilians of German attacks. Fortunately, the British air force shot down enough German

"Come on in. I'll treat you right. I used to know your Daddy": 1936 pro-isolation cartoon reminding Americans of what happened in World War I

planes to cause Hitler to call off the invasion. Even so, Great Britain struggled alone for months as the last foe of nazism to resist conquest.

Gradual United States Involvement

The outbreak of war and the success of the German drive caused a sharp turnaround in U.S. public opinion. There was now much greater willingness to assist a democratic Great Britain in its battle against the dictators. Most Americans understood that German victories in Europe would threaten U.S. security.

Neutrality Act of 1939   In order to assist Great Britain once the war began, President Roosevelt moved quickly to change the earlier Neutrality Acts. According to the original law, only nonmilitary goods could be shipped to belligerent nations on a cash-and-carry basis. Military goods (weapons and ammunition) could not be sold to belligerent nations at all. Roosevelt persuaded Congress to pass a new Neutrality Act in 1939. It provided that U.S.-made war supplies could be sold to belligerents if they were paid for in cash and carried on the purchaser's own ships.

Destroyer Deal and Lend-Lease Act   To help the British defend themselves against crippling submarine attacks, President Roosevelt in 1940 agreed to transfer to Britain 50 U.S. destroyers (ships for use against submarines). In exchange, the United States was given eight British naval and air bases extending from Newfoundland in Canada to a British colony in South America (British Guiana). The exchange was called the "destroyers-for-bases" deal.

Under the pressure of daily German attacks, the British needed more war supplies than could be obtained by the cash-and-carry program. Recognizing this fact, Roosevelt persuaded Congress to authorize the lending, or leasing, of war supplies to Great Britain. He argued that the United States should act as the *arsenal of democracy*. The passage of the *Lend-Lease Act* in 1941 meant that the former policy of neutrality was now abandoned. Although the United States was not yet at war, it was committing much of its economic resources to help Great Britain fight off the German assault.

Moral Dimension: The Atlantic Charter

In August 1941, on a battleship anchored off the coast of Newfoundland (Canada), President Roosevelt met with British Prime Minister Winston Churchill. Together they formulated a statement of common war aims known as the *Atlantic Charter*. These aims included:

★ recognition of the right of all nations to *self-determination* (the right of a people to choose their own government)

★ U.S.-British understanding that neither power would seek to gain territory from the war

★ the disarmament (removal of weapons) of aggressor nations

★ a "permanent system of general security" in the future.

"Hands Across the Sea": FDR with a fist for Hitler and the helping hand of Lend-Lease for Britain

★ In Review

1. Define and explain the importance of isolationism, fascism, appeasement, Neutrality Acts, FDR's Quarantine speech, Lend-Lease Act, and the Atlantic Charter.
2. Give one example of an aggressive act committed in the 1930s by (a) Germany, (b) Italy, and (c) Japan.
3. Describe the causes that led the United States to change its policy from isolationism in 1939 to involvement in 1940 and 1941.

The United States in World War II

In 1941 the United States was committed to British defense. But the U.S. did not officially enter the war until the Japanese attack on the U.S. naval base in Hawaii gave it no choice.

Pearl Harbor

The attack came as a result of a fundamental conflict between the goals of Japan and the United States. Throughout the 1930s, U.S. foreign policy makers had been alarmed by Japan's acts of aggression in China. They viewed such acts as violations of the U.S. Open Door policy. To limit Japan's capacity for making war, the United States in 1940 placed an embargo (stoppage of trade) on a list of U.S. exports that Japan needed to maintain its war machine. Under the embargo, Japan could no longer purchase U.S. oil, aviation gasoline, scrap iron, and steel. Next, President Roosevelt froze all Japanese assets in U.S. banks. In other words, Japan could no longer use these bank deposits to purchase U.S. goods.

In 1941 Japanese military leaders believed that the United States might soon enter the war to oppose Japan's planned invasion of Indonesia. Therefore, the fateful decision was made to launch a surprise attack on the U.S. fleet in the Pacific. If the attack succeeded in destroying the fleet, Japan's generals hoped that the U.S. Navy might take a long time recovering from the blow—too long to stop Japan from achieving all of its war aims.

Early on Sunday morning, December 7, 1941, hundreds of Japanese planes strafed and bombed a fleet of ships docked at the U.S. naval base at Pearl Harbor, Hawaii. In addition to eight battleships and 11 other ships that were either sunk or disabled, about 150 U.S. planes were destroyed and 2,335 soldiers and sailors were killed.

The next day, President Roosevelt asked Congress for a declaration of war against Japan. December 7, he said, was "a date which will live in infamy." Congress voted overwhelmingly for war. Then Japan's allies in Europe—Germany and Italy—declared war on the United States. Now that

President Franklin Roosevelt addressing the nation over radio two days after the Japanese attack on Pearl Harbor

★ ★ ★ ★ ★

A FIRESIDE CHAT BY PRESIDENT ROOSEVELT, DECEMBER 9, 1941

Two days after the Pearl Harbor attack, President Roosevelt spoke to the American people over the radio. The following are excerpts from his "fireside chat" of December 9, 1941.

On the road ahead there lies hard work—grueling work—day and night, every hour and every minute. I was about to add that ahead there lies sacrifice for all of us. But it is not correct to use that word. The United States does not consider it a sacrifice to do all one can, to give one's best to our nation when the nation is fighting for its existence and its future life.

In these past few years—and, most violently, in the past few days—we have learned a terrible lesson. It is our obligation to our dead—it is our sacred obligation to their children and our children—that we must never forget what we have learned.

And what we all have learned is this: There is no such thing as security for any nation—or any individual—in a world ruled by the principles of gangsterism. There is no such thing as impregnable defense against powerful aggressors who sneak up in the dark and strike without warning. We have learned that our ocean-girt hemisphere is not immune from severe attack—that we cannot measure our safety in terms of miles on any map.

U.S. territory had been attacked, the American people put aside their isolationist feelings of the past and rallied to the war effort.

Human Dimensions of the War

U.S. victory in World War II depended almost as much on the work of civilians as on the fighting of the armed forces. During nearly four years of U.S. participation in the war, all Americans had to adjust to the unusual demands of wartime.

"Arsenal of Democracy" Allied hopes for victory depended largely on the speed with which U.S. factories could turn out war goods. Government officials encouraged companies in every industry to stop producing consumer goods and start producing ships, planes, bombs, bullets, and other military supplies. As the chief supplier of war materials for the Allied cause, the United States acted as "the arsenal of democracy."

Role of Women As young men were called into service, trained, and shipped overseas, women took up the slack in the workforce. During wartime, a great variety of jobs were open to women—jobs that had previ-

"Rosie the Riveter Steps Out," in defiance of her traditional role as homemaker

ously been reserved for men. The number of women in the U.S. labor force went from about 15 million in 1941 to about 19 million in 1945. A popular song of World War II, "Rosie the Riveter," celebrated the new status of women as key producers of ships, aircraft, and other war supplies.

American women also made contributions in the military by enlisting in support units (but not in combat units) in all of the services—Army, Navy, Marines. For example, women who joined the Women's Army Corps (WACs) served in the United States and overseas as drivers, radio operators, office staff, and even supply pilots. Military nurses were almost always women. Many retired workers who were too old to go to war returned to work at factories and plants where they replaced younger male workers going off to war.

Mobilization   Even before the United States entered the war, Congress enacted a selective service law, or *draft*, in September 1940. This law passed by only one vote in the House of Representatives. Every man between the ages of 21 and 35 was required to register for possible induction into the armed forces. By 1945 a total of 12.5 million men and women were in uniform—approximately one out of three of the eligible group.

More than a million African Americans served in the U.S. armed forces during World War II, about half overseas. Once again, their hopes for equal treatment were disappointed when they were placed in segregated units.

Women learning to weld and solder during an industrial course in war work

On the home front, black civilians found employment in relatively high-paying jobs in defense plants in the North. The availability of such jobs greatly increased the migration of African Americans from southern farms to northern cities.

Financing the War   The cost of the war was staggering. The United States spent billions of dollars on the war effort. With the government debt growing each day, citizens were encouraged to buy war bonds. Many Hollywood stars campaigned around the country promoting the sale of bonds. The works of the composer Irving Berlin heightened feelings of patriotism. His song "God Bless America" was introduced by the singer Kate Smith in 1942. In concerts around the country, Smith's singing of this patriotic song helped to sell millions of dollars of war bonds. Hollywood stars such as Bob Hope organized shows that took movie and recording stars around the globe to entertain U.S. soldiers. One of the most popular songs among the soldiers of World War II was Irving Berlin's "White Christmas" sung by Bing Crosby.

Rationing at Home   With American industry shifting from peacetime consumer production to wartime production, many goods were in short supply. Products such as clothing, sugar, and meat, rubber for tires, and gasoline for cars were all *rationed*. Americans received coupon books which allowed the purchase of rationed items in accordance with the number of coupons they had received for that product. A special government agency, the Office of Price Administration, checked retail prices to ensure that the prices of products in short supply did not exceed allowable limits and cause inflation.

Experience of Military Service   The experience of men and women in military service is far different from those who do not serve. Service people are often far from home and live in regulated and sometimes harsh conditions. They are exposed to new surroundings and a variety of people and cultures. Each moment of those in battle brings the fear of death in combat. The death of friends and even killing the enemy may leave psychological scars that do not easily heal. Those who came home wounded would often live their remaining lives with physical disabilities. For most, the end of the war meant a return to civilian lives. Adjustment, however, was often difficult. Many of those who returned could not talk about the war and suffered internally, unable to share their feelings. However, all those in the U.S. military service understood that this was a war to save democracy and stop totalitarianism.

Allied Strategy and Leadership

The major goal of Allied strategy was to defeat Nazi Germany first and then focus on Japan and Asia. Allied forces were split between the European and Pacific fronts.

Assistance to the Soviet Union   On June 22, 1941, several months before Pearl Harbor, Hitler broke his nonaggression pact with Stalin by launching a massive assault against the Soviet Union (present-day Russia and neighboring countries). Thus, as 1942 began, Hitler faced three formidable foes: the United States, the Soviet Union, and Great Britain. His days of easy victory were over. Almost immediately after Hitler attacked the Soviet Union, the United States provided military aid to the Soviet Union. This aid was soon followed by assistance under the Lend-Lease Program. As a result, a wave of U.S. military equipment made its way to the Soviet Union. This equipment was crucial in the Soviet Union's defense of its homeland and its subsequent attack on German troops.

Europe First Although Pearl Harbor had been attacked by Japan, Allied strategy required that Nazi Germany be defeated first. It took the Allies more than three years (1942–1945) to win back the territories conquered by German and Italian armies in the first two years of war. The single most

Military and Civilian Deaths in World War II

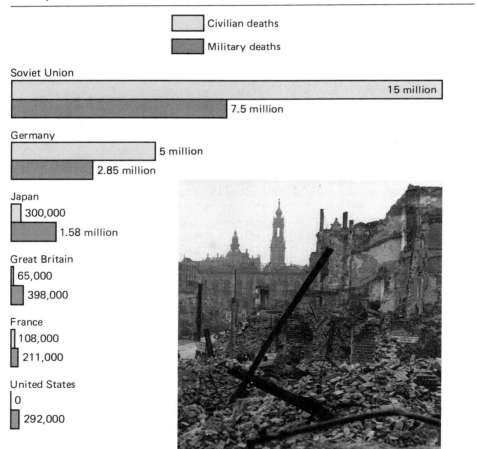

Civilian deaths

Military deaths

Soviet Union
15 million
7.5 million

Germany
5 million
2.85 million

Japan
300,000
1.58 million

Great Britain
65,000
398,000

France
108,000
211,000

United States
0
292,000

important turning point was Hitler's decision to invade the Soviet Union—a decision that proved to be a fatal blunder.

After initial successes, the German invaders in the Soviet Union suffered a crushing defeat at the Battle of Stalingrad (1942 to 1943). Meanwhile, in the North African desert, a British force under General Bernard Montgomery defeated the Germans in a tank battle at El Alamein. Soon after, in 1943, combined assaults by British and American armies forced the surrender of the German army in North Africa. From their African bases, the Allies invaded the Mediterranean island of Sicily and then began a long and bloody campaign to liberate Italy.

On June 6, 1944 (code name: D-Day), Allied forces left England in a massive drive to liberate France. The invading force included 11,000 planes, 600 warships, and 176,000 men. It was the largest amphibious (sea-to-land) assault in history. Crossing the English Channel, the assault force achieved its objective of securing beachheads on the coast of Normandy (northern France). From there Allied forces under U.S. General Dwight Eisenhower, the Supreme Allied Commander in Western Europe, fought for

World War II in Europe, 1943–1945

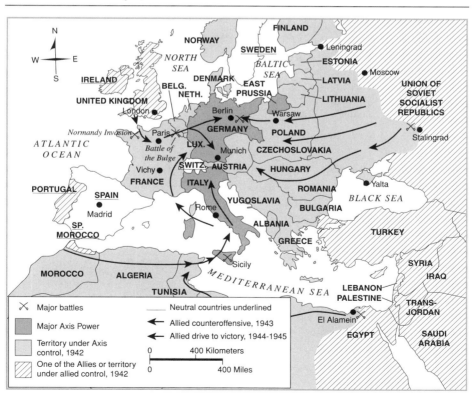

control of Normandy and then all of France. They liberated Paris in August and pushed eastward into Germany.

From the other direction Soviet troops also moved rapidly toward Berlin. In April 1945, American and Soviet troops met for the first time on German territory near the Elbe River. Seeing that the end was near, Hitler committed suicide. Germany surrendered unconditionally on May 7, 1945 (V-E Day), ending the war in Europe.

Two-Front War   As the Germans gobbled up huge pieces of Europe, the Japanese also made rapid gains in Asia. By 1941 much of northern China was under Japanese occupation. Naval and air assaults by Japan quickly brought the islands of the Netherlands East Indies, now Indonesia, under its control. After France fell to Germany, the French colony of Indochina (present-day Vietnam, Laos, and Cambodia) fell to Japan. Early in 1942 the British colony of Malaya also fell to the invader. In early May, U.S. forces in the Philippines surrendered to the Japanese. Japan now controlled much of Asia and the islands of the South Pacific. Although the United States followed a Europe-first policy, Japanese successes forced the U.S. to fight a two-front war against both Germany and Japan.

In the Pacific, U.S. naval and military leaders developed a strategy known as "island hopping." In order to get within striking distance of Japan, American forces would concentrate on winning only the most strate-

World War II in the Pacific, 1941–1945

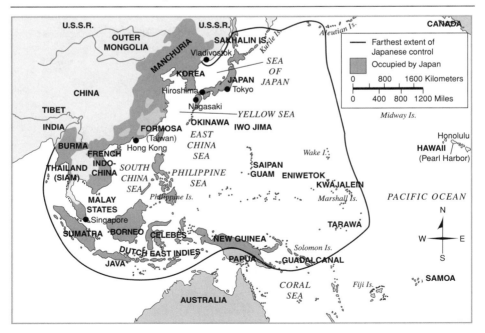

gically located islands, while leaving others under Japanese control. The fighting on each targeted island was fierce and bloody. Casualties on both sides were high.

In the crucial contest between two strong navies, American ships and planes defeated Japanese forces in several major battles. A turning point in the war at sea was the U.S. victory at the Battle of Midway (1942), which probably saved Hawaii from enemy occupation.

The Atomic Bomb

In April 1945, President Roosevelt died. His successor, Vice President Harry S. Truman, had to decide what to do with a newly developed, immensely destructive weapon: the atomic bomb.

Manhattan Project   The great scientist Albert Einstein had left Germany for the United States after Hitler turned against the Jews. Fearing that Germany would develop an atomic bomb, Einstein wrote a letter to President Roosevelt recommending that the United States develop such a bomb first. Although he was a pacifist, Einstein feared that an atomic bomb in the hands of Germany would lead to the defeat of the Allies. Soon after, Roosevelt committed U.S. funds to the *Manhattan Project* (code name for the project to develop an atomic bomb). Based in Los Alamos, New Mexico, scientists who had fled Europe and American scientists worked together to develop an atomic bomb before Germany did. Thus, unwittingly, Hitler's policies helped to create the diverse group of scientists who succeeded in developing the nuclear weapon.

Decision to Use the Bomb   Whether to use the atomic bomb would be a difficult decision for President Truman. At the time, Truman and his military advisers were planning to invade the Japanese homeland in order to achieve final victory. They believed that such an invasion would result in the loss of hundreds of thousands of American soldiers.

If the president decided to use the new bomb, American lives might be saved. On the other hand, thousands of Japanese civilians would be condemned to death. Truman decided to use the bomb. He reasoned that the bomb's destructiveness might force Japan to surrender, and the planned U.S. invasion could then be canceled. On August 6, 1945, a single U.S. plane dropped an atomic bomb on the city of Hiroshima. Three days later a second atomic bomb was dropped on the city of Nagasaki. The two explosions instantly killed more than 100,000 Japanese civilians. Many thousands of others died later from the effects of nuclear radiation.

As Truman hoped, the use of the atomic bomb convinced Japan to surrender. General Douglas MacArthur presided over the ceremony of formal surrender aboard the U.S. battleship *Missouri* on September 2, 1945. Thus ended the most destructive war in history. (The total death toll for all nations: 17 million military deaths and probably more than twice that number in civilian deaths. The U.S. death toll: about 400,000.)

Was the United States morally justified in dropping atomic bombs on Japan? Even to this day, the question continues to be debated. The following facts and possibilities should be considered when making your judgment:

★ Although more than 100,000 people died from the atomic explosions, there might have been many times that number of deaths (including Japanese civilians and soldiers) from the planned U.S. invasion of Japan.

★ Instead of dropping atomic bombs on civilian targets, the United States could have demonstrated the new weapon's destructive power by dropping it over the ocean close to the Japanese shore.

★ After dropping a bomb on Hiroshima, the United States waited less than a week before dropping a bomb on Nagasaki. It could have waited longer to give Japan's government a chance to surrender before dropping the second bomb.

United States Occupation of Japan

After their nation was defeated in war in 1945, the Japanese people surprised the U.S. occupying army with their willingness to cooperate. U.S. General Douglas MacArthur was the supreme commander of the occupation. Acting on instructions from the U.S. government, MacArthur carried out the enormous task of transforming Japan from a military power into a nation without any military weapons.

Besides demilitarizing the country, MacArthur was also responsible for democratizing it. He supervised Japan's adoption of a new constitution (1947) that took away all political power from the Japanese emperor and guaranteed free elections and representative government. The constitution also banned the raising of an army and navy and declared that Japan would never again go to war.

The economic reconstruction, or rebuilding, of Japan required millions of dollars of U.S. aid. By 1955, only ten years after the war, Japan was again a prosperous nation closely allied with the Western nations that had defeated it.

War crime trials were held in Japan. More than 700 Japanese officers were executed for *war crimes*, including the notorious leader of wartime Japan, Hideki Tojo.

Impact of War on Minorities in the United States

Incarceration of West Coast Japanese Americans After Japan's attack on Pearl Harbor, many Americans treated citizens of Japanese descent with great suspicion and hostility. Thousands of Japanese Americans served loyally in the U.S. armed forces. Even so, their families suffered throughout the war from prejudice and discrimination. President Roosevelt yielded to the general prejudice by authorizing in *Executive Order 9066* the removal of all Japanese Americans from their homes in California and other western states. In 1942 the U.S. army seized 110,000 Japanese Americans and transported them to barracks within barbed-wire compounds called "relocation centers." Most were released before the war's end, but those suspected of disloyalty (about 18,000) were kept in a relocation center in California until Japan surrendered.

According to historian Arthur Link, the treatment of Japanese Americans in World War II was "the greatest single violation of civil rights in American history." But the Supreme Court did not see it that way. In a case decided in 1944, *Korematsu* v. *United States*, the Court determined that the removal of Japanese Americans was justified as a matter of military necessity. In recent years, however, many Japanese Americans who suffered loss and humiliation during World War II have received official apologies from the U.S. government as well as small sums of money to partly compensate them for damages.

Racial Segregation in the Military African Americans served in segregated military units during World War II. At the time, the heavyweight champion of the world was Joe Louis, an African American. Although Joe Louis fought many exhibition fights to help bolster the morale of soldiers, he was forced to serve in a segregated army unit. Even African American pilots served in segregated units. Segregation in the armed forces would not end until after World War II.

The Nazi Holocaust

As U.S. troops moved across Germany, they came upon concentration camps whose inmates were in a pitiful condition. They were mainly European Jews who had barely survived a policy of *genocide* (the extermination of an entire people) begun by Hitler in 1941. The survivors told horrifying stories of the Nazi practice of capturing Jews in all occupied countries of Europe and systematically either murdering them or working them to death in concentration camps. About 6 million Jews were killed in the *Holocaust* (systematic destruction of Jews by the Nazis).

Thousands who died in the Holocaust might have survived if the United States had changed its immigration policy. After Hitler had come to power in the 1930s and had begun to persecute the Jewish minority, many refugees from Nazi Germany hoped to gain admission to the United States. About 175,000 immigrants from German-controlled territory were accepted. But hundreds of thousands more were denied entry even though the immigrant quota for Germany was not filled.

Nuremberg War Crimes Trials For nearly an entire year (November 1945–October 1946), a unique series of trials took place in Nuremberg, Germany. The defendants were former military and political leaders of the defeated Nazi government. They were accused of war crimes, especially the mass murder of Jews in Nazi concentration camps. Judges at the *Nuremberg trials* represented the victorious nations of World War II, including the United States. Of 24 defendants, 19 were convicted, and ten of these were executed. In addition, other military trials in Germany led to lesser punishments for some 500,000 former Nazis. Some Nazis who escaped capture were later found and brought to trial. For example, Adolph Eichmann was executed in Israel and Klaus Barbie was imprisoned for life in France. The Nuremberg Tribunal established the precedent that national leaders could be held responsible for "crimes against humanity."

Demobilization: The Late 1940s

As soon as the war ended, the American public eagerly awaited the return of U.S. troops. *Demobilization* (cutting back the armed forces in peacetime) proceeded rapidly. In just two years, 1945 to 1947, some 11 million GI's (the World War II nickname for American soldiers) were released from service.

Inflation and Strikes Just as troops were demobilized in 1945 and 1946, so too was the wartime economy. During the war, the U.S. government had tried to prevent inflation (higher and higher prices for consumer goods) by regulating the prices businesses could charge for products. Such regulations are called price controls.

At war's end, most business owners wanted price controls removed. Reluctantly, President Truman agreed. The result was predictable—sudden jumps in the prices of everything in the marketplace. Consumers were in a buying mood for goods that had been in short supply during the war. Automobiles, gasoline, and rubber products were available again, and demand for them was enormous. Without controls in place, prices increased by 25 percent in just one year (mid-1945–mid-1946).

Businesses showed greater interest in raising prices than in raising wages. Demanding higher pay, labor unions called one strike after another. They argued that consumer prices were rising while workers' incomes were declining. (One reason for the decline was that in peacetime there was less opportunity for overtime pay.) President Truman was normally a supporter of labor's objectives. But strikes in critical industries—steel, automobiles, coal, and railroads—threatened to cripple the economy. In 1946 Truman moved boldly to prevent economic disaster. In response to the coal strike, he ordered U.S. troops to operate the coal mines. In response to a railroad strike, he asked Congress for power to draft striking railroad workers into the Army and have them work the mines as soldiers.

GI Bill: Impact on Education and Housing Since the normal course of their lives had been interrupted by military service, millions of young Americans returning from the war needed help in adjusting to civilian life. Congress had already enacted in 1944 a measure known as the *GI Bill of Rights*. Under this law, veterans were entitled to receive (1) free hospital care if they were sick or wounded, (2) grants and loans to pay for college, and (3) federally guaranteed loans for buying homes and investing in businesses.

The GI Bill of Rights had a positive impact, not only on war veterans, but also on colleges, universities, and the housing industry. Under the law, any veteran could apply for federal aid to pay for tuition, books, and other costs at a college or vocational school. Eight million veterans—about half of those who had served in the armed forces in World War II—took advantage of these educational benefits at a cost to the government of about $13.5 billion. Also under the law, veterans could apply for federally guaranteed, low-interest loans for buying a home or investing in a farm or business. The GI Bill of Rights also made it possible for millions of young families to own their own homes.

Truman's Fair Deal A senator from Missouri in the 1930s and 1940s, Harry Truman did not expect to be president. In the 1944 election, he had been the successful Democratic candidate for vice president when President Franklin Roosevelt was reelected to a fourth term. Nobody—least of all Truman—was prepared for the shocking news of Roosevelt's death in April 1945 (less than four months after his inauguration). Truman, though unprepared, knew his constitutional duties and showed great courage in leading the nation through the last months of World War II.

Truman was elected president in his own right in 1948. In his inaugural address of 1949, Truman said he would try to achieve a "fair deal" for the American people. Truman's domestic program, known as the *Fair Deal*, added to the reform ideas of Franklin Roosevelt's New Deal. The Congress elected in 1948 passed some parts of the Fair Deal while rejecting other parts.

Congress approved the following measures:

★ An increase in the minimum wage from 40 cents an hour to 75 cents an hour

★ An extension of Social Security benefits to 10 million people not covered under the original law

★ Federal funds for the construction of low-income housing and slum clearance

★ Increased federal funds for flood control, irrigation projects, and electric-power projects.

Congress rejected these measures:

★ A national health insurance plan
★ Federal aid to education
★ A law protecting the civil rights of African Americans.

Partisan Problems With Congress After the war, the Republicans won control of Congress and often battled with the Democratic president.

Over Truman's veto, Congress enacted a law intended to limit the power of labor unions. The *Taft-Hartley Act* of 1947 provided for the following:

★ Union officials had to sign a loyalty oath declaring that they were not Communists and did not advocate the violent overthrow of the government.

★ A labor union could no longer demand a *closed shop*—an arrangement in which the employer agrees to hire only dues-paying members of one union.

★ A labor union could not conduct a *secondary boycott*. In a boycott, striking workers refuse to buy their employer's products. In a secondary boycott, strikers also refuse to buy products from firms that do business with their employer.

★ An employer had the right to sue a union for breach of contract (failure to carry out the terms of a contract).

★ The president could call for an 80-day "cooling-off" period to delay a strike that threatened the U.S. economy or national security.

The passage of the Taft-Hartley Act brought an end to the prolabor legislation that had marked the New Deal years. For years afterward, labor unions lobbied to repeal the Taft-Hartley law, which they viewed as unfair.

Republicans and Democrats in Congress had generally cooperated during the war emergency. In other words, the war years had been characterized by *bipartisanship* (two parties acting together for the national good). But during Truman's presidency, Republicans and Democrats were at odds over almost every domestic issue.

As a Democrat, Truman proposed reform laws similar to the New Deal programs of Franklin Roosevelt. He favored (1) a national health insurance program, (2) federal aid to education, (3) an expanded public housing program, and (4) greater Social Security benefits.

But the Republican majority in Congress rejected every one of Truman's proposals. The president launched his campaign for election in 1948 by telling voters that the Republicans had created a "do-nothing" Congress.

Minorities' Problems When World War II ended, African Americans in the South had lived for many decades under Jim Crow laws that denied them equal rights. In northern cities, too, they had suffered from discrimination in housing and jobs. In the South, schools were legally segregated on the basis of race. This is known as *de jure segregation*. In the North, housing patterns often led to segregated schools. This is known as *de facto segregation*. Thus, in both the South and the North, segregation continued to exist after World War II.

Truman's Upset Victory in 1948 In 1948 Republicans thought they had an excellent chance of winning the presidency, which had not been in Republican hands since Herbert Hoover's election in 1928. Election polls showed that their candidate, Governor Thomas E. Dewey of New York, was far ahead.

Opposition to Truman came not only from Republicans but also from within the ranks of his own party. In fact, two groups in the Democratic party were so opposed to his policies that they both organized independent parties. A liberal group led by former vice president Henry Wallace thought Truman's foreign policy was too tough on the Soviets. A conservative group led by Governor Strom Thurmond of South Carolina objected to Truman's support of civil rights bills for African Americans. The southern conservatives who backed Thurmond for president were known as Dixiecrats.

Truman fought an uphill battle. Opinion polls showed a Dewey victory to be almost certain. But Truman had a fighting spirit that impressed many voters. During his "whistle-stop" campaign he traveled from one end of the country to the other and gave short speeches from the rear platform of his train. "Give 'em hell, Harry," people would say when the president hammered away at the "do-nothing" Congress.

The election was close, but Truman won it. His energetic campaign and the strong support of labor unions, farmers, and minorities had helped carry him to victory. The Republicans and newspaper writers were astonished. The morning after the election, a grinning president held up the front page of the *Chicago Tribune*. "DEWEY DEFEATS TRUMAN," read the headline. The newspaper had made the mistake of relying on election polls and early voting returns instead of the final vote.

Truman and Civil Rights More than any president before him, Truman recognized that a country claiming to be a democracy could not deny fundamental rights to a large group of its citizens. He did not like the long-time policy in the U.S. armed forces of segregating troops according to race. Therefore, one of his first acts as president was to issue an executive order ending racial segregation in the armed forces. At the same time, Truman established a Fair Employment Board to ensure that African Americans were given an equal opportunity to hold civil service jobs in the U.S. government.

As an important part of his Fair Deal, Truman urged Congress to enact *civil rights laws* that would (1) abolish the poll tax and (2) punish those guilty of lynching African Americans. Congress failed to enact the civil rights laws proposed by the president. Even so, Truman's strong support for civil rights paved the way for the laws adopted later in the 1950s and 1960s. According to the historian Arthur Schlesinger, Jr., Truman's repeated efforts to make progress in civil rights represented his "boldest initiative in the domestic field."

★ In Review

1. Identify the following and give the significance of each: Pearl Harbor, "arsenal of democracy," D-Day, "island hopping," the Manhattan Project, *Korematsu* v. *United States*, the Holocaust, Nuremberg trials, the GI Bill, Truman's Fair Deal, and Taft-Hartley Act.

2. How did the need to wage "total war" alter the nature of American society?

3. Describe how each of the following were moral issues that grew out of the war experience: (a) integration of African Americans (b) morality of nuclear warfare, (c) rights of Japanese Americans, (d) U.S. reaction to the Nazi Holocaust, and (e) treatment of war criminals.

Chapter Review

MULTIPLE-CHOICE QUESTIONS

Refer to the cartoon on page 386 and answer questions 1 and 2.

1. The umbrella in the cartoon is a symbol of
   (1) an act of war
   (2) an unsuccessful policy
   (3) resistance to Nazi Germany
   (4) international cooperation.

2. Which of the following statements is most clearly implied by the cartoon?
   (1) World War II could have been prevented by further appeasement.
   (2) Peaceful nations have usually been exploited.
   (3) Appeasement did not prevent war.
   (4) Human beings make progress despite war.

Refer to the cartoon on page 387 and answer questions 3 and 4.

3. Which of the following would the cartoonist most likely have sup-ported at the outbreak of World War II?
   (1) Lend-Lease
   (2) ending World War II quickly by a U.S. entry on the side of the Allies
   (3) special privileges for soldiers on leave
   (4) avoiding any participation in the war.

4. The event that the cartoonist is referring to is
   (1) the Spanish-American War
   (2) the Boxer Rebellion
   (3) the Philippine Incursion
   (4) World War I.

5. An immediate result of President Roosevelt's Quarantine speech of 1937 was
   (1) isolationist criticism
   (2) the rapid decline of isolation-ist feeling in the United States
   (3) increased military aid to the democracies of Europe
   (4) Japan's decision to stop its in-vasion of China.

Use the cartoon on page 391 to answer question 6.

6. The cartoon shows that, as a result of World War II,
   (1) women became less interested in having children
   (2) changes took place in the traditional roles of women
   (3) divorces increased
   (4) men stopped working in factories.

Refer to the bar graph on page 394 to answer questions 7 and 8.

7. The graph shows that the Soviet Union and Germany differed from the rest of the listed nations in that they suffered more
   (1) physical destruction
   (2) civilian but fewer military deaths
   (3) combined civilian and military deaths
   (4) military and fewer civilian deaths.

8. The graph shows that as a result of World War II,
   (1) France had more total losses than Great Britain

(2) the United States had the fewest military losses of the Allied powers
(3) Japan had more civilian losses than Germany
(4) more civilians than military personnel were killed in Germany and the Soviet Union.

9. The policy of removing Japanese Americans from their homes during World War II was closely related to the problem of
   (1) a labor shortage during the war
   (2) racial prejudice
   (3) effects of the Great Depression
   (4) imperialism in Latin America.

10. A major goal of Truman's Fair Deal was to
    (1) improve economic benefits for working people
    (2) extend postwar trading privileges to Germany and Japan
    (3) limit the power of labor unions
    (4) shift the funding of education from state and local governments to the federal government.

THEMATIC ESSAYS

1. **Theme:** Fighting World War II: the War Experience and Morality

   The experience of fighting World War II caused Americans to face a number of moral issues.

   Task: Select two issues of morality that World War II brought into focus. For each issue selected:

   ★ Show how the circumstances of World War II made the issue a major moral question.
   ★ Describe the decision that was made in dealing with each issue and the reasons given for reaching that decision.

You may wish to consider issues such as the use of atomic weapons, bringing war criminals to justice, and the conflict between national security and the rights of Japanese Americans.

2. **Theme:** The United States and the Coming of World War II

Necessity demanded that the United States government under the presidency of Franklin D. Roosevelt practice a diplomacy (foreign policy) of neutrality while, in fact, assisting the British and preparing for its own entry into the war.

Task: Specifically describe how the United States government practiced a policy of neutrality while preparing itself for and becoming involved in World War II.

You may wish to include in your answer the Neutrality Acts, the Lend-Lease program, public opinion, and the influence of Charles Lindbergh.

DOCUMENT-BASED QUESTION

*Read each document and answer the question that follows it. Then read the **Task** and write your essay. Essays should include references to most of the documents along with additional information based on your knowledge of United States history and government.*

Historical Context: The opening hostilities of World War II left the United States in a position of deciding whether to aid the democratic nations that were engaged in fighting the forces of dictatorship, oppression, and militarism.

Document 1 From the agreement forming the Rome-Berlin-Tokyo Axis, 1937:

The governments of Germany, Italy, and Japan consider it a condition precedent of a lasting peace, that each nation of the world be given its own proper place. . . .

ARTICLE 1. Japan recognizes and respects the leadership of Germany and Italy in the establishment of a new order in Europe.

ARTICLE 2. Germany and Italy recognize and respect the leadership of Japan in the establishment of a new order in Greater East Asia.

ARTICLE 3. Germany, Italy, and Japan agree to cooperate in their efforts on the aforesaid basis. They further undertake to assist one another with all political, economic, and social means, if one of the three

Contracting Parties is attacked by a Power at present not involved in the European war or in the Chinese-Japanese conflict.

Question: Why was President Franklin D. Roosevelt concerned about the agreement between Germany, Italy, and Japan?

Document 2   From an address by President Franklin D. Roosevelt, 1941:

Suppose my neighbor's home catches fire, and I have a length of garden hose four or five hundred feet away. If he can take my garden hose and connect it up with his hydrant, I may help him to put out his fire. Now, what do I do? I don't say to him before that operation, "Neighbor, my garden hose cost me $15; you have got to pay me $15 for it". . . . I don't want $15—I want my garden hose back after the fire is over. All right. If it goes through the fire all right, intact, without any damage to it, he gives it back to me and thanks me. . . . But suppose it gets smashed up—holes in it—during the fire, . . . He says, "All right, I will replace it." Now, if I get a nice garden hose back, I am in pretty good shape.

In other words, if you lend certain munitions and get the munitions back at the end of the war, if they are intact . . . you are all right. If they have been damaged . . . it seems to me you come out pretty well if you have them replaced by the fellow to whom you have lent them.

Question: What was President Roosevelt suggesting we do to help the British in their fight against the German Nazis?

Document 3   Refer to the cartoon on page 388.

Question: How does the cartoon show the influence of President Franklin D. Roosevelt's Lend-Lease Act?

Document 4   Charles Lindbergh, as quoted in *The New York Times*, April 24, 1941:

We have weakened ourselves for many months, and still worse, we have divided our own people, by this dabbling in Europe's wars. While we should have been concentrating on American defense, we have been forced to argue over foreign quarrels. We must turn our eyes and our faith back to our own country before it is too late. And when we do this, a different vista opens before us.

Practically every difficulty we would face in invading Europe becomes an asset to us in defending America. Our enemy, and not we, would then have the problems of transporting millions of troops across the ocean and landing them on a hostile shore. . . .

Question: Why did Charles Lindbergh feel that the United States should remain neutral?

Document 5 Editorial in *The New York Times*, April 30, 1941, in answer to Charles Lindbergh:

> . . . That conqueror [Hitler] does not need to attempt at once an invasion of continental United States in order to place this country in deadly danger. We shall be in deadly danger the moment British sea power fails; the moment the eastern gates of the Atlantic are open to the aggressor; the moment we are compelled to divide our one-ocean Navy between two oceans simultaneously. . . .

Question: Why did the editor of *The New York Times* disagree with Charles Lindbergh?

Task

> ★ Explain the arguments that both supported and rejected U.S. neutrality during the opening years of World War II.
> ★ Describe how the United States participated in World War II prior to formally entering the war as a combatant.

Chapter 15
Peace With Problems: 1945–1960

★ **Objectives**

★ To compare U.S. involvement in the United Nations after World War II with U.S. rejection of the League of Nations after World War I.

★ To describe the global commitments of U.S. foreign policy after World War II.

★ To explain the origins of the cold-war rivalry between the United States and the Soviet Union.

★ To compare U.S. policy toward Asia with U.S. policy toward Europe in the postwar period.

★ To describe cold-war conflicts in Berlin, China, and Korea.

★ To analyze the impact of the cold war on domestic policy.

By the end of 1945, after almost four years of war, the United States was finally at peace. Americans had passed through many years of crisis—a worldwide depression in the 1930s followed by a world war in the 1940s. Now they looked forward to a time of peace and prosperity. But as they were soon to find out, these postwar years presented new troubles and challenges.

International Peace Efforts

Having fought in two horribly destructive world wars, the United States and its allies wanted to ensure that future world peace would be built on a firm foundation.

Formation of the United Nations

Hoping to build a more peaceful future, the United States and its allies sent representatives to a conference in San Francisco in April 1945. Their purpose was to replace the League of Nations with a new peacekeeping organization. The *United Nations (UN)*, as it was called, would be similar in purpose to the League. Representatives from the member nations would meet to settle disputes and stop acts of aggression like those that had led to World War II.

According to the UN Charter (the constitution of the United Nations), all member nations were entitled to vote in the UN *General Assembly* on almost any international issue. A smaller body, the UN *Security Council*, could call on member nations to take military action in a crisis. But such a decision had to be approved by all five permanent members on the Security Council. The permanent members were the Soviet Union (now Russia), Great Britain, France, China, and the United States. Six non-permanent members of the Security Council—a number later increased to ten—would serve for two-year terms.

Special UN agencies were established for various purposes. An Economic and Social Council would attempt to reduce hunger and improve health care in the poorer countries of the world. A Trusteeship Council would make decisions concerning the colonies given up by Germany and Japan. An International Court of Justice would decide legal questions referred to it by disputing nations.

In 1945, by a vote of 82 to 2, the U.S. Senate approved U.S. membership in the United Nations. In doing so, the United States signaled to the world that it would not again return to a policy of isolationism. As the world's most powerful nation—and also, briefly, the only nation with atomic weapons—the United States was now prepared to play a leading role in world affairs.

United Nations Universal Declaration of Human Rights

In 1948, the United Nations General Assembly approved a document called the *Universal Declaration of Human Rights*. (See page 412.) The list of rights included in this document was based largely on earlier documents that were important to the development of Western democracies (for example, the British Magna Carta of 1215 and the U.S. Declaration of Independence of 1776). The UN document, however, went beyond the earlier documents by including not only civil and political rights but also economic and social rights.

The Declaration of Human Rights included such civil and political rights as freedom of speech and religion, freedom of movement and asylum (protection granted by a government to a political refugee from another country), equality before the law, the right to a fair trial, the right to participate in government, and the right not to be subjected to torture. The document also included such economic, social, and cultural rights as the right to have food, clothing, housing, and medical care, to receive an education, to benefit from social security and a decent standing of living, to work, to

A cartoonist comments on the sorry state of the planet after an atomic war.

get equal pay for equal work, to form labor unions, to marry and raise a family, and to maintain one's culture.

Eleanor Roosevelt's Role   In 1945, the year of Franklin D. Roosevelt's death, Eleanor Roosevelt was appointed the United States representative to the newly formed United Nations, where she served until 1951. In 1946, she was elected chairman of the UN's Human Rights Commission. Eleanor Roosevelt's concern for humanity and her leadership on the commission won the respect of her male colleagues at the UN and led to the passage of the Universal Declaration of Human Rights in 1948.

Displaced Persons: Refugee Aid Efforts   The widespread fighting during World War II forced many people to flee from their homes out of fear for their lives and liberty. These displaced persons were known as *refugees*. These are people who have fled their countries because of a fear of persecution based on their ethnicity, religion, nationality, or political affiliation, and who cannot or do not want to return. As a result, the UN General Assembly in 1951 created the United Nations High Commissioner for Refugees to provide needed assistance for refugees. Such assistance included safeguarding the well-being and rights of refugees, assisting refugees in returning to their own country or settling in another country, and coordinating international action for the resolution of refugee problems.

★ ★ ★ ★ ★

THE UNITED NATIONS UNIVERSAL DECLARATION OF HUMAN RIGHTS

Adopted in 1948, the UN Declaration of Human Rights consists of 30 main articles. Quoted below are Articles 1–5, which list political rights, and Articles 23–24, which list economic rights.

Article 1
All human beings are born free and equal in dignity and rights. They are endowed with reason and conscience and should act towards one another in a spirit of brotherhood.

Article 2
Everyone is entitled to all the rights and freedoms set forth in this Declaration, without distinction of any kind, such as race, color, sex, language, religion, political or other opinion, national or social origin, property, birth or other status.

Furthermore, no distinction shall be made on the basis of the political, jurisdictional or international status of the country or territory to which a person belongs, whether it be independent, trust, non-self-governing or under any other limitation of sovereignty.

Article 3
Everyone has the right to life, liberty and security of person.

Article 4
No one shall be held in slavery or servitude; slavery and the slave trade shall be prohibited in all their forms.

Article 5

No one shall be subjected to torture or to cruel, inhuman or degrading treatment or punishment.

. . .

Article 23

(1) Everyone has the right to work, to free choice of employment, to just and favorable conditions of work and to protection against unemployment.

(2) Everyone, without any discrimination, has the right to equal pay for equal work.

(3) Everyone who works has the right to just and favorable remuneration ensuring for himself and his family an existence worthy of

human dignity, and supplemented, if necessary, by other means of social protection.

(4) Everyone has the right to form and to join trade unions for the protection of his interests.

Article 24

Everyone has the right to rest and leisure, including reasonable limitation of working hours and periodic holidays with pay.

Expansion and Containment in Europe

During the last years of war, the leaders of the United States, Great Britain, and the Soviet Union arranged two meetings to discuss both military strategy and plans for dealing with the postwar world.

Summitry: Yalta and Potsdam

Franklin Roosevelt, Winston Churchill, and Joseph Stalin met at a "big three" conference at Yalta (in the Soviet Union) in 1945. After the death of Roosevelt (and soon afterward, the surrender of Germany), President Harry Truman represented the United States at a conference at Potsdam (in Germany) in July 1945. At these conferences, the "big three" agreed to a number of principles for treating a defeated Germany and a defeated Japan:

★ Germany would be disarmed.

★ Germany would be divided into four zones of occupation (British, American, French, and Soviet). Berlin, the former capital, would also be divided into zones of occupation.

★ "War criminals" in both Japan and Germany would be put on trial.

★ Japan would be occupied chiefly by U.S. troops.

★ Polish territory would be granted to the Soviet Union.

The agreement concerning Poland was made at Yalta. Critics of the agreement at the Yalta Conference accused Franklin Roosevelt of conceding too much to the Soviet Union, practically inviting the Soviets to occupy Poland and dominate the countries of Eastern Europe as "spheres of influence." Defenders of Roosevelt argued that the Soviet Union also made an important concession at Yalta. The Soviets agreed that, after the defeat of Germany, they would begin to wage war against Japan. Furthermore, Soviet troops were in Eastern Europe when the Yalta Conference took place. Roosevelt did not "give away" Eastern Europe to the Soviets; in effect, the region was already theirs.

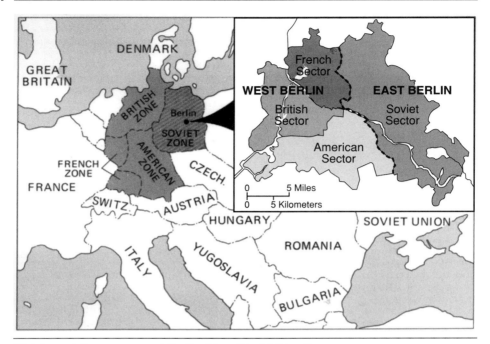

Division of Germany and Berlin After World War II

Origins of the Cold War

By far the major U.S. worry of the postwar years concerned the ambitions of the Soviet Union. Leaders of the Western democracies believed that the Soviet Union was intent on expanding its power by supporting Communist revolutions and gaining control over other nations.

For its part, the Soviet government also had reasons to fear U.S. power. In 1945 the United States was the only nation with atomic, or nuclear, weapons. It had dropped two atomic bombs on Japan. Also Soviet leaders distrusted the United States and other Western democracies because they were capitalist states.

The postwar hostility between the Soviet Union and United States was based on two opposing ideologies (belief systems). The two nations' rivalry in the postwar period was known as the *cold war*. The conflict was "cold" in the sense that Soviet and U.S. armies never fought each other. But the Soviet Union and the United States fought in many other ways, including:

★ An arms race: Attempting to build more powerful nuclear weapons than those of the enemy

★ Local and regional wars: Giving military aid either to rebel forces or government forces, depending on which side in a civil war leaned toward communism

★ Espionage: Spying on each other

★ Propaganda: Creating and distributing messages that condemned the opposing nation and its way of life

★ Space race: Attempting to impress world public opinion by being the first to make gains in space exploration

★ Disputes in the United Nations: Using meetings of the UN General Assembly and Security Council to condemn actions of the rival power.

These cold-war tactics dominated world politics for about 44 years (from 1945 to 1989). This chapter describes only the first phase of the cold war, from 1945 to 1963.

Soviet Satellites in Eastern Europe

As soon as World War II ended, the Soviet Union used occupation troops in Eastern Europe to achieve political control of that region. Angry U.S. reaction marked the beginning of the cold war.

At wartime conferences at Yalta and Potsdam, Soviet leader Joseph Stalin had agreed that postwar governments of Eastern Europe should be elected freely and fairly. In 1945 and 1946, elections took place in Poland, Romania, Bulgaria, and Hungary. However, the elections were far from free. Communist parties in each of these countries had the support of the occupying Soviet army. In each country, Communists took control of the police, the newspapers, and the radio stations. Elections were rigged ("fixed") and Communist candidates elected. Only in Czechoslovakia did free elections take place—until 1948. In that year, Communists forced the Czech leaders to leave office. Thus, Czechoslovakia too fell to the country's Soviet-backed Communist party.

After coming to power, the Communist party of each Eastern European country took orders from the Communist party of the Soviet Union. In effect, seven Eastern European states were now Soviet *satellites*—countries whose policies were dictated by a foreign power, the Soviet Union. An eighth nation, Yugoslavia, was also under Communist rule but managed to remain free of Soviet control.

Counted among the seven satellites was the part of Germany assigned to Soviet control. Originally, at the end of the war, Americans expected Germany to be occupied briefly and then united under a democratically elected government. Instead, because of the conflict between the Soviet Union and the other occupying powers, Germany remained divided into two parts: a freely elected western part (West Germany) and a Communist-controlled Soviet satellite (East Germany).

The Iron Curtain

Soviet domination of the Eastern European countries meant that they were cut off from contact with the West. East Europeans could not travel and

Soviet Satellites in Eastern Europe After World War II

were forbidden to have Western publications or listen to broadcasts from the West. In a speech at Fulton, Missouri, in 1946, the great British wartime leader Winston Churchill said that an "iron curtain" had descended across the continent of Europe. In other words, Soviet control of Eastern Europe was so strong that there might as well have been a fence or curtain separating the East from the West.

Postwar Uses for United States Power

After the end of the war in 1945, as in the post–World War I period, many Americans wanted to leave Europe to resolve its own problems. However, President Truman and congressional leaders believed that the lack of U.S. involvement would leave Europe wide open to Soviet domination.

What was the United States to do if the Soviet Union continued to support Communist uprisings in various countries of the world? American scholar and diplomat George Kennan proposed an answer in an article written in 1947. Kennan argued that "the main element of any United States policy toward the Soviet Union must be that of a long-term, patient but firm and vigilant containment of Russian expansive tendencies. . . ."

The word *containment* was picked up by U.S. policymakers in Washington, including President Truman. It was a good label, or name, for U.S. policy toward the Soviet Union in the postwar period.

The Truman Doctrine Truman used Kennan's idea of containment almost immediately. In 1947 the government of Greece was in serious danger of

★ ★ ★ ★ ★

THE TRUMAN DOCTRINE

On March, 12, 1947, President Truman delivered a speech to Congress about the need for giving U.S. economic aid to Greece and Turkey. The part of the speech quoted below gives Truman's view of the state of the world in 1947.

> The peoples of a number of countries of the world have recently had totalitarian regimes forced upon them against their will. The Government of the United States has made frequent protests against coercion and intimidation . . . in Poland, Rumania and Bulgaria. I must also state that in a number of other countries there have been similar developments.

> At the present moment in world history nearly every nation must choose between alternative ways of life. The choice is too often not a free one.

> One way of life is based upon the will of the majority, and is distinguished by free institutions, representative government, free elections, guarantees of individual liberty, freedom of speech and religion, and freedom from political oppression.

> The second way of life is based upon the will of the minority forcibly imposed upon the majority. It relies upon terror and oppression, a controlled press and radio, fixed elections, and the suppression of personal freedoms.

> I believe that it must be the policy of the United States to support free peoples who are resisting attempted subjugation by armed minorities or by outside pressures.

> I believe that we must assist free peoples to work out their own destinies in their own way.

> I believe that our help should be primarily through economic and financial aid which is essential to economic stability and orderly political processes.

being overthrown by a force of Greek Communists. If Greece fell, then Turkey too could be in danger of being swept into the Soviet orbit. Truman decided to contain the Communist pressure. He asked Congress for $400 million in U.S. military aid for Greece and Turkey. In his statement to Congress, known as the *Truman Doctrine*, Truman said: "The free people of the world look to us for support in maintaining their freedoms. If we falter in our leadership we may endanger the peace of the world—and we shall surely endanger the welfare of our own Nation." Congress granted Truman's request in a *foreign aid* bill—the first of many foreign aid bills in the cold war. As hoped, U.S. aid to Greece and Turkey helped these countries deal successfully with the Communist threat.

The Marshall Plan In 1947 the economies of the nations of Western Europe were still in desperate shape from the destructive effects of war. Communist parties in France and Italy made the most of people's discontent and won large numbers of supporters in both countries. To contain the rising tide of communism and Soviet influence, Truman's secretary of state George Marshall proposed an ambitious program of foreign aid. From 1948 to 1951, Congress approved $12 billion of economic assistance to Europe, a huge sum for that time. The *Marshall Plan*, as the aid program was called, helped to bring about European recovery. By 1951 Communist control of France and Italy was no longer a serious possibility, although the Communist party in both countries remained strong. (The United States had offered Marshall Plan aid to all nations in Europe, but it was refused by the Soviet Union and its satellites.)

A cartoonist's view of America's international alliances and commitments after World War II

The originator of the assistance plan, George Marshall, had been a leader in war as well as peace. As the armed forces' chief of staff during World War II, Marshall had been in charge of planning overall military strategy. In recognition of his postwar strategy for peace (the Marshall Plan), Marshall received the Nobel Peace Prize in 1953.

European Recovery The major goal of Western European countries after World War II was to rebuild their shattered economies. Eventually, they succeeded in restoring prosperity. The most important factors in Western Europe's recovery were: (1) economic aid from the United States in the form of the Marshall Plan; (2) Western Europe's skilled work force; (3) a strong regional demand for consumer goods, such as new cars and appliances; and (4) the reduction of trade barriers within the region.

Many Western Europeans believed that prosperity would come sooner if their governments reduced regional trade barriers. As a result, in 1952, France, West Germany, the Netherlands, Belgium, Luxembourg, and Italy formed the European Coal and Steel Community. It removed tariffs between member countries on coal, iron ore, and steel. It also regulated production of these goods in the community.

In 1957 the same six countries expanded the concept by creating the *European Economic Community (EEC, or Common Market)*. It was designed to eliminate all tariff barriers among member states. Eventually, the organization grew as Great Britain, Greece, Portugal, Spain, Ireland, Denmark, Austria, Finland, and Sweden joined.

European Community and European Union The initial success of the Common Market led member nations to set up a more ambitious plan known as the *European Community (EC)*. Its goals include the free flow of goods, services, people, and capital among member nations. Plans were also discussed for a single European currency, a single European bank, and eventual political union. In 1991, leaders of the member nations met in Maastricht, the Netherlands, and agreed to launch a common currency (the euro), establish common foreign policies through a European Parliament, and lay the groundwork for a common defense policy. In 1994 the European Community became known as the *European Union (EU)*. In 1998 a European Central Bank was established. In 2002, 11 of the 15 European Union countries are scheduled to change over completely to the euro as common currency. The goal of a united Europe faces major opposition within a minority of countries, including Great Britain, where there is a reluctance to give up national sovereignty.

Berlin Airlift Truman and Marshall's containment policy took a slightly different form in Berlin. Recall that the victors of World War II had divided both Germany and Berlin into zones of occupation. Berlin happened to be within the zone under Soviet control. In 1948 the Soviet Union announced that the British, French, and Americans could no longer use the land routes to Berlin that passed through the Soviet zone of occupation.

This meant that food and other vital supplies could not reach the people living in West Berlin. Truman announced that the United States would not abandon West Berlin, as the Soviets had hoped. But he did not use ground troops to break the land blockade for fear of starting a war. Instead, he ordered the U.S. Air Force to bring supplies to West Berlin by air. This operation, known as the *Berlin Airlift*, flew in supplies day after day for almost a year. Finally, in 1949, the Soviets yielded to Western determination and ended their blockade of land routes to West Berlin.

North Atlantic Treaty Organization (NATO) By 1949 U.S. policymakers recognized that the Soviet Union and its *bloc* (group) of Communist states in Eastern Europe threatened the security of Western Europe. For the first time in its history, the United States committed itself to a permanent military alliance in peacetime. In 1949 the president signed and the Senate approved a treaty with 11 nations (Great Britain, France, Italy, Belgium, the Netherlands, Denmark, Norway, Iceland, Portugal, Luxembourg, and Canada). The treaty created an alliance called the *North Atlantic Treaty Organization (NATO)*.

In the treaty, the allies agreed that "an armed attack against one or more of them in Europe or North America shall be considered an attack against all." The common defense of the NATO nations rested on a shield-and-sword concept. European and American ground troops would act as a "shield" against any Soviet attack. U.S. atomic weapons would act as a "sword." The purpose of the NATO alliance was to deter the Soviet Union from aggression and thus to avoid war.

★ In Review

1. Explain the significance of the Senate vote approving U.S. membership in the United Nations.
2. Summarize the origins of the cold war.
3. Define and explain the significance of each of the following: UN Declaration of Human Rights, refugees, Yalta and Potsdam conferences, satellite nation, iron curtain, containment, Truman Doctrine, Marshall Plan, Common Market.

Containment in Asia, Africa, and Latin America

The cold-war rivalry between the United States and the Soviet Union extended to all parts of the world, including Asia, Africa, and Latin America. (For the United States and Japan, see Chapter 14.)

The United States and China

China was a U.S. wartime ally. After Japan was defeated, U.S. policymakers hoped that China would eventually become a strong and prosperous democracy. But this hope for a democratic China was soon threatened. China was in serious danger of falling under the control of a Communist government. From the U.S. point of view, this was an alarming development.

Rise of Mao Zedong to Power China, the most populous nation in the world, had a huge population of peasants who toiled in poverty. A discontented young peasant named Mao Zedong decided in the 1920s that the time had come for the Chinese working class (industrial workers and peasants) to take control of their government and adopt a Communist system. Through the 1920s and 1930s, a rebel army under Mao's leadership fought with the government's army. The government leader was General Jiang Jieshi (old spelling Chiang Kai-shek), head of a ruling party known as the Nationalists. Mao's Communists and Jiang's Nationalists stopped fighting their civil war during World War II in order to fight the Japanese. But as soon as Japan was defeated, the civil war resumed.

Flight of Jiang Jieshi to Taiwan (1949) President Truman and his advisers knew that the Chinese Communists received military aid from the Soviet Union. To contain and defeat Mao's forces, the U.S. Congress voted large amounts of economic aid and military supplies to support Jiang Jieshi and the Nationalists. Unfortunately, Jiang made himself unpopular with the Chinese people by misusing government funds and failing to improve conditions of life for the common people. Jiang ignored U.S. advice to change his ways. At the same time, Mao's army attracted peasant recruits by the millions. The Communist forces scored one victory after another. In 1949 Jiang and his Nationalist supporters fled to the island of Taiwan, off the Chinese coast. The Communists took control of the government of mainland China.

The Soviet Union: A-Bomb Test (1949)

In 1949 the Soviet Union exploded its first atomic bomb. Suddenly the United States was no longer the only nation to possess the most destructive weapon ever made. Since the United States had dropped the two atomic bombs on Japan to end World War II, the world lived in fear that someday such weapons might be used in a war capable of destroying all life on the planet.

In 1952 the United States announced that it had developed a weapon thousands of times more destructive than the atomic bomb, or A-bomb. Its new weapon was the *hydrogen bomb*, or *H-bomb*. But only one year later, the Soviet Union announced that it too had developed and tested an H-bomb. The world now entered a frightening time when the two most powerful nations competed with each other to produce more and more nuclear weapons.

"Hot War" in Asia: Korean War

Only five years after the end of World War II, the United States became involved in a war in Korea. One of this war's underlying causes was U.S. op-

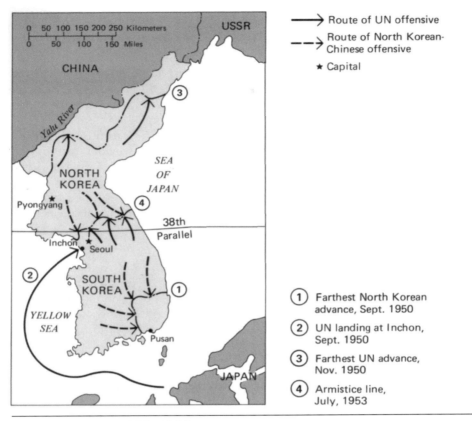

The Korean War, 1950–1953

position to communism. The immediate cause was a sudden attack by a North Korean army against the territory of South Korea.

Korea, a proud nation with an ancient past, had lost its independence in 1910 when Japanese armies occupied the country. At the end of World War II, the Japanese were driven out of Korea by Soviet armies arriving from the north and American armies arriving from the south. Soviets and Americans agreed that the 38th parallel of latitude should be the temporary dividing line between their zones of occupation. After the cold war began, the 38th parallel seemed more like a permanent border between North Korea, with its Soviet-backed Communist government, and South Korea, with its U.S.-supported government. The United Nations had helped to organize the South Korean government. Hoping that the United Nations could manage Korea's problems, U.S. troops left the country in 1949.

In June 1950, a North Korean army marched across the 38th parallel into South Korea. This was precisely the kind of aggressive act that the U.S. policy of containment was supposed to prevent. Truman did not hesitate. He ordered U.S. troops into South Korea and called on the United Nations to undertake the defense of the South Korean government. Coincidentally, the Soviet Union had previously withdrawn its representative from the United Nations and thus, for the time being, had lost its veto power in the Security Council. Although many nations contributed troops to the UN-sponsored defense of South Korea, by far the largest number came from the United States and, of course, South Korea.

Truman did not ask Congress to declare war. Instead, he used his power as commander in chief to conduct an undeclared war in Korea, which he called a *police action*.

China Enters the War The commander of the UN forces was U.S. General Douglas MacArthur. At first, MacArthur's forces suffered a series of defeats. But then a surprise attack behind enemy lines pushed the North Koreans back toward the Chinese border. MacArthur's decision to pursue them caused China to come to the aid of North Korea. Thousands of Chinese soldiers crossed the Yalu River, driving UN forces south. Overwhelmed by the Chinese assault, the UN forces and the South Koreans retreated south of the 38th parallel.

UN Efforts: MacArthur, Truman, and "Limited War" MacArthur urged President Truman to permit him to bomb Chinese bases in Manchuria, a part of China, in order to stop the Chinese attack. Truman refused to give his permission, wishing to pursue a "limited war" in Korea. He feared that bombing China would probably result in a far larger and more dangerous war.

MacArthur conveyed his thoughts to congressional leaders and continued to campaign for the bombing of Chinese territory. At this point in 1951, President Truman removed MacArthur as the commander of UN forces in Korea. Truman concluded that he could not allow MacArthur to challenge the president's authority as commander in chief.

The decision to remove MacArthur took courage because the general was popular with the American people. Returning to the United States, MacArthur received a hero's welcome in a huge ticker-tape parade in New York City. In a speech to Congress, he delivered a statement that became famous: "Old soldiers never die, they just fade away."

Despite MacArthur's popularity, most Americans supported President Truman's policy of avoiding a full-scale war with China.

Point Four Aid

The first president to use economic aid to fight the cold war was Harry Truman. In his inaugural address of 1949, Truman listed several points as the basis for his foreign policy. Most important was his fourth point concerning world poverty. Truman said: "More than half the people of the world are living in conditions approaching misery. Their food is inadequate. They are victims of disease. Their economic life is primitive and stagnant. I believe that we should make available the benefits of our store of knowledge in order to help them realize aspirations for a better life." The foreign aid voted by Congress for developing countries in Asia, Africa, and Latin America was known as Truman's *Point Four Program*.

Cold War at Home

Communism was on the march in the postwar years. In just five years (1945–1950), Communists took over the governments of an entire region, Eastern Europe, and also won control of the world's most populous nation, China. In this time of Communist expansion, many Americans wondered whether their own country might be a target of Communist plots. They feared that Communist spies and Communist sympathizers might be anywhere, working as secret agents of the Soviet government.

Thus, the cold war abroad led to a cold war at home. During the presidencies of Truman and Eisenhower (Truman's successor), the U.S. government took measures to determine whether civil service employees and others might be "disloyal" to the United States. Many of the actions taken by the government restricted freedom of speech. This section illustrates the tension that may develop when a government's concern about national security comes into conflict with a citizen's basic rights.

Government Loyalty Checks

In 1946, newspapers reported that several workers employed in Canada's government had been giving secrets about the American atomic bomb to the Soviet Union. To prevent this from happening in the United States, President Truman began a system of *loyalty checks* of federal employees. To determine whether an employee was likely to be loyal or disloyal, Truman ordered the Federal Bureau of Investigation (FBI) and the Civil Service Commission to find out about the employee's past associations. Had the person ever belonged to a Communist or subversive organization as defined by the U.S. government? (*Subversive* means "seeking to overthrow [the government].") The U.S. attorney general listed 90 organizations whose members *might* be disloyal or subversive. Many of these organizations, however, were never proved to advocate the overthrow of the U.S. government.

Between 1947 and 1951, some 3 million government workers were investigated. More than 200 of them lost their jobs as "security risks." In addition, 2,900 civil servants resigned for various reasons. Some resigned in protest, believing that the loyalty checks violated their constitutional rights. Others resigned to avoid being investigated.

Anti-Communist Laws and Investigations

In addition to loyalty checks, the cold war at home led to the utilization of two anti-Communist laws: the Smith Act (1940) and the Internal Security Act, or McCarran Act (1950).

Smith Act   Congress had enacted this law even before U.S. entry into World War II. The law prohibited any group from advocating or teaching the violent overthrow of the U.S. government and also prohibited any person from belonging to such a group. In effect, since U.S. Communists advocated the overthrow of capitalist governments (although not necessarily by violence), the Smith Act made it illegal for U.S. citizens to join the Communist party.

The First Amendment guarantees a citizen's right to freedom of speech and freedom of association. Did the Smith Act violate the First Amendment? The first important court case to test the law was *Dennis et al.* v. *United States* (1951). Eugene Dennis and ten others admitted to having been members of the Communist party in the 1940s. Dennis had made a number of speeches that, in the government's view, threatened the national security. He and his associates had been arrested and convicted under the Smith Act. They appealed to the Supreme Court, which decided that their First Amendment rights had not been violated. The Supreme Court noted that a speech may be prohibited if it presents a clear and present danger of overthrowing the government by force and violence. Dennis's speeches, in the Court's view, did present such a danger to the national security.

In a later case, *Yates* v. *United States* (1957), the Supreme Court shifted from its position on the Smith Act. For the law to be violated, said the Court, a speaker must encourage people to do something, not merely believe in something. Any idea could be advocated so long as the speaker did not urge people to commit dangerous acts.

McCarran Act   Congress passed a second anti-Communist law in 1950. The Internal Security Act, or McCarran Act, was aimed primarily at "Communist-front" organizations. Such groups did not identify themselves as Communists but were accused of either receiving support from Communists or including Communist members. The law required all Communist and Communist-front organizations to file membership lists and financial statements with the U.S. attorney general. It also prohibited (1) the employment in national defense plants of Communists or members of Communist-front organizations and (2) the entry into the United States of Communists or former Communists.

House Un-American Activities Committee   In the 1940s, a special committee of the House of Representatives—the House Un-American Activities Committee (HUAC)—held a number of hearings on disloyalty. Testimony at these hearings received much attention in the press.

Called before the House committee, a labor organizer named John Watkins answered questions about his own dealings with Communist groups. But he refused to answer questions about the activities of other persons he knew. He believed that such questions were not relevant to the committee's work. Watkins was convicted of violating a federal law that made it a crime to refuse to answer a congressional committee's questions. Watkins appealed to the Supreme Court.

In *Watkins* v. *United States* (1957), the Supreme Court decided that Watkins's conviction was not valid. The Court ruled that a witness at a congressional hearing may properly refuse to answer any committee question that does not relate to the committee's lawmaking task.

The Hiss Case   The most sensational case of suspected disloyalty in the 1940s involved a former member of the U.S. State Department, Alger Hiss. In 1945 Hiss had accompanied Franklin Roosevelt to the Yalta Conference. He had then resigned from the State Department to direct a private organization for world peace. Few people had heard of Alger Hiss until 1948. In that year, a magazine editor and a former Communist, Whittaker Chambers, appeared before the House Un-American Activities Committee. Chambers testified that Hiss had been a Communist spy in the 1930s and had provided Chambers with secret government documents. Hiss denied Chambers's accusations. Nevertheless, a federal court convicted Hiss of perjury (lying under oath) and sentenced him to five years in prison.

The Rosenberg Case   One of the greatest fears of government officials and the American public was that the Soviet Union might learn how to build an atomic bomb. Only the United States had this weapon during the first postwar years.

In 1950, a year after the Soviet Union tested its first atomic bomb, a married couple named Julius and Ethel Rosenberg were arrested and charged with passing secrets about the bomb to the Soviet Union. At their trial they were found guilty of conspiracy to commit espionage (spying). The Rosenbergs maintained that they were innocent and appealed to both the Supreme Court and President Eisenhower. Despite worldwide appeals on their behalf, including ones from Pope Pius XII and Albert Einstein, the Rosenbergs were executed in 1953.

Loyalty and Dissent: The Oppenheimer Case   Dr. J. Robert Oppenheimer, a brilliant physicist, had been one of the scientists responsible for building the atomic bomb at Los Alamos, New Mexico, in 1945. Oppenheimer later opposed the U.S. development of the hydrogen bomb. He feared that this weapon would lead to an uncontrolled arms race and the ultimate destruction of the world. The U.S. government reacted negatively to Oppenheimer's public stand against the H-bomb. The government accused him of being a Communist and labeled him a security risk. In 1954 it withdrew his security clearance.

McCarthyism

Fear of Communist influences and subversion was especially intense during the years that the Korean War was being fought, 1950 to 1953. The person most responsible for arousing public fears was a U.S. senator from Wisconsin, Joseph McCarthy.

In 1950 Senator McCarthy gave a speech in which he claimed that he held in his hand a list of known Communists who worked for the U.S. State Department. A Senate subcommittee found no evidence to support his accusations. Nevertheless, because McCarthy skillfully played on the anti-

Communist fears and suspicions of the American public, he soon became an extremely powerful person. Other public officials began to fear Mc-Carthy's accusations even more than communism.

McCarthy portrayed himself as a patriotic defender of American security. He conducted Senate committee hearings in which he accused many government officials of being "Communist sympathizers." McCarthy's committee investigated actors, writers, educators, and others and accused them of being either Communists or Communist sympathizers. Their constitutional rights were disregarded, and many lost their jobs because of false charges. They had trouble finding new employment because businesses would "blacklist" (refuse to hire) those under investigation.

★   ★   ★   ★   ★

A SPEECH AGAINST McCARTHYISM

Margaret Chase Smith was a Republican senator from Maine. She was the only woman to have served in both the U.S. House of Representatives (1940 to 1949) and the U.S. Senate (1949 to 1973). Senator Joseph McCarthy was also a Republican, but this did not stop Senator Smith from criticizing McCarthy's methods of investigating those he labeled as Communists. On June 1, 1950, Senator Smith invited members of the press into her Senate office and delivered the speech quoted below.

I think that it is high time that we remembered that we have sworn to uphold and defend the Constitution. I think that it is high time that we remembered that the Constitution, as amended, speaks not only of the freedom of speech but also of trial by jury instead of trial by accusation.

Whether it be a criminal prosecution in court or a character prosecution in the Senate, there is little practical distinction [difference] when the life of a person has been ruined.

Those of us who shout the loudest about Americanism in making character assassinations are all too frequently those who, by our own words and acts, ignore some of the basic principles of Americanism: the right to criticize; the right to hold unpopular beliefs; the right to protest; the right of independent thought. . . .

The American people are sick and tired of being afraid to speak their minds lest they be politically smeared as "Communists" or "Fascists" by their opponents. Freedom of speech is not what it used to be in America. It has been so abused by some that it is not exercised by others.

Early in 1954 McCarthy began to look for Communists in the Army. The Army counterattacked by accusing McCarthy of seeking special favors for one of his former Senate aides. McCarthy demanded that his committee investigate the Army. These committee hearings, unlike earlier ones, were televised.

Between April and June 1954, a TV audience of some 20 million people watched the Army-McCarthy hearings. For the first time, many people saw McCarthy in action. They did not like what they saw. He interrupted and bullied witnesses and made reckless use of unsubstantiated charges. These tactics offended the American sense of fair play. As public opinion turned against him, McCarthy soon lost both his supporters and his power. In December 1954, the Senate voted to censure (officially criticize) McCarthy for improper conduct that damaged the reputation of the Senate.

The term *McCarthyism* has come to mean "the use of reckless and unfair accusations in the name of suppressing political disloyalty."

Politics of the Cold War

The cold-war rivalry between the United States and the Soviet Union was complicated by events in China and Korea.

Loss of China There were now two Chinese governments—Mao's Communist government on the mainland (known as the People's Republic of China) and Jiang's Nationalist government on Taiwan. Each contended that it was the only legitimate government for the Chinese nation. Most Americans were shocked by the "loss of China" to communism. President Truman sided with Jiang, and so did his successors, Eisenhower and Kennedy. Through the 1950s and 1960s, the United States recognized only one Chinese government as legitimate—Jiang's Nationalist government. The United States refused to recognize Mao's Communist government.

Because Jiang's government had controlled China when the United Nations was formed in 1945, Nationalist China continued to be a UN member through the 1950s and 1960s. Communist China (the People's Republic of China) was excluded from UN membership. The United States and its NATO allies firmly opposed attempts by the Soviet Union to unseat the Nationalists.

During the Eisenhower's presidency, two small islands under Taiwan's control—Quemoy and Matsu—were bombarded by guns from the mainland. The United States stood ready to defend its ally, Jiang. But Mao stopped short of invading Quemoy and Matsu, and the crisis passed. By the end of the 1950s, an uneasy peace had developed between the "two Chinas."

Stalemate and Truce in Korea (1953) The war in Korea dragged on through 1951 and 1952. Despite much loss of life, neither side could win decisive victories, and the war became stalemated near the 38th parallel. Truce talks started in July 1951 and continued on and off into 1953. The Republican candidate for president in 1952—General Dwight Eisenhower—promised to "go to Korea," if elected, to end the fighting. As president-elect, he carried out his promise in 1952. An armistice was finally signed in June 1953. It established the 38th parallel as the line between the opposing forces.

Truman's Falling Popularity As the election of 1952 drew near, there was widespread dissatisfaction with the Truman administration. First, Truman was blamed for the stalemate in Korea, where negotiations for an armistice had been dragging on for over a year. Second, the country was suffering from an inflationary cycle, which was caused by the expense of the war as well as Truman's failure to settle a steelworkers' strike in 1952. Third, Truman was blamed for the victory of communism in China, and Americans were alarmed by Senator McCarthy's charges that Communists had infiltrated the government. Fourth, there were accusations of corruption among some of Truman's friends. Finally, Truman suffered political damage after he removed the popular General MacArthur from his command in Korea. All of these problems led to a Republican victory in 1952. Eisenhower became the next president.

★ In Review

1. Describe one success and one failure of U.S. foreign policy in Asia between 1945 and 1955.
2. Explain how the United States responded to the Communist threat at home.
3. Identify and explain the significance of each of the following: Mao Zedong, Jiang Jieshi, Yalu River, Point Four Program, Smith Act, House Un-American Activities Committee, *Watkins* v. *United States*, Alger Hiss case, Rosenberg trial, J. Robert Oppenheimer, McCarthyism.

Chapter Review

MULTIPLE-CHOICE QUESTIONS

Use the cartoon on page 411 to answer questions 1 and 2.

1. The cartoonist believes that the United States
   (1) must join the United Nations
   (2) should outlaw atomic weapons
   (3) would be wise to install an international "hot line" telephone to prevent the accidental occurrence of an atomic war
   (4) can never depend on other nations to maintain peace.

2. The cartoonist is expressing the viewpoint that
(1) new weapons technology will make warfare too horrible to sustain
(2) if World War II had continued, there would have been only one survivor
(3) after the next war the only surviving technology will be the telephone
(4) World War III will result in the end of humankind.

Refer to the map on page 414 and answer question 3.

3. The map shows that after the end of World War II,
(1) Germany became a colony of the Soviet Union and the United States
(2) Germany and Berlin were at first divided between the major Allied Powers
(3) France had the most control of Germany
(4) United States policy toward Germany was opposed by three hostile world powers.

Refer to the map on page 416 and answer questions 4 and 5.

4. The map shows that
(1) the Soviet Union was concerned about being attacked from its western borders
(2) Yugoslavia became a democratic nation
(3) the United States had an increasingly strong influence among nations that were not Soviet satellites
(4) there was no question that the Soviet Union was attempting to take over all of Europe.

5. A comparison of this map with the one on page 414, entitled "Division of Germany and Berlin After World War II," shows that
(1) the British, French, and U.S. zones became West Germany while the Soviet Union retained control of East Germany
(2) all of Berlin came under Soviet control
(3) Germany became one nation shortly after the end of World War II
(4) communism had little impact in France and Italy.

Use the cartoon on page 418 to answer questions 6 and 7.

6. In the cartoon, the figure of "Americanism" stands for
(1) isolationism
(2) imperialism
(3) anticommunism
(4) internationalism.

7. The cartoonist is being critical of
(1) loyalty oaths
(2) strikes conducted by organized labor following World War II
(3) the Marshall Plan
(4) the House Un-American Activities Committee (HUAC).

8. Korea was divided in 1945 as a result of
(1) popular elections
(2) a civil war
(3) a compromise political solution reflecting cold-war realities
(4) a dispute in the United Nations.

9. In the early 1950s, the American people were *most* divided over the issues of
(1) nationalistic loyalty versus an individual's right to dissent

(2) improving schools versus saving tax dollars
(3) the need for nuclear power versus fear of radiation effects
(4) the growth of big business versus its impact on the environment.

10. Critics of McCarthyism in the 1950s stressed the idea that

(1) the government should always be on guard against Communist subversion
(2) fears of subversion can lead to the erosion of constitutional liberties
(3) loyalty oaths can prevent espionage
(4) communism is likely to gain influence in times of prosperity.

THEMATIC ESSAYS

1. **Theme:** Containment of Communism

Immediately after World War II, the United States under President Harry S. Truman faced the new challenge of an expanding communism.

Task: Describe two methods employed by the Truman administration to halt or contain the spread of communism throughout Europe and the rest of the world. For each method:

★ Explain the program.
★ Illustrate the program as it applied to a specific area or nation.
★ Describe the ultimate impact of the program upon limiting the spread of communism.

Consider utilizing the Truman Doctrine, Marshall Plan, Point Four Program, and the formation of the North Atlantic Treaty Organization (NATO) as possible examples for your discussion.

2. **Theme:** Security and Democracy During the Late 1940s and 1950s

The threat of global communism led to a fear on the part of many Americans that Communist traitors were influencing and betraying our government and seriously undermining the interests and well-being of the United States.

Task

★ Describe two examples of how the federal government became involved in a hunt for Communists within American society.
★ Show how, in at least one case, one of our constitutional values or individual rights was sacrificed in response to the Communist menace. (You may use one of the examples that you used in the first part of your answer or choose a new example.)

Suggestions include, but are not limited to, a discussion of the use of loyalty checks, J. Robert Oppenheimer, the Smith Act, actions of the House Un-American Activities Committee (HUAC), the case of *Watkins* v. *United States*, the Alger Hiss case, and the activity of Senator Joseph McCarthy.

3. **Theme:** McCarthyism and the Witch Hunt

   The attempt of Senator Joseph McCarthy and others to expose and eliminate Communists from the U.S. government and key areas of society had precedents in a number of "witch hunts" in U.S. history in which a group was singled out and blamed for the problems of the time.

   Task: Compare and contrast the activities of Senator Joseph McCarthy and others during the late 1940s and 1950s to the blame and witch hunting against a specific group of people in a different era of U.S. history.

   You may include in your comparison such situations as the Palmer Raids of 1919–1920, the Copperheads during the Civil War, and the Salem witch trials during the colonial period. You are not, however, limited to these situations.

4. **Theme:** The Cold War

   The cold war was a war of ideology and beliefs that pitted the United States and the Soviet Union against each other in conflicts that mainly involved a third nation or area.

   Task

   ★ Discuss how the peace agreements between the United States and the Soviet Union helped create the situation that led to the cold war.
   ★ Demonstrate how two events that took place during the post–World War II period helped increase tension between the United States and the Soviet Union.

   The outcomes of the summit meetings at Yalta and Potsdam should be discussed in the answer to the first section. For the second section, consider a discussion of the rise of Mao Zedong and the Chinese Communists, Soviet testing of an atomic bomb, the formation of NATO, and the development of a "hot war" in Korea as possible responses.

DOCUMENT-BASED QUESTION

*Read each document and answer the question that follows it. Then read the **Task** and write your essay. Essays should include references to most of the documents along with additional information based on your knowledge of United States history and government.*

Historical Context: World War II left the world with two major super-powers struggling for global dominance in what came to be known as the cold war. One of the earliest tests of will between communism and the United States was over Korea. The fighting of this war, however, led to a dispute between President Harry S. Truman and the commander of UN forces, General Douglas MacArthur, the result of which was the dismissal of MacArthur.

Document 1 President Harry S. Truman, as quoted in *The New York Times*, April 12, 1951:

> So far by fighting a limited war in Korea, we have prevented aggression from succeeding and bringing on a general war. . . . We have taught the enemy a lesson. He has found out that aggression is not cheap or easy. . . .
> We do not want to see the conflict in Korea extended. We are trying to prevent a world war—not start one. . . .
> But you may ask: "Why can't we take other steps to punish the aggressor?" Why don't we bomb Manchuria and China itself? Why don't we assist Chinese Nationalist troops to land on the mainland of China?
> If we were to do these things, we would be running a very grave risk of starting a general war . . . we would become entangled in a vast conflict on the continent of Asia and our task would become immeasurably more difficult all over the world.
> What would suit the ambitions of the Kremlin [Soviet Union] better than for our military forces to be committed to a full-scale war in Red China?

Question: Why did President Truman wish to fight a "limited" war in Korea?

Document 2 General Douglas MacArthur, as quoted in *The New York Times*, April 19, 1951:

> . . . The Communist threat is a global one. Its successful advance in one sector threatens the destruction of every other sector. . . .
> I made it clear that if not permitted to destroy the enemy build-up [of] bases north of the Yalu [River], if not permitted to utilize [the] friendly Chinese force of some 60,000 men on Formosa [Nationalist China], if not permitted to blockade the China coast to prevent the Chinese Reds from getting succor [help] from without, and if there were to be no hope of major reinforcements, the position of the command from the military standpoint forbade victory. . . .
> War's very object is victory, not prolonged indecision.
> In war there can be no substitute for victory.

Question: Why did General MacArthur disagree with President Truman's conduct of the Korean War?

Document 3 President Harry S. Truman in the *Congressional Record* for the 82nd Congress, April 10, 1951:

> With deep regret I have concluded that General of the Army Douglas MacArthur is unable to give his wholehearted support to the policies of the United States government and of the United Nations in matters pertaining to his official duties . . . I have, therefore, relieved General MacArthur of his commands. . . .
>
> Full and vigorous debate on matters of national policy is a vital element in the constitutional system of our free democracy. It is fundamental, however, that military commanders must be governed by the policies and directives issued to them in the manner provided by our laws and Constitution. In time of crisis, this consideration is particularly compelling.

Question: Why did President Truman remove General MacArthur from his command in Korea?

Document 4 Refer to the map on page 422.

Question: What was the result of the Korean War?

Task

- ★ Describe the conflicting strategies of President Truman and General MacArthur regarding the conduct of the Korean War.
- ★ Evaluate the wisdom of President Truman's dismissal of General MacArthur in light of the results of the war and the president's constitutional powers as commander in chief.

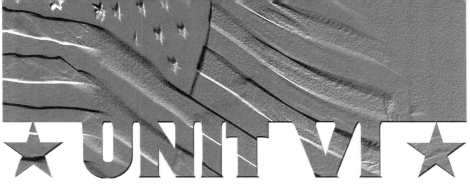

★ UNIT VI ★

The World in Uncertain Times

Chapter 16

Toward a Postindustrial World:
Living in a Global Age

★ Objectives

- ★ To understand the increasingly interdependent nature of the world.
- ★ To explain how the United States is changing from an industrial to a postindustrial nation.
- ★ To describe current changes in technology and their impact on both the United States and the world.
- ★ To recognize that the nations of the world are closely linked in a global economy of trade and electronic communications.

The Industrial Revolution, which began about 1750, continued to change the world for some 200 years. Beginning in the 1950s, there were signs in the United States and other industrialized countries that a new economic revolution was underway. People observed that the world was entering into a new era. As this era moves into the 21st century, much of the world is undergoing rapid change.

Social scientists have proposed different names for this revolutionary age of new technology and new economic systems. Some call it the *information age* and others the *postindustrial age*. The changes that are occurring in this age affect not only the United States but the entire world. This chapter briefly describes the forces that transformed our nation and the world during the last half of the 20th century.

Changes Within the United States

Energy Sources

The industrial age had relied for its energy on the burning of two fuels, coal and oil. Throughout much of the 20th century, people in industrialized nations daily consumed huge quantities of these energy sources. Automobiles, trucks, and airplanes could not operate without oil. In fact, the entire industrial economy depended on oil for fueling its factories, heating its buildings, and supplying the raw materials for making everything from tires to T-shirts.

However, the supply of oil is limited. Scientists predicted that the earth might use up its last gallon of oil sometime in the 21st century. In the 1970s, nations around the world became aware that the days of burning oil at home and gasoline on the road might soon come to an end. In the postindustrial age, what new forms of energy could be substituted for the oil supply that is running out?

Nuclear Power   One answer to this question was to generate energy and heat by splitting the uranium atom. In the 1950s, both the U.S. government and electric power companies had high hopes that nuclear power plants might be the energy source of the future. Such plants did not pollute the air with smoke. They produced electric power cheaply and efficiently. But there was always the danger of an accident that would send harmful substances into the atmosphere. Furthermore, nuclear power plants have not yet been able to solve the problem of what to do with the radioactive byproducts of power generation.

Energy From the Sun and the Wind   Scientists recognized that an ideal substitute for oil would need to be both safe to the environment and practical to use. The light and heat from the sun offered one possibility. Nothing could be safer than trapping the sun's rays to heat a home or to provide power for a small automobile. Unfortunately, the devices created so far to harness solar energy have only limited uses. The same is true of modern windmills and other energy technologies for tapping the forces of nature (winds, tides, and underground heat).

Materials: Plastics, Light Metals

The postindustrial world is largely made of plastic. Consider these things that you may own—calculators, computers, compact discs, wristwatch bands, car seats, radios, cameras, and carpets. These and millions of other items are made entirely or in part from various plastics that did not exist before 1900. In fact, except for cellophane (invented in 1908), most plastics came into common use only in the 1940s and 1950s.

Another symbol of the new age is the throwaway aluminum can. Aluminum is the metal of the late 1900s (just as steel had been the chief metal of the late 1800s). Consumers have been wrapping their food in aluminum foil ever since its invention in 1947. They have been drinking from aluminum cans (instead of glass bottles) ever since the 1960s. Lightweight

An early 20th-century cartoonist's view of the world in the year 2023

cars made from aluminum alloys came into use in the 1970s. The lighter cars made it easier to save gas.

Automation

In the 1950s and 1960s the U.S. economy surged ahead with spectacular gains in productivity. A chief reason for U.S. economic growth in those decades was *automation*—a new method of manufacturing products. Automation is a process in which one set of machines regulates other machines. This enables manufactured goods to be assembled almost automatically, with a minimum need for human labor. Not only does automation increase the speed of production, but it also reduces the possibility of human error.

Though generally benefiting the U.S. economy, automation worried factory workers and labor unions. Automation reduced the number of factory jobs, especially those repetitive jobs that required little education or skill. It became obvious that unskilled jobs would decrease.

New Technology: Computers

The automation of American industries depended in part upon the invention of an electronic device known as the *computer*. The origins of this device go back to 1890. In that year an inventor named Herman Hollerith created a tabulating machine (or counting machine) to speed the process for taking the census.

To help the U.S. armed forces after World War II make rapid calculations, an immense computer weighing 30 tons began operating in 1946. Known as ENIAC (Electronic Numerical Integrator and Calculator), it consisted of 18,000 vacuum tubes. As an electric current flowed through the tubes, the machine performed thousands of mathematical calculations in only a few seconds. Technology advanced so rapidly, however, that this "first generation" of electronic computers was replaced in the 1960s by a new and more powerful type of computer.

Instead of the vacuum tube, the basic electronic building block of the "second generation" computer was a transistor. Less then one-tenth the size of the vacuum tube, the transistor could perform the same functions with even greater speed and reliability.

Another breakthrough in 1969 enabled more powerful computers to be made at lower cost. Replacing the little metallic transistor was an even smaller and more compact "chip"—a thin square of silicon with electronic circuits printed on it. The goal among computer engineers was to invent ways for computers to process and store more information at higher speeds for less cost in smaller machines.

Daniel Bell, a social scientist at Harvard University, observed in the 1960s that the United States was fast becoming a "postindustrial society." Bell observed that in the postindustrial society, "Information is power. Control over communication services is a source of power. Access to communication is a condition of freedom." In the past, almost all information took the form of words and numbers printed in books and documents. In the postindustrial age, however, more and more information was electronic in form. People in this new age learned to store information, or data, on computer discs and transmit it to other computers over telephone lines or through electronic signals using space satellites.

The computer is only the means to access a whole band of knowledge on the Internet (network of computers using the World Wide Web). This has led to a new type of industry as companies have created Web sites to provide everything from information to retail sales. As the 21st century opens, this World Wide Web is only beginning to realize its potential.

New Corporate Structures

The light metal cars and plastic computers of the postindustrial world were not made in just one nation. The corporations that manufactured them had plants and selling outlets in many countries. Such globe-straddling firms were known as *multinational corporations* (MNCs). Leading examples of such firms were General Motors (GM)—automobiles—and International Business Machines (IBM)—computers.

U.S. firms would typically keep their office headquarters in U.S. cities but open manufacturing plants in developing nations. Wage rates outside the United States were usually far below American rates. It was therefore cheaper for manufacturing companies to make goods abroad. By the 1980s, the largest U.S. corporations had turned themselves into multinational firms. By the 1990s, hundreds of U.S. companies operated in six or more countries.

The Internet and World Wide Web are contributing to globalization as communications expand the ability of individuals and corporations to communicate with one another. These businesses can hold conferences that reach out beyond the meeting room. As a result of U.S. leadership on the Internet, English is rapidly becoming the language of business throughout the world.

The trend of businesses becoming multinational has had both beneficial and harmful effects on the U.S. economy. On the positive side, it has vastly increased world trade and opened up world markets for U.S. goods and services. On the negative side, it has resulted in the closing of U.S. factories and the loss of manufacturing jobs for American workers.

Nature of Employment

Daniel Bell, the Harvard social scientist, observed in his book *Coming of Post-Industrial Society* (1973) that by the second half of the 20th century, most Americans had changed the way they earned a living. In the past, they had worked at making products—either growing crops on a farm or manu-

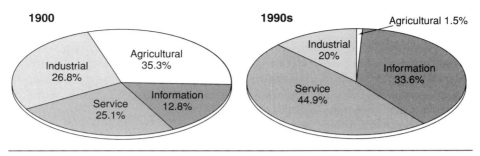

The Changing American Labor Force, 1900 and 1990s

facturing goods in a factory. But beginning in the 1950s, there was an entirely new emphasis. Instead of making products, most workers in the United States provided services of one kind or another.

There were services of a traditional kind—for example, barbering, hairdressing, gardening, and waiting on tables. Even more common were services dealing with information. Teachers transmitted information to their students. Postal clerks transmitted information by mail. Office clerks stored information either in paper files or in computers. People in banks, business offices, medical laboratories, universities, libraries, and hundreds of other institutions did little else but record and interpret information. By 1993 only one out of five workers in the U.S. labor force produced goods in a factory or on a farm. Four out of five workers either dealt with information (creating it, transmitting it, or storing it) or performed some other service such as selling or transportation.

Problems of the Environment

In the second half of the 20th century, rapid technological and industrial growth created environmental problems that had not been anticipated and were difficult to resolve.

Nuclear Waste Disposal Although nuclear power appeared to be a cheap and efficient means to generate energy, a major question was whether nuclear plants could also supply energy safely. Because they were radioactive, the waste materials from nuclear plants presented a risk to the environment. The greatest risk of all was the possibility of an accident causing the nuclear core of a power plant to burn through the plant's protective walls. If such a "meltdown" occurred, the area near the plant could become radioactive for miles around. A disaster like this almost happened in 1979 at a nuclear power plant at Three Mile Island in Pennsylvania. The accident at this plant, although it did not lead to a "meltdown," made people aware of the dangers of nuclear power.

For years afterward, groups of citizens successfully fought power companies' attempts to build more nuclear plants. They became even more de-

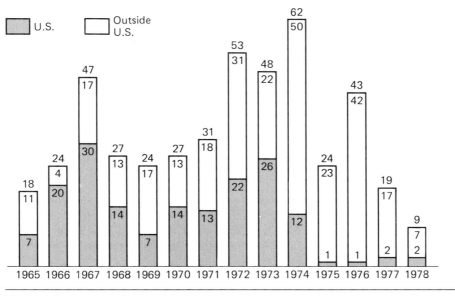

Nuclear Reactor Orders, 1965–1978

termined after a disastrous accident occurred in the Soviet Union in 1986. A nuclear power plant near the Soviet city of Chernobyl caught fire and sent radioactive smoke streaming into the air. Winds carried the radiation across Europe. Millions of people around the world feared that radioactive dust blown from Chernobyl might contaminate their own land.

Air and Water Pollution In the 1960s, Americans became aware that industrial wastes and exhaust fumes from millions of cars and trucks were causing terrible damage to the natural environment. Americans began to understand the dangers to their environment after the publication in 1962 of *Silent Spring*, an alarming book by Rachel Carson. Carson wrote: "Along with the possibility of the extinction of mankind by nuclear war, the central problem of our age has . . . become the contamination of man's total environment." The author pointed out how the pesticide DDT, a chemical spray widely used by farmers to kill insects, caused the deaths of enormous numbers of birds and fish. She also explained the damaging effects to the entire environment if wildlife vanished as a result of chemical pollution. In response to Carson's book, an environmental movement gained strength.

Sewage and industrial waste in America's rivers has long been a problem. Sewage and factory waste had polluted bodies of water such as the Hudson River in New York and the Great Lakes. Wastes also contaminated sources of drinking water in some areas. As late as 1989, water pollution again emerged as a major issue when the oil tanker *Exxon Valdez* spilled more than 10 million gallons of oil in the waters off the coast of Alaska. As a result, much of the fish and the wildlife dependent on fish died. The waters took years to clean up.

Greenhouse Effect   In the 1980s, scientists warned that the burning of forests and fossil fuels and exhaust fumes from motor vehicles might cause a condition similar to what happens in a greenhouse. As more and more carbon dioxide entered the earth's atmosphere, the sun's infrared rays would become trapped. The likely result would be the *greenhouse effect*—a gradual increase in the earth's average temperatures. Such a change in climate could melt the polar ice caps, flooding coastal cities, and generally harming all forms of plant and animal life, including human life. The United States is among the world's leading producers of carbon dioxide.

Ozone Depletion   Another environmental worry that developed in the 1980s concerned a layer of gas high above the earth's surface. This ozone layer blocks the sun's ultraviolet light, which is harmful to living things. Such light can cause skin cancer. The ozone layer's protection against ultraviolet light may cease to exist if aerosol sprays, Styrofoam cups and packaging materials, and chemicals used in refrigerators and air conditioners continue to emit an ozone-destroying gas into the atmosphere. Canada, the United States, and the nations of Western Europe have agreed to try to prevent further damage to the ozone layer. They pledged to ban all production of the damaging substances (chlorofluorocarbons) by the year 2000.

Acid Rain   Lakes and streams around the world are threatened by another environmental danger known as *acid rain*. The chief sources of the prob-

Predictions of a Warmer Planet, 1990–2020

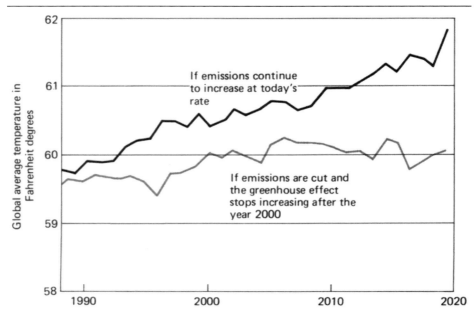

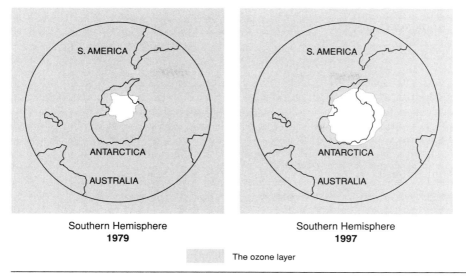

Southern Hemisphere
1979

Southern Hemisphere
1997

The ozone layer

Hole in the Antarctic Ozone Layer, 1979 and 1997

lem are the factory chemicals and automobile exhaust fumes that enter the air as vapor and fall to the earth in rain. The pollutants make the rain more acidic than normal. Bodies of water become acidic, causing the death of fish. Growth of forests and other plants is stunted.

Like other environmental hazards, acid rain recognizes no national boundaries. Wind currents carry the source of pollution for hundreds and even thousands of miles. For example, half of the acid rain that falls in Canada originates in the United States.

Growing Energy Use   By the mid-1990s, energy use in the United States had increased by more than 100 percent since 1960. As a result, the nation was forced to rely on imported sources of petroleum to reduce the gap between production and consumption.

Resource Depletion   Increasing consumption of oil has led to increased domestic production of crude oil and increased imports of oil. This accelerating demand for oil has led to depleted oil reserves and an even greater reliance on foreign petroleum. As the 21st century began, prices of imported oil had increased significantly.

Waste Disposal   Making products out of plastics, aluminum, and glass had negative side effects on the environment. Plastic wrappings and containers do not readily decompose when thrown away. Nor do glass and metal products. Millions of tons of discarded products piled up over the years. Finding ways to dispose of this type of garbage has become a nearly insoluble problem. Many communities have turned to recycling to reduce the waste that must be disposed of. Through recycling, materials can be reused or turned into other products.

79.4	109.3	129.4	143.0	174.8
1960	1970	1980	1986	2000 (estimate)

Source: U.S. Environmental Protection Agency

The Garbage Crisis in the United States (in millions of metric tons)

The production of light metals like aluminum posed a different problem. The process for manufacturing aluminum consumed huge amounts of energy. In order to reduce these energy requirements, efforts have been made to reuse products made of aluminum.

★ In Review

1. Identify two characteristics of a postindustrial society that distinguish it from an industrial society.
2. Define multinational corporation and explain the ways in which it depends on modern technology.
3. Define and explain the significance of the following: greenhouse effect, ozone layer, and acid rain.

Chapter Review

MULTIPLE-CHOICE QUESTIONS

Use the 1923 cartoon on page 437 to answer question 1.

1. The cartoon shows that
   (1) cartoonists and writers will someday be replaced
   (2) technological advances have taken place only in the last several years

(3) new ideas and inventions were important throughout the 20th century
(4) someday we will not need to work.

2. Which products are most a part of the postindustrial world?
   (1) steel and iron

(2) plastics and aluminum
(3) steel and aluminum
(4) plastics and iron.

3. A negative effect of new technologies on U.S. industry is
(1) a decline in the number of well-paid factory jobs
(2) a decline in the number of service jobs
(3) a high failure rate among multinational corporations
(4) a consumer revolt against the use of new technologies.

4. One consequence of the formation of multinational corporations is
(1) increased risk of a major war
(2) a decline in U.S. manufacturing jobs
(3) increased poverty of underdeveloped countries
(4) further depletion of the ozone layer.

Study the pie graphs on page 440 and answer questions 5–7.

5. The two pie graphs show that during the 20th century,
(1) the demands of the workforce have been subject to little change
(2) there has been an increasing need for manual labor
(3) the skills most in demand have changed
(4) the greatest decrease in the workforce has been in the area of industrial labor.

6. The two pie graphs indicate that
(1) industrial and agricultural employment will completely disappear
(2) service careers will gradually give way to those that deal with information
(3) the information sector is taking over the sectors of industry, service, and agriculture

(4) preparation for a career today differs greatly from earlier times.

7. Which of the following is the most accurate statement that can be made about the information given in the pie graphs?
(1) The computer has vastly changed the workforce in the United States.
(2) Information industries have little to do with other sectors of the U.S. economy.
(3) The use of the computer will bring about a resurgence of the agricultural sector of the workforce.
(4) There will always be a demand for minimally skilled labor in our factories.

Refer to the bar graph on page 441 to answer questions 8 and 9.

8. Which is a valid conclusion based on the data in the graph?
(1) Nuclear reactors are an unsafe source of energy.
(2) Orders for nuclear reactors reached their peak in the early 1970s.
(3) Inflation is chiefly responsible for the variations in the numbers of nuclear reactors ordered.
(4) Nations have become less dependent upon nuclear reactors as an energy source because of the popularity of solar converters.

9. Which development would be most likely to help reverse the trend in nuclear reactor orders since the early 1970s?
(1) discovery of major new oil reserves in the Atlantic Ocean
(2) an agreement by all nations with nuclear arms capabilities on a nuclear arms limitation treaty

(3) expansion of solar energy applications
(4) development of safer means of producing nuclear power and disposing of nuclear wastes.

Refer to the illustration on page 444 and answer question 10.

10. The problem presented in the illustration has been caused by

(1) shorter working hours for sanitation workers
(2) increased purchasing power of average U.S. citizens
(3) introduction and increasing use of plastics and light metals
(4) inadequate efforts at recycling on the part of the federal, state, and local governments.

THEMATIC ESSAYS

1. Theme: The Computer and Society

The development of the computer has changed the very nature of how we live and work.

Task

★ Show two ways in which the computer has changed our society.
★ Describe one problem *and* one benefit that has resulted from the changes you have described.

You may use, but are not limited to, changes such as access to information, improved communication, and convenience.

Problems that may be addressed include issues of privacy, information overload (access to more information than necessary), and the introduction of computer viruses.

2. Theme: The Postindustrial World

The emerging of a postindustrial world has created new demands, opportunities, and challenges.

Task

★ Describe one way in which a current problem can be solved in a postindustrial society.
★ Explain one problem that has developed in the transition from an industrial to a postindustrial society. This problem may already exist or become apparent in the future.

You may cite, but are not limited to, a discussion of energy and the development of new materials such as aluminum and plastic.

Some problems to consider involve waste management, pollution, and unemployment.

DOCUMENT-BASED QUESTION

*Read each document and answer the question that follows it. Then read the **Task** and write your essay. Essays should include references to most of the documents along with additional information based on your knowledge of United States history and government.*

Historical Context: Beginning around the 1950s, the United States and the other industrial nations began to undergo changes that indicated the emergence of a new and very different postindustrial world. This is becoming more apparent as we move into the new millennium and the impact of postindustrialism is being felt worldwide. This new world will create demands on the leadership of the United States and new problems that will challenge it to find innovative solutions.

Document 1   From the magazine *L'Express*, Paris, France, May 17, 1976:

> The Russians depend on American agriculture in order to feed themselves and without American technology, Siberia would remain barren. The European leftists who demonstrated against the Vietnam War were dressed in jeans and listened to Bob Dylan every night.

Question: How has the new technology increased the influence of the United States throughout much of Europe and the world?

Document 2   Babatunde Jose, Jr., as quoted in *Sunday Tide*, Port Harcourt, Nigeria, July 3, 1976:

> Though the [the United States] has not been a major participant in the African scene, she has nonetheless demonstrated her desire to help in the building up of the continent. American technological, scientific, educational, and cultural aid is what Africans want from America. We want the cooperation of [the United States] in the development of our friendships.
>   What we Africans do not want, however, is American imperialism and domination. . . .

Question: How can technological assistance from the United States be both helpful and harmful to many of the nations of Africa?

Document 3 Refer to the line graph on page 442.

Question: Why is there concern about the trend indicated on the graph?

Document 4 Refer to the maps on page 443.

Question: According to the maps, what is happening to the protective ozone layer of the Antarctic atmosphere?

Task

★ Explain how the influence of the United States has expanded as the world has continued to move through the early stages of the postindustrial age.
★ Describe three postindustrial problems facing the United States and the rest of the world. At least *one* of the problems described should be a different one from those referred to in the documents.
★ Show how the United States can exercise its leadership in solving either of the problems that you have described.

Chapter 17
Containment and Consensus: 1945–1960

* ★ To describe the foreign policies of the postwar period under the Eisenhower administration.
* ★ To describe victories in African Americans' struggle for civil rights.
* ★ To examine changes in American society in the 1950s.

The United States policy of containment emerged soon after the defeat of Germany and Japan in World War II. This policy launched a new set of power relationships.

Emerging Postwar Power Relationships

East/West

As you recall from Chapter 15, the Nationalists in China, led by Jiang Jieshi, were defeated by the Communists, led by Mao Zedong. Soon afterward, the Nationalists fled to the island of Taiwan. With a new Communist government in China, there was fear of a Chinese-Soviet alliance. Such an alliance could have created a powerful opponent, given the combination of China's population and the industrial and military strength of the Soviet Union. Thus, the United States, which had long protected Chinese interests against a powerful Japan, now sought to develop a new relationship with Japan in order to contain China and the Soviet Union.

In 1949, the United States developed a military alliance (NATO) to protect the nations of Western Europe from an attack by the Soviet Union. In addition, the Marshall Plan helped countries in Western Europe rebuild their economies in order to better contain the influence of communism within them.

North/South

In the 1950s it became common to view the world as divided into three groups of nations. Anticommunist nations of the West were the *first world*. Communist nations allied with the Soviet Union were the *second world*. Newly independent and economically underdeveloped nations of Asia and Africa were the *third world*. Also included in the third world were older nations of Latin America whose economies were underdeveloped or not industrialized.

U.S. policymakers feared that poverty in the third world countries might lead to political unrest, which in turn might lead to Communist uprisings. U.S. foreign aid for the third world was intended to bring about economic growth and thereby contain the spread of communism.

A huge gap exists between the so-called "have" nations of the world (developed and industrialized) and the "have-not" nations (developing and industrializing). It so happens that most of the industrialized nations occupy the northern part of the globe. (Exceptions are Australia and New Zealand.) Most of the developing countries lie to the south near the equator. Roughly speaking then, "have" nations tend to be in the north and "have-not" nations in the south.

Ever since World War II, the United States and other developed countries have given economic aid to less developed countries in the form of (1) loans, (2) outright grants, and (3) technical assistance (expert advice). In addition, multinational corporations have invested heavily in the poorer countries of Asia, Africa, and Latin America. They have opened up factories and mines and given employment to millions, though at wage rates far below U.S. standards. The United States and other developed countries have benefited from this relationship. The raw materials and labor that they can purchase cheaply in third world countries enable companies to sell goods for relatively low prices. The high standard of living enjoyed by the citizens of industrialized countries is largely due to this fact.

The relationship between rich countries and poor ones is far from equal. Because of development loans that they have often been unable to pay back, many developing countries are heavily in debt to the industrialized nations of Europe and to Canada, the United States, and Japan. The burden of debt grows heavier every year. More and more of a poor nation's governmental budget must be used to pay interest on its international debts. Thus, the gap between rich nations and poor nations continues to widen. The poorer nations resent the economic dominance of the richer nations. In the United Nations, they demand that the industrialized countries change their policies in order to provide the developing countries with relief from the crushing burden of debt.

The division between north and south, rich and poor, grows more serious every day as the world's population keeps increasing. Population growth in the United States and other industrialized countries has decreased in recent years. On the other hand, a high birthrate in Africa and

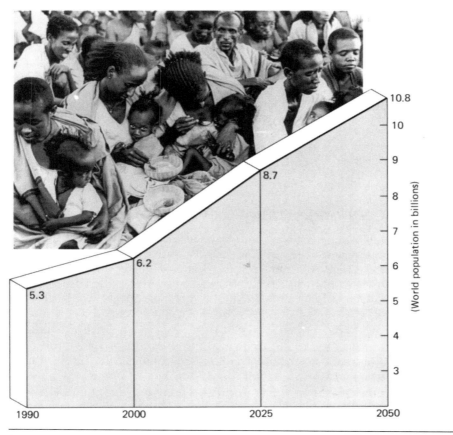

10.8
10
9
8
7
6
5
4
3

8.7

6.2

5.3

(World population in billions)

1990   2000   2025   2050

Projected World Population Growth, 1990–2050

other developing regions means that the population of the poorer part of the world is growing much faster than that of the richer part.

Eisenhower's Foreign Policies

A war hero, Dwight D. Eisenhower was the Republican candidate for president in 1952. During World War II, Eisenhower had been the supreme commander of Allied forces in Europe. In the postwar years, he had been president of Columbia University in New York City and then head of NATO. Popularly known as "Ike," the Republican candidate easily defeated his Democratic opponent, Governor Adlai Stevenson of Illinois. In 1956 President Eisenhower won election to a second term, defeating Stevenson by an even greater margin.

When Eisenhower became president in 1953, he faced two major foreign policy problems. First, how could he stop Soviet aggression? Second, how could he avoid a nuclear showdown with the Soviet Union?

The End of the Korean War

As you recall, the war in Korea had not been won by the time Eisenhower became president. In 1953 a permanent truce was finally agreed to by both sides and the war came to an end. The final act was an exchange of prisoners. Even today, the 38th parallel separates South Korea from North Korea. Thus, the Korean War was not a war for total victory but a war to contain Chinese and Soviet power.

Domino Theory and Massive Retaliation

In the early 1950s, the cold war had reached an intense stage. Chinese Communists under Mao Zedong had taken control of mainland China. Also, with UN backing, the United States had fought a war to prevent a Communist takeover of South Korea. When the French pulled out of Vietnam in 1954, this Asian country seemed about to fall to Communist forces. If this happened, President Eisenhower feared what he called a *domino effect*. He compared the countries of Southeast Asia to a lineup of falling dominoes. If Vietnam fell to communism, for example, other "dominoes" in the region (Cambodia, Laos, and Thailand) might also fall. This domino theory was developed by Secretary of State John Foster Dulles.

Dulles used forceful language to impress the Soviet Union with U.S. determination to stop Soviet aggression in Europe. Any aggressive move, he said, would be met by *massive retaliation*. Dulles did not mention nuclear weapons as such, but they were clearly implied. This willingness to threaten the use of nuclear weapons and risk war has been called *brinksmanship*.

The Hydrogen Bomb; Atoms for Peace

The year of the NATO treaty, 1949, was also the year that the Soviet Union tested its first atomic bomb. Suddenly, the United States was no longer the only nation to possess the most destructive weapon ever made. In 1952 the United States announced that it had developed a weapon thousands of times more destructive than the atomic bomb, or A-bomb. Its new weapon was the *hydrogen bomb*, or *H-bomb*. Just one year later, the Soviet Union announced that it too had developed and tested an H-bomb.

The world now entered into a frightening time. Its two most powerful nations competed with each other to produce more and more nuclear weapons. People in the 1950s soon recognized that much of the world might be destroyed if the cold war ever turned into a hot, nuclear war. Therefore, in 1953, President Eisenhower proposed an atoms-for-peace plan to the United Nations. Under this plan, nations would pool their atomic resources for peaceful purposes. When the Soviet Union refused to participate, the United States launched a limited version of the plan with Canada and its European allies. Thus Western nations would now pursue peaceful uses for atomic power, such as the production of electricity.

Summit Meetings and U-2s

U.S. prestige suffered a setback in 1960 when the Soviet Union shot down a U.S. spy plane, the U-2. During the *U-2 incident*, the Soviet leader, Nikita Khrushchev, angrily charged that the only purpose of the U-2 plane was to spy on the Soviet Union. Eisenhower at first denied that this was true but later admitted that U-2 planes were commonly used for spying. The American pilot, Gary Powers, survived the crash of his plane and was later exchanged for a Soviet spy. As a result of the U-2 incident, Khrushchev canceled a summit conference with President Eisenhower, and cold war tensions increased.

Southeast Asia Treaty Organization (SEATO)

In 1954 the United States formed an alliance in Southeast Asia similar to the NATO alliance in Europe. It was known as the *Southeast Asia Treaty Organization*, or *SEATO*. Treaty members were Great Britain, France, the United States, Australia, New Zealand, Pakistan, Thailand, and the Philippines. (The Philippines had been granted independence from U.S. control in 1946.)

U.S. alliances in both Asia and Europe were based on a single assumption, which was generally accepted at the time. The assumption was that the Soviet Union masterminded Communist movements in all countries of the world. Thus, Americans viewed communism as a single force. Only later, in the 1960s and 1970s, did U.S. policymakers begin to realize that the Chinese Communists and North Korean Communists had national goals different from those of Soviet leaders in Moscow.

Egypt: Aswan Dam and Suez Canal

In 1956 Egypt under General Gamal Abdel Nasser asked for assistance from the United States to build a dam along the Upper Nile River. The dam was expected to generate electricity and provide irrigation for Egypt's desert land. The United States refused partly because of Egypt's anti-Israel stand. Nasser turned to the Soviets, who agreed to help. Soon afterward, Nasser decided to take over the Suez Canal that ran through his nation. It was owned by the British and French. During the *Suez Crisis*, Nasser *nationalized* the canal. (This means that a property formerly belonging to either a colonial power or a private company is seized by a government.)

Seeking to regain control of the canal, Great Britain, France, and Israel carried out a joint attack against Egypt. Furious with his allies for acting without U.S. approval, President Eisenhower condemned the attack. Eisenhower was worried that the Soviet Union might enter the conflict on Egypt's side. As a result of U.S. pressure, the invading forces withdrew, and a UN force moved in to keep the peace. The Suez Canal remained under Egyptian control.

Uprisings in Poland and Hungary

In 1956 anti-Soviet riots broke out in the East European countries of Poland and Hungary. The Soviet Union agreed to loosen slightly its control of the Polish government. In Hungary, however, Soviet tanks rolled into the capital city of Budapest and quickly crushed the uprising.

While he sympathized with the Hungarian freedom fighters, President Eisenhower offered them no military assistance. Eisenhower recognized that the Soviet Union had established a sphere of influence in Eastern Europe. In response to NATO, the Soviets had arranged a military alliance of its own with its Eastern European satellites—an alliance known as the *Warsaw Pact*. To avoid war, Eisenhower was careful not to interfere in the So-

Cold-War Military Alliances—NATO and the Warsaw Pact

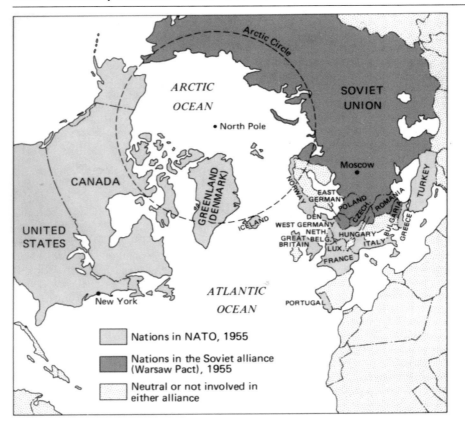

viet sphere of influence. At the same time, the Soviet Union did not challenge the NATO alliance.

Eisenhower Doctrine

Most Arab nations objected to U.S. support of Israel, even though they too received U.S. economic aid. Arab resentment against both Israel and the United States led to growing Soviet influence in the Middle East, especially in Syria. To prevent Soviet influence from spreading further, President Eisenhower in 1957 stated that the United States would send troops to any Middle Eastern nation that requested such help against communism. This policy, known as the *Eisenhower Doctrine*, was first applied in Lebanon. In 1958 the presence of U.S. troops in Lebanon helped that country's government deal successfully with a Communist threat.

Sputnik: Initiating the Space Race

In 1957 the cold war literally reached into outer space. In that year, the Soviet Union launched *Sputnik*, a small metal sphere that orbited Earth. It came as a shock to the American people and their government that the first artificial satellite into space was Soviet-made, not American-made. Both Eisenhower and his successor, John F. Kennedy, wanted to show the world that U.S. space technology was superior to Soviet space technology. Under their leadership, Congress committed vast resources to the race for space. Between 1957 and 1963, the United States launched many satellites and began training astronauts for Earth-orbiting missions. At the same time, the shock from the Sputnik setback caused the U.S. government to spend large sums on science education.

★ In Review

1. Define each of the following terms: "have"/"have-not" nations, domino theory, brinksmanship, H-bomb, and Suez Crisis.
2. Explain how each of the following built on and extended the policy of containment: massive retaliation, SEATO, and the Eisenhower Doctrine.
3. For each Soviet action listed, state how the United States responded: sending troops into Hungary to put down a revolt, 1956; launching the Sputnik satellite, 1957; shooting down the U-2 spy plane, 1960.

Domestic Policies and Constitutional Issues

When Eisenhower moved into the White House in 1953, he was the first Republican president in 20 years. As a Republican, would he make major changes in the domestic programs established by Democratic presidents Roosevelt and Truman? Or would he leave the programs of the New Deal and the Fair Deal largely intact? It soon became clear that the new president wished only to trim and modify the programs of his predecessors. He did not favor drastic change.

The Eisenhower Peace

The end of the Korean War meant that President Eisenhower could focus on important domestic issues.

Return to a Peacetime Economy On domestic issues Eisenhower tended to be conservative. In other words, he believed that private businesses should be allowed a large amount of freedom from government control. He also believed in restoring to the states some of the power exercised by the federal government.

In the early 1950s, oil wells off the coasts of Texas, Louisiana, and California were producing large quantities of oil. The governments of these states claimed that it was within their power to regulate and tax the oil drilled a short distance from their coastlines. During his presidency, Harry Truman had argued that offshore oil rights were under the authority of the federal government. But Eisenhower sided with the states. In 1953 he signed legislation allowing states to control the oil rights within their territorial waters.

Cartoon criticizing President Eisenhower's apparent indifference to U.S. problems in the 1950s

From HERBLOCK: A CARTOONIST'S LIFE (Macmillan, 1993)

Eisenhower also sided with private power companies and spoke critically about the U.S. government's own power projects run by the Tennessee Valley Authority (TVA). He said the TVA was an example of "creeping socialism." The president even favored the idea of having the TVA stop being a supplier of electric power. This proposal, however, was widely criticized and soon abandoned.

While favoring business interests, Eisenhower disagreed with those Republicans who wished to cut back the social programs begun by the Democrats. To show that the Republican party also cared about people's welfare, Eisenhower persuaded Congress to enact the following laws and programs:

★ Increasing the minimum wage from 75 cents an hour to one dollar an hour

★ Increasing Social Security benefits for retired persons and bringing many more workers under the protection of the Social Security system

★ Creating a new cabinet-level department of the executive branch—the Department of Health, Education, and Welfare. (To head the new department, Eisenhower chose a woman, Oveta Culp Hobby.)

★ Granting government loans to students attending college.

Interstate Highway Act (1956) The Eisenhower administration persuaded Congress to pass an ambitious program for building 42,000 miles of inter-

Earl Warren, Chief Justice
of the United States, 1953–1969

state highways to link the major cities of the country. The highway system could also be used by the military in case of a national emergency. The federal government would supply 90 percent of the funds, with the remainder coming from the states. (Of course, the billions of federal dollars spent on new highways gave a tremendous boost to a number of important industries—automobiles, housing, tourism, trucking, and others.)

Suburbanization The new highways made possible the creation of more and more communities at a distance from the workplaces in cities. The suburbs, as the outlying communities were known, attracted people who wanted more open space than city housing could provide.

The Warren Court Within society, there is always tension between balancing the protection of the rights of the accused with the need to protect society. Earl Warren, the governor of California, was appointed chief justice of the United States by President Eisenhower. Under Chief Justice Earl Warren (1953–1969), the Supreme Court made several controversial decisions concerning clauses of the Bill of Rights. (See Chapter 18 for a full discussion of these cases.)

The Modern Civil Rights Movement

Like President Truman before him, President Eisenhower soon found himself involved in the battle for equal rights for African Americans. World War II had given African Americans an expectation of change. After all,

Former prisoners of war returning from Korea (illustrating the integrated U.S. Army of the 1950s)

they reasoned, many thousands of African Americans had fought in the war and played a significant role in liberating other peoples in Asia and Europe. If worldwide freedom and democracy were among the goals of the U.S. war effort, then it was surely time for equal rights and freedom from racial discrimination to be won at home.

When World War II ended, African Americans had lived for many decades under Jim Crow laws in the South that denied them equal rights. In northern cities, too, they had suffered from discrimination in housing and jobs. After the war, discriminatory laws and customs began to break down. The civil rights movement, begun by W. E. B. Du Bois and others early in the century, became a significant force for social change during the presidencies of Truman and Eisenhower.

Jackie Robinson Breaks the Baseball Color Barrier

The most dramatic and widely publicized breakthrough in the 1940s was achieved by a talented and courageous baseball player, Jackie Robinson. When Robinson joined the Brooklyn Dodgers in 1947, he was the first African American athlete to play for a major league baseball team. At first

Jackie Robinson, playing for the Brooklyn Dodgers— the first African American in the baseball major leagues

Robinson had to endure the jeers of whites in the crowd and the racial insults of many white ballplayers on his own team as well as on opposing teams. He also had to stay in segregated motels and rooming houses when his Brooklyn team (now the Los Angeles Dodgers) played in other cities. But his talents as an athlete and his determination to keep calm, in spite of all obstacles, won him the admiration of millions. An outstanding ballplayer, Robinson in 1962 was elected to the Baseball Hall of Fame—the first of many African Americans to win the honor. Robinson's breaking of the color barrier in major league baseball quickly led to other teams acquiring African American players. Thus, Larry Doby of the Cleveland Indians became the first African American ballplayer in the American League.

Brown v. Board of Education of Topeka, 1954

More than any event of the 20th century, a Supreme Court decision in 1954 marked a turning point in the movement for civil rights for African Americans. The landmark case of Brown v. Board of Education of Topeka came before the Court shortly after Earl Warren became its new chief justice.

In earlier cases concerning racial segregation, the Supreme Court had determined that railroads, schools, hotels, and other facilities could be segregated under the Constitution if those facilities were "separate but equal." In other words, segregation was allowed if the separate facilities for the use of African Americans were roughly equal to the facilities set aside for whites. The "separate but equal" rule had originated in 1896 in the Supreme Court case of Plessy v. Ferguson.

In the early 1950s, the school system of Topeka, Kansas, was segregated by law. A young African American named Linda Brown lived closer to one of Topeka's all-white elementary schools than to an all-black elementary school. Her father attempted to enroll her in the white elementary school, but school officials turned him down. Aided by the National Association for the Advancement of Colored People (NAACP), Linda Brown's father brought suit against the Topeka Board of Education. A lower federal court rejected Brown's suit on the grounds that Topeka's schools were properly "separate but equal." Brown and the NAACP then appealed to the U.S. Supreme Court.

The main lawyer representing Brown was an African American employed by the NAACP—Thurgood Marshall. Marshall and his associates used not only legal arguments but also psychological evidence from the studies of Kenneth Clark, an African American psychologist. The studies demonstrated that African American children tended to feel inferior as a direct result of living in a segregated society.

The Supreme Court's decision in the Brown case reversed its previous position. It declared that segregated schools could not be equal, because of the psychological damage that they inflicted on minority children. Led by Warren, all justices on the Supreme Court agreed that segregation on the basis of race deprived children of equal educational opportunities. The

★ ★ ★ ★ ★

BROWN V. BOARD OF EDUCATION OF TOPEKA (1954)

Writing for a unanimous Court, Chief Justice Earl Warren gave several arguments for desegregating the nation's schools. One of his arguments is presented below.

Today, education is perhaps the most important function of state and local governments. Compulsory school attendance laws and the great expenditures for education both demonstrate our recognition of the importance of education to our democratic society. It is required in the performance of our most basic public responsibilities, even service in the armed forces. It is the very foundation of good citizenship. Today it is a principal instrument in awakening the child to cultural values, in preparing him for later professional training, and in helping him to adjust normally to his environment. In these days, it is doubtful that any child may reasonably be expected to succeed in life if he is denied the opportunity of an education. Such an opportunity, where the state has undertaken to provide it, is a right which must be made available to all on equal terms.

We come then to the question presented: Does segregation of children in public schools solely on the basis of race, even though the physical facilities and other "tangible" factors may be equal, deprive the children of the minority group of equal educational opportunities? We believe that it does.

Court concluded that Topeka's school system and others like it violated the Fourteenth Amendment's guarantee of equal protection of the laws.

Shortly afterward, the Supreme Court ruled that any segregated school system in the country would have to become racially desegregated with "all deliberate speed." Thurgood Marshall, the lawyer who had helped achieve this breakthrough for civil rights, was appointed to the Supreme Court in 1967.

Schools were only one institution that began to change in response to the civil rights movement. Other institutions—segregated buses, lunch counters, and movie theaters—also began to change.

Rosa Parks and the Montgomery Bus Boycott

The civil rights movement gained momentum from an incident in Montgomery, Alabama, in 1955. As in many southern cities, it was the rule in Montgomery for African Americans to sit in the rear section of a bus. Re-

Rosa Parks sits in the front of a bus in Montgomery, Alabama, at a time when southern segregation laws required African Americans to sit in the back.

turning home from work one afternoon, an NAACP official named Rosa Parks refused to give up her seat in the front of the bus to a white person. She was arrested and charged with violating the segregation laws. Protesting Rosa Park's arrest, a 26-year-old Baptist minister, Dr. Martin Luther King, Jr., urged African Americans in Montgomery to boycott the city's buses by refusing to ride in them. The bus boycott lasted for more than a year and was extremely effective. It hurt both the bus system and business in general. Under the pressure of the boycott, the city of Montgomery gave in and agreed to desegregate its transportation system.

Little Rock School Desegregation

Many southern whites opposed the Supreme Court's ruling to desegregate their school systems. The first major challenge to the Court's decision occurred in Little Rock, Arkansas, in 1957. This city's board of education had drawn up a desegregation plan and ordered a formerly all-white high school to admit a few African American students.

Arkansas's governor, Orval Faubus, posted units of the Arkansas National Guard around the Little Rock high school to stop African American students from entering the building. Faubus explained that the state troops were there to maintain order. A federal court responded by reaffirming the students' right to enter the school and forbidding the governor to interfere. Faubus finally did remove the troops but only after a mob of whites had stopped the African American students from entering the high school.

Little Rock, Arkansas: Federal troops protect the right of African American students to attend a formerly all-white high school.

President Eisenhower was reluctant to become involved in the crisis. He recognized, however, that Governor Faubus's actions challenged the authority of the national government and the U.S. Supreme Court. He called the Arkansas National Guard into federal service and ordered it back to the high school, this time to protect the right of the African American students to enter the building. In addition, he sent hundreds of U.S. soldiers to Lit-

A crowd of white persons protest racial integration of Little Rock Central High School.

tle Rock to keep order and to prevent any further trouble. Although Governor Faubus referred to these measures as an "occupation," most Americans supported the president's actions.

Segregation in Public Transportation Ruled Unconstitutional

The Supreme Court in 1896 had established the doctrine of "separate but equal" in *Plessy* v. *Ferguson*. Although the case concerned segregation in railroad cars, this ruling, which upheld the constitutionality of *de jure segregation*, was applied to education. (De jure means by law.)

After the 1954 decision in *Brown* v. *Board of Education of Topeka* ended de jure segregation in education, many people concluded that it could apply to transportation as well. However, it was not until the Montgomery bus boycott in 1955 that the issue of segregated transportation caught the attention of the nation. After various appeals, the Supreme Court ruled in 1956 that segregation in transportation was unconstitutional. Thus, Alabama as well as other southern states were in clear violation of the Constitution.

Sit-ins: Nonviolent Tactic

A student group that believed in nonviolent protest called itself the Student Nonviolent Coordinating Committee (SNCC). Beginning in 1960, college students belonging to SNCC organized sit-in demonstrations in major cities of the South. They would walk into a restaurant that practiced segregation and sit at the counter waiting to be served. As expected, the restaurant would refuse to serve them, and they in turn would refuse to leave their seats. Many of the demonstrators were arrested. But combined with the powerful tactic of boycotting segregated businesses, the sit-ins led several cities, including Dallas, Atlanta, and Nashville, to do away with segregation.

Civil Rights Act of 1957

Ever since Reconstruction ended in the 1870s, African Americans in the South had difficulty exercising their constitutional right to vote in elections. State laws were especially designed to discriminate against them. Also many had reason to fear for their lives and property if they appeared at the local polling place and asked for a ballot. To a majority of lawmakers in Congress, a federal law to protect the voting rights of southern blacks seemed long overdue.

In 1957 Congress enacted a civil rights law that called on the U.S. Justice Department to stop any illegal practices designed to prevent African Americans from voting. In 1960 another civil rights law called for the use of federal "referees" in situations where voting rights were being denied. These two laws were weak and failed to provide real protection for African American voters. Even so, they were the first civil rights laws passed since Reconstruction. They prepared the way for stronger laws that would follow in the 1960s (described in Chapter 18).

★ In Review

1. Identify and explain the significance of each of the following: Interstate Highway Act (1956), Jackie Robinson, Rosa Parks, sit-ins, Civil Rights Act of 1957.
2. Summarize the background, the facts, and the Supreme Court decision in *Brown* v. *Board of Education of Topeka*, 1954. Explain its long-term significance.

The American People in the Postwar Era

The post–World War II period brought with it new affluence and new values. People became more concerned with acquiring newly available goods and services. "Keeping up with the Joneses" became a major goal for many Americans.

Prosperity and Consumption

In the depression decade of the 1930s, the American people had been chiefly concerned with economic security. U.S. entry into World War II in 1941 brought back prosperity, as factories strained to turn out increasing quantities of war goods. Many consumer goods were unavailable or in short supply during the war. But when the war ended, Americans had plenty of money to spend—and they spent it on all the things that they had lived without during the Great Depression and the war. Their purchases of new homes, appliances, cars, and televisions created a new society of middle-class consumers tending the lawns of their new suburban homes and spending hours watching their favorite TV shows. Their urge to acquire more and more possessions was known as *consumerism*.

Autos, Homes, and Television In the postwar years, millions of Americans bought new cars. Automobile sales spurred the growth of other industries that supplied the raw materials—such industries as steel, rubber, and glass. Spending on travel, restaurants, and motels increased, as people took to the open road in record numbers. Filling the tank with gas was no problem in the 1950s when gasoline was both plentiful and cheap (about 30 cents a gallon).

Suburban homes of the 1950s were often built in large developments in which one home looked almost exactly like every other. The advantage of such homes was that they could be bought at relatively low prices. Middle-income families in the suburbs filled their homes with the latest electrical equipment—washing machines, clothes dryers, dishwashing machines, and air conditioners.

Television was a new consumer item of the postwar years that profoundly influenced American society. Though developed by several inventors during the 1920s, television sets became common in American homes only in the early 1950s. By 1953 more than half the households in the United States had at least one television. Most TV images in the early 1950s were in black and white (even though color technology was available as early as 1951).

Television was partly like the radio because its regularly scheduled programs were paid for by advertisers. It was also partly like the movies because it was a visual medium that showed old movies as part of its featured programming. Most of the early TV shows were broadcast "live" (as they happened). Much as filmmakers had to make the challenging transition from "silents" to "talkies," radio stars tried to adapt to the demands of being seen as well as heard. Through the medium of television, TV stars such as Lucille Ball, Milton Berle, and Jackie Gleason became household names.

Every TV show had a commercial "sponsor"—a corporation whose purpose in paying for the show was to advertise its products to a huge audience. Because of their visual impact, TV ads were even more effective than radio ads in promoting the sale of automobiles, electrical appliances, and other consumer goods. Often a TV show included the name of its corporate sponsor—for example, "The Kraft Television Theater" and "The Palmolive Comedy Hour."

The most important effect of television was its influence on the tastes and habits of the American people. Watching TV for hours at a time became a daily habit of millions. Most people turned on the television for light entertainment in the form of sports, comedy shows, and adventure movies. Programs of a more serious and educational nature tended to be much less popular. People who watched many hours of TV a week had fewer leisure hours for more meaningful activities such as reading books or going on family outings. Critics of television in the 1950s and later decades believed that television had a generally negative effect on the values and habits of those who watched it most—young, school-age Americans. On the other hand, millions of Americans now had daily access not only to a free form of entertainment but also to some excellent cultural programs (plays, concerts, news commentary, and documentaries).

New Educational Opportunities   The GI Bill of Rights had a positive impact not only on war veterans but also on colleges, universities, and the U.S. housing industry. Under the law any veteran could apply for federal aid in paying for tuition, books, and other costs at a college or vocational school. Eight million veterans—about half of those who had served in the armed forces in World War II—took advantage of these educational benefits at a cost to the government of about $13.5 billion. Also under the law veterans could apply for federally guaranteed, low-interest loans for buying a home or investing in a farm or business. The GI Bill of Rights made it possible for millions of young families to own their own homes.

The Baby Boom and Its Effects

In the time of prosperity that followed World War II, married couples decided to have more children than in the prewar period. The result was a dramatic increase in the birthrate known as the *baby boom*. (Between 1945

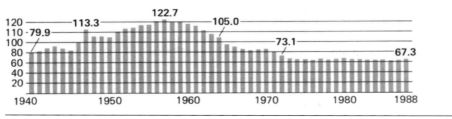

Baby Boom—and Baby Bust: U.S. Birthrate, 1940–1988

and 1960, some 50 million babies were born.) The greater number of children was one reason for increased sales of homes, cars, and appliances as well as children's toys and teen clothing. Cities and suburbs built new schools to make room for the growing youth population.

Migration and Immigration

While middle-class Americans moved from the cities into the suburbs, African Americans from the South and new immigrants from Latin America moved into the cities. By the 1950s, African Americans and Hispanics had become significant and growing minorities in the North.

Suburbanization: Levittowns Following World War II, builders, urged on by the demand for new homes, created new suburban communities. One such community was established in Levittown, New York, where many returning soldiers bought their first homes for little money. The use of the same design for each home encouraged mass production and resulted in lower costs. Levittown was named after the builder who developed the mass-production techniques in housing.

Cities in Decline As African Americans and immigrants from Latin America moved into the central cities, ethnic groups that had long made up the majority population began to move out. Thus, cities increased in minority populations while ethnic groups such as the Irish, Italians, and Jews moved to the suburbs. In general, these minority populations were less affluent than the middle-income groups that moved to the suburbs. As a result, there was a decline in the tax base within the cities and a need for greater services by local government. By the 1970s, many cities were close to bankruptcy and needed help from the federal government.

New Immigration Patterns: Latin American Focus

Most of the newcomers from Latin America came from Mexico, Cuba, and Puerto Rico.

After World War II, poverty in Mexico and economic opportunity in the United States caused many thousands of Mexicans to seek work in California, Texas, and other states of the Southwest. Most Mexicans came to the

United States as *braceros* (a Spanish word meaning "laborers") to harvest the crops on southwestern farms. Many entered the United States legally in compliance with the immigration laws. Others, however, crossed the border illegally.

The Caribbean island of Puerto Rico became a U.S. territory as a result of the Spanish-American War of 1898. The U.S. Congress granted the Puerto Rican people full U.S. citizenship in 1917 and granted their island country special status as a commonwealth in 1952. Commonwealth status meant that Puerto Ricans could elect their own governor and did not have to pay federal taxes. Immigration laws did not apply to Puerto Ricans who, as U.S. citizens, could enter or leave any part of the United States at will. After World War II, many Puerto Ricans migrated to New York and other cities of the Northeast in search of jobs.

Fidel Castro's Communist revolution in Cuba in 1959 caused hundreds of thousands of Cubans to flee to the United States. Many settled in Miami and other Florida cities. Most of the Cuban immigrants were from middle-income and upper-income groups.

★ In Review

1. Define each of the following: consumerism, baby boom, Levittown, bracero.
2. Explain the significance of television as a force for change in American society.
3. Describe the new immigration patterns of the 1950s.

MULTIPLE-CHOICE QUESTIONS

Refer to the graph on page 451 and answer questions 1 and 2.

1. The graph indicates that
   (1) the rest of the world has lagged behind the United States in birth control
   (2) Africa and the Middle East currently have the highest birthrates in the world
   (3) between 1990 and 2050, the population of the world is expected to double
   (4) the development of urban areas throughout the world has resulted in couples having increasing numbers of children.

2. An examination of the graph shows that

(1) the world food supply should be adequate for the next 25 years, after which it will rapidly deplete
(2) there will be increasing demand on the world's resources
(3) the moon and the planets Venus and Mars will be colonized in order to support the growing population of the globe
(4) sex education has been unsuccessful and should be eliminated.

Use the map on page 454 to answer question 3.

3. The map illustrates a situation similar to that
(1) in Europe prior to World War I
(2) on the eve of the Spanish-American War
(3) in Asia at the time of the Boxer Rebellion
(4) in Africa at the beginning of the 20th century.

Refer to the cartoon on page 456 and answer question 4.

4. The cartoonist believed that there was
(1) overwhelming public support for the policies of President Eisenhower
(2) President Eisenhower appeared to be indifferent to many problems of the time
(3) President Eisenhower personally worked out the solutions to the problems facing Americans in the 1950s
(4) air travel was becoming increasingly popular at the time.

5. The significance of the civil rights laws of 1957 and 1960 was that they
(1) succeeded in ending discrimination in public facilities
(2) were the first civil rights laws passed since Reconstruction
(3) opened the doors to equal opportunity in employment
(4) protected women as well as racial minorities.

Base your answer to questions 6 and 7 on the following song lyrics:

Little Boxes

Little boxes on the hillside, little
boxes made of ticky tacky,
Little boxes on the hillside, little
boxes all the same,
There's a green one and a pink one,
and a blue one and a yellow one.
And they're all made out of ticky tacky,
and they all look just the same.

And the people in the houses
All went to the university,
Where they were put in boxes
And they came out all the same,
And there's doctors and lawyers,
And business executives,
And they're all made out of ticky tacky
And they all look just the same.

Malvina Reynolds,
"Little Boxes," 1962

6. The song tells us that during the postwar years
(1) homes were built with substandard materials
(2) there was an overemphasis on education
(3) businessmen ignored the rights of workers in spite of the gains made by organized labor
(4) there was an alarming degree of conformity among Americans.

7. Which of the following most likely alleviated the problems with which Malvina Reynolds was concerned?
(1) a national school curriculum

(2) an increase in the amount of inexpensive mass-produced goods
(3) immigration from Asia, Latin America, and the West Indies
(4) a decrease in the amount of new housing construction.

Use the graph on page 461 to answer questions 8 and 9.

8. Which was an immediate result of the change in birthrate during the late 1940s and 1950s shown in the graph?
(1) a rise in social security benefits paid
(2) overcrowded classrooms
(3) women entering the workforce
(4) increasing cold-war tensions.

9. The probable cause for the birth statistics of the late 1940s and 1950s was that

(1) there was little knowledge of birth control during the period
(2) the number of marriages and families increased after World War II
(3) the marriage rate dropped after World War II
(4) divorces increased during the 1950s.

10. The increased immigration from Mexico and migration from Puerto Rico in the post–World War II period was fueled primarily by
(1) the desire for political freedom
(2) the increase in bilingual education
(3) the desire for better economic opportunity
(4) an appreciation for the popular culture of the United States.

THEMATIC ESSAYS

1. **Theme:** U.S. Foreign Policy, 1945–1960

The U.S. commitment to contain communism resulted in a period of peace with tension.

Task

★ Describe one example of how the United States, during years 1945–1960, promoted peace or kept itself out of a potential conflict.

★ Describe one incident that increased cold-war tensions.

Consider using examples such as the conclusion of the Korean War, the policies of Secretary of States John Foster Dulles, the development of the hydrogen bomb, the "atoms for peace" program, the U-2 incident, formation of new alliances such as NATO and SEATO, the Suez Crisis, the anti-Communist uprising in Hungary, the Eisenhower Doctrine, and the launching of a man-made satellite (*Sputnik*) by the Soviet Union. You are not, however, limited to these examples.

2. Theme: The United States in the 1950s: Conformity and Change

Some historians view the people in the United States of the 1950s as conformists. Others, however, view the period as a time of great change in American society.

Task

★ Describe one way in which Americans during the 1950s sought to conform.

★ Demonstrate one example of how change was, in fact, taking place simultaneously with conformity in the 1950s.

You may use, but are not limited to, such examples as the creation of the interstate highway system, the development of suburbs, early civil rights actions, television, the automobile, consumerism, the baby boom, the decline of cities, and immigration patterns.

DOCUMENT-BASED QUESTION

*Read each document and answer the question that follows it. Then read the **Task** and write your essay. Essays should include references to most of the documents along with additional information based on your knowledge of United States history and government.*

Historical Context: In spite of some small gains for African Americans during the late 1940s and 1950s, it was apparent that implementation of equal rights for black people would be a long and difficult process.

Document 1 Refer to the photograph on page 458.

Question: What does the photograph show about the armed services in the 1950s?

Document 2 Refer to the photograph on page 459.

Question: How did Jackie Robinson serve as a symbol of hope to many African Americans?

Document 3 Refer to the reading on page 461.

Question: What was the chief justice saying about segregated school facilities?

Document 4 Refer to the photograph on page 462.

Question: How did the actions of Rosa Parks help to promote integration in Montgomery, Alabama?

Document 5   Refer to the two photographs on page 463.

Question: Why was it difficult to integrate Central High School in Little Rock, Arkansas?

Task

★ Give one example of how hope for a better future was provided for African Americans during the post–World War II period (late 1940s and 1950s).

★ Show how, in spite of the gains already made, the average African American in the 1950s was still a second-class citizen.

Chapter 18
Decade of Change: the 1960s

★ **Objectives**

- ★ To understand the changes that occurred in the 1960s in American society and politics.
- ★ To compare the leadership of two presidents of the 1960s, Kennedy and Johnson.
- ★ To note the achievements of African Americans in their movement for civil rights.
- ★ To describe other movements for social justice by persons with disabilities, women, Hispanic Americans, and Native Americans.
- ★ To analyze landmark cases of the Supreme Court that redefined civil rights.

The 1960s were years of great change and turmoil. In some respects, the changes were positive. U.S. society became more democratic in the 1960s, as minorities, the handicapped, and women made significant progress toward equality. Also, the Supreme Court made decisions that expanded the protections of the Bill of Rights. Astonishing gains in science and technology enabled the United States to land a man on the moon in 1969.

In other respects, the 1960s was a tragic decade. Assassinations took the lives of a president (John Kennedy), a presidential candidate (Robert Kennedy), and three African American leaders (Medgar Evers, Dr. Martin Luther King, Jr., and Malcolm X). Racial tensions caused riots to erupt in almost every major U.S. city. Drug use among American youths increased. Large numbers of college students took part in massive demonstrations protesting the war in Vietnam.

The Vietnam War and the protest against it will be treated in the next chapter. This chapter focuses chiefly on the positive aspects of change—the progress achieved by women and minorities in their movement for equal rights.

The Kennedy Years

In many respects, the brief presidency of John F. Kennedy was unique. Elected in 1960 at the age of 43, he was the youngest candidate to win the presidency and the first president born in the 20th century. (Theodore Roosevelt was 42 when he took office in 1901, but he became president as a result of President McKinley's assassination.) Kennedy was also the first Roman Catholic to be elected president.

Kennedy came from a wealthy Irish American family in Massachusetts that had long been active in politics. After fighting in World War II and winning a medal for bravery, Kennedy won election to the U.S. House of Representatives and then to the U.S. Senate. A well-financed campaign, an effective speaking style, and a likable personality helped him to win the Democratic nomination for president in 1960. His Republican opponent, Richard Nixon, was better known by most voters, having served as vice president under President Eisenhower for eight years. But Kennedy caught up with Nixon in the opinion polls after debating him on television.

Watching the first of four decades on their TV screens, most Americans thought Kennedy looked more self-assured and confident than his Republican rival. The Kennedy-Nixon debates showed the amazing power of television to sway voter opinion. If these debates had not occurred, Kennedy would probably have lost the election. His margin of victory in the 1960 election was slight—303 electoral votes for Kennedy to 219 votes for Nixon.

The youthful president inspired the American nation—especially the youth of America—with his forceful inaugural address of 1961. His most memorable phrase appealed to the idealism of American youth: "Ask not what your country can do for you. Ask what you can do for your country."

Domestic Policy: The New Frontier

In the tradition of his Democratic predecessors Roosevelt and Truman, President Kennedy gave a name to his reform program. His *New Frontier* included proposals for federal aid to education, greater Social Security benefits, assistance to Appalachia (a poverty-stricken region of the Southeast), protection of African Americans' civil rights, and public health insurance for the elderly.

Even though both houses of Congress had Democratic majorities, Kennedy succeeded in winning passage of only a few of his New Frontier programs. Among those passed were:

★ Federal funds for urban renewal (the rebuilding of rundown city neighborhoods)

★ An increase in the minimum wage to $1.25 an hour

★ Federal loans to aid impoverished families in the Appalachian Mountains and other "distressed areas."

Among the programs rejected were:

★ Federal grants to the states for school construction and teachers' salaries

★ Medicare, or public health insurance, for elderly Americans through the Social Security system

★ A new civil rights law to enable the federal government to take bolder action in cases of racial discrimination and segregation.

Even though Kennedy's most important programs were defeated by conservative Republicans and conservative Democrats, they were later adopted during the presidency of Lyndon Johnson.

Civil Rights Actions

President Kennedy was a Democrat with liberal views on racial issues. As such, he gave encouragement to African Americans' struggle to end segregation.

Desegregating Interstate Buses When President Kennedy took office, he appointed his brother Robert Kennedy as U.S. attorney general. Both the president and the attorney general had to deal with a new tactic in the civil rights movement: freedom rides. By crossing state lines on interstate buses, the freedom riders, whites and blacks of all ages, demonstrated that segregation on buses involved the interstate commerce clause of the U.S. Constitution. Therefore, it was a federal matter, not one limited to local laws. Robert Kennedy urged the Interstate Commerce Commission (ICC) to desegregate the buses. The ICC did so when it ruled that segregation in interstate bus travel must end.

James Meredith at the University of Mississippi In 1962 a young African American, James Meredith, attempted to enroll as a student at the University of Mississippi. This university had previously admitted only white students. Mississippi's governor told Meredith that he could not enroll. But Meredith was determined to do so, despite a huge crowd of whites who threatened to attack him. To contain the crowd and protect Meredith's rights, President Kennedy ordered 400 federal marshals to the university campus. Thus protected, Meredith became the first African American to attend classes and finally to graduate from the University of Mississippi. Soon other southern colleges and universities began admitting African American students.

Public Career of Dr. Martin Luther King, Jr.

One result of the bus boycott in Montgomery (see Chapter 17) was the rise of a supremely gifted leader and speaker, Martin Luther King, Jr.

King believed in nonviolent public demonstrations. He believed that groups of protesters who joined together to disobey unjust laws would eventually prevail. This approach, known as *civil disobedience*, had been

Drawing of African Americans on a nonviolent march for civil rights

taught by earlier reformers. In the 1840s, the American writer Henry David Thoreau had advocated civil disobedience as a method for opposing slavery and the Mexican War. In the 1930s and 1940s, India's great leader Mohandas Gandhi had demonstrated the power of civil disobedience in opposing British rule. Now in the 1950s and 1960s, Martin Luther King, Jr., effectively applied the philosophy of nonviolence and civil disobedience to protesting the segregation laws of the South.

Birmingham Protest ("Letter From Birmingham Jail")   In the early 1960s, several cities in the South decided to do away with their segregation laws. But the city of Birmingham, Alabama, was not one of them. Protesters led by Martin Luther King, Jr., went to Birmingham to participate in a peaceful march through the center of the city. The Birmingham police attacked the marchers with dogs, powerful jets of water from fire hoses, and electric cattle prods. Television cameras brought the confrontation to a national audience. Among the marchers arrested and jailed in Birmingham was their leader, Martin Luther King, Jr. Writing from jail, King explained his reasons for breaking laws that he considered unjust.

> One who breaks an unjust law must do so openly, lovingly, and with a willingness to accept the penalty. I submit that an individual who breaks a law that conscience tells him is unjust and who willingly accepts the penalty of imprisonment in order to arouse the conscience of the community over its injustice is in reality expressing the highest respect for law.

Assassination of Medgar Evers

Medgar Evers was known for his contributions to the civil rights movement in Mississippi. At a young age, he became a leader of the NAACP, organizing economic boycotts, marches, and picket lines. Racial tensions in the 1960s led to his assassination in 1963 by a white supremacist. The accused killer, Byron De La Beckwith, stood trial twice in the 1960s, but in both cases all-white juries could not reach a verdict. Finally, in a third trial in 1994 (31 years after Evers' murder), Beckwith was convicted and sentenced to life in prison.

March on Washington in 1963

In the summer of 1963, Martin Luther King, Jr., and other civil rights leaders organized a huge demonstration in the nation's capital. This *March on Washington*, as it was called, was to alert Congress and the American people to the need for stronger civil rights laws. More than 200,000 people came to Washington, D.C., and heard Martin Luther King deliver a powerful and inspiring speech. (See page 478.) King's words reached out to the nation. It was now apparent that the civil rights movement had grown into a powerful force for change.

Foreign Policy and Cold-War Crises

In foreign policy, President Kennedy's goal was to continue to apply the cold-war policy of containment.

Martin Luther King, Jr., in Washington, D.C., 1963, when he delivered his "I have a dream" speech

★ ★ ★ ★ ★

"I HAVE A DREAM"

On August 28, 1963, Martin Luther King, Jr., stood on a speaker's platform near the Lincoln Memorial in Washington, D.C., and addressed a crowd of more than 200,000 people as well as a huge TV audience. In the most famous part of his speech, the civil rights leader spoke of his dream for a democratic nation.

I still have a dream. It is a dream deeply rooted in the American dream.

I have a dream that one day this nation will rise up and live out the true meaning of its creed. We hold these truths to be self-evident that all men are created equal.

I have a dream that one day out in the red hills of Georgia the sons of former slaves and the sons of former slaveowners will be able to sit down together at the table of brotherhood.

I have a dream that one day even the state of Mississippi, a state sweltering with the heat of oppression, will be transformed into an oasis of freedom and justice.

I have a dream that my four little children will one day live in a nation where they will not be judged by the color of their skin but by their character. . . .

This is our hope. This is the faith that I will go back to the South with. With this faith we will be able to hew out of the mountain of despair a stone of hope.

With this faith we will be able to transform the jangling discords of our nation into a beautiful symphony of brotherhood.

With this faith we will be able to work together, to pray together, to struggle together, to go to jail together, to climb up for freedom together, knowing that we will be free one day.

Cuba: Bay of Pigs Invasion

In 1959 the U.S. policy of containment suffered a setback in Cuba. A young Cuban revolutionary named Fidel Castro overthrew the government of a military dictator, Fulgencio Batista. At first, the United States thought the change in government might be beneficial, because Batista had ruthlessly suppressed Cuban liberties. But Castro promptly seized American-owned properties in Cuba and established a Communist regime similar to the one in the Soviet Union. Suddenly, U.S. policymakers realized that Cuba—a nation only 90 miles from U.S. shores—had fallen under Soviet influence.

What could the United States do to remove Castro from power and thus remove a threat to U.S. security? Military advisers to President Eisenhower thought the best method would be to provide training and support to a band of Cuban exiles in Guatemala. These Cubans were enemies of Castro and wished to lead a revolt against him. When Kennedy became president in 1961, he supported the plan for assisting in an invasion of Cuba. But he rejected the idea of supporting the invasion with U.S. air power. Kennedy hoped that the Cuban exiles could succeed without such air support. The invasion was launched in April 1961, off Cuba's southern coast, an area known as the *Bay of Pigs*. It was a complete failure. Castro's forces easily overcame the invading force of 1,500 men, most of whom were killed or captured. For the young president, John Kennedy, the poorly planned and executed invasion was a great embarrassment.

Vienna Summit and Berlin Wall

Almost as soon as Kennedy moved into the White House in 1961, he was tested by Nikita Khrushchev, the leader of the Soviet Union. The test concerned the future status of the German city of Berlin. Recall that Berlin had been divided in 1945 into an eastern section under Soviet control and a western section supported by the British, French, and Americans. By 1961 West Germany had become far more prosperous than Soviet-controlled East Germany. It now appeared as if Germany might be permanently divided into two different nations. In 1955 West Germany had joined the NATO alliance, and East Germany had joined the Warsaw Pact.

The German situation embarrassed the Soviet Union because East Germans were constantly leaving East Germany and East Berlin to enjoy the greater freedom and prosperity of West Germany. As a result, Khrushchev again threatened to sign a peace treaty with East Germany, which would allow the East German Communists to cut off all the food that came to West Berlin by land.

In June 1961, President Kennedy met Khrushchev at a summit conference in Vienna, Austria. Little was accomplished, as Kennedy stood firm on Berlin.

In August 1961, the Soviets and their East German allies startled the world by erecting a wall of concrete blocks and barbed wire all along the border between East Berlin and West Berlin. The purpose of the *Berlin Wall* was to prevent East Berliners from moving into the western section of the city. But many East Berliners defied the barrier by trying to climb over the wall, tunnel under it, or even swim around it. Some succeeded, while others were shot by East German guards. The Berlin Wall served as a grim reminder of the iron curtain and of Soviet inability to meet people's economic and political needs.

Kennedy's response to the Berlin Wall was to travel to West Berlin to assure the people there that the United States would never give in to Soviet pressures. West Germans roared their approval when he told them: *"Ich bin ein Berliner"* (I am a Berliner). By this he meant that any threat against West Berlin would be viewed as a threat against the United States.

Cuban Missile Crisis

In October 1962, another crisis involving Cuba nearly led to war between the Soviet Union and the United States. Photographs of Cuba taken from U.S. spy planes showed the presence of Soviet missiles (nuclear weapons). The missiles, so close to the shores of the United States, posed a direct threat to U.S. security. Kennedy considered many options including an air strike against Cuba. He finally decided to send U.S. Navy ships into Cuban waters to intercept Soviet ships that might be carrying missiles. In a message to Soviet leader Nikita Khrushchev, Kennedy demanded that Soviet ships carrying missiles to Cuba turn around and that the missiles already in Cuba be removed. Kennedy announced his actions in a televised speech to the American people that caused great concern. People wondered what would happen if Soviet ships tried to break through the U.S. naval blockade. Would shots be fired, and if so, would this trigger an exchange of nuclear weapons between the superpowers?

Fortunately, Khrushchev backed down. He agreed to order the Soviet ships to turn around and later to remove the missiles from Cuba. In return Kennedy agreed that the United States would not again support an invasion of Cuba. Kennedy's handling of the *Cuban missile crisis* was considered to

The Caribbean and Central America

Cartoon of American
and Soviet warships
in showdown over
the Soviet missiles
in Cuba

be the greatest success of his presidency (just as the Bay of Pigs invasion was its greatest failure). After the crisis passed safely, there seemed less danger of a nuclear confrontation. Both the Soviet Union and the United States became more cautious in their dealings with each other. Neither wanted to provoke another crisis like the one that almost led to world disaster.

Indochina: Vietnam and Laos

The origins of the war in Vietnam go back to World War II and the revolution that broke out in Vietnam as soon as that war ended.

Civil War   Vietnam is part of a region once known as Indochina, which is located in Southeast Asia just south of China. The region fell under French control during the imperialist era of the late 1800s. It remained a French colony until World War II, when invading Japanese armies occupied it. After the Japanese left Indochina in 1945, Ho Chi Minh, a national Vietnamese leader, proclaimed the independence of his people from colonial rule. But the French regained military control of the region. Ho, who was also a Communist, led his followers to the northern part of Vietnam, where they began a guerrilla war against the French. In *guerrilla warfare*, small bands of soldiers conduct quick hit-and-run attacks against larger but less mobile forces. In such a war, advanced technology has only limited effectiveness.

Beginning of U.S. Involvement   The French encountered great resistance from the Vietnamese guerrillas. After losing a major battle at Dien Bien Phu in 1954, the French decided to withdraw from Indochina. The region now consisted of three separate nations: Cambodia, Laos, and Vietnam. Each nation had problems adjusting to independence, as Communists competed with other factions to win political control.

One of the nations created from French Indochina was Laos. With the secret help of the U.S. Central Intelligence Agency (CIA)—a government agency that gathered information on foreign matters affecting national security—a pro-Western ruling group was put into power in Laos. The Communists, as well as those wishing to remain neutral between the Soviet Union and the United States, tried to overthrow this regime. To avoid war, President Kennedy agreed to a compromise, and a truce was arranged. In 1962 a "coalition" government was formed in which all three warring factions in Laos had a part in the government. A treaty was signed promising to keep the country neutral. However, two years later, the Communist faction (Pathet Lao) withdrew from the coalition, and the country once again became a battleground.

In 1954 a conference took place in Geneva, Switzerland, to resolve the conflicts in Indochina. The United States took part in the conference as an "observer," not as a full participant. French, Vietnamese, and other diplomats agreed to divide Vietnam at the 17th parallel of latitude into a Communist north and a non-Communist south. They further agreed that, within two years, elections would be held to unite the two halves of Vietnam under a single government.

The nationwide elections never took place. Instead, a civil war broke out in the south between forces supporting Ho Chi Minh and forces backing South Vietnam's government led by Ngo Dinh Diem.

To prevent a Communist victory in the civil war, President Eisenhower decided to increase U.S. support of South Vietnam's government. During his second term, Eisenhower sent U.S. military advisers to Vietnam to help train South Vietnamese soldiers loyal to Diem.

Deeper Involvement Under President Kennedy When John Kennedy became president in 1961, he adopted Eisenhower's policy of supporting South Vietnam's government with military aid. He increased the number of U.S. military advisers from 2,000 in 1961 to 16,000 in 1963. He hoped that U.S. support would enable Diem's government to prevent a Communist takeover. He also hoped Diem would take steps to reduce poverty and make democratic reforms.

Instead, Diem, a Roman Catholic, acted ruthlessly to crush Buddhist opposition to his regime. He ordered his soldiers to arrest Buddhist priests and raid Buddhist temples. As oppression increased, so did opposition to Diem's rule. In 1963 Diem was assassinated by South Vietnamese military leaders.

Latin America and the Alliance for Progress

Kennedy wanted a plan of economic aid that would do for Latin America what the Marshall Plan had done for Europe. He hoped an ambitious program of aid would (1) promote economic growth in a region whose people suffered from poverty and (2) contain the threat of communism spreading from Cuba to other Latin American countries. Kennedy called his aid program for Latin America the *Alliance for Progress*. Under this program, the United States offered to provide all Latin American nations, except Cuba, $20 billion in aid over a ten-year period.

The program did not work out as planned. Latin America lacked the democratic tradition of Western Europe. Instead of helping the poor, aid dollars tended to be used for political purposes to support a country's ruling class. Eventually, Congress allowed the program to die out.

Peace Corps

In his 1961 inaugural address, John F. Kennedy inspired the nation with a call to patriotic service. "Ask not what your country can do for you," said Kennedy. "Ask what you can do for your country." Later, Kennedy suggested a way for idealistic young Americans to serve their country. In a foreign aid program called the *Peace Corps*, volunteers would go abroad to assist the people of an African, Asian, or a Latin American country. They would help others to help themselves by teaching the skills of reading and writing and modern methods of agriculture and health care. In addition to teaching needed skills, the Peace Corps also aimed to build goodwill for the United States through person-to-person contact with citizens of developing countries.

Launching the Race to the Moon

President Kennedy announced in 1961 that he intended the United States to be the first nation to land a human being on the moon. The goal was in fact achieved before the 1960s ended.

Shocked that the Soviets had scored a space triumph with Sputnik in 1957, President Eisenhower signed the Space Act of 1958. It created a new agency, the National Aeronautics and Space Administration (NASA). This agency aimed to compete with the Soviets in space. In 1961, however, the Soviet Union scored again in the space race by sending Yuri Gagarin into orbit as the first human to circle the Earth in outer space.

Less than a month after Gagarin's journey through space, a NASA rocket at Cape Canaveral, Florida, lifted an American astronaut, Alan Shepard, into space. Although he did not orbit the Earth, Shepard returned safely in his space capsule. The U.S. manned space program had its first triumph.

After Shepard's flight, other breakthroughs soon followed. In February 1962, an astronaut named John Glenn spent five hours in space orbiting the Earth. His dramatic achievement matched that of the Soviets and thrilled millions of Americans who followed reports of Glenn's voyage on television. Glenn later became a U.S. senator from Ohio.

Not every rocket launching was a success. Practicing for a space launching in 1967, three astronauts (Virgil Grissom, Edward White, and

Astronaut Edwin E. Aldrin, Jr., walking on the moon, in 1969

Roger Chaffee) lost their lives when a fire broke out in their space capsule. Subsequently, three other astronauts circled the moon and photographed it.

In July 1969, a spacecraft known as *Apollo 11* carried three astronauts from Earth to the moon. While Michael Collins remained behind in the spacecraft, Neil Armstrong and Edward Aldrin set off for the surface of the moon in a small capsule called a lunar module. Through television, millions of people around the world watched in amazement as Armstrong set foot on the gray lunar surface. President Kennedy's promise had been kept. The United States had landed a man on the moon before the end of the decade.

Few people who viewed the event will forget Neil Armstrong's words as he stepped out of the spacecraft onto the moon. Said Armstrong, "That's one small step for a man, one giant leap for mankind." Nor should the world forget the plaque left on the moon at the end of the historic voyage. It read simply, "We came in peace."

Nuclear Test-Ban Treaties in 1963, 1967; Hot Line

One sign of improved U.S.-Soviet relations was the signing of a nuclear test-ban treaty in 1963. The two superpowers agreed to end the testing of nuclear weapons in the atmosphere, in outer space, and underwater. Underground tests were still permitted. In 1967, another treaty banned putting nuclear weapons in orbit around the Earth or on the moon or other planets.

A direct telephone line—or "hot line"—was established between the office of the U.S. president and that of the Soviet premier to enable the two leaders to communicate quickly in a time of crisis.

From HERBLOCK: A CARTOONIST'S LIFE (Macmillan, 1993)

Cartoon of President Kennedy and Premier Khrushchev attempting to contain the spread of nuclear weapons

Movement for Rights of Disabled Citizens

The law defines a disabled person as an individual who has a physical or mental impairment which substantially limits a major life activity. People who have disabilities are sometimes referred to as handicapped. As recently as the 1950s, popular attitudes toward disability were characterized by ignorance, fear, and superstition. In ancient times, people believed that the birth of a disabled child represented a curse on the family, a punishment for evil deeds in the past. Others believed that evil spirits caused a disability and that children with a disability were possessed by the devil. During the Middle Ages, people regarded disabled people with suspicion, and many were burned as witches.

Emergence of 19th-Century Humanitarian View

The movement for handicapped, or disabled, persons had its origins in reforms of the 19th century. Attitudes toward people with disabilities began to change. Many began to pity the disabled and wanted to treat them with special care. Education and training were also stressed. Prominent social reformers included Thomas Hopkins Gallaudet, who established a school for the hearing-impaired in Hartford, Connecticut, in 1817; John Dix Fischer, who began the New England Asylum for the Blind in Boston in 1829; and Dorothea Dix (active 1840–1860), who believed that the best way to treat handicapped persons was to place them in large and humane institutions such as public mental hospitals. In 1865 President Lincoln signed a law establishing Gallaudet College, which continues to this day as a major institution of higher learning for hearing-impaired students.

Development of the Concept of Normalization

In the early 20th century, emphasis began to shift to a policy of "normalization." The new goal was to help disabled persons to enter into the mainstream of society and lead normal lives as much as possible. After World War I, as thousands of disabled veterans returned to the United States, demands rose for federal aid to the handicapped. As a result, the Vocational Rehabilitation Act of 1920 was passed, which established the first major federal program to assist disabled persons. Services included counseling and guidance as well as job training and placement. This law was made permanent by the Social Security Act of 1935, which also provided federal funds to help persons cope with various disabilities (loss of sight and hearing, for example).

Kennedy Administration, 1961–1963

President's Council on Mental Retardation President Kennedy increased public awareness of the problems and abilities of handicapped persons. He created a President's Council on Mental Retardation. As the brother of a mentally retarded woman, President Kennedy had personal knowledge of the need for greater national action. In 1962 he created the President's Committee on Employment of the Handicapped to call attention to the job needs and capabilities of disabled persons, and to encourage businesses to hire the disabled.

Special Olympics During the Kennedy administration, a sports program called the Special Olympics was started for mentally retarded children and adults. It provides sports training and competitive events for participants. Each of the 50 states has a Special Olympics program, as do some 150 countries around the world. Winter and summer Special Olympics games are held periodically at sites around the world.

Litigation and Legislation: 1960–Present

People with physical disabilities protested in the 1960s that federal and state laws treated them unfairly. These people also suffered from discrimination in the job market.

Two court cases of the early 1970s were especially important in protecting the rights of children with mental handicaps.

P.A.R.C. v. Commonwealth of Pennsylvania (1971) The question in this case was whether the state of Pennsylvania could prevent mentally retarded children in the state from participating in a free public education program.

The U.S. district court ruled against the state's action. It argued that equal protection of the laws required a state to provide appropriate programs for the educational needs of mentally retarded children.

Mills v. *Board of Education of District of Columbia* (1972)   This U.S. Supreme Court case established the right of all children, including those with emotional and mental disabilities, to receive public schooling. It declared that no child between the ages of 7 and 16 could be excluded from regular classes unless the school district provided a program suited to the child's special needs.

Beginning in the 1960s, several acts of Congress went a long way toward protecting the rights of disabled persons.

Education of the Handicapped Act, 1966   In 1965 the Elementary and Secondary Education Act (ESEA) was passed to improve the educational opportunities for economically disadvantaged students.   Through special funding known as Title I, the law provided large amounts of federal aid to meet the special needs of educationally deprived children.   The law recognized that children from low-income homes required more educational services than children from more affluent homes.   In 1966 an amendment to the Elementary and Secondary Act provided federal grants for "handicapped" children.

Rehabilitation Act of 1973   Section 504 of the Rehabilitation Act of 1973 prohibited discrimination against the physically disabled in any federal program and in any state program supported by federal funds.   Under this law, the federal government issued a number of regulations to ensure that handicapped persons had full access to all buildings.   It required, for example, (1) ramp accesses in public buildings, (2) specially equipped buses for passengers in wheelchairs, (3) suitable bathroom facilities in public places, and (4) sign-language communication for the hearing-impaired on public television stations.

Education for All Handicapped Children Act, 1975   This act provided strong support for children with learning disabilities.   This law provided for testing to identify handicaps, a list of rights for handicapped children and their parents, and funds to assist states and local school districts in providing programs in special education.   Specifically, it guaranteed children with disabilities between the ages of 3 and 21 a free and appropriate public education in the least restrictive environment and required that all special education services be documented in an individualized education plan (IEP). Parent involvement was included to the extent that they would be notified of findings and involved in decision making.   Many educators view this act as a "bill of rights" for handicapped children and their parents.

Americans With Disabilities Act, 1990   This act was passed to make American society more accessible to people with disabilities.   The law was considered landmark federal legislation that gave protection against discrimination to 43 million mentally and physically impaired Americans. Under the new law, businesses were required to make employment available to disabled persons by providing "reasonable accommodations," such as restructuring jobs, changing the layout of workstations, or altering equipment. All new construction of public accommodations, such as hotels, restaurants, retail stores, and transit systems (public and private), were required to be accessible to individuals with disabilities. For existing facilities, barriers to services were to be removed if "readily achievable."

From Dependence to Independence

During the 1970s, there were several efforts to provide more equality and independence for the physically and mentally disabled.

Activism by Disabled Veterans   As wounded veterans of the Vietnam War returned home, there was increased public awareness of the needs of people with amputated or paralyzed limbs. The doors and stairs of courthouses, schools, and other public buildings made no allowance for the needs of people in wheelchairs. To protest these conditions, disabled persons organized demonstrations in front of buildings that had no access ramps and therefore, in effect, shut them out. In response, the federal government issued regulations that every public building have at least one entrance for wheelchairs, that some telephone booths and toilets be accessible for use by the handicapped, and that new buses be designed to enable passengers in wheelchairs to board.

Deinstitutionalization   The mentally ill were often locked away for years in state mental hospitals and received little treatment. In 1975 the Supreme Court ruled that mentally ill people who were not dangerous to themselves or others could not be confined against their will. As a result, there was an effort to release mentally ill persons from state hospitals and return them to their communities. Support for the mentally ill was to be provided through new medicines and federal aid to local communities.

Many of those released, however, became homeless. They lacked skills and could not find jobs. By the late 1980s and 1990s, the homeless were attracting wide attention on the streets of the nation's cities.

Mainstreaming   As the idea of integrating disabled persons into the general society gained support, so did attempts to educate disabled children in the public schools. In the past, disabled children were often placed in segregated, special schools. However, many people believed that such an approach had negative effects on a child's self-image and ability to learn. As a result, through a series of laws and court decisions during the 1970s, the federal government provided greater educational opportunities to all qualified mentally and physically handicapped students. The states were required to provide special education services in regular classrooms, so that disabled children and non-disabled children could be educated together.

This strategy of integrating children with disabilities into regular school programs was known as *mainstreaming*. Such an approach took the handicapped out of segregated settings and brought them into the mainstream of American life. Special classrooms or separate schools were to be provided only if a child's disability was so severe that mainstreaming was impossible.

Kennedy Assassination in Dallas

In late November 1963, President Kennedy and his wife, Jacqueline Kennedy, traveled to Dallas, Texas, for a political event. While riding in an open car through Dallas, the president was killed instantly by bullets fired from a high-rise building. The police arrested Lee Harvey Oswald for the crime. But another assassin killed Oswald before his case could come to trial. Thus, there is still a mystery surrounding the death of President Kennedy. Why did it happen? Did Oswald act alone, or were others involved in the crime?

The American nation went into a state of deep shock and mourning over the sudden death of its youthful leader. The assassination proved to be the first of a series of violent episodes (involvement in war, protests against war, racial unrest, more assassinations) that marked the decade of the 1960s.

★ In Review

1. Summarize the domestic policies of President Kennedy.
2. Explain how each of the following created a cold-war crisis under President Kennedy: (a) Bay of Pigs invasion; (b) Berlin Wall; (c) Cuban missile crisis; and (d) Indochina—Vietnam and Laos.
3. Define and evaluate the philosophy of Martin Luther King, Jr., as it has been used to protest unjust laws.

Lyndon Johnson and the Great Society

After Kennedy was assassinated, he was succeeded by Vice President Lyndon Johnson, an experienced politician. Before his election as vice president in 1960, Lyndon Johnson had served several terms in the U.S. Senate and had become a master of the lawmaking process. Johnson's personality and political style contrasted sharply with Kennedy's. Johnson was a southerner from Texas (not a New Englander from Massachusetts). He had grown up on a farm and lived close to poverty (unlike Kennedy's wealthy urban background). As a Democrat, however, Johnson shared Kennedy's belief in liberal reforms. Using his boundless energy and shrewd political tactics, President Johnson managed to push through Congress more important legislation than any other president since Franklin D. Roosevelt. He called this domestic program the *Great Society*.

Johnson was elected president in his own right in 1964. His Republican opponent, Senator Barry Goldwater from Arizona, wanted voters to understand that he was deeply committed to conservative ideas. Goldwater, however, was out of touch with the liberalism of the times. President Johnson won by a landslide, 486 electoral votes to only 52 for Goldwater.

Expansion of the Kennedy Social Programs

Johnson's far-reaching Great Society program affected all areas of American life, including health, education, housing, employment, immigration, and civil rights. Johnson's ideas for social legislation were not new. They had been proposed by other Democratic presidents, Truman and Kennedy. But Congress had rejected many of the earlier proposals of the Fair Deal and the New Frontier. Now in 1965 Johnson managed to persuade a Democratic Congress to enact many new laws.

War on Poverty; VISTA   Finishing the term begun by Kennedy, Johnson was quick to show his skills as a legislative leader. First, he persuaded Congress to enact the most important civil rights law in U.S. history (see page 496). Second, he announced an "unconditional" *War on Poverty*. Johnson said that a country as prosperous as the United States should be able to eliminate poverty. As the first step toward this goal, he persuaded Congress to pass the Economic Opportunity Act (1964), which authorized one billion dollars of federal money for antipoverty programs.

Another aspect of the war on poverty was the VISTA program (Volunteers in Service to America). Modeled on the concept of John F. Kennedy's Peace Corps, volunteers were sent to poor rural and urban areas as well as Native American reservations to provide teaching and technical support.

Medicare   To help senior citizens pay for the high costs of hospital care, doctor care, and other medical needs, Congress established a public health insurance program known as *Medicare*, which became part of the Social Security system in 1964. Under the program, persons over 65 were insured for a large part of the costs of health care. Also, states received federal grants to pay the medical bills of needy persons. Such grants of outright aid were known as *Medicaid*.

Aid to Education   To provide federal funds for schools with large numbers of children from low-income families, Congress passed the Elementary and Secondary Education Act in 1965. It authorized the spending of $1.3 billion on educational programs such as *Head Start* (giving instruction to preschool children from disadvantaged backgrounds). To enable qualified students from low-income families to attend college, Congress in 1965 passed the Higher Education Act, which authorized the granting of federal scholarships to capable students.

Environmental Issues

Americans began to understand the dangers to their environment after the publication in 1962 of *Silent Spring*, an alarming book by Rachel Carson. Carson wrote: "Along with the possibility of the extinction of mankind by nuclear war, the central problem of our age has . . . become the contamination of man's total environment." The author pointed out how the pesticide DDT, a chemical spray widely used by farmers to kill insects, caused the deaths of enormous numbers of birds and fish. She also explained the damaging effects to the entire environment if wildlife vanished as a result of chemical pollution.

In response to Carson's book, an environmental movement gained strength. Under presidents Kennedy and Johnson, Congress enacted several laws to control pollution and protect the nation's land, air, and water. For example, in 1965, Congress passed the Water Quality Act, which attempted to establish standards for clean water. The Clean Air Act of 1963 was a first step toward later tougher legislation. It provided funds for states to call conferences to help focus more attention on air quality and pollution. In 1965 the Motor Vehicle Air Pollution Control Act provided for the federal government to establish automobile emission standards.

Continuation
of the Civil Rights Movement

When the 1960s began and John Kennedy moved into the White House, the civil rights movement was already a major force for change. Dr. Martin Luther King, Jr., had emerged as a civil rights leader during the 1950s. Also, the Supreme Court had declared segregated schools to be unconstitutional. During the presidency of Johnson, the civil rights movement grew stronger and achieved some remarkable victories.

African Americans Appointed to High Positions More than any president since Lincoln, President Johnson attempted to assist African Americans and other minorities in their struggle to achieve both economic advancement and equal voting rights. The Civil Rights Act of 1964 and the Voting Rights Act of 1965 (discussed on pages 496–498) probably would not have passed without the strong backing of the Great Society president. In addition, Johnson made sure that African Americans were appointed to high-level positions in government. In 1966 he appointed Robert C. Weaver to be the secretary of a newly created cabinet department—the Department of Housing and Urban Development (HUD). Weaver was the first African American to serve in a president's cabinet. In 1967 a vacated seat on the Supreme Court gave Johnson the opportunity to appoint Thurgood Marshall as the first African American to serve on the nation's highest court.

Black Protest, Pride, and Power

A large number of organizations took part in the civil rights movement. Some were moderate in their goals and methods. They wanted equal rights under the U.S. Constitution and a fair chance to participate in the political and economic system. Other groups were more radical, stressing "black pride" and "black power."

★ NAACP, Urban League Organized in the early 1900s, the NAACP acted as the legal arm of the civil rights movement. It concentrated on winning victories for racial justice by arguing cases in court. The NAACP was chiefly responsible for winning the landmark case of *Brown* v. *Board of Education of Topeka* in 1954. Allied closely with the NAACP, the Urban League sought to end discrimination in employment and housing and to increase job opportunities for African Americans.

★ SNCC (Student Nonviolent Coordinating Committee) The students who joined this organization participated in sit-ins and other peaceful demonstrations against Jim Crow laws in the South.

★ SCLC (Southern Christian Leadership Conference) Dr. King founded this organization in 1957 to coordinate the segregation efforts of African American leaders to end segregation in the South. Its nonviolent methods of protesting racial injustice included boycotts, sit-ins, and marches.

★ CORE (Congress of Racial Equality) Organized during World War II, CORE activists carried out peaceful demonstrations against racial discrimination in both the North and the South. During the 1960s, under the leadership of James Farmer, CORE started a dramatic form of protest known as the *freedom ride*. Protesters against Jim Crow laws would ride in long-distance buses to make sure that bus terminals in the South were not segregated. Freedom riders included both white Americans and African Americans. Members of CORE were willing to suffer attacks and beatings by angry mobs of racists without fighting back. This willingness to endure punishment for a good cause without resorting to violence is called passive resistance.

Testing Segregation Laws

During the 1960s, segregation laws were challenged throughout the South. As you recall from Chapter 17, Rosa Parks had challenged segregation on the buses in Birmingham, Alabama. Segregation had also been successfully challenged in the historic 1954 decision, *Brown* v. *Board of Education of Topeka*. Throughout the 1950s and 1960s, African Americans fought for the right to vote, to end the poll tax, to serve on juries, to be served in restaurants and motels, and to enjoy nonsegregated seating in public theaters and parks. Often, they faced violent opposition to their efforts.

CORE freedom riders faced attacks on their buses as well as other grave personal dangers.

Black Muslims and Malcolm X; Black Panthers

In the mid-1960s, new organizations arose that called for "black power." Nonviolence as a method for change was attacked by those dissatisfied with the pace of progress. Leaders among the radicals—Eldridge Cleaver, Stokely Carmichael, and Angela Davis—spoke of the need for a racial revolution. Said Cleaver in his book, *Soul on Ice*: "We shall have our manhood. We shall have it, or the earth will be leveled by our attempts to gain it."

Two groups committed to the cause of black power were the *Black Muslims* and the *Black Panthers*.

Black Muslims are African American followers of Islam, one of the world's major religions. The founder of the Black Muslims was Elijah Muhammad. He advocated the separation of races, a separate African American state within the United States, and pride in being black. One of the best-known Black Muslims was *Malcolm X*, who broke from the main body of Muslims to form his own group in 1963. Malcolm X rejected passive resistance and urged his followers to fight back against those who violently abused them. "We don't teach you to turn the other cheek," he said. "We teach you to obey the law . . . But at the same time, we teach you that anyone who puts his hands on you, you do your best to see that he doesn't put it on anybody else." Malcolm X was assassinated by black opponents in 1965.

A famous convert to the Nation of Islam was the heavyweight champion of the world, Cassius Clay, who took the Islamic name of Muhammad Ali. In 1967, during the Vietnam War, Muhammad Ali refused induction into the armed forces, saying that he was a minister of Islam and a conscientious objector to war. He was convicted of draft evasion, and the boxing championship was taken from him. In 1970, however, his conviction was overturned. He then resumed his boxing career, once again winning the heavyweight championship.

Organized in 1966, the Black Panthers advocated the use of force to achieve "black power." Violence by whites, they said, should be answered with violence by blacks. For this purpose they formed a semi-military organization, wore a kind of uniform (leather jackets and black belts), and carried rifles. They also called for "better education, better medical care, and better housing" for African Americans. Their chief spokesman was their minister of information, Eldridge Cleaver.

Civil Unrest and Violence

The civil rights movement challenged long-established customs in the South. Activists in the movement could expect strong and even violent opposition from white defenders of segregation. In several tragic episodes, the violence ended in the deaths of innocent people.

Two weeks after the March on Washington in 1963, a bomb exploded in a Baptist church in Birmingham, Alabama. Four African American girls died in the explosion. Before the 1960s ended, more than 30 African American churches were bombed.

Among those who died in the fight for civil rights were three young activists who had traveled to Mississippi in 1964 to register African American voters. James Chaney was a southern black, while his two coworkers, An-

Cartoon of a white person protesting the speed of African Americans' progress in civil rights

From HERBLOCK: A CARTOONIST'S LIFE (Macmillan, 1993)

drew Goodman and Michael Schwerner, were white Jewish students from New York. The three were killed in a Mississippi town by unknown assailants. Although the Ku Klux Klan was thought to be responsible for the murders, the case was never solved.

In another violent episode in 1965, civil rights marchers in Selma, Alabama, were attacked and beaten by the police. To rally support for registering African American voters in Alabama, Dr. King organized a long-distance march from Selma to the state capital of Montgomery. The marchers were beaten by state troopers and harassed by hostile crowds. The marchers finally reached Montgomery only after President Johnson sent federal troops to protect them. One of the protesters, an Italian American woman from the North named Viola Liuzzo, was killed shortly after the march had reached its goal.

In cities of the North, most African Americans lived in crowded neighborhoods where poverty and unemployment were all too common. While aware that civil rights laws helped southern blacks, African Americans living in northern cities saw no immediate benefits from these laws in improving the quality of their lives. Also, as they followed the news of churches being bombed and civil rights marchers being attacked and killed, many young African Americans became increasingly angry and distrustful of whites. The result was a violent outburst of discontent. The first riots took place in the Watts neighborhood of Los Angeles in 1965. Rioting lasted six days and resulted in the deaths of 28 people and damage to property totaling about $200 million.

A Montgomery, Alabama, civil rights marcher
is attacked by a police dog, in 1965.

Riots erupted again in the summer of 1966 and the summer of 1967. More than 167 cities were affected by these outbreaks. Among the worst hit were Detroit, Michigan, and Newark, New Jersey.

Investigating the causes of the rioting, a national commission called the *Kerner Commission* issued a controversial report. It noted that the United States was rapidly becoming two "separate but unequal" societies, one black and one white. It recommended that the government adopt major programs to relieve urban poverty and increase the job opportunities of African American youths.

Assassinations of Civil Rights Leaders

Racial tensions in the 1960s also led to the violent deaths of three African American leaders. Medgar Evers, a leader of the NAACP in Mississippi, was killed in 1963, by white racists. Malcolm X was killed in 1965. Three Black Muslims were convicted for the slaying.

The most shocking assassination of all was the killing of Martin Luther King, Jr., in Memphis, Tennessee, in 1968. The civil rights leader had gone to Memphis to support the demands of sanitation workers for higher wages. While standing on the terrace of his motel room, he was shot by a southern white, James Earl Ray. (In the 1990s, some questioned whether Ray was the actual killer.) News of his death touched off riots in many cities. Throughout the nation Americans paid tribute to the man who had so courageously led the struggle for racial justice and democratic reform.

Legislative Impact of the Civil Rights Movement

President Kennedy strongly supported both the March on Washington and a civil rights bill that Congress was then considering. Kennedy expected to lead the fight for the bill's passage. But less than three months after the march, he was assassinated. Lyndon Johnson, as the new president, pledged to see that Kennedy's civil rights bill passed into law. In 1964 he kept his pledge by persuading Congress to adopt the most important civil rights law since Reconstruction. A constitutional amendment of 1964 and a voting rights law of 1965 were additional triumphs of the civil rights movement in the Johnson years.

Civil Rights Act of 1964   This act authorized the U.S. attorney general to bring suit if an individual's civil rights were violated. It also prohibited various forms of racial discrimination. Discrimination is the act of denying an individual equal opportunity because of some factor other than ability, such as race, ethnicity, gender, or religion. These were the discriminatory practices banned by the Civil Rights Act of 1964:

★ No discrimination in the services provided by such businesses as restaurants, hotels, motels, and gas stations

★ No discrimination in the use of government-operated facilities such as public parks and pools

★ No discrimination in federally supported programs (such as urban renewal and antipoverty programs)

★ No discrimination either by employers of 100 or more workers or by labor unions of 100 or more members (a number later reduced to 25).

In effect, this far-reaching law meant that all Jim Crow laws and practices of the past were now abolished. Race could no longer be a reason to deny anyone equal rights or opportunities.

The Civil Rights Act of 1964 was upheld by the Supreme Court in *Heart of Atlanta Motel, Inc.* v. *United States*, 1964. In this case, a motel owner had challenged the right of Congress to pass legislation outlawing discrimination in motels. The Court ruled that Congress had the right to enact this type of legislation under the powers of the interstate commerce clause of the Constitution.

Twenty-fourth Amendment In 1964 an amendment previously proposed by Congress was ratified by the necessary number of states. The Twenty-fourth Amendment banned the use of the poll tax in elections for president, vice president, and Congress. (A poll tax is a fee charged to voters). This amendment was especially important to African Americans in the South, many of whom were too poor to pay the poll tax required to vote. The amendment applied to federal elections only. Soon afterward, however, many states abolished the poll tax as a requirement for voting in state and local elections.

Voting Rights Act, 1965 Another major victory of the civil rights movement was the passage in 1965 of a law to give greater federal protection to African American voters in the South. The *Voting Rights Act* prohibited the practice of using literacy tests to keep African Americans from voting. Furthermore, the new law authorized the U.S. government to identify places in the South where only a small percentage of African Americans had registered to vote.

★ **Estimated Percentages of Voting-Age African Americans Registered in 1960 and 1968** ★

State	1960	1968
Alabama	13.7	56.7
Arkansas	37.3	67.5
Florida	38.9	62.1
Georgia	29.3	56.1
Louisiana	30.9	59.3
Mississippi	5.2	59.4
N. Carolina	38.1	55.3
S. Carolina	15.6	50.8
Tennessee	58.9	72.8
Texas	34.9	83.1
Virginia	22.8	58.4
Total	29.1	62.0

Federal registrars would then go to these places to assist African Americans in registering. Only one year after the law was passed, the number of southern blacks registered to vote increased from 870,000 to 1,289,000—an increase of about 50 percent.

Fair Housing Act of 1968   This important act declared that the practice of discriminating against minorities in the rental or sale of homes was illegal.

Court Decisions Upholding or Modifying Equal Rights

One of the most important allies of the civil rights movement was Judge Frank M. Johnson, who served as a federal judge in Alabama. Born and bred in Alabama, Judge Johnson ruled against segregation in a number of cases, earning the hostility of many whites in that state. In most of his decisions, he applied the reasoning of the Supreme Court in *Brown* v. *Board of Education of Topeka* to halt segregation in all aspects of public life in Alabama.

Educational Equity

The Supreme Court began to rule against segregation on a national level in the 1950s. In 1950, the Supreme Court declared in *Sweatt* v. *Painter* that a black student, Herman Sweatt, must be accepted by the law school at the University of Texas because the law school established for African Americans was considered unequal. This principle was applied again in that same year when a black student challenged the right of the University of Oklahoma to have him sit separately from white students in classes and in the cafeteria. The Supreme Court ruled in *McLaurin* v. *Oklahoma State Regents* that a state may not treat a student differently from others solely because of his race.

Following these cases, *de jure* segregation in education was ended throughout the South in *Brown* v. *Board of Education of Topeka* in 1954. In the following year, the Supreme Court ruled that segregated schools must be desegregated with "all due deliberate speed." Still dissatisfied with the slow pace of desegregation, the Supreme Court ruled in 1964 that schools in Prince Edward County in Virginia could not use public funds to support private schools established for white students.

In the 1970s, the Supreme Court challenged *de facto* segregation in the North, where education was segregated as a result of housing patterns. (*De facto* means actual, as the result of an existing situation.) In several cases, the Supreme Court ruled that busing should be used to desegregate neighborhood schools. At times, as in Boston, Massachusetts, the ruling led to violence by whites who objected to the arrival of black students in their formerly all-white schools.

Affirmative Action

Starting with the presidency of Lyndon Johnson, the U.S. government adopted a policy known as *affirmative action*. The purpose of the policy was to make sure that past discrimination against women and ethnic minorities did not continue into the future. To accomplish its purpose, the government encouraged businesses to increase job opportunities for women and minorities. Government also encouraged colleges and universities to admit more students who were female or nonwhite. A college failing to adopt an affirmative action plan for recruitment would lose financial aid. A business failing to adopt such plans would lose its government contracts.

One of the first decisions of the Supreme Court involving affirmative action in education was *Regents of the University of California* v. *Bakke* (1978). Allan Bakke, a white man, had twice applied to the medical school of the University of California. Both times the university rejected Bakke's application even though his overall scores on standard entrance requirements were higher than those of many students who had been admitted. The university argued that it had set aside 16 out of 100 openings for minority students in order to fulfill its affirmative action goals. Bakke sued the university, arguing that its quota system violated the equal-protection clause of the Fourteenth Amendment.

Ruling in favor of Bakke, the Supreme Court declared that the university's approach to affirmative action was unconstitutional because it involved racial quotas. However, it said in the Bakke case that race could be one factor, but not the only factor, in deciding whom to admit to a university program.

Preferential Treatment in Employment

In 1971 the Supreme Court ruled against discrimination in employment on the basis of race. A power company in North Carolina was no longer allowed to demand that applicants who did not have high school diplomas be required to take a intelligence test. The Court ruled that an intelligence test requirement violated the Civil Rights Act of 1964 as well as the Fourteenth Amendment, which called for equal treatment under the law.

The case of *Kaiser Aluminum and Chemical Corporation* v. *Weber* (1979) involved an affirmative action plan for correcting racial imbalance in the workforce at the Kaiser Aluminum and Chemical Corporation. The workers at Kaiser had been almost exclusively white. To change this situation, both the steelworkers union and the company agreed to develop a special training program in which half of the trainees would be African Americans. At a Kaiser plant in Louisiana, a white worker named Brian Weber was rejected for the training program even though he had greater *seniority* (years of service) than the African Americans who were selected. Weber brought suit, claiming that he had been discriminated against for reasons of race.

The Supreme Court ruled against Weber. It argued that the affirmative action plan at Kaiser was a reasonable means for correcting racial imbalance. The Court approved the plan because it was only temporary and did not result in white workers losing their jobs.

In the case of *Fullilove* v. *Klutznick* (1980), the Supreme Court voted in favor of federal legislation that established an affirmative action requirement that 10 percent of federal funds for local public works projects be used to acquire services or supplies from minority-owned businesses. The Court stated that Congress has the right to pass such legislation under the equal-protection clause of the Fourteenth Amendment.

Not all decisions of the Supreme Court favored affirmative action in employment. In a case involving the firefighters of Memphis, Tennessee, the Court ruled that African American workers hired to reduce racial imbalance could be first to be laid off if they had less seniority than white coworkers. And in 1995 the Court ruled against favoritism being shown to women and minority businesspeople who bid on government contracts.

Equal Access to Housing

In the case *Jones* v. *Alfred H. Mayer Co.* (1968), the Supreme Court voted in favor of equal access to housing by ruling that the Thirteenth Amendment, which ended slavery, implied that all citizens should be treated equally with regard to private property ownership. Thus, this decision supported the open housing provisions of the Civil Rights Act of 1968, which provided that there could be no discrimination in the sale or rental of housing.

Travel and Accommodations

The Supreme Court in *Heart of Atlanta Motel, Inc.* v. *United States* (1964) ruled that Congress had the right to pass legislation outlawing discrimination in public accommodations. (See page 497.)

Voting Rights

In the case *Baker* v. *Carr* (1962), the Supreme Court ruled that all legislative districts must have approximately the same number of persons. Thus, individual districts in African American areas could no longer be larger in population than voting districts in white areas. (See page 508.)

Women's Demands for Equality

African Americans were not the only group in the United States who suffered from discrimination. Women and other groups who felt that they were not always given fair treatment organized reform movements of their own.

The Modern Women's Movement

Recall that an earlier movement for women's rights had focused on winning the right to vote. When the women's suffrage amendment (the Nineteenth

Amendment) was adopted in 1920, it seemed to many men that equal rights for women had been fully achieved. In fact, women had a long way to go to attain equal rights in the workplace, not just equal rights in the voting booth.

In the 1920s, urbanization and the automobile were partly responsible for allowing women greater social freedom. During the Depression of the 1930s, women continued to enter the workforce in large numbers to earn income desperately needed by their families. After U.S. entry into World War II in the 1940s, millions of women took jobs in factories and ship-yards—jobs vacated by men called to service in the war. Women also volunteered for military service in the various branches established for women (WACS, Army; WAVES, Navy; WAFS, Air Force).

When the war ended, many women left their jobs, as ex-servicemen returned to the workforce in large numbers. During the 1950s, most women living in middle-income homes believed that their most important role was to stay at home for the benefit and care of their families. Their husbands would provide the family's income while they looked after the house and children. This traditional view of a woman's role as mother and home-maker was challenged in the 1960s by women known as *feminists*.

Kennedy Commission and the Civil Rights Act, 1963–1964 President Kennedy established a commission to investigate and review the role of women in the United States. Its first chairperson was former first lady Eleanor Roosevelt. The commission stated that women are entitled to participate equally with men in American society. Thus, one of the goals of the Civil Rights Act of 1964 was to make it illegal for employers to discriminate on the basis of a person's sex.

Education—Title IX (1972) Amendments to an education act included a provision known as Title IX. Its purpose was to promote equal treatment in schools for female staff and students. It stated that "no person in the United States shall, on the basis of sex, be excluded from participation in, be denied the benefits of, or be subjected to discrimination under any education program or activity receiving Federal financial assistance." An important consequence of this act was that schools and colleges greatly increased their sports programs for girls and young women. Previously, athletic programs in most schools had concentrated on supporting male teams in all sports, while restricting female athletes to only a few sports.

NOW (1966) to Present In 1966 feminist leaders formed the *National Organization for Women (NOW)*. Goals of the organization included equal pay for equal work, day-care centers for the children of working mothers, and the passage of antidiscrimination laws. Another goal was to increase the awareness of women and men about the various ways that men unfairly dominated their lives.

Many members of NOW had been active in the struggle to win civil rights for African Americans. Drawing on this experience, they organized

Drawing by Dana Fradon; © 1972 The New Yorker Magazine, Inc.

"How Come No Founding Mothers?" A cartoonist's view of women's complaints about their exclusion from history

marches and demonstrations and thereby attracted national attention. NOW also supported female candidates for office and lobbied for changes in the laws. Able spokespersons for women's rights such as Gloria Steinem and Bella Abzug became nationally known. In the 1970s, Azbug won election to Congress as a representative from a district in New York City. Gloria Steinem founded the magazine *Ms.* that focused on feminist issues.

NOW still functions as a pressure group to help expand the political and economic rights of women. Despite progress, it is still concerned with the goal of equal pay for equal work, and issues such as a woman's right to have an abortion. In order to achieve its goals, it maintains strong political involvement on both state and national levels.

Issues: Shifting Roles and Images

The question of the role and image of women was addressed in a 1963 book by Betty Friedan entitled *The Feminine Mystique.* Friedan was a college-educated woman who, as a suburban housewife in the 1950s, began to question the traditional assumptions concerning women's roles. Her book criticized the common assumption that women are happiest at home rather than in the workplace. She argued that women, far from being the "weaker sex," were as capable as men in all respects and should have equal opportunity to pursue high-level jobs in business and the professions. Widely read and discussed, Friedan's book challenged women to redefine their role in society and to break away from a limited view of themselves.

Equal Rights Amendment

In 1972 Congress proposed a controversial amendment to the Constitution. Called the *Equal Rights Amendment (ERA)*, it stated: "Equality of rights under the law shall not be denied or abridged by the United States or any state on account of sex." For ten years, NOW and other feminist organizations campaigned for ERA to be ratified by the necessary number of states. By 1977 they had won ratification by 35 states, just three states short of their goal. But opposition to the ERA was also strong. Some women feared that the ERA might spell the end of their exemption from military service and might permit divorced men to neglect financial responsibilities to their former wives. Opponents of the ERA eventually prevailed. In 1982, the last year that the ERA could have been ratified according to Congress's deadline, supporters failed to persuade the required number of state legislatures to ratify the proposed amendment.

Even without an equal rights amendment, lawyers for NOW could argue that discrimination against women violated the equal protection clause of the Fourteenth Amendment. According to this clause, no state may "deny to any person within its jurisdiction the equal protection of the laws." Feminist lawyers used this clause successfully to challenge government support of all-male public schools, such as Stuyvesant High School in New York City.

Right to Privacy: *Roe* v. *Wade*, 1973

In the case of *Roe* v. *Wade*, a pregnant young woman living in Texas wanted to have an abortion but could not do so because of Texas's law prohibiting abortions. The Supreme Court decided that the Texas law was unconstitutional because it violated a woman's constitutional right to privacy. The Court ruled that a woman could choose whether or not to have an abortion during the first six months of pregnancy. During the last three months of pregnancy, however, a state may ban an abortion to protect the unborn child, or fetus, since at this stage the fetus may be considered a person.

The decision in *Roe* v. *Wade* sparked controversy that still has not been resolved. Supporters argued that the right to privacy applies to a woman's body. Opponents argued that even during the first six months of pregnancy, the fetus is a person who has a right to life equal to that of any person after birth.

Equality in the Workplace

If women's preferred role was in the workplace, then career opportunities for women should be equal to opportunities for men. But as Friedan and other feminists pointed out, male employers tended to favor male workers and discriminate against female workers. Median (average) income for men in the mid-1960s was $7,500 a year, compared to only $5,600 a year for women. Most women found it difficult to obtain high-level positions in finance and management. When applying to law and medical schools, male applicants were generally given preference over female applicants.

The Equal Employment Opportunity Act (1972) required that employers give equal pay for equal work. It also banned discriminatory practices in hiring, firing, promotions, and working conditions. Thus, the act attempted to reduce the inequality in pay between men and women.

Today, many women confront a "glass ceiling" in private corporations—an invisible barrier of discrimination which limits their ability to achieve equal opportunity for the highest positions in a corporate structure. Some women prefer to spend part of their time raising families rather than spending all of their time in their chosen profession. This compromise often means that they will not reach the highest level in the corporate workplace. However, the fact remains that in the year 2000, women still earned only about 75 percent of the salary paid to men in the same jobs.

Increased Focus on Domestic Abuse

Women have long suffered domestic abuse. In the last decades of the 20th century, many women turned to the courts for protection orders. They also received aid from private foundations and women's shelters. This increased focus has reduced the likelihood of women accepting domestic abuse because they have nowhere to turn for help.

Rising Consciousness of Hispanic and Native Americans

The concern for the civil rights of African Americans and women has aided the rising consciousness of Hispanic and Native Americans.

"Brown Power" Movement

Just as African Americans began to speak of black power, Hispanic Americans organized a movement for "brown power." A gifted and determined leader of the movement was a labor organizer named Cesar Chavez.

Organizing Farm Labor Like thousands of other Mexican Americans in the Southwest, Chavez had worked long hours for low pay as a migrant farm laborer. He observed that employers often exploited migrant workers whose need for work at any wage was great. Migrant workers had no permanent residence and were therefore extremely difficult to organize into a labor union for group action. Despite the difficulties, Chavez succeeded in organizing a strong union of migrant workers called the United Farm Workers.

For five years, from 1965 to 1970, Chavez's union struggled for *La Causa*—the goal of winning both better pay and greater respect for migrant farm laborers from California's landowners who employed them in harvesting grapes. The union conducted a strike against the grape growers and also urged the American people not to buy California grapes. Like Martin Luther King, Jr., Chavez insisted that the movement be completely nonviolent. Eventually, the strike and the boycott put enough pressure on California's grape growers to win major concessions for the union and workers. In 1970 the largest grape growers in the state agreed to sign a contract with Chavez's union.

Cuban and Haitian Immigration

While middle-class Americans moved from the cities into the suburbs, new immigrants from Latin America moved into the cities. By the 1950s, the Hispanic (Spanish-speaking) part of the U.S. population had become a significant and growing minority.

Fidel Castro's revolution in Cuba in 1959 caused hundreds of thousands of Cubans to flee to the United States. Many settled in Miami and other Florida cities. Most of the Cuban immigrants were from middle-income and upper-income groups. This immigration continued into the 1980s, when large numbers of Cubans fled in boats, risking their lives to reach U.S. soil.

Throughout the 1960s, Haiti was ruled by "Papa Doc" Duvalier. Duvalier formed his own private military force and threatened or executed those who opposed his rule. As a result, the 1960s saw a surge in immigration from Haiti, primarily to Florida and New York. Continuing political and economic dislocation led to large increases in illegal immigration in the 1980s and 1990s, as many Haitians attempted to reach Florida by boat.

Increasing Hispanic American Presence in Politics

The increase in Spanish-speaking immigrants has led to increased Hispanic involvement in the political process in states with large Hispanic minorities, such as Florida, Texas, California, and New York. For example, in the 1980s, Miami elected its first Cuban-born mayor, Xavier Suarez, and Florida elected a Hispanic American governor, Bob Martinez. In 1988 President Reagan appointed Lauro Cavazos to lead the U.S. Department of Education. Cavazos thus became the first Hispanic American member of the Cabinet. In New York City, Hispanic Americans such as Nathan Quinones, Joseph Fernandez, and Ramon Cortines all served in the position of chancellor (chief executive officer) of the city's huge school system.

Native Americans' Demands for Equality

Native Americans had long-standing grievances against the U.S. government, which had taken away their lands in the 18th and 19th centuries. Inspired by the civil rights movement, Native Americans from different reservations joined forces in an attempt to assert "red power."

Grievances and Goals   An organization called the National Congress of American Indians complained bitterly about the government agency that supervised Native American life on the reservations. The U.S. Bureau of Indian Affairs (BIA) had failed for decades to raise living standards. A 1960 study found that Native Americans had a life expectancy of only 46 years, compared with 70 years for the U.S. population as a whole. Native Americans suffered from higher rates of malnutrition and unemployment than any other ethnic minority.

Activists in the movement for Native American rights wanted the following:

★ Less supervision by the BIA and greater freedom to manage reservation life as Native Americans saw fit. As one Native American put it, "We simply want to run our lives our own way."

★ The return of fishing and hunting rights that they had once enjoyed, even if this meant changing state game laws for their benefit

★ Greater economic assistance in combating problems of poverty

★ The return of lands that had once belonged to their ancestors and that U.S. treaties had guaranteed would not be taken from them.

Occupation of Alcatraz   In 1969, a small group of Native Americans took control of Alcatraz, an island in San Francisco Bay. On the island was a former federal prison from which escape was virtually impossible. When Native Americans took over the island, it was unlikely that they knew they would remain for almost two years. The Native Americans believed that a treaty dating back to the 1860s gave them the right to seize federal lands no longer in use. The main purpose, however, was to highlight injustices toward the Native Americans. In time, more than 600 persons occupied the island, calling themselves "Indians of All Nations." They insisted that the island was a perfect place for a reservation because, like other reservations on which Native Americans had been forced to move, it was barren. In time, most of the Native Americans left the island as communications and electricity were cut. Finally, those who remained were removed by the federal government. However, their protest had entered the consciousness of the nation.

Wounded Knee, 1973   Though united in their goals, Native Americans disagreed on how best to achieve them. Some favored peaceful protest, while others resorted to the use of armed force. In 1972 a radical group, the American Indian Movement (AIM), occupied the offices of the BIA in Washington, D.C., and demanded that the U.S. government honor treaties signed a century or more earlier. The next year, 1973, more than 200 members of AIM took up arms and gained control of the village of Wounded Knee on a Sioux reservation in South Dakota. Wounded Knee had been the site of the massacre of Indians by U.S. troops in 1890. For two months, the invaders of Wounded Knee held the village and demanded that old treaty rights be granted. Even though they won no concessions, they may have prepared the way for the court victories later won by several Native American tribes.

Court Victories Through the 1970s, Native Americans from Maine to California went to court to sue for lands promised to them by treaties in earlier centuries. One court granted the Narragansett Indians of Rhode island the return of 1,800 acres. The Penobscots of Maine won both thousands of acres and millions of dollars. The Sioux of South Dakota won another case, in which a court ruled that seven million acres of land had been taken from their people illegally.

Supreme Court Decisions on Rights

As you recall from Chapter 17, Earl Warren, the former governor of California, was appointed Chief Justice of the United States by President Eisenhower. Soon, conservatives and liberals disagreed about the many important decisions regarding rights of the accused made by the Warren Court. Americans with conservative views accused the Warren Court of interfering with law enforcement and the police powers of the states. Countering that view, people with liberal views generally applauded the Court's decisions. They argued that fair police procedures are required by the Fourth, Fifth, and Sixth amendments. Could evidence obtained by the police without a search warrant be used in court? Could a trial be fair if the defendant had no lawyer to represent him or her? The Warren Court gave its answers to these and other questions in the landmark cases summarized below.

Mapp v. *Ohio,* 1961 This case involved the Fourth Amendment's protection against "unreasonable searches and seizures" of a suspected person's property. A court in Cleveland, Ohio, had convicted a woman named Dollree Mapp of a crime on the basis of evidence that the police had obtained without a search warrant. The Supreme Court ruled that the accused person's rights had been violated. It said that evidence wrongly obtained by the police could not be admitted as evidence in the suspect's trial.

Gideon v. *Wainright,* 1963 This case involved the Sixth Amendment's guarantee that a citizen accused of a crime shall "have the assistance of counsel for his defense." Accused of breaking into a Florida poolroom, Gideon was too poor to pay for a lawyer at his trial. Florida provided lawyers for defendants in capital cases (those punishable by death) but not in minor criminal cases like Gideon's. The Supreme Court ruled that Gideon's rights to a fair trial had been violated. It said that a state must provide lawyers to indigent (poor) defendants in criminal cases whether or not the crime is a capital one.

Escobedo v. *Illinois,* 1964 This case also involved the Sixth Amendment's guarantee of an accused person's right to counsel (or his or her right to be defended by a lawyer). The police in Illinois arrested Danny Escobedo as a suspect in a murder. During questioning, the police refused to grant Escobedo's request to see a lawyer. Escobedo made statements to the police that were later used at his trial to convict him of murder. The Supreme Court ruled that Escobedo's right to counsel under the Sixth Amendment had been violated.

Miranda v. *Arizona,* 1966   One difference between the Miranda case and the Escobedo case was that the suspect Miranda did not ask to see a lawyer when questioned by the Arizona police. After two hours of questioning, Miranda signed a written confession of his crime (kidnapping and rape). Later, however, a lawyer representing Miranda appealed the case to the Supreme Court. The Court ruled that the police cannot question someone about a crime before informing that person of his or her constitutional rights. The Supreme Court's decision stated: "Prior to any questioning, the person must be warned that he has a right to remain silent, that any statement he does make may be used as evidence against him, and that he has a right to the presence of an attorney." These warnings are now known as "Miranda rights." The police now read the warnings to arrested suspects before questioning.

Legislative Reappointment: *Baker* v. *Carr,* 1962   One of the most important decisions to emerge in the 1960s was the Supreme Court decision in *Baker* v. *Carr* (1962). Commonly known as "one person, one vote," the decision gave the federal courts the power to review representation in state legislatures to ensure that each election district included approximately the same number of people. Thus, each individual's vote in electing representatives to the state legislature would have equal value. This decision on legislative reapportionment expanded the concept of democratic representation. Prior to *Baker* v. *Carr*, many state legislatures were dominated by representatives from rural areas. As a consequence of this decision, the number of representatives from urban areas increased. Also, minority group representation increased in state legislatures.

★ In Review

1. Why was Johnson more successful than Kennedy in translating social programs into legislation?
2. Identify the goals of reformers in each of the following movements: (a) women's rights, (b) rights of Hispanic Americans, and (c) rights of Native Americans.
3. How did the civil rights movement influence the demands for equality on the part of Hispanic Americans and Native Americans?
4. Select three landmark U.S. Supreme Court cases decided under the Warren Court. For each case, (a) identify the constitutional issue involved and (b) summarize the Supreme Court's decision.

Chapter Review

MULTIPLE-CHOICE QUESTIONS

Base your answer to question 1 on the following excerpt from the inaugural address of John F. Kennedy concerning the cold war with the Soviet Union:

> Let every nation know, whether it wishes us well or ill, that we shall pay any price, bear any burden, meet any hardship, support any friend, oppose any foe, to assure the survival and the success of liberty.

1. John F. Kennedy was declaring that the government of the United States would
   (1) actively support voting rights for African Americans
   (2) attack Cuba
   (3) work to prevent the spread of communism
   (4) support the state of Israel against neighboring countries that wished to destroy it.

Use the map on page 480 to answer questions 2 and 3.

2. The map illustrates that concern over communism in Cuba was especially great because of Cuba's
   (1) size
   (2) nearness to the United States
   (3) easy access to the Soviet Union
   (4) location near other Communist nations.

3. A key concern of the U.S. government regarding the revolution in Cuba led by Fidel Castro was that

(1) Cuba could become a base for spreading communism throughout Latin America
(2) recent immigrants from Cuba would leave the United States
(3) Cuba provided a port for Soviet ships competing for U.S. trade in Latin America
(4) the lucrative U.S.–Cuban tourist trade would come to an abrupt end.

4. Both the New Frontier and the Great Society shared the idea that
   (1) foreign trade should be cut to a minimum
   (2) the federal government should meet the economic and social needs of the less fortunate
   (3) taxes should be raised to stimulate consumer spending
   (4) key industries should be nationalized.

Refer to the cartoon on page 494 and answer question 5.

5. The cartoon shows that
   (1) the American public was not ready for true civil rights
   (2) some white Americans complained that civil rights activists wanted too much too soon
   (3) equality of opportunity was not as available in professional careers as in industry
   (4) no matter what the situation, there will always be prejudice against black Americans.

Refer to the table on page 497 and answer questions 6 and 7.

6. By 1968, the southern state with the poorest African American voter registration
   (1) was the same one as in 1960
   (2) increased its registration percentage of 1960 by only 5 percentage points
   (3) had registered less than half of its eligible black voters
   (4) had registered slightly more than half of its eligible black voters

7. To accurately evaluate the statistics in the table, a historian would need to compare them with voter registration statistics for
   (1) previous years
   (2) other minority groups in each state during 1960 and 1968
   (3) African Americans in northern states during 1960 and 1968
   (4) white voters during the corresponding years in each state.

Use the cartoon on page 502 to answer question 8.

8. Which is a valid generalization that can be drawn from the cartoon?

   (1) Women have not had an important role in U.S. history.
   (2) Women have become more appreciative of American art.
   (3) Women have become more conscious of their role in American society.
   (4) Women artists are demanding greater respect for their contributions to the field.

9. In what respect was the civil rights movement of Native Americans similar to the movement of African Americans?
   (1) Both concerned treaty rights.
   (2) Both concerned the unfair treatment of an ethnic minority.
   (3) Both were inspired by the women's movement of the 19th century.
   (4) Both movements were ignored by the white majority.

10. In the United States, informing suspects of their legal rights during an arrest procedure is required as a result of
    (1) customs adopted from English common law
    (2) state legislation
    (3) decisions of the U.S. Supreme Court
    (4) laws passed by Congress.

THEMATIC ESSAYS

1. **Theme:** Federal Activism

   From the 1950s through the 1970s, the U.S. government took an active role in creating change and reform, which benefited great numbers of people.

   Task

   ★ Choose one example of federal legislation and one Supreme Court decision from the 1950s through the 1970s. Explain how each created positive change for a specific group.

★ Evaluate the degree of success of each of the two examples that you selected.

Examples of federal legislation that you might use involve the handicapped, voting rights, health care, civil rights, and poverty.

Examples of Supreme Court decisions that you might use involve integration, rights of the accused, voting, and affirmative action.

Please note that you are not confined to the suggestions given. The specific names of the federal law and the Supreme Court case are not necessary so long as detailed descriptions are given.

2. **Theme:** Public Opinion and the Civil Rights Movement

The 1960s were a time when public opinion influenced the federal government to begin ensuring greater equality for African Americans.

Task

★ Describe two specific examples of how leaders of the civil rights movement were able to use public opinion in their fight to promote greater equality for black Americans.

★ Describe how the media (television, radio, newspapers, etc.) helped to promote or influence public opinion about either the civil rights or the antiwar movement.

★ Evaluate the degree of success of either of the two examples that you described.

You may use examples from areas such as integration of facilities, voter registration, equality of educational opportunity, and the March on Washington. You are not, however, confined to these particular areas.

DOCUMENT-BASED QUESTION

Read each document and answer the question that follows it. Then read the **Task** *and write your essay. Essays should include references to most of the documents along with additional information based on your knowledge of United States history and government.*

Historical Context: The civil rights movement of the 1960s utilized a variety of tactics to achieve its objective of creating a more equitable society.

Document 1 Martin Luther King, Jr., in a letter from a Birmingham jail, April, 1963:

Nonviolent direct action seeks to create such a crisis and establish such creative tension that a community that has consistently refused to negotiate is forced to confront the issue. It seeks so to dramatize the issue that it can no longer be ignored. I just referred to the creation of tension as a part of the work of the nonviolent register. This may sound rather shocking. But I must confess that I am not afraid of the word tension. I have earnestly worked and preached against violent tension, but there is a type of constructive nonviolent tension that is necessary for growth.

Question: Why did Martin Luther King, Jr., recommend nonviolent direct action?

Document 2 Refer to the cartoon on page 476.

Question: Why would the artist who created this 1963 cartoon have agreed with the speech by Martin Luther King, Jr., as excerpted on page 478?

Document 3 Refer to the photograph on page 495.

Question: What happened to many people in the South who demanded their civil rights?

Document 4 Stokely Carmichael in "What We Want," 1966:

But our vision is not merely of a society in which all black men have enough to buy the good things of life. When we urge that black money go into black pockets, we mean the communal pocket. We want to see money go back into the community and used to benefit it. We want to see the cooperative concept applied in business and banking. We want to see black ghetto residents demand that an exploiting store keeper sell them, at minimal cost, a building or a shop that they will own and improve cooperatively; they can back their demand with a rent strike, or a boycott, and a community so unified behind them that no one else will move into the building or buy at the store. The society we seek to build among black people, then, is not a capitalist one. It is a society in which the spirit of community and humanistic love prevail.

Question: What new tactics did Stokely Carmichael suggest that black Americans use to improve their lives?

Document 5 Statement by the minister of defense of the Black Panthers, May 2, 1967:

The Black Panther Party for Self-Defense calls upon the American people in general and the black people in particular to take careful note of the racist California Legislature which is now considering legislation aimed at keeping the black people disarmed and powerless at the very same time that racist police agencies throughout the country are intensifying the terror, brutality, murder, and repression of black people.

Black people have begged, prayed, petitioned, demonstrated, and everything else to get the *racist* power structure of America to right the wrongs which have historically been perpetrated against black people. All of these efforts have been answered by more repression, deceit, and hypocrisy. As the aggression of the racist American government escalates in Vietnam, the police agencies of America escalate the repression of black people throughout the ghettoes of America. Vicious police dogs, cattle prods, and increased patrols have become familiar sights in black communities. City Hall turns a deaf ear to the pleas of black people for relief from this increasing terror.

The Black Panther Party for Self-Defense believes that the time has come for black people to arm themselves against this terror before it is too late.

Question: How did the Black Panther party feel African Americans should respond to conditions in the United States?

Task

★ Describe the different tactics suggested by various civil rights activists as the decade of the 1960s progressed.

★ Explain why civil rights leaders changed their strategies at various intervals of the 1960s.

Chapter 19
The Limits of Power—Turmoil at Home and Abroad: 1965–1973

★ Objectives

★ To understand that the American political system is subject to a variety of public pressures.

★ To realize that modern war technology is not always effective in dealing with nationalistic uprisings.

★ To explore the consequences of U.S. involvement in Vietnam.

★ To analyze and compare the policies of two presidents, Lyndon Johnson and Richard Nixon.

No war in U.S. history was as controversial as the one fought in the Asian country of Vietnam between 1965 and 1973. It came as a shock to the American people that their country's armed forces—although better equipped than any military force in history—could not achieve victory in the jungles of a relatively small nation. Many people, particularly students in high school and college, questioned whether it was necessary to fight in Vietnam. Public protests against the war were one reason that Lyndon Johnson surprised the world in 1968 by announcing that he would not seek reelection.

The next president to deal with Vietnam, Richard Nixon, also faced student unrest and the growing discontent of the American people about the war's cost and destructiveness. Nixon adopted a policy of pulling U.S. troops out of Vietnam.

Vietnam: Sacrifice and Turmoil

The war in Vietnam began long before the presidency of Lyndon Johnson in the 1960s. Its origins go back to World War II and the revolution that broke out in Vietnam as soon as that war ended.

514

Early U.S. Involvement

The Southeast Asian region known as Indochina is made up of three countries: Cambodia, Laos, and Vietnam. They were French colonies until the mid-1950s. The Japanese occupation of this area during World War II inspired nationalist groups to challenge French rule. After the war, guerrillas in Vietnam, led by the Communist-nationalist Ho Chi Minh, pushed the French out. The United States had backed the French in this conflict, and the Soviet Union had aided Ho. (See Chapter 17 for more details.)

An agreement at the 1954 peace conference in Geneva, Switzerland, divided Vietnam at the 17th parallel of latitude. Ho Chi Minh headed the Communist government of North Vietnam. The government of South Vietnam under Ngo Dinh Diem had the support of the United States.

Anti-Diem factions in the South, many aided by the Communist North, tried to bring down Diem's government. Their aim was to reunite the two parts of Vietnam. South Vietnam asked for help from the United States. In response, the Eisenhower administration sent a few hundred military advisers. President Kennedy later increased the number of advisers to a few thousand.

The repressive actions of Diem's government led to Diem's assassination. Successive governments were no more popular. By the mid-1960s, the Communist opposition appeared to be gaining strength.

United States and the Spread of Communism

As you recall from Chapter 17, President Eisenhower and his secretary of state, John Foster Dulles, feared what they called a *"domino effect."* They compared the countries of Southeast Asia to a lineup of falling dominoes. If Vietnam fell to communism, for example, other "dominoes" in the region (Cambodia, Laos, and Thailand) might also fall. In addition, they believed that U.S. failure to respond to the Communist challenge in Indochina would lessen the credibility of U.S. commitments in other parts of the world during the cold war.

Johnson and Americanization of the War

Lyndon Johnson, who became president after Kennedy's assassination in 1963, promised "no wider war" in Vietnam. But he soon changed this policy when it became clear that the new leaders of South Vietnam were even less capable than Diem of winning the civil war against the Communists.

South Vietnam Under Threat In 1964 President Johnson concluded that South Vietnam's government was in danger of losing control of the country to the Viet Cong (the Communist guerrillas in South Vietnam). To counter the strong support given to the Viet Cong by the North Vietnamese government, Johnson decided that the use of U.S. troops was now necessary. He and many of his advisers wanted to prevent the Vietnam "domino" from

Asia in 1954

falling to communism so as to save the rest of Southeast Asia from the same fate.

An incident in August 1964 provided President Johnson with a specific reason for sending U.S. troops into combat. There were reports, which later proved inaccurate, that two U.S. ships had been attacked by North Vietnamese gunboats in the Gulf of Tonkin off the coast of North Vietnam. President Johnson used this event to ask Congress for a resolution supporting increased military aid to South Vietnam. The resolution authorized the president "to take all necessary measures to repel any armed attack against the forces of the United States and to prevent further aggression."

Congress approved the *Tonkin Gulf Resolution* overwhelmingly, with only two senators voting against it. In effect, the resolution turned over to the president the power to use the armed forces in Vietnam in any way he

"Snow White and the Seven Experiments," a 1970 cartoon targeting U.S. hypocrisy in supporting military regimes in Asia

saw fit. For several years afterward, Congress entrusted the president with the power to make war. Thus, like the earlier war in Korea, the Vietnam War was fought without a formal declaration of war by the U.S. Congress.

Escalation and the Tet Offensive President Johnson waited until after the election of 1964 to begin a major military assault against North Vietnam. Early in 1965, U.S. planes began bombing enemy targets in the North. At the same time, U.S. combat troops arrived in South Vietnam by the thousands. In little more than three years, the number of U.S. troops in Vietnam rose from 184,000 in 1965 to 536,100 in 1968. TV and newspaper reports referred to the steady buildup of American forces in Vietnam as a policy of *escalation*. The administration assumed that increased bombing, especially in North Vietnam, as well as the increased number of American troops, would lead to a quick victory for the United States and the government of South Vietnam. Underlying U.S. policy was another assumption: that the two Communist powers, China and the Soviet Union, had plans to take control of much of Asia.

In January 1968, Communist forces launched an all-out attack against targeted cities in South Vietnam. TV news reports showed major Communist gains and the capital of Saigon in peril of being taken. Eventually, the attackers were pushed back, but the Communists' so-called Tet Offensive had dramatically demonstrated their strength. It also forced Americans to recognize the possibility that the war could go on for much longer.

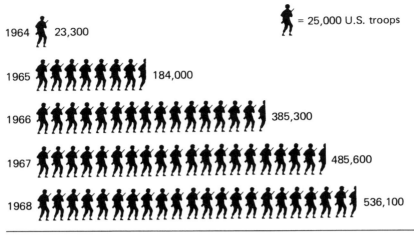

U.S. Troop Buildup in Vietnam, 1964–1968

Controversy Over the War

Arguments for the War As U.S. involvement in the war escalated, Americans wanted to know "why are we in Vietnam?" In a 1965 speech at Johns Hopkins University, President Johnson gave these reasons:

★ "We are there," said the president, "because we have a promise to keep." Ever since 1954 the United States had pledged to help South Vietnam.

★ To end U.S. commitments to South Vietnam would cause other nations to doubt whether they could trust U.S. commitments to them.

★ A Communist victory in South Vietnam would threaten neighboring countries in Southeast Asia and foster Communist aggression throughout the region.

★ The Communist government of the People's Republic of China supported North Vietnam's war effort as part of "a wider pattern of aggressive purposes."

Arguments Against the War Opponents of U.S. involvement in Vietnam argued as follows:

★ The Communist nation of North Vietnam did not take orders from China or the Soviet Union. In fact, China and Vietnam had a long history of hostility and distrust toward one another. North Vietnam was fighting for nationalistic reasons.

★ The war was being fought in a distant area that was not vital for U.S. security. Nor were Vietnam's economic resources vital to the U.S. economy.

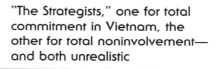

"The Strategists," one for total commitment in Vietnam, the other for total noninvolvement— and both unrealistic

★ It was terribly costly for U.S. troops to be bogged down in a land war on the Asian continent.

★ The South Vietnam government was corrupt and undemocratic.

★ South Vietnam's army was not capable of fighting successfully against the Viet Cong guerrillas and the highly disciplined troops of North Vietnam. (North Vietnamese soldiers had begun fighting in South Vietnam in 1963.)

★ Thousands of Americans were being killed and wounded.

Student Protests

Draft Protesters and Political Radicals As more and more young Americans were drafted into military service and sent to fight in Vietnam, many people raised questions about Johnson's war policy. They began to doubt whether the United States was fighting for a worthwhile cause. They objected to fighting a war against an enemy on the other side of the world— an enemy that posed little threat to the United States. Many college students adopted various strategies for protesting the war policy. They gathered in groups and publicly set fire to their draft cards. They occupied buildings on college campuses and chanted defiant slogans such as "Hey, hey, LBJ, how many kids did you kill today?" Among those who used radical methods of protest on college campuses were the Students for a Democratic Society (SDS). In addition, thousands escaped the draft law by moving to Canada.

The radical methods of the protesting students angered conservative groups who rallied to the flag and defended the U.S. war effort. By 1966, the nation was sharply divided between "doves" (those opposed to war) and "hawks" (those favoring even greater use of U.S. military power in Vietnam).

1968: Year of Turmoil

Cultural Radicals As 1968 began, a new movement among the nation's youth was in full swing. People in the movement were against the war and preached love and nonviolence. In addition, some students on college campuses adopted a style of life and dress that offended the older generation of their parents. Many people thought of radical students as those who wore their hair long and took drugs, although only a minority did either of these things. Rebellious youths valued personal honesty and creativity as ideals and generally opposed the norms of American culture—marriage, patriotism, and business. The radical lifestyle was known as the *counterculture*. Those adopting an extremely original lifestyle were known as "hippies" and "flower children." Some of them lived and worked together in what they called a communal family. These communes were generally located in rural areas.

Social Impact of the Vietnam War The Vietnam War created deep divisions within American society. Many members of the previous generation who had fought in World War II believed strongly that the right to disagree did not justify the antiwar protests or draft evasions. They believed that Americans should serve their country patriotically and objected to the actions of radical students and to the counterculture of the hippies. Returning Vietnam veterans. They did not understand why they were not given the same positive welcome that soldiers in prior wars had received.

Opponents of the war believed strongly that they had a responsibility to protest against a war that they believed to be immoral and that served no national interest. They challenged the trust that others placed in elected officials. They also challenged the view that the United States should act as the "policeman of the world."

The president and his military advisers stated many times that U.S. and South Vietnamese forces would eventually win the war. Many Americans, however, no longer accepted official reports about the war. They were more impressed by news reports on television, which showed that most villages in the South Vietnamese countryside were still under Viet Cong control. The commitment of more and more U.S. ground troops did not seem to make much difference. Members of the press spoke of a "credibility gap" between the government's view of the war and the public's view. Increasing numbers of people questioned the government's policy, and opposition to the war increased.

Long-term Causes of U.S. Involvement

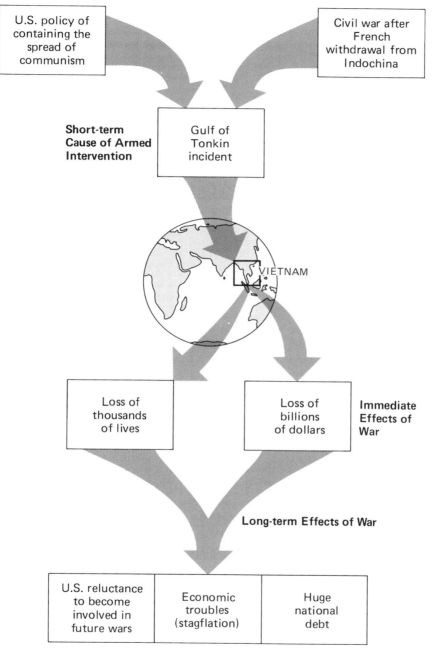

The Vietnam War: Causes and Effects

Johnson's Decision Not to Seek Reelection   The beginning of 1968 was also the beginning of campaigns for the presidency. Most Americans assumed that President Johnson would be nominated for reelection by the Democratic party. But young people rallied to the support of an antiwar candidate, U.S. Senator Eugene McCarthy of Minnesota. In an early primary in New Hampshire, McCarthy surprised the nation by winning more than 40 percent of the vote. Another challenger to Johnson's leadership, President John Kennedy's brother Robert, announced his candidacy for the Democratic nomination. Following these events, President Johnson made a television address to the American people. He said that, in the interests of peace, he was ending the bombing of North Vietnam and opening up peace negotiations with the enemy. At the same time, to prevent politics from interfering with the success of his peace plan, Johnson announced that he would neither seek nor accept the nomination of his party for reelection.

Assassinations: Martin Luther King, Jr./Robert Kennedy   In April 1968, an assassin shot and killed Martin Luther King, Jr. Many black communities across the nation showed their frustration and anger by erupting into riots.

Just two months later in June, while Robert Kennedy was campaigning in California, he was shot and killed by an Arab nationalist named Sirhan Sirhan. The nation now mourned the second Kennedy to be killed by an assassin. Many believed that Robert Kennedy, if he had lived and won the presidency, could have helped to unite the country and overcome the divisions between young and old, blacks and whites.

Democratic Convention   The Democratic National Convention in 1968 took place in Chicago. Although Eugene McCarthy was popular with antiwar Democrats, he did not have enough support to win the nomination for president. Johnson's vice president, Hubert Humphrey, won the nomination instead. Antiwar demonstrators led by well-known radicals Abbie Hoffman and Bobby Seale gathered in a Chicago park to protest the Democrats' choice of Humphrey. The Chicago police overreacted to verbal abuse and charged into the crowd of protesters. On television, people watched in dismay as the image on their screen flashed back and forth from the nomination of Humphrey inside the convention hall to the battle in the streets between the police and the protesters.

Election of Richard Nixon   The violence associated with the Democratic convention and Humphrey's support of the war effort helped the Republicans and their candidate, Richard Nixon. A third-party candidate from Alabama, George Wallace, promised to take away thousands of votes in the South from both major candidates. Although Nixon was well ahead early in the campaign, Humphrey gained steadily in the opinion polls. On Election Day, Nixon emerged as the winner in one of the closest elections in U.S. history.

Nixon and Vietnam

When sworn into office in January 1969, President Nixon was confronted with a double problem: how to deal with the war in Vietnam and how to deal with the antiwar movement at home.

President Johnson had carried out his 1968 promise to send U.S. diplomats to Paris to discuss peace terms with representatives from North Vietnam. The peace talks continued under President Nixon, but so did the war in Vietnam.

New Proposal for Peace   Nixon and his national security adviser, Henry Kissinger, proposed that both North Vietnam and the United States pull their troops out of South Vietnam at the same time. (Formerly, Johnson had proposed that the United States would withdraw troops only after the North Vietnamese did so.) The North Vietnamese in Paris rejected the U.S. proposal.

Vietnamization and Heavy Bombing   As his military strategy in Vietnam, Nixon announced that U.S. troops would gradually be withdrawn from

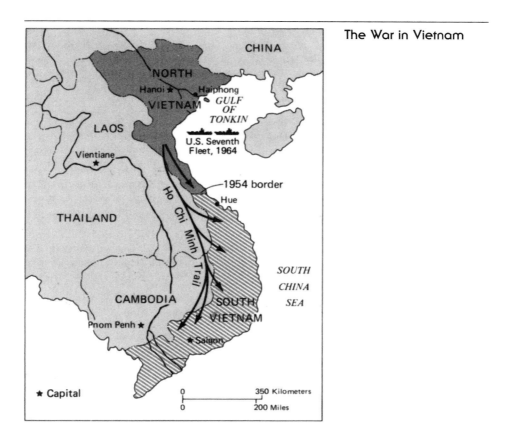

The War in Vietnam

Vietnam. At the same time, South Vietnamese troops would receive intensive training to carry on the war by themselves. This strategy was called *Vietnamization.*

To avoid public debate and criticism, Nixon carried out another part of his strategy in secret. He ordered a series of bombing raids over Cambodia. His purpose in doing so was to cut off Cambodian roads and supply routes that the North Vietnamese relied on for sending men and materials to the South. The U.S. military argued that the bombing of North Vietnam could not be effective unless U.S. planes also bombed the trails over which enemy troops and supplies traveled. So secret was the bombing of Cambodia that even Congress was unaware of it at first.

More Protests   Many Americans who had previously supported the U.S. war effort began to join the antiwar movement. On October 15, 1969, antiwar groups throughout the United States participated in a full day of peaceful protest. On November 15, 1969, more than 250,000 protesters gathered in Washington, D.C., and marched from the Washington Monument to the White House. Shortly afterward, President Nixon appeared on television and appealed to the "silent majority" to support his efforts to end the war. In response to this appeal, many thousands of Americans sent telegrams of support to the White House.

Opposition continued, however, especially after the nation learned of the bombing of Cambodia. News of the bombing touched off protests on college campuses across the country. In May 1970 at Kent State University in Ohio, the National Guard opened fire on a peaceful demonstration to break it up. Four students were killed and several wounded.

Pentagon Papers   In 1971, after the invasion of Cambodia, Daniel Ellsberg, an official in the Department of Defense, released a secret Pentagon study of U.S. involvement in Vietnam to several newspapers, including *The New York Times*. Believing that this study would damage U.S. support for the war, President Nixon demanded that the *Times* not publish these documents. In a major decision known as *New York Times* v. *United States* (1971), the Supreme Court upheld the right of newspapers to publish the documents, which became known as the Pentagon Papers. In this ruling, the Supreme Court rejected President Nixon's argument that the national security of the United States was at stake. The *Times* and other papers exercised their First Amendment right of freedom of the press and published the Pentagon Papers.

Withdrawal From Vietnam   In 1972, as more U.S. troops left Vietnam, Nixon ordered the continuous bombing of North Vietnam. Its capital, Hanoi, was bombed for the first time in the war. Moreover, its harbor of Haiphong was mined to cut off shipments of oil and other supplies. At the same time, South Vietnamese forces lost ground to the Communists.

"Middle Course"—the State Department's Vietnam policy of commitment, but not full commitment

In Paris, Henry Kissinger continued to negotiate with the North Vietnamese. Finally, in early 1973, he and President Nixon agreed to terms that had the approval of South Vietnam, North Vietnam, and the United States. According to this agreement:

★ The last U.S. troops (down to less than 50,000 in 1972) would leave Vietnam.

★ North Vietnamese forces in South Vietnam would be permitted to remain.

★ South Vietnam's government would remain in place until elections could determine the South's future.

★ the Vietcong would return all American prisoners of war and provide a full accounting for Americans missing in action (MIAs).

This agreement meant the end of U.S. involvement in Vietnam. However, the civil war in Vietnam continued for almost two more years.

North Vietnamese Victory Without U.S. troop support, South Vietnam's government could not long survive. In 1975, a combined force of Vietcong and North Vietnamese swept into the South's capital of Saigon and thus won control of all of Vietnam. Also in 1975, Cambodia and Laos fell to Communist forces. The loss of South Vietnam, despite U.S. military power and financial aid, demonstrated both the limits on the presidency and the limits on national power.

Consequences of the Vietnam War

The Vietnam War had a profound effect on U.S. public opinion, the U.S. economy, and U.S. foreign policy.

Casualties and Costs About 58,000 Americans died in the Vietnam War, and 365,000 were wounded. A memorial in Washington, D.C., honors those Americans who died fighting in the war by engraving their names on a huge black marble wall. Each year millions of people visit the Vietnam Memorial and are emotionally moved by the experience.

The Vietnam War also had long-term medical and psychological effects on returning veterans. Some soldiers who were imprisoned and tortured or involved in harsh combat suffered from post-traumatic stress disorder (PTSD) in which they had recurring flashbacks and nightmares. Other soldiers suffered medical problems believed to be associated with Agent Orange, a poisonous defoliant chemical (used to remove the protective covering of leaves from trees). There was also an increase in drug dependency among some veterans.

Economically, the cost of the war to the United States came to a staggering sum—about $150 billion. Government spending on the war was so great that it put a severe strain on the U.S. economy. Because the government was also spending vast sums for domestic programs (Johnson's Great Society), the government had to borrow billions of dollars. The national debt (the total sum owed by the government to purchasers of its bonds) jumped to a record figure. Inflation also became a serious problem both during and after the war.

Impact on U.S. Foreign Policy Only a minority of Americans actively protested the war. But millions of others doubted the wisdom of involving

"Passing the Buck": Sorting out responsibility among five presidents and one secretary of state

U.S. armed forces in a distant conflict. The 1950s policy of containing communism everywhere in the world came under criticism. Partly because of Vietnam, President Nixon tried to modify the U.S. approach to the cold war. To this day, both the American people and Congress have been reluctant to become involved in another foreign conflict.

Congress and the War Powers Act   Many members of Congress regretted the Tonkin Gulf Resolution, which had given total war-making power to President Johnson. To limit the president's power in the future, Congress passed the *War Powers Act* in 1973. These were the act's major provisions:

★ Within 48 hours of sending troops into combat, the president must inform Congress of the reasons for the action.

★ If U.S. troops are involved in fighting abroad for a period of more than 90 days, the president must obtain Congress's approval for continuing the use of troops. If Congress does not approve, the president must bring the troops home.

★ In Review

1. Identify the following and explain the significance of each: Ho Chi Minh, Tonkin Gulf Resolution, Tet Offensive, doves, hawks, hippies, credibility gap, Vietnamization, Pentagon Papers, War Powers Act.
2. Summarize the arguments for and against the Vietnam War.
3. Evaluate both the short-term and long-term effects of the Vietnam War on the United States.

Chapter Review

MULTIPLE-CHOICE QUESTIONS

Use the cartoon on page 517 to answer questions 1–3.

1. The cartoon criticizes U.S. foreign policy
   (1) all over the world
   (2) in Latin America
   (3) in Asia
   (4) in Europe.

2. The cartoon accuses the United States of
   (1) imperialism
   (2) contradicting its ideals
   (3) poor leadership
   (4) starting wars.

3. The cartoonist probably feels that the situation depicted in the cartoon was caused by
(1) expansionists in Congress
(2) paranoia about the spread of communism
(3) the resurgence of nazism and fascism
(4) a rise in terrorist actions in various parts of the world.

Refer to the chart on page 521 and answer questions 4 and 5.

4. The chart shows that the Gulf of Tonkin incident
(1) was the main cause of the Vietnam War
(2) resulted in the U.S. policy of containment
(3) led directly to increased U.S. participation in the Vietnam War
(4) led to the French withdrawal from Vietnam.

5. A conclusion that can be drawn from an examination of the chart is that the Vietnam War
(1) affected the United States only several years after its conclusion
(2) was caused by a single incident
(3) was the fault of the United States
(4) had long- and short-term causes as well as long- and short-term effects.

Use the cartoon on page 519 to answer questions 6 and 7.

6. The cartoonist feels that
(1) winning the war in Vietnam regardless of cost was the ladder to containing communism in Southeast Asia

(2) the United States stood a better change of containing communism in the deserts of the Middle East than in Asia
(3) the United States should have attacked communism at its real source—the Soviet Union
(4) neither those supporting escalation or withdrawal truly understood the situation in Vietnam.

7. The cartoonist was probably most in favor of the United States
(1) gradually eliminating its troops from the conflict
(2) slowly increasing U.S. involvement
(3) adding military advisers but eliminating fighting men
(4) continuing U.S. participation until it was clear that a strong, stable non-Communist government was able to prevent the spread of communism.

Refer to the cartoon on page 525 to answer questions 8 and 9.

8. The point of view of the cartoon is that the U.S. State Department
(1) was having a difficult time resolving a border dispute between North and South Vietnam
(2) was conducting a limited war in Vietnam
(3) was secretly supporting opponents of President Johnson
(4) was contemplating a military withdrawal from Vietnam in 1968.

9. During which other war would a similar cartoon have most likely been drawn?
(1) the Spanish-American War
(2) World War I
(3) World War II
(4) the Korean War.

10. The War Powers Act of 1973 was passed mainly in response to concern that presidents Johnson and Nixon
    (1) had made treaties without informing the Senate
    (2) could involve the nation's armed forces in combat without congressional approval
    (3) had failed to control harmful antiwar protests
    (4) had refused to present military budgets to Congress.

THEMATIC ESSAYS

1. **Theme:** The United States Versus Communism in Asia

   The United States, a nation that was originally founded upon the idea of ending its colonial status and achieving independence, ironically and unwittingly found itself in the role of a great power attempting to prevent the independence of a colonial people.

   Task

   ★ Describe how the United States became involved in the Vietnam conflict after 1954.

   ★ Show how the development of Communist movements in Asia led the United States to a great commitment in Vietnam.

   In answering the first part of the question, you may wish to refer to the rise of nationalism in Vietnam during World War II, the war between Vietnamese nationalists and French imperialists, and the peace treaty agreed upon at Geneva in 1954.

   In answering the second part of the question, you may wish to show how the United States government was influenced by the rise of Mao Zedong in China, the Korean War, the theory of the domino effect, and the lack of popularity of the South Vietnamese government.

2. **Theme:** The Vietnam War and U.S. Domestic Policies

   The Vietnam War had an impact on the United States in ways that were not foreseen when it entered the conflict. As a result of extended U.S. participation in Vietnam, there were significant changes at home.

   Task

   ★ Describe two ways in which the war in Vietnam changed the United States.

   ★ Show how one of the changes that you have discussed had an impact on the United States that lasts to this day.

You may discuss, but are not limited to, the effects of the Vietnam War on the presidential election of 1968, Lyndon Johnson's Great Society program, the attitude of the American public toward government, the soldiers who fought in the war, and students in high school and college.

DOCUMENT-BASED QUESTION

*Read each document and answer the question that follows it. Then read the **Task** and write your essay. Essays should include references to most of the documents along with additional information based on your knowledge of United States history and government.*

Historical Context: The commitment of troops to the fighting of the war in the Southeast Asian nation of Vietnam became one of the most hotly protested federal actions in the history of the United States. Many Americans, most particularly students in high school and college, questioned the wisdom of U.S. involvement.

Document 1 Refer to the illustration on page 516.

Question: Why were many Americans fearful of a Communist victory in Vietnam?

Document 2 Refer to the illustration on page 578.

Question: How did the United States become further involved in the Vietnam War between 1964 and 1968?

Document 3 Refer to the map on page 523.

Question: What were the Communist North Vietnamese able to do throughout South Vietnam?

Document 4 From an undated handbill entitled "An Appeal to the Conscience of the American People":

> Opponents of the administration's policies point out that the many Saigon governments have been military dictatorships.
> None of the many Saigon governments were elected by the Vietnamese people. The United States refused to permit the elections provided by the Geneva Agreement of 1954 and installed Ngo Diem. South Vietnam has been ruled by military dictatorship supported by United States' dollars ever since. Opposed by the majority of the people of South Vietnam, it has changed 14 times since January 1964.

Question: Why did the writer of the handbill oppose U.S. support of South Vietnam (Saigon)?

Document 5 President Lyndon B. Johnson in his state of the union message, January 12, 1966:

> We will stay because a just nation cannot leave to the cruelties of enemies a people who have staked their lives and independence on America's solemn pledge—a pledge which had grown through the commitment of three American Presidents.
>
> We will stay because in Asia—and around the world—are countries whose independence rests, in large measure, on confidence in America's word and in American protection. To yield to force in Viet-Nam would weaken that confidence, would undermine the independence of many lands, and would whet the appetite of aggression. We would have to fight in one land, and then we would have to fight in another—or abandon much of Asia to the domination of Communists.

Question: Why did President Lyndon Johnson feel that the United States should maintain its commitments in Vietnam?

Task

★ Explain the arguments supporting and opposing the involvement of the United States in the Vietnam War.

★ Give specific reasons why one of the two sides had the better argument.

Chapter 20
The Trend Toward Conservatism: 1969–1980

★ Objectives

★ To understand that periods of upheaval in history are often followed by conservative reactions.

★ To assess the impact of the Watergate Affair on the presidency.

★ To compare and contrast the domestic policies of presidents Nixon, Ford, and Carter.

★ To identify and evaluate presidential responses to foreign policy challenges.

★ To explain how domestic policies are influenced by global interdependence.

$\mathbf{T}$he 1960s was a decade of liberal reform (civil rights, Great Society programs) as well as radical protest (the antiwar movement). The decades that followed, the 1970s and 1980s, were strikingly different. The American people largely abandoned the liberal hopes that had stirred them in the 1960s. The majority now expressed conservative tastes in their private lives and conservative choices in their public lives as citizens. (In general, liberals believe that the federal government should guide the economy and help people in need. Conservatives, on the other hand, prefer to keep the government's role in the economy and society to a minimum.)

Nixon as President, 1969–1974

Richard Nixon, who had served as vice president under Eisenhower, was elected president for the first time in 1968. The election was held in the midst of anti-Vietnam War protests and a growing distrust of government officials and policies. Nixon's popularity increased while in office and he easily won reelection in 1972.

Domestic Policies and Events

President Nixon judged many of the programs of the Great Society to be wasteful and unworkable. However, in some ways, he expanded the role of the federal government in domestic policies and events.

Modifications to Great Society Programs In an attempt to modify Great Society programs, President Nixon reduced the amount of federal money spent on aid to education, housing, job training, and welfare assistance. He persuaded Congress to eliminate the Office of Economic Opportunity, which had administered many of Johnson's programs for aiding the poor.

One new program established by President Nixon was the *Occupational Safety and Health Administration (OSHA)*, which provided for the inspection of workplaces to see that they met safety and health standards.

Another new agency was the *Drug Enforcement Agency (DEA)*. The increased use of drugs in the 1960s led to a greater concern about the illegal sale and distribution of controlled substances. The Drug Enforcement Agency, which is part of the Justice Department, coordinates efforts to reduce the sale and use of illegal drugs in the United States. Drug enforcement agents are sometimes assigned to countries that export illegal drugs into the United States.

In 1970, the Sierra Club and other environmental groups organized a nationwide demonstration called Earth Day. Hundreds of thousands of Americans who took part in the demonstration wanted to raise the consciousness of the nation and pressure the government to enact tougher anti-pollution laws. President Nixon responded by persuading Congress to establish the *Environmental Protection Agency (EPA)*. This agency, created in 1970, had the power to enforce 15 previously enacted federal programs for protecting the environment against various hazards. Under a Clean Air Act of 1970, the EPA could set federal standards for monitoring the quality of the air. Under a Clean Water Act of 1972, the new agency could assist states and local governments in funding projects for cleaning up polluted rivers and lakes. During Nixon's administration, the use of DDT was also banned. (DDT is the pesticide blamed by Rachel Carson for the death of birds and fish.)

The food stamp program began in 1964 during the Johnson administration. During the Nixon years, the program was greatly expanded. It provides coupons to the poor that can be exchanged for food. The program is administered by the Department of Agriculture, which also provides subsidized school lunches for the poor as well as meals for older poor Americans. (In 1996, Congress voted to make legal immigrants ineligible for the program but partially reversed itself in 1998 by restoring food stamps to those who had arrived before the 1996 legislation.)

Revenue Sharing Conservatives applauded a policy that Nixon called the *New Federalism*. Arguing that the states understood the needs of their people better than the national government, Nixon proposed giving the states much greater freedom to decide how to use federal funds. In other words, he wanted the federal government to "share" its revenues with state and local governments. In 1971, Congress approved the idea of *revenue sharing* by passing a number of bills that permitted a state or community to use federal funds for whatever purpose it wished.

Supreme Court Appointments Nixon had a major opportunity to affect the future of the Supreme Court when Chief Justice Earl Warren announced his retirement in 1969. To fill the place of the liberal chief justice, Nixon selected a conservative judge, Warren Burger. Later in his presidency, three other vacancies arose on the nation's highest court. The Senate rejected two of Nixon's nominees to the Court. But those judges who finally won Senate approval (Harry Blackmun, Lewis Powell, and William Rehnquist) were conservative in their views. As Nixon hoped, the decisions of the Burger Court in the 1970s tended to be far more conservative than those of the Warren Court in the 1960s.

The Moon Landing In July 1969, Neil Armstrong and Edwin E. Aldrin, Jr., walked on the moon. The United States had landed a man on the moon before the end of the decade, as promised by President Kennedy. For President Nixon, the landing on the moon was a welcome change from the protest marches against the Vietnam War.

Self-Determination for Native Americans Recognizing the poverty on the Native American reservations, President Nixon attempted to provide greater self-determination for American Indians. A major goal was the protection of hunting and fishing rights and the restitution of land. One action taken by the president was the return of traditional lands to the Taos people in New Mexico. At the same time, the president increased the number of Native Americans employed in the Bureau of Indian Affairs. In 1975, soon after President Nixon left office, the Indian Self-Determination and Educational Assistance Act was passed. This law increased the role of Native Americans in directing their own education and government.

Ratification of the Twenty-Sixth Amendment In 1971, the Twenty-sixth Amendment was added to the Constitution. This amendment states that "the right of citizens of the United States, who are 18 years of age or older, to vote shall not be denied or abridged by the United States or by any state on account of age." This amendment in part was a response to the number of young Americans who were considered old enough to fight in the Vietnam War but not yet old enough to vote.

Title IX—Equal Education Access In 1972, Congress passed an education act that included a provision known as Title IX. The purpose of Title IX was to ensure that gender discrimination would be considered illegal in determining participation in educational programs. As a result of Title IX, athletic activities for women expanded greatly. For example, if a school had a men's basketball team, it would now also be required to have a women's basketball team. As a result, women's participation in sports programs has increased greatly since 1972. In addition, specialized, once all-male schools, such as Stuyvesant High School in New York City, had to open their doors to both sexes.

Nixon's Internationalism

During the 1950s, as Eisenhower's vice president, Richard Nixon had often expressed hostility to the Soviet Union, China, and other Communist nations. However, after becoming president in 1969, Nixon adopted policies that were designed to lessen cold-war tensions and to scale back U.S. military commitments.

In making foreign policy, Nixon depended on the advice of his assistant for national security affairs, Henry Kissinger. In 1973, Nixon appointed Kissinger secretary of state.

Nixon and Kissinger believed that U.S. foreign policies should have a single goal—supporting the national self-interest of the United States. Kissinger argued that all nations pursued their own self-interests. Therefore, he thought, the United States should do the same in order to devise realistic and successful policies. This approach to world policies, which focuses on realities rather than ideals, is known as *realpolitik*.

During his years as president (1969–1974), Nixon attempted to apply realpolitik and to reshape U.S. relations with the major Communist powers, the Soviet Union and China.

Nixon Doctrine In Chapter 19, you read about Nixon's policy of winding down U.S. involvement in Vietnam by withdrawing troops and negotiating an agreement with North Vietnam. To avoid U.S. involvement in other Asian wars, the president announced a policy known as the *Nixon Doctrine*. In the future, Nixon said, the nations of Asia would have to carry the main burden of their own defense. They would no longer be able to rely on the United States to supply massive amounts of military aid or large numbers of ground forces.

Opening to China The most dramatic change in U.S. policy during Nixon's presidency concerned the two governments that claimed to rule China. Recall from Chapter 14 that the United States had refused to recognize the Communist government of China established by Mao Zedong in 1949. The United States recognized instead the Chinese government on the island of Taiwan—a government established by Mao's anti-Communist rival, Jiang Jieshi. (Jiang's Nationalist party had ruled China in the 1930s and 1940s.)

During the 1960s, Mao's Communist government in China began denouncing the Soviet Union. This surprised many Americans, who had assumed that Communist nations were tightly bound together as allies and

President Nixon and
Chairman Mao
exchange greetings
in China, 1972

would follow identical policies. Nixon perceived that China was growing extremely suspicious of its giant northern neighbor, the Soviet Union. Under these circumstances, he and Kissinger believed that the time had come to establish normal relations with the People's Republic of China (the Chinese Communists' name for their nation).

In 1971, Kissinger traveled on a secret mission to Beijing, China's capital. His goal was to prepare the way for improved U.S. relations with the People's Republic. Following Kissinger's trip, President Nixon surprised the world by announcing that he would go to China to seek an understanding with its Communist leaders. The president's trip to China in 1972 succeeded in bringing about a major shift in U.S. policy. In effect, the United States stopped taking the side of the anti-Communist government on the island of Taiwan. Instead, it stressed the importance of fostering trade and good relations with mainland China.

After Nixon's trip, China and the United States exchanged performing troupes and athletic teams. But they did not exchange ambassadors until 1979, when the United States formally recognized the People's Republic of China.

Détente: SALT and Grain   Nixon's attempt to reduce, or relax, cold-war tensions and to improve U.S.-Soviet relations was known as the policy of *détente*, a French word meaning the relaxation of tensions. A principal goal of détente was to set limits on the production of nuclear weapons. During Nixon's first term as president, diplomats from the United States and the Soviet Union held a series of talks called the *Strategic Arms Limitation Talks (SALT I)*. They negotiated an important breakthrough in the arms race by setting fixed limits on both long-range nuclear missiles, or intercontinental ballistic missiles (ICBMs), and defensive missiles, or antiballistic missiles (ABMs).

In 1972, Nixon traveled to the Soviet Union where he met with Soviet Premier Leonid Brezhnev. The leaders of the two superpowers signed the

"Let's talk about not watering them": U.S. and Soviet diplomats negotiate a nuclear arms reduction.

SALT agreement. The president also agreed to end a U.S. trade ban of 1949, which had prohibited the shipment of U.S. goods to the Soviet Union. To help the Russian people through a bad food shortage, Nixon offered (and Congress later approved) the sale to the Soviets of $750 million worth of U.S. wheat. The U.S.–Soviet "grain deal," as it was called, pleased not only the Soviet Union but U.S. farmers as well.

The United Nations proposed another disarmament agreement in 1972. The 100 nations that signed this Seabed Agreement pledged never to place nuclear weapons on the ocean floor. Both the Soviet Union and the United States were among the signers.

Kissinger and the Middle East   A crisis erupted in the Middle East in October 1973. Arab nations of the Middle East launched a surprise attack against Israel. Their immediate objective was to take from Israel the territories it had won during an Arab-Israeli war in 1967. Henry Kissinger traveled to the warring nations of the Middle East in an effort to arrange a cease-fire. At stake was not only the security of Israel but also U.S.-Soviet relations. The United States supported Israel in the conflict, while the Soviet Union supported the Arab nation of Syria. A cease-fire was finally arranged after Israeli troops had successfully crossed into Egyptian territory.

The end of the military crisis led immediately to the beginning of an economic crisis. Angered by U.S. support of Israel, several Arab nations announced an embargo on the shipment of oil to the United States and its Western allies. The United States response to this embargo is treated later in the chapter.

In Moscow, President Nixon and Secretary of State Kissinger share a toast to détente while a smiling Premier Brezhnev (center) chats with diplomats.

The Presidency in Crisis

The American people had not completely trusted the military policy and public statements of Lyndon Johnson. Their distrust grew even greater during Richard Nixon's second term in office. The reason stemmed from his involvement in a political crisis and scandal known as the *Watergate Affair*.

Resignation of Spiro Agnew In 1973, the elected vice president, Spiro Agnew, resigned his office after he had fallen under suspicion of having taken bribes while serving as governor of Maryland. Nixon then appointed Gerald Ford, a congressman from Michigan, as vice president in accordance with a section of the Twenty-fifth Amendment. (The section reads: "Whenever there is a vacancy in the office of the vice president, the president shall nominate a vice president who shall take the office upon confirmation by a majority of both houses of Congress.")

Watergate Affair and the Constitution The crime that caused the crisis occurred early in the Republican party's campaign to elect Nixon to a second term. In 1972, the Democratic party had nominated George McGovern, a

In this 1974 cartoon, President Nixon, weighed down by Watergate, leaves foreign policy to Secretary of State Kissinger.

liberal senator from South Dakota, as its candidate for president. The Democrats' campaign was being run from an office in Washington, D.C., in a building called the Watergate. To get information about the Democrats' campaign, five men tried to break into the Democrats' office late at night. A watchman on duty called the police, who arrested the burglars.

In the November election, President Nixon won by a huge margin. But no sooner had he begun his second term than the Watergate crisis broke. In 1973, the newspapers and TV news were full of stories about the Watergate break-in of the previous summer. The news reports suggested that the crime might have been planned by members of the White House staff and perhaps by the president himself. The Federal Bureau of Investigation (FBI) began investigating the Watergate Affair. An unofficial investigation by two reporters for the *Washington Post* revealed that suspicions about certain officials close to the president might be well founded.

The most dramatic investigation was conducted by a Senate committee and televised to the nation. The witnesses who answered the committee's questions were members of the president's White House staff. Throughout 1973, Nixon stated again and again that he had no previous knowledge of the break-in and that he had not attempted to cover it up.

United States v. Nixon During the course of its investigation, the Senate committee learned that the president had taped every conversation that took place in his White House office. The committee requested that the president turn over the tapes as evidence for its hearings. Nixon released some tapes and offered summaries and transcripts of others. But he refused to turn over certain tapes on the principle that it was his *executive privilege* to keep possession of them. Nixon argued that he would be violating separation of powers if he turned over the tapes to a Senate committee or even to a special prosecutor.

In the case *United States v. Nixon* (1974), the Supreme Court ruled that due process of law is more important than executive privilege. The president then released the requested tapes. They revealed that, only a few days after the Watergate break-in, Nixon had participated in an effort to protect those responsible for the crime. His actions, if he were convicted of them, would be criminal, because to cover up a crime is itself a crime.

Impeachment Process and Resignation According to the U.S. Constitution, impeachment consists of a two-part process. First, the House of Representatives may charge a federal official, including the president, with misconduct. This requires a majority vote. Second, the Senate may find the accused guilty of misconduct. This requires a two-thirds vote and may result in removal from office. The Chief Justice of the United States serves as the judge during the Senate trial. Only two presidents have been impeached (Andrew Johnson in 1867 and William Jefferson Clinton in 1998), but neither was found guilty by the Senate.

In 1974, a committee of the House of Representatives voted to recommend that President Nixon be impeached. Republican advisers urged

Nixon to resign and thus prevent the possibility that Congress might remove him by impeachment and trial. He reluctantly agreed. On August 8, 1974, he announced on television that he would resign his office and turn over the presidency to the newly appointed vice president, Gerald Ford. It was the first time in U.S. history that a living president had left office before the end of his term.

In the last week of July 1974, the House Judiciary Committee had voted to recommend the articles of impeachment quoted below. Do you think the three reasons given by the committee are strong enough to justify the removal of a president from office?

Assessment Until the Watergate Affair, there had been a steady increase in presidential power. Beginning with Franklin Roosevelt's strong presidency

★ ★ ★ ★ ★

ARTICLES OF IMPEACHMENT

ARTICLE I: On June 17th, 1972, . . . agents of the Committee for the Reelection of the President: Committed unlawful entry of the headquarters of the Democratic National Committee . . . for the purpose of securing political intelligence. . . . Richard M. Nixon, using the powers of his high office, engaged personally and through his subordinates and agents in a course of conduct or plan designed to delay, impede, and obstruct the investigation of such unlawful entry; to cover up, conceal, and protect those responsible; and to conceal the existence and scope of other unlawful covert activities.

ARTICLE II: Richard M. Nixon . . . has repeatedly engaged in conduct violating the constitutional rights of citizens, impairing the due and proper administration of justice in the conduct of lawful inquiries; or contravening the laws of government agencies of the executive branch and the purposes of these agencies.

ARTICLE III: Richard M. Nixon . . . has failed without lawful cause or excuse to produce papers and things as directed by duly authorized subpoenas issued by the Committee on the Judiciary of the House of Representatives. . . .

In all this Richard M. Nixon has acted in a manner contrary to his trust as President and subversive of constitutional government, to the great prejudice of the cause of law and justice and to the manifest injury of the people of the United States.

Wherefore, Richard M. Nixon by such conduct warrants impeachment and trial and removal from office.

in the 1930s, the power exercised from the White House was enormous, especially in times of war (World War II, the Korean War, and the Vietnam War). Historian Arthur Schlesinger, Jr., published a book in 1973 warning the nation that the growth in presidential power was beginning to get out of hand. He said that presidents such as Johnson and Nixon acted as if they could ignore both Congress and the American people.

The Watergate Affair and Nixon's resignation brought an end to the *imperial presidency* (as Schlesinger called the abuse of presidential power). Congress, the Supreme Court, and an independent press had fully asserted themselves in checking Nixon's power. Americans breathed a sigh of relief to see the constitutional system of checks and balances work as it had been intended to work. Congress had forced a president to leave office because of that president's abuse of his power. Nixon's fall was a lesson for later presidents not to overstep the limits on power that are basic to the U.S. system of government.

★ In Review

1. Identify and explain the significance of the following: Occupational Safety and Health Administration (OSHA), Drug Enforcement Administration (DEA), Environmental Protection Agency (EPA), revenue sharing, Twenty-sixth Amendment, Title IX, realpolitik, détente, SALT I.
2. Describe how President Nixon changed U.S. foreign policy with regard to China and the Soviet Union.
3. Explain how the system of checks and balances applied to the Watergate Affair.

Appointive Presidency

Nixon's resignation led to Vice President Gerald Ford taking over as his successor. Like his predecessor, President Ford followed policies that were moderately conservative.

Gerald Ford was in an unusual situation when he took the oath of office as the new president. The American people had not elected him to either the vice presidency or the presidency. In a televised speech to the nation, Ford promised to restore trust in the U.S. government. "Our national nightmare is over," he said. But memories of Watergate lingered for years afterward.

Another issue concerned the vice presidency. Now that Ford had moved into the presidency, who was to replace him as vice president? He selected the former governor of New York, Nelson Rockefeller. A Senate committee conducted a long and probing investigation of Rockefeller before finally recommending that his nomination be approved. At last, the United States had both a president and a vice president—both unelected—who could be trusted to carry out their constitutional duties.

Domestic Policy Issues

Pardon for Nixon   Only a month after becoming president, Ford announced that he was pardoning ex-President Nixon for any crime committed in the Watergate Affair. Critics of this action wondered if the pardon was even legal since no court had even charged Nixon with a crime. President Ford defended his action by saying that it was time for the nation to put the Watergate Affair aside and move forward. The power for a president to pardon individuals and release them from punishment is contained in Article II, Section 2, of the Constitution.

Although Nixon was pardoned, other members of his White House staff were less fortunate. Among those convicted and imprisoned for covering up the Watergate Affair and committing *perjury* (lying under oath) were Nixon's former attorney general, John Mitchell, and key White House aides.

First Oil Crisis

Recall that Americans first became aware of their dependence on foreign oil when an Arab-Israeli war broke out in 1973. The Arabs used their control of oil fields in the Middle East to punish the United States for its support of Israel. Saudi Arabia, Iraq, Iran, and other nations placed an embargo on the sale of their oil to the United States and its allies.

"You're like a bunch of . . . of . . . of . . . CAPITALISTS!": Uncle Sam outraged at OPEC's control of the oil market

The Arab oil embargo of 1973 added to the woes of the American economy. Between 1973 and 1974, the price of a barrel of oil jumped from $3 to $11. The price increases affected not only the price of gasoline but also the price of almost all other manufactured products because factory equipment cannot operate without oil. The U.S. automobile industry was badly hurt as American consumers bought fewer American cars and more of the smaller, fuel-efficient imports from Japan and Europe.

The embargo made Americans realize that a significant percentage of the oil they used came from the Middle East, where the price of oil and its output were controlled by Arab members of the *Organization of Petroleum Exporting Countries (OPEC)*. (Japan and Western Europe depended almost totally on OPEC oil.) OPEC's 1973 embargo made worldwide oil prices soar. The oil shortage, or *energy crisis*, also led to long lines at gas stations. OPEC lifted its embargo in 1974 but continued to limit production and keep oil prices high.

Presidents Nixon and Ford both urged Americans to conserve energy in their homes and on the road. When the crisis passed, however, the nation became even more dependent on foreign oil.

Carter's Presidency

Election of 1976

Honesty in government was an important issue in the presidential election of 1976. More than a dozen Democrats entered the race for their party's nomination. Each hoped to convince voters that, because of the Watergate Affair, Republican leadership in the White House was suspect. The candidate who eventually won the Democratic nomination was Jimmy Carter, a former governor of Georgia. Although few people outside Georgia had ever heard of Carter, they soon became familiar with his winning smile on TV debates and news shows. Carter's campaign stressed his honesty and lack of previous involvement in the politics of Washington, D.C. Millions of Democratic voters found Carter to be an attractive, likable, and trustworthy candidate.

The Republican nominee, President Gerald Ford, started his campaign well behind Carter in the opinion polls. But after debating Carter on television, Ford closed the gap. The results of the election were close. Carter emerged with 297 electoral votes to Ford's 240 votes. For the first time since the election of Zachary Taylor in 1848, the United States was to have a president from the South.

Carter's Style of Leadership

Carter proved to be a hardworking, honest, and dedicated president. There was never much doubt about his good intentions and concern for human rights. There was some doubt, however, about his effectiveness as a leader. At times, he would tell Congress and the American people that a certain law was urgently needed. But then he would not follow through on his proposals to make sure that the Democratic majority in Congress voted for them. He angered and frustrated lawmakers in his own party by sometimes changing his policies at the last minute. Public opinion polls during his four years in office (1977 to 1981) showed a decline in his popularity, especially after he failed to deal forcefully with a second energy crisis, in 1979, and failed to win the release of American hostages in Iran (see pages 546–547).

Domestic Policy Issues

Amnesty for Draft Evaders In 1977, President Carter provided an *amnesty* (a general or blanket pardon) for Vietnam War draft evaders. Many of these young men had fled to Canada rather than allow themselves to be drafted into the army. The amnesty was intended to bring an end to the disagreements that still existed about how these young men should be treated. The decision caused controversy, as many families that had suffered the loss of a loved one in the war were opposed to the amnesty. Nevertheless, the amnesty provided a solution to the issue.

Second Oil Crisis President Carter had to deal with an even worse energy crisis than had President Ford. In 1979, a revolution in Iran caused a major cutback in that country's production of oil. Oil prices climbed from about $11 a barrel to $40 a barrel. The shock to the world economy was severe. At U.S. gas stations, motorists waited in long lines to refill their tanks and then had to pay more than a dollar a gallon for gas (compared to about 80 cents a gallon before the oil shortage). People became frustrated and angry over having to start or end their workday in long gas lines.

The second oil crisis reminded Americans that they were at the mercy of OPEC and upheavals in the Middle East. President Carter had already persuaded Congress to set up a new cabinet department, the Department of Energy. Now he urged that the department expand its search for practical forms of energy other than oil. In 1980, Congress voted $20 billion in research funds to develop synthetic fuels.

Environmental Concerns Environmental concerns increased greatly during the 1970s. The partial meltdown of a nuclear power plant at Three Mile Island in Pennsylvania in 1979 reminded people that accidents at nuclear power plants could cause dangerous amounts of radioactive materials to be released into the atmosphere. At the same time, pollutants that caused acid rain and radioactive toxic wastes were also creating hazards to the environment. Thus, concerns for the environment were increasing throughout the United States.

Foreign Policy Issues

The United States faced a number of foreign policy issues during the Carter administration. They included conflicts in the Middle East, the Soviet invasion of Afghanistan, and a hostage crisis in Iran.

Middle East in Turmoil   The history of the Middle East in modern times has been marked by civil wars, revolutions, assassinations, invasions, and border wars. In dealing with each conflict, U.S. policymakers tried to balance three main interests: (1) giving support to the democratic state of Israel, (2) giving support to Arab states to ensure a steady flow of Middle Eastern oil to the United States and its allies, and (3) preventing the Soviet Union from increasing its influence in the region.

From 1947 to 1973, Israel fought four wars with Arab neighbors. First, from 1948 to 1949, Arab states attacked Israel in a failed attempt to crush the independence of the new Jewish state. Second, in the Suez Crisis of 1956, Israel joined France and Great Britain in attacking Egypt. (After the United States condemned the attack, Israel withdrew.) Third, in 1967, Israel took only six days to defeat Jordan, Syria, and Egypt.

As a result of the 1967 Six-Day War, Israel forces occupied the bordering territories of the Golan Heights (taken from Syria), the Sinai Peninsula and Gaza Strip (taken from Egypt), and the West Bank of the Jordan River (taken from Jordan). Israel refused to give back these territories, which helped secure its borders against future attack. The embittered Arab nations hoped to regain the territories in yet another war.

A fourth conflict, called the Yom Kippur War, broke out in October 1973. Arab nations, seeking to win back territories lost in 1967, launched a surprise attack against Israel on the Jewish holy day of Yom Kippur. After fierce fighting and initial Arab victories, Israel drove back the Arabs in a successful counterattack. The United States, fearful of Soviet intervention, used its influence to negotiate a cease-fire.

Middle East Mediation   After the Yom Kippur War, presidents Ford and Carter attempted to reduce tensions between Israel and its Arab neighbors. In 1978, President Carter persuaded Egypt's president Anwar Sadat and Israel's prime minister Menachem Begin to travel to the United States and informally discuss peace at Camp David, Maryland. Most world leaders doubted that peace would result from these talks. They were therefore surprised when the Egyptian and Israeli leaders announced at Camp David that they had reached an *accord* (agreement) on resolving problems dividing their countries. Later, Egypt and Israel signed a treaty of peace based on the Camp David Accords. The treaty of 1979 provided for the following:

★ Israel was to return the Sinai Peninsula to Egypt.

★ Egypt formally recognized Israel as an independent nation.

★ Israel and Egypt pledged to respect the border between them.

Many Egyptians and other Arabs bitterly condemned Sadat for making peace with Israel. Begin also faced severe criticism within his country for returning the Sinai Peninsula to Egypt. For their courage in agreeing to make peace with a former enemy, Anwar Sadat and Menachem Begin received the Nobel Peace Prize in 1978. Sadly, however, his peace policy cost Sadat his life. In 1981, the Egyptian leader was assassinated by Muslim extremists.

Soviet Invasion of Afghanistan   President Nixon had initiated a policy of détente with the Soviet Union. This policy changed after the Soviet invasion of Afghanistan, a Muslim nation located on the Soviet Union's southern border. A rebellion broke out in Afghanistan in 1978 against the Soviet-backed Communist government. The Soviets invaded Afghanistan in December 1979 in an attempt to crush the rebellion.

The movement of Soviet troops alarmed President Carter and his advisers, who feared that the Soviets might use Afghanistan as a base to seize oil fields in the Persian Gulf. To punish the Soviets for their aggression, Carter cut back the U.S. grain shipments to the Soviet Union. He also announced that U.S. athletes would not go to Moscow in 1980 to participate in the Summer Olympics there. In effect, because of the Soviet invasion of Afghanistan, the United States suspended its policy of détente.

Iranian Hostage Crisis   A low point in the history of U.S. foreign relations occurred during the Carter presidency. In 1979, Iranian revolutionaries, in violation of international law, broke into the U.S. Embassy in Iran's capital, Teheran. They captured 62 Americans, and held 52 as hostages (captives held until ransom is paid or demands are met) for over a year.

Many Iranians were angered by past U.S. policies toward their country. Since 1953, the United States had supported the regime of Iran's monarch, Shah Mohammad Reza Pahlavi. In return for U.S. military aid, the shah had let the United States use Iran as a base for spying on the Soviet Union. The shah had also employed secret police to ruthlessly suppress dissent. Fundamentalist Muslims condemned the shah for modernizing Iran rather

Blindfolded American hostages being held in Iran, 1979

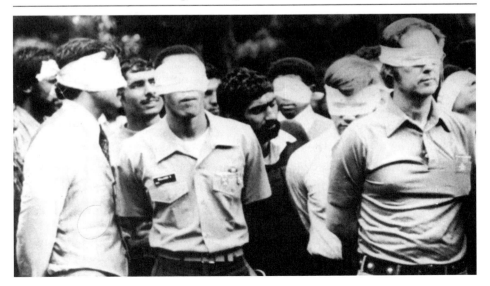

than following Muslim religious laws and customs strictly. A leader of these fundamentalists was the Ayatollah Khomeini. (Ayatollah is a Muslim title for an advanced religious scholar.)

In 1979, Khomeini led a successful revolution against the shah, who went into exile. President Carter allowed the ailing shah to enter the United States for medical treatment. This action so angered Iranian revolutionaries that some of them seized the Americans in the U.S. Embassy and demanded the return of the shah for trial. Carter refused and demanded release of the hostages.

In April 1980, Carter decided to attempt a military rescue of the hostages. Unfortunately, the U.S. helicopters carrying U.S. troops broke down in the Iranian desert, and the rescue effort failed. Months passed without any change in the hostage situation, except for the death of the shah in July. Running for reelection in 1980. President Carter suffered political damage from his inability to free the hostages. He lost the election partly because of *stagflation* (inflation coupled with high unemployment) and partly because of the frustrating situation in Iran.

On the day when Carter left office, January 20, 1981, Iran announced the release of the hostages, 444 days after their capture. The hostage crisis injured U.S. prestige. Coming only a few years after the loss of the Vietnam War, the crisis made many Americans wonder whether the nation was beginning to decline as a world power.

T. R. "I took Panama" Roosevelt does a double take in outrage at President Carter's Panama Canal "give-away."

Changing Relations With Panama   Ever since 1903, when Panama gained its independence, the United States has had a special relationship with that country. Panama's first government signed a treaty granting the United States the right to own and operate a canal through Panama and also to own a ten-mile-wide strip of land bordering the canal (the Panama Canal Zone). At first, the people of Panama welcomed U.S. efforts to build and protect the canal. Beginning in the 1960s, however, many Panamanians protested the U.S. presence in their country. The time had come, they said, for the United States to give control of the canal to Panama.

As a Democrat, President Carter favored the Good Neighbor policy of a Democratic predecessor, Franklin Roosevelt. He believed that the presence of U.S. troops in the Panama Canal Zone not only angered the Panamanian people but also offended other people of Latin America. Therefore, Carter negotiated two treaties with Panama in 1977. According to the first treaty, the United States promised to transfer ownership of the canal and canal zone to Panama, which took place in the year 2000. According to the second treaty, the United States and Panama agreed that the canal would always be neutral territory. If threatened by an outside power, the United States could use military force to defend it.

The Panama Canal treaties stirred much controversy in the United States. Many Americans were reluctant to have their country give up the

Vietnamese boat people, fleeing their homeland, arrive in Hong Kong.

canal. President Carter, however, managed to persuade two-thirds of the Senate to ratify both treaties. It was one of the major political victories of his presidency.

Carter and Human Rights During his presidency (1977–1981), Jimmy Carter insisted that the United States could and should use its influence to stop oppressive governments from abusing the human rights of their citizens. He knew that some violators (South Africa) were aligned with the West, while others (Cuba and Poland) were Communist countries. He felt that the United States, as a freedom-loving country, should require friend and foe alike to respect the basic rights of their citizens.

In Latin America (as in other regions of the world), human rights abuses were extensive. Military regimes in Argentina and Chile arrested many thousands of people and either imprisoned them without trial or killed them. The victims' only crime—or alleged crime—was often joining political groups opposed to the regime. In Central America, El Salvador's friendly government and Nicaragua's hostile Communist government were both guilty of mistreating and killing citizens who opposed their policies.

At Carter's urging, Congress reduced or eliminated U.S. economic aid to countries such as Argentina and Chile. Unwilling to reform, they accused Carter of meddling in their internal affairs.

Oppressed peoples were better helped by being admitted into the United States as refugees from tyranny. From the end of the Vietnam War in 1975 into the 1990s, there was a steady stream of refugees from Vietnam fleeing reprisals by the Communist government there. During Carter's presidency, Fidel Castro let thousands of Cubans go. Thousands of Haitians also left their island nation in a desperate effort to escape harsh laws and extreme poverty. Both of the Caribbean groups sailed to Florida. Many Americans wanted to turn the "boat people" away because many were poor and unskilled, but Carter let them make the United States their new home.

★ In Review

1. Explain the significance of the Ford presidency.
2. How did President Carter respond to each of the following issues: the second oil crisis, environmental concerns, the Middle East conflicts, the Soviet invasion of Afghanistan, the Iranian hostage crisis, relations with Panama.
3. Evaluate the appropriateness of President Carter's emphasis on human rights considerations in the conduct of U.S. foreign policy.

Chapter Review

MULTIPLE-CHOICE QUESTIONS

Base your answers to questions 1 and 2 on the cartoon on page 537.

1. The main idea of the cartoon is that preserving world peace depended largely on the
   (1) balance of terror
   (2) agreement by the superpowers to stop the arms race
   (3) adoption of isolationist policies by the nuclear powers
   (4) formation of military alliances between the United States and the Soviet Union.

2. The cartoon was most likely drawn to comment on the
   (1) conflict in Vietnam
   (2) negotiation of a SALT agreement
   (3) grain deal between the United States and the Soviet Union
   (4) outbreak of a war in the Middle East.

Read the following headline and answer question 3.

NIXON MUST SURRENDER TAPES, SUPREME COURT RULES, 8 TO 0; HE PLEDGES FULL COMPLIANCE

3. Which feature of the U.S. constitutional system is best illustrated by the headline?
   (1) checks and balances
   (2) executive privilege
   (3) power to grant pardons
   (4) federalism.

Use the cartoon on page 542 to answer question 4.

4. The cartoon shows that in 1974
   (1) the United States demanded that oil production be drastically cut
   (2) the Organization of Petroleum Exporting Countries was born
   (3) oil-producing nations were able to manipulate oil prices
   (4) the United States was able to ignore the rise in petroleum prices by producing more of its own oil.

5. A major goal of U.S. foreign policy in the Middle East has been to bring about
   (1) a peaceful settlement of Arab-Israeli issues
   (2) an end to U.S. cooperation with Arab nations
   (3) ownership of oil resources by Western nations
   (4) permanent UN control of disputed territories.

Use the photograph on page 546 to answer questions 6 and 7.

6. The photograph shows that
   (1) U.S. citizenship does not guarantee safety overseas
   (2   American interference in foreign countries endangers its citizens abroad
   (3) by the end of the 1970s, the policies of the United States were unpopular throughout the world

(4) Americans were advised to avoid overseas travel during the years 1979 and 1980.

7. The hostage situation depicted in the photograph resulted from
    (1) U.S. support of Israel
    (2) the refusal of the U.S. government to turn over the shah of Iran to the new Iranian government
    (3) President Carter's negotiation of the Camp David Accords
    (4) Vietnamese support for the Iranian Revolution.

Use the cartoon on page 547 to answer questions 8 and 9.

8. The cartoonist felt that
    (1) there was historical precedent for the U.S. return of the canal to Panama
    (2) the return of the Panama Canal would result in better relations between the United States and Panama
    (3) President Carter should have rethought his idea for returning the canal to Panama
    (4) the return of the canal to Panama would prevent a revolution there.

9. The cartoonist felt that President Theodore Roosevelt would have
    (1) been upset over the return of the canal to Panama
    (2) approved of the return of the Panama Canal
    (3) negotiated a better treaty before returning the canal to the Panamanians
    (4) invoked the Roosevelt Corollary before returning the Panama Canal.

Refer to the photograph on page 548 and answer question 10.

10. Which problem does the photograph most anticipate for the United States?
    (1) training of Vietnamese refugees for a new assault on the Communist government of Vietnam
    (2) immigration and resettlement of Vietnamese refugees in U.S. society
    (3) relocating of Vietnamese refugees in other nations
    (4) negotiating a peaceful return of Vietnamese refugees to their homeland.

THEMATIC ESSAYS

1. **Theme:** "Stagflation" During the 1970s

   The end of U.S. participation in the Vietnam War, coupled with an oil embargo by Arab producers and explorers of petroleum, led to a unique economic hardship for the people of the United States called "stagflation" (a combination of economic recession and inflation).

   Task

   ★ Describe how the end of U.S. involvement in the Vietnam War resulted in a decline in production and employment that caused an economic recession.

★ Explain why the Arab oil embargo took place.

★ Demonstrate why the Arab oil embargo resulted in rising prices (inflation).

★ Show why the problem of "stagflation" was unusual and extremely difficult to solve.

You should consider in your discussion the relationship of the Vietnam War to production (the law of supply and demand), the 1973 Yom Kippur War between Israel and its Arab neighbors, and the relationship that prices have to production (another application of the law of supply and demand).

2. **Theme:** The United States in an Interdependent World

Events of the 1970s showed that the nations of the world were becoming increasingly interdependent. This meant that after many years of trying to be neutral or isolationist, the people and government of the United States would have to adopt new strategies for existing in a constantly changing global environment.

Task

★ Describe two examples of how, during the 1970s, the federal government was forced to respond to events going on in others parts of the world.

★ Show how both problems that you described illustrate that the United States must adapt to a new, more interdependent world.

★ Suggest one strategy that the federal government can adopt to coexist in a world that is more interdependent than ever before.

You may discuss, but are not limited to, events such as the Iranian Revolution, the Arab oil embargo, the end of the Vietnam War, the Soviet invasion of Afghanistan, and the economic and political conditions of neighbors in Latin America and the Caribbean.

DOCUMENT-BASED QUESTION

Read each document and answer the question that follows it. Then read the Task and write your essay. Essays should include references to most of the documents along with additional information based on your knowledge of United States history and government.

Historical Context: In spite of a number of diplomatic successes, President Richard Nixon's second term in office was plagued by the issues of the Watergate scandal, which erupted during the 1972 presidential election campaign.

Document 1 From Article I of the impeachment against President Richard Nixon, 1974:

Article I

In his conduct of the office of President of the United States, Richard M. Nixon, in violation of his constitutional oath faithfully to execute the office of President of the United States and, to the best of his ability, preserve, protect, and defend the Constitution of the United States, and in violation of his constitutional duty to take care that the laws be faithfully executed, has prevented, obstructed, and impeded the administration of justice, in that:

On June 17, 1972, and prior thereto, agents of the Committee for the Re-election of the President committed unlawful entry of the headquarters of the Democratic National Committee in Washington, District of Columbia, for the purpose of securing political intelligence. Subsequent thereto, Richard M. Nixon, using the powers of his high office, engaged personally and through his subordinates and agents, in a course of conduct or plan designed to delay, impede, and obstruct the investigation of such unlawful entry; to cover up, conceal and protect those responsible; and to conceal the existence and scope of other unlawful covert activities.

Question: Why was the House Judiciary Committee recommending that President Nixon be impeached?

Document 2 From President Richard Nixon's address to the nation, January 23, 1973:

Good evening. I have asked for this radio and television time tonight for the purpose of announcing that we today have concluded an agreement to end the war and bring peace with honor in Vietnam and in Southeast Asia. . . .

We must recognize that ending the war is only the first step toward building the peace. All parties must now see to it that this is a peace that lasts, and also a peace that heals, and a peace that not only ends the war in Southeast Asia, but contributes to the prospects of peace in the whole world.

This will mean that the terms of the agreement must be scrupulously adhered to.

Question: What announcement did President Nixon make to the nation on January 23, 1973?

Document 3 Refer to the photographs on pages 536 and 538.

Question: Why did President Nixon travel to Communist China and the Soviet Union?

Document 4   Refer to the cartoon on page 538.

Question: What does the cartoon say about President Nixon's ability to carry out foreign affairs (the other figure in the cartoon is Secretary of State Henry Kissinger)?

Task

- ★ Describe two examples of the conduct of foreign affairs during the administration of President Richard Nixon.

- ★ Describe how President Nixon increasingly had to concern himself with the Watergate scandal.

- ★ Evaluate the effect that the Watergate scandal had on President Nixon's conduct of foreign affairs.

Chapter 21

The New Outlook of the Reagan Years: 1981–1988

★ **Objectives**

★ To assess the impact of the new federalism on domestic policies.

★ To understand the impact of Supreme Court decisions on schools.

★ To evaluate the government's response to the problems of farmers, the poor, the new immigrants, and the elderly.

★ To explain how U.S. foreign policy affected Caribbean and Central American nations and the Soviet Union.

Jimmy Carter was defeated for reelection in 1980 by a former movie star and two-term governor of California, Ronald Reagan. Reagan was elected governor of California in 1966 and reelected in 1970. As a rising star in the Republican party, he almost won that party's nomination for president in 1976 but was narrowly defeated by President Gerald Ford. Reagan won the Republican nomination easily in 1980 and went on to defeat the Democrats' choice, President Carter, in a landslide victory.

Reagan proved to be an extremely popular president. As an experienced entertainer, he knew how to use the TV medium to project a pleasing personality to a mass audience. Unlike Jimmy Carter, Reagan took a firm stand on domestic issues. He believed in reducing taxes, reducing government spending on social programs, and increasing government spending on defense. His policies had both a positive effect on business and a negative effect on the poor.

In the election of 1984, Reagan's popularity was demonstrated by an overwhelming victory over his Democratic challenger, Walter Mondale, vice president under Carter. In the electoral college, the president won the votes of 49 states. (The one state voting for Mondale was his own home state of Minnesota.)

A cartoonist's view of Washington's "new look" in the 1980s: The White House and the Capitol have only right wings (that is, they are very conservative).

Reagan—the New Federalism and Growth of Conservatism

A major issue that arose under the Reagan presidency was whether it was primarily the job of the federal government or of the state governments to combat crime, reform schools, and provide for the general welfare. The Republican presidents elected in the 1970s and 1980s (Nixon, Ford, Reagan, and Bush) believed that the chief responsibility for social welfare lay with state and local authorities. Nixon used the term New Federalism to describe his plan for giving the states freedom to decide how to use federal grants. (See page 534.) Reagan adopted the same policy and urged the states to take more responsibility for solving social and economic problems.

Through the 1980s, as the federal government trimmed its own budget and cut back social programs, the states did increase their spending on everything from police salaries to hospital beds. But they soon reached a limit on new programs, when citizens objected to paying higher taxes for improved public services. Candidates for election added to the public outcry against taxes by promising not to raise taxes either at the federal or the state level.

Supply-Side Economics

In 1974, the year that Ford replaced Nixon as president, the U.S. inflation rate climbed to a frightening 11 percent. Subsequently, the inflation rate increased to 13 percent under President Carter. The problem was partly the result of government spending on the Vietnam War. It was also the result of high oil prices caused by an Arab oil embargo. Both Ford and Carter attempted to bring inflation under control, but neither succeeded. The failure of these presidents to find a cure for inflation was one reason that neither was elected to a second term.

"Wall Flowers": social programs are left out of the government's budget—they receive far fewer funds than defense.

Reagan's efforts to deal with inflation solved this problem only to create huge budget deficits. Reagan's approach to the economic muddle was based on a theory called *supply-side economics*. Conservatives who supported this theory believed that the economy would benefit if government spent less money and businesses spent more. The best way to arrange this, according to the supply-siders, was to cut federal taxes. Businesses would then have more money to invest in productive enterprises, and consumers would receive more income from this economic boom to buy goods and services. At the same time, the government would make major cuts in welfare programs, which were considered wasteful by Reagan and other conservatives.

In 1981 Reagan persuaded Congress to enact the largest income tax cut in U.S. history. The Economic Recovery Tax Act (ERTA) provided for a 25 percent reduction in personal income taxes over a period of about three years. It also allowed general tax credits for corporations.

At the same time, the Federal Reserve decided to keep interest rates at a high level. Its anti-inflation policy began to have an effect during Reagan's first two years in office. The inflation rate dropped to 6 percent in 1982 and less than 4 percent in 1983. Unfortunately, another cause of the lower inflation was a severe business recession. By late 1982 about 11 percent of the labor force had no jobs.

Prosperity returned in 1984 and continued for the remainder of the decade. Inflation ceased to be a serious problem. But another problem took its place: that of staggering budget deficits.

Tax Policy and Budget Deficits

Tax Policy For obvious reasons, lowering taxes is always more popular with voters than raising them. Having already cut taxes in his first term, Reagan decided to reform the tax system during his second term. At his urging, Congress passed the Tax Reform Act in 1986. Previous tax laws had

"Trickle-Down Economics"—the cartoonist believes that Reagan's tax reforms were generous for the rich, but left little for the poor.

divided taxpayers into several brackets, according to their earned income. The higher the taxable income, the higher the percentage of income paid in taxes. The new law created only two tax brackets. Lower-income people were taxed at 15 percent of taxable income and upper-income people at 28 percent.

People with very high incomes benefited most from this reform law. Instead of being taxed at a 50 percent rate, as formerly, they paid just 28 percent. Thus, a millionaire was in the same tax bracket as a person earning $30,000 a year. The new law closed some "loopholes" in the old tax code so that wealthy taxpayers could not deduct as much from their income to lower their taxes.

Budget Deficits Every year the executive branch of the U.S. government submits a budget to Congress. The budget is a document listing both what the government expects to spend for the year ahead and what it expects to receive in income. If the government spends more than it collects in taxes, it ends the year with a *deficit*. (The opposite result—more money received than money spent—is known as a *surplus*.)

Beginning with the Depression years of the 1930s, the U.S. government almost always ended its *fiscal year* (budget year) with a deficit. To make up the difference between expenses and income, it had to borrow millions and even billions of dollars each year. In other words, the government went heavily into debt. The debt was kept at a reasonably manageable level through the early 1960s. After the Vietnam War, however, the national debt exceeded $500 billion and rapidly climbed to nearly $1 trillion when Ronald Reagan submitted his first budget to Congress in 1981.

Effects of "Reaganomics" Critics of President Reagan's economic policy warned that "Reaganomics" (as they called the supply-side theory) would

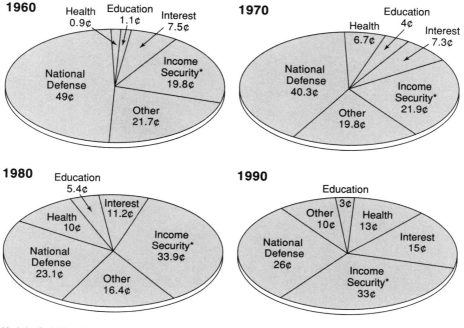

* Includes Social Security payments to the elderly and disabled, unemployment compensation, and welfare.

Federal Budgets, 1960–1990: Percentages of Spending, by Major Categories

result in huge deficits. They were right. Reagan's tax cuts of 1981 meant lower government revenues. At the same time, increased spending for defense meant higher government expenditures. The result: record deficits for eight years in a row and a national debt well above $2 trillion by the end of the 1980s.

Many economists were alarmed by these runaway budget deficits. They pointed out that, as deficits rose, so did the burden of paying interest on the national debt. By 1990 interest payments cost the government about $150 billion annually. Partly because of the debt burden, the government was less able to spend adequate sums for urgent national needs such as highway repair and health care.

Deregulation of Business

The 20h century began with the Progressive Era and the founding of regulatory agencies to protect consumers. In the late 1970s and 1980s, conservative presidents argued that regulation of business had gone too far. Carter and Reagan adopted policies to deregulate the economy. Deregulation meant removing many governmental rules that had limited and controlled business competition.

★ Federal Debt, 1970–1998 ★
(billions of $)

Year	Debt	As Percent of Gross Domestic Product
1970	$ 380.9	38.7
1975	$ 541.9	35.9
1980	$ 909.0	34.4
1982	$1,137.3	36.4
1984	$1,564.6	42.3
1986	$2,120.6	50.3
1988	$2,601.3	54.1
1990	$3,206.5	58.5
1992	$4,002.1	67.6
1994	$4,643.7	70.0
1996	$5,181.9	68.0
1998	$5,478.7	65.2

President Carter was responsible for deregulating four industries: oil, natural gas, airlines, and trucking. The prices of oil and natural gas to the American consumer were kept artificially low by government price controls. Carter decided to phase out such price controls in order to encourage U.S. companies to expand their search for new sources of oil and natural gas. In 1978 the president persuaded Congress to eliminate the Civil Aeronautics Board (CAB), which had regulated the airline industry for 40 years. The CAB had limited competition by assigning the routes that airlines could use and the rates they could charge. The CAB scaled back its rulemaking and rate setting and in 1985 went out of existence. U.S. airlines were then free to compete for customers without restriction (except for observing federal safety standards). Many small airlines could not compete and went out of business. Consumers had fewer low-cost fare options to choose from.

President Reagan went even further than Carter in calling for deregulation. He ordered the dozens of regulatory agencies in the executive branch to cut back their rulemaking and allow businesses greater freedom. Reagan weakened a number of regulatory agencies by appointing opponents of regulation to head the agencies. The Reagan years saw a huge increase in business mergers because little was done to enforce the antitrust laws. Also, President Reagan speeded up the deregulation of the oil industry (a policy begun by Carter).

Environmental and Civil Rights Policies

President Reagan's belief in reduced involvement by the federal government led to decreased support for environmental measures during his administration. For example, strip mining for coal increased. Laws protecting wildlife were enforced less vigorously. President Reagan believed that business must be encouraged if the high U.S. unemployment rate was to be reduced. He believed that environmental efforts would lead to higher costs for business and higher prices for consumers.

President Reagan's philosophy of reduced federal involvement and his support of "states' rights" led to a change of policy with regard to civil rights. President Johnson's Great Society had initiated the strongest civil rights legislation in the 20th century. President Reagan, on the other hand, decreased federal support for remedies to end discrimination such as busing and affirmative action. However, President Reagan did sign into law a bill establishing Martin Luther King, Jr., Day as a national holiday, the only nonpresident to be so honored.

Effects on Minorities President Reagan's policy of reducing government spending on social programs represented a setback for the poor during the 1980s. Because minorities made up a disproportionate share of those in poverty, major cuts in social programs meant that such groups as African Americans and Hispanic Americans did not benefit equally from the Reagan Revolution. In addition, minorities also suffered a setback by the decreased emphasis on affirmative action to end discrimination. As a result of Reagan's policies, the income gap between white and black Americans increased.

Continuing Political Progress for Minorities

However, even during this period, African Americans and Hispanic Americans made great political progress. In cities such as Atlanta, Detroit, Chicago, Los Angeles, and Philadelphia, African Americans were elected as mayors. In addition, Hispanic Americans were elected as mayors in cities such as San Antonio, Texas, and Miami, Florida. Hispanic Americans were also elected as governors in New Mexico and Florida.

In the 1980s, civil rights leader the Reverend Jesse Jackson recognized that ethnic minorities were a growing force in U.S. politics. After winning a strong following as a leader of African Americans, Jackson began to broaden his appeal and reach out to other minorities, women, and discontented farmers and workers. He referred to this multiracial and multicultural blend of peoples as the "Rainbow Coalition." In the election years 1984 and 1988, Jackson campaigned for the Democratic nomination for president. Though he fell short of winning a majority of delegate votes, he won national attention and came closer to being a presidential candidate than any other nonwhite American. In 1992 Jackson supported the election of Bill Clinton.

The Supreme Court and the Schools, 1962–1995

The following cases focus on the extent to which the Bill of Rights applies to students in a school context:

***Engel* v. *Vitale* (1962)**   In this case, the parents of several pupils in New York schools objected to a prayer composed by a state agency, the New York State Board of Regents. The prayer was meant to be nondenominational (neither Christian nor Jewish nor Muslim). The board recommended that students recite the prayer on a voluntary basis in public school classrooms at the beginning of each day. The Supreme Court ruled against the use of the prayer, arguing that it violated the principle of the separation of church and state.

***Abington School District* v. *Schempp* (1963)**   This case involved a Pennsylvania law requiring that at least ten Bible verses be read in public schools at the beginning of each day. The Schempps, a family in Abington, Pennsylvania, sued the school district for relief from this practice. They said that daily Bible readings went against their religious beliefs. The Supreme Court ruled in favor of the Schempps. It declared that reading from the Bible in a public school violated the First Amendment's guarantee against the establishment of religion.

***Tinker* v. *Des Moines School District* (1969)**   In this case, the Supreme Court decided that students could not be penalized for wearing black armbands to school to protest the Vietnam War. The Court argued that students do not "shed their constitutional rights to freedom of speech or expression at the schoolhouse gate."

***New Jersey* v. *TLO* (1985)**   In this case, a high school freshman in New Jersey had been found smoking in the school bathroom. She was made to open her purse. In her purse, school officials found wrapping paper for tobacco or marijuana, a list of students who owed her money, and a substantial amount of cash. The student was found to be delinquent and sentenced to one-year probation. The Supreme Court ruled that the school acted reasonably to maintain order and discipline. It held that reasonable suspicion for searches and seizures in schools need not be based on the "probable cause" provision of the Fourth Amendment.

***Vernonia School District* v. *Acton* (1995)**   In this case, the Supreme Court ruled that a school district has the right to institute a student athletic drug policy that includes the random testing of urine for drugs. The Court held that the policy did not violate the Fourth Amendment right to privacy of the students. It noted that student athletes are already required to take medical tests prior to approval for student teams. Thus, the addition of a drug test need not be based on suspicion of drug use among individual students. The Court held that the state may exercise a greater degree of supervision over students in public schools than it could exercise over adults.

★ In Review

1. Identify the following: supply-side economics, New Federalism, Tax Reform Act of 1986, budget deficits, deregulation.

2. Summarize the economic policies of President Reagan. Why are these policies known as the "Reagan Revolution"?
3. According to the Supreme Court, how does the Bill of Rights apply to students in a school context?

New Approaches to Old Problems

Many problems confronted by the American people in the 1980s and 1990s had their roots in the past. But the new conservatism required new solutions.

The Farmer's Dilemma: Feast or Famine

The history of farm production in the United States is a great American success story. Between 1940 and 1970, farmers doubled the amount of wheat they could grow on a single acre. In the same period, production of all crops per acre increased 66 percent.

At the same time, however, both the number of farms and the number of people engaged in farming steadily declined. In 1994 about 2.5 percent of the American people earned their living as farmers (compared to 38 percent in 1900). The decline of the small family farm was closely linked to the mechanization of farms in the 20th century. Expensive equipment made possible gains in productivity on large and medium-size farms. But farmers with small farms, who could not afford such equipment, found that they could not compete. By 1995 most farm acreage was controlled by large agricultural corporations.

Farm Subsidies Ever since the Great Depression, the federal government had paid subsidies to farmers to help them survive years when crops brought low prices. (A *subsidy* is a grant of money from the government to a private enterprise.) Laws enacted by Congress in 1973 and 1977 established target prices for basic crops such as wheat, corn, and cotton. If the market price for a crop fell below its target price, the U.S. government would pay farmers the difference between the two prices. The government policy encouraged farmers to produce more crops. On the other hand, the government also paid farmers if they used less of their land to raise crops. By the mid-1990s, many in Congress began to oppose farm price supports as too expensive.

Feast in the 1970s Farmers are always subject to sudden changes in the world demand for their crops. Theirs is a business of either feast (high demand, high prices) or famine (low demand, low prices). The 1970s were largely a boom time for American farmers. Prices for farm products were high partly because of increased exports to the Soviet Union and other nations. Encouraged by the federal government, farmers borrowed money to modernize farms and increase production. They made spectacular gains in productivity. In 1972 one American farmer produced enough to feed 53 people; by 1982 the same farmer could feed 78 people.

Famine in the 1980s But feast turned to famine in the 1980s. Farmers became the victims of their own success. When world demand for their crops declined, they were left with millions of tons of unsold grain and received low prices for the rest. Contributing to the lower prices was an embargo on the sale of grain to the Soviet Union. (As explained on page 546, the grain embargo was President Carter's response to the Soviet invasion of Afghanistan in 1979.) Farmers now faced high debts and declining income. Thousands of family farms went bankrupt.

In order to help farmers, President Reagan initiated two programs in the 1980s. The first program was called "Payment in Kind" (PIK). Farmers were paid in surplus crops held by the government for not planting on their land. It was hoped that this would reduce the oversupply that had led to reduced prices for farm products. A second program was made part of the Food Security Act of 1985. Again, in return for not planting crops on their land, farmers would receive payments from the government to help protect them from financial loss. Both federal programs provided aid to farmers at a difficult time, but increased the federal deficit. In the 1990s, exports of grain again helped to increase farm income.

Poverty in an Affluent Society—"The Underclass"

After World War II, most Americans lived comfortably on incomes high enough to sustain an affluent, or prosperous, lifestyle. Even so, during the 1960s, there were still millions of Americans who lived in poverty. President Johnson declared a "war on poverty" in 1964, partly because of an eye-opening book about poverty written by Michael Harrington, *The Other America* (1962). It depicted the lives of the poor in urban neighborhoods and rural communities. Harrington discussed the effect of poverty on the elderly, racial minorities, migrant farm workers, and the homeless. He urged the federal government to assume responsibility for helping the poor overcome the forces that kept them from participating fully in the American economy.

To a certain extent, Johnson's programs of assistance succeeded. Between 1960 and 1969, the number of Americans classified as poor by the government dropped from 40 million to 24 million. However, in the 1970s, the economic condition of stagflation (rising inflation coupled with unemployment) led to increases in poverty. In the 1980s, increasing numbers of homeless people slept in bus terminals and makeshift shelters on the streets of major cities.

Americans who suffered most from poverty included children, single women with children to support, African Americans, Native Americans, Latinos, migrant farm workers, and unemployed factory and mine workers.

Increased poverty was one cause of two other trends: an increase in the crime rate and an increase in the school dropout rate. In the 1980s, an inexpensive addictive drug, crack, worked its way into poor urban neighbor-

The cartoonist comments on the escalating defense budget, which reduced social programs to the status of beggars.

hoods. Drug use, drug wars, and crime made life more difficult for millions living in U.S. cities.

At the other end of the income scale, the wealthiest fifth of the U.S. population commanded a greater and greater share of total national income. In the 1980s, social scientists called attention to this fact and warned of the negative effect on American democracy if the income gap between rich and poor continued to widen.

In 1981 President Reagan argued that government programs to reduce poverty were not a solution but part of the problem. He believed that financial aid to all except the "truly needy" caused the poor to be permanently dependent on government funds. Many Americans, concerned about high taxes and budget deficits, supported the president's efforts to cut back on federal antipoverty programs. Reagan's critics blamed his cuts in welfare programs for the increasing numbers of homeless people. But some social scientists argued that the poor might represent a permanent "underclass" in American society and that no amount of government aid could effectively deal with the problem.

The "New" Immigrants

In 1986 Americans celebrated the 100th anniversary of a great national symbol—the Statue of Liberty. Ever since its completion, this statue had

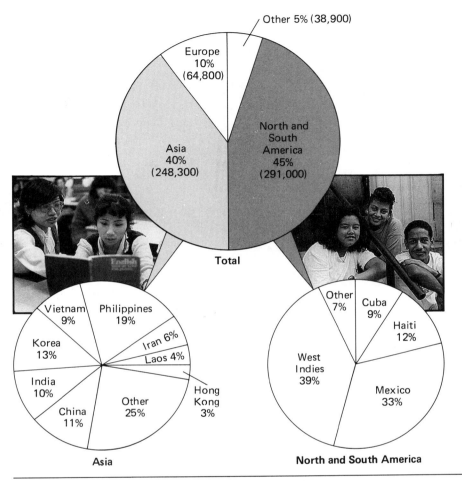

Other 5% (38,900)

Europe
10%
(64,800)

North and
South
America
45%
(291,000)

Asia
40%
(248,300)

Total

Vietnam
9%

Philippines
19%

Iran 6%

Korea
13%

Laos 4%

India
10%

China
11%

Other
25%

Hong
Kong
3%

Asia

Other
7%

Cuba
9%

Haiti
12%

West
Indies
39%

Mexico
33%

North and South America

Sources of Legal Immigration to the United States, 1989

greeted the arrival in New York harbor of immigrants from Europe. In the 1980s (as in the 1880s), the U.S. population changed rapidly as a result of a new wave of immigration. The "new new immigrants," as they were called, did not come from Europe. They came instead from Asia and Latin America. At the same time, immigrants from areas in turmoil (the Soviet Union, Eastern Europe, and Iran), as well as immigrants from India and Pakistan, added to the large number of new arrivals.

Immigration Act of 1965

Between 1921 and 1965, U.S. immigration laws had favored nationalities from western Europe and discriminated against people from other parts of the world. (Review Chapter 8.) This old quota system was ended in 1965 by a new immigration law that set the following criteria for determining who would be admitted as immigrants each year:

★ No more than 20,000 from any one country

★ No more than 120,000 from countries of the Western Hemisphere (Canada and Latin America)

★ No more than 170,000 from countries of the Eastern Hemisphere (Asia, Africa, Europe, and Australia)

★ Preference given to skilled workers and professionals and to those with family ties to U.S. citizens.

Under a 1953 law, the president had the authority to admit refugees fleeing from political oppression. President Ford used this authority to admit hundreds of thousands of Vietnamese, Laotians, and Cambodians after their countries fell to communism.

Illegal Immigrants In addition to the millions of "new new immigrants" admitted legally, there were millions of others who crossed the U.S.-Mexican border illegally. Facing high unemployment and poverty in Mexico, they escaped detection as they waded across the shallow Rio Grande. U.S. employers were often glad to hire them for low wages.

U.S. labor unions feared that the illegal Mexican aliens would undercut American workers by taking jobs for less than the minimum wage. (One report, however, said that three-fifths of the immigrants arrested as illegal workers earned more than the minimum.)

There were other reasons for opposing illegal immigration: (1) Illegal aliens did not pay taxes, and yet, because of their numbers, they placed a strain on city services and added to the cost of city government. (2) To permit illegal immigration to continue would be unfair to those other immigrants who had to wait patiently for years to gain lawful entry to the United States. These were two of the arguments used by members of Congress who wanted to control, and, if possible, eliminate, illegal immigration.

Immigration Reform and Control Act of 1986

Enacted with President Reagan's approval, the *Immigration Reform and Control Act of 1986* (the Simpson-Mazzoli Act) placed heavy fines on employers who knowingly hired illegal aliens. At the same time, the law permitted illegal aliens who had entered the United States before 1982 to remain here as legal residents. Opponents of the law warned about its potentially damaging effects. They argued that employers would fear to hire not just illegal aliens but also the millions of Hispanic Americans who were legal residents because certain proof of legality might be hard to obtain. Whether wise or unwise, the immigration control act has not stopped the flow of illegal immigrants across the Mexican-U.S. border.

Arguments for Encouraging Immigration Many social scientists have pointed out the economic benefits of increased immigration. They note that immigrants add to the economy by (1) purchasing goods and services and (2) paying taxes. In effect, immigrants may create jobs for native-born Americans rather than taking jobs away. Furthermore, if a decreased native birthrate produces a future labor shortage, there will be a growing need for skilled workers from abroad. The diverse backgrounds of immigrants enrich the culture of the United States.

Changing Demographic Patterns

People aged 65 and older are classified as "elderly" or "senior citizens." Because of advances in medicine and health care, the numbers of elderly Americans increased steadily. In 1999 they represented 13 percent of the U.S. population (compared to only 5.5 percent in 1930).

Increased Life Expectancy In 1900 there were no known cures for such common diseases as tuberculosis, influenza, pneumonia, and polio. Over the next 60 years breakthroughs in medical science brought these and other diseases under control. One of the most important discoveries was by a British scientist, Sir Alexander Fleming. In 1928 he discovered that some infections could effectively be treated with penicillin, a bacteria-killing acid derived from a mold. The discovery of penicillin (an antibiotic) and other lifesaving drugs accounted for major gains in life expectancy. In 1900 only 41 out of 100 Americans lived to age 65. By 1990 the number had risen to 79 out of 100. According to some population experts, the average baby born in the year 2010 will live to be 90.

As the number of elderly increased, so did their political influence. They knew that their health problems and medical bills would increase during years of retirement—years when their incomes would be relatively low. Many relied for their support on the monthly Social Security checks mailed to them by the U.S. government. For millions of elderly Americans in the 1970s and 1980s, the most important political issue was the future of the Social Security system.

The elderly organized powerful pressure groups that lobbied Congress for greater Social Security benefits. Two of the best known are the American Association of Retired Persons (AARP) and the Gray Panthers. They wanted higher monthly checks to keep pace with inflation. They also sought wider benefits under Medicare, the government's insurance plan for paying hospital and doctor bills for people 65 and over. Senior citizens won a major legislative victory in 1975 when Congress passed a law linking Social Security benefits to the cost of living. If inflation caused the cost of living to increase, Social Security benefits would also rise automatically. The new provision was known as a cost-of-living adjustment (COLA).

Increased Social Security Taxes Though needed by senior citizens, the increased Social Security benefits were extremely expensive, especially in the inflationary years of the late 1970s. To prevent the Social Security system from going bankrupt, Congress passed two laws:

★ A law of 1977 raising the Social Security tax. (Since the passage of the original Social Security Act of 1935, a Social Security tax has automatically been collected from workers' paychecks and employers. These taxes go into a special fund that pays the benefits of retired workers.)

★ The Social Security Reform Act of 1983. This law saved the Social Security system from financial collapse by (a) speeding up planned increases in Social Security taxes and (b) delaying for six months a scheduled increase in benefits.

Ever since the reform of 1983, money coming into the Social Security system has been enough to pay the benefits to which the elderly are entitled. However, social scientists predict that the system may again be in trouble early in the 21st century as the huge number of baby boomers (those born in the late 1940s and 1950s) retire from the workforce.

Social Security is a help, but life is still difficult for many of the elderly, who are apt to suffer from loneliness and fear of crime. Nursing homes and programs such as "meals on wheels" have attempted to meet their needs. But the quality of nursing-home care is uneven. For many elderly, the term "golden years" is inappropriate.

★ In Review

1. How did President Reagan attempt to solve each of the following problems? (a) the farmer's dilemma and (b) poverty in an affluent society.
2. What were the sources of immigration after 1975? How have these new immigrant groups affected American society?
3. What are the political, economic, and social implications of an increasingly elderly population?

Renewed United States Power Image

Since the beginning of the 20th century, U.S. policy toward Latin America has followed two different paths. Presidents of the Progressive Era (Theodore Roosevelt, William H. Taft, and Woodrow Wilson) followed the path of intervention. Sending U.S. Marines into the Dominican Republic, Haiti, and Nicaragua caused much resentment not only in these countries but also throughout Latin America. The United States reversed its interventionist policies in the 1930s. It then followed the path of the "good neighbor," as Franklin Roosevelt called his Latin American policy.

After World War II the United States tried to follow both the interventionist path and the "good neighbor" path at the same time. U.S. fears of Soviet influence and Communist revolutions caused President Kennedy to give aid to Latin American countries (the Alliance for Progress) and also to support an invasion of Cuba (the Bay of Pigs crisis). From then until the present day, U.S. policy has continued along both paths—economic assistance on the one hand, and military intervention on the other.

Central America and the Caribbean

As president, Ronald Reagan took a different view of politics in Latin America from prior presidents. He believed that the United States should readily intervene with military force if its interests were threatened. It was more important to act decisively in Latin America than to win Latin American's goodwill. This was in line with the traditional containment policy of opposing communism.

The Grenada Invasion   Grenada, an island nation in the Caribbean Sea, has a population of only 94,000. A few hundred American students were attending a medical school on the island when, in 1983, an uprising led to the overthrow of the democratic government by Communist forces. Shortly thereafter, believing that the medical school students were in danger, President Reagan ordered U.S. troops to invade the island. The invasion force quickly defeated the Cuba-backed Communist defenders and restored democratic rule to the island. Opinion polls showed that most Americans were pleased to see U.S. troops win this localized war.

Aid to El Salvador   Throughout the 1980s the Central American nation of El Salvador was torn apart by civil war. Both sides—the government's army and the rebel forces—were guilty of killing innocent people. President Reagan was convinced that the rebels, if successful, would establish a Communist government in El Salvador. To prevent this, he urged Congress to vote millions of dollars in military aid for El Salvador's government. Despite more than $600 million in U.S. aid, the civil war continued. Tens of thousands died in the bloody conflict. Finally, in late 1991, UN negotiators persuaded both sides to agree to a cease-fire and peace settlement.

Aid to the Nicaraguan "Contras"   Meanwhile, in nearby Nicaragua, U.S. aid was helping a rebel group to fight Nicaragua's Communist government. That government, which came to power in 1979, was known as the *Sandinistas*. The anti-Communist, anti-Sandinista forces were known as the *contras*. In 1982 and 1983, President Reagan urged Congress to supply the "contras" with financial and military aid. Congress did so. In 1984, however, Congress granted only financial aid for the "contras" and rejected the president's request for military aid. In 1986 Reagan once again persuaded Congress to approve military aid for the "contras."

The civil war in Nicaragua ended in 1990 when the Sandinista government permitted a free election to be held. The Sandinistas lost the election

Poor Contra goes to bed hungry every night. CONTRA ALSO HAS NO BULLETS FOR HIS GUN, NO ROCKETS, NO GRENADES AND NO FUN AT ALL. BUT WITH YOUR HELP, THERE IS HOPE. FOR JUST 100 MILLION BUCKS YOU CAN ADOPT A CONTRA OF YOUR VERY OWN. AND REMEMBER, YOU'LL NOT ONLY BE NOURISHING A FRAIL LITTLE BODY — YOU'LL BE OVERTHROWING A GOVERNMENT! WRITE YOUR CONGRESSMAN & ASK HOW YOU CAN ADOPT-A-CONTRA

"Adopt a Contra"—a critical view of undercover U.S. aid for military insurgents attempting to overthrow the government of Nicaragua

and peacefully turned over the government to the winning party and its moderately conservative leader. The United States provided aid to the new government. The "contras" disbanded, returning to civilian life.

The Iran-Contra Affair President Reagan did not expect the civil war in Nicaragua to end peacefully. Because Congress had refused to vote military aid for the "contras" in 1984, he had urged supporters of his policies to make private donations to the rebel cause. At the same time, in the Middle East, the president was having trouble freeing U.S. citizens who were being held hostage in Lebanon. What connection could there be between hostages in Lebanon and aid to the "contras" of Nicaragua?

In 1988 members of the press thought that they had found the missing connection. They discovered that U.S. officials had secretly arranged to sell weapons to Iran. This act alone violated a law of Congress banning the sale of U.S. weapons to that country. In addition, members of the press strongly suspected that the arms sale was made with the intention of winning the release of the American hostages in Lebanon. The press referred to this aspect of the affair as the "arms-for-hostages deal." Finally, money from the illegal sale of arms was secretly channeled to the "contras" of Nicaragua. This secret operation was carried out by a presidential aide and Marine lieutenant colonel, Oliver North. Investigating the Iran-Contra Affair, a congressional committee questioned Colonel North about his money-channeling operation. North testified that President Reagan knew nothing about his efforts to pass money from the Iranian arms sale to the "contras."

Although Colonel North's actions may not have been undertaken directly under orders by the president, some Americans compared the scandal to the Watergate Affair. Others believed that North had acted in the interests of his country.

Marines in Lebanon

To the north of Israel is Lebanon. Its population is divided between Christians and various groups of Muslims. Lebanon's constitution provides for the sharing of power among various religious groups. By the 1970s, Lebanon's Muslims outnumbered Christians. Palestinians in Lebanon's refugee camps then began to protest the government's pro-Western policies. In 1975 a fierce civil war erupted between the Christians and the allied Palestinians and Muslims.

Syria intervened by supporting the radical Palestine Liberation Organization (see pages 611–612) while Israel sent troops into southern Lebanon to retaliate for PLO terrorist attacks on Israel. In 1982 Israel bombarded the capital, Beirut, and demanded and won a Palestinian withdrawal from the city. To keep the peace in Beirut and assist in the UN-supervised withdrawal, President Reagan ordered U.S. Marines to the embattled city as peacekeepers, but this effort ended in tragedy. In 1983 a terrorist bomb exploded at the barracks near Beirut, killing 241 Marines. In 1984 President Reagan removed the troops.

Following the departure of the U.S. Marines, Syria assumed control over much of Lebanon, while Israel occupied a strip of southern Lebanon as a security zone to halt attacks against northern Israel. During the 1980s and 1990s, militant groups based in Lebanon launched rocket attacks and suicide raids against Israel, while Israeli forces retaliated with commando raids into southern Lebanon. The United States has urged both sides to resolve the conflict.

Economic Competition, Cooperation, and Boycott

For almost three decades after the end of World War II, U.S. foreign-policy makers tried to contain the advance of communism. In the 1970s, however, the United States became less concerned with Communist expansion and more concerned with economic competition from Japan.

Japan

Early in the 1970s, Americans discovered that they were buying more and more goods from Japan. Japanese cars on U.S. highways were an increasingly familiar sight. Japanese motorcycles, cameras, TV sets, and radios were now standard equipment in millions of American homes. Although consumers benefited from these high-quality imports, U.S. manufacturers and labor unions worried about losing business and jobs to foreign competitors.

Ever since World War I, the United States had been a creditor nation. In other words, the value of U.S.-made goods sold abroad (exports) was greater than the value of foreign-made goods sold in the United States (imports). In each year of the 1980s and 1990s, however, just the opposite occurred. Instead of being the world's largest creditor nation, the United States had become the world's largest debtor nation. By far, the widest gap between exports and imports was in U.S. trade with Japan.

How could the U.S. government help American manufacturers sell more goods abroad, especially in Japan? Since 1947 most nations of the world, including the United States, had participated in a series of diplomatic conferences called the *General Agreement on Tariffs and Trade (GATT)*. Each round of trade talks usually resulted in member nations of GATT lowering their tariffs. Honoring U.S. commitments to GATT, Reagan favored keeping U.S. tariffs low. He feared that raising tariffs to protect U.S. manufacturing would result in tariff wars and hurt both the world and the U.S. economies. The United States, however, continued to pressure Japan's government to change its economic policies. It objected to Japan's practice of placing quotas on the number of foreign goods that it would allow Japanese businesses to buy.

South Africa

During the major part of the cold war (1947–1977), U.S. policy makers were mainly concerned about stopping Communist forces from gaining control of African governments. In later years, beginning with the presidency of Jimmy Carter, the focus shifted to a question of racial justice in South Africa.

The Republic of South Africa was once a Dutch colony. The British took control of the colony after defeating the Dutch settlers in the Boer War (1899–1902). The Afrikaners, as people of Dutch descent called themselves, outnumbered the British and eventually, in 1948, won control of the government. Their republic broke all ties with Great Britain in 1961.

One of the first acts of the Afrikaner government in 1948 was to adopt a policy of strict racial separation. This policy of *apartheid* (an Afrikans word meaning "apartness") separated the people of South Africa into four racial groups: whites, blacks, Asians, and "colored" persons (mixed ancestry). Apartheid applied to all aspects of life. Socially, blacks had to live apart from the other races. Politically, they could not vote. Economically, they could work only in the lowest paying occupations. South African blacks had to carry identification passes and could enter white areas only for a limited time. South Africa's all-white government ordered many blacks to move to "tribal homelands" far from the coastal cities (even though blacks had never lived on the lands assigned to them).

The huge majority of the world's people are nonwhite. They viewed the racist policies of the South African government as an insulting carryover from the days when white Europeans ruled much of Africa and Asia. In the United Nations, a series of resolutions condemning apartheid and calling on UN members to stop trading with South Africa was passed.

Until the 1980s, the U.S. government did very little to oppose apartheid. Many U.S. businesses and even universities invested in South Africa's profitable gold, diamond, and uranium mines. However, the ruthless methods used by the South African government to enforce apartheid were widely reported on TV news shows and dramatized in the movies. At many U.S. colleges, students organized demonstrations against apartheid. A black South African opponent of apartheid, Episcopal Archbishop Desmond Tutu, traveled to U.S. cities to urge that the United States stop trading with South Africa. In 1986 Congress passed (over President Reagan's veto) an act placing an embargo, or ban, on trade with South Africa.

Partly in response to the worldwide pressures being brought to bear on its economy, South Africa in 1990 began to modify its policies. A new South African president, F. W. de Klerk, promised to integrate parks and beaches and to permit South African blacks to vote. In 1990, after spending 27 years in prison for opposing apartheid, black leader Nelson Mandela was released. On a tour of the United States, Mandela urged Americans to continue the U.S. trade embargo until apartheid ended. However, in July 1991, President George Bush pointed to the progress South Africa had made in phasing out racist policies and persuaded Congress to lift the U.S. embargo.

Mandela and De Klerk recognized the need for peaceful transition from white rule to a government elected by people of all races. In April 1994, the first South African elections were held in which all races could vote. Mandela's party—the African National Congress (ANC)—won a majority of seats in the legislature, and Mandela became South Africa's first black president. This transition to multiracial democracy led to an end of all U.S. boycotts of South Africa and increased cooperation between the two nations.

United States–Soviet Relations

The most startling change in world affairs in the last quarter of the 20th century was the end of the cold war between the Soviet Union and the United States. During its final 15 years (1974 to 1989), the cold war went through three phases. First, presidents Ford and Carter tried to improve U.S.-Soviet relations by continuing Nixon's policy of détente. Second, during Reagan's first term as president (1981 to 1985), relations between the superpowers once again became increasingly hostile. Third, after Mikhail Gorbachev came to power in the Soviet Union in 1985, he permitted the countries of Eastern Europe to free themselves from Soviet control. In the Soviet Union as well as in Eastern Europe, many aspects of communism were abandoned as unworkable. In effect, in 1989 and 1990, the Soviets more or less conceded that capitalism and Western-style democracies had their good points after all.

Arms Limitation Efforts

In 1972 President Nixon went to Moscow to meet with the Soviet leader, Leonid Brezhnev, and signed the first Strategic Arms Limitation Talks

Treaty (SALT I). It applied only to the future production of defensive nuclear missiles. Such missiles, which intercepted and destroyed attacking missiles, were known as antiballistic missiles, or ABMs. The United States and the Soviet Union agreed to set an upper limit on the number of ABMs that each would produce. Soviets and Americans alike hoped that this treaty would significantly reduce the risk of nuclear war. Now that defensive missiles were limited, there was less danger of one superpower thinking that it could rely on its defense capabilities in order to defeat the other.

Soviet and American diplomats worked for years to devise a plan for limiting various offensive, or attacking, missiles. In 1979 President Carter and Soviet Premier Brezhnev signed a second strategic arms treaty, SALT II. It established a ceiling on the number of long-range offensive missiles that each superpower could produce. It also limited the number of cruise missiles (low-flying weapons), which could be launched from airplanes and submarines.

Defense Spending and "Star Wars"

Many members of the U.S. Senate feared that the SALT II treaty left the Soviet Union with a military advantage. But the Senate never had a chance to vote either for or against SALT II. Early in 1980 President Carter withdrew the treaty from consideration after he received reports that Soviet troops had invaded Afghanistan.

Carter was especially disappointed in the Soviet Union because he had wanted détente to succeed. Ronald Reagan, on the other hand, had never believed that the Soviet Union could be trusted. In his 1980 campaign for the presidency, Reagan promised to increase military spending so that the United States could once again take the lead in the arms race. He kept his promise. In his first year in office, 1981, he asked Congress to approve huge increases in the defense budget for building new weapons systems. He wanted $1.5 trillion spent over a five-year period on new bombers, submarines, and missiles. While rejecting or trimming some of Reagan's program, Congress approved most of it.

"Star Wars": A cartoonist views the Reagan administration's planned missile-defense shield as a costly computer game.

The most ambitious and controversial of Reagan's proposals was to develop a "space shield"—the *Strategic Defense Initiative (SDI)*. Critics of the idea thought it sounded like the popular movie *Star Wars*. The weapons, as conceived by defense experts, would orbit the Earth and, from outer space, shoot down Soviet missiles before they could reach U.S. targets. Though skeptical about SDI's cost and practicality, Congress voted funds to explore the idea. Despite increased tensions, U.S.-Soviet relations generally improved. In 1993, the first defense budget of the Clinton administration cut off the SDI program after 10 years of development and an outlay of $30 billion. (The possibility of reviving the missile shield occupied the Clinton administration in the years 1999–2000.)

Gorbachev and Soviet-American Relations

Leonid Brezhnev, the Soviet leader since 1964, died in 1982. He had presided over the slow decline of his country's economy. His first successor died after only 15 months in office, the second after 13 months. In March 1985, the Soviet Communist party selected as leader Mikhail Gorbachev. Relatively young and energetic, he recognized national problems and proposed sweeping reforms to revitalize the Soviet system.

First, he told the people to speak their minds openly about public issues and not to fear penalties. (In the past, critics of government policy were arrested and imprisoned.) Gorbachev's new policy was called *glasnost* (openness).

The average Soviet shopper in the 1980s faced severe shortages of food and consumer goods.

Reagan (right) and Gorbachev sign an arms-reduction treaty.

A second policy—for economic reform—was called *perestroika* (restructuring). Gorbachev encouraged local bureaucrats and factory managers to make their own decisions rather than take orders from the central government. He wanted more privately owned businesses that could decide how to produce goods and make profits. Perestroika was a move away from a command economy toward a mixture of private businesses and government welfare.

Gorbachev realized that the Soviet economy could not improve if a large percentage of the nation's resources went to its armed forces. He observed that, because of Reagan's arms buildup, the United States might

A cartoonist's view of what Reagan and Gorbachev were really thinking when they met to discuss arms reduction.

soon be far ahead in the arms race. His country could no longer afford to strain its economic resources in an attempt to match U.S. armaments. Gorbachev was therefore eager to meet with U.S. leaders and reduce the costly and dangerous arms race. On three occasions he met with President Reagan to discuss arms control and other issues. At their third meeting in Washington, D.C. (December 1987), the two leaders made a significant breakthrough by signing a treaty to reduce missiles in Europe. These were missiles of intermediate range that could travel hundreds of miles (compared with longer-range ICBMs that could cross oceans). The Intermediate-range Nuclear Forces Treaty (INF Treaty) went far beyond the SALT treaties. Instead of just limiting future production of weapons, the INF Treaty provided that all intermediate-range missiles in Europe be removed and dismantled. Gorbachev and Reagan established 1990 as the year when Europe would be completely free of intermediate-range nuclear weapons.

★ In Review

1. Identify and explain the significance of each of the following: Grenada, *Sandinistas*, "contras," Iran-Contra Affair, trade deficit, apartheid, Nelson Mandela, SALT II, Strategic Defense Initiative, Mikhail Gorbachev, glasnost, perestroika, INF Treaty.
2. Explain how each of the following posed a challenge to U.S. foreign policy: El Salvador, Nicaragua, civil war in Lebanon, South Africa.
3. To what extent did Reagan's foreign policy represent a return to traditional themes of cold war and power politics?

Chapter Review

MULTIPLE-CHOICE QUESTIONS

Use the cartoon on page 556 to answer questions 1 and 2.

1. The cartoon shows that after the 1980 election,
   (1) there were no more liberals or progressives in the federal government
   (2) the executive branch had become liberal while the legislative branch had become more conservative
   (3) conservatives captured the presidency and much of Congress
   (4) the Supreme Court was making more conservative decisions to appease President Reagan.

2. The most likely explanation for the situation depicted in the cartoon was
(1) greater public sympathy for affirmative action programs
(2) the desire of Americans to return to an isolationist foreign policy
(3) the narrowing of economic opportunity during the 1970s
(4) a more youthful electorate.

Base your answers to questions 3 and 4 on the following excerpt from President Reagan's first inaugural address:

> . . . . it is not my intention to do away with the government. It is rather to make it work—work with us, not over us; to stand by our side, not ride on our back. . . .

3. In making this statement, President Reagan was appealing to a philosophy that would have been most approved by
(1) Thomas Jefferson
(2) John F. Kennedy
(3) Franklin D. Roosevelt
(4) Lyndon B. Johnson.

4. President Reagan was attempting to appeal to the American tradition of
(1) equality
(2) democracy
(3) individual freedom
(4) big government.

Refer to the cartoon on page 558 and answer questions 5 and 6.

5. The cartoon is referring to President Reagan's
(1) stand against government regulation of business
(2) position on affirmative action programs

(3) opposition to the Sandinista government in Nicaragua
(4) economic policy.

6. The cartoonist felt that
(1) benefits for the wealthy would eventually benefit the middle class and the poor
(2) Reagan's economic policy would have the greatest benefit for the middle class
(3) the poor would get fewer but adequate benefits from Reagan's economic policy
(4) Reagan's economic philosophy would benefit the rich and have progressively smaller benefits for the middle class and the poor.

Base your answers to questions 7 and 8 on the cartoon on page 571.

7. The cartoon deals with U.S. foreign policy toward
(1) Eastern Europe
(2) the Far East
(3) Latin America
(4) Africa.

8. The cartoonist was suggesting that the United States should
(1) attempt to overthrow foreign governments
(2) submit international disputes to the United Nations for binding arbitration
(3) provide foreign nations with military aid
(4) not interfere with the internal affairs of another nation.

Use the cartoon on page 575 to answer questions 9 and 10.

9. The cartoon depicts the proposal for the Strategic Defense Initiative ("Star Wars") as
(1) realistic
(2) impractical

(3) in need of more research
(4) easy to accomplish.

10. The taxpayer in the cartoon is
(1) enthusiastic about SDI
(2) in need of more information about SDI

(3) concerned over the potential cost of SDI
(4) demanding that SDI be abandoned to safeguard Social Security funds.

THEMATIC ESSAYS

1. Theme: "Reaganomics," a Conservative Revolution

The election of Ronald Reagan to the presidency of the United States marked a change in federal economic policy that has been called no less than a "conservative revolution."

Task

★ Describe two aspects of the Reagan philosophy of dealing with the U.S. economy (Reaganomics).

★ Describe two specific examples of how President Reagan applied the principals of Reaganomics to the economy of the United States.

★ Show a specific effect of one of the applications that you selected on a specific group.

You may use, but are not limited to, examples dealing with various federal social programs, taxation, federal regulation of business and industry, and relations with organized labor.

2. Theme: President Reagan and Military Spending

In spite of a conservative economic policy, the administration of President Reagan significantly increased the defense budget.

Task

★ Describe one reason why President Reagan increased the defense budget at the same time that he was reducing spending in most other areas.

★ Discuss one specific economic effect of added defense spending on the U.S. economy.

★ Evaluate the wisdom of increased defense spending in light of the specific impact that it had on other aspects of the U.S. economy.

In your answer to the first part of the question, you may use, but are not limited to, a discussion of the Strategic Defense Initiative (SDI or "Star Wars") and President Reagan's foreign policy.

In answering the second part of the question, you may wish to discuss the national debt or the costs of increased military spending on other specific segments of the national budget.

DOCUMENT-BASED QUESTION

*Read each document and answer the question that follows it. Then read the **Task** and write your essay. Essays should include references to most of the documents along with additional information based on your knowledge of United States history and government.*

Historical Context: Many people credit or blame President Reagan for substantially changing the nature of the United States as well as the world in which it exists.

Document 1 Refer to the cartoon on page 557.

Question: What does the cartoon say about President Reagan's priorities in the federal budget?

Document 2 From a 1982 address by President Reagan to the American people concerning political developments in Central America:

My fellow Americans, I must speak to you tonight about a mounting danger in Central America that . . . will grow worse . . . if we fail to take action now.

. . . With over a billion dollars in Soviet-bloc aid, the Communist Government of Nicaragua has launched a campaign to subvert and topple its democratic neighbors.

Using Nicaragua as a base, the Soviets and Cubans can . . . threaten the Panama Canal, interdict our vital Caribbean sea lanes and, ultimately, move against Mexico. Should that happen, desperate Latin peoples by the millions would begin fleeing north into the cities of the southern United States, or to wherever some hope for freedom remained.

The United States Congress has before it . . . an aid package of $100 million for the more than 20,000 freedom fighters struggling to . . . eliminate this Communist menace at its source. . . . We are not asking for a single dime in new money. We are asking only to be permitted to switch a small part of our present defense budget—to the defense of our own southern frontier. . . .

Question: What was President Reagan asking Congress and the American people to do regarding the Sandinista government in Nicaragua?

Document 3 Refer to the cartoon on page 577.

Question: According to the cartoon, what difficulties were going on at the Reagan-Gorbachev summit meeting?

Document 4 Refer to the cartoon on page 565.

Question: What was the cartoonist saying about spending priorities during the Reagan administration?

Document 5   Refer to the table on page 560.

Question: What happened to the federal debt during the Reagan years (1981–1989)?

Document 6   Refer to the photograph on page 576.

Question: What does the photograph show about the economy of the Soviet Union prior to its collapse?

Task

★ Describe and evaluate the success of President Reagan's foreign and domestic policies.

★ Explain what the long-term results of President Reagan's foreign and domestic policies are on the United States of today.

Chapter 22
Approaching the New Century:
1989–2000

★ Objectives

★ To examine the domestic issues that arose during the presidencies of George Bush and Bill Clinton.

★ To identify the forces and events leading to the end of the cold war and the dissolution of the Soviet Union.

★ To analyze the role of the United States in the global economy.

★ To evaluate presidential responses to foreign policy challenges in the Persian Gulf, Somalia, Haiti, the Middle East, Bosnia, Yugoslavia, Iraq, North Korea, and Russia.

The approach of the 21st century turned American interest toward the future. As the Reagan era ended, Americans became more concerned with domestic programs such as Social Security, Medicare, and tax reduction. In addition, disagreements over such issues as abortion, affirmative action, campaign finance reform, and gun control became more pronounced. Americans realized that the policies established over the next decade would serve as a bridge to the next century.

The Bush Presidency

Reagan's conservative policies were carried into the 1990s by his successor, George Bush. As Reagan's vice president for eight years, Bush was closely identified with Reagan's basic philosophy. Before becoming vice president, Bush had gained wide and varied experience as a congressman from Texas, director of the Central Intelligence Agency (CIA), and U.S. ambassador to the United Nations.

The Election of 1988

George Bush had no trouble winning the Republican nomination for president in 1988 and not much trouble defeating the Democrats' candidate, Governor Michael Dukakis of Massachusetts. Bush's vice president was Senator Dan Quayle of Indiana.

Effects of Demographics The election of George Bush demonstrated the growing importance of the suburbs in national elections. As incomes rose and people moved from urban areas to the suburbs, they became more concerned about such issues as lowering taxes, reducing government spending, reducing crime, and curbing the sale and use of illegal drugs. These issues were strongly supported by Republicans. As a result, many suburbanites who had formerly voted for Democratic party candidates changed their votes to Republican party candidates. (The people who changed parties were sometimes referred to as "Reagan Democrats.") In his campaign, Bush promised to fight crime and drugs and improve education without raising taxes. He depicted Michael Dukakis as being soft on crime. Voters responded to Bush's message and gave him 53 percent of the popular vote and 426 of 538 electoral votes.

Influence of Political Action Committees Many special interest groups form *political action committees (PACs)* to contribute money to presidential campaigns. Examples of special interest groups include farmers, senior citizens, labor unions, tobacco companies, gun lobbies, and oil companies. These groups contribute indirectly to the campaigns of candidates who are believed to be in agreement with their positions. They are forbidden by federal law to give money to individual candidates. The money goes to efforts to get out the vote and promotion of issues favored by the group and the candidates. With the cost of campaigns increasing because of the expense of buying television time for political advertisements, candidates and parties

President George Bush

began to rely more heavily on political action committees and their efforts to promote issues. If issue advertisements were being paid for by PACs, a candidate would not have to buy television time to publicize the same issue.

Domestic Issues

As president, Bush called for states to assume a larger role in domestic programs. In so doing, he was following Reagan's New Federalism.

Environmental Concerns   As you recall from pages 441–442, a major oil spill by the oil tanker *Exxon Valdez* occurred by 1989 off the shores of Alaska. Many environmentalists complained that the federal government reacted too slowly to clean up the spill. As a result, much of the wildlife in the region perished. Further, President Bush continued President Reagan's policy of deregulation in order to make businesses more competitive with foreign companies. These reduced regulations weakened enforcement of such environmental measures as the Clean Air Act.

Economic Concerns   A business boom in the 1980s was marked by heavy consumer spending, high interest rates, and a low savings rate. The general prosperity ended in 1991 as the economy slipped into recession. Layoffs in most industries pushed the unemployment rate up to 7 percent. The federal government cautiously tried to effect a recovery. Hoping to increase consumer and business borrowing, the Federal Reserve Board reduced the discount rate (interest charged to member banks).

Tax Increases   During his election campaign of 1988, George Bush was often asked whether he would ever raise taxes in order to reduce the budget deficit. "Read my lips," he would always say, "no new taxes." President Bush remained true to his campaign pledge until the summer of 1990, when he stated that new taxes might be necessary after all.

Crisis Over Deficit Reduction   As the federal deficit continued to rise, neither the president nor Congress could avoid raising taxes any longer. According to the 1985 *Gramm-Rudman-Hollings Act*, measures had to be taken to balance the federal budget by the early 1990s. If Congress failed to devise a plan for reducing deficits to zero, the law provided for automatic budget cuts in all departments of the executive branch.

In 1990, after months of debate, President Bush and Congress agreed on a deficit-reduction plan that raised taxes and cut federal spending. The income tax rate for the wealthy was raised from 28 to 31 percent. Federal excise taxes on cigarettes, alcoholic beverages, and gasoline also went up. The plan provided for large cuts in military spending and smaller cuts in a number of social programs.

Conservatives and liberals alike objected to the new tax law. Conservatives criticized President Bush for agreeing to new taxes, thereby violating his campaign pledge. Liberals attacked Bush's unwillingness to make the very wealthy bear more of the tax burden.

Bailout of Savings and Loan Associations   Another heavy burden on the government and the economy was the failure of hundreds of *savings and loan associations (S&Ls)*. The problem was caused by unwise, reckless, and perhaps illegal investment and loan decisions by S&L owners. Because the U.S. government insured the savings deposited in the bankrupt businesses, it was obligated to pay depositors. To recover its losses, the government took over and tried to sell property of the failed S&Ls. The bailout cost taxpayers more than $300 billion. They were outraged.

Social Concerns: Supreme Court Cases

***Texas* v. *Johnson*, 1989**   If a person burned a U.S. flag in public, could that person be arrested and punished under a state law? This question was answered by the Supreme Court in 1989 in the case of *Texas* v. *Johnson*. The Court ruled that the First Amendment right to freedom of speech applied to a U.S. citizen who had burned the U.S. flag as an act of protest. Therefore, Texas's law against desecrating (harming) the U.S. flag was declared unconstitutional. In 2000 the U.S. Senate narrowly failed to pass a constitutional amendment outlawing the burning of the American flag.

***Cruzan* v. *Director, Missouri Department of Health*, 1990**   This case involved the issue of termination of life-support systems for persons in a vegetative state. A young woman, Nancy Cruzan, had suffered major injuries in an automobile accident and was lying in a vegetative state in a Missouri hospital. Her parents wished to terminate her life-support system because there was no evidence of brain function, but the hospital refused to honor this request. The case eventually reached the Supreme Court, which ruled that a state may require that there be clear and convincing evidence that an individual did not want to be sustained by a life-support system before terminating the system. This evidence may be in the form of a living will.

***Planned Parenthood of Southeastern Pennsylvania, et al.* v. *Casey*, 1992**   In this case, five abortion clinics in Pennsylvania challenged the state's law requiring teenagers to obtain their parents' consent for an abortion. The Supreme Court upheld this law as constitutional. On the other hand, it said that its original ruling in *Roe* v. *Wade* was still valid. A state could limit but could not ban abortions.

The Family in Crisis

In the last decades of the 20th century, one change stood out as supremely important for the future of American society. In little more than a generation, between 1960 and 1990, the American family weakened and lost some of its ability to care for children's economic and emotional needs.

In 1966 the divorce rate was twice as high as in 1950. Divorce became so common that two out of every five children born during the 1970s could expect to see their parents' marriage break up before these children turned 16. By the 1990s, half of all marriages ended in divorce.

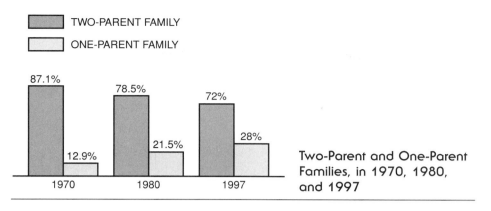

TWO-PARENT FAMILY

ONE-PARENT FAMILY

87.1%

78.5%

72%

28%

21.5%

12.9%

1970   1980   1997

Two-Parent and One-Parent
Families, in 1970, 1980,
and 1997

The high divorce rate severely affected two groups: women and children. As single parents, divorced women suffered income loss and emotional strain. Some children suffered emotionally from seeing their parents separate. If they lived with their mother, which most did, they shared her economic plight, which worsened when fathers withheld child support. Government at all levels tried to find ways to make sure fathers paid court-awarded child support.

Married women sought employment outside the home in record numbers during the 1970s and 1980s. By 1990, 60 percent of married women were in the labor force (compared to just 25 percent in 1950). Also in the labor force were thousands of single mothers. Women worked outside the home because they wanted to use their talents and education. Growing numbers, though, worked to help pay family expenses because one income was not enough.

Mothers who worked outside the home had to make arrangements for all-day care of preschool children and after-school care of youngsters in elementary school. Many older children had to spend time alone until a parent or caregiver arrived.

As the 1990s began, the number of mothers of preschool children working for wages was about equal to the number staying home. Traditionally, men and women alike had assumed that child care was the mother's responsibility. Feminists questioned this traditional assumption, asking why fathers should be relieved of the hundreds of tasks involved in the care of children and the home. Although some men tried to adopt new habits in the home, most of them left the burden of child care and other domestic chores to their wives. Thus, whether they were married or divorced, women with children at home and a job outside the home were badly overburdened. The day-care centers to which they brought their young children were seldom ideal or even adequate. In addition child care was costly. Through the 1980s the women's movement focused on winning the support of federal and state lawmakers and businesses for providing satisfactory day-care and nursery-school centers.

Effects of Drug Abuse

The use of illegal drugs has been a problem in the United States since the late 1940s. On college campuses in the 1960s, increasing numbers of students smoked marijuana and adopted the slogan, "Tune in, turn on, and drop out." At the same time, teenagers and even preteens began buying and selling illegal drugs as part of a widening network of organized crime. Drug abuse increased further in the 1980s with the sale of a low-priced drug, crack.

The effects of illegal drugs on U.S. society were devastating. City police departments and state and federal courts had to devote more and more of their resources to arresting and prosecuting "pushers" (sellers) of illegal drugs. But because of the demand for drugs among people of every social class, law enforcement officials found it nearly impossible to stop or even reduce the illegal sale of drugs in major cities. Fulfilling a campaign promise, President Bush in 1989 declared an all-out "war on drugs" involving the expenditure of more than $7 billion a year.

Addiction to drugs was partly responsible for increases in violent crime (murder, rape, robbery, and assault) and property crime (burglary, larceny, and auto theft). In the 1980s, the rate of violent crime went up by nearly 30 percent. Law enforcement officials ascribed much of the increase to the widespread use of illegal drugs.

Drug abuse also contributed to the AIDS epidemic. Unknown before 1981, AIDS (acquired immunodeficiency syndrome) had caused the deaths of more than 200,000 people by the mid-1990s. The two most common ways for the AIDS virus to enter a person's body was through sexual contact and the practice of sharing needles to inject an illegal drug into the bloodstream.

Foreign Policy Issues

During the 1990s, violent struggles for power challenged U.S. allies and U.S. interests. The United States responded to a number of crises, including an invasion of Panama and a war against Iraq. A weakened Soviet economy, Gorbachev's policies, and long-suppressed nationalism brought an end to the cold war and led to both peaceful revolution and violent civil strife in Eastern Europe.

Invasion of Panama During his first year as president, George Bush decided to use U.S. troops to remove from power the Panamanian dictator, Manuel Noriega. After coming to power in the late 1980s, Noriega had regularly violated the human rights of Panamanian citizens. He was also suspected of being involved in the smuggling of illegal drugs into the United States. Two U.S. grand juries indicted Noriega on drug trafficking charges. In December 1989, President Bush decided to treat Noriega as an international outlaw. He ordered a surprise attack and invasion of Panama in order to drive Noriega from power and prevent the Panama Canal from

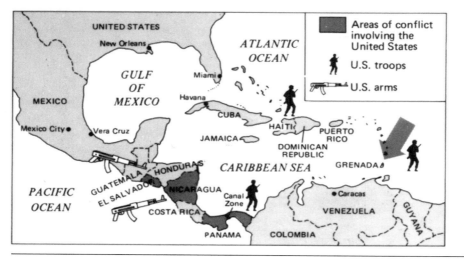

U.S. Interventions in Latin America in the 1980s and 1990s

falling under Noriega's control. The invading U.S. forces met little resistance. They captured Noriega and brought him to the United States for trial. Their task accomplished, most U.S. troops returned home. (Noriega was convicted in a federal court and sentenced to jail in the United States.)

Some troops remained to oversee a free election. The new government of Panama was friendly to the United States and received U.S. aid. Leaders of other Latin American countries, however, condemned the U.S. invasion as an act of aggression.

The Decline of Communism

Dramatic proof of the decline of communism occurred with amazing suddenness. In June 1989, Poland held free elections, and the Communists lost. Because Gorbachev favored reform and openness, the Soviet Union accepted the result of the Polish election.

Soon, one country after another in Eastern Europe followed Poland's example. The people of Hungary, Czechoslovakia, and Romania held mass demonstrations and demanded free elections and the end of Communist rule. In Romania, the long-time ruler, Nicolae Ceausescu, launched a bloody attack on demonstrators, vowing to remain in power. Within days he was overthrown and executed. In most of Eastern Europe, the people voted to replace the Communist system with multiparty systems.

Fall of the Berlin Wall and German Reunification (1990) East Germany was the last country behind the "iron curtain" (under Communist and Soviet control). In 1989 the Communist grip on power showed signs of weakening. In an effort to save itself, East Germany's government permitted East German citizens to travel freely to West Germany.

The fall of the Berlin Wall in 1989 is celebrated by joyous Berliners.

In November 1989, Germans on both sides of the Berlin Wall, a hated symbol of German division and the cold war, tore it down, and East Germans crossed directly into West Berlin. Soon, the West German government was accepted by East Germans as the government for all of Germany. The World War II allies—Great Britain, France, the United States, and the Soviet Union—agreed to a reunited Germany, which became official in October 1990. The government of the new Germany, meeting in Berlin, pledged never again to take military action against its European neighbors.

For the first time since the beginning of World War II, the nations of Eastern Europe were free from outside control. The "iron curtain" dividing Europe into two hostile camps had collapsed.

End of the Cold War

George Bush began his presidency in 1989, the year that communism collapsed in Eastern Europe. On a ship near the Mediterranean island of Malta, he and Gorbachev held their first summit. Most observers now believed that cold-war politics had passed into history. There were signs of a new world order. One was U.S. willingness to provide food and economic aid to the Soviet Union. Another was Soviet willingness to support U.S. policy against Iraq, which was threatening its neighbors.

Besides the decline of communism and the dismantling of nuclear weapons systems in Europe, there was greater cooperation in the United Nations. During the cold war, the Security Council had usually been deadlocked by superpower rivalry. Now, the Security Council could pass important resolutions. In 1990, for example, it voted to condemn Iraq for its invasion of Kuwait. (See pages 592–595.) President Bush noted that the end of the cold war freed the United Nations to do its intended job—keep the peace.

Dissolution of the Soviet Union

In December 1991, after months of turmoil, the Soviet Union ceased to exist as a single nation. In its place were 15 independent republics, most of which joined a loose confederation called the *Commonwealth of Independent States (CIS)*.

There were both economic and political reasons for the collapse of the former superpower:

Economic Failure Gorbachev had hoped that his reform policies of *glasnost* and *perestroika* would spur economic growth. Instead, the Soviet economy continued its rapid decline. Fewer goods reached the marketplace, and long lines formed to buy the goods that were available. Critics called for an end to the old system.

Yeltsin's Rise to Power Chief among those impatient with Gorbachev's policies was a radical reformer, *Boris Yeltsin*. In 1987 he broke with Gorbachev and resigned from the Communist party (then the only legal one). In 1990 Yeltsin and several other non-Communists were elected to the newly created legislature, the Congress of People's Deputies. In 1991 Yeltsin was elected president of the Russian republic. His demands for reform and his openness made him a popular figure.

Failed Coup Attempt Increasingly, Gorbachev allied himself with conservatives in the Communist party. However, in August 1991, these hard-liners tried to oust Gorbachev and seize control of the government. Their attempted *coup* (seizure of power) was quickly defeated when Moscow's citizens, led by Yeltsin, blocked the path of Soviet troops. The troops refused to attack the crowd. Those who plotted the coup were arrested. Yeltsin's decision to risk his life fighting the coup leaders made him a national hero.

Independence for the Republics In 1991 all 15 republics in the Soviet Union demanded their independence. The first to succeed were the republics of Lithuania, Latvia, and Estonia, which had been taken over by the Soviet Union during World War II. Independence for the remaining republics became official on December 8, 1991, when the presidents of Russia, Ukraine, and Byelorussia (or Belarus) declared that the Soviet Union was "dead." They formed the new Commonwealth of Independent States (CIS), open to all republics. Shortly afterward, Gorbachev resigned as Soviet president.

Effects on U.S. Foreign Policy   In a meeting at Camp David, in February 1992, President Bush and Boris Yeltsin declared that the cold war had officially ended.   The two leaders also agreed to make deep cuts in their arsenals of long-range nuclear weapons. Yeltsin assured the United States that nuclear missiles of the former Soviet Union would remain safely under central control. The United States joined other Western nations in pledging to give emergency aid to the struggling Russian economy.

Crisis in Bosnia

A major problem facing the Bush administration in Eastern Europe was the breakup of Yugoslavia and the ensuing civil war in Bosnia, one of its former republics.   Founded after World War I, Yugoslavia consisted of six republics. One of these republics, Serbia, exercised the most control. In 1991 Bosnia declared itself independent. The following year, the United States recognized Bosnia's independence. Bosnia consisted of three major ethnoreligious groups—Bosnian Muslims, Serbian Orthodox Christians, and Croatian Roman Catholics.

Because the Serbs dominated Yugoslavia, they opposed the breakup of the country. In addition, many Bosnian Serbs were opposed to Bosnian independence because they feared living as a minority within a Bosnian state. The Serbs' opposition to this move led to a brutal civil war involving the three groups. Serbs killed thousands of Muslims and engaged in "ethnic cleansing" (expulsion of Muslims and non-Serbs from areas under Bosnian Serb control). The civil war resulted in thousands of deaths on all sides. Millions of Bosnian Muslims and others became refugees.

Crisis in the Persian Gulf

In the 1980s, the four major producers of oil in the Middle East were Saudi Arabia (the largest), Kuwait, Iran, and Iraq. All four are located on the shores of the Persian Gulf. Between 1980 and 1988, Iran and Iraq fought a costly and brutal war. Iraq won small gains in territory.

Iraq's Invasion of Kuwait   Shortly after the Iran-Iraq War, Iraq's military dictator, Saddam Hussein, accused Kuwait of taking an unfair share of oil revenues. In August 1990, claiming that Kuwait was a part of Iraq, he invaded and occupied it. The invasion and occupation received wide news coverage around the world and led to a third energy crisis in 1990 that caused the price of gasoline and heating oil to increase sharply. To pressure Iraqi forces to withdraw, the United States and the United Nations voted to place an embargo on Iraqi oil. The resulting drop in oil supplies quickly led to even higher fuel prices.

The Iraqi invasion alarmed President Bush and other world leaders for three reasons. First, it was an act of aggression by a strong nation against a weaker one. (Iraq in 1990 had the fourth largest military force in the

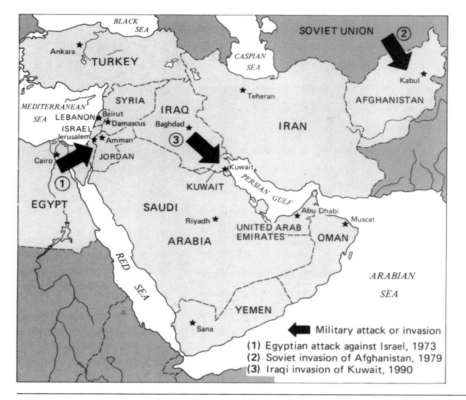

Invasions in the Middle East, 1973–1990

world.) Second, the taking of Kuwait opened the way to an Iraqi conquest of the world's largest oil producer, Saudi Arabia. Third, Iraq's military power and aggressive actions would allow it to dominate the other countries of the Middle East.

To prevent further aggression, President Bush ordered U.S. troops to Saudi Arabia. "We have drawn a line in the sand," said the president, as he announced a defensive effort called Operation Desert Shield. U.S. troops were joined by forces from a UN-supported coalition of 28 nations, including Great Britain, France, Saudi Arabia, Syria, Turkey and Egypt.

Members of the UN Security Council, including both the United States and the then Soviet Union, voted for a series of resolutions concerning Iraq's aggression. One UN resolution demanded Iraq's unconditional withdrawal from Kuwait. Other resolutions placed an international embargo on trade with Iraq and authorized UN members to use force if Iraqi troops did not leave Kuwait by January 15, 1991. As the January deadline neared, members of Congress debated whether or not to authorize the president to send U.S. troops into combat in the Persian Gulf. Both houses voted in favor of the war resolution.

U.S. forces in the Persian Gulf War

Operation Desert Storm After the deadline expired, thousands of planes from allied bases in Saudi Arabia took part in massive air strikes against military targets in Iraq and Kuwait. There was no effective resistance and little loss of life among U.S. and allied forces.

The major Iraqi response was to launch Scud (Soviet-made) missiles against both Saudi Arabia and Israel. The missiles did little damage. Recognizing that Saddam Hussein wanted to win Arab support by provoking an Israeli counterattack, Israel did not retaliate.

After more than a month of round-the-clock bombing attacks, U.S. and allied forces launched a massive ground attack against Iraqi positions in both Kuwait and southern Iraq. The demoralized Iraqis offered little resistance. They surrendered by the tens of thousands as allied tanks swept

Cartoon of Saddam Hussein protesting his innocence while stockpiling chemical weapons

Cartoon showing that rising oil prices cause pain and hardship for many consumers

across the desert toward Kuwait City and into Iraq itself. Saddam Hussein was now forced to concede defeat. In accordance with the UN resolution, all Iraqi forces not captured by the allies withdrew from Kuwait. On the evening of February 27, 1991—six weeks after the first air strike and only 100 hours after the ground war began—President Bush went on television to announce that the war had been won. He said, "Kuwait is liberated. Iraq's army is defeated. Our military objectives are met." Operation Desert Storm, as Bush called the U.S. war effort, had ended in a rapid and over-whelming victory.

As part of the cease-fire agreement, Iraq agreed to eliminate all poison gas and germ weapons and allow UN observers to inspect weapons-storage sites. To enforce the agreement, the UN imposed trade sanctions (penalties) that were to remain in effect until Iraq complied with all terms. Another concern was that Hussein would order air attacks against Iraq's minority Kurdish population in the north. In order to prevent this and show hu-manitarian concern, the United States created safe havens for the Kurds in-side Iraq and established a "no-fly" zone in northern Iraq.

Effects of the War   The Persian Gulf War liberated Kuwait and ruined Sad-dam Hussein's ambitions to control Mideast oil prices and supplies. The war also demonstrated military cooperation between the nations of West-ern Europe and the United States. Russia supported U.S. resolutions in the UN. Saddam Hussein, however, remained in power as Iraq's dictator. Bush was criticized for not sending troops into the Iraqi capital to oust the dic-tator. UN inspection teams in Iraq suspected that Hussein was acquiring nuclear, chemical and biological weapons.

★ In Review

1. Identify each of the following and explain its significance: political action committee, savings and loan bailout, ethnic cleansing, Oper-ation Desert Storm.

2. For each of the following Supreme Court cases, identify the constitutional issue involved and summarize the decision: (a) *Texas v. Johnson*, 1989; (b) *Cruzan v. Director, Missouri Department of Health*, 1990; and (c) *Planned Parenthood of Southeastern Pennsylvania, et al. v. Casey*, 1991.
3. Discuss the role of economics and political leadership in bringing about an end to the cold war.

The Clinton Presidency

The economy remained sluggish as the Republicans nominated President Bush and Vice President Quayle for reelection in 1992. Bush cited the U.S. victory in the Gulf War and the end of the cold war as major achievements of his administration and blamed the Democratic majority in Congress for stalling his economic programs. The Democratic nominee, Governor Bill Clinton of Arkansas and his running mate, Senator Albert Gore of Tennessee, blamed economic ills on Bush and said it was "time for a change." The biggest voter turnout in 20 years elected Clinton after 12 years of conservative Republican leadership.

In 1996 Clinton was elected to a second term. Americans now felt optimistic about the improving economy and the president's increasingly moderate approach to social and economic issues. Clinton won 379 electoral votes to 159 for his opponent, Kansas Senator Robert Dole. Republicans, however, kept their majorities in both houses, which they had established in the 1994 congressional election. Clearly, many voters felt unable to endorse fully the positions of either party.

Third-Party Candidate   Texas billionaire H. Ross Perot, an independent candidate for president in the election of 1992, spent millions of dollars buying TV time to present his programs. He promised to end the deficit and revive U.S. global competitiveness. His early following decreased after he dropped out of the race, only to reenter it later. However, he succeeded in capturing about 19 percent of the popular vote.

Domestic Issues

Following his election in 1992, President Clinton supported some liberal legislation (health care reform, gun control), but as a fiscal conservative, cut federal spending, federal jobs, and the budget deficit.

The election of Democrat Bill Clinton in 1992 marked a shift away from the conservative policies of presidents Reagan and Bush. After his inauguration, Clinton moved quickly to fulfill his campaign promises to address many social and economic problems. Working with Democratic majorities in both houses of Congress, Clinton succeeded in getting a family and medical leave bill passed. It granted employees 12 weeks of unpaid leave from

President Bill Clinton, speaking at a town meeting, presents his proposals for a national health plan.

work to care for newborn infants and family members who are ill. He also pushed through approval for a program called Americorps (modeled on the Great Society program VISTA) for enlisting young people in community service projects. In addition, President Clinton dealt with issues such as health care, education, welfare reform, and the Social Security system.

Health Care How to help individuals pay for the rising costs of modern medicine was a problem Clinton wanted to tackle. He assigned his wife, Hillary Rodham Clinton, to head a task force to propose a plan for reforming the U.S. health care system. The plan that the Clintons proposed to Congress had two main objectives: (1) to ensure that all Americans were covered by health insurance and (2) to prevent the total costs of medical care from consuming more and more of the national wealth. Various groups, such as small businesses and the insurance industry, vigorously opposed the plan. Their views were widely reflected in Congress. By mid-1994, it was clear that legislative action on health care reform would be indefinitely delayed. In fact, no major health care legislation would pass for the remainder of the Clinton administration.

Education Throughout the 20th century, Americans placed enormous stress on the benefits of public education. But since the early 1970s, educators have issued alarming reports about low levels of student performance on standardized tests. Few agreed about how to improve schools and student performance. Conservatives urged a "back to basics" approach (more math, reading, and writing). Liberals proposed restructuring schools to make teachers, parents, and students part of the decision-making process. Government at all levels lacked funds for ambitious programs.

Nevertheless, in the mid-1990s, a reformist goal of achieving national standards in education set off debate among conservatives, moderates, and liberals. In this debate, President Clinton clearly favored national standards and increased federal aid to schools. The president's proposals had an impact on state governments, which began to increase local standards. In New York, for example, new standards called for three years of mathematics and the sciences, and the passing of related Regents exams in order to be eligible for a Regents-endorsed diploma.

Welfare Reform In 1996 President Clinton signed into law a welfare reform bill that made sharp cuts in the amount of money that the federal government spent for welfare programs. The new law provided federal welfare funding in the form of block grants to states and required welfare recipients to work. The legislation was strongly supported by the Republican Congress. As it was implemented, welfare costs dropped nationwide.

Stability of the Social Security System Ever since the reform of 1983, money coming into the Social Security system has been enough to pay the benefits to which the elderly are entitled. However, social scientists predict that the system may again be in trouble when the aging baby boomers begin to retire from the workforce. At that time, it is anticipated that the number of younger workers who will be funding the Social Security system will de-

A cartoonist contrasts American students' poor skills with the highly developed ones of students in other lands.

crease. In addition, those who collect Social Security receive increases in payments when the cost of living increases. Thus, there is concern that by 2030, the Social Security system may not be sufficiently funded.

Gays in the Military   One of the first policy changes that President Clinton made when he began his term of office was to remove the long-standing ban against homosexuals serving in the armed forces. To make the military more comfortable with the change, Clinton said that gays could serve but only if they remain silent about their sexual preferences ("don't ask, don't tell"). The policy stirred up controversy in both the military and civilian sectors.

Women in Government   In order to carry out a campaign promise, President Clinton appointed a number of women to top posts. For example, in 1993 Janet Reno became the attorney general and Ruth Bader Ginsburg was appointed to the U.S. Supreme Court. In 1997 Madeleine K. Albright was appointed secretary of state. Women also gained stronger representation in Congress after the election of 1992. Barbara Boxer and Dianne Feinstein of California, Carol Moseley-Braun of Illinois, and Patty Murray of Washington won Senate seats. The number of women in the House increased from 28 to 47.

Economic Concerns in the 1990s

The U.S. economy received more attention than any other domestic issue in the conservative era from 1974 to 2000. Americans were aware that their entire society was undergoing economic change in those years.

Role of Technologies   Technological changes occurred so rapidly in the postindustrial age that nobody—not even scientists—could keep up with all that was happening. The following account gives only a small sampling of new technologies and their effect on U.S. society.

Of all the new technologies, computers were the most revolutionary. By the 1990s the personal computer was widely recognized as a powerful communications tool with nearly infinite uses—as a tool of instruction in the classroom, a word processor, a keeper of records, a calculator and problem solver, and a means for tapping into information files known as data bases. A vast computer network, the *Internet*, became a major attraction for personal computer users and speculative business entrepreneurs eager to exploit the new technology for profit. Increasingly, consumers used the Internet to make purchases of all types of services and products, and E-mail became an important means of communication, often replacing letter writing and telephone calls.

One problem with computerized files of information was that they might permit businesses and government agencies to invade a person's privacy. For a small user's fee, almost anyone could look at a data base listing names of people who had, for example, once been arrested or failed to pay a debt. What was to stop strangers from gaining access to embarrassing or harmful information? Should there be laws regulating the use of computerized records? By the mid-1990s, citizens were gradually becoming aware of this potential threat to their basic rights to privacy.

By the year 2000, companies producing new technological products and services were replacing older corporations as the businesses with the greatest market value.

Additional technological developments in science led to *cloning* (reproduction of offspring from only one parent without fertilization) and the development of genetically altered foods. By the late 1990s, scientists were able to clone animals such as sheep. They were also able to produce new forms of genetically altered soybeans and corn. In addition, in 2000 scientists engaged in genome research were able to identify the complete sequence of human DNA.

Impact of the Baby Boom Generation   The term "baby boom generation" refers to those who were born soon after World War II ended. With many soldiers returning from the war, an end to the Great Depression, and increased prosperity, Americans began to have more children in the late 1940s and in the 1950s than the generations preceding and following them. These baby boomers will reach retirement age early in the 21st century. As a result, there is concern that the contributions of the current generation to the Social Security system will not be sufficient to continue to pay Social Security benefits at the same level as retirees now receive. Thus, legislation was passed that gradually raised the age for collecting full Social Security benefits from 65 to 67 years of age. Other effects of the aging of the baby boom generation have been the growth of retirement facilities and an increased sale of prescription drugs and vitamins.

Coping with Budget Deficits   The national debt doubled from $1 trillion to $2 trillion during the Reagan presidency in the 1980s. During the Bush years, the problem of the federal deficit did not go away. How to deal with the problem was a major issue in the presidential election of 1992. One of Bill Clinton's first acts as president was to submit to Congress a comprehensive plan for reducing the deficit. Because his plan called for higher taxes, it was opposed by every Republican in Congress and by many Democrats. But in August 1993, the deficit-reduction bill passed by one vote each in the Senate and House. The measure provided for (1) an increase in the top income tax rate (to 36 percent), (2) a slight increase in the federal tax on gasoline, (3) spending cuts, and (4) a deficit reduction totaling $496 billion over five years.

By 1994 the recession's end was signaled by a significant decline in unemployment. This economic upturn occurred despite layoffs of employees by major corporations and several interest rate increases by the Federal Reserve Board to curb inflation. By 1995 the economy appeared to be healthy, and Clinton claimed that he was the first president in the last 12 years to reduce the federal deficit. Nevertheless, the deficit was more than $4 trillion and still a matter of national concern.

From HERBLOCK ON ALL FRONTS (New American Library, 1980)

In a cartoonist's view, the computer now keeps a watchful eye over its human creators.

President Clinton reduced both federal spending and federal employment. He and Vice President Albert Gore promised to examine every federal expenditure to determine if it was necessary and wise. They called this program the "reinvention of government."

Republican Midterm Victories By 1994, there was increasing dissatisfaction with the Clinton administration. Some Americans believed he was too liberal on social issues. Others were disappointed with his leadership and his failed national health plan. As a result, Republicans won control of both the House and the Senate for the first time in 40 years.

In these congressional elections, the Republicans campaigned on a platform known as the "Contract With America." They pledged to pass within 100 days legislation on a balanced-budget amendment, term limits for Congress, and welfare reform. They argued that the federal bureaucracy was wasteful and that the federal government's spending was out of control. They wanted a small central government, with many of its functions and powers transferred to the states.

By eliminating federal guidelines and reducing the federal bureaucracy, Republicans hoped to cut government spending. President Clinton opposed major portions of the Contract With America because he feared they would hurt the poor and the middle classes.

Stock Market Trends: The Bull Market A period of rising stock prices is referred to as a *bull market*. From 1987 through the end of the 1990s, the investment sector surged forward in a strong bull market. For example, in 1987 the Dow Jones average (a grouping of the stock of 30 major companies) stood at 2,000. By 1999 the Dow Jones average had increased to more than 10,000, a five-fold increase. One of the major reasons for this increase was the growth in new technology businesses. The United States became a world leader in the production of computers, computer chips, and operating systems. The value of these technology companies also rose rapidly.

One consequence of the new bull market was the increased wealth of those who were heavily invested in stocks and those who worked for the new technology-based corporations. As wealth increased in the late 1990s, Federal Reserve chairman Alan Greenspan, fearful of possible inflation, began to slowly raise interest rates in an attempt to slow the economy and the stock market buying and selling.

The general public seemed confident that the economic boom would continue and kept up their spending for all types of products. They were also reassured by the lowest unemployment rate—4 percent—in 40 years.

Political Concerns in the 1990s

The Republican congressional victory in 1994 led to conflicts with President Clinton over political issues. These conflicts were not ones that could be easily resolved.

Senate Whitewater Investigations Prior to his election as president, Bill Clinton had been governor of Arkansas. While serving as governor, he and his wife, Hillary Rodham Clinton, had taken loans from an Arkansas bank and purchased land in the Whitewater region in Arkansas. It was believed that the value of land in this area would greatly increase. Questions arose regarding both the loans and the purchase of the land. A special Whitewater committee was established in the Senate to determine if Clinton had acted improperly and violated the law. Soon afterward, there were allegations that both the president and his wife were attempting to keep important documents from the committee.

After more than a year of investigation, the committee reached no conclusions regarding the president's role in Whitewater. Further investigation was left to a special prosecutor appointed by Attorney General Janet Reno. In September 2000, the investigation ended without charges.

Gun Control The issue of gun control is related to the Second Amendment of the Constitution. On one side are those who cite the statement in the amendment that says "the right of the people to keep and bear arms shall not be infringed." On the other side are those who note that the right to bear arms refers to a "well-regulated militia," another phrase in the Second Amendment. In 1993 Congress passed and the president signed the Brady Bill that called for a five-day waiting period and background checks by local officials before a handgun could be sold. (James Brady had been wounded in an assassination attempt on President Reagan in 1981.) However, in 1996, the Supreme Court held that local officials could not be required by Congress to conduct background checks. The Court cited the division of powers between the federal and state governments.

As a result of increasing violence involving guns in the United States, the issue of gun control became even more controversial. Advocates for gun control pointed to events such as the shootings in Littleton, Colorado, in April 1999. In that terrible event, two teenagers armed with guns killed 13 of their fellow students and a teacher and wounded 30 others in Columbine High School. Despite the tragedy, Congress could not agree on gun legislation. The National Rifle Association (NRA), the main lobbying group opposed to gun control, argued that people rather than guns kill people. Others, such as Long Island, New York, Representative Carolyn McCarthy, whose husband had been shot and killed on the Long Island Railroad, argued that guns must be made more difficult to obtain.

As a result of several lawsuits against gun manufacturers, a major gun company announced in March 2000 that it would place child safety locks on all handguns sold in the United States. In return, the federal government and some cities agreed to drop their lawsuits against the company.

Campaign Finance Reform The amount of money spent on elections by the two major political parties has long been an issue of concern to many Americans. In 1974 a federal law was passed that established disclosure requirements for campaign contributions and set specific limits on donations to individual candidates. Unlimited contributions to political parties or organizations for party-building and issue-education activities were allowed. (These contributions are called "soft money.") In spite of the restrictions on soft money, these funds were often used to benefit specific candidates. The 1974 law also began public financing of presidential elections and created a Federal Election Commission. In 1976 aspects of the campaign finance law were declared unconstitutional by the Supreme Court in *Buckley* v. *Valeo*. In this decision, the Supreme Court ruled that placing mandatory spending limits on federal candidates and limiting the spending by supporters on behalf of federal candidates is unconstitutional. The Court declared that these limitations reduced freedom of expression as guaranteed in the First Amendment as well as the ability to communicate ideas with regard to political issues. The Court noted that "every means of communicating ideas in today's mass society requires the expenditure of money."

In the presidential election of 1996, more than $2.5 billion was spent by both parties, a record for campaign expenditures. On December 1, 1998, auditors for the Federal Election Commission ruled that both major parties had violated campaign finance laws by spending party funds on the specific campaigns of the presidential candidates. However, the Federal Election Commission did not accept the auditors' report. Subsequently, several individuals were convicted of making illegal contributions to the Clinton-Gore campaign. In fact, the Democratic party was forced to return approximately $1 million in contributions.

Part of the problem in financing campaigns is the high cost of television advertising. There is also the long campaign process, starting with the primaries and ending with the general election. Expenses for polling, travel, and staff mount up over the months, particularly in a presidential campaign. So far, efforts to pass a campaign finance reform bill in Congress have been unsuccessful.

Impeachment and Acquittal A special prosecutor had been appointed by Attorney General Janet Reno to investigate President Clinton's involvement in the Whitewater Affair. Eventually, in 1998, the investigation turned from Whitewater to President Clinton's sexual involvement with a White House intern. Despite the president's denials, evidence was found that such an involvement had occurred.

At the same time, an Arkansas woman brought a sexual harassment lawsuit against the president, claiming that while governor of Arkansas, Clinton had made unwanted sexual advances toward her. Although the president wanted to delay the case until he finished his term, the Supreme Court ruled unanimously that the case must proceed. As a result, President Clinton reached an agreement with the special prosecutor to provide testimony on videotape rather than in open court. In his testimony in the harassment case, the president denied any sexual involvement on his part with the intern or the Arkansas woman. These denials led to a call for impeachment charges based on the evidence that the president did have a sexual involvement with the intern.

In November 1998, President Clinton settled the harassment lawsuit, but he admitted no wrongdoing. In December 1998, the House of Representatives, controlled by Republicans, voted to impeach Clinton on two charges, the first impeachment charges since those brought against Andrew Johnson in 1868. The president was charged with perjury (providing false and misleading testimony under oath before a grand jury) in the harassment case and obstruction of justice (attempting to influence others to conceal his relationship with the intern). The accusations were not specifically about the affair but about the president's response to the allegations. The proceeding then moved to the Senate. As specified in the Constitution, the chief justice, William Rehnquist, presided over the trial. On February 12, 1999, the Senate failed to find President Clinton guilty of the charges. With 67 votes required to convict on either count, the perjury charge failed, with 55 voting against and 45 in favor, while the obstruction of justice charge tally was 50 voting against and 50 in favor. As a result, President Clinton was acquitted and remained in office.

THE AMERICAN PEOPLE
Changes at the Millennium

★ POPULATION

One thing about the people of the United States—they do not stand still. They are always moving about, leaving one city or state, settling down somewhere else. Moreover, as a group, they keep getting a makeover. They get older or younger, richer or poorer, more male or more female. Ethnically and religiously, they tend to get more diverse. So what's new? That's the way it has been for centuries—not just in the United States, but all over the world. It's just a fact of life: populations change. Everywhere.

Geographic Shifts

One of the most obvious ways in which the U.S. population has changed is in where it lives.

Westward Ho When the Revolutionary War ended in 1783, the population was concentrated in 13 states along the Atlantic seaboard. For the next two centuries, the population has shifted westward. The United States has extended its boundaries to the Pacific and acquired Alaska, Hawaii, and distant possessions.

To the Sun Belt Since the 1960s, the shift has been as much to the South as to the West. Until well after World War II, the Northeast and the Midwest had prospered as centers of industrial growth. But many steel mills and factories fell behind as their equipment aged and newer industries with the latest technology sprang up in other countries and in other parts of the United States. Able to produce more goods at

States With Fastest-Growing Populations in the 1990s

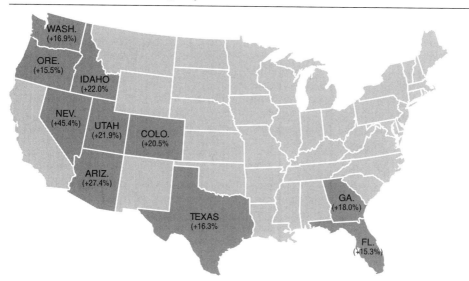

WASH. (+16.9%)
ORE. (+15.5%)
IDAHO (+22.0%)
NEV. (+45.4%)
UTAH (+21.9%)
COLO. (+20.5%)
ARIZ. (+27.4%)
TEXAS (+16.3%)
GA. (+18.0%)
FL. (+15.3%)

★ Population by Region, 1960–2000 ★
(in thousands)

	1960	1970	1980	1990	2000 (est.)
Northeast	44,678	49,041	49,135	50,809	51,800
Midwest	51,619	56,572	58,866	59,669	59,600
South	54,973	62,795	75,372	85,446	96,900
West	28,053	34,804	43,172	52,786	59,400

lower cost, the newer industries seized the lead and many older ones had to close. As factories fell into disuse, people began calling the older centers of industry the *Rust Belt*.

Newer industries thrived in the South and West, where the cost of living was lower and employer-friendly laws helped to keep wages down. Job seekers moved to where the jobs were. The population of the Sun Belt (as people began calling the South and West) grew faster and faster.

A Mobile Population Americans have always had the reputation of footloose wanderers who do not stay put. In early days it was the availability of land on the frontier that often drew people away from their homes. Nowadays, it is likely to be the lure of a better job or less traffic congestion or a shorter commute. Each year, just over 15 percent of the U.S. people move to a new home, down from about 18 percent in the late 1960s. Two times out of three, movers stay in the same state and the same county. But about 5 percent of U.S. residents each year move farther afield, to another county or state.

Who's Rich? Who's Poor?

Wealth and poverty are not evenly distributed across the United States. Economic distinctions occur along geographic, racial, ethnic, and other lines.

Geographical Differences Some communities and states have concentrations of wealth or poverty—or both. Fairfield County, Connecticut, for example, has a per capita (for each person) income that is roughly twice the national average. Other places with unusually high per capita incomes include such major cities as New York and San Francisco and certain suburbs in major metropolitan areas. Just because per capita income is high does not mean a place has little poverty, though. Both New York City and San Francisco have concentrations of extreme poverty not far from their wealthiest neighborhoods.

On a statewide basis, the richest states are Connecticut, New York, and Massachusetts. The poorest are Mississippi, West Virginia, and Arkansas.

Poverty Level Since the 1960s, the federal government has defined a poverty level based on assumptions about how much money a person or a family of various sizes needs to meet basic needs. The threshold (or dividing line) is adjusted each year to reflect changes in the cost of living. For a family of four, the poverty threshold is now about $17,000. Nationally, about 13 percent of people fall below this level, but the proportion is much higher in some states. The states with the highest percentage of people below the poverty level (21 to 17 percent) are New Mexico, Louisiana, and Arkansas. But the highest rate of all (22 percent) is in the District of Columbia.

Racial and Ethnic Differences Wealth and poverty also divide along racial and ethnic lines. White people are more likely than black people or Hispanics to be wealthy—and less likely to be poor. In the late 1990s, 10.5 percent of whites, 26.1 percent of blacks, and 25.6 percent of Hispanics fell below the poverty level. Other groups with high rates of poverty include Native Americans and Pacific islanders. Nonetheless, the typical American living in poverty is white, with 23 million poverty-level whites compared to 9 million African Americans and 8 million Hispanic Americans.

A Widening Gap? Some reports in recent years have shown a widening gap between the wealthiest and the poorest segments of the population. Back in 1970, the wealthiest 5 percent of Americans received 15.6 percent of all income. Nowadays that figure has grown to 20.7 percent. In contrast, the poorest 20 percent of the population— a group four times as large as the wealthy 5 percent group—received 5.4 percent of the nation's income in 1970. It is now down to 4.2 percent. Reasons

for the trend include tax cuts that have favored wealthier people more than poorer people, a decline in high-paying factory jobs, and an increase in the proportion of service jobs (such as hamburger flipper or bank teller) that pay relatively low wages.

Diversity of Religious Beliefs

One defining characteristic of the U.S. population is the variety of religious beliefs that people hold. A sizable majority of the population (86 percent) identifies itself as Christian—some 59 percent being Protestant and 27 percent Catholic. (Protestants themselves are divided among hundreds of denominations and sects.) Another 2 percent of the population is Jewish, and 5 percent express a preference for other religions, such as Muslim, Buddhist, or Black Muslim. The remaining 7 percent of the population either has no religious beliefs or declines to specify a preference.

Generations on the March

Since the generation of baby boomers appeared after World War II, Americans

Births in the United States, 1946–1996

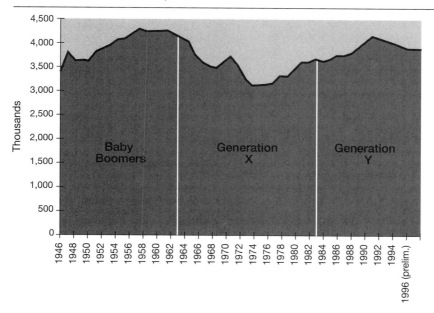

have paid close attention to the succession of generations. Companies that sell products to young people are always eager to know when a new bulge in population is coming. After all, they want to sell as many trendy athletic shoes or soft drinks or game machines as they can. In the final decade of the 20th century, the up-and-coming generation was called Generation X. These were defined as people born between 1964 and 1983. Now that most Gen X'ers have passed out of their teens, marketers are targeting Generation Y, or people born since 1983. *Business Week* called the Gen Y'ers "a generation that rivals the baby boom in size—and will soon rival it in buying clout."

Each successive generation has been more racially diverse than the one before. About two-thirds of Gen Y'ers are white and one-third are of another race.

The 2000 Census

Much of what we know about the U.S. population comes from a census that is conducted every ten years by the U.S. Bureau of the Census. The 2000 census gathered both basic information (how many people live in each household?) and more specific details (how many people had jobs? how did they travel between home and work?). After each census, the latest population figures are used to make adjustments in how many representatives each state sends to Congress and to redraw the districts from which members of Congress and state legislators are elected. Thus, the census results have very real effects on Americans' lives.

★ HOUSEHOLDS

As U.S. families have undergone rapid change in recent years, the very definition of "family" has begun to blur. Nowadays people sometimes place nontraditional living arrangements (homosexual partners, for example) in with other types of "families." So just where do we stand? How common are the various types of living arrangements in the United States today?

The Household

The basic unit in which people organize their living arrangements is called the household. A household often contains a group of individuals related by blood or marriage or adoption—in other words, a family in the traditional sense. But a household is not necessarily a family. A household may be a single person living alone. It may be two or more unrelated individuals living together—college roommates, for example. Or it may be a combination of related and unrelated people sharing a home.

The size of the average U.S. household has been steadily dropping over the years. In 1940, the average household held 3.67 persons. Since 1985 the average has hovered between 2.7 and 2.6 persons. Of course, if fewer people live in each housing unit, then more housing units must be created. Older homes and apartments have been divided into multiple dwellings, and builders have scrambled to put up new apartments and houses.

A Place for Children

Almost all children under the age of 18 live in a household with someone to whom they are related. Seven out of ten children (68 percent) live with two parents, biological or adoptive, while most of the rest (27 percent) live with a single parent. Between 5 and 6 percent of children live with grandparents—often with one or both parents as well.

In recent years there has been a sharp rise in the number of children being reared by a single parent (usually a mother) who has never been married—or by two parents who have never been married. This fact is a reflection of four wider social trends—a tendency of couples to marry later in life than in the past, an increase in divorce, an increase in cohabitation (the living together of unmarried couples), and a rise in out-of-wedlock births.

Living arrangements for young people over the age of 18 have been changing too. In the face of high costs for renting an apartment or buying a home, and with marriages coming later than in the past, more and more young adults are staying on with their parents. Nowadays roughly 12 percent of 25- to 34-year-olds live with their parents, up from 8 percent in 1970.

Living Alone
The proportion of U.S. residents who live alone has been on the rise. As recently as 1960, roughly 13 percent of all households contained just one person. Nowadays single people make up 25 percent of all households. Those most likely to live alone are older people (mainly women) who have divorced or whose spouses have died.

Gay Couples
A nontraditional type of household is the sort formed by two people of the same sex who consider themselves to be a couple. Such homosexual unions have become more visible since the start during the 1970s of the gay rights movement, patterned on the civil rights movement.

Gay males and lesbians have campaigned for laws prohibiting discrimination on the basis of sexual orientation—and a handful of cities and states have passed such laws. A number of companies now provide gay couples with "family" job benefits such as health insurance for a nonworking domestic partner. In addition, some states provide for ways in which gay couples can adopt and rear children. And the clergy of some U.S. religious groups perform marriage ceremonies

Adults Living Alone, by Age Group, in the Late 1990s

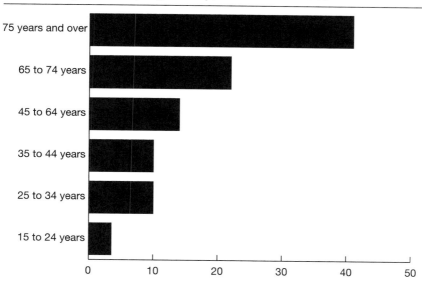

for same-sex couples. In 2000, Vermont became the first state to create a type of civil marriage for gays, with such benefits as tax breaks, inheritance, and the right to make medical decisions for a partner. About half the states have laws barring official recognition of gay unions, however.

"Empty Nesters"

Older couples whose children have grown up and moved away are known as "empty nesters." With improvements in health care and other factors, people now live longer than in the past. Thus, empty nesters represent an increasing proportion of the population.

What Does the Future Hold?

Demographers have made predictions about what further changes we can expect. They see the following trends:

★ A continued increase in the age at which people marry—but a slower increase than in the recent past. This will mean a continuing decline in the proportion of households containing married couples.

★ A modest decline in the divorce rate, which has already dropped slightly after reaching a peak in 1979. This may help to slow the rate of increase in the proportion of children raised by single parents.

★ In the future, children who live with a single parent are somewhat more likely than now to be living with their father, although most single-parent families will continue to be headed by women.

★ CITIES

In 1900, St. Louis had a population of 575,000 and was the fourth largest city in the United States. One hundred years later, the population of St. Louis had shrunk to 339,000, and it was no longer in the top 10 or even the top 40 U.S. cities. By the end of the 20th century, it ranked a mere 50th, behind such Sun Belt cities as Phoenix, Arizona; San Jose, California; and El Paso, Texas.

St. Louis was not the only U.S. city to experience falling population in the late 20th century. Other cities that ranked in the top five in 1900—New York, Chicago, Philadelphia, and Boston—did manage to close the century with more people than they began with. But all lost population over the second half of the century.

In fact, the years from 1950 to 2000 saw many old-line cities shrink as newer cities—some of which had originally been suburbs of larger cities—grew rapidly and moved up in rank. Two of the fastest-growing cities in the country have been Henderson, Nevada, and Plano, Texas—cities that have grown up in the shadow of Las Vegas and Dallas. Henderson (with more than 150,000 residents) and Plano (with more than 200,000) are now larger than such old-line cities as Syracuse, New York, and Providence, Rhode Island. Unlike the gritty industrial cities of the Northeast, the newer cities have few old-style "smokestack industries" or factories. Instead, they feature neighborhoods of single-family homes interspersed with office parks and shopping malls.

Urban Decline and Revival

For a time in the 1970s, Americans seemed ready to give up on big cities. Massive traffic jams clogged streets and freeways. Slums expanded as middle-class families moved out to suburbs and landlords boarded up apartment buildings or rented shabby rooms to low-income families. Many jobs migrated to the suburbs too. With people and businesses leaving and urban properties deteriorating, tax revenue dropped and city governments slashed their budgets. Meanwhile, urban crime rates soared.

By the dawn of the 21st century, however, crime rates were sharply lower and many cities were taking on a new luster. Construction crews were busily putting up new office towers and downtown sports stadiums—for example, San Francisco's PacBell Park and Detroit's Comerica Park. In some cities, civic centers and chic shops and trendy restaurants had restored nightlife to downtowns that had been shutting down at the close of the business day. Warehouse districts and empty lots had "morphed" into sleek residential neighborhoods occupied by professional singles and couples. Many older neighborhoods also spruced up as higher-income people replaced poorer people—a process known as *gentrification* (being taken over by "the gentry," or "the upper class").

Many of the reviving cities had shrunk to a smaller version of their previous selves, with populations down by 20 percent, 30 percent, and more. U.S. cities seemed to be proud of their makeovers. "Less can be more, if the 'less' are affluent singles and couples that replace families. They pay taxes and have no dependents," said a researcher of urban trends.

Not everyone welcomed the gentrification process, however. Advocates for the poor and for minorities argued that gentrification often meant the conversion of apartment buildings into single-family homes. That reduced the supply of housing for poorer people, they said, and led to increased crowding of poor people into other neighborhoods.

Attack on Urban Problems

Efforts to attack urban problems have undergone a considerable evolution in recent years.

Urban Renewal From the 1930s to the 1970s, federal, state, and local governments sponsored a variety of programs known as *urban renewal*. The focus was on bulldozing run-down neighborhoods and replacing them with new government buildings or parks or freeways. Efforts were made to find or build new housing for people whose homes were torn down. Often, however, those people ended up in worse housing than before. African Americans sometimes complained that urban renewal amounted to "black removal."

Cities like Chicago and St. Louis built blocs of multistory apartment buildings that tended to isolate the poor and concentrate their social problems. Notorious housing projects like Pruitt-Igoe in St. Louis and Cabrini-Green in Chicago became crime-filled ghettos. (Pruitt-Igoe was demolished in 1972. Twenty-eight years later, plans were announced to dynamite Cabrini-Green.)

Increased Federal Role The creation of the U.S. Department of Housing and Urban Development (HUD) in 1965 marked a new stage in federal involvement in urban life. HUD distributed funds to local governments to replace run-down housing with subsidized apartments for the poor. In recent years it has promoted mixed-income townhouses and low-rise apartments in place of the high-rise tenements of the past.

Attracting Businesses and Private Investors Recent efforts to rebuild downtown neighborhoods and revive city life have involved a mixture of public and private investments. By offering tax breaks to private investors, cities like Detroit have lured major corporate offices and new retail businesses into the downtown area.

Urban revival in downtown Boston, Mass., uses the buildings of an earlier time for present-day purposes.

Both Republicans and Democrats have supported some form of subsidy to businesses that invest in depressed areas. An *enterprise zone* program was started under President Reagan in 1986. Its purpose was to offer tax credits for investments in housing. In 1993, President Clinton proposed and Congress passed a new program. The aim of the legislation was to link tax breaks for businesses to job-training and other social programs. Detroit is one of six cities and three rural areas designated as *empowerment zones* under the 1993 program.

Mixed-Use Development The goal of many urban redevelopment efforts these days is *mixed-use development*. That means a combination of residential, business, and entertainment opportunities. In cities like Albuquerque,

New Mexico, and Dayton, Ohio, for example, civic officials and investors have announced plans for such new downtown facilities as apartments, multiroom hotels, a performing arts center, a multiplex cinema, improved public parking and transportation, a minor league baseball stadium, and a riverfront park and skating rink. Many other cities have launched or completed similar projects.

The Future? Many experts are optimistic that the revival already seen in some cities will spread to others as well. No one expects such urban problems as crime, crowding, poverty, and racial strife to be easily overcome. But cities that can spruce up their look and entice new industries and new residents offer a more promising future than seemed likely a few decades ago.

Foreign Policy Issues

United States–Middle East Relations   Complicating the Arab-Israeli conflict was the problem of Palestinian refugees and their demands for a nation of their own. After Israel's victories in the wars of 1948 and 1967, large numbers of Palestinians found temporary homes in refugee camps in neighboring Arab nations (Syria, Lebanon, and Jordan). The poverty of the refugee camps and nationalist feelings of the Palestinians gave rise to a political movement called the *Palestine Liberation Organization (PLO)*. Its goal was to eliminate Israel as a nation and turn it into a homeland for Palestinians. The PLO's leader was Yasir Arafat, and its main weapon was *terrorism* (the use of violence to spread fear and to disrupt the normal operations of government). To the PLO, terrorism meant killing Israelis. Palestinian terrorists regularly attacked Israeli settlements, buses, beaches, and airplanes. They even carried their terrorism to countries outside the Middle East.

Among the territories taken by Israel in the 1967 war were the Gaza Strip (formerly part of Egypt) and the West Bank (formerly part of Jordan). More than a million Palestinians lived in these two captured territories. Beginning in 1987, Palestinian youths protested the presence of Israeli troops by throwing stones at them. Israeli forces occasionally responded to the stone throwing by firing at their assailants. Many young Palestinians were wounded, and some were killed. The *Intifadah*, as the Palestinians called their protest uprising, attracted international attention.

In a major diplomatic breakthrough in 1993, Israeli Prime Minister Yitzhak Rabin and PLO leader Yasir Arafat signed a historic "land for peace" agreement in Washington, D.C. Israel agreed to gradually withdraw from parts of the West Bank and the Gaza Strip. In return, the PLO recognized Israel's right to exist and made a commitment to end terrorism. In 1994 a formal peace treaty between Jordan and Israel officially ended nearly five decades of a state of war. In 1995 an agreement between Israel and the PLO expanded Palestinian self-rule in the West Bank, reconfirmed Israel's right to exist, and upgraded Palestinian antiterrorism measures to enhance Israeli security. Thus, a period of peaceful relations between Israel and its Arab neighbors seemed possible.

Arab and Jewish extremists, however, challenged the peace process. In 1994 a Jewish gunman fired on a mosque in Hebron, killing 29 Arab worshippers before he himself was killed. In 1995, during a peace rally in Tel Aviv, Prime Minister Rabin was assassinated by an Orthodox Jewish Israeli who was opposed to the peace process.

Support for Rabin's successor, Shimon Peres, was weakened by a new Palestinian movement, *Hamas*, which used bombings and suicide attacks against Israelis to undermine Israeli-PLO talks on expanding Palestinian self-rule. The bombings swayed Israeli public opinion against the peace accords. As a result, Benjamin Netanyahu, a conservative candidate who emphasized security issues, was elected prime minister in 1996.

In 1997 Israel and the PLO agreed on an Israeli withdrawal from most of the West Bank city of Hebron. In 1998 an interim agreement arranged by President Clinton and signed by Prime Minister Netanyahu and PLO leader Arafat returned additional West Bank territory to the Palestinians, in exchange for new security guarantees. Negotiations broke down, however, and full implementation of the agreement did not begin until September 1999. In the meantime, in May 1999, a general election was held in Israel in which the Labor party candidate, Ehud Barak, became prime minister by defeating Netanyahu in a landslide victory. Barak's promise to revive the Middle East peace process appealed to many Israelis who had become upset by the freeze in Mideast peacemaking. He followed through on his promise by transferring a portion of the West Bank to partial Palestinian control. Israel also decided to withdraw its troops from Lebanon and start peace talks with Syria.

The United States in the Global Economy

North American Free Trade Agreement   Low wages and scarce jobs led many Mexicans to enter the United States illegally in search of a better life. There was also growing concern about the number of U.S. businesses moving production facilities to Mexico to take advantage of lower wages and weaker environmental rules there. In response, President Clinton completed negotiations begun by President Bush for the *North American Free Trade Agreement (NAFTA)* with Mexico and Canada. When it went into effect in 1994, the agreement created the Western Hemisphere's largest free trade zone. The treaty provided for the immediate elimination of tariffs on some goods and the gradual removal of other tariffs. Thus, a business in the United States, Canada, or Mexico gained a potential market of 380 million customers for its products. It was hoped that an expanded market would increase production and create jobs and that better economic conditions in Mexico would reduce illegal immigration to the United States. Many workers in Canada and the United States, however, worried that jobs would be lost if businesses moved to Mexico to take advantage of a lower-paid workforce. In the future, countries in Central and South America may become part of the free-trade zone.

General Agreement on Tariffs and Trade; World Trade Organization   After World War II, the major economic powers of the world set up rules to reduce and limit trade barriers and to settle trade disputes. These rules were called the *General Agreement on Tariffs and Trade (GATT)*. Periodically, trade negotiations were carried out, and each round of trade talks usually resulted in member nations of GATT lowering their tariffs. In 1995 GATT changed its name to the *World Trade Organization (WTO)*. Consisting of 135 member nations, the WTO is the major body overseeing international trade.

In 1999 the World Trade Organization met in Seattle, Washington, for a new round of trade negotiations to increase global trade. The opening of the talks was delayed by thousands of protesters, who paralyzed the city by demonstrating against unrestricted trade and the power of the WTO. The protesters charged that the WTO promoted unrestricted trade chiefly in the interests of large multinational corporations at the expense of workers' rights and the environment. To meet the demands of the protesters, President Clinton called on the WTO to expand its agenda to include the protection of labor rights and the environment. However, the governments of most developing nations opposed any linkage of trade with labor or environmental standards, fearing that the imposition of such standards would excessively burden their economies or be used by other countries as an excuse to exclude their goods. In addition, critics of the WTO said that it infringed on a nation's sovereignty because the WTO could act as a court in trade disputes and impose sanctions if it found a country's policies in violation of the group's agreements. Supporters of the WTO maintained that free trade led to greater global prosperity. By the end of the meetings in Seattle, sharp divisions among the WTO's members resulted in a failure to set an agenda for a new round of talks.

U.S. Trade With China, Japan, the Pacific Rim, and Latin America

China As the world's most populous nation (about 1.2 billion people), China offers potentially the greatest market in the world for U.S. goods. China's violations of human rights, however, have posed a barrier to full-scale trade with the United States. Ever since President Nixon's trip to China in 1972, the United States has tried to establish normal relations with China's Communist government. The road to improved relations, however, has not been smooth.

Between 1978 and 1989, the Communist leaders adopted a number of liberal and economic reforms. They permitted students to criticize government policies and suggest ideas for making the government more democratic. They encouraged people to organize their own small businesses. They opened their country to Western tourists and invited experts from the West to advise them on methods of improving their economy.

The spring of 1989 saw a brutal end to the days of reform and openness in China. Some hundred thousand students had gathered in Tiananmen Square, a huge public square in the capital of Beijing, to demonstrate peacefully and urge the government to make democratic reforms in the Communist system. In reply, the government ordered troops to fire on the demonstrators. In a few hours, several thousand protesters were killed. Thousands were arrested.

The United States joined other nations in protesting the massacre. For the most part, however, President Bush followed much the same policy toward China as before. He did not carry out the economic sanctions voted by Congress. The president wanted to avoid antagonizing the government of China. He argued that the United States could best help the Chinese people by keeping on good terms with China's government.

President Clinton continued this policy of keeping on good terms with China even while Chinese dissidents favoring democratic reforms were being arrested. The administration believed that increased trade with a prospering China would lead it to adopt a better human rights policy sooner than would economic sanctions. In order to achieve this goal, the president sought to have Congress approve permanent most-favored-nation status for China. This would effectively allow China to export goods to the United States at lower tariff rates. These tariff rates would be the same as those applied to goods from Europe. Congress has approved this status for China periodically. Critics of giving China trade concessions believe that it must first demonstrate significant improvement in human rights. A second reason for opposition is the $56 billion trade deficit with China. Until China opens up its markets more to U.S. goods, the argument goes, we should not give favored treatment to its goods.

Japan In 1992 President Bush and U.S. business leaders traveled to Japan to urge the Japanese to increase U.S. imports. The Japanese agreed only to "targets" rather than specific increases. Incensed, some U.S. business leaders and government officials called for a return to the traditional policy of raising U.S. tariffs and quotas on Japanese products. Others opposed such economic protectionism and stressed the need for U.S. businesses to become more productive and competitive.

President Clinton continued to press Japan to import more American products, and his efforts achieved minor success. In mid-1995, he threatened a 100 percent rise in import duties on certain popular, high-priced Japanese cars if Japan did not ease its foreign trade policies. U.S. and Japanese negotiators then worked out a compromise agreement by which Japan pledged to open its market for U.S. cars somewhat. Some observers thought the agreement was more a compromise than an economic victory. Japan continues to export more to the United States than it imports.

Countries of the Pacific Rim Japan is not the only Asian country whose businesses compete strongly with those of the United States. On the East Asian coastline, or *Pacific Rim*, industry and trade grew rapidly in the 1980s and 1990s in South Korea, Taiwan, Thailand, Singapore, Malaysia, and Hong Kong. The clothing, shoes, electric appliances, and steel produced in these areas sold well in foreign markets, including the United States. In 1993 the total value of U.S. imports from these countries of the Pacific Rim almost equaled that of U.S. imports from Japan. Like Japan, South Korea and other Pacific Rim nations formerly had trade barriers against U.S. products. In 1994 President Clinton signed an agreement with the Pacific Rim countries to eliminate these trade barriers and move toward free trade over a period of several years.

The economic downturn in this area in the late 1990s made products from the Pacific Rim nations even cheaper for Americans to buy. But American products became too costly for Asians, and imports slowed.

Latin America   During the Clinton presidency, Latin America continued to be one of the largest trading partners of the United States, exporting traditional products such as coffee, bananas, copper, and tin to this country. New products such as televisions and videocassette recorders, mainly from Mexico, were increasingly exported to the United States. Other exports include textiles and automobiles. For example, U.S. imports of passenger cars from Mexico increased from 13,000 in 1985 to more than 580,000 in 1998. In 1999 the United States trade deficit with all of South and Central America was $13 billion.

In 1995 a crisis developed when the peso (the Mexico currency) steeply declined in value. With increased fear of inflation and unemployment in Mexico, President Clinton provided $20 billion to support the peso by guaranteeing the value of Mexican bonds. Many opposed this action.

The United States maintains trade relations with all of Latin America except for Cuba. Hoping to bring down the Communist leader of Cuba, Fidel Castro, the United States imposed a trade embargo in 1962. Cuba traded mainly with the Communist nations of Europe. With the collapse of the Soviet Union in 1991 and the ongoing U.S. embargo on Cuban products, the Cuban economy was badly damaged. Fidel Castro resisted political and economic change, so thousands of Cubans left their homes and attempted to enter the United States illegally. As the exodus of "boat people" rose rapidly, the United States announced that Cuban refugees would be detained rather than granted free entry, as in the past. Later, the United States announced that it would intercept and turn back boats leaving Cuba. In 1994 a new U.S.-Cuba agreement ended the exodus and raised the yearly quota of Cubans allowed to enter the United States legally. In 2000 an issue arose over the fate of a young Cuban boy, Elián González. Elián was rescued from a boat that capsized on its way from Cuba to the United States. Although the immigration service ruled that Elián was in the United States illegally, relatives of Elián opposed his return to Cuba. Castro supported the father of the boy, who wanted him to live in Cuba. The issue strained relations between Cuba and the United States even further.

Interventions in Somalia, Haiti, Bosnia, Yugoslavia, and Iraq

Somalia   During the last year of the Bush presidency, the United States provided humanitarian aid to Somalia, an African nation suffering from famine and civil war. In addition, U.S. troops joined a multinational UN force to help bring peace to the region. After significant multinational casualties, the United States withdrew its troops in 1994. By 1995 all UN forces had left Somalia. The war and famine continue.

Haiti   In 1990 Father Jean-Bertrand Aristide was elected president of Haiti. Less than a year later, Aristide was ousted in a military coup and fled to the United States. In response to the illegal takeover, the United Nations imposed an oil and arms embargo on Haiti in 1993.

As political and economic conditions worsened in Haiti, the number of refugees trying to reach the United States soared. Some of them were returned to Haiti, others were held in detention centers, and still others were allowed to emigrate to welcoming countries.

In spite of the oil embargo, Haiti's military government continued to engage in violence and human rights violations. The military leaders refused to step down and return Aristide to office. In 1994 the UN authorized an invasion by a multinational force. With U.S. forces already on the way, the invasion was averted when the military leaders agreed to let Aristide resume office. As part of the agreement, thousands of U.S. troops were stationed in Haiti to restore order. Aristide returned and resumed office in October 1994. In 1995 U.S. forces were replaced by a UN peacekeeping force, which exercised responsibility in Haiti until 1997. Although Haiti has a democratic form of government, its economy has barely improved.

Bosnia In 1994 Muslims and Croatians in Bosnia agreed to create a Muslim-Croat confederation. Heavy Muslim-Serb fighting continued, with many civilian casualties. Bosnian Serbs controlled more than 70 percent of the country. However, as fighting continued in 1995, the balance of power began to shift toward the Muslim-Croat alliance. Heavy NATO air strikes at Bosnian Serb targets and a Croat-Muslim offensive recaptured significant territory from the Bosnian Serbs. In 1995 the leaders of Bosnia, Croatia, and Serbia signed a treaty in Dayton, Ohio, to end Bosnia's nearly four-year-old civil war. The peace agreement divided Bosnia into two autonomous (self-governing) regions, a Muslim-Croat federation controlling 51 percent of the country and a Serb republic holding 49 percent. To maintain the peace, the North Atlantic Treaty Organization (NATO) stationed approximately 60,000 troops in Bosnia, including 20,000 American soldiers. In 1996 the NATO force was reduced to 30,000 troops, with 8,000 from the United States. Meanwhile, a United Nations tribunal in the Netherlands began bringing charges against suspected war criminals. Today, Bosnia is an independent nation, and several thousand U.S. troops are stationed there to ensure that war does not break out again.

Yugoslavia Ethnic and religious conflict also led to war in Kosovo, a province in southern Yugoslavia. Approximately 90 percent of the residents in the province are ethnic Albanians, most of whom are Muslim. (The remaining 10 percent are Serbs, most of whom are Orthodox Christian.) Until 1989 Kosovo functioned as an autonomous province within Yugoslavia with its own elected officials and Albanian language schools. In that year, President Slobodan Milosevic of Yugoslavia took away Kosovo's autonomy by forcing elected officials to step down and reinstating Serbo-Croatian, rather than Albanian, as the official language. As a result, ethnic Albanians in Kosovo began a series of demonstrations demanding full political independence, which led to severe and often violent countermeasures by Serbian officials. Violence increased when the Kosovo Liberation Army

(KLA) was formed in 1996. The KLA, made up of ethnic Albanians, used guerrilla warfare to achieve its goal of establishing Kosovo's independence.

In an attempt to suppress the independence movement, Milosevic in 1998 authorized the execution of dozens of ethnic Albanian separatists in Kosovo. In addition, Serbian police burned the homes of thousands of residents, many of whom fled to neighboring Albania. Full-scale war resulted, causing many more casualties.

Fearful that the Serbs were engaging in "ethnic cleansing" tactics, as they had in Bosnia, the United Nations called on ethnic Albanians and Serbs to announce an immediate cease-fire or face NATO air strikes. Although the Albanians in Kosovo signed the peace plan, the Serbs rejected it because it called for the stationing of a NATO peacekeeping force in Kosovo. When Milosevic refused to comply, NATO launched a massive air war against Yugoslavia and Serbian forces in Kosovo between March and June 1999. The Serbs retaliated by terrorizing the Albanian residents of Kosovo and forcing hundreds of thousands to flee, mostly to Albania and Macedonia. In May 1999, the United Nations war crimes tribunal indicted Milosevic for "crimes against humanity" for causing this forcible deportation. In June 1999, Milosevic accepted a peace plan that included a NATO occupation force. As a result, Serbian forces withdrew from Kosovo and NATO suspended the air strikes. A 50,000-member multinational force entered Kosovo, and most of the refugees returned by September. But relations between the Serbs and ethnic Albanians remained uneasy.

Iraq Iraq's defeat in the Persian Gulf War in 1991 led to UN trade sanctions and an agreement to permit UN observers to inspect suspected weapons sites within Iraq. These inspection teams were to monitor Iraq's destruction of its missiles and chemical and biological weapons. However, Iraq resisted unrestricted UN access to its sites and ended its cooperation with the UN weapons inspectors in 1998. As a result, the inspectors left Iraq, and the crisis culminated in intensive U.S. and British bombardment of Iraqi military targets.

In 1999 U.S. and British warplanes continued to bomb Iraq on a regular basis—whenever violations of the peace agreement occurred. In the meantime, Iraq rejected a UN proposal that would have permitted resumption of UN arms inspections inside Iraq in return for a more generous food-for-oil arrangement. (In 1996 the UN had allowed Iraq to begin selling limited amounts of oil for food and medicine.)

North Korea and Nuclear Concerns

After communism had collapsed elsewhere, the Communist regime of dictator Kim Il Sung and his son and successor, Kim Jong Il, still ruled North Korea. In the early 1990s, there was growing concern that North Korea was developing nuclear weapons. While denying the charge, North Korea refused to allow the UN to inspect its nuclear power plants. Reacting to threats of UN economic sanctions, North Korea, in 1994, reached an agreement with the United States to freeze its nuclear program in exchange for two light-water reactors and economic and diplomatic concessions. (Light-water reactors make the production of nuclear weapons much more difficult.) Nevertheless, fears that North Korea might still be engaging in secret nuclear activities continued to cloud U.S.-North Korean relations.

United States–Russian Relations, 1991 to the Present

Since the end of the cold war and the emergence of Russia as an independent state in December 1991, the United States has developed a broad-based relationship with Russia, seeking to expand areas of cooperation and resolving differences without confrontation. In a meeting at Camp David in February 1992, President Bush and President Boris Yeltsin of Russia declared that the cold war had officially ended. At that time, the United States joined other Western nations in pledging to give emergency aid to the struggling Russian economy. In return, Russia began a series of economic reforms.

As a first step, Russia eliminated state subsidies (financial assistance) of most goods and services and launched a drive to *privatize* (put up for public sale) thousands of large and medium-sized stated-owned businesses. Unfortunately, many of these state-owned businesses came under the control of a small number of individuals. Prices soared far beyond what ordinary Russians could afford, and Russia suffered periodic economic crises. For example, in 1998, Russia devalued its currency, the ruble, causing its value to plunge and the country to default on its debt. To assist Russia, the Clinton administration continued to give emergency loans on condition that Russia make further economic reforms. As the largest foreign investor, the United States encouraged Russia to make changes, including reducing its budget deficit and improving its tax collection system, to create a more favorable climate for foreign and domestic investors.

The United States has also worked with Russia to reduce the nuclear arsenals of both sides and on measures to prevent the spread of weapons of mass destruction to other countries. For example, in 1992 the United States and Russia ratified a Strategic Arms Reduction Treaty (START I) to reduce strategic nuclear arms by about 30 percent over 7 years. In 1993 the United States and Russia signed a second Strategic Arms Reduction Treaty (START II), which would reduce strategic nuclear weapons on each side by more than two-thirds of their current levels, eliminate multiple-warhead intercontinental ballistic missiles (ICBMs), and disable and dismantle launching systems. Although the United States ratified the START II in 1996, the Russian parliament has yet to ratify the treaty. In 1996 the United States and Russia signed the Comprehensive Test Ban Treaty (CTBT), which banned all nuclear weapon tests and other nuclear explosions. It is intended to help prevent the nuclear powers from developing more advanced weapons, while limiting the ability of other countries to acquire such devices. The U.S. Senate rejected the CTBT in 1999, making the United States the only nuclear power not to ratify it. The United States, however, is working with Russia to dismantle hundreds of Russian nuclear weapons.

Despite these areas of agreement, the United States and Russia continue to differ on a number of issues. For example, the United States objected to Russia's excessive use of force in subduing Chechnya. In 1994 the Russian government sent troops into the breakaway Muslim republic of Chechnya after it declared itself independent from the rest of Russia. Grozny, the Chechen capital, fell in 1995, but Chechen rebels did not give in. After heavy fighting that continued for almost two years, Russia and the Chechen leaders finally signed a peace accord in 1996. However, in 1999 a series of explosions in Russia were blamed on Chechen Islamic terrorists. As a result, the conflict between Russia and Chechnya heated up again. A full-scale Russian invasion of Chechnya took place, causing more than 100,000 civilians to flee into neighboring republics. By February 2000, after weeks of bitter fighting, the Russian army was victorious.

Meanwhile, Boris Yelstin, in a surprise move, had resigned from the Russian presidency on December 31, 1999, probably owing to failing health. He named Vladimir Putin as his successor. (Putin had been largely responsible for Russia's successful military strategy against Chechnya.) Putin solidified his position by winning a new presidential election in March 2000 by a slender majority.

Another area of disagreement concerned Russia's cooperation with Iran's missile program. The United States considers Iran an enemy state that promotes international terrorism and is trying to build nuclear weapons. However, despite strong opposition from the United States, Russia has agreed to build a nuclear power plant in Iran. The United States fears that this action will transfer sensitive nuclear and weapons technology to Iran. The Russian government claims that it will monitor the building of the plant to ensure that Iran would not have access to nuclear weapons and that the type of reactors being sold to Iran are not designed to process the uranium needed for nuclear weapons.

Other areas of disagreement included Russia's opposition to the expansion of NATO to include countries in Eastern Europe, Russia's desire to immediately end UN sanctions against Iraq, and Russia's strong opposition to NATO's bombing of Yugoslavia, a traditional ally of Russia.

United States–European Relations

The major goal of Western European countries after World War II was to rebuild their shattered economies. Eventually, they succeeded in restoring prosperity. One of the most important factors in Western Europe's recovery was the reduction of trade barriers within the region.

European Union (EU) Many Western Europeans believed that prosperity would come sooner if their governments reduced regional trade barriers. As a result, in 1957 France, West Germany, the Netherlands, Belgium, Luxembourg, and Italy created the European Economic Community (EEC) or *Common Market*. It was designed to eliminate all tariff barriers among member states. Eventually, the organization grew to 15 nations, as Great Britain, Greece, Portugal, Spain, Ireland, Denmark, Austria, Finland, and Sweden joined.

The initial success of the Common Market led member nations to set up a more ambitious plan known as the European Community (EC). Its goals included the free flow of goods, services, people, and capital among member nations. Plans were also discussed for a single European currency, a single European bank, and eventual political union. If such a union is achieved, it would, among other things, set a common foreign policy for all member nations. These goals face major opposition among many Western Europeans, who are reluctant to give up their national sovereignty.

In 1994 the European Community became known as the *European Union (EU)*. The member nations agreed to launch a common currency (the euro) for at least some nations by 1999 (Britain and, later, Denmark and Sweden "opted out" of joining), sought to establish common foreign policies, and laid the groundwork for a common defense policy. In 1998 the European Central bank was established. The EU is also making provisions to include qualified East European nations in its trade network. The United States believes that the EU will reduce the likelihood of war again erupting in Europe. It does, however, look upon the EU as an economic rival.

North Atlantic Treaty Organization (NATO) With the collapse of the Soviet Union in 1991 and the end of the cold war, NATO members put greater stress on creating a rapid deployment force to react to local crises. By the mid-1990s, 27 nations, including Russia and other former Soviet republics, established a friendly relationship with NATO known as the "Partnership for Peace," which provided for limited joint military exercises, peacekeeping missions, and information exchange. A NATO-led multinational force was deployed in Bosnia in 1995 and in Kosovo in 1999.

NATO has worked gradually toward extending full membership to qualified East European nations. In 1997 NATO and Russia concluded a "Founding Act" that increased Russian cooperation with NATO and paved the way for NATO to admit East European states.

★ In Review

1. Describe (a) three social concerns, (b) three economic concerns, and (c) two political concerns that arose during the Clinton presidency.
2. Summarize the issues involved in the (a) movement for campaign finance reform and (b) the impeachment of President Clinton.
3. Explain how each of the following posed a challenge to U.S. foreign policy during the 1990s: (a) Middle East, (b) Somalia, (c) Haiti, (d) Bosnia, (e) Yugoslavia, (f) Iraq, and (g) Russia.

Chapter Review

MULTIPLE-CHOICE QUESTIONS

1. Bill Clinton was able to defeat President Bush in the 1992 presidential election primarily because of
(1) the failure of the U.S. military to oust Saddam Hussein from power in Iraq
(2) discontent over an economic recession
(3) the 1986 *Challenger* space shuttle disaster
(4) the signing of the START I treaty with Russia.

2. President Clinton was unable to establish a national health care program because of
(1) public opposition
(2) a Supreme Court ruling that such a program would be unconstitutional
(3) opposition from Congress, insurance companies, and other pressure groups
(4) its endorsement by fringe radical organizations.

Base your answers to questions 3 and 4 on the following cover headline from Newsweek, *April 3, 2000:*

**THE NEW MIDDLE AGE—
A BOOMER'S GUIDE TO HEALTH,
WEALTH & HAPPINESS**

3. The headline refers to
(1) Americans who were born in the years following World War II
(2) the group known as "Generation X"
(3) octogenarians (people 80 years old and older)
(4) children born during the 1990s.

4. Which of the following projections can be drawn from the headline?
(1) More college and university professors will need to be hired.
(2) Blue-collar workers will be in more demand that white-collar workers.
(3) Cancer and heart disease are being conquered.
(4) New demands and challenges will be made on Social Security and other services to the elderly.

Base your answer to question 5 on the following cover headline from Newsweek, *April 24, 2000:*

**IS THE BULL MARKET
REALLY OVER?**

5. The headline expresses concern that
(1) a second Great Depression is about to take place
(2) the unprecedented rise in stocks during the second half of the 1990s may have ended
(3) high-tech stocks have decreased in value as a result of successful federal antitrust challenges
(4) domestic issues have for too long been given priority over foreign affairs.

6. What would be an expected result of the public financing of election campaigns?
(1) Personal income taxes would be reduced.
(2) Political parties would no longer be necessary.
(3) People or organizations able to contribute large amounts of money would lose their influence over politicians.
(4) Incumbents would be guaranteed reelection.

7. During President Clinton's impeachment proceedings, the House of Representatives
(1) dismissed the original charges
(2) approved several articles of impeachment
(3) brought President Clinton up on charges in the Supreme Court
(4) used the impeachment proceedings of Andrew Johnson and Richard Nixon to form the basis of the charges.

Base your answer to question 8 on the following table:

Cold War	1990s and Beyond
NATO	NATO
Warsaw Pact	NAFTA
SEATO	GATT/World Trade
Common	Organization
Market	European Union (EU)

8. Which of the following situations best explains the change shown in the right column?
(1) Military alliances still dominate the world scene.
(2) Nations no longer form military alliances.
(3) The United Nations has outlawed military alliances.
(4) Economic alliances tend to predominate over military alliances.

9. In the late 1990s, congressional opposition to granting a more favorable trade status to China was based primarily on China's
(1) nuclear buildup
(2) high-priced exports
(3) history of unstable governments
(4) disregard for human rights.

10. Restoring Jean-Bertrand Aristide as president of Haiti was important in order to show
(1) Cuba's power in the Caribbean
(2) that democratically elected officials should be allowed to hold office
(3) the weakness of UN peacekeeping forces
(4) that Haiti was a major Caribbean country.

THEMATIC ESSAYS

1. **Theme:** The Impeachment Process

   During his second term in office, President Clinton became only the second president in U.S. history to be impeached.

   Task

   ★ Describe the specific constitutional charges against President Clinton.

★ Compare and contrast the result of the impeachment of President Andrew Johnson with that of President Clinton.

Be sure to confine your treatment to specific violations of the Constitution for which President Clinton was impeached.

2. **Theme:** Presidential Decision Making in the 1990s and Beyond

The president of the United States must make decisions, often very quickly, regarding emergencies and issues that have serious implications for or are crucial to the well-being and security of the nation.

Task

★ Describe one problem faced by President Bush and another problem faced by President Clinton.

★ For each problem, discuss the *options* and *final decision* made by the president in office.

★ Evaluate the implications of the decision made by each president.

You may wish to use in your discussion of President Bush examples such as the crisis in Bosnia, the Persian Gulf Crisis, and his response regarding the collapse of communism in the Soviet Union and Eastern Europe.

Your discussion of the decisions made by President Clinton may include his support of the North American Free Trade Agreement (NAFTA), advocacy of a national health care program, and intervention in nations undergoing severe crises, such as Somalia, Bosnia, Yugoslavia, and Haiti.

In your discussion of presidential decision making, you are not limited to any of the suggestions given.

DOCUMENT-BASED QUESTION

*Reach each document and answer the question that follows it. Then read the **Task** and write your essay. Essays should include references to most of the documents along with additional information based on your knowledge of United States history and government.*

Historical Context: As the United States begins the new millennium, it faces, as in the past, a number of challenging problems whose solutions will affect it and the other nations of the world for many years to come.

Document 1 Refer to the cartoon on page 600.

Question: What problem, according to the cartoon, has resulted from the increasing use of computers?

Document 2 Refer to the graph on page 559.

Question: How did the nature of immigration change in the 1980s?

Document 3 Refer to the cartoon on page 598.

Question: How does the cartoonist feel about education in the United States as compared with other nations?

Document 4 Refer to the map on page 589.

Question: What does the map illustrate about recent U.S. relations with its Latin American and Caribbean neighbors?

Document 5 Refer to the cartoon on page 595.

Question: What does the cartoon say about the ability of the U.S. government to control oil prices?

Task

★ Describe two problems that the United States is currently facing.

★ Discuss the options for each problem and suggest a potential solution.

★ Explain the outcome that you anticipate from your suggested solutions to the problems.

The Declaration of Independence

Note: Capitalization, spelling, punctuation, and paragraphing have been modernized. In addition, the signers' names have been rearranged and grouped alphabetically by state.

In Congress, July 4, 1776

The Unanimous Declaration of the Thirteen United States of America

When in the course of human events, it becomes necessary for one people to dissolve the political bands which have connected them with another, and to assume, among the powers of the earth, the separate and equal station to which the laws of nature and of nature's God entitle them, a decent respect to the opinions of mankind requires that they should declare the causes which impel them to the separation.

We hold these truths to be self-evident: that all men are created equal; that they are endowed by their Creator with certain unalienable rights; that among these are life, liberty, and the pursuit of happiness.

That to secure these rights, governments are instituted among men, deriving their just powers from the consent of the governed. That, whenever any form of government becomes destructive of these ends, it is the right of the people to alter or to abolish it, and to institute new government, laying its foundation on such principles, and organizing its powers in such form, as to them shall seem most likely to effect their safety and happiness. Prudence, indeed, will dictate that governments long established should not be changed for light and transient causes; and, accordingly, all experience hath shown that mankind are more disposed to suffer, while evils are sufferable, than to right themselves by abolishing the forms to which they are accustomed. But when a long train of abuses and usurpations, pursuing invariably the same object, evinces a design to reduce them under absolute despotism, it is their right, it is their duty, to throw off such government, and to provide new guards for their future security.

Such has been the patient sufferance of these colonies; and such is now the necessity which constrains them to alter their former systems of government. The history of the present King of Great Britain is a history of repeated injuries and usurpations, all having in direct object the establishment of an absolute tyranny over these states. To prove this, let facts be submitted to a candid world.

He has refused his assent to laws the most wholesome and necessary for the public good.

He has forbidden his governors to pass laws of immediate and pressing importance, unless suspended in their operation till his assent should be obtained; and, when so suspended, he has utterly neglected to attend to them.

He has refused to pass other laws for the accommodation of large districts of people, unless those people would relinquish the right of representation in the legislature—a right inestimable to them and formidable to tyrants only.

He has called together legislative bodies at places unusual, uncomfortable, and distant from the depository of their public records, for the sole purpose of fatiguing them into compliance with his measures.

He has dissolved representative houses repeatedly, for opposing, with manly firmness, his invasions on the rights of the people.

He has refused, for a long time after such dissolutions, to cause others to be elected; whereby the legislative powers, incapable of annihilation, have returned to the people at large for their exercise; the state remaining, in the meantime, exposed to all the dangers of invasion from without and convulsions within.

He has endeavored to prevent the population of these states; for that purpose obstructing the laws for naturalization of foreigners, refusing to pass others to encourage their migration hither, and raising the conditions of new appropriations of lands.

He has obstructed the administration of justice by refusing his assent to laws for establishing judiciary powers.

He has made judges dependent on his will alone for the tenure of their offices and the amount and payment of their salaries.

He has erected a multitude of new offices and sent hither swarms of officers to harass our people and eat out their substance.

He has kept among us, in times of peace, standing armies, without the consent of our legislatures.

He has affected to render the military independent of, and superior to, the civil power.

He has combined with others to subject us to a jurisdiction foreign to our constitution and unacknowledged by our laws, giving his assent to their acts of pretended legislation:

For quartering large bodies of armed troops among us;

For protecting them, by a mock trial, from punishment for any murders which they should commit on the inhabitants of these states;

For cutting off our trade with all parts of the world;

For imposing taxes on us without our consent;

For depriving us, in many cases, of the benefits of trial by jury;

For transporting us beyond seas to be tried for pretended offenses;

For abolishing the free system of English laws in a neighboring province, establishing therein an arbitrary government and enlarging its boundaries, so as to render it at once an example and fit instrument for introducing the same absolute rule into these colonies;

For taking away our charters, abolishing our most valuable laws, and altering fundamentally the forms of our governments;

For suspending our own legislatures, and declaring themselves invested with power to legislate for us in all cases whatsoever.

He has abdicated government here by declaring us out of his protection and waging war against us.

He has plundered our seas, ravaged our coasts, burned our towns, and destroyed the lives of our people.

He is, at this time, transporting large armies of foreign mercenaries to complete the works of death, desolation, and tyranny already begun with circumstances of cruelty and perfidy scarcely paralleled in the most barbarous ages, and totally unworthy the head of a civilized nation.

He has constrained our fellow citizens taken captive on the high seas to bear arms against their country, to become the executioners of their friends and brethren, or to fall themselves by their hands.

He has excited domestic insurrections among us, and has endeavored to bring on the inhabitants of our frontiers the merciless Indian savages, whose known rule of warfare is an undistinguished destruction of all ages, sexes, and conditions.

In every stage of these oppressions we have petitioned for redress in the most humble terms. Our repeated petitions have been answered only by repeated injury. A prince whose character is thus marked by every act which may define a tyrant is unfit to be the ruler of a free people.

Nor have we been wanting in attentions to our British brethren. We have warned them, from time to time, of attempts by their legislature to extend an unwarrantable jurisdiction over us. We have reminded them of the circumstances of our emigration and settlement here. We have appealed to their native justice and magnanimity; and we have conjured them, by the ties of our common kindred, to disavow these usurpations, which would inevitably interrupt our connections and correspondence. They, too, have been deaf to the voice of justice and consanguinity. We must, therefore, acquiesce in the necessity which denounces our separation, and hold them, as we hold the rest of mankind, enemies in war, in peace friends.

We, therefore, the representatives of the United States of America, in General Congress assembled, appealing to the Supreme Judge of the world for the rectitude of our intentions, do, in the name and by authority of the good people of these colonies, solemnly publish and declare: that these united colonies are, and of right ought to be, free and independent states; that they are absolved from all allegiance to the British crown, and that all political connection between them and the state of Great Britain is, and ought to be, totally dissolved; and that, as free and independent states, they have full power to levy war, conclude peace, contract alliances, establish commerce, and to do all other acts and things which independent states may of right do. And for the support of this declaration, with a firm reliance on the protection of Divine Providence, we mutually pledge to each other our lives, our fortunes, and our sacred honor.

**[Signed by]   John Hancock
[Massachusetts]**

[Connecticut]
Samuel Huntington
Roger Sherman
William Williams
Oliver Wolcott

[Delaware]
Thomas McKean
George Read
Caesar Rodney

[Georgia]
Button Gwinnett
Lyman Hall
George Walton

[Maryland]
Charles Carroll
of Carrollton
Samuel Chase
William Paca
Thomas Stone

[Massachusetts]
John Adams
Samuel Adams
Elbridge Gerry
Robert Treat Paine

[New Hampshire]
Josiah Bartlett
Matthew Thornton
William Whipple

[New Jersey]
Abraham Clark
John Hart
Francis Hopkinson
Richard Stockton
John Witherspoon

[New York]
William Floyd
Francis Lewis
Philip Livingston
Lewis Morris

[North Carolina]
Joseph Hewes
William Hooper
John Penn

[Pennsylvania]
George Clymer
Benjamin Franklin
Robert Morris
John Morton
George Ross
Benjamin Rush
James Smith
George Taylor
James Wilson

[Rhode Island]
William Ellery
Stephen Hopkins

[South Carolina]
Thomas Heyward, Jr.
Thomas Lynch, Jr.
Arthur Middleton
Edward Rutledge

[Virginia]
Carter Braxton
Benjamin Harrison
Thomas Jefferson
Francis Lightfoot Lee
Richard Henry Lee
Thomas Nelson, Jr.
George Wythe

The Constitution
of the United States
# of America

Note: Footnotes, headings, and explanations have been added to aid the reader. The explanations within the body of the text are enclosed in brackets [ ]. The parts of the Constitution that are no longer in effect are printed in *italic* type. Capitalization, spelling, and punctuation have been modernized.

PREAMBLE

We the people of the United States, in order to form a more perfect Union, establish justice, insure domestic tranquility,[1] provide for the common defense, promote the general welfare, and secure the blessings of liberty to ourselves and our posterity [descendants], do ordain [issue] and establish this Constitution for the United States of America.

ARTICLE 1. CONGRESS

Section 1. Legislative Power All legislative powers herein granted shall be vested in a Congress of the United States, which shall consist of a Senate and House of Representatives.

Section 2. House of Representatives [1] The House of Representatives shall be composed of members chosen every second year by the people of the several states, and the electors [voters] in each state shall have the qualifications requisite [required] for electors of the most numerous branch of the state legislature.

[2] No person shall be a representative who shall not have attained to [reached] the age of twenty-five years and been seven years a citizen of the United States, and who shall not, when elected, be an inhabitant of that state in which he shall be chosen.

---

[1] "Insure domestic tranquility" means *assure peace within the nation*.

[3] Representatives and direct taxes[1] shall be apportioned [divided] among the several states which may be included within this Union according to their respective numbers [population], *which shall be determined by adding to the whole number of free persons, including those bound to service for a term of years* [indentured servants], *and excluding Indians not taxed, three-fifths of all other persons.*[2] The actual enumeration [census] shall be made within three years after the first meeting of the Congress of the United States, and within every subsequent term of ten years, in such manner as they shall by law direct. The number of representatives shall not exceed one for every thirty thousand, but each state shall have at least one representative; *and until such enumeration shall be made, the State of New Hampshire shall be entitled to choose three, Massachusetts eight, Rhode Island and Providence Plantations one, Connecticut five, New York six, New Jersey four, Pennsylvania eight, Delaware one, Maryland six, Virginia ten, North Carolina five, South Carolina five, and Georgia three.*[3]

[4] When vacancies happen in the representation from any state, the executive authority [governor] thereof shall issue writs of election[4] to fill such vacancies.

[5] The House of Representatives shall choose their Speaker and other officers; and shall have the sole power of impeachment.[5]

Section 3. Senate [1] The Senate of the United States shall be composed of two senators from each state, *chosen by the legislature thereof,*[6] for six years; and each senator shall have one vote.

[2] *Immediately after they shall be assembled in consequence of the first election, they shall be divided as equally as may be into three classes. The seats of the senators of the first class shall be vacated at the expiration of the second year, of the second class at the expiration of the fourth year, and of the third class at the expiration of the sixth year,*[7] *so that one-third may be chosen every second year; and if vacancies happen by resignation, or otherwise, during the recess of the legislature of any state,*

[1] Modified by Amendment XVI, which granted Congress the power to levy a direct tax on individual incomes rather than on the basis of state populations.

[2] "Other persons" refers to slaves. Amendment XIII abolished slavery; Amendment XIV specifically eliminated the three-fifths formula.

[3] Temporary provision.

[4] "Issue writs of election" means *call a special election.*

[5] "Power of impeachment" means *right to charge federal officials with misconduct.*

[6] Replaced by Amendment XVII, which provided for popular election of senators.

[7] Temporary provision, designed to organize the first Senate in such a way that, thereafter, only one-third of its members would be subject to replacement at each successive election.

the executive [governor] *thereof may make temporary appointments until the next meeting of the legislature, which shall then fill such vacancies.*[1]

[3] No person shall be a senator who shall not have attained to the age of thirty years and been nine years a citizen of the United States, and who shall not, when elected, be an inhabitant of that state for which he shall be chosen.

[4] The vice president of the United States shall be president of the Senate, but shall have no vote, unless they be equally divided [tied].

[5] The Senate shall choose their other officers, and also a president pro tempore [temporary presiding officer], in the absence of the vice president, or when he shall exercise the office of president of the United States.

[6] The Senate shall have sole power to try all impeachments.[2] When sitting for that purpose, they shall be on oath or affirmation.[3] When the president of the United States is tried, the chief justice [of the United States] shall preside; and no person shall be convicted without the concurrence [agreement] of two-thirds of the members present.

[7] Judgment in cases of impeachment shall not extend further than to removal from office, and disqualification to hold and enjoy any office of honor, trust, or profit under the United States; but the party convicted shall nevertheless be liable and subject to indictment, trial, judgment, and punishment, according to law.

Section 4. Elections and Meetings of Congress [1] The times, places, and manner of holding elections for senators and representatives shall be prescribed [designated] in each state by the legislature thereof; but the Congress may at any time by law make or alter such regulations, except as to the places of choosing senators.

[2] The Congress shall assemble at least once in every year, *and such meeting shall be on the first Monday in December,*[4] unless they shall by law appoint a different day.

Section 5. Rules and Procedures of the Two Houses [1] Each house shall be the judge of the elections, returns, and qualifications of its own

---

[1]Modified by Amendment XVII, which permits a governor to select a temporary replacement to fill the vacancy until the next election.

[2] "To try all impeachments" means *to conduct the trials of officials impeached by the House of Representatives*. When trying such cases, the Senate serves as a court.

[3] If taking an oath violates a member's religious principles, that person may "affirm" rather than "swear."

[4]Amendment XX changed this date to January 3.

members,[1] and a majority of each shall constitute a quorum[2] to do business; but a smaller number may adjourn from day to day, and may be authorized to compel the attendance of absent members, in such manner, and under such penalties, as each house may provide.

[2] Each house may determine the rules of its proceedings, punish its members for disorderly behavior, and with the concurrence of two-thirds, expel a member.

[3] Each house shall keep a journal [record] of its proceedings, and from time to time publish the same, excepting such parts as may in their judgment require secrecy; and the yeas [affirmative votes] and nays [negative votes] of the members of either house on any question shall, at the desire of one-fifth of those present, be entered on the journal.

[4] Neither house, during the session of Congress, shall, without the consent of the other, adjourn for more than three days, nor to any other place than that in which the two houses shall be sitting.

Section 6. Members' Privileges and Restrictions [1] The senators and representatives shall receive a compensation [salary] for their services, to be ascertained [fixed] by law and paid out of the treasury of the United States. They shall in all cases except treason, felony [serious crime], and breach of the peace [disorderly conduct], be privileged [immune] from arrest during their attendance at the session of their respective houses, and in going to and returning from the same; and for any speech or debate in either house, they shall not be questioned in any other place.[3]

[2] No senator or representative shall, during the time for which he was elected, be appointed to any civil office under the authority of the United States, which shall have been created, or the emoluments [salary] whereof shall have been increased, during such time; and no person holding any office under the United States shall be a member of either house during his continuance in office.

Section 7. Lawmaking Procedures [1] All bills for raising revenue shall originate [be introduced] in the House of Representatives; but the Senate may propose or concur with [approve] amendments as on other bills.

[2] Every bill which shall have passed the House of Representatives and the Senate shall, before it becomes a law, be presented to the president of the United States; if he approve, he shall sign it, but if not, he shall return it, with his objections, to that house in which it shall have originated, who shall enter the objections at large on their journal, and proceed to reconsider it. If after such reconsideration two-thirds of

---

[1]This provision empowers either house, by a majority vote, to refuse to seat a newly elected member.

[2]A "quorum" is the *number of members that must be present in order to conduct business.*

[3] "They shall not be questioned in any other place" means that *they may not be sued for slander or libel.* Freedom from arrest during congressional sessions and freedom of speech within the halls of Congress—two privileges granted to members of Congress—are known as *congressional immunity.*

that house shall agree to pass the bill, it shall be sent, together with the objections, to the other house, by which it shall likewise be reconsidered, and, if approved by two-thirds of that house, it shall become a law. But in all such cases the votes of both houses shall be determined by yeas and nays, and the names of the persons voting for and against the bill shall be entered on the journal of each house respectively. If any bill shall not be returned by the president within ten days (Sundays excepted) after it shall have been presented to him, the same shall be a law, in like manner as if he had signed it, unless the Congress by their adjournment prevent its return, in which case it shall not be a law[1]

[3] Every order, resolution, or vote to which the concurrence of the Senate and House of Representatives may be necessary (except on a question of adjournment) shall be presented to the president of the United States; and before the same shall take effect, shall be approved by him, or, being disapproved by him, shall be repassed by two-thirds of the Senate and House of Representatives, according to the rules and limitations prescribed in the case of a bill.

Section 8. Powers of Congress The Congress shall have power:

[1] To lay and collect taxes, duties, imposts, and excises,[2] to pay the debts and provide for the common defense and general welfare of the United States; but all duties, imposts, and excises shall be uniform [the same] throughout the United States;

[2] To borrow money on the credit of the United States;

[3] To regulate commerce with foreign nations, and among the several states, and with the Indian tribes;

[4] To establish a uniform rule of naturalization [admitting to citizenship], and uniform laws on the subject of bankruptcies throughout the United States;

[5] To coin money, regulate the value thereof, and of foreign coin, and fix [set] the standard of weights and measures;

[6] To provide for the punishment of counterfeiting[3] the securities and current coin of the United States;

[7] To establish post offices and post roads;

[8] To promote the progress of science and useful arts by securing for limited times to authors and inventors the exclusive right to their respective writings and discoveries;[4]

[9] To constitute tribunals [establish courts] inferior to [lower than] the Supreme Court;

[1] If Congress adjourns before the ten-day period is up, the president can kill a bill by ignoring it ("putting it in his pocket"). Therefore, this type of presidential rejection is called a *pocket veto*.

[2] "Duties, imposts, and excises" are forms of taxation. Duties and imposts are taxes on imports. Excises are taxes on goods produced or services performed within a country.

[3] Making an imitation with the intent of passing it as the genuine article.

[4] Copyright and patent laws, passed by Congress on the basis of this clause, protect the rights of authors and inventors.

[10] To define and punish piracies and felonies committed on the high seas[1] and offenses against the law of nations [international law];

[11] To declare war, grant letters of marque and reprisal,[2] and make rules concerning captures on land and water;

[12] To raise and support armies, but no appropriation of money to that use shall be for a longer term than two years;

[13] To provide and maintain a navy;

[14] To make rules for the government and regulation of the land and naval forces;

[15] To provide for calling forth the militia[3] to execute [carry out] the laws of the Union, suppress [put down] insurrections [rebellions], and repel [drive back] invasions;

[16] To provide for organizing, arming, and disciplining [training] the militia, and for governing such part of them as may be employed in the service of the United States, reserving to the states respectively the appointment of the officers, and the authority of training the militia according to the discipline [regulations] prescribed by Congress;

[17] To exercise exclusive legislation in all cases whatsoever, over such district[4] (not exceeding ten miles square) as may, by cession of particular states, and the acceptance of Congress, become the seat of government of the United States, and to exercise like authority over all places purchased by the consent of the legislature of the state in which the same shall be, for the erection of forts, magazines, arsenals, dockyards, and other needful buildings; and

[18] To make all laws which shall be necessary and proper for carrying into execution the foregoing powers and all other powers vested by this Constitution in the government of the United States, or in any department or officer thereof.[5]

Section 9. Powers Denied to the Federal Government [1] *The migration or importation of such persons as any of the states now existing shall think proper to admit shall not be prohibited by the Congress prior to the year 1808; but a tax or duty may be imposed on such importation, not exceeding ten dollars for each person.*[6]

[1]Open ocean; waters outside the territorial limits of a country.

[2]Letters of marque and reprisal are government licenses issued to private citizens in time of war authorizing them to fit out armed vessels (called *privateers*) for the purpose of capturing or destroying enemy ships.

[3]Citizen soldiers who are not in the regular armed forces but are subject to military duty in times of emergency; for example, the National Guard.

[4] "To exercise exclusive legislation ... over such district" means *to be solely responsible for making the laws for a designated area.*

[5]This is the so-called "elastic clause" of the Constitution, which allows Congress to carry out many actions not specifically listed.

[6]This temporary provision prohibited Congress from interfering with the importation of slaves ("such persons") before 1808.

[2] The privilege of the writ of habeas corpus[1] shall not be suspended, unless when in cases of rebellion or invasion the public safety may require it.

[3] No bill of attainder[2] or ex post facto law[3] shall be passed.

[4] No capitation [head] or other direct tax shall be laid, unless in proportion to the census or enumeration herein before directed to be taken.[4]

[5] No tax or duty shall be laid on articles exported from any state.

[6] No preference shall be given by any regulation of commerce or revenue to the ports of one state over those of another; nor shall vessels bound to, or from, one state be obliged to enter, clear, or pay duties in another.

[7] No money shall be drawn from the treasury, but in consequence of appropriations made by law; and a regular statement and account of the receipts and expenditures of all public money shall be published from time to time.

[8] No title of nobility shall be granted by the United States; and no person holding any office of profit or trust under them shall, without the consent of the Congress, accept of any present, emolument, office, or title, of any kind whatever, from any king, prince, or foreign state.

Section 10. Powers Denied to the States [1] No state shall enter into any treaty, alliance, or confederation; grant letters of marque and reprisal; coin money; emit bills of credit;[5] make anything but gold and silver coin a tender [legal money] in payment of debts; pass any bill of attainder, ex post facto law, or law impairing the obligation of contracts,[6] or grant any title of nobility.

[2] No state shall, without the consent of the Congress, lay any imposts or duties on imports or exports, except what may be absolutely necessary for executing its inspection laws; and the net produce [income] of all duties and imposts, laid by any state on imports or exports, shall be for the use of the treasury of the United States; and all such laws shall be subject to the revision and control of the Congress.

[3] No state shall, without the consent of Congress, lay any duty of

---

[1]A "writ of habeas corpus" is a court order obtained by a person taken into custody, demanding to know the reasons for imprisonment. If the court rules that the reasons are insufficient, the prisoner is released.

[2]A law that deprives a person of civil rights without a trial.

[3]A law that punishes a person for a past action that was not unlawful at the time it was committed.

[4]Modified by Amendment XVI.

[5]"Emit bills of credit" means issue paper money.

[6]"Impairing the obligation of contracts" means *weakening the obligations persons assume when they enter into legal agreements.*

tonnage,[1] keep troops[2] or ships of war in time of peace, enter into any agreement or compact with another state or with a foreign power, or engage in war unless actually invaded or in such imminent [threatening] danger as will not admit of delay.

ARTICLE II. THE PRESIDENCY

Section 1. Executive Power [1] The executive power shall be vested in a president of the United States of America. He shall hold his office during the term of four years,[3] and, together with the vice president, chosen for the same term, be elected as follows:

[2] Each state shall appoint, in such manner as the legislature thereof may direct, a number of electors, equal to the whole number of senators and representatives to which the state may be entitled in the Congress; but no senator or representative, or person holding an office of trust or profit under the United States, shall be appointed an elector.

[3] *The electors shall meet in their respective states, and vote by ballot for two persons, of whom one at least shall not be an inhabitant of the same state with themselves. And they shall make a list of all the persons voted for, and of the number of votes for each; which list they shall sign and certify, and transmit sealed to the seat of the government of the United States, directed to the president of the Senate. The president of the Senate shall, in the presence of the Senate and House of Representatives, open all the certificates, and the votes shall then be counted. The person having the greatest number of votes shall be the president, if such number be a majority of the whole number of electors appointed; and if there be more than one who have such majority, and have an equal number of votes, then the House of Representatives shall immediately choose by ballot one of them for president; and if no person have a majority, then from the five highest on the list the said House shall in like manner choose the president. But in choosing the president, the votes shall be taken by states, the representation from each state having one vote; a quorum for this purpose shall consist of a member or members from two-thirds of the states, and a majority of all the states shall be necessary to a choice. In every case, after the choice of the president, the person having the greatest number of votes of the electors shall be the vice president. But if there should remain two or more who have equal votes, the Senate shall choose from them by ballot the vice president.*[4]

[4] The Congress may determine the time of choosing the electors, and the day on which they shall give their votes; which day shall be the same throughout the United States.

---

[1] "Duty of tonnage" means a tax based upon a vessel's cargo-carrying capacity.
[2] Other than militia.
[3] Amendment XXII limits a president to two terms.
[4] Replaced by Amendment XII.

[5] No person except a natural-born citizen, *or a citizen of the United States at the time of the adoption of this Constitution*,[1] shall be eligible to the office of president; neither shall any person be eligible to that office who shall not have attained to the age of thirty-five years and been fourteen years a resident within the United States.

[6] In case of the removal of the president from office, or of his death, resignation, or inability to discharge the powers and duties of the said office, the same shall devolve on the vice president, and the Congress may by law provide for the case of removal, death, resignation, or inability, both of the president and vice president, declaring what officer shall then act as president, and such officer shall act accordingly, until the disability be removed, or a president shall be elected.[2]

[7] The president shall, at stated times, receive for his services a compensation, which shall neither be increased nor diminished [decreased] during the period for which he shall have been elected, and he shall not receive within that period any other emolument from the United States, or any of them.

[8] Before he enter on the execution of his office, he shall take the following oath or affirmation:

"I do solemnly swear (or affirm) that I will faithfully execute the office of President of the United States, and will, to the best of my ability, preserve, protect, and defend the Constitution of the United States."

Section 2. Powers of the President [1] The president shall be commander in chief of the army and navy [all the armed forces] of the United States, and of the militia of the several states, when called into the actual service of the United States; he may require the opinion in writing of the principal officer in each of the executive departments upon any subject relating to the duties of their respective offices; and he shall have power to grant reprieves[3] and pardons[4] for offenses against the United States except in cases of impeachment.

[2] He shall have power, by and with the advice and consent of the Senate, to make treaties, provided two-thirds of the senators present concur; and he shall nominate, and, by and with the advice and consent of the Senate, shall appoint ambassadors, other public ministers and consuls, judges of the Supreme Court, and all other officers of the United States whose appointments are not herein otherwise provided for and which shall be established by law; but the Congress may by law vest the appointment of such inferior officers as they think proper in the president alone, in the courts of law, or in the heads of departments.

[3] The president shall have power to fill up all vacancies that may

---

[1] Temporary provision.

[2] Modified by Amendments XX and XXV.

[3] A "reprieve" is a postponement of the execution of a sentence.

[4] A "pardon" is a release from penalty.

happen during the recess of the Senate, by granting commissions which shall expire at the end of their next session.

Section 3. Duties and Responsibilities of the President He shall, from time to time, give to the Congress information of the state of the Union, and recommend to their consideration such measures as he shall judge necessary and expedient [advisable]; he may, on extraordinary [special] occasions, convene both houses, or either of them, and in case of disagreement between them with respect to the time of adjournment, he may adjourn them to such time as he shall think proper; he shall receive ambassadors and other public ministers; he shall take care that the laws be faithfully executed, and shall commission [appoint] all the officers of the United States.

Section 4. Impeachment The president, vice president, and all civil officers[1] of the United States, shall be removed from office on impeachment for, and conviction of, treason, bribery, or other high crimes and misdemeanors [offenses].

ARTICLE III. THE SUPREME COURT AND OTHER COURTS

Section 1. Federal Courts The judicial power of the United States shall be vested in one Supreme Court, and in such inferior [lower] courts as the Congress may from time to time ordain and establish. The judges, both of the Supreme and inferior courts, shall hold their offices during good behavior, and shall, at stated times, receive for their services a compensation, which shall not be diminished during their continuance in office.

Section 2. Jurisdiction of Federal Courts [1] The judicial power shall extend to all cases in law and equity[2] arising under this Constitution, the laws of the United States, and treaties made, or which shall be made, under their authority; to all cases affecting ambassadors, other public ministers, and consuls; to all cases of admiralty and maritime jurisdiction;[3] to controversies [disputes] to which the United States shall be a party; to controversies between two or more states, between a state and citizens of another state,[4] between citizens of different states, between citizens

---

[1] "Civil officers" include executive and judicial officials, but not members of Congress or officers in the armed forces.

[2] "Cases in law" refers mainly to disputes that arise from the violation of, or the interpretation of, federal laws, treaties, or the Constitution. "Equity" is a branch of the law that deals more generally with the prevention of injustice.

[3] Legal disputes involving ships and shipping on the high seas, in territorial waters, and on the navigable waterways within the country.

[4] Modified by Amendment XI, which provides that a state may not be sued in the federal courts by a citizen of another state (or by a citizen of a foreign country). A state, however, retains the right to sue a citizen of another state (or a citizen of a foreign country) in the federal courts.

of the same state claiming lands under grants of different states, and between a state, or the citizens thereof, and foreign states, citizens, or subjects.[1]

[2] In all cases affecting ambassadors, other public ministers, and consuls, and those in which a state shall be a party, the Supreme Court shall have original jurisdiction.[2] In all the other cases before mentioned, the Supreme Court shall have appellate jurisdiction,[3] both as to law and fact, with such exceptions and under such regulations as the Congress shall make.

[3] The trial of all crimes, except in cases of impeachment, shall be by jury; and such trial shall be held in the state where the said crimes shall have been committed; but when not committed within any state, the trial shall be at such place or places as the Congress may by law have directed.

Section 3. Treason [1] Treason against the United States shall consist only in levying [carrying on] war against them, or in adhering to [assisting] their enemies, giving them aid and comfort. No person shall be convicted of treason unless on the testimony of two witnesses to the same overt [open; public] act, or on confession in open court.

[2] The Congress shall have power to declare the punishment of treason, but no attainder of treason shall work corruption of blood or forfeiture except during the life of the person attainted.[4]

ARTICLE IV. INTERSTATE RELATIONS

Section 1. Official Acts and Records Full faith and credit shall be given in each state to the public acts, records, and judicial proceedings of every other state.[5] And the Congress may, by general laws, prescribe the manner in which such acts, records, and proceedings shall be proved, and the effect thereof.

Section 2. Mutual Obligations of States [1] The citizens of each state shall be entitled to all privileges and immunities of citizens in the several states.

[2] A person charged in any state with treason, felony, or other crime, who shall flee from justice and be found in another state, shall, on

---

[1] Modified by Amendment XI (see footnote 4, page 640).

[2] "Original jurisdiction" means the authority of a court to hear cases that have not previously been tried by lower courts.

[3] "Appellate jurisdiction" means the authority of a court to review cases that have previously been tried by lower courts.

[4] Punishment imposed on someone for treason may not be extended to that person's children or heirs.

[5] The official acts of each state must be accepted by the other states. The "full faith and credit" clause applies to court judgments, contracts, marriages, corporation charters, etc.

demand of the executive authority of the state from which he fled, be delivered up, to be removed to the state having jurisdiction of the crime.[1]

[3] *No person held to service or labor in one state, under the laws thereof, escaping into another, shall, in consequence of any law or regulation therein, be discharged from such service or labor, but shall be delivered up on claim of the party to whom such service or labor may be due.*[2]

Section 3. New States and Territories [1] New states may be admitted by the Congress into this Union; but no new state shall be formed or erected within the jurisdiction of any other state; nor any state be formed by the junction [joining] of two or more states, or parts of states, without the consent of the legislatures of the states concerned as well as of the Congress.

[2] The Congress shall have power to dispose of and make all needful rules and regulations respecting the territory or other property belonging to the United States; and nothing in this Constitution shall be so construed [interpreted] as to prejudice [damage] any claims of the United States, or of any particular state.

Section 4. Federal Guarantees to the States The United States shall guarantee to every state in this Union a republican form of government, and shall protect each of them against invasion; and on application of the legislature, or of the executive (when the legislature cannot be convened), against domestic violence [riots].

ARTICLE V. AMENDING THE CONSTITUTION

The Congress, whenever two-thirds of both houses shall deem [think] it necessary, shall propose amendments to this Constitution, or, on the application of the legislatures of two-thirds of the several states, shall call a convention for proposing amendments, which, in either case, shall be valid, to all intents and purposes, as part of this Constitution when ratified by the legislatures of three-fourths of the several states, or by conventions in three-fourths thereof, as the one or the other mode [method] of ratification may be proposed by the Congress; provided *that no amendment which may be made prior to the year 1808 shall in any manner affect the first and fourth clauses in the ninth section of the first article; and*[3] that no state, without its consent, shall be deprived of its equal suffrage in the Senate.

ARTICLE VI. MISCELLANEOUS PROVISIONS

Section 1. Public Debts All debts contracted and engagements [agreements] entered into before the adoption of this Constitution shall be as

[1]The delivery by one state or government to another of fugitives from justice is called *extradition*.

[2]Since the phrase "person held to service or labor" refers to a slave, this clause was nullified by Amendment XIII.

[3]Temporary provision.

valid [binding] against the United States under this Constitution as under the Confederation.

Section 2. Federal Supremacy This Constitution, and the laws of the United States which shall be made in pursuance thereof, and all treaties made, or which shall be made, under the authority of the United States, shall be the supreme law of the land; and the judges in every state shall be bound thereby, anything in the constitution or laws of any state to the contrary notwithstanding.[1]

Section 3. Oaths of Office The senators and representatives before mentioned, and the members of the several state legislatures, and all executive and judicial officers, both of the United States and of the several states, shall be bound by oath or affirmation to support this Constitution; but no religious test shall ever be required as a qualification to any office or public trust under the United States.

ARTICLE VII. RATIFICATION

The ratification of the conventions of nine states shall be sufficient for the establishment of this Constitution between the states so ratifying the same.

Done in convention, by the unanimous consent of the states present, the 17th day of September, in the year of our Lord 1787, and of the independence of the United States of America the twelfth. In witness whereof we have hereunto subscribed our names.

Signed by   George Washington
[President and Deputy
from Virginia]
and 38 other delegates

---

[1]This "supremacy clause" means that federal laws always override state legislation in cases of conflict.

Amendments to the Constitution

Note: The first ten amendments to the Constitution, adopted in 1791, make up the Bill of Rights. The year of adoption of later amendments (11 to 27) is given in parentheses.

AMENDMENT I.   FREEDOM OF RELIGION, SPEECH, PRESS, ASSEMBLY, AND PETITION

Congress shall make no law respecting an establishment of religion, or prohibiting the free exercise thereof;[1] or abridging [reducing] the freedom of speech or of the press; or the right of the people peaceably to assemble, and to petition the government for a redress [correction] of grievances.

AMENDMENT II.   RIGHT TO BEAR ARMS

A well-regulated militia being necessary to the security of a free state, the right of the people to keep and bear arms shall not be infringed [weakened].

AMENDMENT III. QUARTERING OF TROOPS

No soldier shall, in time of peace, be quartered [assigned to live] in any house without the consent of the owner, nor in time of war, but in a manner to be prescribed by law.

AMENDMENT IV. SEARCHES AND SEIZURES

The right of the people to be secure [safe] in their persons, houses, papers, and effects [belongings] against unreasonable searches and seizures shall not be violated; and no [search] warrants shall issue but upon probable caused supported by oath or affirmation, and particularly describing the place to be searched, and the persons or things to be seized.

AMENDMENT V.   RIGHTS OF THE ACCUSED; PROPERTY RIGHTS

No person shall be held to answer for a capital or otherwise infamous crime unless on a presentment or indictment of a grand jury,[3] except in cases arising in the land or naval forces, or in the militia, when in actual service in time of war or public danger; nor shall any person be subject

---

[1] "The free exercise thereof" refers to freedom of worship.

[2] "Probable cause" means *a reasonable ground of suspicion*.

[3] "A capital or otherwise infamous crime" refers to serious offenses punishable by death or by imprisonment. Before someone may be tried for such a crime, a grand jury must decide that sufficient evidence exists to bring that person to trial.

for the same offense to be twice put in jeopardy of life or limb;[1] nor shall be compelled in any criminal case to be a witness against himself; nor be deprived of life, liberty, or property without due process of law;[2] nor shall private property be taken for public use without just compensation.[3]

AMENDMENT VI.   OTHER RIGHTS OF THE ACCUSED

In all criminal prosecutions [trials], the accused shall enjoy the right to a speedy and public trial by an impartial [fair] jury of the state and district wherein the crime shall have been committed, which district shall have been previously ascertained by law; and to be informed of the nature and cause of the accusation; to be confronted with the witnesses against him; to have compulsory process for obtaining witnesses in his favor[4] and to have the assistance of counsel for his defense.

AMENDMENT VII. CIVIL SUITS

In suits at common law[5] where the value in controversy shall exceed twenty dollars, the right of trial by jury shall be preserved, and no fact tried by a jury shall be otherwise reexamined in any court of the United States, than according to the rules of the common law.

AMENDMENT VIII. BAILS, FINES, AND PUNISHMENTS

Excessive bail shall not be required, nor excessive fines imposed, nor cruel and unusual punishments inflicted.

AMENDMENT IX.   RIGHTS NOT LISTED

The enumeration [listing] in the Constitution of certain rights shall not be construed to deny or disparage [weaken] others retained by the people.

AMENDMENT X.   POWERS RESERVED TO THE STATES AND PEOPLE

The powers not delegated to the United States by the Constitution, nor prohibited by it to the states, are reserved to the states respectively, or to the people.

[1] A person may not be tried twice for the same offense (*double jeopardy*).

[2] "Due process of law" means proper legal procedure.

[3] The government has the *power of eminent domain*, or the right to take private property for public use. This provision requires the government to pay the owner a fair price for such property.

[4] The accused person has the right to request the court to issue an order, or *subpoena*, compelling a witness to appear in court.

[5] "Common law" is law based on custom and precedent (past decisions made in similar cases). Originating in England, it was brought to the English colonies by the early settlers and became the foundation of the American legal system.

AMENDMENT XI.   SUITS AGAINST STATES (1798)

The judicial power of the United States shall not be construed to extend to any suit in law or equity, commenced or prosecuted against one of the United States by citizens of another state, or by citizens or subjects of any foreign state.

AMENDMENT XII.   ELECTION OF PRESIDENT AND VICE PRESIDENT (1804)

[1] The electors shall meet in their respective states, and vote by ballot for president and vice president, one of whom at least shall not be an inhabitant of the same state with themselves; they shall name in their ballots the person voted for as president, and in distinct [separate] ballots the person voted for as vice president; and they shall make distinct lists of all persons voted for as president, and of all persons voted for as vice president, and of the number of votes for each, which lists they shall sign and certify, and transmit sealed to the seat of the government of the United States, directed to the president of the Senate.

[2] The president of the Senate shall, in the presence of the Senate and House of Representatives, open all the certificates, and the votes shall then be counted; the person having the greatest number of votes for president shall be the president, if such number be a majority of the whole number of electors appointed; and if no person have such majority, then from the persons having the highest numbers not exceeding three on the list of those voted for as president, the House of Representatives shall choose immediately, by ballot, the president. But in choosing the president, the votes shall be taken by states, the representation from each state having one vote; a quorum for this purpose shall consist of a member or members from two-thirds of the states, and a majority of all the states shall be necessary to a choice. And if the House of Representatives shall not choose a president whenever the right of choice shall devolve upon them, *before the fourth day of March next following,*[1] then the vice president shall act as president, as in the case of the death or other constitutional disability of the president.

[3] The person having the greatest number of votes as vice president shall be the vice president, if such number be a majority of the whole number of electors appointed; and if no person have a majority, then, from the two highest numbers on the list, the Senate shall choose the vice president; a quorum for the purpose shall consist of two-thirds of the whole number of senators, and a majority of the whole number shall be necessary to a choice. But no person constitutionally ineligible to the office of president shall be eligible to that of vice president of the United States.

[1]Changed to January 20 by Amendment XX.

AMENDMENT XIII. ABOLITION OF SLAVERY (1865)

Section 1. Slavery Forbidden Neither slavery nor involuntary servitude [compulsory service], except as a punishment for crime whereof the party shall have been duly convicted, shall exist within the United States, or any place subject to their jurisdiction.

Section 2. Enforcement Power Congress shall have power to enforce this article [amendment] by appropriate [suitable] legislation.

AMENDMENT XIV. CITIZENSHIP AND CIVIL RIGHTS (1868)

Section 1. Rights of Citizens All persons born or naturalized in the United States, and subject to the jurisdiction thereof, are citizens of the United States and of the state wherein they reside.[1] No state shall make or enforce any law which shall abridge the privileges or immunities of citizens of the United States; nor shall any state deprive any person of life, liberty, or property, without due process of law;[2] nor deny to any person within its jurisdiction the equal protection of the laws.[3]

Section 2. Apportionment of Representatives In Congress Representatives shall be apportioned among the several states according to their respective numbers, counting the whole number of persons in each state, excluding Indians not taxed.[4] But when the right to vote at any election for the choice of electors for president and vice president of the United States, representatives in Congress, the executive and judicial officers of a state, or the members of the legislature thereof, is denied to any of the *male* inhabitants of such state, being *twenly-one* years of age and citizens of the United States, or in any way abridged, except for participation in rebellion or other crime, the basis of representation therein shall be reduced in the proportion which the number of such *male* citizens shall bear to the whole number of *male* citizens *twenty-one* years of age in such state.[5]

Section 3. Persons Disqualified From Public Office No person shall be a senator or representative in Congress, or elector of president and

---

[1]This clause made the former slaves citizens.

[2]The primary purpose of this clause was to protect the civil rights of the former slaves. However, after the Supreme Court broadened the meaning of the word "person" to include "corporation," the clause began to be used to protect business interests as well.

[3]The "equal protection" clause has served as the legal basis for many civil rights cases.

[4]This clause nullifies the three-fifths formula of Article 1, section 2.

[5]Italicized words in this section were invalidated by Amendments XIX and XXVI.

vice president, or hold any office, civil or military, under the United States, or under any state, who, having previously taken an oath, as a member of Congress, or as an officer of the United States, or as a member of any state legislature, or as an executive or judicial officer of any state, to support the Constitution of the United States, shall have engaged in insurrection or rebellion against the same, or given aid or comfort to the enemies thereof. But Congress may, by a vote of two-thirds of each house, remove such disability.

Section 4. Valid Pubilc Debt Defined The validity [legality] of the public debt of the United States, authorized by law, including debts incurred for payment of pensions and bounties [extra allowances] for services in suppressing insurrection or rebellion, shall not be questioned. But neither the United States nor any state shall assume or pay any debt or obligation incurred in aid of insurrection or rebellion against the United States, or any claim for the loss or emancipation [liberation] of any slave; but all such debts, obligations, and claims shall be held illegal and void.

Section 5. Enforcement Power The Congress shall have power to enforce, by appropriate legislation, the provisions of this article.

AMENDMENT XV. RIGHT OF SUFFRAGE (1870)

Section 1. African Americans Guaranteed the Vote The right of citizens of the United States to vote shall not be denied or abridged by the United States or by any state on account of race, color, or previous condition of servitude [slavery].

Section 2. Enforcement Power The Congress shall have power to enforce this article by appropriate legislation.

AMENDMENT XVI. INCOME TAXES (1913)

The Congress shall have power to lay and collect taxes on incomes, from whatever source derived, without apportionment among the several states, and without regard to any census or enumeration.

AMENDMENT XVII. POPULAR ELECTION OF SENATORS (1913)

[1] The Senate of the United States shall be composed of two senators from each state, elected by the people thereof, for six years; and each senator shall have one vote. The electors [voters] in each state shall have the qualifications requisite for electors of the most numerous branch of the state legislatures.[1]

[1]This amendment changed the method of electing senators as given in Article 1, Section 3.

[2] When vacancies happen in the representation of any state in the Senate, the executive authority of such state shall issue writs of election to fill such vacancies: Provided, that the legislature of any state may empower [authorize] the executive thereof to make temporary appointments until the people fill the vacancies by election as the legislature may direct.

[3] *This amendment shall not be so construed as to affect the election or term of any senator chosen before it becomes valid as part of the Constitution.*[1]

AMENDMENT XVIII. PROHIBITION (1919)[2]

Section 1. Intoxicating Liquors Prohibited *After one year from the ratification of this article, the manufacture, sale, or transportation of intoxicating liquors within, the importation thereof into, or the exportation thereof from the United States and all territory subject to the jurisdiction thereof, for beverage purposes, is hereby prohibited.*

Section 2. Enforcement Power *The Congress and the several states shall have concurrent power to enforce this article by appropriate legislation.*

Section 3. Conditions of Ratification *This article shall be inoperative unless it shall have been ratified as an amendment to the Constitution by the legislatures of the several states, as provided in the Constitution, within seven years from the date of the submission hereof to the states by the Congress.*

AMENDMENT XIX.   WOMEN'S SUFFRAGE (1920)

[1] The right of citizens of the United States to vote shall not be denied or abridged by the United States or by any state on account of sex.

[2] Congress shall have power to enforce this article by appropriate legislation.

AMENDMENT XX.   PRESIDENTIAL AND CONGRESSIONAL TERMS[3] (1933)

Section 1. Terms of Office The terms of the president and vice president shall end at noon on the 20th day of January, and the terms of senators and representatives at noon on the 3d day of January, of the

---

[1]Temporary provision designed to protect those elected under the system previously in effect.

[2]This entire amendment was repealed in 1933 by Amendment XXI.

[3]This amendment is often called the "Lame Duck" Amendment because it shortened the period (from four months to two) between the elections in November and the time when defeated officeholders or officeholders who do not run again (known as "lame ducks") leave office.

years in which such terms would have ended if this article had not been ratified; and the terms of their successors[1] shall then begin.

Section 2. Convening Congress The Congress shall assemble at least once in every year, and such meeting shall begin at noon on the 3d day of January, unless they shall by law appoint a different day.[2]

Section 3. Presidential Succession If, at the time fixed for the beginning of the term of the president, the president-elect[3] shall have died, the vice president-elect shall become president. If a president shall not have been chosen before the time fixed for the beginning of his term, or if the president-elect shall have failed to qualify, then the vice president-elect shall act as president until a president shall have qualified; and the Congresss may by law provide for the case wherein neither a president-elect nor a vice president-elect shall have qualified, declaring who shall then act as president, or the manner in which one who is to act shall be selected, and such person shall act accordingly until a president or vice president shall have qualified.

Section 4. Selection of President and Vice President The Congress may by law provide for the case of the death of any of the persons from whom the House of Representatives may choose a president whenever the right of choice shall have devolved upon them, and for the case of the death of any of the persons from whom the Senate may choose a vice president whenever the right of choice shall have devolved upon them.

Section 5. Effective Date *Sections 1 and 2 shall take effect on the 15th day of October following the ratification of this article.*[4]

Section 6. Conditions of Ratification *This article shall be inoperative unless it shall have been ratified as an amendment to the Constitution by the legislatures of three-fourths of the several states within seven years from the date of its submission.*[5]

AMENDMENT XXI. REPEAL OF PROHIBITION (1933)

Section 1. Amendment XVIII Repealed The Eighteenth Article of amendment to the Constitution of the United States is hereby repealed.

Section 2. Shipment of Liquor Into "Dry" Areas The transportation or importation into any state, territory, or possession of the United States

---

[1] A "successor" is a person who is elected or appointed to replace another in a public office.

[2] This section changed the date given in Article 1, Section 4.

[3] A "president-elect" is a person who has been elected to the presidency but has not yet assumed office.

[4] Temporary provision.

[5] Temporary provision.

for delivery or use therein of intoxicating liquors in violation of the laws thereof is hereby prohibited.[1]

Section 3. Conditions of Ratification *This article shall be inoperative unless it shall have been ratified as an amendment to the Constitution by conventions in the several states,[2] as provided in the Constitution, within seven years from the date of the submission hereof to the states by the Congress.[3]*

AMENDMENT XXII. LIMITING PRESIDENTIAL TERMS (1951)

Section 1. Limit Placed on Tenure No person shall be elected to the office of the president more than twice, and no person who has held the office of president, or acted as president, for more than two years of a term to which some other person was elected president shall be elected to the office of the president more than once. *But this article shall not apply to any person holding the office of president when this article was proposed by the Congress, and shall not prevent any person who may be holding the office of president, or acting as president, during the term within which this article becomes operative from holding the office of president or acting as president during the remainder of such term.[4]*

Section 2. Conditions of Ratification *This article shall be inoperative unless it shall have been ratified as an amendment to the Constitution by the legislatures of three-fourths of the several states within seven years from the date of its submission to the states by the Congress.[5]*

AMENDMENT XXIII. SUFFRAGE FOR WASHINGTON, D.C. (1961)

Section 1. D.C. Presidential Electors The district constituting [making up] the seat of government of the United States shall appoint in such manner as the Congress may direct:

A number of electors of president and vice president equal to the whole number of senators and representatives in Congress to which the district would be entitled if it were a state, but in no event more than

---

[1]This section allowed individual states to prohibit the use of intoxicating liquors if they wished to.

[2]This was the first amendment to be submitted by Congress for ratification by state conventions rather than state legislatures.

[3]Temporary provision.

[4]Temporary provision.

[5]Temporary provision.

the least populous state;[1] they shall be in addition to those appointed by the states, but they shall be considered, for the purposes of the election of president and vice president, to be electors appointed by a state; and they shall meet in the district and perform such duties as provided by the Twelfth Article of amendment.[2]

Section 2. Enforcement Power The Congress shall have power to enforce this article by appropriate legislation.

AMENDMENT XXIV. POLL TAXES (1964)

Section 1. Poll Tax Barred The right of citizens of the United States to vote in any primary or other election for president or vice president, for electors for president or vice president, or for senator or representative in Congress, shall not be denied or abridged by the United States or any state by reason of failure to pay any poll tax or other tax.

Section 2. Enforcement Power The Congress shall have the power to enforce this article by appropriate legislation.

AMENDMENT XXV. PRESIDENTIAL SUCCESSION AND DISABILITY (1967)

Section 1. Elevation of Vice President In case of the removal of the president from office or his death or resignation, the vice president shall become president.

Section 2. Vice Presidential Vacancy Whenever there is a vacancy in the office of the vice president, the president shall nominate a vice president who shall take the office upon confirmation by a majority vote of both houses of Congress.

Section 3. Temporary Disability Whenever the president transmits to the president pro tempore of the Senate and the Speaker of the House of Representatives his written declaration that he is unable to discharge the powers and duties of his office, and until he transmits to them a written declaration to the contrary, such powers and duties shall be discharged by the vice president as acting president.

Section 4. Other Provisions for Presidential Disability [1] Whenever the vice president and a majority of either the principal officers of the executive departments, or of such other body as Congress may by law provide, transmit to the president pro tempore of the Senate and the Speaker of the House of Representatives their written declaration that the president is unable to discharge the powers and duties of his office, the vice president shall immediately assume the powers and duties of the office as acting president.

[1]At the present time, the District of Columbia is entitled to three electors.

[2]By providing for electors, this amendment gave residents of Washington, D.C., the right to vote for president and vice president.

[2] Thereafter, when the president transmits to the president pro tempore of the Senate and the Speaker of the House of Representatives his written declaration that no inability exists, he shall resume the powers and duties of his office unless the vice president and a majority of either the principal officers of the executive department, or of such other body as Congress may by law provide, transmit within four days to the president pro tempore of the Senate and the Speaker of the House of Representatives their written declaration that the president is unable to discharge the powers and duties of his office. Thereupon Congress shall decide the issue, assembling within 48 hours for that purpose if not in session. If the Congress, within 21 days after receipt of the latter written declaration, or, if Congress is not in session, within 21 days after Congress is required to assemble, determines by two-thirds vote of both houses that the president is unable to discharge the powers and duties of his office, the vice president shall continue to discharge the same as acting president; otherwise, the president shall resume the powers and duties of his office.

AMENDMENT XXVI. VOTE FOR 18-YEAR-OLDS (1971)

Section 1. Lowering the Voting Age The right of citizens of the United States, who are 18 years of age or older, to vote shall not be denied or abridged by the United States or by any state on account of age.

Section 2. Enforcement Power The Congress shall have power to enforce this article by appropriate legislation.

AMENDMENT XXVII. CONGRESSIONAL PAY RAISES (1992)

No law varying the compensation for the services of the Senators and Representatives shall take effect until an election of Representatives shall have intervened.

Index

Photo Credits

Page 30: Ben Franklin, *Philadelphia Gazette*, May 9, 1754 / Page 35: Courtesy of the John Carter Brown Library at Brown University / Page 36: Courtesy, American Antiquarian Society / Page 37: Library of Congress / Page 49: Stock Montage, Inc. / Page 76 left: The Liaison Agency Network © Lee Celano / Page 76 rt: The Liaison Agency Network © Porter Gifford / Page 83: Corbis-Bettmann / Page 95: Washington: © Hulton Getty/Liaison Agency / Page 95: Cabinet: © Bettmann/Corbis / Page 100: "Peter Pencil," 1809 (Houghton Library, Harvard) / Page 101: New-York Historical Society / Page 102: Corbis-Bettmann / Page 103: © Hulton Getty/Liaison Agency / Page 104: Giraudon/Art Resource / Page 114: Corbis-Bettmann / Page 115: Historical Pictures Service / Page 123: Corbis-Bettmann / Page 124: The Nelson-Atkins Museum of Art, Kansas City, Missouri / Page 126: Woolaroc Museum, Bartlesville, Oklahoma / Page 128: Corbis-Bettmann / Page 129: © Bettmann/ Corbis / Page 130: Corbis-Bettmann / Page 131: Stowe: © Bettmann/Corbis / Douglass: Corbis/Bettmann/UPI / Tubman, Brown: © Hulton/Getty/Liaison Agency / Garrison: Corbis / Page 144: © Hulton Getty/Liaison Agency / Page 145: North Wind Picture Archives / Page 149: *Yankee Doodle*, 1847 / Page 151: *Punch* (London), 1846 / Page 155: Corbis/Bettmann / Page 167: Corbis-Bettmann / Page 177: *Harper's Weekly*, November 16, 1867 / Page 179: Archives of the Rutherford B. Hayes Library / Page 182: © Hulton Getty/ Liaison Agency / Page 183: © Hulton Getty/Liaison Agency / Page 184: Corbis/Bettmann / Page 185: © Bettmann/Corbis / Page 189: North Wind Picture Archives / Page 201: New-York Historical Society / Page 204: Library of Congress / Page 207: Corbis-Bettmann / Page 208: Culver Pictures / Page 209: Library of Congress / Page 211: Library of Congress / Page 218: © Bettmann/Corbis / Page 221: Culver Pictures / Page 234 left: Corbis-Bettmann / Page 234 rt: Corbis/Bettmann-UPI / Page 249: Corbis/Bettmann / Page 250: Gamma Liaison Network © Roger Viollet Gamma Presse / Page 251: New York Public Library, Prints Division, Astor, Lenox, and Tilden Foundations / Page 256: Corbis-Bettmann / Page 260: © Hulton Getty/Liaison Agency / Page 269: © Amsco School Publications / Page 275: Library of Congress / Page 277: Corbis/Bettmann / Page 282: Library of Congress / Page 288: UPI/Corbis-Bettmann / Page 295: Louis Dalrymple, *Judge*, 1895 / Page 300: © Amsco School Publications / Page 312: *Los Angeles Daily Times*, 1917 / Page 316: Corbis-Bettmann / Page 319: Library of Congress / Page 322: © copyright Chicago Tribune Company. All rights reserved. / Page 323: Jay N. Darling, *The Des Moines Register*, 1926 / Page 335: *Dallas News* (1921) / Page 338: *No source in USGO (Essex Coach ad)* / Page 340: © Stock Montage, Inc. / Page 341: Library of Congress / Page 342: Corbis-Bettmann / Page 343: *The Best of H. T. Webster* (Simon & Shuster, 1953) / Page 347: © Hulton Getty/Liaison Agency / Page 361 (both): Corbis-Bettmann / Page 364: Corbis-Bettmann / Page 369: Fred O. Seibel Collection, University of Virginia / Page 383: Corbis-Bettmann / Page 391: Corbis-Bettmann / Page 386: *Straight Herblock* (Simon & Shuster, 1964) / Page 387: C.D. Batchelor, *New York Daily News*, 1936 / Page 388: Orr in *Scottish Daily Record* [Glasgow], 1941 / Page 391: Historical Pictures Service / Page 392: Library of Congress / Page 394: Corbis-UPI/Bettmann / Page 411: Jay N. Darling, *Des Moines Register*, 1945 / Page 418: Joseph Parrish, *Chicago Tribune*, 1949 / Page 437: *The Best of H. T. Webster* (Simon & Shuster, 1953) / Page 456: *Herblock's Special for Today* (Simon & Shuster, 1958) / Page 457: Corbis/Bettmann-UPI / Page 458: © Bettmann/Corbis / Page 459: UPI/Bettmann / Page 462: © Bettmann/Corbis / Page 463 top: Corbis/Bettmann-UPI / Page 463 bot.: UPI-Corbis-Bettmann / Page 476: Illingworth © *London Daily Mail* / Page 477: © Bettmann/Corbis / Page 481: © Amsco School Publications / Page 484: National Aeronautics and Space Administration / Page 488: Herblock, *A Cartoonist's Life* (Macmillan, 1993) / Page 493: UPI/Corbis-Bettmann / Page 494: *Straight Herblock* (Simon & Shuster, 1964) / Page 495: Black Star © 2000 Charles Moore / Page 502: Dana Fradon © 1972 The New Yorker Magazine, Inc. / Page 517: Corky Trinidad, *Honolulu Star-Bulletin*, 1970 / Page 519: Bill Mauldin © 1966 *Chicago Sun Times* / Page 525: Cal Alley, *The Commercial Appeal* (Memphis, Tenn.), 1968 / Page 526: © 1975 Jules Feiffer; Universal Press Syndicate / Page